THE COINAGE OF THE PHOENICIAN CITY OF TYRE
IN THE PERSIAN PERIOD

ORIENTALIA LOVANIENSIA
ANALECTA
——— 188 ———

STUDIA PHOENICIA
XX

THE COINAGE
OF THE PHOENICIAN CITY OF TYRE
IN THE PERSIAN PERIOD
(5th-4th cent. BCE)

by

J. ELAYI and A.G. ELAYI

UITGEVERIJ PEETERS and DEPARTEMENT OOSTERSE STUDIES
LEUVEN — PARIS — WALPOLE, MA
2009

A CIP record for this book is available from the Library of Congress.

CJ
1379
.E539
2009

© 2009, Peeters Publishers & Department of Oriental Studies
Bondgenotenlaan 153, B-3000 Leuven/Louvain (Belgium)
All rights reserved, including the rights to translate or to
reproduce this book or parts thereof in any form.

ISBN 978-90-429-2202-0 (Peeters, Leuven)
D. 2009/0602/49

CONTENTS

Introduction	7
Chapter I: Catalogue of the Tyrian coins	25
1. Group I: Dolphin (third quarter of the 5th century)	28
2. Group II: Deity riding on seahorse (around 425-333/2 BCE)	47
3. Group III: Unclassified series	176
4. Mint of Tyre?	200
Chapter II: Study of dies and relative chronology	201
1. Group I: Dolphin	201
2. Group II: Deity riding on seahorse	205
3. Group III: Unclassified series	215
4. Mint of Tyre?	219
Chapter III: Analysis of the monetary inscriptions	221
1. The monetary inscriptions	224
2. The monetary graffiti	238
3. The monetary countermarks	240
4. Palaeographical analysis of the Tyrian monetary inscriptions	241
5. Sociocultural aspects of the Tyrian monetary script	249
Chapter IV: Analysis of iconography	253
1. The owl	253
2. The dolphin	258
3. The seahorse	262
4. The deity	265
5. The shell	272
6. The head of lion	273
7. The head of ram	276
8. The rosette	277
9. The crescent-shaped countermark	279

Chapter V: The Tyrian monetary workshop 281
1. The monetary metals 281
2. The flans 284
3. The dies 289
4. Striking 297
5. Alterations not related to the manufacturing process 302
6. Workshop operations 303
Chapter VI: Metrological study 311
1. Terminology and methodology 312
2. Illustration of the method determining the modified standard 316
3. The problem of the addition of copper 317
4. Metrological analysis of the Tyrian silver coinage 318
5. Metrological analysis of the Tyrian bronze coinage 321
Chapter VII: The coinage of Tyre and the history of the city 323
1. Tyre before the inauguration of her coinage 323
2. The inauguration of Group I.1 of Tyrian coinage (around 450 BCE) 328
3. Group I.2 (last part of the third quarter of the 5th century) 336
4. Group II.1.1 (around 425-394 BCE) 338
5. Group II.1.2 (around 393-358 BCE) 345
6. Group II.2 (around 357-333/2 BCE) 365
Conclusion 391
Appendix I: Hoards containing Tyrian coins 397
Appendix II: False or dubious Tyrian coins 403
Abbreviations 405
Bibliography 411
Index of public and private collections 431
Index of sale catalogues 437
Index of hoards 453
Index of geographic names 455
Figures 461
Plates 519

INTRODUCTION

This book represents the second of the four corpora on Phoenician coinages minted under Persian rule in this area, that is to say before Alexander's conquest of the Phoenician cities in 333/332 BCE.[1] The first corpus, covering the Sidonian coinage was published in 2004.[2] Let us recall that the four main Phoenician mints at that time were, from North to South, the mint of Arwad/'RWD (now 'Arwād in Syria), of Byblos/GBL (Gbeil), of Sidon/ṢDN (Saida) and of Tyre/ṢR (Sour) (Fig. 1), these last three cities being located in Lebanon.[3]

Despite the traditional view, other Phoenician cities had minted coins during the Persian period, but these mints are not well-known as we showed in 1993.[4] There was probably a mint in the IVth century in Tripolis (Tripoli/Trablous, Lebanon), 'TR in Phoenician and Atri in Akkadian.[5] But the ancient city, located under the modern town, has not yet been excavated.[6] If the coins of Tripolis have not circulated out of the city as was the case for Byblos, this coinage would have remained almost completely unknown[7]. As far as the mint of Ascalon is concerned, the first problem consists in her political status in the Persian period which is far from clear: an autonomous city under the rule of Tyre?[8] The existence of a mint in Ascalon is based on the interpretation of the Phoenician monetary inscription 'N or ' alone, sometimes in a retrograde writing, as an abbreviation of '[ŠQL]N.[9] In the recent catalogue of 'Philistian' coinage, 50

---

1. Cf., in particular, Elayi, *Sidon*, pp. 137-159; *id.*, 'Les cités phéniciennes entre liberté et sujétion', *DHA* 16, 1990, pp. 93-113; *id.*, 'La domination perse sur les cités phéniciennes', in *ACFP* II, Roma 1991, pp. 77-85.
2. Elayi-Elayi, *Monnayage de Sidon* I-II.
3. We use in this book the toponyms usual in Phoenician studies: Arwad, Byblos, Sidon and Tyre.
4. Cf. Elayi-Elayi, *Trésors*, pp. 11-13.
5. J. Elayi and A.G. Elayi, 'La première monnaie de 'TR/Tripolis (Tripoli, Liban)?', *Trans* 4, 1991, pp. 143-151.
6. Cf. H. Salamé-Sarkis, 'Chronique archéologique du Liban-Nord', *BMB* 24, 1971, pp. 91-100; *id.*, 'Chronique archéologique du Liban-Nord II: 1973-1974', *BMB* 26, 1973, pp. 98-99; *id.*, *Contribution à l'histoire de Tripoli et de sa région à l'époque des Croisades*, Paris 1980, pp. 45-48.
7. Elayi-Elayi, *Trésors*, pp. 354-355 and fig. 22.
8. Ps.-Scyl., *Périple* 104 (πόλις Τυρίων καὶ Βασιλεία).
9. Cf. C. Lambert, 'Egypto-arabian, Phoenician, and other Coins of the fourth Century B.C. found in Palestine', *QDAP* 2, 1933, p. 3; Y. Meshorer, 'The Mints of Ashdod and Ascalon during the Late Persian Period', *ErIs* 20, Jerusalem 1989, *Vol. Y. Yadin*, pp. 287-291; G. Finkielsztejn, 'Phanébal, déesse d'Ascalon', in T. Hackens and G. Moucharte eds, *Numismatique et histoire économique phéniciennes et puniques*, Studia Phoenicia IX, Louvain-la-Neuve 1992, pp. 52-54; A. Lemaire, 'Épigraphie et numismatique palestiniennes', in E.-M. Laperrousaz and A. Lemaire dirs, *La Palestine à l'époque perse*, Paris 1994, p. 284; H. Gitler, 'Achaemenid Motifs in the Coinage of

'Athenian-styled' and 4 'Philistian-styled' coins are listed for the mint of Ascalon, most of them bearing this inscription.[10] None of these 54 coins were found in regular excavations, 38 are unpublished and only 4 of them were acquired a long time ago by the collections of the British Museum and Cabinet des Médailles.[11] A hoard of 31 divisionary coins (obols?) was recently found in regular excavations of Ascalon and published in 1996, but they are different from the previous 54 coins: they are 'pseudo-Athenians' with profiled-eye Athena and therefore not necessarily minted in the site.[12] Therefore, for the moment we have to consider the existence of an Ascalonite mint at that time as a hypothesis in need of confirmation. We have still less information about Myriand(r)us in the Persian period, a Phoenician harbour according to classical sources, possibly located in Alexandrette/Iskanderun in Turkey.[13] The hypothesis of a mint in Beirut at the same time remains unproven.[14] It would be surprising that Sidon had allowed Beirut, a mere town in her territory, to mint her own coins.[15] The hypothesis of a mint in Dor, as proposed by E. Stern, has not been proven either.[16] The ancient hypothesis of a mint in Akko also has no foundation.[17] As for Beirut, Sidon probably did not allow Dor, a town in her territory, to mint coins. It was the same for Akko who belonged to Tyre. Al-

---

Ashdod, Ascalon and Gaza from the Fourth Century BC', *Trans* 20, 2000, pp. 73-87; L. Mildenberg, 'Über die Münzbildnisse in Palästina und Nordwest Arabien zur Perserzeit', in C. Uehlinger ed., *Images as Media, Sources for the Cultural History of the Near East and Eastern Mediterranean (First Millennium BCE)*, OBO 175, Fribourg 2000, p. 376 and n. 4; J. Elayi and A. Lemaire, 'Numismatique', *Trans* 25, 2003, p. 90; H. Gitler and O. Tal, *The Coinage of Philistia of the Fifth and Fourth Centuries BC. A Study of the Earliest Coins of Palestine*, Milano-New York 2006, pp. 39-40, 96-113 (with bibl.).

10. Gitler-Tal, *ibid.*, pp. 96-113.
11. *Ibid.*, no. III 3Da (Babelon, *Perses*, pl. VIII, 8), III 4Dc (*BMC Palestine*, pl. xix, 10), III 9Oc (Babelon, *Traité*, pl. CXXIII, 19) and IV 1Db (Babelon, *Perses*, pl. VIII, 18).
12. H. Gitler, 'New Fourth-Century BC Coins from Ascalon', *NC* 156, 1996, pp. 1-9; Gitler-Tal, *op. cit.* (n. 9), pp. 39, 53 and 153.
13. Cf. Elayi-Elayi, *Trésors*, p. 12 (with bibl.).
14. U. Finkbeiner and H. Sader, 'Bey 020 Preliminary report of the excavations 1995', *BAAL* 2, 1997, p. 150; Exhibition of the Institut du Monde arabe, Paris 27 Oct.-2 May 1999, no. 25 333 (National Museum of Beirut); cf. Elayi-Sayegh, *Beyrouth II*, pp. 334-335; *id.*, *Beyrouth I*, pp. 295-297. Z. Sawaya now attributes this coin to Tyre: "Les trouvailles monétaires de Beyrouth datées de l'époque perse", in Conférences de l'ASPEP, Paris 28-11-2007; possibly it belongs to our Series III.2.4.
15. On the political status of Phoenician cities in the Persian period, cf. J. Elayi, 'Studies in Phoenician Geography during the Persian Period', *JNES* 41, 1982, pp. 83-110; *id.*, *Économie*, pp. 9-30; on the territory of Sidon, cf. Elayi-Sayegh, *Beyrouth II*, pp. 336-337 (with bibl.).
16. E. Stern, 'Dor à l'époque perse', in Laperrousaz-Lemaire dirs, *op. cit.* (n. 9), pp. 110-111 ('Nous sommes convaincus que des monnaies de ce type étaient aussi frappées à Dor, à cause de l'importance de la cité en tant que capitale d'une province et port non moins important qu'Ashdod'); *id.*, *Dor Ruler*, p. 194 and fig. 128; Y. Meshorer, in *id.*, *Dor Final Report*, pp. 461, 462, fig. 10, and 466, no. 10 ('Coin No. 10, published here for the first time, may well be of the mint of Dora').
17. U. Hübner, 'Die Münzprägungen Palästinas in alttestamentlicher Zeit', in *Trumah, Zeitschrift der Hochschule für Jüdische Studien* 4, 1994, pp. 119-145; cf. J. Elayi and A. Lemaire, 'Numismatique', *Trans* 17, 1999, p. 142.

though the knowledge of the so-called 'pseudo-Athenian' or 'Philistian' coins has much progressed, however the identification of their mints, among which could be some Phoenician, is still uncertain.[18] Therefore we do not see any significant new element to change our 1993 position: 'All things considered, because of the uncertainty which still characterises these other possible Phoenician coinages, we consider their study as premature and we devote this book only to the coinages of Arwad, Byblos, Sidon and Tyre, relatively well-known and well-represented'.[19]

As is the case for many other coinages, some coins which are different from the known types and difficult to attribute, are presented as 'uncertain' Phoenician coins.[20] There are some attempts to attribute them to the Tyrian mint that we shall examine, or attribution of Tyrian coins to other mints.[21] As for the borrowings from the Phoenician types by the so-called 'philisto-Arabian' or 'Philistian' coinages, they are outside the scope of this book and they have recently been studied by H. Gitler and O. Tal, without resolving all the difficulties.[22] Bringing together the four Phoenician coinages in a single corpus would have facilitated comparisons and avoided repetitions, but such a book would have been too voluminous and not easy to use. In order to provide more convenience and greater clarity, we have decided to publish the corpus of the coinages of Sidon, Tyre, Arwad and Byblos separately. The corpus of the Sidonian coinage was published first because it is the best known of the four main Phoenician coinages[23] and therefore provides chronological benchmarks which can be used in order to complete our lack of knowledge of the three other coinages.

Instead of studying the complete history of the Tyrian mint, we have selected one period only: the Persian period. It does not mean that the other periods are less interesting or less important. Hopefully other corpora devoted to the Tyrian mint during the Hellenistic, Roman, Byzantine and Medieval periods will be issued after our corpus related to the Persian period. We have focused

---

18. J. Elayi and A.G. Elayi, 'Nouveau trésor de monnaies aradiennes, athéniennes et pseudo-athéniennes', *Trans* 18, 1999, pp. 75-84; H. Nicolet-Pierre, 'Tétradrachmes athéniens en Transeuphratène', *Trans* 20, 2000, pp. 107-119; J. Elayi and J. Sapin, *Quinze ans de recherches (1985-2000) sur le Transeuphratène à l'époque perse*, Paris 2000, pp. 169-170; Gitler, *loc. cit.* (n. 12), pp. 1-9; Gitler-Tal, *op. cit.* (n. 9), with bibl.: according to these authors, it could be an 'inter-city monetary system that operated probably under a central minting authority' (p. 51), but we do not see exactly what they mean.

19. Elayi-Elayi, *Trésors*, p. 12.

20. See, for example, Babelon, *Perses*, pp. LV-LXVII; *BMC Phoenicia*, pp. cxliii-cxlv; *Catalogue De Luynes*, pp. 163-165.

21. See, for example, coins no. 241 and 242 attributed to 'incerti di Samaria': Meshorer-Qedar, *Samarian Coinage*, p. 125 and pl. 31, no. IC3 and IC4.

22. Gitler-Tal, *op. cit.* (n. 9), pp. 211-218; cf. also Mildenberg, *loc. cit.* (n. 9), pp. 375-392; S.N. Gerson, 'Fractional Coins of Judea and Samaria in the fourth Century BCE', *NEA* 64, 2001, pp. 106-121; Elayi-Sapin, *op. cit.* (n. 18), pp. 179-183.

23. For different reasons, mainly because of its annual dating: cf. Elayi-Elayi, *Le monnayage de Sidon*, pp. 635-637.

on this period because it is already a major task since a quantity of 1,814 coins have been assembled in the catalogue. Another reason for the choice of this period is that it is perfectly integrated into our research programme: the history of the Phoenician cities during the Persian period. The first stage was, in 1990, a first approach to the economic history of these cities under Persian rule.[24] As we do not have the huge mass of Mesopotamian economic tablets at our disposal, it was necessary to use all kinds of information, including numismatic, thereby enabling the main problems of economic history to be solved. The second stage involved, in 1993, collecting and analysing all the hoards including, partly or totally, Phoenician coins dated from the Persian period, and also the coins from excavations.[25] This study resulted in important conclusions concerning the monetary circulation, the various aspects of monetary economy as a function of periods and areas, the phenomenon of hoarding and the issue of monetary alterations (graffiti, countermarks and other alterations related with control or falsification). The third stage consisted, in 1997, of an investigation of Phoenician weights[26] that we have collected and analysed from different points of view: epigraphical, iconographical, technological, economic and metrological. We have used an original method, also suitable to numismatic studies, adapting the statistical models to these weights and allowing us to establish cautious and solid foundations for Phoenician metrology. Following an old, somewhat forgotten idea,[27] recent works have underlined that it would be interesting to study the possible relation between the standard of weighed metal and the monetary standard.[28] Besides these three main stages, preliminary to the corpora on Phoenician coinages, we have devoted many articles to specific numismatic problems, several of them concerning the Tyrian mint: the inauguration date of its coinage,[29] the series of shekels with dolphin,[30] the series of divisionary coins with dolphin,[31] the series with the rosette,[32] the bronze series with the lion's head and shell,[33] the typology of the dolphin and shell,[34] the

---

24. Elayi, *Économie*.
25. Elayi-Elayi, *Trésors*.
26. *Id., Poids phéniciens.*
27. V. Queipo, *Essai sur les systèmes métriques des anciens peuples* I, Paris 1859, pp. 335-336; cf. *DAGR*, s.v. 'pondus', p. 548 and n. 13.
28. N.F. Parise, 'Unità ponderali e circolazione metallica nell'Oriente mediterraneo', in T. Hackens *et al.* eds, *A Survey of Numismatic Research 1985-1990*, Brussels 1991, pp. 32-34 (with bibl.)
29. Elayi, *Phénomène monétaire*, pp. 59-76.
30. *Id.*, 'Les sicles de Tyr au dauphin', *NAC* 21, 1992, pp. 37-49.
31. J. Elayi and A. Lemaire, 'Les petites monnaies de Tyr au dauphin avec inscription', *NAC* 19, 1990, pp. 99-116; J. Elayi and A.G. Elayi, 'Nouvelles monnaies divisionnaires de Tyr au dauphin avec inscription', *BCEN* 27, 1990, pp. 69-74.
32. J. Elayi and A.G. Elayi, 'Les monnaies de Tyr au dauphin et à la rosette', *Annotazioni Numismatiche* 3, 1991, pp. 38-42.
33. *Id.*, 'La dernière série tyrienne en bronze aux types civiques', *NAC* 27, 1998, pp. 1-11.
34. J. Elayi, 'Étude typologique des sicles de Tyr au dauphin', *Cahiers Numismatiques* 108, 1991, pp. 11-17.

methodology of monetary iconographical study,[35] the epigraphical study of monetary inscriptions,[36] the system of abbreviations,[37] the graffiti and countermarks,[38] the circulation of Tyrian coins[39] and new hoards containing Tyrian coins.[40] It should also be stated that this programme of research concerning the history of the Phoenician cities in the Persian period is part of a larger programme, concerning Transeuphratene during the same period,[41] which is an indispensable reference for understanding, for example, monetary circulation or trading exchanges.

This corpus of the Tyrian coinage will also permit us to update our book on Phoenician hoards, thanks to the new discoveries of hoards and isolated coins,[42] and to the important conclusions obtained here concerning in particular the typology, iconography, epigraphy and political history.[43] The Tyrian corpus will also enable the study of Phoenician economic history to be completed and the relations between the metrology of weights and of coins to be established with greater precision.[44]

The Tyrian shekels of Phoenician standard (13.56g and 20-25mm in diameter) were not as spectacular as the Sidonian double shekels (28.02g until 366 BCE and 30-35mm in diameter). They have always interested numismatists, but they have almost always – until today – been included in Greek numismat-

---

35. *Id.*, 'Remarques méthodologiques sur l'étude iconographique des monnaies phéniciennes', in *Mélanges* J.-P. Rey-Coquais, *MUSJ* 59, 2006 (in press).
36. *Id.*, 'Étude paléographique des légendes monétaires phéniciennes d'époque perse', *Trans* 5, 1992, pp. 24-25 and 38-39, Table II.
37. J. Elayi and A.G. Elayi, 'Systems of Abbreviations used by Byblos, Tyre and Arwad in their pre-Alexandrine Coinages', *JNG* 37-38, 1987-88, pp. 14-18.
38. A. Lemaire and J. Elayi, 'Graffiti monétaires ouest-sémitiques', in Hackens-Moucharte eds, *op. cit.* (n. 9), pp. 59-76; Elayi-Lemaire, *Graffiti*, pp. 42, no. 18, 45, no. 32, 54, no. 87, 129, no. 138, 136, no. 180.
39. J. Elayi, 'La diffusion des monnaies phéniciennes en Palestine', in Laperrousaz-Lemaire dirs, *op. cit.* (n. 9), pp. 289-309.
40. J. Elayi and A.G. Elayi, 'Nouveaux trésors de monnaies phéniciennes (*CH* VIII)', *Trans* 11, 1996, pp. 101-113.
41. On this programme, cf. J. Elayi and J. Sapin, *Nouveaux regards sur la Transeuphratène*, Brepols, Turnhout 1991 (*Beyond the River. New Perspectives on Transeuphratene*, JSOT.S 250, Sheffield 1998); *id.*, *op. cit.* (n. 18), pp. 7-15 (with bibl.).
42. Elayi-Elayi, *loc. cit.* (n. 40), pp. 95-114; *id.*, 'Suplemento al corpus de tesoros de monedas fenicias', in *ACFP* IV, Cádiz 2000, pp. 483-486; *id.*, 'Nouveaux trésors de monnaies phéniciennes (*CH* IX)', *Trans* 26, 2003, pp. 105-117; J. Elayi and A. Lemaire, 'Numismatique', *Trans* 1, 1989, pp. 155-159; *Trans* 4, 1991, pp. 119-376; *Trans* 10, 1995, pp. 151-177; *Trans* 17, 1999, pp. 117-141; *Trans* 25, 2003, pp. 65-87; *Trans* 33, 2007, pp. 21-25.
43. We shall complete the questions that have been shelved (Elayi-Elayi, *Trésors*, pp. 17-18 and 384).
44. Cf. *id.*, 'Nouveaux poids phéniciens (I)', *Trans* 17, 1999, pp. 35-43. As far as we know, the publications announced by P. Bordreuil and P.-L. Gatier for more than twenty years have not yet been issued (cf. Elayi-Elayi, *Poids phéniciens*, pp. 12-15 and nn. 22-23).

ics.[45] Following the works of J.P. Six,[46] J. Rouvier established a first catalogue of Phoenician coins, including Tyrian ones, mainly based on his large personal collection.[47] He was a connoisseur of these coins and a man of good sense. Unfortunately, his collection was widely scattered and the plates of his publications are not of a sufficiently good quality to permit the necessary checks. However, we were lucky to find a part of the Rouvier collection in the American Numismatic Society in New York, which was acquired through the Newell collection.[48] The collections of Phoenician coins in the Cabinet des Médailles of the Bibliothèque de France in Paris were published by E. Babelon in 1893 and 1910[49], and by J. Babelon in 1930.[50] Those of the British Museum in London were published by G.F. Hill in 1910.[51] The catalogues of E. Babelon (*Perses achéménides* and *Traité*) are still useful today because of the completeness of their collections and the detailed presentation of the coins, although the classification and chronology are quite obsolete and the comments out of date. In fact, there was no book that could replace them, until the issue of our last corpus on the Sidonian coinage. Several other collections were partly published between 1968 and 1982: the collection of the American University of Beirut by D. Baramki, that of the National Museum of Beirut by M. Chéhab, and that of the American Numismatic Society of New York by J.W. Betlyon.[52] But these books are very succinct compared with the E. Babelon and G.F. Hill catalogues. However, the small book of J.W. Betlyon takes the last finds and publications partly into account, and contains some interesting ideas, but it also contains too many errors and lacks and needs to be used with caution. In this respect, the experts of sale catalogues are not mistaken and continue to refer mainly to the catalogues of E. Babelon and G.F. Hill. There was a first wave of specific works on Phoenician coinages, in particular Tyrian, during the second half of the 19th century, with the publications of T.E. Mionnet, H. de Luynes, J. Brandis, B.V. Head, J.P. Six, E. Babelon and J. Rouvier.[53] The second wave

45. Cf., for example, Kraay, *Greek Coins*; C. Morrisson and B. Kluge eds, *A Survey of Numismatic Research 1990-1995*, Berlin 1997, p. 102; C. Alfaro and A. Burnett, *A Survey of Numismatic Research 1996-2001*, Madrid 2003, pp. 151-152.
46. J.P. Six, 'Observations sur les monnaies phéniciennes', *NC* 17, 1877, pp. 177-241; *id.*, 'L'ère de Tyr', *NC* 3rd series 26, 1886, pp. 106-110.
47. J. Rouvier, 'L'ère d'Alexandre le Grand en Phénicie', *REG* 12, 1899, pp. 376-377; *id.*, 'Numismatique des villes de la Phénicie: Tyr', *JIAN* 6, 1903, pp. 269-332.
48. We have mentioned it in the catalogue, every time that we could obtain the information or that we have recognized a coin.
49. E. Babelon, *Perses*; *id.*, *Traité*.
50. *Catalogue De Luynes*.
51. *BMC Phoenicia*.
52. Baramki, *Coins AUB*; *id.*, *The Coin Collection of the American University of Beirut Museum*, Beirut 1974; Chéhab, *Monnaies*; Betlyon, *Coinage of Phoenicia*.
53. T.E. Mionnet, *Description de Médailles antiques, grecques et romaines*, vol. 5, Paris 1808, pp. 643-644, no. 15-25; Suppl. au vol. 8, pl. XIX, no. 5; H. de Luynes, *Essai sur la numismatique des Satrapes de la Phénicie*, Paris 1846, pp. 69-82; J. Brandis, *Das Münz-, Mass- und Gewichtswesen in Vorderasien bis auf Alexander den Grossen*, Berlin 1866, pp. 376-377, 513-

occurred only after 1950, sporadically until 1985 and more systematically afterwards with the publications of H. Seyrig, P. Naster, L. Sole, N. Vismara, R. Martini, A. Destrooper-Georgiades,[54] and our publications.[55] As for the publications of hoards, coins from excavations, isolated coins and sale catalogues, we refer to our above-mentioned corpus of Phoenician hoards, to the six bulletins entitled 'Numismatique' by J. Elayi and A. Lemaire, published in the *Transeuphratène* series, and to the book of J. Elayi and J. Sapin, which is an analysis of fifteen years of research (1985-2000), in particular numismatic, in Transeuphratene during the Persian period.[56]

The coinage of Tyre does not bear any explicit mention such as the name of the city or the name of a king which could ensure its attribution to the Tyrian mint. In this respect, P. Naster used to say: 'The attributions (of coins) to Arados, Sidon and Tyre, even if likely, are always conjectural, we often forget it since the publications of J.P. Six, E. Babelon and J. Rouvier dated between 1877 and the beginning of this century. Only the attribution to Gebal/Byblos is certain thanks to the explicit monetary legend which does not need to be interpreted, but just read'.[57] Among the old publications, T.E. Mionnet for example attributed all Phoenician coinages to the kings of Persia, distinguishing between Persian and non-Persian iconography.[58] H. de Luynes confused the coins of Kition and Tyre.[59] However, the so-called 'murex'[60] was reputed to be the 'Tyrian symbol *par excellence* '[61] and helped in the identification of the Tyrian mint, whereas it is hard to identify the Sidonian mint. Today, we can confirm

---

514; Head, *Coinage of Lydia*, pp. 31-32; Six, *loc. cit.* (n. 46) 1877, pp. 177-241 and 1886, pp. 106-110; Rouvier, *loc. cit.* (n. 47) 1899, pp. 376-377 and 1903, pp. 269-332. Cf. also the Tyrian coins in general books: Head, *Historia Numorum*, p. 799; Gardner, *History of Ancient Coinage*, pp. 345-347; E. Babelon, *Les monnaies grecques. Aperçu historique*, Paris 1921, pp. 52-53. Cf. also the introductions to the catalogues of E. Babelon and G.F. Hill, mentioned above.

54. H. Seyrig, 'Sur une prétendue ère tyrienne', *Syr.* 34, 1957, pp. 93-98; P. Naster, 'La technique des revers partiellement incus des monnaies phéniciennes', in *Centennial Publication of the American Numismatic Society*, New York 1958, pp. 503-511; *id.*, 'Le développement des monnayages phéniciens avant Alexandre, d'après les trésors', in A. Kindler ed., *The patterns of the monetary development in Phoenicia and Palestine in Antiquity, International Numismatic Convention. Jerusalem 1963*, Jerusalem 1967, pp. 3-24 (= P. Naster, *Scripta Nummaria. Contributions à la méthodologie numismatique*, Louvain-la-Neuve 1983, pp. 178-196); L. Sole, 'Le emissioni monetali della Fenicia prima di Alessandro-I', *SEAP* 16, 1997, pp. 75-125; *id.*, 'Le emissioni monetali della Fenicia prima di Alessandro-II', *SEAP* 18, 1998, pp. 81-147; N. Vismara and R. Martini, 'Ripostigli con monete della Lycia, di Cyprus e della Phoenicia. Spunti per una discussione', *Trans* 20, 2000, pp. 45-60; A. Destrooper-Georgiades, in V. Krings ed., *La civilisation phénicienne et punique. Manuel de recherche*, Leiden *et al.* 1995, pp. 151-154.

55. Cf. above, nn. 4 and 29-40.
56. Cf. above, nn. 18 and 42.
57. Naster, *loc. cit.* (n. 54) 1958, pp. 510-511 (=*id.*, *op. cit.* [n. 59], p. 29); *id.*, *loc. cit.* (n. 59) 1967, pp. 3-4 (= *id.*, *op. cit.* [n. 54], pp. 178-179).
58. Mionnet, *op. cit.* (n. 53), pp. 640-644.
59. De Luynes, *op. cit.* (n. 53), pp. 69 and 82.
60. Cf. Elayi, *loc. cit.* (n. 34), pp. 13-17.
61. Brandis, *loc. cit.* (n. 53), pp. 376-377; Six, *loc. cit.* (n. 46) 1877, p. 189.

this hypothesis of attribution, taking into account the new discoveries and the progress of research. First of all, two coins (no. 667 and 668) bear two letters: Ṣ and probably R, which seem to represent the name of the city: ṢR, 'Tyre'. This reading is confirmed by significant and converging indications. Several hoards containing Tyrian coins were found in the territory of Tyre: hoards TXXVI from Khirbet el-Kerak, TXXXIII and XXXIV from the area of Akko, TXXXV from Tell Abu Hawam, TXXXVI from the north of Galilee, TXXXVII from Safed and TLII from the Moshav Dalton[62]. The frequent association of coins from the neighbouring mints of Tyre and Sidon in hoards has also to be pointed out.[63] In the same way, the main discoveries of isolated coins were made in sites probably belonging to Tyre: for example Akko, Tel Nahariya, Tell Keisan, Haifa, Miṣpe-Yamim, Meiron, Sasa and Gush Ḥalav.[64] The sites where bronze coins have been discovered are also in the same area (Akko, Tell Keisan, Kibboutz Ḥanita): it means that the issuing mint was very close since the bronze coins did not usually leave the territory of the minting city.[65] Moreover, the abbreviation used on the last Tyrian series corresponds to the name of a king of Tyre known from other sources.[66] Finally, the traditions of writing are more or less the same in the cities of Tyre and Sidon.[67] Therefore, we can today consider the attribution of this coinage to the city of Tyre as having been established.

Our corpus on the Tyrian coinage is firstly, and basically, a traditional numismatic study, as systematic and elaborate as possible. But it is at the same time a study in all the other fields of research enlightened by numismatic studies: in particular metrology, iconography, epigraphy, technology, political and economic history, history of religions, etc. This research is made easier by the fact that this corpus forms part of a group of carefully planned and self-explanatory studies, and that it benefits from the first corpus on Sidon. In return, the Tyrian corpus will complete the conclusions of the Sidonian corpus.

As usual, the introduction of a corpus has to inform readers of its genesis. The difficulties are inherent first in the nature of the corpus itself. Unlike a catalogue, a corpus must in principle be almost exhaustive, which is impossible in the case of Tyre for several reasons. As a matter of fact, for an important mint such as Tyre, the number of coins is very high. Moreover they are scattered in public and private collections all around the world, mainly because of

---

62. Cf. Elayi-Elayi, *Trésors*, pp. 139-147 (TXXVI), 163-168 (TXXXIII), 168-170 (TXXXIV), 171-185 (TXXXV), 185-186 (TXXXVI), 187-189 (TXXXVII) and 240 (TLII); for the hoard TXXXVI, cf. now *id., loc. cit.* (n. 40), p. 101.
63. Cf. *id., Trésors*, pp. 367-368.
64. *Ibid.*, fig. 251.
65. *Ibid.*, fig. 27 and pp. 365-367. A Tyrian coin was maybe too found at Beirut; cf. *supra*, n. 14.
66. See further, Chapters III and VII.
67. Cf. Elayi, *loc. cit.* (n. 36), pp. 31-32.

the Lebanese war of 1975-1985 and the state of insecurity of the whole area which aided salvage excavations and thefts of all kinds. It was necessary to find the collections containing Tyrian coins, then to be allowed to study them and then to embark on a lot of travelling. As far as the sale catalogues are concerned, and which we have ceased consulting since the beginning of 2006, their photographs are not always of good quality. Some catalogues, mainly the old ones, provide only a brief description, sometimes erroneous: in this case, we have only taken into account those descriptions that appear serious. Our corpus is not exhaustive because of the particular difficulties of this mint and for lack of resources as we shall see later on. But is there any exhaustive corpus, even if it has been made in the best possible conditions? What is important, in our opinion, is not to be exhaustive – which is always unrealistic – but to collect representative specimens of coins, an objective we think we have achieved.

The second difficulty encountered while preparing a corpus is the following: is it possible to collect only the coins found in regular excavations? This would be the ideal since the coins could be studied in their context and all of them would be genuine. Even if this method is more satisfactory from a scientific point of view, just one example will suffice in understanding that this is impossible. The 'Numismatics' bulletin of *Transeuphratène* covering the period 1989-2006 recorded only 34 Tyrian coins found in regular excavations, and 483 coins from the Antiquities market, among which 251 coins of hoards discovered in salvage excavations and 232 coins in sale catalogues.[68] It is obvious that the number of coins found in regular excavations is very restricted, and that most of them are known only by the antiquities market. Moreover, coins from excavations are often worn and damaged, whereas those put on sale have generally been selected among the well-preserved specimens. The reality dictates a method: all the coins have to be taken into account, including those found in salvage excavations and published in sale catalogues.

Another difficulty comes from the deficiency of excavations in Tyre in the Persian levels, from the looting and from the lack of interest on the part of the archaeologists for numismatics. The successive excavations in the area of Tyre did not take into account the discoveries of coins. Unlike Sidon, which was surrounded by vast gardens in the suburbs, the continual rebuilding of Tyre was responsible for the destruction of a lot of archaeological material. E. Renan, who was first to excavate there in 1861, wrote: 'One can call Tyre a city of ruins built out of ruins'.[69] He opened some trenches inside the island part of the city and excavated the areas of Tell el-Maʿshuq and 'Kabr-Hiram' near Qana, focusing mainly on Greek, Roman and Byzantine remains. In 1903, T.C. Macridy Bey found several Roman sarcophagi and sent them to Constantin-

---

68. Cf. Elayi, in *Trans* 1, 1989, pp. 155-159; 4, 1991, pp. 119-126; 10, 1995, pp. 151-177; 17, 1999, pp. 117-141; 25, 2003, pp. 63-87; 33, 2007, pp. 21-25.
69. E. Renan, *Mission de Phénicie*, Paris 1864, pp. 529-608, in particular 530.

ople.[70] In 1921, D. Le Lasseur resumed Renan's excavations in the city, unearthing a lot of Persian period material, with a very limited interest for the coins[71], and starting exploration of the harbour. This exploration was continued between 1924 and 1936 by A. Poidebard.[72] From 1947 onwards, Tyre was systematically excavated by M. Chéhab, exclusively interested in Greek, Roman and Byzantine levels,[73] that is not at all in Persian period Tyrian coinage. Later on, H. Frost, P.M. Bikai, I. Kawkabani, M.E. Aubet, C. Morhange, I. Noureddine, N. Carayon, M. El-Amouri and M. El-Hélou were neither interested in Persian levels nor coins.[74] The interesting preliminary report of I. Kawkabani on the Persian period temple of Jahr el-Bass excavated in 1972 is also very disappointing with respect to the coins since the excavator was only interested in the stamped written handles.[75]

The Lebanese civil war and the bad economic situation also explain why coins found by chance in the area of Tyre have often been neglected or sold. Ideology, at a local level, has also probably played a role in the treatment of the coins found in this area. As a matter of fact, for some people, the place of the Phoenicians in the ancient history of Lebanon has been minimised, and even obliterated. For other people, it has been exaggerated, and sometimes, Tyre is located in the 'Land of Bible'.[76] Beyond the local level, collectors seem in general to be much more interested in Greek coins than in Phoenician coins, Tyrian in particular. When they are interested in Tyrian coins, only the most beautiful series of shekels are concerned, not the divisions, especially if they are in bronze. The lack of gold coins reduces also the commercial value of the Tyrian coinage of the Persian period. If we consider the aesthetic point of view, the typology is relatively standardised with little variety of types, and with only a few series having been worked by skilful engravers, such as series II.1.1.1.a for example. As we shall see later, the set character of the typology was at least partly a decision of the mint authority.

70. T. Macridy Bey, 'Fouilles exécutées dans la région de Tyr en 1903', *Syr.* 3, 1922, pp. 131-133, in D. Le Lasseur, 'Mission archéologique à Tyr (avril-mai 1921)', *Syr.* 3, 1922, pp. 116-133.
71. Le Lasseur, *ibid.*, pp. 6, 21-22, 24-25 and fig. 14.
72. A. Poidebard, *Un grand port disparu: Tyr*, Paris 1939.
73. See, for example, M. Chéhab, 'Chronique', *BMB* 6, 1942-43, p. 86; 8, 1946-48, pp. 160-161; 9, 1949-50, p. 108; 12, 1955, pp. 47-48; 18, 1965, 112-113; 21, 1968, 10-84; *id.*, *Tyr à l'époque des croisades*, *BMB* 31-32, 1978-79; *Fouilles de Tyr*, *BMB* 33-36, 1983-86.
74. See, for example, H. Frost, 'Recent Observations on the Submerged Harbourworks at Tyre', *BMB* 24, 1971, pp. 103-111; P.M. Bikai, *The Pottery of Tyre*, Warminster 1978; C. Doumet and I. Kawkabani, 'Les tombes de Rachidieh: remarques sur les contacts internationaux et le commerce phénicien au VIIIe siècle av. J.-C.', in *ACFP* III/2, Tunis 1995, pp. 379-395; F. Denise and L. Nordiguian, *Une aventure archéologique: Antoine Poidebard photographe et aviateur*, Beirut 2004, pp. 310-317; M.E. Aubet, *The Phoenician cemetery of Tyre-Al Bass: excavations 1997-1999*, Beirut 2004; C. Morhange and M. Saghieh-Beydoun, *La Mobilité des Paysages Portuaires Antiques du Liban*, BAAL Hors-Série II, Beirut 2005, pp. 7-132.
75. I. Kawkabani, 'Les estampilles phéniciennes de Tyr', *AHL* 21, 2005, pp. 1-79.
76. Elayi-Sapin, *op. cit.* (n. 18), p. 179, n. 187.

The Coinage of Tyre in the Persian period 17

Another difficulty, a serious one, not specific to Tyrian coinage, is the problem of forgeries. As a matter of fact, the profession of coin forger dates back to the time when coinage was invented because it is lucrative and relatively easy to forge a coin. Ancient forged coins can provide a lot of varied information on the history of the period. As we have written elsewhere,[77] the large-scale development of modern forged coins is connected with the unprecedented rise of coin discoveries in the Middle East from the 1960s onwards, but mainly during the last two decades. We have identified this rise by studying the history of coin hoards.[78] This rise can be explained in particular by the more widespread avaibility and improved quality of metal detectors, by a confused political situation making their use possible on a large scale, by the absence of State control, by the economic difficulties which have encouraged hoard diggers, and by the numerous reconstructions of buildings destroyed in fighting, and digging deep foundations in line with modern construction techniques. The extensive development of this new market which has caused a marked increase in the prices of the coins has very likely encouraged, in its turn, the forgers. In addition to this favourable context, the unprecedented degree of technological development has placed at the forgers' disposal the most sophisticated forgery techniques, that make fakes more and more difficult to detect, even for the most experienced numismatists. If he is rigorous, a specialist should not adopt a position regarding an object he has not seen, only engaging his responsibility for an object that he has examined and for which he has requested the appropriate analyses. But for a corpus, this ethic can only be partially respected because it is not possible to examine all the coins collected, especially those from ancient collections now scattered and from sale catalogues, nor to request analyses for all dubious coins. As we have written elsewhere, it is no longer possible 'to suppress the problem by saying that we shall only consider in our research the coins found in regular excavations, the authenticity of which is in principle assured: in this way we would miss about 98% of the Phoenician numismatic documentation for example (75 coins from excavations, 3,040 registered coins from illicit excavations and 801 coins published in sale catalogues)'.[79] In this Tyrian corpus, only 14 coins out of 1,814 come from regular excavations![80] We have to be lucid and honest enough to say that there are possibly fakes among the coins collected in this corpus, as well as in any other corpus. We have tried to eliminate the fakes as much as possible and we have presented some of the most representative of them in Appendix II, in order to show what they can be like, at least as regards Tyrian coins. But we must say that not all fakes will have the same consequences for historical research. We have proposed distinguishing

---

77. *Ibid.*, pp. 179-180.
78. Elayi-Elayi, *Trésors*, pp. 14-16 and fig. 3.
79. Elayi-Sapin, *op. cit.* (n. 18), p. 180.
80. We take into account only the coins published, clearly identified as Tyrian and described.

two categories of fakes: 'the fakes which are copies of known models and the fakes which invent new monetary types'. The making of fakes of this second category can be very prejudicial since the forgers invent new inscriptions and types, frequently displaying remarkable research and quite a good knowledge of the context: they have led incautious scholars to rewrite history on the basis of false information. This category of fakes is relatively easy to detect for a good specialist and must be strongly criticised: it is rare in Phoenician numismatics and we try to criticise it when necessary.[81] The fakes of the first category are less easy to detect, mainly on photographs, but if they are not detected, they are less damaging for research since the forgery mainly concerns the weights and the number of coins and dies used for calculating the volume of production and the money supply in circulation. It would only create a problem if the proportion of fakes was such that the numerical conclusions were to be really changed: this is not the case today in Phoenician numismatics, Tyrian in particular.

In addition to the above-mentioned difficulties, important but, let us say, normal, we have encountered other difficulties, abnormal in a scientific milieu, that we are obliged to mention so as not be accused of shortcomings in our corpus. Elaborating a numismatic corpus costs a lot of money, because of the amount of travelling needed to study public and private collections all around the world, and because of the numerous photographs to be ordered or to be taken (when curators grant permission). Despite the scientific support of French numismatists, the CNRS only provided a very small part of the budget, in 1989-1990, 1985-1986, 2004 and 2006.[82] Otherwise we have taken advantage of some photographs and casts, generously offered by curators of museums and colleagues. But most of the funding for this corpus fell to us personally.

As is the custom when elaborating a corpus, we have written to all the curators of public numismatic collections who were likely to have Tyrian coins. We have obtained four kinds of answers: positive answers the senders of which we shall thank later on, negative answers concerning the Tyrian coins the senders of which we shall also thank, no answer (at the end of the 'Introduction' we give the list of the collections concerned and which are not to be considered responsible for any possible shortcomings), and one answer refusing access to the collection.[83] This last answer is all the more incomprehensible since it is the main collection of Phoenician coins, in this case Tyrian: the collection of the

---

81. Cf., for example, J. Elayi and A.G. Elayi, 'Remarques sur les deux premières monnaies en or de Sidon', *BSFN* 48, 1991, pp. 99-101; J. Elayi, 'Un dromadaire sur une galère aradienne!', *Annotazioni Numismatiche*', 2002, pp. 1090-1091.

82. Cf. Elayi-Elayi, *Monnayage de Sidon*, p. 22. This small aid was provided by C. Brixhe, A. Laronde, F. Baratte and J.-M. Durand.

83. We mention the persons with whom we have been in contact. If some of them have been omitted, it is because we could not read their signature. In some cases, we could not order photographs because we had no grant.

National Museum of Beirut, to which we were refused access without any explanation by the current General Director of Antiquities, F. Al-Hosseini, S. Hakimian being Director of the Museum.[84] When we were preparing our book on Phoenician weights published in 1997,[85] access to the Museum of Beirut's collection, the main collection of weights concerned, had been also refused to us by C. Asmar, previous General Director of Antiquities, and S. Hakimian. However, the explanation given then, namely that the collection was still not available because of the Lebanese war, was understandable. But the recent unjustified refusal of access to the collection of coins cannot be understood.

Once again, we have tried to overcome these difficulties as best as possible, something which would probably have dissuaded any other researcher from completing this book. We apologise to our readers for the failings caused by the concealment of documents and information, and the impossibility of checking the coins published, and for any imperfections in presentation due to the near absence of financial support. But we assume responsibility for all the other imperfections that may be present herein. Just as with other specialised books, this corpus of Tyrian coinage represents a stage in our research and our conclusions will probably be supplemented and supported by further precisions by the publication of the next two Phoenician corpora (of Arwad and Byblos), and by any new discoveries that may be made.

At the beginning of our book, after the Introduction, we present in Chapter I the corpus of Persian period Tyrian coins which constitutes the basis of the book and to which the other chapters frequently refer. We have tried to make it easier to consult by its presentation and by the directions for use given at the beginning of Chapter I. Chapter II is devoted to the numismatic part itself: justification of the classification adopted, elements of relative chronology and study of dies. Chapter III is related to the analysis of monetary inscriptions, graffiti and countermarks, from the point of view of their reading and meaning (political and socio-cultural) and of the writing. Chapter IV is concerned with iconography as regards the personal interpretation of the engravers as well as the interpretation of the minting authority's messages. Chapter V deals with the different manufacturing techniques, the functioning of the workshop and the ancient falsifications. The aim of Chapter VI is to study the metrology of the Tyrian coins, its relation with the metrology of weights and its place among the contemporary weights systems of the Near East. Finally, Chapter VII presents the historical conclusions about the city of Tyre and the Near East drawn from the study of the Tyrian coinage, the results obtained from the study of the Sidonian coinage in furnishing important reference points for absolute chronology, as well as from all other available sources. Correct dating of the coins is very

---

84. Letter in date of 29-1-2002.
85. Elayi-Elayi, *Poids phéniciens*, p. 14.

important for archaeologists who often base the dating of buildings on them.[86] Two Appendices are devoted to additional subjects, which have no place in the exposition of the book: Appendix I: Hoards containing Tyrian coins; Appendix II: False or dubious Tyrian coins.

ACKNOWLEDGMENTS

Our thanks go to the numerous persons who, all over the world and during the last 25 years, have helped us in the elaboration of this corpus, all in their different ways: our colleagues who gave us photographs and information, the curators of public collections who sent us casts and photographs, the private collectors and professional numismatists who allowed us to study their coins and provided us with information.

We are especially indebted to M. Amandry (Cabinet des Médailles, Bibliothèque de France, Paris), M. Kampmann (ex-Maison Platt, Paris), A. Lemaire (Ecole Pratique des Hautes Etudes, IVe section, Paris), G. Le Rider (Institut de France, Paris), P. Naster (Université Catholique, Louvain-la-Neuve), A. Spaer (Jerusalem) and N. Vismara (Civici Musei, Pavia).

Valuable assistance was also offered by: H. Bartlett Wells (Lexington), C. Brixhe (University of Nancy), E. Culasso Gastaldi (University of Padova), A. Davesne (CNRS, Paris), A. Destrooper-Georgiades (Ecole Française d'Athènes), D. Gedalje (La monnaie de Paris), H. Gitler (Israel Museum, Jerusalem), B. Gouyon (La monnaie de Paris), E. Gubel (Musées Royaux d'Art et d'Histoire, Bruxelles), S. Hurter (Leu Numismatik, Zurich), V. Klagsbald (Paris), F.L. Kovacs (San Mateo, Californie), B. Métivier (Muséum National d'Histoire Naturelle, Paris), L. Mildenberg (Leu Numismatik, Zurich), F. Petter (Muséum National d'Histoire Naturelle, Paris), F. Poplin (Muséum National d'Histoire Naturelle, Paris), M. Prieur (Paris), S. Qedar (Jerusalem), N. Shahaf (Haifa), M. Tranier (Muséum National d'Histoire Naturelle, Paris), H. Voegtli (Basel), J.-F. Voisin (Muséum National d'Histoire Naturelle, Paris) and C. Walker (British Museum, London).

Finally we thank the curators of public collections of museums and institutions without the help of whom our work could not have been completed:

Those who have answered positively and given us access to their collections:

— Beirut, Lebanon: American University of Beirut Museum (L. Badre)

---

86. Cf., for example, L. Porat and Z. Gal, "Nahariyya", *ESI* 19, 1999, p. 8*: "The numismatic finds ... provide a date for the building in the 4th century BCE".

The Coinage of Tyre in the Persian period

- Berlin, Germany: Staatliche Museum (H.-D. Schultz, S. Schultz and B. Weisser)
- Birmingham, United Kingdom: Museum and Art Gallery (D. Simons)
- Bologna, Italy: Museo Civico Archeologico (L. Canali)
- Boston, U.S.A.: Museum of Fine Arts (M.B. Comstock)
- Brussels, Belgium: Bibliothèque Royale Albert Ier, Cabinet des Médailles (J. Lallemand and F. de Callataÿ)
- Budapest, Hungary: Magyar Nemzeti Múzeum (M. Torbágyi)
- Cambridge, United Kingdom: Fitzwilliam Museum (T. Volk)
- Cambridge: Harvard University, Sackler Museum (C. Ratte)
- Copenhagen, Denmark: Nationalmuset (A. Kromann and J. Zahle)
- Haifa, Israel: National Maritime Museum (N. Kashtan)
- Istanbul, Turkey: Istanbul Arkeoloji Müzeleri Müdürlüğü, Kültür ve Turizm Bakanliği (N. Olcay and A. Pasinli)
- Jerusalem, Israel: Hebrew University, Institute of Archaeology (D.P. Barag)
- Jerusalem: Israel Museum, Department of Coins (Y. Meshorer and H. Gitler)
- Jerusalem: Rockefeller Museum (A. Sussmann)
- Kibboutz Hanita Museum, Israel (through A. Lemaire)
- Leiden, Netherlands: Rijksmuseum, Het Koninklijk Penningkabinet (J.P.A. van der Vin)
- London, United Kingdom: British Museum, Department of Coins (M.J. Price and U. Wartenberg)
- Madrid, Spain: Museo Arqueológico Nacional, Departamento de Numismática y Medallistica (C. Alfaro Asins)
- Munich, Germany: Staatliche Münzsammlung (D. Klose)
- Munster, Germany: Westfälisches Landesmuseum für Kunst und Kulturgeschichte (P. Ilisch)
- New York, U.S.A.: American Numismatic Society (C. Arnold-Biucchi and N. Waggoner)
- Nicosia, Cyprus: Archaeological Museum (I. Nicolaou)
- Oslo, Norway: Universitetet, Myntkabinettet (H. Ingvaldsen and J.H. Nordbø)
- Oxford, United Kingdom: Ashmolean Museum, Heberden Coin Room (C.J. Howgego)
- Paris, France: Bibliothèque de France, Cabinet des Médailles (M. Amandry, D. Gérin and H. Nicolet-Pierre)
- Princeton, U.S.A.: Princeton University Libraries (B.E. Levy)
- Rome, Italy: Bibliotheca Apostolica Vaticana, Medagliere Vaticano (G. Alteri)
- Stockholm, Sweden: Royal Coin Cabinet, National Museum of Monetary History (U. Westermark)
- Tel Aviv, Israel: Kadman Numismatic Museum (A. Kindler)
- Toronto, Canada: Royal Ontario Museum (A.H. Easson)

- Vienna: Kunsthistorisches Museum, Sammlung von Medaillen, Münzen und Geldzeichen (G. Dembski)
- Warsaw, Poland: Museum Narodowe (A. Krzyzanowska)

Those who have made negative answers because their collections did not contain Tyrian coins:
- Aachen, Germany: Museen der Stadt (E.G. Grimme)
- Aberdeen, United Kingdom: Anthropological Museum, Marischal College (C. Hunt)
- Amman, Jordan: Archaeological Museum (F. Zayadine)
- Amorbach, Germany: Fürstlich Leiningensche Verwaltung (D. Oswald)
- Ann Arbor, U.S.A.: University of Michigan, Kelsey Museum of Ancient and Mediaeval Archaeology (M. Cool Root)
- Antioch, Turkey: Archaeological Museum (through A. Davesne)
- Athens, Greece: Nomismatiko Mouseio (M. Oeconomides)
- Avellino, Italy: Museo Irpino (C. Grella)
- Baltimore, U.S.A.: Johns Hopkins University (S. Tripp)
- Barcelona, Spain: Gabinet Numismàtic de Catalunya (M. Campo)
- Basel, Switzerland: Historiches Museum (B. Schärli)
- Beirut, Lebanon: Museum of University Saint Joseph (L. Nordiguian)
- Berkeley, United Kingdom: Lowie Museum of Anthropology (T. Babineau and F.A. Norick)
- Bienne, Switzerland: Museum Schwab (M. Bourquin)
- Bonn, Germany: Akademisches Kunstmuseum der Universität (C. Grunwald)
- Bratislava, ex-Czechoslovakia: Slovenské Národné Múseum (E. Minarovičová)
- Brescia, Italy: Civici Musei d'arte e storia (B. Passamani)
- Brindisi, Italy: Museo Archeologico Provinciale (B. Sciarra)
- Bristol, United Kingdom: Museum and Art Gallery (J. Steward)
- Bryn Mawr, U.S.A.: Bryn Mawr College (L. Houghtalin)
- Cardiff, United Kingdom: National Museum of Wales (E.M. Besly and G.B. Boon)
- Cleveland, U.S.A.: Saint Louis Art Museum (S.M. Goldstein)
- Copenhagen, Denmark: Ny Carlsberg Glyptotek (F. Johansen)
- Detroit, U.S.A.: National Bank of Detroit (L.M. Stark)
- Dresden, Germany: Staatliche Kunstsammlungen, Münzkabinett (P. Arnold)
- Dublin, Eire: University of Dublin, Weingreen Museum of Biblical Antiquities (J.R. Bartlett)
- Dunedin, New Zealand: University of Otago (C. Ehrhardt)
- Frankfurt/Main, Germany: Historisches Museum (M. Caspers and G. Förschner)
- Frankfurt/Main: Johann Wolfgang Goethe-Universität (H. Schubert)
- Frankfurt/Main: Museum für Vor- und Frühgeschichte, Archäologisches Museum (D. Antzinger)

- Geneva, Switzerland: University of Geneva (R.F. Stucky)
- Gent, Belgium: Rijksuniversiteit, Centrale Bibliotheek (G. Milis-Proost)
- Gotha, Germany: Museen der Stadt Gotha, Schlossmuseum, Münzkabinett (W. Steguweit and U. Wallenstein)
- Graz, Austria: Landes-Museum Joanneum Graz (O. Burböck)
- Haifa, Israel: Dagon Museum (R. Hecht)
- Hanover, Germany: Kestner-Museum (F. Berger)
- Helsinki, Finland: Coin Cabinet, Museovirasto (T. Talvio)
- Karlsruhe, Germany: Badisches Landesmuseum (P.-H. Martin)
- Kassel, Germany: Staatliche Kunstsammlungen (P. Geroki)
- Klagenfurt, Germany: Landesmuseum für Kärnten (F. Glazer)
- Koblenz, Germany: Mittlerhein-Museum
- Köln, Germany: Römisch-Germanisches Museum (F. Naumann)
- Krakow, Poland: Muzeum Naradowe, Gabinet Numizmatyczny (J. Bezwinska and J. Bodzek)
- Lausanne, Switzerland: Cabinet des Médailles du canton de Vaud (A. Geiser)
- Leipzig, Germany: Karl-Marx-Universität Universitätsbibliothek (R. Jäger)
- Liege, Belgium: Musée Curtius (L. Engen)
- Lisbon, Portugal: Museum of the Foundation Calouste Gulbenkian (M.C. Hipolito)
- Liverpool, United Kingdom: Liverpool Museum (C. Longworth and A.R. Millard)
- Lund, Sweden: Lunds Universitets, Historika Museum
- Luxembourg: Musée d'Etat, Cabinet des Médailles (R. Weiller)
- Mainz, Germany: Städtisches Münzkabinett (Dr. Falck)
- Manchester, United Kingdom: University, Manchester Museum (K. Sugden)
- Milan, Italy: Castello Sforzesco, Gabinetto Numismatico (R. Martini)
- Naples, Italy: Medagliere del Museo Nazionale (E. Pozzi)
- Newcastle, United Kingdom: University of Newcastle upon Tyne (D.A. Spawforth)
- North Terrace, Australia: Art Gallery of South Australia (B. Fargher)
- Padua, Italy: Museo Bottacin (A. Saccocci)
- Palermo, Italy: Museo Archeologico Regionale (C.A. Di Stefano)
- Paris: Institut Catholique, Musée Bible et Terre Sainte (J. Briend)
- Perpignan, France: Musée de Numismatique J. Puig (J. Joussemet)
- Philadelphia, U.S.A.: University Museum of Archaeology/Anthropology (J.B. Klein and D.G. Romano)
- Prague, ex-Czechoslovakia: Narodni Muzeum (J. Haskova and K. Kurz)
- Providence, U.S.A.: Brown University, Center for Old World Archaeology and Art (R. Holloway)
- Ravenna, Italy: Museo Nazionale, Medagliere (F. Zurli)
- Rome, Italy: Medagliere dei Musei Capitolini (L. Travaini)
- Rome: Museo di Villa Giulia (P. Pelagatti)

- Rome: Museo Nazionale Romano (S. Balbi de Caro)
- Saint-Louis, U.S.A.: Cleveland Museum of Art (A.P. Kozloff)
- Sao Paulo, Brazil: Museu de Arqueologia e Etnologia da Universidade de Sao Paulo (M.B. Borba Florenzano)
- Sassari, Italy: Medagliere del Museo Nazionale G.A. Sanna (F. Lo Schiavo)
- Seville, Spain: Museo de l'Ayuntamiento
- Sofia, Bulgaria: Archaeological Institut (K. Dimitrov)
- Szczecin, Poland: Muzeum Naradowe (W. Filipowiak)
- Turin, Italy: Museo Civico (A.S. Fava and S. Pennestri)
- Vienna, Austria: Universität Wien, Institut für Numismatik (W. Szaivert)
- Wageningen, Netherlands: Gelderse Archaelogische Stichting
- Washington, U.S.A.: Smithsonian Institution, National Museum of History and Technology, Numismatic Department (D.G. Mitten and E. Clain-Stefanelli)
- Winterthur, Switzerland: Münzkabinett der Stadt Winterthur (C. Zindel)
- York, United Kingdom: Yorkshire Museum (M. Mays)
- Zagreb, ex-Yugoslavia: Arkheološki Muzej (I. Mirnik)
- Zurich, Switzerland: Musée National Suisse (H.-U. Geiger)

On the contrary, we have not received any answer from the following museums and institutions:
- Alexandria, Egypt: Greek-Roman Museum, Department of Coins and Medals
- Charleville-Mézières, France: Musée de l'Ardenne
- Damascus, Syria: National Archaeological Museum
- Geneva, Switzerland: Art Museum, Department of Coins
- Stuttgart, Germany: Württembergisches Landesmuseum
- Tehran, Iran: National Museum
- Valetta, Malta: Archaeological Museum

And we have not been allowed to consult the following collection:
- Beirut: National Museum

CHAPTER I

CATALOGUE OF THE TYRIAN COINS

The elaboration of a catalogue of corpora has to follow special rules and we refer to good examples, published more or less recently, in the parallel field of archaic and classical Greek coinages.[1] These catalogues certainly provide precious information on the procedure to be followed, but every coinage has its own specificity and cannot enter into a pre-established mould. In our opinion, the catalogue must take into account all the particular aspects of the coinage studied. In this corpus (as in our previous corpus of the Sidonian coinage)[2], we have decided to include all the Tyrian pre-Alexandrine coinage, both the large denominations as well as the small ones including the minute coins, incorporating both silver and bronze coins (there were no Tyrian gold coins in the Persian period). The study of dies was carried out, not only for large denominations but as far as possible on all kinds of small denominations. We have identified the dies only on relatively well-preserved coins or when they could be spotted by a defect or a characteristic detail. However, in spite of this caution, everybody knows that there is always an element of subjectivity in any study of dies. We have taken into consideration in the catalogue all the coins brought to our knowledge whether our information is complete or not, whether the coins are illustrated or not and whatever their state of preservation may be. Far from being merely an attractive catalogue of the well-preserved large denominations, our catalogue also includes all the coins, even the minute and poorly preserved ones. However, the coins which seemed to us to be false or dubious have been excluded from the catalogue and some of them have been presented in Appendix II.

---

1. For example G. Le Rider, *Antioche de Syrie sous les Séleucides, Corpus des monnaies d'or et d'argent, I. De Séleucos I à Antiochos V c. 300-161*, Paris 1999; id., *Le monnayage d'argent et d'or de Philippe II*, Paris 1977; R.T. Williams, *The Silver Coinage of Velia*, London 1992; U. Westermark and K. Jenkins, *The Coinage of Gela*, Berlin 1970.
2. Elayi-Elayi, *Monnayage de Sidon*.

Our aim was to present a catalogue of the Tyrian coinage, being at the same time as complete and as clear as possible for the users of this corpus. Therefore we have neither classified the coins according to the metal composition[3] nor by separating large and small denominations. We have tried to present a chronological classification according to a relative chronology established from the die links, the overstrikings, and the evolution of the defects on the dies and from any other source of information. In order to facilitate the use of this corpus, we already indicate our classification proposals according to an absolute chronology that we shall justify in Chapter VII. The catalogue is presented first by groups based on chronological order, for example 'Group I: Dolphin (third quarter of the 5th century)', then by decreasing denominations, for example 'I.1.1. Shekels AR', 'I.1.2. Quarters of shekel AR', 'I.1.3. Sixteenths of shekel AR'. The denominations are designated in a conventional and approximate way, for example 'I.1.4. Halves of sixteenth of shekel AR'. But we refer to Chapter VI for all the necessary metrological details.

Each catalogue number represents a coin: this numbering by coin, instead of the frequently used numbering by die couple,[4] seemed to us easier for referring to it in the text and for listing the coins for which the dies study was impossible. The number of the coin is followed by the die couple (for example 'O3-R8'), then by the weight, the diameter and the die axis when they are known. As regards the dies study, each series has its own numbering for obverse and reverse dies. The re-cut dies are not given a new number but bear the mention ' (R7 and R7'). However, it is difficult to identify re-cuttings due to the poor state of preservation of the coins in general.[5] The weight can be slightly different depending on the available source of information.[6] As far as the coins from the BNF, Cabinet des Médailles, of Paris are concerned, the weights indicated in the catalogue are those that we have checked personally. For the coins published in several sale catalogues, we have selected the most recent weight, considering that in principle the weighing should become more precise because of the improvement in scales. We have kept only two figures after the comma, rounding up to the nearest figure; the few mentions still in grains have been converted into grams. The diameter mentioned in the catalogue is the maximum diameter indicated in the publications or that we have measured ourselves directly on the coins or on the casts. These indications on the die couple, weight,

---

3. See the remarks of L. Mildenberg, *The Coinage of the Bar Kokhba War*, Aaran *et al.* 1984, pp. 59, n. 134 and 119, n. 314 (with bibl.).

4. Cf., for example, G. Le Rider who has used the two processes for two different coinages: *op. cit.* (n. 1) 1977 and *op. cit.* (n. 1) 1999.

5. Die links are proposed in some publications: we have kept only those which seemed to be correct.

6. In a corpus, everybody knows that it is impossible to examine many coins and that there is no other way than to accept the weights mentioned, on the assumption that the coins have been weighed with precision.

diameter and die axis are followed by a description of the new obverse and reverse dies, with their possible defects, the traces of overstriking, the alterations and the possible technical characteristics.

Afterwards various items of information are indicated concerning the bibliography, the present location and the provenance of the coin. The location in a public collection mentions first the town, then the institution, the inventory number or the number of reference to a catalogue, and the present and/or previous collection in which the coin is/was, for example: 'New York, ANS, no. N9 (ex Newell coll.)'. The list of public and private collections is given at the end of the book.[7] The name of the collector is mentioned if permission has been given or otherwise anonymous; the place of the collection is indicated wherever possible. Sometimes we mention only 'Antiquities market' whith the name of the country or town and the date of examination of the coin if possible. The bibliographical references to the catalogues of collections or to the main studies are abbreviated in order to save space and the list of abbreviations is given at the end of the book. The sale catalogues are mentioned as succinctly as possible with the name of the expert or the company, the place of the sale, the number and the date of the sale, and the number of the coin in the sale catalogue, for example 'Noble, Sydney, 62, 17-18/11/1999, no. 1932'. A list of the sale catalogues is given at the end of the book. We have not considered it useful to distinguish between the different kinds of sale (lists, catalogues, auction sales, bid sales, etc.) because the number and date of the sale are enough to identify it. When a coin has been sold several times, we have first mentioned its last known sale, then the successive sales in reverse chronological order. Likewise the successive transfers of a coin through various collections have been mentioned. When we have seen a coin in the stock of a company, we mention the name of the company and the place, together with the date of our visit. The place of discovery is also indicated for excavation coins, the place where the hoard was purchased when the coins belonged to a hoard, for example: 'Akko excavations', 'bought in Jerusalem' or 'Jordan hoard TLIII' following the number of our corpus for Phoenician hoards.[8] A list of hoards containing Tyrian coins is given at the end of the present book (Appendix I).

The order of the couples of dies depends on the sequences determined by the internal chronology of the coin production when it is detectable. When it is not, the couples of dies have been presented by groups, from the largest onwards. When the obverse or/and reverse dies of a coin have not been identified, it is classified at the end of the series. Group III (Unclassified series) encompasses all the series which could not be classified chronologically in the present state of documentation. The last group (4) is reserved for some coins for which

---

7. We have not considered it useful to distinguish between ancient and present collections.
8. Elayi-Elayi, *Trésors*.

an attribution to the mint of Tyre has sometimes been proposed but remains questionable for the moment.

Concerning the illustrations of the coins, an asterisk placed after an obverse or reverse die ('O1*-R1*') means that the die is illustrated in the plates. We have tried to illustrate, as far as possible, all the obverse and reverse dies in each different series by selecting the best illustrations. But their quality is very unequal because of their various origins: photographs of the coins, of the casts, of the photographs of sale catalogues, often of poor quality. Since most of the photographs were taken or obtained around twenty years ago, they have not benefited from current photographic technologies. When the scale or diameter was not indicated in sale catalogues, we have been obliged to select a supposed approximate scale. Some coins, in particular the small divisions, have been illustrated by an enlarged photograph with the mention of the scale (for example '1x3'). As we have said, our aim in this corpus was not to select only the large and beautiful coins but to take into account all the Tyrian coins. Thus in our opinion, the scientific advantages greatly outweigh the aesthetical disadvantages.

1. Group I: Dolphin (third quarter of the 5th century)

I.1. Without incuse impression on the reverse (first part of the third quarter of the 5th century)

I.1.1. Shekels AR

1.	O1* - R1* 13.61g 20mm 11h	O: winged dolphin, to right, over triple line of waves; ŠL̥[above; border of dots partly off the flan. R: owl standing to right, head facing; over its left shoulder, crook and flail; shallow incuse impression. Paris, BNF, no. 1982; Babelon, *Perses*, no. 1982 and pl. XXXVI, 4; *id.*, *Traité*, no. 985; Elayi, *NAC* 21, 1992, p. 38, no. 1.
2.	O2* - R1 13.64g 20mm	Same as 1. O: ŠLŠN above dolphin; border of dots partly off the flan. Beirut, NM, no. 1315; Chéhab, *Monnaies*, no. 1315 and pl. LIII, 2; Elayi, *NAC* 21, 1992, p. 38, no. 2.
3.	O3 - R2* 13.86g 20mm 9h	Same as 1. O: ŠL̥[above dolphin. R: owl slightly decentred top-wards. Oxford, AM, no. 98; Kraay, *Greek Coins*, pl. 61, no. 1047; Kraay-Moorey, *RN* 10, 1968, p. 191 and pl. XXI; Elayi, *NAC* 21, 1992, p. 38, no. 3 (Jordan

4. O3* - R3* hoard TLIII).
   13.59g 19mm Same as 1. Somewhat irregular and thick flan.
   6h O: slightly worn; ŠLŠN̊ above dolphin; border off the flan.
   New York, ANS, no. N9; Elayi, *NAC* 21, 1992, pp. 38 and 46, no. 5 (ex Newell coll.).
5. O3 - R4* Same as 1. Slightly worn.
   13.72g 19mm O: ŠL̊[above dolphin.
   11h Copenhagen, NatMus, no. 295; *SNG Copenhagen*, no. 295 and pl. 8; Naville, Geneva, 7, 23-24/6/1924, no. 1741 (ex Bément coll. = ex Weber coll.); Elayi, *NAC* 21, 1992, pp. 38 and 46, no. 4.
6. O4* - R4 Same as 1.
   13.16g 21mm O: slightly worn. Š[above dolphin, partly off the flan; no border visible.
   Rouvier, *JIAN* 6, 1903, p. 269, no. 1775 and pl. XVIII, 2; Elayi, *NAC* 21, 1992, p. 38, no. 6.
7. O5* - R5* Same as 1.
   13.64g O: ŠLŠN̊ above dolphin; border of dots partly off the flan.
   R: slightly decentred to left.
   Baldwin, London, 34, 13/10/2003, no. 535 = Classical Numismatic Group, Lancaster-London, 42, 29-30/5/1997, no. 586.

I.1.2. Quarters of shekel AR

8. O1* - R1* O: winged dolphin, to right, over double line of waves; MḤ ṢGR̊ above; border of dots.
   3.17g 13mm
   9h R: owl standing to right, head facing; over its left shoulder, crook and flail; shallow incuse impression.
   Paris, BNF, no. 111; Elayi-Lemaire, *NAC* 19, 1990, pp. 100-101 and 113, no. 3 (ex De Vogüé coll.).
9. O2* - R1 Same as 8.
   3.35g 13mm O: MḤ ṢG̊R̊ above dolphin; border of dots partly off the flan.
   Kindler, *ErIs* 8, 1967, p. 323, no. 2, and pl. 46 (who reads MHS SWR); Elayi-Lemaire, *NAC* 19, 1990, pp. 100 and 113, no. 2.
10. O3* - R2* Same as 8. Chisel-cut.
    3.30g 12mm O: MḤ ṢGR above dolphin; border of dots partly off the flan.
    2h New York, ANS, no. 1977.158, 755; Elayi-Elayi, *BCEN* 27, 1990, pp. 69 and 72, no. 1.

11. O4* - R2   Same as 8.
     2.91g   O: *JḤ ṢGR* above dolphin; border of dots partly off
                           the flan.
                           R: rather worn.
                           Münzen und Medaillen, Basel, 484, January 1986,
                           no. 21.
12. O5* - R3*   Same as 8.
     3.22g 14mm   O: *M ḤṢGR̊* above dolphin; border of dots partly
                           off the flan.
                           London, BM, no. 1913-7-14 3; Elayi-Lemaire, *NAC*
                           19, 1990, pp. 101 and 113, no. 4; Elayi-Elayi,
                           Trésors, p. 267, no. 2; Spink, London, 14/7/1913 =
                           Hirsch, Munich, 32, 14-15/11/1912, no. 587 (South
                           Turkey hoard TLXII).
13. O6* - R4*   Same as 8.
     3.35g 14mm   O: *JḤ̊ṢGR̊* above dolphin; border of dots partly off
     4h   the flan.
                           Boston, MFA, no. 66.317; Elayi-Lemaire, *NAC* 19,
                           1990, pp. 100 and 113, no. 1.
14. O? - R?   Same as 8. Rather worn and plated.
     2.50g 13mm   O: *JṢ̊GR̊* above dolphin; border of dots partly off
                           the flan.
                           Elayi-Lemaire, *NAC* 19, 1990, pp. 101 and 113, no.
                           5; Rouvier, *JIAN* 6, 1903, p. 270, no. 1779 and pl.
                           XVIII, 4 (ex Rouvier coll.).

I.1.3. Sixteenths of shekel AR

15. O1* - R1*   O: winged dolphin, to right, over one line of waves;
     0.56g 8mm   *MR̊* above dolphin; border of dots.
     1h   R: owl standing to right, head facing; over its left
                           shoulder, crook and flail; shallow incuse impression.
                           New York, ANS, no. N6; Elayi-Elayi, *BCEN* 27,
                           1990, pp. 70 and 72, no. 3 (ex Newell coll.).
16. O2* - R2*   Same as 15.
     0.41g 8mm   O: *MR̊* above dolphin; border of dots partly off the
                           flan.
                           Private coll.; Elayi-Lemaire, *NAC* 19, 1990, pp. and
                           101 and 113, no. 6.
17. O3* - R3*   Same as 15.
     0.35g 8mm   O: inscription off the flan; border of dots partly off
     3h   the flan.
                           Berlin, SM, no. 8 (ex Prokesch-Osten coll.).
18. O4* - R?   Same as 15. Slightly worn.

		0.52g 8mm	O: MR̊ above dolphin.
		3h	Berlin, SM, no. 9 (ex Fox coll.).
19.	O? - R4*		Same as 15. Slightly worn.
		0.58g 8mm	O: MR̊ above dolphin; border of dots partly off the flan.
		2h	New York, ANS, no. 52.142; Elayi-Elayi, *BCEN* 27, 1990, pp. 70-72 and 72, no. 2 (ex Gunther coll.).

I.1.4. Halves of sixteenth of shekel AR

20.	O1* - R1*	O: dolphin, to right, over one line of waves; inscription off the flan; border of dots partly off the flan.
	0.16g 6mm	R: rosette with eight petals; concave type.
		Paris, BNF, no. 1965/829-29; Elayi-Elayi, *AN* 1, 1991, pp. 39-40, no. 6 (ex Seyrig coll.).
21.	O2* - R2*	Same as 20.
	0.19g 7mm	O: square border of dots; two (?) illegible letters.
		London, BM, no. 1979.6-10.8; Elayi-Elayi, *AN* 1, 1991, pp. 39-40, no. 5.
22.	O3* - R3*	Same as 20.
	0.21g 6mm	O: dolphin and border of dots partly off the flan.
		Paris, BNF, no. 1965/829-30; Elayi-Elayi, *AN* 1, 1991, pp. 39-40, no. 4 (ex Seyrig coll.).
23.	O? - R4*	Same as 20. Slightly worn.
	0.28g	O: border of dots partly off the flan.
		New York, ANS, no. N8; Elayi-Elayi, *AN* 1, 1991, pp. 39-40, no. 3 (ex Newell coll.).
24.	O? - R?	Same as 20. Rather worn.
	0.30g	Rouvier, *JIAN* 6, 1903, p. 270, no. 1783 and pl. XVIII, 7; Elayi-Elayi, *AN* 1, 1991, pp. 39-40, no. 1.
25.	O? - R?	Same as 20. Rather worn.
	0.28g	O: border of dots partly off the flan; two (?) illegible letters.
		New York, ANS, no. N7; Elayi-Elayi, *AN* 1, 1991, pp. 39-40, no. 2 (ex Newell coll.).

I.1.5. Tenths of sixteenth of shekel AR

26.	O1* - R1*	O: dolphin, to right, over one line of waves; Š above dolphin; border of dots partly off the flan.
	0.06g 4mm	R: owl standing to right, head facing; over its left shoulder, crook and flail; shallow incuse impression.
	11h	Paris, BNF, no. 1965/829-27; Elayi-Lemaire, *NAC* 19, 1990, pp. 101 and 113, no. 7 (ex Seyrig coll.). Found on the beach of Byblos.

27.	O? - R2* 0.06g 4mm 11h	Same as 26. Slightly worn. O: letter off the flan. New York, ANS, no. N28; Elayi-Elayi, *BCEN* 27, 1990, pp. 70 and 72, no. 4 (ex Newell coll.).
28.	O? - R? 0.07g 4mm	Same as 26. Rather worn. O: letter off the flan. Paris, BNF, no. 1987/469.

I.2. With incuse impression on the reverse (last part of the third quarter of the 5th century)

I.2.1. Shekels AR

29.	O1 - R1* 13.27g 20mm 4h	O: dolphin, to right, over triple line of waves; below, shell; ŠL[above dolphin; cable border partly off the flan. R: owl standing to right, head facing; over its left shoulder, crook and flail; incuse impression surrounding type; all in shallow incuse square. Berlin, SM, no. 10179; Elayi, *NAC* 21, 1992, p. 39, no. 19.
30.	O1 - R2 13.42g 6h	Same as 29. O: ŠL[above dolphin. Glendining, London, 10/12/1986, no. 339.
31.	O1* - R3* 13.68g	Same as 29. Small cracks on the edge. O: ŠL[above dolphin; cable border partly off the flan. Private coll.; Elayi, *NAC* 21, 1992, pp. 39 and 46, no. 17.
32.	O1 - R4* 13.71g 12h	Same as 29. Small cracks on the edge. O: inscription off the flan. New York, ANS, no. N1; Elayi, *NAC* 21, 1992, pp. 39 and 46, no. 18 (ex Newell coll.).
33.	O2 - R4 13.47g	Same as 29. Slightly worn. O: ŠLŠ[over dolphin; cable border partly off the flan. Hirsch, Munich, 161, 22-24/2/1989, no. 347 = 158, 4-6/5/1988, no. 156.
34.	O2* - R4 12.48g	Same as 29. Slightly worn. O: ŠLŠN over dolphin. Malter, Encino, 27, 10/6/1984, no. 28.
35.	O3* - R2* 13.52g 6h	Same as 29. Small cracks on the edge. O: JN over dolphin; cable border partly off the flan. Sotheby's, New York, 19-20/6/1991, no. 473 =

		NFA, Beverly Hills, 2, 25-26/3/1976, no. 298.
36.	O3 - R4	Same as 29. Flan slightly irregular.
	13.63g 23mm	O: ŠL̊[over dolphin; cable border partly off the flan.
	12h	
		Beirut, AUB Museum, no. 1259A; Baramki, *Coins AUB*, p. 220, no. 1 and pl. XXVII, 1; Elayi, *NAC* 21, 1992, p. 39, no. 20.
37.	O3 - R4	Same as 29. Flan slightly irregular.
	13.57g	O: ŠLŠ[over dolphin; cable border partly off the flan.
		Peus, Frankfurt/Main, 321, 27-29/4-2/5/1988, no. 235.
38.	O3 - R5*	Same as 29.
	13.44g	O: ŠLŠN̊ over dolphin; cable border partly off the flan.
	3h	
		Oxford, AM, no. 85; Elayi, *NAC* 21, 1992, pp. 39 and 47, no. 23.
39.	O3 - R6*	Same as 29.
	12.58g	O: ŠLŠ̊N̊ over dolphin; cable border partly off the flan.
	12h	
		Cambridge, FM, no. 6081; *SNG Cambridge*, no. 6081; Glendining, London, 12, 21-23/2/1961, no. 2674; Elayi, *NAC* 21, 1992, p. 39, no. 24 (ex Lockett coll.).
40.	O3 - R7*	Same as 29. Slightly worn.
	13.68g	O: ŠLŠ̊N̊ over dolphin; cable border partly off the flan.
		Numismatica Ars Classica, Zurich, E, 4/4/1995, no. 2409.
41.	O3 - R8*	Same as 29. Small cracks on the edge.
	13.58g	O:]L̊Š̊N̊ over dolphin.
	3h	
		New York, ANS, no. N3; Elayi, *NAC* 21, 1992, pp. 39 and 46, no. 21 (ex Newell coll.).
42.	O4* - R8	Same as 29. Small cracks on the edge.
	13.52g	O: ŠLŠ̊[over dolphin; cable border partly off the flan.
		Künker, Osnabrück, 94, 27-28/9/2004, no. 1458 = Monetarium, Schweizerische Kreditanstalt, Zurich, 31, April 1980, no. 56 = NFA, Beverly Hills, 2, Jan.-Feb. 1979, no. 40 = Malloy, New York, 13, 8/12/1978, no. 96.
43.	O4 - R9*	Same as 29. Flan partly irregular.
	12.67g	O: inscription almost obliterated; cable border partly

		off the flan.
		Monetarium, Schweizerische Kreditanstalt, Zurich, Spring 1995, no. 95.
44.	O4 - R10	Same as 29. Slightly worn.
	13.41g	O: ŠLŠ[above dolphin; cable border partly off the flan.
		Paris, BNF, no. 283 (ex Seyrig coll.).
45.	O5* - R3	Same as 29.
	13.60g 22mm	O: ŠLŠN above dolphin; cable border partly off the flan.
	3h	
		Rome, VM, no. 199b.
46.	O5 - R11*	Same as 29.
	13.30g 21mm	O: Š[above dolphin; dolphin and cable border partly off the flan.
	12h	
		Rome, VM, no. 199c.
47.	O6 - R10*	Same as 29. Small cracks on the edge.
	12.95g	O: ŠLŠN above dolphin.
	9h	Leu, Zurich, 83, 6-7/5/2002, no. 398 = Berk, Chicago, 84, 19/1/1995, no. 324.
48.	O6 - R11	Same as 29.
	13.30g 26mm	O: inscription and cable border partly off the flan.
	12h	NFA, Beverly Hills, 2/12/1985, no. 270 = Hess-Leu, Lucerne-Zurich, 31, 6-7/12/1966, no. 528 = Hirsch, Munich, 34, 5/5/1914, no. 507; Elayi, *NAC* 21, 1992, pp. 40 and 47, no. 31 (ex German private coll.).
49.	O6 - R12*	Same as 29.
	13.58g 24mm	O: ŠLŠ[above dolphin; cable border partly off the flan.
	5h	
		Paris, BNF, no. 1980; Babelon, *Perses*, no. 1980; id., *Traité*, no. 981; Elayi, *NAC* 21, 1992, p. 40, no. 30.
50.	O6* - R13*	Same as 29.
	13.53g 24mm	O: ŠL[above dolphin; cable border partly off the flan.
	5h	
		Stockholm, RCC, no. 102; Münzen und Medaillen, Basel, 19, 5-6/6/1959, no. 556; Kraay-Hirmer, *Greek Coins*, no. 681; W. Schwabacher, *Griechische Münzkunst*, Mainz 1974, no. 32; Elayi, *NAC* 21, 1992, pp. 40 and 47, no. 32 (ex King Gustaf VI Adolf coll. no. 102 = ex Swiss private coll.).
51.	O7* - R13	Same as 29.
	13.63g	O: inscription obliterated; cable border partly off the flan.

The Coinage of Tyre in the Persian period

		R: deep chisel-cut.
		Numismatica Ars Classica, New York, Triton II, 1-2/12/1998, no. 501.
52.	O8 - R14*	Same as 29. Overstruck. Slightly worn.
	13.54g	O: ŠLŠN above dolphin. Relatively small die.
		Baldwin, London, 33, 7/12/2000, no. 166.
53.	O8* - R15*	Same as 29. Small cracks on the edge and chisel-cut.
	13.57g	O: ŠLŠN above dolphin; cable border partly off the
	2h	flan.
		New York, ANS, no. N2; Naville, Geneva, 7, 23-24/6/1924, no. 1740; Elayi, *NAC* 21, 1992, p. 39, no. 16 (ex Newell coll. = ex Bément coll. = ex Mathey coll.).
54.	O8 - R15	Same as 29. Irregular flan.
	13.56g	O: inscription almost obliterated; cable border partly off the flan.
		Stack's, New York, Autumn 1991, no. 83.
55.	O9 - R15	Same as 29. Chisel-cut.
	13.13g 22mm	O: Š[above dolphin.
	9h	Berlin, SM, no. 2; Elayi, *NAC* 21, 1992, p. 39, no. 14 (ex Imhoof-Blumer coll.).
56.	O9* - R16*	Same as 29. Small cracks on the edge.
	13.22g 20mm	O: inscription almost obliterated; cable border partly
	3h	off the flan.
		London, BM, no. 15114; *BMC Phoenicia*, p. 227, no. 2 and pl. XXVIII, 10; Elayi, *NAC* 21, 1992, pp. 39 and 46, no. 15.
57.	O10* - R16	Same as 29. Small cracks on the edge.
	13.62g 23mm	O: ŠLŠN above dolphin; cable border partly off the
	4h	flan.
		Paris, BNF, no. 78; Kraay-Moorey, *RN* 10, 1968, p. 218 and pl. XXVII, 78; Elayi-Elayi, *JNG* 37-38, 1987-88, pl. 3, 3; *Trésors*, p. 243, no. 15; Elayi, *NAC* 21, 1992, p. 39, no. 25 (Massyaf hoard TLIV).
58.	O10 - R17	Same as 29.
	13.38g	O: ŠLŠN above dolphin; cable border partly off the flan.
		Freeman & Sear, New York, Triton V, 15-16/1/2002, no. 1512 = Tradart, New York, 1, 13/12/1982, no. 152 = NFA, Encino, 7, 6/12/1979, no. 302 = Glendining, London, 11/12/1974, no. 122; Elayi, *NAC* 21, 1992, pp. 39 and 47, no. 26.
59.	O10 - R18*	Same as 29. Slightly worn.
	13.35g 21mm	O: ŠLŠN above dolphin; cable border partly off the

		flan. Private coll.; Elayi, *NAC* 21, 1992, pp. 39 and 47, no. 27.
60.	O11* - R17* 13.46g 24mm 7h	Same as 29. Irregular flan. O: ŠLŠN above dolphin; cable border partly off the flan. R: deep chisel-cut. Berk, Chicago, 137, 31/3/2004, no. 203 = Myers, Ariadne Galleries, New York, 9/12/1981, no. 296 = Superior Stamp and Coin, Beverly Hills, 17-23/6/1974, no. 321 = Leu, Lucerne, 27/3/1956, no. 326; *Catalogue Jameson*, no. 1775; *Catalogue Rosen*, no. 756; Elayi, *NAC* 21, 1992, pp. 39-40 and 47, no. 28 (ex Rosen coll. = ex Jameson coll.).
61.	O11 - R19	Same as 29. Slightly worn. O: ŠL̊[above dolphin; cable border partly off the flan. Glendining, London, 5/3/1970, no. 124 (reverse photograph upside down); Elayi, *NAC* 21, 1992, p. 40, no. 29.
62.	O12* - R19* 13.64g 22mm	Same as 29. Slightly worn. O: ŠL[above dolphin; dot above its head; shell and cable border partly off the flan. Classical Numismatic Group, Lancaster-London, 53, 15/3/2000, no. 658.
63.	O13 - R20* 13.26g 24mm 7h	Same as 29. Slightly worn. O: inscription obliterated; cable border partly off the flan. Berlin, SM, no. 1.13; Elayi, *NAC* 21, 1992, p. 38, no. 8.
64.	O13 - R21* 13.69g 22mm	Same as 29. Slightly worn. O: ŠL[above dolphin; cable border partly off the flan. Beirut, NM, no. 2709; Chéhab, *Monnaies*, no. 2709 and pl. LIII, 1 (wrong weight); Elayi, *NAC* 21, 1992, p. 39, no. 12 ; Elayi-Elayi, *Trésors*, p. 92, no. 439 (3rd Byblos hoard).
65.	O13 - R22* 9.62g 20mm 12h	Same as 29. Damaged. O: ŠLŠ[above dolphin; shell and cable border partly off the flan. Paris, BNF, no. 79; Kray-Moorey, *RN* 10, 1968, p. 218, no. 79; Elayi-Elayi, *Trésors*, p. 243, no. 16; Elayi, *NAC* 21, 1992, p. 39, no. 13 (Massyaf hoard TLIV).

66. O13* - R23*   Same as 29.
    13.82g 21mm   O: ŠL̊[above dolphin; cable border partly off the
    6h   flan.
                   London, BM, no. BNK 868; *BMC Phoenicia*, p.
                   227, no. 1 and pl. XXVIII, 9; Rouvier, *JIAN* 6, 1903,
                   p. 269, no. 1775; Elayi, *NAC* 21, 1992, p. 38, no. 11
                   (Massyaf hoard TLIV).
67. O14* - R23   Same as 29.
    13.32g   O: ŠLŠN̊ above dolphin; cable border partly off the
    12h   flan.
                   Leu, Zurich, 28/5/1974, no. 170; Elayi, *NAC* 21,
                   1992, pp. 38 and 46, no. 7.
68. O14 - R24*   Same as 29.
    13.40g 22mm   O: inscription off the flan.
    3h   Paris, BNF, no. 3208; Babelon, *Perses*, no. 1979;
                   id., *Traité*, no. 980; Elayi, *NAC* 21, 1992, p. 38, no.
                   9 (ex De Luynes coll.).
69. O14 - R25*   Same as 29.
    13.43g 21mm   O: ŠLŠN above dolphin; cable border partly off the
    6h   flan.
                   Paris, BNF, no. 110; Elayi, *NAC* 21, 1992, p. 38, no.
                   10 (ex De Vogüé coll.).
70. O15* - R25   Same as 29.
    13.60g   O: ŠLŠ[above dolphin; shell and cable border partly
    3h   off the flan.
                   Sotheby's, New York, 21-22/6/1990, no. 605.
71. O16* - R26*   Same as 29.
    13.58g   O: Š̊L̊Š̊N̊ above dolphin; cable border partly off the
    9h   flan.
                   Troxell-Spengler, *ANSMN* 15, 1969, p. 7, no. 20 and
                   pl. II; *IGCH*, no. 1820; NFA, Beverly Hills, 14-
                   19/11/1984, no. 188; Elayi, *NAC* 21, 1992, p. 40, no.
                   36; Elayi-Elayi, *Trésors*, p. 280, no. 1 (Balkh hoard
                   TLXIX).
72. O17* - R27*   Same as 29. Small cracks on the edge.
    13.50g   O: ŠLŠN above dolphin; cable border partly off the
    12h   flan.
                   SNG ANS, no. 1434; Numismatic Art & Ancient
                   Coins, 4, 17/4/1986, no. 278 (ex Berry coll.).
73. O1 - R?   Same as 29. Slightly worn.
    13.76g   O: inscription almost obliterated; cable border partly
                   off the flan.
                   Spink, London, 96, 31/3/1993, no. 108.
74. O2 - R?   Same as 29. Slightly worn.

	13.70g 22mm 11h	O: ŠL[above dolphin; cable border partly off the flan. Rome, VM, no. 199a.
75.	O2 - R? 13.29g	Same as 29. Slightly worn. O: ŠL̊[above dolphin; cable border partly off the flan. Elsen, Brussels, 78, 20/3/2004, no. 106 = Superior Galleries, Beverly Hills, 11-12/6/1986, no. 1416.
76.	O4 - R?	Same as 29. Slightly worn. O: ŠL̊[above dolphin; cable border partly off the flan. Jidejian, *Lebanon, its Gods*, p. 1 (reverse not illustrated).
77.	O6 - R? 13.45g 12h	Same as 29. Irregular flan. Small cracks on the edge. Slightly worn. O: inscription obliterated and partly off the flan. *SNG Cambridge*, no. 6082; Münzen und Medaillen, Basel, 13, 17-19/6/1954, no. 1206; Elayi, *NAC* 21, 1992, pp. 40 and 47, no. 34.
78.	O6 - R? 13.38g	Same as 29. Slightly worn. O: ŠL̊[above dolphin, partly off the flan. Védrines, Paris, 5/7/1985, no. 111 = Bourgey, Paris, 5-6/12/1977, no. 125 = Glendining, London, 9, 3/6/1976, no. 55; Elayi, *NAC* 21, 1992, p. 40, no. 35.
79.	O6 - R? 12.90g 24mm 10h	Same as 29. Irregular flan. Overstruck. Slightly worn. O: Š̊L̊Š̊N̊ above dolphin; cable border partly off the flan. New York, ANS, no. 1977.158, 751; Elayi, *NAC* 21, 1992, pp. 40 and 47, no. 33.
80.	O18* - R? 12.74g	Same as 29. Slightly worn. O: ŠLŠN̊ above dolphin; cable border partly off the flan. Rubinger, Antiqua, Woodland Hills, 10, 2001, no. 78.
81.	O? - R4 12.58g	Same as 29. Slightly worn. O: ŠLŠN̊ above dolphin; cable border partly off the flan. Myers, Ariadne Galleries, New York, 7/12/1982, no. 158.
82.	O? - R13 13.17g	Same as 29. Small cracks on the edge. Slightly worn. O: Š̊L̊Š̊N̊ above dolphin; cable border partly off the

		flan. Monetarium, Schweizerische Kreditanstalt, Zurich, 45, Spring 1986, no. 49.
83.	O? - R28* 13.24g 24mm 12h	Same as 29. Irregular flan. Small cracks on the edge. Slightly worn. O: ŠL[above dolphin; cable border partly off the flan. Spaer coll., Jerusalem; Peus, Frankfurt/Main, 323, 1-4/11/1988, no. 893 = 300, 3-4 and 9/11/1987, no. 1224; Elayi, *NAC* 21, 1992, pp. 40 and 47, no. 37.
84.	O? - R? 13.79g	Same as 29. Irregular flan. Rather worn. O: inscription off the flan. Cahn, Frankfurt/Main, 71, 14/10/1931, no. 572; Elayi, *NAC* 21, 1992, pp. 40 and 47, no. 38.
85.	O? - R? 13.64g	Same as 29. Irregular flan. Rather worn. O: ŠL[above dolphin; cable border partly off the flan. R: re-struck. Baldwin, London, 34, 13/10/2003, no. 536.
86.	O? - R? 13.61g	Same as 29. Irregular flan. Rather worn. O:]LŠN above dolphin; cable border partly off the flan. Deep chisel-cut. Lanz, Munich, 26, 5/12/1983, no. 298.
87.	O? - R? 13.40g	Same as 29. Rather worn. O: ŠLŠN above dolphin; cable border partly off the flan. Kurpfälzische Münzhandlung, Mannheim, 42, June 1992, no. 316.
88.	O? - R? 12.53g 20mm 5h	Same as 29. Rather worn. O: ŠL[above dolphin; cable border partly off the flan. Mildenberg-Hurter, *Dewing Collection*, no. 2669; Oleson, *Dewing Collection*, no. 54b (ex Dewing coll.).
89.	O? - R? 7.19g 21mm 6h	Same as 29. Fragmentary. Rather worn. O: inscription obliterated. Paris, BNF, no. 80; Kraay-Moorey, *RN* 10, 1968, p. 216, no. 80 and pl. XXVII; Elayi-Elayi, *Trésors*, p. 243, no. 17; Elayi, *NAC* 21, 1992, p. 40, no. 39 (Massyaf hoard TLIV).
90.	O? - R?	Same as 29. Fragmentary. Rather worn. O: inscription obliterated. Beirut, NM; Kraay-Moorey, *RN* 10, 1968, p. 218, no. 81 and pl. XXVII; Elayi-Elayi, *Trésors*, pp. 243-

		244, no. 18; Elayi, *NAC* 21, 1992, p. 40, no. 40 (Massyaf hoard TLIV).
91.	O? - R?	Same as 29. Small cracks on the edge. Rather worn.
		O: ŠLŠŇ above dolphin; cable border partly off the flan.
		R: re-struck.
		Berk, Chicago, 89, 14/2/1996, no. 190 = 87, 13/9/1995, no. 185 = 84, 19/1/1995, no. 325.
92.	O? - R?	Same as 29. Rather worn.
		O: ŠLŠN above dolphin.
		Dunand, *Byblos II*, no. 7115 and fig. 45; Elayi-Elayi, *Trésors*, p. 88, no. 11 (Byblos hoard TX).
93 - 109		Same as 29.
		Robinson, *Iraq* 12, 1950, p. 50; Schlumberger, *Argent grec*, p. 53 (1 Tehran Museum, 3 Pozzi coll., 1 Seyrig coll., 1 Godard coll.); Elayi-Elayi, *Trésors*, p. 278, no. 33-49 (Malayer hoard TLXVIII).
110 - 181		Same as 29.
		Schlumberger, *Argent grec*, p. 53 (Tehran Museum); Elayi-Elayi, *Trésors*, p. 278, no. 50-121 (Malayer hoard TLXVIII).

I.2.2. Quarters of shekel AR

182.	O1* - R1* 3.92g 14mm	O: dolphin, to right, over double line of waves; below, shell; MḤṢGR above dolphin; cable border partly off the flan.
		R: owl standing to right, head facing; over its left shoulder, crook and flail; incuse impression surrounding type; all in shallow incuse square. Defect on the scepter.
		Private coll.; Münzen und Medaillen, Basel, 32, 20/10/1966, no. 154 (who reads *MCHZUR*); Elayi-Lemaire, *NAC* 19, 1990, pp. 102 and 114, no. 8 and pl. XII.
183.	O1 - R1 3.07g 14mm	Same as 182.
		O: MḤṢGR above dolphin; cable border partly off the flan.
		R: defect on the scepter.
		Vinchon, Paris, 7/11/2001, no. 70 = Elsen, Brussels, 38, 11/2/1995, no. 144; 28, 20/2/1993, no. 298 (who reads *MCHZUR*).
184.	O1 - R2* 3.39g	Same as 182.
		O: MḤṢGR̊ above dolphin.

Classical Numismatic Group, Lancaster-London, 33, 15/3/1995, no. 396 = 19/3/1994, no. 131.

185. O1 - R3*
3.26g 14mm
9h

Same as 182.
O: *MḤṢGR̊* above dolphin. Scratched in cleaning.
NFA, Los Angeles, 29, 13/9/1992, no. 181 = Leu, Zurich, 53, 21-22/10/1991, no. 160.

186. O2* - R4*
2.84g

Same as 182. Deep chisel-cut.
O: *MḤṢGR̊* above dolphin. Trace of compass in the center.
Maly, Lucerne, Nomos 99, 6, Autumn 1975, no. 20; Elayi-Lemaire, *NAC* 19, 1990, pp. 104, no. 20, and 114, pl. II.

187. O3* - R4
3.31g 13mm
3h

Same as 182.
O: *MḤṢGR̊* above dolphin; cable border partly off the flan. Trace of compass under the cable border.
Paris, BNF, no. 1981a; Babelon, *Perses*, no. 1981a; *id.*, *Traité*, no. 983 and pl. CXXII, 3; Elayi-Lemaire, *NAC* 19, 1990, pp. 102, no. 11, and 114, pl. II.

188. O4* - R5*
3.04g 14mm

Same as 182.
O: *M̊ḤṢGR̊* above dolphin, partly off the flan.
London, BM, no. 1922-4-3-6; Forrer, *Weber Collection*, no. 8082; Elayi-Lemaire, *NAC* 19, 1990, p. 103, no. 17 and 114, pl. II (ex Weber coll.).

189. O4 - R6*
3.10g
12h

Same as 182.
O: *MḤ̊[* above dolphin; cable border partly off the flan.
Brussels, NM, no. 1745; Naster, *Collection De Hirsch*, no. 1745; Elayi-Lemaire, *NAC* 19, 1990, pp. 103, no. 13, and 114, pl. II (ex De Hirsch coll.).

190. O5* - R7*
3.16g 14mm
12h

Same as 182.
O: *MḤṢGR* above dolphin.
New York, ANS, no. N5; Elayi-Elayi, *BCEN* 27, 1990, pp. 70 and 72, no. 5 (ex Newell coll.).

191. O6* - R8*
2.98g 13mm
1h

Same as 182.
O: *M̊ḤṢGR̊* above dolphin; cable border partly off the flan.
New York, ANS, no. N4; Elayi-Elayi, *BCEN* 27, 1990, pp. 70 and 72, no. 6 (ex Newell coll.).

192. O7* - R9*
3.00g 15mm
3h

Same as 182.
O: *MḤ̊[* above dolphin. Defect on the tail.
Paris, BNF, no. 1981; Babelon, *Perses*, no. 1981 and pl. XXX, 3; *id.*, *Traité*, no. 983b and pl. CXXII, 4; *Catalogue De Luynes*, p. 157, no. 3209 and pl.

		CXV; Elayi-Lemaire, *NAC* 19, 1990, pp. 103, no. 18, and 114, pl. II (ex De Luynes coll.).
193.	O8* - R10* 2.33g 15mm 12h	Same as 182. O: *JḤṢGR* above dolphin. Beirut, AUB Museum, no. 1259A; Baramki, *Coins AUB*, p. 220, no. 2 and pl. XXVII, 2; Elayi-Lemaire, *NAC* 19, 1990, pp. 104, no. 21, and 118, pl. III.
194.	O9* - R11* 3.10g 14mm 9h	Same as 182. O: *MḤṢGR* above dolphin; cable border partly off the flan. Defect on the shell. Berlin, SM, no. 702/1903; Elayi-Lemaire, *NAC* 19, 1990, pp. 103, no. 14, and 114, pl. II (ex Weber coll.).
195.	O10* - R12* 3.40g 13mm 6h	Same as 182. O: *MḤṢG[* above dolphin; cable border partly off the flan. NFA, Los Angeles, 26, 14/9/1991, no. 131.
196.	O11* - R13* 3.06g 3h	Same as 182. O: *MḤṢGR* above dolphin. Demirjian, Ridgefield, Spring 1980, no. 44 = Hess-Leu, Lucerne-Zurich, 24, 16/4/1964, no. 242; Elayi-Lemaire, *NAC* 19, 1990, pp. 103, no. 14, and 114, pl. II.
197.	O12* - R14* 3.37g	Same as 182. Small cracks on the edge. O: *MḤṢGR* above dolphin; cable border partly off the flan. Defect on the shell. Paris, BNF, no. 284 (ex Seyrig coll.).
198.	O13* - R15* 2.83g	Same as 182. O: *MḤṢGR* above dolphin. Hirsch, Munich, 168, 22-24/11/1990, no. 363.
199.	O2 - R? 3.06g	Same as 182. Slightly worn. O: *JḤṢGR* above dolphin; cable border partly off the flan. Münzen und Medaillen, Weil/Rhein, 16, 19-20/5/2005, no. 977.
200.	O2 - R? 2.30g 13mm	Same as 182. Slightly worn. O: *M[* above dolphin. Brüder Egger, Vienna, 26/11/1909, no. 425; Elayi-Lemaire, *NAC* 19, 1990, pp. 104, no. 22, and 115, pl. III.
201.	O4 - R? 3.08g 13mm	Same as 182. Slightly worn. O: *M[* above dolphin. Albrecht-Hoffmann, Köln, 43, 27-30/4/1981, no.

The Coinage of Tyre in the Persian period

202.	O4 - R?	205 = Münzen und Medaillen, Basel, January 1968, no. 17; Elayi-Lemaire, *NAC* 19, 1990, pp. 103, no. 15, and 114, pl. II.
		Same as 182. Irregular flan. Slightly worn.
	3.33g 14mm	O: $M\overset{\circ}{H}\overset{\circ}{S}G\overset{\circ}{R}$ above dolphin; cable border partly off the flan.
	11h	R: chisel-cut.
		Spaer coll., Jerusalem; Elayi-Lemaire, *NAC* 19, 1990, pp. 102, no. 10, and 114, pl. II.
203.	O5 - R?	Same as 182. Slightly worn.
	3.36g	O: $J\overset{\circ}{S}\overset{\circ}{G}\overset{\circ}{R}$ above dolphin; cable border partly off the flan.
		Münzen und Medaillen, Basel, February 1964, no. 23.
204.	O14* - R?	Same as 182. Slightly worn.
	3.06g 14mm	O: overstruck; $M\overset{\circ}{H}\overset{\circ}{S}\overset{\circ}{G}\overset{\circ}{R}$ above dolphin.
	11h	R: overstruck.
		Leiden, RM, no. 8080; Elayi-Lemaire, *NAC* 19, 1990, p. 116.
205.	O15* - R?	Same as 182. Slightly worn.
	2.87g 14mm	O: $M\overset{\circ}{H}\overset{\circ}{S}\overset{\circ}{G}\overset{\circ}{R}[$ above dolphin; cable border partly off the flan.
	4h	
		Spaer coll., Jerusalem; Elayi-Lemaire, *NAC* 19, 1990, pp. 104, no. 19, and 114, pl. II (bought in Jerusalem).
206.	O16* - R?	Same as 182. Slightly worn.
	2.69g 13mm	O: inscription almost obliterated.
	6h	New York, ANS, no. 48.19; Elayi-Elayi, *BCEN* 27, 1990, pp. 70 and 72, no. 7 (ex Gauthier coll.).
207.	O? - R16*	Same as 182. Slightly worn.
	3.19g 14mm	O: inscription almost obliterated; cable border partly off the flan.
	5h	R: deep chisel-cut.
		Paris, BNF, no. 82; Kraay-Moorey, *RN* 10, 1968, p. 218 and pl. XXVII, 82; Elayi-Lemaire, *NAC* 19, 1990, pp. 102-103, no. 12, and 114, pl. II; Elayi-Elayi, *Trésors*, p. 244, no. 19 (Massyaf hoard TLIV).
208.	O? - R17*	Same as 182. Slightly worn.
	3.01g	O: $\overset{\circ}{M}\overset{\circ}{H}\overset{\circ}{S}\overset{\circ}{G}\overset{\circ}{R}$ above dolphin; cable border partly off the flan.
		Rubinger, Antiqua, Woodland Hills, 10, 2001, no. 79 = Sternberg, Zurich, 34, 22-23/10/1998, no. 140.

209.	O? - R? 3.40g 14mm 7h	Same as 182. Rather worn. O: inscription almost obliterated; cable border partly off the flan. *Catalogue McClean* III, p. 376, no. 9516 and pl. 352, 6; Elayi-Lemaire, *NAC* 19, 1990, pp. 102, no. 9, and 114, pl. II (ex McClean coll.).
210.	O? - R? 2.80g	Same as 182. Rather worn. O: $M\overset{\circ}{H}\overset{\circ}{S}G\overset{\circ}{R}$ above dolphin; cable border partly off the flan. Rauch, Vienna, 7, 4-5/6/1971, no. 83.
211.	O? - R? 3.39g 13mm	Same as 182. Rather worn. O: inscription almost obliterated. Cambridge, FM, no. 1977-38.
212.	O? - R? 3.38g	Same as 182. Rather worn. Ratto, Geneva, 26/4/1909, no. 5171.
213.		Same as 182. Tehran, NM; Schlumberger, *Argent grec*, p. 52; Elayi-Elayi, *Trésors*, p. 278, no. 122, not illustrated (Malayer hoard TLXVIII).
214- 221		Same as 182. Tehran, NM; Schlumberger, *Argent grec*, p. 52; Elayi-Elayi, *Trésors*, p. 278, no. 123-130, not illustrated (Malayer hoard TLXVIII).

I.2.3. Eighth of shekel AR?

222.	O1* - R1* 1.55g 14mm 7h	O: dolphin, to right, over double line of waves; below, shell; $MH\dot{S}G\overset{\circ}{R}$ above dolphin; cable border. Small die. R: owl standing to right, head facing; over its left shoulder, crook and flail; incuse impression surrounding type; all in shallow incuse square. Chisel-cut. Vienna, KHM, no. 34755; Elayi-Lemaire, *NAC* 19, 1990, pp. 104, no. 23, and 115, pl. III.

I.2.4. Sixteenths of shekel AR

223.	O1 - R1* 0.67g	O: dolphin, to right, over one line of waves; below, shell; *MR* above dolphin; cable border partly off the flan. R: owl standing to right, head facing; over its left shoulder, crook and flail; incuse impression surrounding type; all in shallow incuse square. Classical Numismatic Group, Lancaster-London, 60,

		22/5/2002, no. 936 = Vecchi, London, 14, 5/2/1999, no. 692.
224.	O1* - R2 0.64g 9mm 7h	Same as 223. O: inscription almost obliterated; cable border? London, BM, no. 1863-12-20 3; Rouvier, *JIAN* 6, 1903, p. 269, no. 1777 and pl. XVIII, 3; *BMC Phoenicia*, p. 227, no. 3 and pl. XXVIII, 11; Elayi-Lemaire, *NAC* 19, 1990, pp. 105, no. 26 and 115, pl. III.
225.	O2 - R2* 0.58g	Same as 223. O: *MR* above dolphin; cable border? Sternberg, Zurich, 34, 22-23/10/1998, no. 141.
226.	O2* - R3* 0.57g 8mm 3h	Same as 223. O: *MR̊* above dolphin; cable border partly off the flan. Fulco, *RB* 82, 1975, p. 234, no. 1 and pl. XVIII; Briend-Humbert, *Tell Keisan*, p. 235 and pl. 133, 1; Elayi-Lemaire, *NAC* 19, 1990, pp. 105, no. 29 and 115, pl. III (Tell Keisan excavations).
227.	O3* - R3 0.67g 2h	Same as 223. O: inscription out off the flan; cable border partly off the flan. Hauck & Aufhäuser, Münzen und Medaillen, Deutschland, 18, 5-6/10/2004, no. 365; Klein, *Sammlung*, no. 725 (ex Klein coll.).
228.	O4* - R4* 0.58g 8mm 3h	Same as 223. O: *MR* above dolphin; cable border partly off the flan. New York, ANS, no. 65.217; Betlyon, *Coinage of Phoenicia*, pl. 4, no. 7 (wrong reference); Elayi-Elayi, *BCEN* 27, 1990, pp. 70 and 72, 8; Elayi-Lemaire, *NAC* 19, 1990, pp. 105, no. 28, and 115, pl. III.
229.	O5* - R5* 0.64g 10h	Same as 223. O: inscription off the flan; cable border partly off the flan. Leu, Zurich, 54, 28/4/1992, no. 177.
230.	O6* - R6* 0.55g 8mm	Same as 223. O: *MR* above dolphin; cable border partly off the flan. Kibboutz Ḥanita Museum, no. 204; Elayi-Lemaire, *NAC* 19, 1990, pp. 105, no. 30, and 115, pl. III.
231.	O2 - R? 0.58g 7mm	Same as 223. Slightly worn. O: *MR* above dolphin; cable border partly off the

	6h	flan. Spaer coll., Jerusalem; Elayi-Lemaire, *NAC* 19, 1990, pp. 105, no. 27, and 115, pl. III (bought in Beirut).
232.	O7* - R? 0.70g	Same as 223. Slightly worn. O: $\overset{\circ}{M}\overset{\circ}{R}$ above dolphin; cable border partly off the flan. Münzen und Medaillen, Basel, 32, 20/10/1966, no. 155; Elayi-Lemaire, *NAC* 19, 1990, pp. 105, no. 25, and 115, pl. III.
233.	O7 - R? 0.69g	Same as 223. Slightly worn. O: inscription off the flan; cable border partly off the flan. Classical Numismatic Group, Lancaster-London, 45, 18/3/1998, no. 576 = 42, 29-30/5/1997, no. 587.
234.	O? - R7 0.47g 8mm 7h	Same as 223. Slightly worn. O: $\overset{\circ}{M}\overset{\circ}{R}$ above dolphin; cable border? Tel Aviv, KNM, no. 1669; Kindler, *ErIs* 8, 1967, p. 324, no. 23 and pl. 46, 23; Elayi-Lemaire, *NAC* 19, 1990, pp. 106, no. 32, and 115, pl. III (found in Akko).
235.	O? - R? 0.77g 5h	Same as 223. Rather worn. O: inscription off the flan; cable border partly off the flan. *SNG Copenhagen*, p. 37, no. 294 and pl. 8; Elayi-Lemaire, *NAC* 19, 1990, pp. 104, no. 24, and 115, pl. III.
236.	O? - R? 0.48g 8mm 2h	Same as 223. Rather worn. O: inscription obliterated; cable border partly off the flan. Tel Aviv, KNM, no. 1671; Elayi-Lemaire, *NAC* 19, 1990, pp. 106, no. 31, and 115, pl. III (found in Akko).
237.	O? - R? 0.45g 7mm 5h	Same as 223. Rather worn. O: inscription off the flan; cable border partly off the flan. Tel Aviv, KNM, no. 6795; Elayi-Lemaire, *NAC* 19, 1990, pp. 106, no. 33, and 115, pl. III.
238.	O? - R?	Same as 223. Rather worn. O: $\overset{\circ}{M}\overset{\circ}{R}$ above dolphin; cable border partly off the flan. Malloy, New York, 13, 8/12/1978, no. 97.

I.2.5. Halves of sixteenth of shekel AR

239.	O1* - R1* 0.23g 6mm	O: dolphin, to right, over one line of waves; below, shell; *H Y̊/M̊* above dolphin; cable border partly off the flan. R: head of lion, to right; all in incuse square. London, BM, no. 1985.5-20-3; Elayi-Lemaire, *NAC* 19, 1990, pp. 106, no. 35, and 115, pl. III; Elayi-Elayi, *Trésors*, p. 94, no. 2 and pl. V (Byblos hoard TXIII-XV).
240.	O2* - R2* 0.36g 6mm	Same as 239. O: *H Y̊/M̊* above dolphin; border obscure. Berk, Chicago, 50, 18/11/1987, no. 250.
241.	O3* - R3* 0.31g 6mm 12h	Same as 239. O: *H Y̊/M̊* above dolphin. Meshorer-Qedar, *Samarian Coinage*, p. 125 and pl. 31, no. IC3 ('Incerti of Samaria).
242	O4* - R4* 0.17g 6mm 12h	Same as 239. O: *H Y̊/M̊* above dolphin. Meshorer-Qedar, *Samarian Coinage*, p. 125 and pl. 31, no. IC4 ('Incerti of Samaria').
243.	O5* - R? 0.36g 6mm	Same as 239. Slightly worn. O: *H Y̊/M̊* above dolphin. Dothan, *BASOR* 224, 1976, p. 27, fig. 28; Elayi-Lemaire, *NAC* 19, 1990, pp. 106, no. 36, and 115, pl. III (Akko excavations).
244.	O? - R? 0.28g 6mm	Same as 239. Rather worn. O: inscription almost obliterated; cable border partly off the flan. Tel Aviv, KNM, no. 1335; Kindler, *ErIs* 8, 1967, p. 324 and pl. 46, 24; Elayi-Lemaire, *NAC* 19, 1990, pp. 106, no. 34, and 115, pl. III (from Akko).
245.	O? - R? 0.13g 6mm 12h	Same as 239. Rather worn. O: dolphin to right? R: head of lion to right? New York, ANS, no. N22; Elayi-Elayi, *BCEN* 27, 1990, p. 71, no. 9 (ex Newell coll.).

2. Group II: Deity riding on seahorse (around 425-333/2 BCE)

II.1. Phoenician standard

II.1.1. Anepigraphic (around 425-394 BCE)

II.1.1.1. Shekels AR

II.1.1.1.a. Flat fabric

246. O1* - R1*
      13.72g 24mm
      9h
      O: deity, bearded, riding on seahorse with curled wing, to right; holding reins in right hand and an arched bow in left hand; below, two lines of waves and dolphin, to right; guilloche border.
      R: owl standing to right, head facing; over its left shoulder, crook and flail; guilloche border.
      Leu, Zurich, 28/5/1974, no. 227 = Sotheby's, London, 3-11/2/1909, no. 772 (ex Montagu coll. = ex Sartiges coll.).

247. O1 - R1
      12.65g 24mm
      9h
      Same as 246. Yellowish colour (plated?). Slightly worn.
      New York, ANS, Hunt Fund, Constantine 9/3/09.

248. O2 - R1
      13.45g 25mm
      Same as 246. Small cracks on the edge.
      O: deep chisel-cut; guilloche border partly off the flan.
      Noble, Sydney, 62, 17-18/11/1999, no. 1932.

249. O2* - R2
      12.53g 24mm
      Same as 246.
      Coin Galleries, New York, 12/2/1992, no. 252 = 6, Myers-Adams, New York 6/12/1973, no. 241 = Glendining, London, 23/5/1963, no. 1070.

250. O3* - R1
      13.63g 25mm
      12h
      Same as 246.
      London, BM, no. 1906-7-13 1; *BMC Phoenicia*, p. 230, no. 19 and pl. XXIX, 6; Regling, *Sammlung Warren*, no. 1306; Head, *A Guide*, no. 58 (ex Warren coll.).

251. O4* - R1
      13.27g 22mm
      9h
      Same as 246. Small cracks on the edge.
      O: guilloche border partly off the flan.
      Paris, BNF, no. 1997; Babelon, *Perses*, no. 1997.

252. O5* - R2
      13.53g 24mm
      Same as 246.
      O and R: guilloche border partly off the flan.
      Princeton, PUL, no. 5-553.

253. O6* - R2*
      25mm
      Same as 246. Several small cracks on the edge.
      O: guilloche border partly off the flan.
      Baranowsky, Milan, 25/2/1931, no. 764 (ex Traverso-Martini coll.).

254. O6 - R3*
      13.64g 23mm
      5h
      Same as 246.
      O and R: guilloche border partly off the flan.
      Paris, BNF, no. R2748; Diebolt-Nicolet-Pierre, *RSN*

56, 1977, pl. 26, no. 18; Elayi-Elayi, *Trésors*, p. 266, no. 2 (Cilicia hoard TLXI).

255. O7 - R2　　Same as 246.
　　　13.65g 26mm　O: slightly worn; guilloche border partly off the flan.
　　　10h　　R: two chisel-cuts.
　　　　　Istanbul, KTB, no. 11451.

256. O7* - R4*　Same as 246. Irregular flan.
　　　12.69g 27mm　O and R: guilloche border partly off the flan.
　　　11h　　Berlin, SM, no. 18.

257. O7 - R4　Same as 246. Broken.
　　　12.62g 26mm　O: guilloche border partly off the flan.
　　　　　Lanz, Munich, 64, 7/6/1993, no. 306.

258. O8* - R4　Same as 246.
　　　13.50g 24mm　O: deity and guilloche border partly off the flan.
　　　　　Peus, Frankfurt/Main, 300, 3-4 and 9/11/1987, no. 1226.

259. O9* - R4　Same as 246. Small cracks on the edge.
　　　25mm　O and R: guilloche border partly off the flan.
　　　　　NFA, Beverly Hills, 18/11/1947, no. 1319.

260. O10 - R5*　Same as 246.
　　　13.41g 25mm　O: defect on the dolphin; guilloche border partly off the flan.
　　　　　R: guilloche border partly off the flan.
　　　　　Freeman & Sear, Chatsworth, 1, 10/3/1995, no. 224 = NFA, Los Angeles, 33, Spring 1994, no. 1449.

261. O10* - R6*　Same as 246.
　　　13.24g 24mm　O: defect on the dolphin; guilloche border partly off the flan.
　　　　　R: guilloche border partly off the flan.
　　　　　Poinsignon Numismatique, Strasbourg, 19-20/6/1984, no. 197 = Bonhams, London, 1, 21-22/5/1980, no. 208 = Hess, Lucerne, 249, 13/11/1979, no. 227.

262. O10 - R6　Same as 246.
　　　13.19g 24mm　O: defect on the dolphin; guilloche border partly off the flan.
　　　9h
　　　　　Hess-Divo, Zurich, 289, 24-25/10/2001, no. 31 = Glendining, London, 10/12/1986, no. 340 = 21-23/2/1961, no. 2675 (ex Lockett coll.).

263. O10 - R6　Same as 246.
　　　24mm　O: defect on the dolphin; guilloche border partly off the flan.
　　　　　Gibbons, London, 8, Autumn 1975, no. 43.

264. O11 - R6　Same as 246.

		23mm	O and R: guilloche border partly off the flan. Information from N. Vismara 16/11/1998 (Lebanon hoard).
265.	O11* - R8*		
	13.18g 23mm		O and R: guilloche border partly off the flan. Naville, Geneva, December 1928, no. 2011.
266.	O12 - R6		Same as 246.
	13.37g 24mm		O: defect below the dolphin; guilloche border partly off the flan. London, BM, no. 1948-12-2 1; Robinson, *Iraq* 12, 1950, p. 46, no. 16 and pl. XXIV; Jenkins, *BMQ* 28, 1964, no. B; Kraay-Hirmer, *Greek Coins*, no. 682; Reade, *Iran* 24, 1986, p. 80 and pl. I, 16; Jenkins, *Greek Coins*, no. 219; Elayi-Elayi, *Trésors*, p. 269, no. 3 (Babylon hoard TLXIII).
267.	O12* - R7*		Same as 246. Minor chisel-cut on the edge.
	13.53g 24mm		O: defect below the dolphin. Leu, Zurich, 79, 31/10/2000, no. 767 = Freeman & Sear, New York, 3/11-1/12/1999, no. 623.
268.	O13 - R9		Same as 246.
	13.51g 25mm		O: guilloche border partly off the flan.
	12h		Cambridge, FM, no. 1777:43; *SNG Cambridge*, no. 6084.
269.	O13 - R9*		Same as 246.
	13.48g 28mm		O: guilloche border partly off the flan.
	4h		Brussels, NM, no. 1746; Naster, *Collection De Hirsch*, no. 1746 (ex De Hirsch coll.).
270.	O13 - R9		Same as 246.
	13.18g 25mm		R: defect above the owl.
	6h		Paris, BNF, no. 3217; *Catalogue De Luynes*, no. 3217 (ex De Luynes coll.).
271.	O13* - R10*		Same as 246.
	13.27g 24mm		O and R: guilloche border partly off the flan.
	2h		New York, ANS, no. N33 (ex Newell coll.).
272.	O14* - R10		Same as 246. Small cracks on the edge.
	13.65g 24mm		Dürr-Michel, Numisart, Geneva, 16/11/1998, no. 487.
273.	O15* - R11*		Same as 246. Slightly irregular flan.
	13.28g 24mm		O and R: guilloche border partly off the flan.
	3h		New York, ANS, no. N20 (ex Newell coll.).
274.	O15 - R12*		Same as 246.
	13.46g 25mm		O: guilloche border partly off the flan.
	6h		R: chisel-cut. Defect on the leg of the owl. Berlin, SM, no. 17 (ex Fox coll.).

275.	O16 - R13 13.63g 24mm	Same as 246. Sotheby's, London, 3-11/2/1909, no. 771 (ex Benson coll.).
276.	O16* - R13* 13.38g 25mm 3h	Same as 246. Small cracks on the edge. O: guilloche border partly off the flan. London, BM, no. RPK, p.164.C1; *BMC Phoenicia*, p. 230, no. 20; Rouvier, *JIAN* 6, 1903, no. 1788; Head, *Historia Numorum*, no. 352; Gardner, *History of Ancient Coinage*, no. 8.
277.	O16 - R13 12.93g 24mm	Same as 246. Slightly irregular flan. O and R: guilloche border partly off the flan. Stockholm, RCC, no. 29392.
278.	O17* - R13 13.08g 27mm 3h	Same as 246. Small cracks on the edge. O: guilloche border partly off the flan. Berlin, SM, no. 19 (ex Löbbecke coll.).
279.	O18* - R14* 13.57g 23mm 1h	Same as 246. O and R: guilloche border partly off the flan. Paris, BNF, no. 1998; Babelon, *Perses*, no. 1998.
280.	O19* - R15* 12.60g 23mm 2h	Same as 246. Partly broken. O and R: guilloche border partly off the flan. New York, ANS, no. 1977.158,754.
281.	O20* - R16* 13.40g 23mm 1h	Same as 246. Irregular flan. O and R: guilloche border partly off the flan. Naville, Geneva, 7, 23-24/6/1924, no. 1743 = Feuardent, Paris, 18-19/12/1919, no. 408 (ex Bément coll. = ex Collignon coll.).
282.	O21* - R17* 12.24g 28mm 2h	Same as 246. Small cracks on the edge. Relatively small dies. O: big dolphin. New York, ANS, no. 47.97 (ex Petrie coll.).
283.	O22* - R18* 13.71g 28mm 12h	Same as 246. Irregular flan. O and R: guilloche border partly off the flan. Oxford, AM, no. 92; Kraay, *Greek Coins*, no. 1050 (ex Robinson coll.).
284.	O22 - R18 13.27g 24mm	Same as 246. Small cracks on the edge. O: guilloche border partly off the flan. Leiden, RM, no. 3285 (ex Van Rede coll.).
285.	O23* - R19* 12.98g 23mm	Same as 246. O: guilloche border partly off the flan. Hirsch, Munich, 156, 25-27/11/1987, no. 249 = 152, 26-29/11/1986, no. 248 = Kricheldorf, Stuttgart, 7, 12-13/11/1959, no. 106.
286.	O24* - R20* 12.10g 25mm	Same as 246. O and R: guilloche border partly off the flan.

		Schlessinger, Berlin-Charlottenburg, 4/2/1935, no. 1500.
287.	O25* - R21* 13.25g 25mm 9h	Same as 246. Irregular flan. O: seahorse and guilloche border partly off the flan. Defect above the dolphin. R: guilloche border partly off the flan. Paris, BNF, no. 1973.1.442 (ex Seyrig coll.).
288.	O26* - R22* 13.64g 25mm	Same as 246. Small cracks and chisel-cut on the edge. R: graffito on the right. Classical Numismatic Group, Lancaster-London, 63, 21/5/2003, no. 675.
289.	O27* - R23* 13.25g 24mm	Same as 246. Jerusalem, AI, no. 28; Ratto, Lugano, 4/4/1927, no. 2655.
290.	O28* - R24* 12.93g 23mm 12h	Same as 246. Partly broken. O and R: guilloche border partly off the flan. London, BM, no. 151 14; *BMC Phoenicia*, p. 230, no. 22, not illustrated.
291.	O28 - R25* 12.93g 22mm 5h	Same as 246. O and R: guilloche border partly off the flan. Paris, BNF, no. 1996; Babelon, *Perses*, no. 1996.
292.	O28 - R26 12.80g 23mm	Same as 246. Irregular flan. O and R: guilloche border partly off the flan. Peus, Frankfurt/Main, 315, 28-30/4 and 2/5/1986, no. 168 = 314, 30-31/10, 1 and 4/11/1985, no. 175.
293.	O29 - R26 13.55g 27mm 7h	Same as 246. Slightly irregular flan. O and R: guilloche border partly off the flan. Istanbul, KTB, no. 11450.
294.	O29* - R27* 11.63g 24mm	Same as 246. O: guilloche border partly off the flan. R: deep chisel-cut. Partly incuse impression surrounding type. Leiden, RM, no. 8081; *SNG VIII, Hart Collection*, no. 1097g; Schlessinger, Berlin-Charlottenburg, 4/2/1935, no. 1501 = Ratto, Lugano, 4/4/1927, no. 2656 = Ratto, Milano, 15, no. 250 (ex Hart coll.).
295.	O30* - R28* 13.91g 25mm 5h	Same as 246. Cambridge, FM, no. 1777:40; *Catalogue McClean*, no. 9518 and pl. 352, 8 (ex McClean coll.).
296.	O30 - R28 13.11g 26mm 8h	Same as 246. O and R: guilloche border partly off the flan. Paris, BNF, no. 2002; Babelon, *Perses*, no. 2002.
297.	O30 - R29*	Same as 246.

	13.73g 27mm	O: flan flaw. Classical Numismatic Group, Lancaster-London, 54, 14/6/2000, no. 813 = Numismatica Ars Classica, New York, Triton II, 1-2/12/1998, no. 502 (Lebanon hoard).
298.	O31 - R25 13.68g 25mm	Same as 246. O: dolphin and guilloche border partly off the flan. Markov, New York, 11, 2-3/9/2003, no. 96 = Rubinger, Antiqua, Woodland Hills, 10, 2001, no. 80.
299.	O31 - R28 13.41g 25mm 5h	Same as 246. O: guilloche border partly off the flan. Leu, Zurich, 61, 17-18/5/1995, no. 166.
300.	O31 - R30* 13.47g 26mm 9h	Same as 246. *SNG Copenhagen*, no. 301 (ex Webster coll.).
301.	O31 - R31* 13.15g 28mm	Same as 246. Small cracks on the edge. Irregular flan. Ratto, Lugano, 9/10/1934, no. 246.
302.	O31* - R33* 13.47g 25mm 2h	Same as 246. O: relatively small die. New York, ANS, no. N31; Betlyon, *Coinage of Phoenicia*, pl. 5, 4 (ex Newell coll.).
303.	O32 - R31 12.99g 27mm 6h	Same as 246. Slightly irregular flan. R: guilloche border partly off the flan. London, BM, no. 15114; *BMC Phoenicia*, p. 230, no. 21, not illustrated.
304.	O32 - R31 12.98g 25mm	Same as 246. Slightly irregular flan. R: guilloche border partly off the flan. Agora, Tel Aviv, 21/5/1975, no. 262.
305.	O32* - R32* 13.63g 25mm	Same as 246. O: guilloche border partly off the flan. Private coll.; Florange-Ciani, 17-21/2/1929, no. 1069 (ex Allotte de la Füye coll.).
306.	O32 - R35* 13.27g 25mm 3h	Same as 246. Paris, BNF, no. 3216; *Catalogue De Luynes*, no. 3216; Babelon, *Traité*, pl. CXXII, 16 (ex De Luynes coll.).
307.	O33 - R32 13.33g 25mm	Same as 246. Small cracks on the edge. O and R: guilloche border partly off the flan. Vecchi, London, 12, 5/6/1998, no. 401 = Gorny, Munich, 67, 2/5/1994, no. 346.
308.	O33* - R33* 12.40g 26mm 6h	Same as 246. New York, ANS, no. N32 (ex Newell coll.).

309.	O34* - R33 13.46g 24mm	Same as 246. Hess, Lucerne, 15/2/1934, no. 515.
310.	O34 - R33 12.62g 23mm	Same as 246. Small cracks on the edge. O: slightly worn. Ratto, Milan, 15, no. 252.
311.	O34 - R34* 24mm	Same as 246. Some cracks on the edge. R: defect on the right of the owl. Bourgey, Paris, 3-5/12/1928, no. 122.
312.	O35 - R35 13.46g 24mm	Same as 246. O: guilloche border partly off the flan. Münzen und Medaillen, Basel, 583, February 1995, no. 18.
313.	O35* - R35 12.62g 23mm	Same as 246. Rather square flan. Slightly broken. O and R: guilloche border partly off the flan. Ratto, Lugano, 4/4/1927, no. 2654 = Naville, Geneva, 7, 23-24/6/1924, no. 1742 = Hirsch, Munich, 25, 29/11/1909, no. 3025 (ex Bément coll. = ex Philipsen coll.).
314.	O35 - R36 13.24g 25mm 10h	Same as 246. Small cracks on the edge. Leu, Lucerne, 36, 17-18/4/1968, no. 334 = Leu, Zurich, and Schulman, Amsterdam, 1966, no. 3066 = Florange-Ciani, Paris, 1925, no. 513 = Naville, Geneva, 1, 1921, no. 3066 (ex Pozzi coll.).
315.	O35 - R36* 13.20g 23mm	Same as 246. Peus, Frankfurt/Main, 323, 1-4/11/1988, no. 894 = 300, 3-4 and 9/11/1987, no. 1227.
316.	O35 - R37* 12.38g 22mm	Same as 246. Small cracks on the edge. O: guilloche border partly off the flan. Private coll.
317.	O36* - R37 12.19g 22mm	Same as 246. O: guilloche border partly off the flan. R: slight scratch. Elsen, Brussels, December 1987, no. 28 = 40, January 1982, no. 32 = Peus, Frankfurt/Main, 303, 20-22/10/1981, no. 191.
318.	O30 - R40 13.28g 23mm 3h	Same as 246. Slightly irregular flan. Slightly worn. O and R: guilloche border partly off the flan. CGB, Paris, 31/12/2002, no. 71.
319.	O32 - R? 11.29g 26mm 3h	Same as 246. Slightly worn. O and R: guilloche border partly off the flan. Istanbul, KTB, no. 11452.
320.	O54 - R? 12.45g 26mm	Same as 246. Irregular flan. Slightly worn. O and R: guilloche border partly off the flan. Coin Galleries, New York, 5, 1964, no. E109.

321.	O55* - R? 27mm	Same as 246. Slightly worn. Thompson, *ADAJ* 17, 1972, pp. 57-58 and 144, pl. VII, 2, no. J-12942; *id.*, *BASOR* 227, 1977, p. 31; *id.*, *BA* 50, 1987, pp. 101-104; Elayi-Elayi, *Trésors*, pp. 352-353 (Khirbet el-Hajjar excavations).
322.	O? - R30 12.97g 23mm	Same as 246. Slightly worn. O: guilloche border partly off the flan. Hirsch, Munich, 171, 25-28/9/1991, no. 450 = 167, 26-29/9/1990, no. 569.
323.	O? - R55* 13.80g 22mm 6h	Same as 246. Slightly worn. O: guilloche border partly off the flan. R: three chisel-cuts. Vienna, KHM, no. 33.280.
324.	O? - R56* 13.54g 24mm	Same as 246. Slightly worn. O: dolphin and guilloche border partly off the flan. Classical Numismatic Group, Lancaster-London, 67, 22/9/2004, no. 912 = Baldwin, London, 34, 13/10/2003, no. 542.
325.	O? - R57* 13.05g 23mm	Same as 246. Slightly corroded. Small chisel-cut. O and R: guilloche border partly off the flan. Védrines, Paris, 5/7/1985, no. 112 = Bourgey, Paris, 5-6/12/1977, no. 126.
326.	O? - R58* 13.78g 26mm 6h	Same as 246. Slightly worn. Deep chisel-cut. Toronto, ROM, no. 922.44.19; Milne, *RA*, 1905, p. 258, no. 2; Elayi-Elayi, *Trésors*, p. 293, no. 21 and pl. XXXVI (Beni Hassan hoard TLXXV).
327.	O? - R63* 13.08g 25mm 11h	Same as 246. Slightly worn. Vienna, INUW, no. 8101.

II.1.1.1.b. Thick fabric

328.	O37* - R37* 13.51g 24mm 12h	Same as 246. Rather thick fabric. Slightly irregular flan. O and R: guilloche border partly off the flan. Brussels, NM, no. 14.
329.	O38* - R38* 12.98g 23mm	Same as 246. Rather thick fabric. Irregular flan. O: countermark with Phoenician letters on the seahorse. R: guilloche border partly off the flan. Elsen, Brussels, 70, 15/6/2002, no. 111 = Schulten, Köln, 18-20/10/1989, no. 165 = Müller, Solingen, 62, 19-20/5/1989, no. 123.
330.	O39* - R38 13.11g 23mm	Same as 246. Rather thick fabric. O and R: guilloche border partly off the flan.

	3h	Cambridge, FM, no. 1777:39; *Catalogue McClean*, III, no. 9517 and pl. 352, 7 (ex McClean coll.).
331.	O39 - R39*	Same as 246. Thick fabric. Chisel-cut.
	12.70g 21mm	O and R: guilloche border partly off the flan.
	7h	Shahaf coll., Haifa, no. 6 (bought in Akko).
332.	O40 - R39	Same as 246. Thick fabric. Small cracks on the edge.
	12.24g 21mm	O and R: guilloche border partly off the flan. Hirsch, Munich, 192, 27-29/11/1996, no. 322 = 183, 20-24/9/1994, no. 652.
333.	O40* - R40*	Same as 246. Rather thick fabric. Small cracks on the edge.
	12.98g 22mm	O and R: guilloche border partly off the flan.
	5h	Paris, BNF, no. 503; Le Rider, *Mission en Susiane*, pp. 79, 87 and pl. II, 7; *id.*, *Fouilles de Suse*, p. 203 and pl. XXXVIII, 503; *id.*, *Iran* 38, 1965, no. 503 (Susa excavations).
334.	O41* - R41*	Same as 246. Thick fabric.
	13.19g 21mm	O: small scratches; guilloche border partly off the flan.
		R: guilloche border partly off the flan.
		Schulman, Amsterdam, 265, 28-29/9/1976, no. 225.
335.	O41 - R42*	Same as 246. Thick fabric. Irregular flan. Chisel-cut.
	12.24g 18mm	O and R: guilloche border partly off the flan.
	12h	Berlin, SM, no. 10.
336.	O42* - R43*	Same as 246. Thick fabric. Irregular flan.
	12.88g 20mm	O: defect below the seahorse; guilloche border partly off the flan.
		R: guilloche border partly off the flan.
		Ratto, Lugano, 4/4/1927, no. 2657 = Ratto, Milan, 15, no. 251.
337.	O43* - R44*	Same as 246. Thick fabric. Small cracks on the edge.
	13.36g 21mm	O and R: guilloche border partly off the flan. Gorny, Munich, 58, 9/4/1992, no. 486.
338.	O44* - R45*	Same as 246. Thick fabric. Irregular flan. Chisel-cut.
	13.04g 23mm	O: seahorse and guilloche border partly off the flan.
	11h	R: guilloche border partly off the flan.
		Jerusalem, RocMus, no. H1.12; Lambert, *QDAP* 1, 1931, p. 15, no. 12 and pl. XIX; Elayi-Elayi, *Trésors*, p. 171, no. 1 and pl. XXVII (Tell Abu Hawam hoard TXXXV).
339.	O45* - R46*	Same as 246. Rather thick fabric.
	13.56g 21mm	O: scratch. Slightly damaged: dolphin blundered.

The Coinage of Tyre in the Persian period

	9h	R: defect before the head; guilloche border partly off the flan. Deep chisel-cut. New York, ANS, no. 1944.100.72670; Newell, *NC*, 1914, p. 20, no. 92 and pl. IV, 4; Elayi-Elayi, *Trésors*, p. 265, no. 5 and pl. XXXV (Cilicia hoard TLX).
340.	O46* - R47* 13.38g 18mm 3h	Same as 246. Thick fabric. Oval flan. O and R: guilloche border partly off the flan. Berlin, SM, no. 12 (ex Löbbecke coll.).
341.	O47* - R48* 11.09g 22mm 9h	Same as 246. Rather thick fabric. Irregular flan. O and R: guilloche border partly off the flan. Argenor Numismatique, Paris, October 2002, no. 363.
342.	O48* - R49* 9.77g 22mm 9h	Same as 246. Rather thick fabric. Plated. O: dolphin and guilloche border partly off the flan. R: guilloche border partly off the flan. Budapest, MNM, no. 24.
343.	O49* - R50* 12.85g 23mm 2h	Same as 246. Rather thick fabric. Oval flan. Slightly broken. O and R: guilloche border partly off the flan. New York, ANS, no. N11; Rouvier, *JIAN* 6, 1903, p. 271, no. 1786 and pl. XVIII, 9 (ex Newell coll. = ex Rouvier coll.).
344.	O50* - R51* 13.21g 22mm 10h	Same as 246. Rather thick fabric. Oval flan. Small cracks on the edge. New York, ANS, no. N10 (ex Rouvier coll.).
345.	O51* - R52* 12.83g 22mm	Same as 246. Rather thick fabric. Small cracks on the edge. O and R: guilloche border partly off the flan. Bourgey, Paris, 2-3/4/2001, no. 294.
346.	O52* - R53* 13.34g 23mm 5h	Same as 246. O: guilloche border partly off the flan. Paris, BNF, no. 3218 ; *Catalogue De Luynes*, no. 3218; Babelon, *Perses*, no. 1999 (ex De Luynes coll.).
347.	O53* - R54* 12.89g 21mm 11h	Same as 246. Small cracks on the edge. R: defect on the left; guilloche border partly off the flan. New York, ANS, no. 1977.158,752.
348.	O38 - R? 12.95g 22mm 6h	Same as 246. Thick fabric. Oval flan. Slightly worn. O and R: guilloche border partly off the flan. New York, ANS, no. N19 (ex Newell coll.).
349.	O45 - R? 12.72g 21mm	Same as 246. Thick fabric. Slightly worn. O and R: guilloche border partly off the flan.

350. O49 - R?
12.89g 20mm
6h

Ratto, Geneva, 26/4/1909, no. 5172.
Same as 246. Thick fabric. Slightly worn.
O and R: guilloche border partly off the flan.
Princeton, PUL, no. 5928.

351. O? - R1
12.97g 23mm
11h

Same as 246. Rather thick fabric. Two deep chisel-cuts. Slightly worn.
O and R: guilloche border partly off the flan.
SNG Copenhagen 1987, no. 466 and pl. 20 (ex Fabricius coll.)

352. O? - R30
12.84g 21mm
9h

Same as 246. Thick fabric. Slightly worn.
O: dolphin and guilloche border partly off the flan.
R: guilloche border partly off the flan.
SNG Copenhagen, no. 298 and pl. 8.

353. O? - R51

Same as 246. Thick fabric. Slightly worn.
O and R: guilloche border partly off the flan.
Information from N. Vismara 16/11/1998 (Lebanon hoard).

354. O? - R59*
13.14g 23mm

Same as 246. Thick fabric. Slightly worn. Plated?
O and R: guilloche border partly off the flan.
Vigne, Paris, September 1986, no. 25 = Florange-Ciani, Paris, 17-21/2/1925, no. 1067 (ex Allotte de la Füye coll.).

355. O? - R60*
19mm

Same as 246. Thick fabric. Irregular flan. Slightly worn. Deep chisel-cut.
O: dolphin and cable border off the flan.
R: cable border off the flan.
Boston, MFA, no. 2202.

356. O? - R61*
13.62g 21mm
6h

Same as 246. Thick fabric. Small chisel-cut.
O: cable border partly off the flan. Rather worn.
R: cable border off the flan.
New York, ANS, no. N18 (ex Newell coll.).

357. O? - R62*
13.09g 23mm
12h

Same as 246. Thick fabric. Oval flan. Slightly worn.
O: dolphin and guilloche border partly off the flan.
R: guilloche border partly off the flan.
Spaer coll., Jerusalem (bought in Cyprus).

358. O? - R63*
13.37g 22mm

Same as 246. Thick fabric. Slightly worn.
O and R: guilloche border off the flan.
Vinchon, Paris, 22-23/5/1995, no. 162.

II.1.1.1.c. Rather indistinct

359. O? - R?
13.73g 22mm
12h

Same as 246. Worn.
O and R: guilloche border off the flan.
Beirut, AUB Museum, no. C1255; Baramki, *Coins AUB*, no. 1255 and pl. XXVII, 6.

360. O? - R?   Same as 246. Worn.
      13.64g   Sotheby's, London, 3-11/2/1909, no. 771 (ex Benson coll.).
361. O? - R?   Same as 246. Worn.
      13.59g 24mm   O and R: guilloche border partly off the flan.
                        Argenor Numismatique, Paris, October 2001, no. 451.
362. O? - R?   Same as 246. Chisel-cut. Worn.
      13.36g 22mm   O and R: guilloche border partly off the flan.
                        Baldwin, London, 34, 13/10/2003, no. 539.
363. O? - R?   Same as 246. Worn.
      13.25g 21mm   O: dolphin and guilloche border partly off the flan.
                        R: guilloche border partly off the flan.
                        Hirsch, Munich, 176, 19-20/11/1992, no. 386 = 172, 27-29/11/1991, no. 357.
364. O? - R?   Same as 246. Worn.
      13.25g 23mm   O and R: guilloche border partly off the flan.
                        Gadoury, Mulhouse, 11-13/10/1981, no. 150.
365. O? - R?   Same as 246. Worn. Irregular flan.
      13.20g 26mm   O and R: guilloche border partly off the flan.
                        Malter, Encino, 1969, no. 151.
366. O? - R?   Same as 246. Worn. Irregular flan.
      13.18g 26mm   O and R: guilloche border partly off the flan.
      3h   New York, ANS, no. 1977.158, 753.
367. O? - R?   Same as 246. Worn. Small cracks on the edge.
      12.98g 24mm   O: guilloche border partly off the flan.
      4h   New York, ANS, no. 1984.66.40 (ex Rosen coll.).
368. O? - R?   Same as 246. Worn.
      12.95g 26mm   O: guilloche border partly off the flan.
                        Hirsch, Munich, 162, 8-10/5/1989, no. 353.
369. O? - R?   Same as 246. Worn.
      12.76g 20mm   O and R: guilloche border partly off the flan.
                        Oslo, UOM, no. 7.
370. O? - R?   Same as 246. Worn. Deep chisel-cut.
      12.76g 26mm   O and R: guilloche border partly off the flan.
      5h   Cambridge, FM, no. 1777:45; *SNG Cambridge*, no. 6083; Elayi-Elayi, *Trésors*, p. 283, no. 2 (Tell el-Mashkuta hoard TLXXI).
371. O? - R?   Same as 246. Worn. Irregular flan.
      12.53g 25mm   O and R: guilloche border partly off the flan.
      3h   Mildenberg-Hurter, *Dewing Collection*, no. 2671 (ex Dewing coll.).
372. O? - R?   Same as 246. Worn.
      12.44g 24mm   Madrid, MAN, no. 21.69.7.

373. O? - R?　　　　　Same as 246. Worn. Irregular flan.
　　　12.38g 24mm　　O and R: guilloche border partly off the flan.
　　　2h　　　　　　　Leiden, RM, no. 3286 (ex Van Rede coll.).
374. O? - R?　　　　　Same as 246. Worn. Small cracks on the edge.
　　　12.30g 21mm　　Chisel-cut. Plated.
　　　6h　　　　　　　O and R: guilloche border partly off the flan.
　　　　　　　　　　　Mildenberg-Hurter, *Dewing Collection*, no. 2670 (ex Dewing coll.).
375. O? - R?　　　　　Same as 246. Worn. Irregular flan.
　　　12.25g 24mm　　O and R: guilloche border partly off the flan.
　　　　　　　　　　　Berk, Chicago, 105, 17/11/1998, no. 275.
376. O? - R?　　　　　Same as 246. Worn.
　　　11.80g 23mm　　Kress, Munich, 174, 8-9/3/1979, no. 493.
377. O? - R?　　　　　Same as 246. Worn.
　　　11.25g 24mm　　O and R: guilloche border partly off the flan.
　　　　　　　　　　　Beirut, NM, no. 1320; Chéhab, *Monnaies*, p. 115, no. 1320 and pl. LIV, 1.
378. O? - R?　　　　　Same as 246. Worn. Irregular flan. Plated.
　　　10.63g 20mm　　O: guilloche border partly off the flan.
　　　12h　　　　　　　R: defect in front of the head; guilloche border partly off the flan.
　　　　　　　　　　　Berlin, SM, no. 10182.
379. O? - R?　　　　　Same as 246. Worn. Pierced. Slightly broken.
　　　10.46g 24mm　　O: guilloche border partly off the flan.
　　　11h　　　　　　　R: guilloche border partly off the flan. Four chisel-cuts.
　　　　　　　　　　　Jerusalem, RocMus, no. 1262.1.
380. O? - R?　　　　　Same as 246. Worn and damaged. Plated.
　　　9.93g 22mm　　 O and R: guilloche border partly off the flan.
　　　12h　　　　　　　Berlin, SM, no. 10181.
381. O? - R?　　　　　Same as 246. Worn.
　　　9.93g 24mm　　 R: guilloche border partly off the flan. Chisel-cut.
　　　　　　　　　　　Vecchi, London, 1, 13/5/1983, no. 86.
382. O? - R?　　　　　Same as 246. Fragment.
　　　7.43g 23mm　　 Toronto, ROM, no. 922.44.5; Milne, *RA*, 1905, p. 258, no. 2; Elayi-Elayi, *Trésors*, p. 293, no. 22 and pl. XXXVI (Beni Hassan hoard TLXXV).
　　　2h
383. O? - R?　　　　　Same as 246. Worn. Irregular flan.
　　　　　　23mm　　　O and R: guilloche border partly off the flan.
　　　　　　　　　　　CH VIII, no. 156, pl. XX, 11; Elayi-Elayi, *Trans* 11, 1996, p. 111, no. 1 and pl. VIII, 64 (Phoenicia hoard TLXXIX).
384. O? - R?　　　　　Same as 246. Worn. Irregular flan.
　　　　　　22mm　　　O and R: guilloche border partly off the flan.

			CH VIII, no. 156, pl. XX, 12; Elayi-Elayi, *Trans* 11, 1996, p. 111, no. 2 and pl. VIII, 65 (Phoenicia hoard TLXXIX).
385.	O? - R?		Same as 246. Worn. Irregular flan.
		25mm	O and R: guilloche border partly off the flan.
			CH VIII, no. 154, pl. XX, 8; Elayi-Elayi, *Trans* 11, 1996, p. 110, no. 3 and pl. VIII, 61 (Phoenicia hoard TLXXVIII).
386.	O? - R?		Same as 246. Worn.
		22mm	O and R: guilloche border partly off the flan.
			Information from N. Vismara 16/11/1998 (Lebanon hoard).
387.	O? - R?		Same as 246. Worn. Overstruck.
		24mm	O and R: guilloche border partly off the flan.
			Information from N. Vismara 16/11/1998 (Lebanon hoard).
388.	O? - R?		Same as 246. Worn.
		22mm	O: dolphin and guilloche border partly off the flan.
			R: guilloche border partly off the flan.
			Ritter, Dusseldorf, 75, October 2005, no. 506 = 68, August 2004, no. 627 = 66, May 2004, no. 287 = 63, August 2003, no. 676 = 60, August 2002, no. 670.
389.	O? - R?		Same as 246. Worn. Irregular flan.
		22mm	O and R: guilloche border partly off the flan.
			Kurpfälzische Münzhandlung, Mannheim, 32, 1-2/6/1987, no. 124.
390.	O? - R?		Same as 246. Worn. Some cracks on the edge.
		21mm	O and R: guilloche border partly off the flan.
			Kurpfälzische Münzhandlung, Mannheim, 17, 10-13/12/1979, no. 179.
391.	O? - R?		Same as 246. Worn.
			O and R: guilloche border partly off the flan.
			O: dolphin off the flan.
			Superior Stamp and Coin, Beverly Hills, 17-23/6/1974, no. 322.
392.	O? - R?		Same as 246. Worn.
		22mm	O and R: guilloche border partly off the flan.
			O: dolphin and forelegs of the seahorse off the flan.
			Parke, Bern, 16-17/10/1968, no. 237.
393.	13.50g		Cahn, Frankfurt/Main, 3-4/11/1913, no. 214, not illustrated.
394.	13.15g		Sotheby's, London, 7/12/1866, no. 627, not illustrated (ex Bunburry coll.).
395.	13.10g		Hirsch, Munich, 175, 23-26/9/1992, no. 536, not

396. 12.94g illustrated.
Regling, *Sammlung Warren*, no. 1307, not illustrated (ex Warren coll.).
397. 12.84g 22mm Hess, Lucerne, 209, 12/4/1932, no. 39, not illustrated.
398. 12.72g Cahn, Frankfurt/Main, 68, 26/11/1930, no. 1575, not illustrated (ex Moritz Simon).
399. 11.15g Rasmussen, Copenhagen, 10-11/3/1970, no. 884 = Hamburger, Frankfurt/Main, 12/6/1930, no. 458, not illustrated (ex Proschowsky coll.).

II.1.1.1.d. Owl to left

400. O1* - R1* Same as 246, but the owl is turned to left.
11.93g 23mm O and R: guilloche border partly off the flan.
Münzen und Medaillen, Basel, 4, 26-27/11/1974, no. 175.

II.1.1.2. Fourths of shekel AR

401. O1* - R1* O: deity, bearded, riding on seahorse with curled wing, to right; holding reins in right hand and an arched bow in left hand; below, two lines of waves and dolphin, to right; guilloche border.
3.18g 14mm
R: owl standing to right, head facing; over its left shoulder, crook and flail; shallow incuse impression.
Private coll.
402. O1 - R1 Same as 401. Small cracks on the edge.
3.14g 16mm O: guilloche border partly off the flan. Restruck.
6h R: guilloche border partly off the flan.
New York, ANS, no. N36 (ex Newell coll.).
403. O1 - R2* Same as 401. Deep chisel-cut.
3.15g 17mm R: guilloche border partly off the flan.
11h Oxford, AM, no. 89.
404. O1 - R3* Same as 401. Small dies.
3.17g 17mm Paris, BNF, no. 2003; Babelon, *Perses*, no. 2003.
12h
405. O2 - R3 Same as 401. Small cracks on the edge.
3.26g Peus, Frankfurt/Main, 380, 3/11/2004, no. 607.
406. O2* - R4 Same as 401. Flaw on the obverse (restruck?). Chisel-cut.
2.97g 17mm
New York, ANS, no. N42 (ex Newell coll.).
407. O3* - R4* Same as 401.
3.06g 19mm O: one line of waves; guilloche border partly off the flan.

		Cambridge, FM, no. 9519; *Catalogue McClean*, no. 9519 (ex McClean coll.).
408.	O3* - R5* 3.04g 15mm	Same as 401. Small cracks on the edge. O: one line of waves; dolphin and guilloche border partly off the flan. Superior Galleries, New York, 31/5/1989, no. 6105 = Superior Stamp and Coin, Beverly Hills, 24/5, Winter 1988/89, no. C44 = Hirsch, Munich, 159, 21-24/9/1988, no. 461.
409.	O3 - R6* 3.42g	Same as 401. Triangular flan. O: one line of waves. R: chisel-cut. Vecchi, London, 2, 12-13/9/1996, no. 550.
410.	O3 - R7* 2.84g 19mm 9h	Same as 401. O: one line of waves. R: defect on the owl. Leiden, RM, no. 8082.
411.	O3 - R8* 3.16g 16mm 7h	Same as 401. Oval flan. O: one line of waves. Paris, BNF, no. 678 (ex Chandon de Briailles coll.).
412.	O4* - R8 3.00g 16mm 9h	Same as 401. O: guilloche border partly off the flan. Berlin, SM, no. 21.
413.	O4 - R9* 2.87g 16mm 9h	Same as 401. Oval flan. Berlin, SM, no. 22.
414.	O5* - R10* 3.05g 16mm	Same as 401. Slightly worn. O and R: guilloche border partly off the flan. Helbing, Munich, 8/11/1928, no. 4098.
415.	O6* - R11* 3.22g 16mm 9h	Same as 401. Irregular flan. Small cracks on the edge. O: one line of waves; guilloche border partly off the flan. Münzen und Medaillen, Basel, January 1968, no. 18 = Leu, Lucerne, 31, 6-7/12/1966, no. 529 = 7, April 1960, no. 252.
416.	O7* - R12* 3.24g	Same as 401. Chisel-cut. O: one line of waves; guilloche border partly off the flan. R: defect in front of the owl. Glendining, London, 21-23/2/1961, no. 2676 = Ratto, Lugano, 4/4/1927, no. 2660.
417.	O8* - R13* 3.14g	Same as 401. R: guilloche border partly off the flan.

		Peus, Frankfurt/Main, 332, 23-25 and 28/10/1991, no. 289 = Superior Galleries, Beverly Hills, 11-12/6/1986, no. 1417 = Sternberg, Zurich, 12, 18-19/11/1982, no. 303.
418.	O6 - R?	Same as 401. Slightly worn.
	3.30g 15mm	O: guilloche border partly off the flan.
		BMC Phoenicia, pl. 44, 3; Hill, *Catalogue Ward*, no. 817.
419.	O8 - R?	Same as 401. Slightly worn.
	3.38g	R: guilloche border partly off the flan.
	1h	*SNG Copenhagen*, no. 304 and pl. 8.
420.	O8 - R?	Same as 401. Slightly worn.
	3.15g	*SNG Copenhagen*, no. 302 and pl. 8.
	5h	
421.	O? - R?	Same as 401. Irregular flan. Rather worn.
	3.30g 16mm	O and R: guilloche border partly off the flan.
		Bologna, ArchM, no. 11.
422.	O? - R?	Same as 401. Rather worn.
	3.19g	O: guilloche border partly off the flan.
		Paris, BNF, no. 285 (ex Seyrig coll.).
423.	O? - R?	Same as 401. Irregular flan. Rather worn.
	3.18g	O and R: guilloche border partly off the flan.
		Baldwin, London, 34, 13/10/2003, no. 541.
424.	O? - R?	Same as 401. Rather worn.
	3.02g 16mm	Jerusalem, IM, no. 3877.
425.	O? - R?	Same as 401. Rather worn.
	2.88g 16mm	Spaer coll., Jerusalem (bought in Jerusalem).
	6h	
426.	O? - R?	Same as 401. Rather worn.
	2.86g 14mm	O: guilloche border partly off the flan.
	11h	Paris, BNF, no. 114 (ex De Vogüé coll.).
427.	O? - R?	Same as 401. Rather worn. Plated.
	2.63g 15mm	O: one line of waves.
	12h	R: guilloche border partly off the flan.
		Jerusalem, RocMus, no. H7.39; Lambert, *QDAP* 2, 1933, p. 7, no. 39 and pl. I; Elayi-Elayi, *Trésors*, p. 214, no. 39 (Abu Shusheh hoard TXLVII).
428.	O? - R?	Same as 401. Rather worn. Plated.
	2.60g	O and R: guilloche border partly off the flan.
	12h	*SNG Copenhagen*, no. 303 and pl. 8.
429.	O? - R?	Same as 401. Rather worn. Plated?
	2.35g 16mm	O and R: guilloche border partly off the flan.
		Kindler, *ErIs* 8, 1967, p. 233 and pl. 46, 4.

II.1.1.3. Sixteenths of shekel AR

430.	O1* - R1* 0.57g 8mm 11h	O: seahorse with curled wing, to left; below, two lines of waves; border of dots. R: owl standing to left, head facing; over its right shoulder, crook and flail; border of dots. Elayi-Elayi, *Trésors*, p. 237, no. 275 and pl. XXXIV (Naplouse hoard TLI).
431.	O1 - R2 0.51g	Same as 430. O and R: border of dots partly off the flan. Elsen, Brussels, 63, 16/9/2000, no. 573.
432.	O2* - R2* 0.55g 8mm 12h	Same as 430. O and R: border of dots partly off the flan. Elayi-Elayi, *Trésors*, p. 237, no. 278 and pl. XXXIV (Naplouse hoard TLI).
433.	O2 - R3* 0.42g 8mm	Same as 430. O and R: border of dots partly off the flan. Jerusalem, IM, no. 3884.
434.	O3* - R3 0.55g	Same as 430. O and R: border of dots partly off the flan. Sternberg, Zurich, 22, 20-21/11/1989, no. 137; Elayi-Elayi, *Trésors*, p. 237, no. 229 (Naplouse hoard TLI).
435.	O4* - R3 0.61g	Same as 430. O and R: border of dots partly off the flan. Hauck & Aufhäuser, Münzen und Medaillen, Deutschland, 18, 5-6/10/2004, no. 366; Klein, *Sammlung*, no. 728 (ex Klein coll.).
436.	O5 - R4*	Same as 430. O and R: border of dots partly off the flan. *CH* VIII, no. 156, pl. XX, 11; Elayi-Elayi, *Trans* 11, 1996, p. 111, no. 11 and pl. VIII, 74 (Phoenicia hoard TLXXIX).
437.	O5 - R5* 0.61g 10mm	Same as 430. O: border of dots partly off the flan. Paris, BNF, no. 1965/751 (ex Seyrig coll.) (from Byblos).
438.	O5* - R6*	Same as 430. *CH* VIII, no. 156, pl. XX, 16; Elayi-Elayi, *Trans* 11, 1996, p. 111, no. 6 and pl. VIII, 69 (Phoenicia hoard TLXXIX).
439.	O6* - R6	Same as 430. O and R: border of dots partly off the flan. *CH* VIII, no. 156, pl. XX, 13; Elayi-Elayi, *Trans* 11, 1996, p. 111, no. 3 and pl. VIII, 66 (Phoenicia hoard

TLXXIX).

440.	O6 - R6	Same as 430. *CH* VIII, no. 156, pl. XX, 14; Elayi-Elayi, *Trans* 11, 1996, p. 111, no. 4 and pl. VIII, 67 (Phoenicia hoard TLXXIX).
441.	O6 - R7* 0.77g 6h	Same as 430. O and R: border of dots partly off the flan. Oxford, AM, no. 99.
442.	O7* - R8* 0.75g 9mm 3h	Same as 430. O: one line of waves. Tel Aviv, KNM, no. K1787 ; Kindler, *ErIs* 8, 1967, no. 25 and pl. 46; Elayi-Elayi, *Trésors*, p. 165, no. 19 (Akko hoard TXXXIII).
443.	O7 - R9 0.49g	Same as 430. O and R: border of dots partly off the flan. Elsen, Brussels, 85, 10/9/2005, no. 117.
444.	O8* - R9* 0.60g 9mm 3h	Same as 430. O: one line of waves; border of dots off the flan. Tel Aviv, KNM, no. K1309.
445.	O9 - R10* 0.50g 9mm 3h	Same as 430. O: one line of waves. Tel Aviv, KNM, no. K1314 (found in Akko).
446.	O9* - R11* 0.68g 9mm 12h	Same as 430. O: one line of waves. R: border of dots partly off the flan. Tel Aviv, KNM, no. K1786 ; Kindler, *ErIs* 8, 1967, p. 324, no. 24 and pl. 46; Elayi-Elayi, *Trésors*, p. 165, no. 21 (Akko hoard TXXXIII).
447.	O10* - R11 0.35g 9mm 4h	Same as 430. Oval flan. O: one line of waves. R: border of dots partly off the flan. Shahaf coll., Haifa, no. 32.
448.	O11* - R12* 0.55g 8mm 3h	Same as 430. O and R: border of dots partly off the flan. Shahaf coll., Haifa, no. 31.
449.	O12* - R12 0.20g 9mm 4h	Same as 430. Slightly broken. O and R: border of dots partly off the flan. Shahaf coll., Haifa, no. 24.
450.	O13* - R13* 0.67g	Same as 430. O: waves and border of dots partly off the flan. R: border of dots partly off the flan. Kovacs, San Mateo, 1988.

451.	O13 - R14* 0.45g 6h	Same as 430. O and R: border of dots partly off the flan. London, BM, no. 1889-6-4 38; *BMC Phoenicia*, p. 233, no. 43 and pl. XXIX, 17.
452.	O14* - R15* 0.45g 9mm 11h	Same as 430. O: owl and border of dots partly off the flan. Spaer coll., Jerusalem.
453.	O15* - R16* 0.48g 8mm 12h	Same as 430. O: seahorse and border of dots partly off the flan. Jerusalem, RocMus, no. H7.41 ; Lambert, *QDAP* 2, 1933, p. 7, no. 41 and pl. I; Elayi-Elayi, *Trésors*, p. 214, no. 41 and pl. XXXIV (Abu Shusheh hoard TXLVII).
454.	O16* - R17* 0.50g 9mm 4h	Same as 430. Shahaf coll., Haifa, no. 19.
455.	O17* - R18* 0.55g 10mm 6h	Same as 430. O: border of dots partly off the flan. R: defect on the right. Shahaf coll., Haifa, no. 17.
456.	O18* - R19* 0.48g 10mm 3h	Same as 430. O and R: border of dots partly off the flan. Shahaf coll., Haifa, no. 13.
457.	O19* - R20* 0.76g	Same as 430. R: defect above. Münzen und Medaillen, Basel, 586, May 1995, no. 22; *CH* VIII, pl. XX, 17; Elayi-Elayi, *Trans* 11, 1996, p. 111, no. 7 and pl. VIII, 70 (Phoenicia hoard TLXXIX).
458.	O20* - R21* 0.56g 9mm 3h	Same as 430. R: defect on the left. Tel Aviv, KNM, no. K1685 (found in Akko).
459.	O21* - R22* 0.56g 9mm 1h	Same as 430. O: border of dots partly off the flan. R: three dots in front of the owl. Tel Aviv, KNM, no. 1777 ; Kindler, *ErIs* 8, 1967, no. 15 and pl. 46, 15; Elayi-Elayi, *Trésors*, p. 165, no. 20 and pl. XXVI (Akko hoard TXXXIII) (bought in Akko).
460.	O22* - R23* 0.51g 9mm	Same as 430. Slightly worn. Plated? O and R: border of dots partly off the flan. Jerusalem, IM, no. 3885.

461.	O23* - R24* 0.60g	Same as 430. O: waves and border of dots partly off the flan. Kovacs, San Mateo, 1988.
462.	O24* - R25* 0.58g 8mm 10h	Same as 430. O: one line of waves. R: defect on the owl. New York, ANS, no. 1977.153,757.
463.	O25* - R26* 0.51g 10mm	Same as 430. O: one line of waves; border of dots partly off the flan. Jerusalem, IM, no. 3888.
464.	O26* - R27* 0.48g	Same as 430. R: border of dots partly off the flan. Numismatic & Ancient Art Gallery, Zurich, 11/4/1991, no. 623.
465.	O27* - R28* 0.39g 1h	Same as 430. O and R: border of dots partly off the flan. Meshorer-Qedar, *Coinage of Samaria*, p. 78, no. SH259, pl. 44; Elayi-Elayi, *Trésors*, p. 228, no. 85 (Samaria hoard TXLIX).
466.	O28* - R29* 0.64g 10mm 7h	Same as 430. Paris, BNF, no. 1969/723 ; Elayi-Elayi, *Trésors*, p. 237, no. 240 and pl. XXXIV (Naplouse hoard TLI).
467.	O29* - R30* 0.53g 9mm 12h	Same as 430. O and R: border of dots partly off the flan. Tel Aviv, KNM, no. K1767 ; Kindler, *ErIs* 8, 1967, p. 324, no. 5; Elayi-Elayi, *Trésors*, p. 165, no. 18, and pl. XXVI (Akko hoard TXXXIII) (bought in Akko).
468.	O30* - R31* 0.30g 10mm 2h	Same as 430. O: defect on the wing. R: border of dots partly off the flan. Shahaf coll., Haifa, no. 21.
469.	O31 - R32 0.66g	Same as 430. O and R: border of dots partly off the flan. Paris, BNF, no. 1973 (ex Seyrig coll.).
470.	O31* - R32* 0.45g 9mm 11h	Same as 430. O and R: border of dots partly off the flan. Shahaf coll., Haifa, no. 14.
471.	O32* - R33* 0.42g 8mm 1h	Same as 430. O and R: border of dots partly off the flan. Leiden, RM, no. 8083.
472.	O33 - R34* 0.56g 9mm	Same as 430. O: waves and border of dots partly off the flan.

The Coinage of Tyre in the Persian period

	1h	R: owl and border of dots partly off the flan.
		New York, ANS, no. 1983.51.720 (ex Rosen coll.).
473.	O34* - R35*	Same as 430. Slightly broken.
	0.46g 9mm	O and R: border of dots partly off the flan.
	10h	New York, ANS, no. N35; Rouvier, *JIAN* 6, 1903, p. 276, no. 1819 and pl. XVIII, 19 (ex Newell coll. = ex Rouvier coll.).
474.	O35 - R35	Same as 430.
	0.50g 10mm	O and R: border of dots partly off the flan.
	1h	Shahaf coll., Haifa, no. 25.
475.	O35* - R36*	Same as 430.
	0.48g 9mm	O: border of dots partly off the flan.
	4h	R: defect on the flail.
		New York, ANS, no. N39 (ex Newell coll.).
476.	O35 - R36	Same as 430. Slightly worn.
	0.40g 9mm	O: seahorse and border of dots partly off the flan.
	4h	R: defect on the flail.
		Tel Aviv, KNM, no. K1684 (bought in Akko).
477.	O35 - R37	Same as 430.
	0.58g 8mm	O: seahorse and border of dots partly off the flan.
	8h	R: head of the owl off the flan.
		Tel Aviv, KNM, no. K1686 (bought in Akko).
478.	O36* - R37*	Same as 430. Slightly worn.
	0.58g	O and R: border of dots partly off the flan.
	5h	Meshorer-Qedar, *Coinage of Samaria*, p. 78, no. SH266, and pl. 45; Elayi-Elayi, *Trésors*, p. 227, no. 79 (Samaria hoard TXLIX).
479.	O4 - R?	Same as 430. Slightly worn.
	0.55g 9mm	O: waves and border of dots partly off the flan.
	7h	R: owl and border of dots partly off the flan.
		Paris, BNF, no. 1969/727; Elayi-Elayi, *Trésors*, p. 238, no. 280 and pl. XXXIV (Naplouse hoard TLI).
480.	O15 - R?	Same as 430. Slightly worn.
	0.50g 10mm	R: deficient striking.
		Jerusalem, IM, no. 3889.
481.	O19 - R?	Same as 430. Slightly worn.
	0.50g	O: waves and border of dots partly off the flan.
		Baldwin, London, 34, 13/10/2003, no. 543.
482.	O19 - R?	Same as 430. Slightly worn.
		Elayi-Elayi, *Trans* 11, 1996, p. 111, no. 5 and pl. VIII, 68.
483.	O26 - R?	Same as 430. Slightly worn.
	0.66g	Berk, Chicago, 135, 10/12/2003, no. 130.
484.	O28 - R?	Same as 430. Slightly worn.

	0.50g 9mm	O: waves and border of dots partly off the flan.
	12h	Tel Aviv, KNM, no. K1310 (bought in Akko).
485.	O34 - R?	Same as 430. Slightly worn.
	0.37g 10mm	O and R: border of dots partly off the flan.
	8h	Berlin, SM, no. 26.
486.	O65* - R?	Same as 430. Slightly worn.
	0.50g 10mm	O and R: border of dots partly off the flan.
		Jerusalem, IM, no. 3886.
487.	O66* - R?	Same as 430. Slightly worn.
	0.79g 8mm	O and R: border of dots partly off the flan.
		Jerusalem, IM, no. 10621.
488.	O65 - R?	Same as 430. Slightly worn.
		CH VIII, 156, 20; Elayi-Elayi, *Trans* 11, 1996, p. 111, no. 9 and pl. VIII, 72 (Phoenicia hoard TLXXIX).
489.	O? - R71*	Same as 430. Slightly worn.
	0.50g 9mm	O: waves and border of dots partly off the flan.
	3h	Shahaf coll., Haifa, no. 16.
490.	O? - R72*	Same as 430. Slightly worn.
	0.40g 9mm	O and R: border of dots partly off the flan.
	10h	Shahaf coll., Haifa, no. 44.
491.	O? - R73*	Same as 430. Slightly worn.
	0.54g 8mm	Jerusalem, IM, no. 10622.
	3h	
492.	O? - R74*	Same as 430. Slightly worn.
	0.49g 9mm	O: border of dots partly off the flan.
	1h	Tel Aviv, KNM, no. K1783; Kindler, *ErIs* 8, 1967, p. 324, no. 21; Elayi-Elayi, *Trésors*, p. 165, no. 23 and pl. XXVI (Akko hoard TXXXIII).
493.	O? - R75*	Same as 430. Slightly worn.
	0.76g	O: seahorse and border of dots partly off the flan.
	3h	Meshorer-Qedar, *Coinage of Samaria*, p. 78, no. SH255 and pl. 43; Elayi-Elayi, *Trésors*, p. 227, no. 72 (Samaria hoard TXLIX).
494.	O? - R75	Same as 430. Slightly worn.
	0.57g	O: border of dots partly off the flan.
	6h	Meshorer-Qedar, *Coinage of Samaria*, p. 78, no. SH258 and pl. 44; Elayi-Elayi, *Trésors*, p. 227, no. 80 (Samaria hoard TXLIX).
495.	O? - R75	Same as 430. Slightly worn.
	0.45g	Meshorer-Qedar, *Coinage of Samaria*, p. 78, no. SH257 and pl. 44; Elayi-Elayi, *Trésors*, p. 228, no. 84 (Samaria hoard TXLIX).
	12h	
496.	O? - R76*	Same as 430. Slightly worn.

	0.55g 6h	O and R: border of dots partly off the flan. Meshorer-Qedar, *Coinage of Samaria*, p. 78, no. SH264 and pl. 45; Elayi-Elayi, *Trésors*, p. 227, no. 81 (Samaria hoard TXLIX).
497.	O? - R77* 0.77g 1h	Same as 430. Slightly worn. O: border of dots partly off the flan. Meshorer-Qedar, *Coinage of Samaria*, p. 78, no. SH261 and pl. 44; Elayi-Elayi, *Trésors*, pp. 226-227, no. 71 (Samaria hoard TXLIX).
498.	O? - R78* 0.54g 10mm 6h	Same as 430. Slightly worn. Paris, BNF, no. 1969/725; Elayi-Elayi, *Trésors*, p. 237, no. 253 and pl. XXXIV (Naplouse hoard TLI).
499.	O? - R79* 0.69g 12h	Same as 430. Rather worn. O: border of dots partly off the flan. Meshorer-Qedar, *Coinage of Samaria*, p. 78, no. SH256 and pl. 44; Elayi-Elayi, *Trésors*, p. 227, no. 74 (Samaria hoard TXLIX).
500.	O? - R80 0.60g 10mm 7h	Same as 430. Slightly worn. O and R: border of dots partly off the flan. Shahaf coll., Haifa, no. 30.
501.	O? - R80* 0.47g 9mm 3h	Same as 430. Slightly worn. Tel Aviv, KNM, no. K1782; Kindler, *Erls* 8, 1967, p. 324, no. 20; Elayi-Elayi, *Trésors*, p. 165, no. 24 (Akko hoard TXXXIII).
502.	O? - R81* 0.63g	Same as 430. Slightly worn. O: seahorse and border of dots partly off the flan. Peus, Frankfurt/Main, 361, 6/11/1999, no. 251.
503.	O? - R? 0.74g 11mm 4h	Same as 430. Irregular flan. Rather worn. Tel Aviv, KNM, no. K1687 (bought in Akko).
504.	O? - R? 0.71g 5h	Same as 430. Rather worn. O: seahorse and border of dots partly off the flan. R: border of dots partly off the flan. Meshorer-Qedar, *Coinage of Samaria*, p. 78, no. SH263 and pl. 44; Elayi-Elayi, *Trésors*, p. 227, no. 73 (Samaria hoard TXLIX).
505.	O? - R? 0.70g 4h	Same as 430. Rather worn. O: seahorse and border of dots partly off the flan. R: owl and border of dots partly off the flan. Meshorer-Qedar, *Coinage of Samaria*, p. 78, no. SH262 and pl. 44; Elayi-Elayi, *Trésors*, p. 228, no. 86 (Samaria hoard TXLIX).
506.	O? - R? 0.69g	Same as 430. Rather worn. O: seahorse and border of dots partly off the flan.

	12h	R: owl and border of dots partly off the flan. Meshorer-Qedar, *Coinage of Samaria*, p. 78, no. SH267 and pl. 45; Elayi-Elayi, *Trésors*, p. 227, no. 75 (Samaria hoard TXLIX).
507.	O? - R? 0.66g 9mm 12h	Same as 430. Irregular flan. Rather worn. O and R: border of dots partly off the flan. Tel Aviv, KNM, no. K1785; Kindler, *ErIs* 8, 1967, p. 324, no. 23; Elayi-Elayi, *Trésors*, p. 165, no. 22 (Akko hoard TXXXIII).
508.	O? - R? 0.66g	Same as 430. Rather worn. O and R: border of dots partly off the flan. Müller, Solingen, 60, 20-21/1/1989, no. 125 = 56, 25-26/9/1987, no. 170.
509.	O? - R? 0.65g 10mm 2h	Same as 430. Rather worn. O: border of dots partly off the flan. Tel Aviv, KNM, no. K1629.
510.	O? - R? 0.63g 1h	Same as 430. Rather worn. Meshorer-Qedar, *Coinage of Samaria*, p. 78, no. SH265 and pl. 45; Elayi-Elayi, *Trésors*, p. 227, no. 76 (Samaria hoard TXLIX).
511.	O? - R? 0.62g 9h	Same as 430. Rather worn. O and R: border of dots partly off the flan. Meshorer-Qedar, *Coinage of Samaria*, p. 78, no. SH253 and pl. 43; Elayi-Elayi, *Trésors*, p. 227, no. 77 (Samaria hoard TXLIX).
512.	O? - R? 0.61g 10mm 9h	Same as 430. Rather worn. Paris, BNF, no. 1969/724; Elayi-Elayi, *Trésors*, p. 237, no. 245 and pl. XXXIV (Naplouse hoard TLI).
513.	O? - R? 0.60g 9mm 3h	Same as 430. Rather worn. O: border of dots partly off the flan. Tel Aviv, KNM, no. K1312 (from Akko).
514.	O? - R? 0.60g 9mm 3h	Same as 430. Rather worn. O: chisel-cut. Tel Aviv, KNM, no. K1317 (from Akko).
515.	O? - R? 0.60g 9mm 12h	Same as 430. Rather worn. Tel Aviv, KNM, no. K1691 (from Akko).
516.	O? - R? 0.59g	Same as 430. Rather worn. O: border of dots partly off the flan. Müller, Solingen, 25, 16-17/2/1979, no. 83.
517.	O? - R? 0.59g	Same as 430. Rather worn. Müller, Solingen, 24, 21-23/9/1978, no. 96.
518.	O? - R? 0.58g	Same as 430. Rather worn. O: one line of waves; border of dots partly off the

The Coinage of Tyre in the Persian period 73

	6h	flan. Meshorer-Qedar, *Coinage of Samaria*, p. 78, no. SH254 and pl. 43; Elayi-Elayi, *Trésors*, p. 227, no. 78 (Samaria hoard TXLIX).
519.	O? - R? 0.57g	Same as 430. Rather worn. Small cracks on the edge. O and R: border of dots partly off the flan. Müller, Solingen, 31, 4-5/2/1981, no. 132.
520.	O? - R? 0.52g	Same as 430. Partly broken and rather worn. O: border of dots partly off the flan. London, BM, no. 1921-7-6 1.
521.	O? - R? 0.51g 3h	Same as 430. Irregular flan. Rather worn. O: border of dots partly off the flan. Meshorer-Qedar, *Coinage of Samaria*, p. 78, no. SH268 and pl. 45; Elayi-Elayi, *Trésors*, p. 227, no. 82 (Samaria hoard TXLIX).
522.	O? - R? 0.51g	Same as 430. Rather worn. R: border of dots partly off the flan. Müller, Solingen, 24, 21-23/9/1978, no. 97.
523.	O? - R? 0.50g 10mm 5h	Same as 430. Rather worn. Chisel-cut. O: border of dots partly off the flan. Tel Aviv, KNM, no. K1690 (from Akko).
524.	O? - R? 0.50g 9mm 12h	Same as 430. Rather worn. Tel Aviv, KNM, no. K1694 (from Akko).
525.	O? - R? 0.50g 10mm 7h	Same as 430. Rather worn. O and R: border of dots partly off the flan. Shahaf coll., Haifa, no. 41.
526.	O? - R? 0.48g 1h	Same as 430. Rather worn. O and R: border of dots partly off the flan. Meshorer-Qedar, *Coinage of Samaria*, p. 78, no. SH260 and pl. 44; Elayi-Elayi, *Trésors*, pp. 227-228, no. 83 (Samaria hoard TXLIX).
527.	O? - R? 0.46g 9mm 12h	Same as 430. Rather worn. Spaer coll., Jerusalem (bought in Beirut).
528.	O? - R? 0.45g 10mm 7h	Same as 430. Partly broken and rather worn. O and R: border of dots partly off the flan. Paris, BNF, no. 678A (ex Chandon de Briailles coll.).
529.	O? - R? 0.45g 9mm 3h	Same as 430. Rather worn. O and R: border of dots partly off the flan. Tel Aviv, KNM, no. K1689.
530.	O? - R?	Same as 430. Rather worn.

	0.44g 9mm	O: waves and border of dots partly off the flan.
	12h	Tel Aviv, KNM, no. K1784; Kindler, *ErIs* 8, 1967, p. 324, no. 22; Elayi-Elayi, *Trésors*, p. 165, no. 25 (Akko hoard TXXXIII) (bought in Akko).
531.	O? - R?	Same as 430. Partly broken and rather worn.
	0.44g 9mm	R: border of dots partly off the flan.
	12h	Fulco, *RB* 2, 1975, p. 234 and pl. 18, 3; Briend-Humbert, *Tell Keisan*, p. 236, no. 3 and pl. 133; Elayi-Elayi, *Trésors*, pp. 344-345 (Tell Keisan excavations).
532.	O? - R?	Same as 430. Rather worn. Small cracks on the edge.
	0.40g 10mm	
	2h	O and R: border of dots partly off the flan.
		Tel Aviv, KNM, no. K1311 (from Akko).
533.	O? - R?	Same as 430. Rather worn. Small cracks on the edge.
	0.40g 9mm	
	2h	O and R: border of dots partly off the flan.
		Tel Aviv, KNM, no. K1692 (bought in Akko).
534.	O? - R?	Same as 430. Rather worn.
	0.35g 10mm	Tel Aviv, KNM, no. K1628 (from Akko).
	12h	
535.	O? - R?	Same as 430. Rather worn.
	0.35g 10mm	O: border of dots partly off the flan.
	6h	Shahaf coll., Haifa, no. 47.
536.	O? - R?	Same as 430. Rather worn.
	0.30g 8mm	Shahaf coll., Haifa, no. 39.
	2h	
537.	O? - R?	Same as 430. Rather worn.
	0.25g 7mm	Kindler, *ErIs* 8, 1967, p. 323 and pl. 46, 7.
538.	O? - R?	Same as 430. Partly broken and rather worn.
	0.23g	O and R: border of dots partly off the flan.
		Jerusalem, IM, no. 852; Elayi-Elayi, *Trésors*, p. 168, no. 1 and pl. XXVII (Akko hoard TXXXIV).
539.	O? - R?	Same as 430. Broken and rather worn.
	0.22g 8mm	O and R: border of dots partly off the flan.
	3h	Tel Aviv, KNM, no. K1688 (bought in Akko).
540.	O? - R?	Same as 430. Very worn.
		O: seahorse and border of dots partly off the flan.
		CH VIII, 156, 22; Elayi-Elayi, *Trans* 11, 1996, p. 111, no. 12 and pl. VIII, 75 (Phoenicia hoard TLXXIX).
541.	O? - R?	Same as 430. Rather worn.
		Malloy, New York, 24, 18/3/1988, no. 137.
542.	O? - R?	Same as 430. Rather worn.

		O and R: border of dots partly off the flan.
		Rauch, Vienna, 7, 4-5/6/1971, no. 85.
543.	O? - R?	Same as 430. Rather worn.
		O: border of dots partly off the flan.
		Rauch, Vienna, 7, 4-5/6/1971, no. 86.
544.	O? - R?	Same as 430. Very worn.
	0.37g 9mm	Sheridan, *Numismatist* 8, 1971, p. 1131, no. 210; Elayi-Elayi, *Trésors*, p. 203, no. 13 (Beirut hoard TXLIII).
545.	O? - R?	Same as 430. Rather worn.
		O and R: border of dots partly off the flan.
		Private coll. (Naplouse hoard TLI?).
546.	0.48g 9mm	Same as 430.
		Fulco, *RB* 2, 1975, p. 235 and pl. 18,4, not illustrated (Tell Keisan excavations).
547.	0.58g	Same as 430.
		Ratto, Lugano, 4/4/1927, no. 2661, not illustrated.
548.		Same as 430.
		Elayi-Elayi, *Trésors*, p. 209, no. 10, not illustrated (Gaza hoard TXLVI).
549-558		Same as 430. Elayi-Elayi, *Trésors*, p. 237, no. 230-239, not illustrated (Naplouse hoard TLI).
559-562		Same as 430. Elayi-Elayi, *Trésors*, p. 237, no. 241-244, not illustrated (Naplouse hoard TLI).
563-569		Same as 430. Elayi-Elayi, *Trésors*, p. 237, no. 246-252, not illustrated (Naplouse hoard TLI).
570-573		Same as 430. Elayi-Elayi, *Trésors*, p. 237, no. 254-257, not illustrated (Naplouse hoard TLI).
574-589		Same as 430. Elayi-Elayi, *Trésors*, p. 237, no. 259-274, not illustrated (Naplouse hoard TLI).
590-591		Same as 430. Elayi-Elayi, *Trésors*, p. 237, no. 276-277, not illustrated (Naplouse hoard TLI).
592.		Elayi-Elayi, *Trésors*, p. 238, no. 279, not illustrated (Naplouse hoard TLI).
593-601		Same as 430. Elayi-Elayi, *Trésors*, p. 238, no. 281-289, not illustrated (Naplouse hoard TLI).
602-		Same as 430.

612   Elayi-Elayi, *Trésors*, p. 238, no. 290-300, not illustrated (Naplouse hoard TLI).

II.1.2. Inscribed (around 393-358 BCE)

II.1.2.1. Shekels AR

II.1.2.1.a. With *M* on the reverse

613. O1 - R1*   Thick fabric.
      13.54g 27mm   O: deity, bearded, riding on seahorse with curled
      5h   wing, to right; holding reins in right hand and an
                         arched bow in left hand; below, two lines of waves
                         and dolphin, to right; guilloche border.
                         R: owl standing to right, head facing; over its left
                         shoulder, crook and flail; *M* in field right; guilloche
                         border.
                         Paris, BNF, no. 3213; Babelon, *Perses*, no. 1990;
                         id., *Traité*, pl. CXXII, 10; *Catalogue De Luynes*, no.
                         3213 (ex De Luynes coll.).
614. O1 - R2*   Same as 613.
      12.42g 20mm   O: guilloche border partly off the flan.
      12h   R: *M* in field right; guilloche border partly off the
                         flan.
                         Berlin, SM, no. 11 (ex Prokesch-Osten coll.).
615. O1* - R3*   Same as 613. Deep chisel-cut.
      13.42g 21mm   O: guilloche border partly off the flan.
      10h   R: *M̊* in field right; guilloche border partly off the
                         flan.
                         New York, ANS, no. N12 (ex Newell coll.).
616. O2 - R3   Same as 613. Irregular flan.
      12.84g   O: dolphin and guilloche border partly off the flan;
                         defect under the seahorse.
                         R: *M̊* in field right; guilloche border partly off the
                         flan.
                         Bishop-Holloway, *Wheaton Collection*, no. 273 (ex
                         Wheaton coll.).
617. O2* - R4*   Same as 613. Irregular flan. Small cracks on the
      12.54g 24mm   edge.
      10h   O: seahorse and guilloche border partly off the flan.
                         R: *M̊* in field right; guilloche border partly off the
                         flan.
                         Jerusalem, RocMus, no. H1.14; Lambert, *QDAP* 1,
                         1931, p. 15, no. 14; Elayi-Elayi, *Trésors*, p. 171, no.
                         3 and pl. XXVII (Tell Abu Hawam hoard TXXXV).

618.	O2 - R5* 13.48g 23mm 5h	Same as 613. Irregular flan. Small cracks on the edge. O: dolphin and guilloche border partly off the flan; defect under the seahorse. R: M in field right; guilloche border partly off the flan. Paris, BNF; Babelon, *Perses*, no. 1995; id., *Traité*, no. 994, pl. CXXII, 11.
619.	O3* - R6* 12.00g 22mm 11h	Same as 613. Slightly worn. Small cracks on the edge. O: guilloche border partly off the flan; defect on the dolphin. R: $\overset{o}{M}$ in field right; guilloche border partly off the flan. Shahaf coll., Haifa, no. 5.
620.	O3 - R7* 12.65g	Same as 613. Irregular flan. Small cracks on the edge. O: guilloche border partly off the flan; defect on the dolphin and waves. R: $\overset{o}{M}$ in field right; guilloche border partly off the flan. Classical Numismatic Group, Lancaster-London, 41, 19/3/1997, no. 703.
621.	O3 - R8* 12.47g 19mm 2h	Same as 613. Irregular flan. Small cracks on the edge. O: guilloche border partly off the flan; defect on the dolphin and waves. R: $\overset{o}{M}$ in field right; guilloche border partly off the flan. Vienna, KHM, no. 33.281.
622.	O4* - R8 13.60g	Same as 613. Small cracks on the edge. O: guilloche border partly off the flan. R: $\overset{o}{M}$ in field right; guilloche border partly off the flan. Müller, Solingen, 66, 28-29/9/1990, no. 107 = Numismatica, Vienna, 13, 9-11/11/1976, no. 367.
623.	O5* - R9* 12.74g 23mm 1h	Same as 613. Irregular flan. Small cracks on the edge. O: guilloche border partly off the flan. R: $\overset{o}{M}$ in field right; guilloche border partly off the flan. Jerusalem, RocMus, no. H1.1; Lambert, *QDAP* 1, 1931, p. 15, no. 1; Elayi-Elayi, *Trésors*, p. 171, no. 2 and pl. XXVII (Tell Abu Hawam hoard TXXXV).

624. O5 - R10*   Same as 613.
12.40g 21mm   O: guilloche border partly off the flan.
7h   R: *M* in field right; guilloche border partly off the flan.
                 Berlin, SM, no. 16 (ex Löbbecke coll.).

625. O6* - R11*   Same as 613. Irregular flan. Small cracks on the edge.
12.70g 22mm   O: guilloche border partly off the flan.
6h   R: *M* in field right; guilloche border partly off the flan.
                 Paris, BNF, no. 112 (ex De Vogüé coll.).

626. O7* - R12*   Same as 613. Irregular flan. Chisel-cut.
12.44g 22mm   O: seahorse and guilloche border partly off the flan.
6h   R: $\overset{o}{M}$ in field right; guilloche border partly off the flan.
                 Spaer coll., Jerusalem (bought in Cyprus).

627. O8* - R13*   Same as 613. Oval flan. Small cracks on the edge.
12.10g 23mm   O: guilloche border partly off the flan.
1h   R: *M* in field right; guilloche border partly off the flan.
                 Jerusalem, RocMus, no. H1.2; Lambert, *QDAP* 1, 1931, p. 15, no. 2 and pl. XIX; Elayi-Elayi, *Trésors*, p. 171, no. 4 and pl. XXVII (Tell Abu Hawam hoard TXXXV).

628. O9* - R14*   Same as 613. Irregular flan.
13.21g 21mm   O: guilloche border partly off the flan. Chisel-cut.
10h   R: *M* in field right; guilloche border partly off the flan. Two chisel-cuts.
                 New York, ANS, no. 1944.100.72 668; Newell, *NC*, 1914, no. 91 and pl. IV, 3; Elayi-Elayi, *Trésors*, p. 265, no. 4 and pl. XXXV (Cilicia hoard TLX).

629. O1 - R?   Same as 613. Irregular flan. Slightly worn. Small cracks on the edge.
12.32g 23mm   O: guilloche border partly off the flan.
10h   R: $\overset{o}{M}$ in field right; guilloche border partly off the flan.
                 Berlin, SM, no. 14 (ex Dannenberg coll.).

630. O10 - R?   Same as 613. Irregular flan. Slightly worn. Chisel-cut.
13.36g   O: guilloche border partly off the flan.
                 R: $\overset{o}{M}$ in field right; guilloche border partly off the flan.
                 Classical Numismatic Group, Lancaster-London, 34, 6/5/1995, no. 197 = England, Quarryville-London,

27, 29/9/1993, no. 748.

631. O? - R5
12.80g
Same as 613. Rather worn. Small cracks on the edge.
O: guilloche border partly off the flan.
R: *M* in field right; guilloche border partly off the flan.
Archaeological Center, Tel Aviv, 22, 28/9/1999, no. 6.

632. O? - R8
12.85g
Same as 613. Rather worn.
O: seahorse and guilloche border partly off the flan.
R: *M* in field right; guilloche border partly off the flan.
Numismatica, Vienna, 21, 20-23/11/1978, no. 144.

633. O? - R8
11.99g 20mm
9h
Same as 613. Rather worn. Chisel-cut. Plated.
R: *M* in field right.
BMC Phoenicia, p. 299, no. 11 and pl. XXVIII, 16; Rouvier, *JIAN* 6, 1903, p. 272, no. 1791 and pl. XVIII, 12; Jenkins, *BMQ* 28, 1964, no. 6; Kraay, *Greek Coins*, no. 1049; Elayi-Elayi, *Trésors*, pp. 271-272, no. 3 and pl. XXXVI (Tigris hoard TLXIV).

634. O? - R13*
13.28g 22mm
Same as 613. Rather worn. Plated?
O: guilloche border partly off the flan.
R: *M* in field right; guilloche border partly off the flan.
Beirut, NM, no. 1318: Chéhab, *Monnaies*, no. 1320 and pl. LIII, 3.

635. O? - R14
13.55g 20mm
2h
Same as 613. Rather worn.
O: dolphin and guilloche border partly off the flan.
R: *M* in field right; guilloche border partly off the flan.
SNG Copenhagen, no. 299 and pl. 8.

636. O? - R46*
11.80g
Same as 613. Rather worn.
O: dolphin and guilloche border partly off the flan.
R: *M* in field right; guilloche border partly off the flan.
Müller, Münz Zentrum-Rheinland, Solingen, 101, 15-18/12/1999, no. 142 = 98, 5-7/5/1999, no. 155.

637. O? - R47*
10.98g 20mm
Same as 613. Irregular flan. Rather worn.
O: guilloche border partly off the flan.
R: *M* in field right; guilloche border partly off the flan.
Jerusalem, IM, no. 3876.

638.	O? - R48* 12.64g 20mm 2h	Same as 613. Rather worn. Small cracks on the edge. O: dolphin and guilloche border partly off the flan. R: M in field right; guilloche border partly off the flan. New York, ANS, no. 55.80.
639.	O? - R? 13.34g	Same as 613. Rather worn. O: guilloche border partly off the flan. R: $\overset{o}{M}$ in field right; countermark below. Y. Yadin et al., *Hazor I*, Jerusalem 1958, pl. CLII, 10 (Hazor excavations).
640.	O? - R? 13.31g	Same as 613. Rather worn. O: deity, seahorse and guilloche border partly off the flan. R: M in field right; guilloche border partly off the flan. Gadoury, Monte-Carlo, 26-27/11/1985, no. 49.
641.	O? - R? 12.20g 22mm	Same as 613. Irregular flan. Rather worn. O: dolphin and guilloche border partly off the flan. R: $\overset{o}{M}$ in field right; guilloche border partly off the flan. Christensen, 7/7/1978, no. 178 = 9/7/1965, no. 82 (ex Parsons coll.).
642.	O? - R? 12.09g	Same as 613. Irregular flan. Rather worn. O: guilloche border partly off the flan. R: M in field right; guilloche border partly off the flan. Hirsch, Munich, 166, 16-19/5/1990, no. 549 = 160, 23-25/11/1988, no. 313.
643.	O? - R? 10.31g 19mm 12h	Same as 613. Rather worn. Plated. R: M in field right; guilloche border partly off the flan. London, BM, no. HPB p164.28 ; *BMC Phoenicia*, p. 229, 12, not illustrated (from Cyprus).
644.	O? - R?	Same as 613. Rather worn. O: seahorse and guilloche border partly off the flan. R: $\overset{o}{M}$ in field right; guilloche border partly off the flan. Malloy, New York, 45, 19/3/1997, no. 175.
645.	11.80g	Same as 613. Plated? R: M in field right. Baldwin, London, 34, 13/10/2003, no. 540, not illustrated.
646-		Same as 613.

651.   R: *M* in field right.
                        Jenkins, *BMQ* 28, 1964, pp. 88-90, Erskine list;
                        Elayi-Elayi, *Trésors*, pp. 272-273, not illustrated
                        (Tigris hoard TLXIV).

II.1.2.1.b. With *MB* on the reverse

652.   O10* - R15   Same as 613. Oval flan.
        12.52g 23mm   O: dolphin and guilloche border partly off the flan.
        12h   R: *B* in field left and *M* right; guilloche border partly
                        off the flan.
                        Beirut, AUB Museum, no. C1254; Baramki, *Coins
                        AUB*, p. 220, no. 7, and pl. XXVII, 4.
653.   O11* - R15*   Same as 613. Oval flan. Small cracks on the edge.
        12.53g 21mm   O: guilloche border partly off the flan.
        12h   R: *B* in field left and *M* right; guilloche border partly
                        off the flan.
                        London, BM, no. 1868-4-7 1 ; Rouvier, *JIAN* 6,
                        1903, p. 272, no. 1792 and pl. XVIII, 13 ; *BMC
                        Phoenicia*, p. 229, no. 13 and pl. XXVIII, 17.
654.   O? - R49*   Same as 613. Irregular flan. Slightly worn.
        12.32g 23mm   O: dolphin and guilloche border partly off the flan.
                        R: *B* in field left and *M* right; owl and guilloche
                        border partly off the flan.
                        Jerusalem, AI, no. 3836.

II.1.2.1.c. With *B* on the reverse

655.   O11 - R16*   Same as 613. Small cracks on the edge.
        12.59g 20mm   O: deity and guilloche border partly off the flan.
                        R: *B* in field right; guilloche border partly off the
                        flan.
                        Hirsch, Munich, 175, 23-26/9/1992, no. 535 = 162,
                        8-10/5/1989, no. 352.
656.   O38 - R?   Same as 613. Slightly worn.
        11.89g   O: guilloche border partly off the flan; countermark
                        on the seahorse.
                        R: $\overset{\circ}{B}$ in field right; guilloche border partly off the
                        flan.
                        Müller, Solingen, 18, 23-25/9/1976, no. 161.
657.   O? - R50*   Same as 613. Irregular flan. Slightly worn.
                        O: guilloche border partly off the flan.
                        R: *B* in field right; guilloche border partly off the
                        flan.
                        Phoenix, London, P96, 1993, no. G395.

II.1.2.1.d. With ṢR on the reverse

658. O12* - R17* Same as 613. Small cracks on the edge.
     13.12g 19mm O: dolphin, waves and guilloche border partly off
     2h   the flan.
                    R: ṢR in field right; guilloche border off the flan.
                    Jerusalem, RocMus, no. H1.13; Lambert, *QDAP* 1,
                    1931, p. 15, no. 13 and pl. XIX; Elayi-Elayi,
                    Trésors, p. 172, no. 5 and pl. XXVII (Tell Abu Ha-
                    wam hoard TXXXV).
659. O? - R44*   Same as 613. Slightly worn. Small cracks on the
     13.02g 19mm edge.
     12h   O: seahorse and guilloche border partly off the flan.
                    R: ṢR in field right; guilloche border off the flan.
                    Paris, BNF, no. 3212; Babelon, *Perses*, no. 1989;
                    id., *Traité*, no. 997; *Catalogue De Luynes*, no. 3212
                    (ex De Luynes coll.).

II.1.2.1.e. With ʿ on the reverse

660. O? - R45*   Same as 613. Slightly worn. Small cracks on the
     12.90g 20mm edge.
     1h   O: seahorse and guilloche border partly off the flan.
                    R: ʿ in field left; guilloche border off the flan.
                    New York, ANS, no. N21 (ex Newell coll.).

II.1.2.1.f. With *I* on the reverse

661. O13 - R18   Same as 613.
     13.36g 17mm O: guilloche border?
     4h   R: *I* in field right; guilloche border partly off the
                    flan.
                    Paris, BNF, no. 3215 (ex De Luynes coll.).
662. O13 - R18   Same as 613. Slightly irregular flan.
     13.28g 21mm O : *I* in field right. Dolphin and part of guilloche
     9h   border off the flan.
                    Paris, BNF, no. 3214; Babelon, *Perses*, no. 1992;
                    id., *Traité*, no. 998 (ex De Luynes coll.).
663. O13* - R18* Same as 613. Slightly irregular flan.
     13.22g 19mm O : guilloche border off the flan.
     9h   R: *I* in field right; guilloche border off the flan.
                    New York, ANS, no. N20 (ex Newell coll.).
664. O14* - R19* Same as 613. Small cracks on the edge.
     13.16g 20mm O : guilloche border partly off the flan.
     5h   R: *I* in field right; guilloche border off the flan.

665. O15 - R20* Same as 613. Chisel-cut.
 13.25g 18mm O : seahorse and dolphin partly off the flan. Defect on the dolphin.
 R: $\overset{o}{I}$ in field right; guilloche border off the flan.
 Bologne, ArchM, no. 11.
 Paris, BNF, no. 677; Kundig, Basel, 8, 22/3/1937, no. 401 = Helbing, Munich, 8/11/1928, no. 4096 (ex Chandon de Briailles coll.).

666. O15* - R21* Same as 613. Slightly irregular flan.
 12.88g 21mm O : dolphin off the flan.
 4h R: *1[* in field right; guilloche border off the flan.
 Shahaf coll., Haifa, no. 20.

667. O16* - R21 Same as 613. Slightly irregular flan.
 12.85g 21mm O : head of the seahorse and guilloche border off the flan.
 7h R: *1[* in field right; guilloche border off the flan.
 Jerusalem, RocMus, no. H1.3; Lambert, *QDAP* 1, 1931, p. 15, no. 3; Elayi-Elayi, *Trésors*, p. 172, no. 6 and pl. XXVII (Tell Abu Hawam hoard TXXXV).

668. O? - R19 Same as 613. Irregular flan. Chisel-cut.
 13.96g 16mm O : head of the seahorse, dolphin and guilloche border off the flan.
 9h R: *1* in field right; guilloche border off the flan.
 Berlin, SM, no. 13.

II.1.2.1.g. With *2* on the reverse

669. O17* - R22* Same as 613. Irregular flan. Slightly worn.
 13.14g 18mm O: head of the deity, dolphin and guilloche off the flan.
 3h R: *2* in field right; guilloche border off the flan.
 Paris, BNF, no. 1996; Babelon, *Perses*, no. 1996.

670. O30 - R? Same as 613. Irregular flan. Slightly worn.
 13.20g O: dolphin and guilloche border off the flan.
 R: *2* in field right; guilloche border off the flan. Chisel-cut.
 Numismatica, Vienna, 21, 20-23/11/1978, no. 145.

671. O? - R21 Same as 613. Irregular flan. Slightly worn.
 O: guilloche border off the flan.
 R: $\overset{o}{2}$ in field right; guilloche border off the flan.
 Glendining, London, 18-20/4/1955, no. 611.

672. O? - R25* Same as 613. Irregular flan. Slightly worn. Chisel-cut.
 13.17g 21mm
 3h O: guilloche border off the flan.

R: *2* in field right; guilloche border off the flan. Overstruck?
London, BM, no. 1908-12-10 196; *BMC Phoenicia*, p. 229, no. 14 and pl. XXIX, 1 (probably from India).

673. O? - R41*
12.85g 20mm
6h

Same as 613. Irregular flan. Slightly worn.
O: guilloche border off the flan.
R: *2[* in field right; guilloche border off the flan.
Jerusalem, RocMus, no. H1.4; Lambert, *QDAP* 1, 1931, p. 15, no. 4; Elayi-Elayi, *Trésors*, p. 172, no. 7 and pl. XXVII (Tell Abu Hawam hoard TXXXV).

II.1.2.1.h. With *3* on the reverse

674. O18* - R23*
13.32g 18mm
12h

Same as 613. Irregular flan.
O: dolphin and guilloche border off the flan.
R: *3* in field right; guilloche border off the flan.
Paris, BNF, no. 1973.1.441 (ex Seyrig coll.).

675. O19* - R24*
13.21g 21mm
3h

Same as 613. Chisel-cut.
O: guilloche border off the flan.
R: *3* in field right; guilloche border off the flan.
New York, ANS, no. N14 (ex Newell coll.).

676. O20* - R24
13.15g 20mm
3h

Same as 613. Chisel-cut.
O: guilloche border off the flan.
R: *3* in field right; guilloche border off the flan.
London, BM, no. 1862-8-6 19; *BMC Phoenicia*, p. 229, no. 15 and pl. XXIX, 2.

677. O21 - R25'*
12.84g 18mm

Same as 613. Irregular flan.
O: head of the deity and guilloche border off the flan.
R: *3* in field right; guilloche border partly off the flan.
NFA, Beverly Hills, 28, 23/4/1992, no. 790.

678. O? - R?
12.50g 19mm
6h

Same as 613. Rather worn. Chisel-cut.
O: head of the deity off the flan.
R: *3[* in field right; guilloche border off the flan.
Spaer coll., Jerusalem (bought in Jerusalem).

679. O? - R?

Same as 613. Rather worn. Irregular flan.
O: guilloche border partly off the flan.
R: *3* in field right; guilloche border partly off the flan.
Malter, Encino, 27-28/9/1980, no. 871.

II.1.2.1.i. With *4* on the reverse

680.	O21 - R26* 13,23g 19mm 7h	Same as 613. Irregular flan. Two chisel-cuts. O: deity and guilloche border partly off the flan. R: *4* in field right; guilloche border partly off the flan. Paris, BNF, no. 1995; Babelon, *Perses*, no. 1995 ; *id.*, *Traité*, pl. CXXII, 14.
681.	O21 - R27* 13,39g 20mm 5h	Same as 613. Irregular flan. O: dolphin and guilloche border off the flan. R: *4* in field right; guilloche border off the flan. Paris, BNF, no. 113 (ex De Vogüé coll.).
682.	O21* - R28* 13.17g 22mm 5h	Same as 613. Irregular flan. Small cracks on the edge. O: guilloche border partly off the flan. R: *4* in field right; guilloche border partly off the flan. Jerusalem, RocMus, no. H1.7; Lambert, *QDAP* 1, 1931, p. 15, no. 7; Elayi-Elayi, *Trésors*, p. 172, no. 9 and pl. XXVII (Tell Abu Hawam hoard TXXXV).
683.	O22* - R29* 13.02g 20mm 1h	Same as 613. Irregular flan. Small cracks on the edge. O: seahorse and guilloche border partly off the flan. R: *4[* in field right; guilloche border off the flan. Jerusalem, RocMus, no. H1.6; Lambert, *QDAP* 1, 1931, p. 15, no. 6; Elayi-Elayi, *Trésors*, p. 172, no. 8 and pl. XXVII (Tell Abu Hawam hoard TXXXV).
684.	O23* - R30* 13.08g	Same as 613. Irregular flan. Small cracks on the edge. O: dot before the head of the seahorse; dolphin off the flan. R: *4[* in field right; guilloche border partly off the flan. Ahlström, Stockholm, 35, 9-10/5/1987, no. 2115 = Numismatica, Vienna, 13, 9-11/11/1976, no. 368.
685.	O34* - R? 12.64g 21mm	Same as 613. Irregular flan. Small cracks on the edge. Slightly worn. O: guilloche border partly off the flan. R: *4?* in field right; guilloche border off the flan. Hirsch, Munich, 168, 22-24/11/1990, no. 362.
686.	O? - R? 13.00g 24mm 12h	Same as 613. Irregular flan. Small cracks on the edge. Rather worn. O: guilloche border partly off the flan. R: *4* in field right; guilloche border partly off the flan.

Paris, MBTS, no. 34 (ex Starcky coll.).

687. O? - R? Same as 613. Oval flan. Rather worn.
O: seahorse, dolphin and guilloche border partly off the flan.
R: *4* in field right; guilloche border partly off the flan.
Hirsch, Munich, 236, 23-25/9/2004, no. 2043.

II.1.2.1.j. With *5* on the reverse

688. O21* - R27'* Same as 613. Irregular flan. Small cracks on the edge.
13.33g 19mm
12h
O: seahorse and guilloche border partly off the flan.
R: *5* in field right; guilloche border off the flan.
London, BM, no. 1888-12-8 15; *BMC Phoenicia*, p. 229, 16 and pl. XXIX, 3.

689. O35* - R? Same as 613. Slightly worn.
O: guilloche border partly off the flan.
R: $\overset{o}{5}${ in field right; guilloche border partly off the flan.
Gans, NFA, 19/4/1960, no. 439 (ex Bauer coll.).

690. O? - R42* Same as 613. Irregular flan. Slightly worn.
13.06g 18mm O: guilloche border off the flan.
R: *5* in field right; guilloche border off the flan.
Albrecht-Hoffmann, Köln, 42, 10-13/11/1980, no. 132 = 23-25/11/1978, no. 208.

II.1.2.1.k. With *10(?)* on the reverse

691. O36* - R? Same as 613. Slightly worn.
O: guilloche border partly off the flan.
R: *10?* in field right.
Sotheby's, London, July 1921, no. 327.

II.1.2.1.l. With *Z* or *20* on the reverse

692. O? - R? Same as 613. Rather worn.
O: cable border (?) partly off the flan.
R: $\overset{o}{Z}$ or $\overset{o}{20}$ in field right; cable border (?) off the flan.
Ritter, Dusseldorf, 60, August 2002, no. 669.

II.1.2.1.m. With *Z1* or *21* on the reverse

693. O37* - R? Same as 613. Slightly worn.
12.25g 21mm O: defect behind the wing; dolphin and guilloche

border partly off the flan.
R: $\overset{\circ}{Z1}$ or $\overset{\circ}{21}$ in field right.
Malter, Encino, 4, 29/10/1978, no. 10.

II.1.2.1.n. With *Z3* or *23* on the reverse

694. O24* - R31*　　　Same as 613.
　　　13.00g 19mm　　O: guilloche border partly off the flan.
　　　　　　　　　　　R: $\overset{\circ}{Z3}$ or $\overset{\circ}{23}$ in field right.
　　　　　　　　　　　Shahaf coll., Haifa, no. 70.
695. O25* - R32*　　　Same as 613. Small cracks on the edge.
　　　12.53g 20mm　　O: guilloche border off the flan.
　　　12h　　　　　　R: *Z3* or *23* in field right; guilloche border off the flan.
　　　　　　　　　　　Oxford, AM, no. 88.

II.1.2.1.o. With *Z4* or *24* on the reverse

696. O25 - R33　　　　Same as 613. Irregular flan.
　　　12.77g　　　　　O: guilloche border partly off the flan.
　　　　　　　　　　　R: *Z4* or *24* in field right; guilloche border off the flan.
　　　　　　　　　　　Hirsch, Munich, 169, 20-22/2/1991, no. 550.
697. O26 - R33*　　　Same as 613. Irregular flan.
　　　12.76g 19mm　　O: dolphin and guilloche border off the flan.
　　　11h　　　　　　R: *Z4* or *24* in field right; guilloche border off the flan.
　　　　　　　　　　　Copenhagen, NatMus, no. 300 ; Forrer, *Weber Collection*, no. 8085 ; *SNG Copenhagen*, pl. 8, no. 300 (ex Weber coll.).

II.1.2.1.p. With *Z5* or *25* on the reverse

698. O26* - R34*　　　Same as 613. Irregular flan. Small cracks on the edge.
　　　12.73g 22mm
　　　9h　　　　　　 O: deity, dolphin and guilloche border partly off the flan.
　　　　　　　　　　　R: *Z5* or *25* in field right; owl and guilloche border partly off the flan.
　　　　　　　　　　　New York, ANS, no. N41 (ex Newell coll.).
699. O26 - R34　　　　Same as 613. Irregular flan. Small cracks on the edge.
　　　12.28g 22mm
　　　1h　　　　　　 O: seahorse, dolphin and guilloche border partly off the flan.
　　　　　　　　　　　R: *Z5* or *25* in field right; guilloche border partly off

the flan.
Jerusalem, RocMus, no. I11.9; Lambert, *QDAP* 1, 1931, p. 15, no. 9; Elayi-Elayi, *Trésors*, p. 172, no. 10 and pl. XXVII (Tell Abu Hawam hoard TXXXV).

II.1.2.1.q. With *Z10* or *30* on the reverse

700. O27* - R35   Same as 613. Irregular flan. Small cracks on the
     12.95g 20mm   edge.
     1h   O: dolphin and guilloche border partly off the flan.
                   R: $\mathring{Z}10$ or $\mathring{30}$ in field right; guilloche border partly off the flan.
                   Jerusalem, RocMus, no. H1.11; Lambert, *QDAP* 1, 1931, p. 15, no. 11; Elayi-Elayi, *Trésors*, p. 172, no. 12 and pl. XXVII (Tell Abu Hawam hoard TXXXV).

701. O28* - R35*   Same as 613. Oval flan. Small cracks on the edge.
     13.11g 21mm   O: dolphin and guilloche border partly off the flan.
     1h   R: *Z10* or *30* in field right; guilloche border off the flan.
                   Jerusalem, RocMus, no. H1.10; Lambert, *QDAP* 1, 1931, p. 15, no. 10 and pl. XIX; Elayi-Elayi, *Trésors*, p. 172, no. 11 and pl. XXVII (Tell Abu Hawam hoard TXXXV).

702. O28 - R35   Same as 613. Oval flan.
     13.01g 21mm   O: seahorse, dolphin and guilloche border partly off the flan.
     12h   R: *Z10* or *30* in field right; guilloche border off the flan.
                   New York, ANS, no. N17; Rouvier, *JIAN* 6, 1903, p. 272, no. 1790 and pl. XVIII, 11 (ex Newell coll. = ex Rouvier coll.).

703. O? - R?   Same as 613. Irregular flan. Rather worn. Chisel-cut.
     12.93g 21mm   O: dolphin and guilloche border off the flan.
                   R: $\mathring{Z}10$ or $\mathring{30}$ in field right; guilloche border off the flan. Two countermarks below.
                   NFA, Encino, 8, 6/6/1980, no. 406 ; Brett, *Greek Coins*, no. 2202 (ex Boston MFA coll. = ex Warren coll. = ex Greenwell coll.).

II.1.2.1.r. With *Z11* or *31* on the reverse

704. O28 - R36*   Same as 613. Chisel-cut.

	12.83g 19mm 6h	O: guilloche border off the flan. R: *Z11* or *31* in field right; guilloche border off the flan. London, BM, no. 1906-7-12 85; *BMC Phoenicia*, p. 230, no. 17 and pl. XXIX, 4.
705.	O29* - R36 13.10g 20mm 5h	Same as 613. Irregular flan. O: dolphin and guilloche border partly off the flan. R: *Z̊11* or *3̊1* in field right; guilloche border off the flan. Paris, BNF, no. R2767 (ex Seyrig coll.).

II.1.2.1.s. With *Z13* or *33* on the reverse

706.	O30* - R37* 13.15g 19mm 9h	Same as 613. Small cracks on the edge. Plated. O: dolphin and guilloche border partly off the flan. R: *Z13* or *33* in field right; guilloche border off the flan. London, BM, no. 1888-12-8 16; *BMC Phoenicia*, p. 230, no. 18 and pl. XXIX, 5; Zeimal, *Monnaies Tadjikistan*, no. 44 (ex Cunningham coll.).
707.	O? - R43* 12.60g 20mm 11h	Same as 613. Small cracks on the edge. O: dolphin, waves and part of the seahorse and guilloche border off the flan. R: *Z̊13* or *3̊3* in field right; guilloche border partly off the flan. New York, ANS, no. N16 (ex Newell coll.).
708.	O? - R? 13.10g 20mm	Same as 613. Irregular flan. Rather worn. Small cracks on the edge. O: dolphin and guilloche border partly off the flan. R: *Z13* or *33* in field right; guilloche border partly off the flan. Kindler, *ErIs* 8, 1967, p. 123, no. 1 and pl. 46.

II.1.2.1.t. With *Z14* or *34* on the reverse

709.	O31* - R40* 11.15g 24mm 4h	Same as 613. Irregular flan. O: cable border (?) partly off the flan. R: *Z14* or *34* in field right; cable border (?) partly off the flan. Spaer coll., Haifa; Gorny, Munich, 38, 30/11/1987, no. 262.

II.1.2.1.u. With *T4* on the reverse

710. O? – R40*
     13.21g 21mm
     7h
     Same as 613. Irregular flan. Slightly worn.
     O: dolphin and guilloche border partly off the flan.
     R: *T* in field left and *4* right; guilloche border off the flan.
     Jerusalem, RocMus, no. H1.5; Lambert, *QDAP* 1, 1931, p. 15, no. 5 and pl. XIX; Elayi-Elayi, *Trésors*, pp. 172-173, no. 13 and pl. XXVII (Tell Abu Hawam hoard TXXXV).

II.1.2.1.v. With *T6* on the reverse

711. O32* - R39*
     13.05g 22mm
     7h
     Same as 613. Irregular flan.
     O: seahorse and guilloche border partly off the flan.
     R: *T* in field left and *6* right; guilloche border partly off the flan.
     Paris, BNF, no. R2766 (ex Seyrig coll.).

712. O32 - R39
     12.90g 20mm
     10h
     Same as 613.
     O: seahorse and guilloche border partly off the flan.
     R: *T* in field left and *6* right; guilloche border partly off the flan.
     Beirut, AUB Museum, no. C1254A; Baramki, *Coins AUB*, no. 1254A and pl. XXVII.

713. O33* - R40*
     13.10g 22mm
     11h
     Same as 613.
     O: guilloche border partly off the flan.
     R: *T* in field left and *6* right; re-cut?
     Jerusalem, RocMus, no. H1.8; Lambert, *QDAP* 1, 1931, p. 15, no. 8 and pl. XIX; Elayi-Elayi, *Trésors*, p. 173, no. 14 and pl. XXVIII (Tell Abu Hawam hoard TXXXV).

714. O33 - R40
     12.70g 21mm
     10h
     Same as 613. Small cracks on the edge.
     O: seahorse and guilloche border partly off the flan.
     R: *T̊* in field left and *6* right; guilloche border partly off the flan.
     Shahaf coll., Haifa, no. 4 (bought in Akko).

II.1.2.2. Sixteenths of shekel AR

II.1.2.2.a. With *M* on the reverse

715. O37* - R38*
     0.50g 9mm
     2h
     Same as 715.
     O: seahorse with curled wing, to left; below, two lines of waves; border of dots.
     R: owl standing to left, head facing; over its right

shoulder, crook and flail; *M* in field left, above the crook; border of dots.
Shahaf coll., Haifa, no. 46.

716. O? - R38 Same as 715. Slightly worn.
0.50g 8mm O: waves and border of dots partly off the flan.
R: *M* in field left, above the crook; border of dots partly off the flan.
Kindler, *ErIs* 8, 1967, p. 324, no. 9 and pl. 46.

II.1.2.2.b. With *I* on the reverse

717. O36* - R39* Same as 715.
0.59g 9mm R: *I* in field left, above the crook; border of dots.
3h Tel Aviv, KNM, no. K1765 ; Kindler, *ErIs* 8, 1967, p. 324, no. 3 ; Elayi-Elayi, *Trésors*, p. 163, no. 2 and pl. XXVI (Akko hoard TXXXIII).

718. O38* - R40* Same as 715.
0.55g R: *Ỉ* in field left, above the crook.
Markov, New York, 11, 2-3/9/2003, no. 97.

719. O38 - R41* Same as 715.
0.77g R: *I* in field left, above the crook.
Elsen, Brussels, 38, 11/2/1995, no. 145 = 34, 23/4/1994, no. 76 = 147, October 1992, no. 58.

720. O39* - R42* Same as 715.
0.37g 9mm O: waves off the flan.
6h R: *Ỉ* in field left, above the crook.
Tel Aviv, KNM, no. K1683 (from Gaza).

721. O40* - R43* Same as 715.
0.51g 9mm O: border of dots partly off the flan.
4h R: *I* in field left, above the crook; border of dots partly off the flan.
Tel Aviv, KNM, no. K1764; Kindler, *ErIs* 8, 1967, p. 324, no. 2 and pl. 46; Elayi-Elayi, *Trésors*, p. 163, no. 3 and pl. XXVI (Akko hoard TXXXIII).

722. O41* - R44* Same as 715.
0.69g 9mm O: one line of waves; border of dots partly off the flan.
4h R: *I* in field left, above the crook; border of dots partly off the flan.
Tel Aviv, KNM, no. K1763; Kindler, *ErIs* 8, 1967, p. 324, no. 1; Elayi-Elayi, *Trésors*, p. 163, no. 1 and pl. XXVI (Akko hoard TXXXIII).

723. O42* - R45* Same as 715.
0.40g 9mm O: border of dots off the flan.

	6h	R: $\stackrel{\text{o}}{I}$ in field left, above the crook; border of dots partly off the flan. Shahaf coll., Haifa, no. 29.
724.	O? - R82*	Same as 715. Slightly worn. O: one line of waves; seahorse and border of dots partly off the flan. R: $\stackrel{\text{o}}{I}$ in field left, above the crook; border of dots partly off the flan. Elayi-Elayi, *Trans* 11, 1996, p. 111, no. 8 and pl. VIII, 71 (Phoenicia hoard TLXXIX).
725.	O? - R82	Same as 715. Slightly worn. O: border of dots partly off the flan. R: *I* in field left, above the crook; border of dots partly off the flan. Elayi-Elayi, *Trans* 11, 1996, p. 111, no. 10 and pl. VIII, 73 (Phoenicia hoard TLXXIX).
726.	O? - R83* 0.80g 9mm 3h	Same as 715. Irregular flan. Slightly worn. O: waves and border of dots partly off the flan. R: $\stackrel{\text{o}}{I}$ in field left, above the crook; border of dots partly off the flan. Tel Aviv, KNM, no. K1695 (bought in Akko).
727.	O? - R? 0.45g 8mm 3h	Same as 715. Rather worn. O: seahorse and border of dots partly off the flan. R: $\stackrel{\text{o}}{I}$ in field left, above the crook; border of dots partly off the flan. Tel Aviv, KNM, no. K1308 (bought in Akko).
728.	O? - R? 0.29g 10mm 1h	Same as 715. Rather worn. Plated. O: waves and border of dots partly off the flan. R: *I* in field left, above the crook; border of dots partly off the flan. Paris, BNF, no. 1969/726 ; Elayi-Elayi, *Trésors*, p. 237, no. 258 and pl. XXXIV (Naplouse Hoard TLI).
729.	0.72g	Same as 715. R: *I* in field left, above the crook. Baldwin, London, 34, 13/10/2003, no. 544, not illustrated.
730.	0.50g	Same as 715. R: *I* in field left, above the crook. Baldwin, London, 34, 13/10/2003, no. 544, not illustrated.
731.	0.59g 9mm 12h	Same as 715. R: *I* in field left, above the crook. Tel Aviv, KNM, no. K1766; Kindler, *ErIs* 8, 1967, p. 324, no. 4, not illustrated; Elayi-Elayi, *Trésors*, p.

163, no. 4 (Akko hoard TXXXIII).

II.1.2.2.c. With *2* above the crook on the reverse

732. O33 - R44'
 0.73g 10mm
 3h
Same as 715. Irregular flan.
O: waves and border of dots partly off the flan.
R: *2* in field left, above the crook; border of dots partly off the flan.
Tel Aviv, KNM, no. K1769; Kindler, *ErIs* 8, 1967, p. 324, no. 7, not illustrated; Elayi-Elayi, *Trésors*, pp. 163-164, no. 5 (Akko hoard TXXXIII).

733. O33* - R46*
 0.62g 9mm
 12h
Same as 715.
O: border of dots partly off the flan.
R: *2* in field left, above the crook; border of dots partly off the flan.
Tel Aviv, KNM, no. K1768; Kindler, *ErIs* 8, 1967, p. 324, no. 6 and pl. 46; Elayi-Elayi, *Trésors*, p. 164, no. 6 (Akko hoard TXXXIII).

734. O43* - R44'
 0.82g
 4h
Same as 715.
O: head of the seahorse and border of dots partly off the flan.
R: *2* in field left, above the crook; border of dots partly off the flan.
Meshorer-Qedar, *Coinage of Samaria*, p. 77, no. SH237 and pl. 41; Elayi-Elayi, *Trésors*, p. 225, no. 55 (Samaria hoard TXLIX).

735. O44* - R44'
 0.60g 9mm
 3h
Same as 715.
O: defect on the waves; border of dots partly off the flan.
R: *2* in field left, above the crook; border of dots partly off the flan.
Tel Aviv, KNM, no. K1696 (bought in Akko).

736. O45* - R47*
 0.67g 9mm
 12h
Same as 715.
O: waves and border of dots partly off the flan.
R: *2* in field left, above the crook; border of dots partly off the flan.
Spaer coll., Jerusalem (bought in Jerusalem).

737. O46* - R48*
 0.62g
 12h
Same as 715.
O: border of dots partly off the flan.
R: *2* in field left, above the crook; border of dots partly off the flan.
Meshorer-Qedar, *Coinage of Samaria*, p. 78, no. SH238 and pl. 41; Elayi-Elayi, *Trésors*, p. 225, no. 56 (Samaria hoard TXLIX).

738. O67* - R?
    0.25g 8mm
    4h

Same as 715. Slightly worn.
O: one line of waves; border of dots partly off the flan.
R: *2* in field left, above the crook; border of dots partly off the flan.
Tel Aviv, KNM, no. K1697 (bought in Akko).

II.1.2.2.d. With *2* below the crook on the reverse

739. O32 - R49*
    0.72g 9mm
    7h

Same as 715.
O: border of dots partly off the flan.
R: *2* in field left, below the crook; border of dots partly off the flan.
Tel Aviv, KNM, no. K1772; Kindler, *ErIs* 8, 1967, p. 324, no. 10, not illustrated ; Elayi-Elayi, *Trésors*, p. 164, no. 9 (Akko hoard TXXXIII).

740. O33 - R50*
    0.54g
    3h

Same as 715.
O: head of the seahorse and border of dots partly off the flan.
R: *2* in field left, below the crook; border of dots partly off the flan.
Meshorer-Qedar, *Coinage of Samaria*, p. 78, no. SH247 and pl. 42; Elayi-Elayi, *Trésors*, p. 226, no. 65 (Samaria hoard TXLIX).

741. O44 - R50
    0.70g
    12h

Same as 715.
O: border of dots partly off the flan.
R: *2* in field left, below the crook; border of dots partly off the flan.
Meshorer-Qedar, *Coinage of Samaria*, p. 78, no. SH244 and pl. 42; Elayi-Elayi, *Trésors*, p. 225, no. 59 (Samaria hoard TXLIX).

742. O47* - R51*
    0.63g 8mm
    11h

Same as 715.
O: waves and border of dots partly off the flan.
R: *2* in field left, below the crook; border of dots partly off the flan.
Sternberg, Zurich, 25-26/11/1976, no. 720.

743. O48* - R52*
    0.55g 9mm
    4h

Same as 715. Oval flan.
O: one line of waves; border of dots partly off the flan.
R: *2* in field left, below the crook; border of dots partly off the flan.
Tel Aviv, KNM, no. K1779; Kindler, *ErIs* 8, 1967, p. 324, no. 9 and pl. 46 ; Elayi-Elayi, *Trésors*, p. 164, no. 10 (Akko hoard TXXXIII).

744.	O49* - R53* 0.76g 9mm 12h	Same as 715. O: border of dots partly off the flan. R: *2* in field left, below the crook; defect on the legs of the owl; border of dots partly off the flan. Tel Aviv, KNM, no. K1773; Kindler, *ErIs* 8, 1967, p. 324, no. 11, not illustrated ; Elayi-Elayi, *Trésors*, p. 164, no. 8 (Akko hoard TXXXIII).
745.	O50* - R54* 0.59g 5h	Same as 715. Small cracks on the edge. R: *2* in field left, below the crook; border of dots partly off the flan. Meshorer-Qedar, *Coinage of Samaria*, p. 78, no. SH245 and pl. 42; Elayi-Elayi, *Trésors*, p. 226, no. 63 (Samaria hoard TXLIX).
746.	O51* - R55* 0.59g 6h	Same as 715. O: border of dots partly off the flan. R: *2* in field left, below the crook; border of dots partly off the flan. Meshorer-Qedar, *Coinage of Samaria*, p. 78, no. SH243 and pl. 42; Elayi-Elayi, *Trésors*, p. 226, no. 62 (Samaria hoard TXLIX).
747.	O52* - R56* 0.73g 12h	Same as 715. O: border of dots partly off the flan. R: *2* in field left, below the crook; border of dots partly off the flan. Meshorer-Qedar, *Coinage of Samaria*, p. 78, no. SH239 and pl. 41; Elayi-Elayi, *Trésors*, p. 225, no. 58 (Samaria hoard TXLIX).
748.	O53* - R57* 0.47g 8mm 7h	Same as 715. O: defect below the waves; border of dots partly off the flan. R: *2* in field left, below the crook; border of dots partly off the flan. Paris, BNF, no. 1966/260 (from Gaza).
749.	O54* - R58* 0.63g 12h	Same as 715. O: one line of waves; border of dots partly off the flan. R: $\overset{8}{2}$ in field left, below the crook; border of dots partly off the flan. Meshorer-Qedar, *Coinage of Samaria*, p. 78, no. SH241 and pl. 42; Elayi-Elayi, *Trésors*, pp. 225-226, no. 61 (Samaria hoard TXLIX).
750.	O? - R54 0.66g 12h	Same as 715. Slightly worn. O: border of dots partly off the flan. R: *2* in field left, below the crook; border of dots

		partly off the flan.

Meshorer-Qedar, *Coinage of Samaria*, p. 78, no. SH246 and pl. 42; Elayi-Elayi, *Trésors*, p. 225, no. 60 (Samaria hoard TXLIX).

751. O? - R54 Same as 715. Slightly worn.
0.53g 9mm O: seahorse and border of dots partly off the flan.
3h R: *2* in field left, below the crook; border of dots partly off the flan.
Tel Aviv, KNM, no. K1774; Kindler, *ErIs* 8, 1967, p. 324, no. 12, not illustrated ; Elayi-Elayi, *Trésors*, p. 164, no. 11 and pl. XXVI (Akko hoard TXXXIII).

752. O? - R58 Same as 715. Slightly worn.
0.61g 9mm O: one line of waves; border of dots partly off the flan.
2h R: *2* in field left, below the crook and defect above; border of dots partly off the flan.
Tel Aviv, KNM, no. K1778; Kindler, *ErIs* 8, 1967, p. 324, no. 16, not illustrated ; Elayi-Elayi, *Trésors*, p. 165, no. 16 and pl. XXVI (Akko hoard TXXXIII).

753. O? - R84* Same as 715. Slightly worn.
0.57g O: seahorse, waves and border of dots partly off the flan.
5h R: *2* in field left, below the crook; border of dots partly off the flan.
Meshorer-Qedar, *Coinage of Samaria*, p. 78, no. SH242 and pl. 42; Elayi-Elayi, *Trésors*, p. 226, no. 64 (Samaria hoard TXLIX).

754. O? - R85* Same as 715. Slightly worn.
0.65g 9mm O: border of dots partly off the flan.
6h R: *2* in field left, below the crook; border of dots partly off the flan.
Tel Aviv, KNM, no. K1315.

755. O? - R? Same as 715. Rather worn.
0.76g O: waves obliterated and border of dots partly off the flan.
12h R: *2* in field left, below the crook; border of dots partly off the flan.
Meshorer-Qedar, *Coinage of Samaria*, p. 78, no. SH240 and pl. 42; Elayi-Elayi, *Trésors*, p. 225, no. 57 (Samaria hoard TXLIX).

756. O? - R? Same as 715. Rather worn.
0.68g 8mm O: one line of waves; seahorse and border of dots partly off the flan.
R: *2* in field left, below the crook; border of dots

		partly off the flan.
		Jerusalem, IM, no. 3883.
757.	O? - R?	Same as 715. Rather worn.
	0.65g 9mm	O: one line of waves; border of dots partly off the flan.
	4h	
		R: $\overset{8}{2}$ in field left, below the crook; border of dots partly off the flan.
		Fulco, *RB* 2, 1975, p. 234 and pl. 18, 2; Briend-Humbert, *Tell Keisan*, p. 236, no. 2 and pl. 133; Elayi-Elayi, *Trésors*, pp. 344-345 (Tell Keisan excavations).
758.	O? - R?	Same as 715. Rather worn.
	0.50g 9mm	O: seahorse and border of dots partly off the flan.
	3h	R: $\overset{8}{2}$ in field left, below the crook; border of dots partly off the flan.
		Tel Aviv, KNM, no. K1776; Kindler, *ErIs* 8, 1967, p. 324, no. 14 ; Elayi-Elayi, *Trésors*, p. 164, no. 7 and pl. XXVI (Akko hoard TXXXIII).
759.	0.47g 8mm	Same as 715.
		R: *2* in field left, below the crook.
		Kindler, *ErIs* 8, 1967, p. 324, no. 13, not illustrated.

II.1.2.2.e. With *10* on the reverse

760.	O55 - R59*	Same as 715.
	0.60g 9mm	O: one line of waves; seahorse and border of dots partly off the flan.
	12h	
		R: $\overset{o}{10}$ in field left, below the crook; border of dots partly off the flan.
		Tel Aviv, KNM, no. K1780; Kindler, *ErIs* 8, 1967, p. 324, no. 18 ; Elayi-Elayi, *Trésors*, p. 164, no. 15 and pl. XXVI (Akko hoard TXXXIII).
761.	O55* - R60*	Same as 715.
	0.35g 10mm	O: one line of waves; border of dots partly off the flan.
	2h	
		R: *10* in field left, below the crook; border of dots partly off the flan.
		Shahaf coll., Haifa, no. 18.
762.	O56* - R61*	Same as 715.
	0.58g	O: one line of waves; seahorse and border of dots partly off the flan.
	12h	
		R: *10* in field left, below the crook; border of dots partly off the flan.
		Meshorer-Qedar, *Coinage of Samaria*, p. 78, no.

763. O57* - R61
0.40g 9mm

SH251 and pl. 43; Elayi-Elayi, *Trésors*, p. 226, no. 66 (Samaria hoard TXLIX).
Same as 715.
O: one line of waves; border of dots partly off the flan.
R: *10* in field left, below the crook; border of dots partly off the flan.
Shahaf coll., Haifa, no. 33.

764. O58* - R62*
0.47g 9mm
9h

Same as 715.
O: one line of waves; border of dots partly off the flan.
R: *1̊0?* in field left, below the crook; border of dots partly off the flan.
New York, ANS, no. N34 (ex Newell coll.).

765. O59* - R63*
0.58g 9mm
6h

Same as 715.
O: seahorse, waves and border of dots partly off the flan.
R: *1̊0?* in field left, below the crook; border of dots partly off the flan.
Tel Aviv, KNM, no. K1770; Kindler, *ErIs* 8, 1967, p. 324, no. 8 ; Elayi-Elayi, *Trésors*, p. 164, no. 13 and pl. XXVI (Akko hoard TXXXIII).

766. O60* - R64*
0.55g 9mm
5h

Same as 715.
O: one line of waves; border of dots partly off the flan.
R: *1̊0?* in field left, below the crook; border of dots partly off the flan.
Tel Aviv, KNM, no. K1771; Kindler, *ErIs* 8, 1967, p. 324, no. 9, not illustrated ; Elayi-Elayi, *Trésors*, p. 164, no. 14 and pl. XXVI (Akko hoard TXXXIII).

767. O40 - R?
0.69g
9h

Same as 715. Slightly worn.
O: one line of waves; border of dots partly off the flan.
R: *1̊0* in field left, below the crook; border of dots partly off the flan.
Meshorer-Qedar, *Coinage of Samaria*, p. 78, no. SH252 and pl. 43; Elayi-Elayi, *Trésors*, p. 226, no. 67 (Samaria hoard TXLIX).

768. O? - R64
0.50g 9mm

Same as 715. Slightly worn.
O: one line of waves; border of dots partly off the flan.
R: *10* in field left, below the crook.
Jerusalem, IM, no. 3887.

769. O? - R86*   Same as 715. Slightly worn.
     0.65g 10mm   O: waves and border of dots partly off the flan.
     11h   R: *10* in field left, below the crook; border of dots partly off the flan.
                     Shahaf coll., Haifa, no. 28.

770. O? - R87*   Same as 715. Slightly worn.
     0.48g 10mm   O: waves obliterated and border of dots partly off the flan.
     12h   R: *10* in field left, below the crook; border of dots partly off the flan.
                     Berlin, SM, no. 25 (ex Löbbecke coll.).

771. O? - R?   Same as 715. Rather worn. Plated.
     0.70g 10mm   O: waves and border of dots partly off the flan.
     6h   R: *1̊0?* in field left, below the crook; border of dots partly off the flan.
                     Shahaf coll., Haifa, no. 45.

772. O? - R?   Same as 715. Rather worn.
     0.64g 9mm   O: waves and border of dots partly off the flan.
     3h   R: *1̊0?* in field left, below the crook; border of dots partly off the flan.
                     Tel Aviv, KNM, no. K1306; Kindler, *ErIs* 8, 1967, p. 324, no. 17 and pl. 46 ; Elayi-Elayi, *Trésors*, pl. XXVI, 13 (Akko hoard TXXXIII).

773. O? - R?   Same as 715. Rather worn.
     0.57g 9mm   O: one line of waves; seahorse and border of dots partly off the flan.
     9h   R: *1̊0* in field left, below the crook; owl and border of dots partly off the flan.
                     Spaer coll., Jerusalem (bought in Jerusalem, probably from Gaza).

774. O? - R?   Same as 715. Rather worn.
     0.40g 8mm   O: waves and border of dots partly off the flan.
     6h   R: *1̊0?* in field left, below the crook; border of dots off the flan.
                     Tel Aviv, KNM, no. K1316 (from Akko).

II.1.2.2.f. With *Z1* or *21* on the reverse

775. O? - R88*   Same as 715. Slightly worn.
     0.45g 8mm   O: waves and border of dots partly off the flan.
     9h   R: *Z* in field left, above the crook and *1̊?* below; border of dots partly off the flan.
                     Shahaf coll., Haifa, no. 23.

776.	O? - R89*	Same as 715. Irregular flan. Slightly worn.
	0.46g	O: one line of waves; border of dots partly off the flan.
		R: $\overset{\circ}{Z}[$ in field left, below the crook; border of dots partly off the flan.
		Numismatica, Vienna, 12, 11-14/5/1976, no. 86.
777.	O? - R?	Same as 715. Rather worn.
	0.60g 10mm	O: border of dots partly off the flan.
		R: $\overset{\circ}{Z}[$ in field left, above the crook; border of dots partly off the flan.
		Shahaf coll., Haifa, no. 34.

II.1.2.2.g. With *Z2* or *22* on the reverse

778.	O31 - R65*	Same as 715.
	0.55g	O: waves and border of dots partly off the flan.
		R: Z in field left, above the crook and 2 below; border of dots partly off the flan.
		Elsen, Brussels, 48, 22/2/1997, no. 206.
779.	O? - R?	Same as 715. Rather worn.
	0.25g 7mm	O: border of dots partly off the flan.
	5h	R: $\overset{\circ}{Z}$ in field left, below the crook and 2 above; border of dots partly off the flan.
		Tel Aviv, KNM, no. K1337.

II.1.2.2.h. With *Z4* or *24* on the reverse

780.	O61* - R66*	Same as 715.
	0.65g 8mm	O: border of dots partly off the flan.
	3h	R: defect in field right; Z in field left, above the crook and 4 below; border of dots partly off the flan.
		Tel Aviv, KNM, no. K1313 (from Akko).
781.	O62* - R66	Same as 715. Slightly damaged.
	0.60g 9mm	O: three dots below the seahorse; border of dots partly off the flan.
	7h	R: defect in field right; Z in field left, above the crook and 4 below; border of dots partly off the flan.
		Tel Aviv, KNM, no. K1693; Kindler, *ErIs* 8, 1967, p. 323, no. 5 and pl. 46 (bought in Akko).
782.	O62 - R66	Same as 715. Small cracks on the edge.
	0.50g 9mm	O: three dots below the seahorse; border of dots partly off the flan.
	8h	R: defect in field right; Z in field left, above the crook and 4 below; border of dots partly off the flan.
		Shahaf coll., Haifa, no. 12.

783. O? - R66   Same as 715. Partly worn.
     0.52g 10mm   O: waves obliterated and border of dots partly off
     1h   the flan.
                     R: defect in field right; Z in field left, above the crook and $\overset{\circ}{4}$ below; border of dots partly off the flan.
                     Paris, BNF, no. 1966/259 (from Gaza).
784. O? - R90*   Same as 715. Partly worn.
     0.65g   O: waves obliterated and border of dots off the flan.
     3h   R: Z in field left, above the crook and *4* below; border of dots partly off the flan.
                     Meshorer-Qedar, *Coinage of Samaria*, p. 78, no. SH249 and pl. 43 (who read *5*); Elayi-Elayi, *Trésors*, p. 226, no. 69 (Samaria hoard TXLIX).
785. O? - R?   Same as 715. Worn.
     0.53g   O: almost all the type off the flan.
     9h   R: Z in field left, above the crook and $\overset{\circ}{4}$ below; border of dots partly off the flan.
                     Meshorer-Qedar, *Coinage of Samaria*, p. 78, no. SH250 and pl. 43 (who read *5*); Elayi-Elayi, *Trésors*, p. 226, no. 70 (Samaria hoard TXLIX).
786. O? - R?   Same as 715. Partly damaged and worn.
     0.46g 9mm   O: waves and border of dots partly off the flan.
     6h   R: Z in field left, above the crook and $\overset{\circ}{4}$ below; border of dots partly off the flan.
                     Spaer coll., Jerusalem (bought in Jerusalem).

II.1.2.2.i. With *Z5* or *25* on the reverse

787. O42 - R67*   Same as 715.
     0.53g 8mm   O: border of dots partly off the flan.
     12h   R: Z in field left, above the crook and *5* below; border of dots partly off the flan.
                     Spaer coll., Jerusalem (bought in Natanyah).
788. O42 - R68*   Same as 715. Slightly damaged.
     0.61g 8mm   O: border of dots partly off the flan.
     7h   R: Z in field left, above the crook and *5* below; border of dots partly off the flan.
                     Tel Aviv, KNM, no. K1775; Kindler, *ErIs* 8, 1967, p. 324, no. 19 and pl. 46; Elayi-Elayi, *Trésors*, p. 165, no. 17 and pl. XXVI (Akko hoard TXXXV).
789. O63* - R69*   Same as 715.
     0.49g 8mm   O: border of dots off the flan.
                     R: Z in field left, above the crook and *5* below; border of dots partly off the flan.

		Sternberg, Zurich, 25-26/11/1976, no. 719.
790.	O64* - R70* 0.61g 10mm 5h	Same as 715. O: border of dots partly off the flan. R: $\overset{\circ}{Z}$ in field left, above the crook and *5* below; border of dots partly off the flan. Tel Aviv, KNM, no. K1781; Elayi-Elayi, *Trésors*, p. 164, no. 12 and pl. XXVI (Akko hoard TXXXV).
791.	O? - R91* 0.70g 12h	Same as 715. Slightly worn. O: waves and border of dots partly off the flan. R: *Z* in field left, above the crook and *5* below; border of dots partly off the flan. Meshorer-Qedar, *Coinage of Samaria*, p. 78, no. SH248 and pl. 43; Elayi-Elayi, *Trésors*, p. 226, no. 68 (Samaria hoard TXLIX).
792.	O? - R91 0.47g 8mm 11h	Same as 715. Slightly worn. O: border of dots partly off the flan. R: *Z* in field left, above the crook and *5* below; border of dots partly off the flan. Spaer coll., Jerusalem (bought in Sebaste).
793.	O? - R91 0.44g 8mm	Same as 715. Slightly worn. O: seahorse, waves and border of dots partly off the flan. R: *Z* in field left, above the crook and *5* below; border of dots partly off the flan. Sheridan, *Numismatist* 8, 1971, p. 113, no. 9 and pl.; Elayi-Elayi, *Trésors*, p. 203, no. 16 (Beirut hoard TXLIII).
794.	O? - R92* 0.70g 10mm 5h	Same as 715. Slightly worn. O: border of dots partly off the flan. R: *Z* in field left, above the crook and $\overset{\circ}{5}$ below; border of dots partly off the flan. Tel Aviv, KNM, no. K1788; Kindler, *ErIs* 8, 1967, p. 324, no. 6 and pl. 46 (who reads *26*).
795.	O? - R93* 0.35g 8mm	Same as 715. Slightly worn. O: seahorse and border of dots partly off the flan. R: $\overset{\circ}{Z}$ in field left, above the crook and *5[* below; border of dots partly off the flan. Shahaf coll., Haifa, no. 40.

II.2. 'Attic' standard (around 357-333 BCE)

II.2.1. Shekels AR

II.2.1.1. With *B1M* on the reverse

796. O1* - R1* O: deity, bearded, riding on seahorse with curled
      20mm   wing, to right; holding reins in right hand and an
                 arched bow in left hand; below, two lines of waves
                 and dolphin, to right; guilloche border.
                 R: owl standing to right, head facing; over its left
                 shoulder, crook and flail; *B1* in field right above the
                 crook and *M* below.
                 Platt, Paris, 1930, no. 643.
797. O1 - R2   Same as 796.
      8.48g   R: *B1* in field right above the crook and *M* below.
                 Classical Numismatic Group, Lancaster-London, 39,
                 18/9/1996, no. 723.
798. O1 - R2*   Same as 796.
      8.81g 21mm O: guilloche border partly off the flan.
                 R: *B1* in field right above the crook and *M* below.
                 Private coll.
799. O1 - R3*   Same as 796.
      8.80g   O: guilloche border partly off the flan.
      12h   R: *B1* in field right above the crook and *M* below.
                 Superior Coins, 8/12/1993, no. 396 = Hess-Leu,
                 Lucerne-Zurich, 31, 6-7/12/1966, no. 530.
800. O1 - R4*   Same as 796. Small cracks on the edge.
      8.86g 20mm O: dolphin and guilloche border partly off the flan.
      12h   R: *B1* in field right above the crook and *M̊* below;
                 guilloche border partly off the flan.
                 Budapest, MNM, no. 25.
801. O1 - R5   Same as 796. Small cracks on the edge.
      8.83g   O: head of the seahorse and guilloche border partly
                 off the flan.
                 R: *B1* in field right above the crook and *M* below.
                 Elsen, Brussels, 13, 10/6/1989, no. 49.
802. O2 - R5   Same as 796.
      8.77g 22mm O: guilloche border partly off the flan.
      12h   R: *B1* in field right above the crook and *M* below;
                 guilloche border partly off the flan.
                 Catalogue McClean, no. 9520 and pl. 352, 10.
803. O2* - R6* Same as 796. Small cracks on the edge.
      8.79g 21mm O: deity, seahorse and guilloche border partly off the

12h flan.
R: *B1* in field right above the crook and *M* below; guilloche border partly off the flan.
New York, ANS, no. N45; Newell, *Tyrus*, no. 12 (ex Newell coll.).

804. O2 - R7*
8.86g 20mm
Same as 796.
O: head of the deity and guilloche border partly off the flan.
R: *B1* in field right above the crook and *M* below; guilloche border partly off the flan.
Glendining, London, 18-20/4/1955, no. 612 = Schulman, Amsterdam, 16/12/1926, no. 203 = Naville, Geneva, 7, 23-24/6/1924, no. 1744 (ex Bément coll.).

805. O3* - R7*
8.83g
Same as 796.
O: guilloche border partly off the flan.
R: *B1* in field right above the crook and *M* below; guilloche border partly off the flan.
Baldwin, London, 34, 13/10/2003, no. 546.

806. O4* - R5*
8.74g 21mm
Same as 796.
O: defect on the waves; guilloche border partly off the flan.
R: *B1* in field right above the crook and *M* below; guilloche border partly off the flan.
London, BM, no. 1892-11-4 1; *BMC Phoenicia*, p. 231, no. 25 and pl. XXIX, 8; Rouvier, *JIAN* 6, 1903, p. 274, no. 1799 and pl. XVIII, 15.

807. O4 - R5
8.72g
Same as 796.
O: defect on the waves; guilloche border partly off the flan.
R: *B̊1* in field right above the crook and *M* below; guilloche border partly off the flan.
Münzen und Medaillen, Basel, 23-24/6/1983, no. 382 = Coin Galleries, New York, 10/4/1991, no. 148 = Hess, Lucerne, 15/2/1934, no. 516 = Cahn, Frankfurt/Main, 26/11/1930, no. 1576 = Santamaria, Rome, 27/3/1928, no. 291 (ex Moritz Simon coll.).

808. O? - R41*
8.84g 21mm
12h
Same as 796. Slightly worn.
O: guilloche border partly off the flan.
R: *B1* in field right above the crook and *M* below; guilloche border partly off the flan.
Paris, BNF, no. 2007; Babelon, *Perses*, no. 2007.

809. O? - R42*
8.82g 22mm
Same as 796. Slightly worn.
R: *B1* in field right above the crook and *M* below;

		11h	guilloche border partly off the flan. Vienna, KHM, no. 32.645.
810.	O? - R?		Same as 796. Rather worn. O: guilloche border partly off the flan. R: *B1* in field right above the crook and *M* below; guilloche border partly off the flan. Sotheby's, London, 16/2/1972, no. 283.
811.	O? - R?		Same as 796. Rather worn. R: *B1* in field right above the crook and *M̊* below; guilloche border partly off the flan. Ratto, Geneva, 26/4/1909, no. 5173.
812-813.			Same as 796. R: *B1* in field right above the crook and *M* below. Elayi-Elayi, *Trésors*, p. 236, no. 133-134 (Naplouse hoard TLI).
814-817.			Same as 796. R: *B1* in field right above the crook and *M* below. Elayi-Elayi, *Trésors*, p. 187, no. 1-4 (Safed hoard TXXXVII).

II.2.1.2. With *M2* on the reverse

818.	O5* - R8* 8.69g 19mm 1h	Same as 796. O: guilloche border partly off the flan. R: *M2* in field right above the crook. Paris, BNF, no. 2008; Babelon, *Perses*, no. 2008; id., *Traité*, pl. CXXII, 20.
819.	O5 - R8	Same as 796. O: guilloche border partly off the flan. R: *M2* in field right above the crook. Sotheby's, London, 1/5/1929, no. 69 (ex Bull coll.).
820.	O6* - R9* 8.66g 22mm	Same as 796. Oval flan. O: guilloche border partly off the flan. R: *M2* in field right above the crook. London, BM, no. 1896-6-1 120; *BMC Phoenicia*, p. 231, no. 26 and pl. XXIX, 9; Rouvier, *JIAN* 6, 1903, p. 274, no. 1801 and pl. XVIII, 16.
821.	O7* - R10* 8.39g 19mm	Same as 796. O: head of the seahorse and guilloche border partly off the flan. R: dot and defect before the owl; *M2* in field right above the crook. London, BM, no. 1902-2-6 165; *BMC Phoenicia*, p. 231, no. 27, not illustrated; Rouvier, *JIAN* 6, 1903, p. 274, no. 1800 (who reads *M1*).

822. O8* - R11*   Same as 796.
     8.58g   O: guilloche border partly off the flan.
                    R: defect before the owl; *M2* in field right above the crook.
                    Hirsch, Munich, 24-26/9/1998, no. 384 = Sternberg, Zurich, June 1998, no. 209.
823. O9* - R12*   Same as 796. Pierced.
     7.90g 21mm   O: defect on the waves.
     1h   R: *M2* in field right above the crook.
                    Jerusalem, RocMus, no. 1266.1.
824. O10* - R13*   Same as 796. Plated. Slightly irregular flan.
     7.82g 20mm   O: defect on the waves; guilloche border partly off the flan.
     11h   R: *M2* in field right above the crook.
                    Paris, BNF, no. 3221; *Catalogue De Luynes*, no. 3221 (ex De Luynes coll.).
825. O11* - R14*   Same as 796. Plated?
     7.64g 20mm   O: guilloche border partly off the flan.
     3h   R: *M2* in field right above the crook; guilloche border partly off the flan.
                    Paris, BNF, no. 2011; Babelon, *Perses*, no. 2011.
826. O12* - R15*   Same as 796.
     8.74g   O: defect on the waves; guilloche border partly off the flan.
                    R: *M2* in field right above the crook; guilloche border partly off the flan.
                    Peus, Frankfurt/Main, 321, 27-29/4 and 2/5/1988, no. 236 = 300, 3-4 and 9/11/1987, no. 1228.
827. O12 - R?   Same as 796. Slightly worn.
     8.05g   O: defect on the waves; guilloche border partly off the flan.
                    R: *M2* in field right above the crook; guilloche border partly off the flan.
                    Numismatica Ars Classica, Zurich, P, 12/5/2005, no. 1595.
828. O? - R43*   Same as 796. Rather crude style. Slightly worn.
     20mm   O: guilloche border partly off the flan.
                    R: *M2̂* in field right above the crook; guilloche border partly off the flan.
                    Elayi-Elayi, *Trésors*, p. 248, no. 2 and pl. XXXIV (Syrian hoard TLVIII?).
829. O? - R44*   Same as 796. Slightly worn.
     8.10g 20mm   R: *M2* in field right above the crook; guilloche border partly off the flan.
     12h

The Coinage of Tyre in the Persian period   107

		New York, ANS, no. N46; Newell, *Tyrus*, no. 13 (ex Newell coll.).
830.	O? - R45* 8.52g 20mm	Same as 796. Small cracks on the edge. Slightly worn. O: guilloche border partly off the flan. R: *M2* in field right above the crook; guilloche border partly off the flan. UBS, Zurich, 45, 15-17/9/1998, no. 299.
831.	O? - R? 8.68g 21mm 2h	Same as 796. Rather worn. O: guilloche border partly off the flan. R: *M2̊* in field right above the crook; guilloche border partly off the flan. New York, ANS, no. N43 (ex Newell coll.).
832.	O? - R? 7.79g 19mm 1h	Same as 796. Rather worn. O: guilloche border partly off the flan. R: *M2* in field right above the crook; guilloche border partly off the flan. Paris, BNF, no. 2010; Babelon, *Perses*, no. 2010.
833.		Same as 796. R: *M2* in field right above the crook. Elayi-Elayi, *Trésors*, p. 236, no. 135 (Naplouse hoard TLI).

II.2.1.3. With *M2'* on the reverse

834.	O13* - R16*	Same as 796. O: guilloche border partly off the flan. R: *M2* in field right above the crook and ' below. Hamburger, Frankfurt/Main, 17/6/1908, no. 630 (ex Suchier coll.).
835.	O14* - R17* 8.54g 17mm 12h	Same as 796. O: guilloche border partly off the flan. R: *M2* in field right above the crook and ' below. Berlin, SM, no. 29 (ex Prokesch-Osten coll.).
836.	O32* - R? 8.55g 19mm 12h	Same as 796. Slightly worn. O: guilloche border partly off the flan. R: *M2̊* in field right above the crook and ' below. New York, ANS, no. N44 (ex Newell coll.).

II.2.1.4. With *M3* on the reverse

837.	O15* - R18* 8.84g 22mm 1h	Same as 796. O: guilloche border partly off the flan. R: defect behind the owl; *M2* in field right above the crook; guilloche border partly off the flan.

		Jerusalem, RocMus, no. H1.22; Lambert, *QDAP* 1, 1931, p. 16, no. 22; Elayi-Elayi, *Trésors*, p. 173, no. 16 and pl. XXVIII (Tell Abu Hawam hoard TXXXV).
838.	O16* - R19* 8.66g 22mm 12h	Same as 796. O: guilloche border partly off the flan. R: *M2* in field right above the crook; guilloche border partly off the flan. New York, ANS, no. N47 (ex Newell coll.).
839.	O17* - R20* 8.85g 19mm	Same as 796. O: one line of waves; head of the horse and guilloche border partly off the flan. R: *M2* in field right above the crook; guilloche border partly off the flan. Overstruck. Peus, Frankfurt/Main, 334, 4/11/1992, no. 527 = Sternberg, Zurich, 8, 16-17/11/1978, no. 198.
840.	O18* - R21* 8.54g	Same as 796. O: defect under the seahorse; guilloche border partly off the flan. R: *M2* in field right above the crook; guilloche border partly off the flan. Lanz, Munich, 125, 1-2/11/2005, no. 496 = Hirsch, Munich, 208, 17-19/2/2000, no. 1864.
841.	O? - R46* 8.59g	Same as 796. Slightly worn. O: overstruck. R: *M2* in field right above the crook; chisel-cut. London, BM, no. 1874-7-16 234; *BMC Phoenicia*, p. 231, no. 28 and pl. XXIX, 10.
842.	O? - R? 8.49g 20mm 12h	Same as 796. Rather worn. O: one line of waves; guilloche border partly off the flan. R: $\overset{\circ}{M}\overset{\text{\textit{?}}}{2}$ in field right above the crook; guilloche border partly off the flan. Vienna, KHM, no. 22.257.

II.2.1.5. With *M3* ˀ on the reverse

843.	O18 - R22* 8.85g 18mm 12h	Same as 796. O: defect under the seahorse; guilloche border partly off the flan. R: *M3* in field right above the crook and ˀ below; guilloche border partly off the flan. Berlin, SM, no. 30.
844.	O19* - R23*	Same as 796.

| | 8.54g 22mm
12h | O: defect on the dolphin; guilloche border partly off the flan.
R: defect on the leg of the owl; *M3* in field right above the crook and ⸥ below.
Jerusalem, RocMus, no. H1.15; Lambert, *QDAP* 1, 1931, p. 15, no. 15 and pl. XIX; Elayi-Elayi, *Trésors*, p. 173, no. 15 and pl. XXVIII (Tell Abu Hawam hoard TXXXV). |
| 845. | O? - R47*
8.76g 21mm
1h | Same as 796. Slightly worn.
O: tail of the seahorse and guilloche border partly off the flan.
R: defect behind the owl; *M3* in field right above the crook and ⸥ below; guilloche border partly off the flan.
Jerusalem, RocMus, no. H1.21; Lambert, *QDAP* 1, 1931, p. 16, no. 21 and pl. XIX; Elayi-Elayi, *Trésors*, p. 173, no. 15 and pl. XXVIII (Tell Abu Hawam hoard TXXXV). |

II.2.1.6. With *1Ṣ* on the reverse

| 846. | O19 - R24
8.82g 21mm
1h | Same as 796.
O: guilloche border partly off the flan.
R: *1* in field right above the crook and *Ṣ* below; guilloche border partly off the flan.
Vienna, KHM, no. 29. |
| 847. | O20* - R25
8.52g 20mm
12h | Same as 796. Small cracks on the edge.
O: forelegs of the seahorse and guilloche border partly off the flan.
R: *1* in field right above the crook and *Ṣ* below; guilloche border partly off the flan.
Copenhagen, NatMus, no. 306; *SNG Copenhagen*, no. 306 and pl. 8. |

II.2.1.7. With *2Ṣ* on the reverse

| 848. | O21 - R26
8.66g 21mm
12h | Same as 796.
O: guilloche border partly off the flan.
R: *2* in field right above the crook and *Ṣ* below; guilloche border partly off the flan.
Paris, BNF, no. 850; Babelon, *Perses*, no. 2012. |
| 849. | O21* - R26*
8.61g 22mm
1h | Same as 796.
O: guilloche border partly off the flan.
R: *2* in field right above the crook and *Ṣ* below; guilloche border partly off the flan. |

		Jerusalem, RocMus, no. H1.16; Lambert, *QDAP* 1, 1931, p. 15, no. 16 and pl. XIX; Elayi-Elayi, *Trésors*, p. 173, no. 18 and pl. XXVIII (Tell Abu Hawam hoard TXXXV).
850.	O21 - R27* 8.48g 22mm	Same as 796. O: guilloche border partly off the flan. R: *2* in field right above the crook and *Ṣ* below. Münzen und Medaillen, Basel, 10, 12-13/6/1979, no. 243.
851.	O21 - R28* 8.59g 21mm	Same as 796. Small cracks on the edge. O: guilloche border partly off the flan. R: *2* in field right above the crook and *Ṣ* below. Myers, Ariadne Galleries, New York, 12, 4/12/1975, no. 262.
852.	O? - R28 8.55g 22mm	Same as 796. Slightly worn. O: guilloche border partly off the flan. R: *2* in field right above the crook and *Ṣ* below. London, BM, no. 1865-11-12 2; *BMC Phoenicia*, p. 231, no. 29 and pl. XXIX, 11.

II.2.1.8. With *3Ṣ* on the reverse

853.	O21 - R24'* 8.85g 22mm 2h	Same as 796. O: guilloche border partly off the flan. R: *3* in field right above the crook and *Ṣ* below. Jerusalem, RocMus, no. H1.17; Lambert, *QDAP* 1, 1931, p. 15, no. 17; Elayi-Elayi, *Trésors*, p. 173, no. 19 and pl. XXVIII (Tell Abu Hawam hoard TXXXV).
854.	O21 - R29* 8.27g 23mm 2h	Same as 796. O: guilloche border partly off the flan. R: *3* in field right above the crook and *Ṣ* below. Jerusalem, RocMus, no. H1.18; Lambert, *QDAP* 1, 1931, p. 15, no. 18; Elayi-Elayi, *Trésors*, pp. 173-174, no. 22 and pl. XXVIII (Tell Abu Hawam hoard TXXXV).
855.	O4 - R30 8.82g 20mm	Same as 796. O: defect under the waves; guilloche border partly off the flan. R: *3* in field right above the crook and *Ṣ* below; guilloche border partly off the flan. Kundig, Basel, 4, 10/10/1935, no. 892.
856.	O22 - R30 9.06g 20mm	Same as 796. O: guilloche border partly off the flan.

	11h	R: *3* in field right above the crook and *Ṣ* below; guilloche border partly off the flan. New York, ANS, no. 1977.158, 758; Glendining, London, 18-20/4/1955, no. 613B.
857.	O22* - R30* 8.52g 21mm 12h	Same as 796. O: defect on the waves; guilloche border partly off the flan. R: *3* in field right above the crook and *Ṣ* below. New York, ANS, no. N48 (ex Newell coll.).
858.	O23* - R31* 8.50g 22mm 12h	Same as 796. O: guilloche border partly off the flan. R: *3* in field right above the crook and *Ṣ* below. Jerusalem, RocMus, no. H1.20; Lambert, *QDAP* 1, 1931, p. 16, no. 20; Elayi-Elayi, *Trésors*, p. 173, no. 20 and pl. XXVIII (Tell Abu Hawam hoard TXXXV).
859.	O23 - R32* 8.49g 23mm 1h	Same as 796. O: guilloche border partly off the flan. R: *3* in field right above the crook and *Ṣ* below; guilloche border partly off the flan. Jerusalem, RocMus, no. H1.19; Lambert, *QDAP* 1, 1931, p. 16, no. 19; Elayi-Elayi, *Trésors*, p. 173, no. 21 and pl. XXVIII (Tell Abu Hawam hoard TXXXV).
860.	O24* - R33* 8.81g 21mm	Same as 796. Small cracks on the edge. O: guilloche border partly off the flan. R: *3* in field right above the crook and *Ṣ* below; guilloche border partly off the flan. London, BM, no. 1910-6-8 14; *BMC Phoenicia*, p. 231, no. 29bis, not illustrated.
861.	O? - R30 8.22g 21mm 12h	Same as 796. Partly worn. O: dolphin obliterated and guilloche border partly off the flan. R: *3* in field right above the crook and *Ṣ* below; legs of the owl obliterated and guilloche border partly off the flan. Berlin, SM, no. 27.
862.	O? - R35* 8.46g 20mm 12h	Same as 796. Slightly worn. O: guilloche border partly off the flan. R: *3* in field right above the crook and *Ṣ* below. Paris, BNF, no. 2013; Babelon, *Perses*, no. 2013.
863.	O? - R33 8.75g	Same as 796. Slightly worn. O: guilloche border partly off the flan. R: *3* in field right above the crook and *Ṣ* below.

Hirsch, Munich, 152, 26-29/11/1986, no. 249.

864. O? - R? Same as 796. Rather worn.
8.84g O: guilloche border partly off the flan.
12h R: *3* in field right above the crook and *Ṣ* below.
SNG Copenhagen, no. 307 and pl. 8.

865. O? - R? Same as 796. Rather worn.
8.83g O: guilloche border partly off the flan.
R: *3* in field right above the crook and *Ṣ* below.
Forrer, *Weber Collection*, no. 8086 (ex Weber coll.).

866. O? - R? Same as 796. Rather worn.
R: *3* in field right above the crook and *Ṣ* below.
Zograf, *Monnaies*, no. 12.

II.2.1.9. With ʿ3Ṣ on the reverse

867. O? - R48* Same as 796. Slightly worn. Plated.
6.95g 19mm O: defect on the waves; tail of the seahorse and guilloche border partly off the flan.
R: ʿ3 in field right above the crook and and *Ṣ* below; guilloche border partly off the flan.
London, BM, no. 1900-7-7 174; *BMC Phoenicia*, p. 232, no. 33, not illustrated.

II.2.1.10. With 4Ṣ on the reverse

868. O25* - R34* Same as 796.
8.80g 21mm O: defect under the waves; guilloche border partly off the flan.
12h R: *4* in field right above the crook and *Ṣ* below; guilloche border partly off the flan.
Berlin, SM, no. 28 (ex Löbbecke coll.).

869. O25 - R35 Same as 796.
8.80g 20mm O: guilloche border partly off the flan.
12h R: *4* in field right above the crook and *Ṣ* below; guilloche border partly off the flan.
Warsaw, NM, no. 219095 (ex Protassowicki coll.).

870. O26* - R36 Same as 796.
8.86g 21mm O: head of the seahorse and guilloche border partly off the flan.
R: *4* in field right above the crook and *Ṣ* below.
Malter, Encino, 34, 13 and 15/12/1986, no. 61 = Gorny, Munich, 32, 12-13/11/1985, no. 126 = Hirsch, Munich, 32, 14-15/11/1912, no. 588; Elayi-Elayi, *Trésors*, p. 267, no. 3 (South Turkey hoard

TLXII).

871.	O27* - R36* 8.93g 20mm 11h	Same as 796. O: dolphin and guilloche border partly off the flan. R: *4* in field right above the crook and Ṣ below. New York, ANS, no. N49; Newell, *Tyrus*, no. 11 (ex Newell coll.).
872.	O28* - R37* 8.71g 20mm 12h	Same as 796. O: guilloche border partly off the flan. R: *4* in field right above the crook and Ṣ below. New York, ANS, no. N50 (ex Newell coll.).
873.	O29* - R38* 8.87g 20mm 12h	Same as 796. O: guilloche border partly off the flan. R: *4* in field right above the crook and Ṣ below; guilloche border partly off the flan. Budapest, MNM, no. 26.
874.	O25 - R? 8.75g 20mm 12h	Same as 796. Slightly worn. O: guilloche border partly off the flan. R: *4* in field right above the crook and Ṣ below; guilloche border partly off the flan. Vienna, KHM, no. 34.065.
875.	O? - R33 8.85g 11h	Same as 796. Slightly worn. O: guilloche border partly off the flan. R: *4* in field right above the crook and Ṣ below. Mildenberg-Hurter, *Dewing Collection*, no. 2672 (ex Dewing coll.).
876.	O? - R36 8.83g 21mm	Same as 796. Slightly worn. O: guilloche border partly off the flan. R: *4* in field right above the crook and Ṣ below; guilloche border partly off the flan. London, BM, no. 1892-11-4 2; *BMC Phoenicia*, p. 231, no. 30 and pl. XXIX, 12.
877.	O? - R? 8.82g 21mm 1h	Same as 796. Rather worn. O: dolphin obliterated and guilloche border partly off the flan. R: *4* in field right above the crook and Ṣ below; guilloche border partly off the flan. Jerusalem, RocMus, no. H1.24; Lambert, *QDAP* 1, 1931, p. 16, no. 23; Elayi-Elayi, *Trésors*, p. 174, no. 23 and pl. XXVIII (Tell Abu Hawam hoard TXXXV).

II.2.1.11. With Ṣ and unclear figure on the reverse

878-
883.
Same as 796.
R: unclear figure in field right above the crook and Ṣ below.
Elayi-Elayi, *Trésors*, p. 236, no. 136-141 (Naplouse hoard TLI).

II.2.1.12. With inscription obliterated

884. O? - R?
7.33g 20mm
Same as 796. Worn.
O: dolphin and guilloche border partly off the flan.
R: guilloche border partly off the flan; inscription obliterated in field right.
Jerusalem, AI, no. 4257.

II.2.1.13. With owl standing to left and *4* on the reverse

885. O30* - R39*
7.70g 22mm
11h
Same as 796, except for the reverse. Rather crude style.
O: guilloche border partly off the flan.
R: owl standing to left; *4* partly obliterated in field left above the crook; guilloche border partly off the flan.
Paris, BNF, no. 66 (ex Smith-Lessouëf coll.).

886. O31* - R40*
8.11g 20mm
Same as 796, except for the reverse. Rather crude style.
O: guilloche border partly off the flan.
R: owl standing to left; *4* in field left above the crook; guilloche border partly off the flan.
London, BM, no. 1891-6-3 204; *BMC Phoenicia*, p. 231, no. 31, not illustrated.

II.2.1.14. ʿOzmilk's shekels with ꜥ3 on the reverse

887. O1* - R1*
19mm
Same as 796.
O: head of the seahorse and guilloche border partly off the flan.
R: ꜥ3 in field right above the crook; guilloche border partly off the flan.
Rollin-Feuardent, Paris, 9/5/1910, no. 647.

888. O2* - R2*
6.80g 21mm
Same as 796. Plated. Split die.
O: guilloche border partly off the flan.
R: ꜥ3 in field right above the crook; guilloche border partly off the flan.

Florange-Ciani, Paris, 17-21/2/1925, no. 1068.

889. O3* - R3* Same as 796.
  8.85g 20mm O: guilloche border off the flan.
  12h R: ʿ3 in field right above the crook; guilloche border partly off the flan.
  Paris, BNF, no. 2014; Babelon, *Perses*, no. 2014.

890. O4* - R4* Same as 796.
  8.86g 20mm O: guilloche border partly off the flan.
  12h R: ʿ3 in field right above the crook; guilloche border partly off the flan.
  New York, ANS, no. N52 (ex Newell coll.).

891. O4 - R5 Same as 796.
  8.83g O: guilloche border partly off the flan.
  R: ʿ3 in field right above the crook; guilloche border partly off the flan.
  Helbing, Munich, 34, October 1927, no. 3147.

892. O5* - R5* Same as 796.
  8.58g 21mm O: guilloche border partly off the flan.
  R: ʿ3 in field right above the crook; guilloche border partly off the flan.
  London, BM, no. 1905-10-18 20; *BMC Phoenicia*, p. 232, no. 32 and pl. XXIX, 13.

893. O6 - R5 Same as 796.
  8.86g 21mm O: guilloche border partly off the flan.
  R: ʿ3 in field right above the crook; guilloche border partly off the flan.
  Birmingham, MAG, no. 371'20; Brüder Egger, Vienna, 26/11/1909, no. 424.

894. O6* - R6* Same as 796.
  9.06g 21mm O: dolphin and guilloche border partly off the flan.
  12h R: ʿ3 in field right above the crook; guilloche border partly off the flan.
  Münster, WL, no. 8624/12 (ex Bieder coll.).

895. O6 - R7* Same as 796.
  8.80g 21mm O: guilloche border partly off the flan.
  R: ʿ3 in field right above the crook; guilloche border partly off the flan.
  Glendining, London, 11/12/1974, no. 123 = Kündig, Münzhandlung, Basel, 4, 1/10/1935, no. 893 = Bourgey, Paris, 14-15/4/1910, no. 213 (ex Norman coll.).

896. O6 - R7 Same as 796.
  8.60g R: ʿ3 in field right above the crook; guilloche border

		partly off the flan.
		Rubinger, Antiqua, Woodland Hills, 10, 2001, no. 81.
897.	O6 - R8*	Same as 796.
	8.74g 21mm	O: guilloche border partly off the flan.
	12h	R: ʿ3 in field right above the crook; guilloche border partly off the flan.
		Jerusalem, RocMus, no. H1.23; Lambert, *QDAP* 1, 1931, p. 16, no. 24 and pl. XIX; Elayi-Elayi, *Trésors*, p. 174, no. 24 and pl. XXVIII (Tell Abu Hawam hoard TXXXV).
898.	O6 - R9*	Same as 796.
	8.59g	O: guilloche border partly off the flan.
		R: ʿ3 in field right above the crook; guilloche border partly off the flan.
		Gorny-Mosch, Giessener Münzhandlung, Munich, 113, 18/10/2001, no. 297.
899.	O7* - R5	Same as 796.
	8.82g 21mm	O: head of the seahorse and guilloche border partly off the flan.
	11h	R: ʿ3 in field right above the crook; guilloche border partly off the flan.
		Münich, SMS, no. 28.
900.	O8* - R10*	Same as 796. Small dies.
	8.53g 22mm	O: guilloche border partly off the flan.
	1h	R: ʿ3 in field right above the crook; guilloche border partly off the flan.
		Jerusalem, RocMus, no. H1.30; Lambert, *QDAP* 1, 1931, p. 16, no. 30 and pl. XIX; Elayi-Elayi, *Trésors*, p. 174, no. 27 and pl. XXVIII (Tell Abu Hawam hoard TXXXV).
901.	O9* - R10	Same as 796. Small dies.
	8.81g	R: ʿ3 in field right above the crook.
	12h	*SNG Copenhagen*, no. 308 and pl. 8.
902.	O10* - R9	Same as 796.
	8.60g 21mm	R: ʿ3 in field right above the crook; guilloche border partly off the flan.
	12h	Leiden, RM, no. 8084.
903.	O10 - R10	Same as 796. Small cracks on the edge.
	8.84g 20mm	O: guilloche border partly off the flan.
		R: ʿ3 in field right above the crook; guilloche border partly off the flan.
		Ratto, Lugano, 4/4/1927, no. 2658.

904. O10 - R11*   Same as 796.
     8.84g 21mm   O: guilloche border partly off the flan.
                   R: ʿ3 in field right above the crook; guilloche border partly off the flan.
                   Martin, London, October 1993, no. G65 = Cahn, Frankfurt/Main, 84, 29/11/1933, no. 425.
905. O6 - R?   Same as 796. Slightly worn.
     8.89g   O: guilloche border partly off the flan.
                   R: ʿ3 in field right above the crook; guilloche border partly off the flan.
                   Leu, Zurich, and Schulman, Amsterdam, 1966, no. 3067 (ex Pozzi coll.).
906. O103* - R?   Same as 796. Slightly worn.
     8.19g 20mm   R: $\overset{8}{\text{ʿ}}\hspace{-0.1em}3$ in field right above the crook; guilloche border partly off the flan.
     1h   Jerusalem, RocMus, no. H1.25; Lambert, *QDAP* 1, 1931, p. 16, no. 25 and pl. XIX; Elayi-Elayi, *Trésors*, p. 174, no. 25 and pl. XXVIII (Tell Abu Hawam hoard TXXXV).
907. O? - R5   Same as 796. Slightly worn.
                   R: ʿ3 in field right above the crook.
                   Haifa, NMM; *Sefunim* 3, 1969-71, pp. 91-92 and pl. XVIII, 3 (obverse not illustrated); Elayi-Elayi, *Trésors*, p. 347 (found in the sea, near ʿAtlit).
908. O? - R7   Same as 796. Slightly worn.
     8.75g 19mm   O: guilloche border partly off the flan; re-struck.
                   R: ʿ3 in field right above the crook; guilloche border partly off the flan.
                   Platt, Paris, 18-19/11/1935, no. 101 (coll. Bougon).
909. O? - R8   Same as 796. Slightly worn. Small dies.
     8.87g   O: guilloche border partly off the flan.
                   R: ʿ3 in field right above the crook.
                   Berk, Chicago, 112, 13/1/2000, no. 245; 65, 26/2/1991, no. 373.
910. O? - R171*   Same as 796. Slightly worn.
     8.70g 21mm   O: guilloche border partly off the flan.
     12h   R: $J\,\overset{8}{\text{ʿ}}\hspace{-0.1em}3$ in field right above the crook; guilloche border partly off the flan.
                   Oxford, AM, no. 93 (ex Cunningham coll.).
911. O? - R?   Same as 796. Rather worn. Deep chisel-cut.
     8.67g   O: guilloche border partly off the flan.
                   R: $\overset{8}{\text{ʿ}}\hspace{-0.1em}3$ in field right above the crook; guilloche border partly off the flan.

		Albrecht-Hoffmann, Köln, 74, 11-13/11/1992, no. 397 = 71, 3-5/6/1991, no. 577.
912.	O? - R?	Same as 796.
		R: ⸢3 in field right above the crook. Graffito.
		Madrid, MAN, no. 3832/42; Elayi-Lemaire, *Graffiti*, p. 45, no. 32.
913.		Same as 796.
		R: ⸢3 in field right above the crook.
		Elayi-Elayi, *Trésors*, p. 187, no. 5, not illustrated (Safed hoard TXXXVII).
914-916.		Same as 796.
		R: ⸢3 in field right above the crook.
		Elayi-Elayi, *Trésors*, p. 236, no. 142-144, not illustrated (Naplouse hoard TLI).

II.2.1.15. ⸢Ozmilk's shekels with ⸢4 on the reverse

917.	O7 - R16*	Same as 796.
	8.51g 20mm	O: guilloche border partly off the flan.
		R: ⸢4 in field right above the crook; scratch; guilloche border partly off the flan.
		London, BM, no. 1900-7-7 175; *BMC Phoenicia*, p. 232, no. 34, not illustrated; Reichardt, London, 1899, no. 257.
918.	O9 - R17*	Same as 796. Small dies.
	8.79g 21mm	O: re-struck.
	1h	R: ⸢4 in field right above the crook, with a dot inside; guilloche border partly off the flan.
		New York, ANS, no. N62; Newell, *Tyrus*, no. 14 (ex Newell coll.).
919.	O9 - R18	Same as 796.
	8.85g 20mm	R: ⸢4 in field right above the crook; letter and guilloche border partly off the flan.
		Vinchon, Paris, 14/4/1984, no. 207 (ex De Behague coll.).
920.	O10 - R12*	Same as 796.
	8.81g 20mm	R: ⸢4 in field right above the crook.
		Leu, Münzen und Medaillen, Basel, 3-4/12/1965, no. 487 (ex Niggeler coll.).
921.	O10 - R12	Same as 796.
	8.77g 20mm	O: guilloche border partly off the flan.
	11h	R: ⸢4 in field right above the crook; guilloche border partly off the flan.
		Jerusalem, RocMus, no. H1.27; Lambert, *QDAP* 1,

1931, p. 16, no. 27 and pl. XIX; Elayi-Elayi, *Trésors*, p. 174, no. 26 and pl. XXVIII (Tell Abu Hawam hoard TXXXV).

922. O10 - R13*
19mm
Same as 796. Small crack on the edge.
R: ᶜ4 in field right above the crook.
Feuardent, Paris, 18/6/1924, no. 137 = Bourgey, Paris, 29-31/5/1911, no. 227.

923. O10 - R14*
8.30g 21mm
11h
Same as 796.
O: guilloche border partly off the flan.
R: ᶜ4 in field right above the crook; guilloche border partly off the flan. Re-struck.
Jerusalem, RocMus, no. H1.26; Lambert, *QDAP* 1, 1931, p. 16, no. 26 and pl. XIX; Elayi-Elayi, *Trésors*, p. 174, no. 29 and pl. XXVIII (Tell Abu Hawam hoard TXXXV).

924. O10 - R15*
8.81g
12h
Same as 796.
O: guilloche border partly off the flan.
R: *J4* in field right above the crook; guilloche border partly off the flan.
Hess-Leu, Lucerne-Zurich, 12-13/4/1962, no. 367.

925. O11* - R18*
23mm
Same as 796. Small dies.
R: ᶜ4 in field right above the crook.
Bourgey, Paris, 20-21/12/1921, no. 54.

926. O12* - R18
8.83g 20mm
12h
Same as 796.
O: guilloche border partly off the flan.
R: ᶜ4 in field right above the crook; guilloche border partly off the flan.
New York, ANS, no. N51 (ex Newell coll.).

927. O12 - R19*
8.87g
12h
Same as 796.
O: guilloche border partly off the flan.
R: ᶜ4 in field right above the crook; guilloche border partly off the flan.
SNG Copenhagen, no. 309 and pl. 8.

928. O13* - R20*
9.25g 21mm
Same as 796. Small dies.
R: ᶜ4 in field right above the crook, with a dot in the letter.
Button, Frankfurt/Main, 28-29/10/1959, no. 112.

929. O14* - R21*
7.34g
Same as 796. Plated?
O: guilloche border partly off the flan.
R: ᶜ4 in field right above the crook.
Hirsch, Munich, 236, 23-25/9/2004, no. 2044.

930. O15* - R22*
8.87g 21mm
Same as 796. Partly worn.
O: head of the seahorse obliterated and guilloche border partly off the flan.

		R: ᶜ4 in field right above the crook; guilloche border partly off the flan.
		Tel Aviv, KNM, no. K1634.
931.	O15 - R22	Same as 796.
	8.44g	O: guilloche border partly off the flan.
		R: ᶜ4 in field right above the crook; guilloche border partly off the flan.
		Münzen und Medaillen, Basel, 448, September 1982, no. 8.
932.	O104* - R?	Same as 796. Slightly worn.
	7.91g	O: dolphin and guilloche border partly off the flan.
		R: ᶜ4 in field right above the crook.
		Hunterian Collection, III, no. 31 (ex Hunterian coll.).
933.	O? - R17	Same as 796. Slightly worn. Cracks on the edge.
	8.00g 21mm	O: waves, dolphin and guilloche border partly off the flan.
	11h	
		R: ᶜ4 in field right above the crook.
		Jerusalem, RocMus, no. H1.28; Lambert, *QDAP* 1, 1931, p. 16, no. 28 and pl. XIX; Elayi-Elayi, *Trésors*, p. 174, no. 30 and pl. XXVIII (Tell Abu Hawam hoard TXXXV).
934.	O? - R172*	Same as 796. Slightly worn.
	8.32g 21mm	O: small die; guilloche border partly off the flan. Restruck.
	12h	
		R: ᶜ4 in field right above the crook.
		Jerusalem, RocMus, no. H1.29; Lambert, *QDAP* 1, 1931, p. 16, no. 29 and pl. XIX; Elayi-Elayi, *Trésors*, p. 174, no. 28 and pl. XXVIII (Tell Abu Hawam hoard TXXXV).
935.	O? - R?	Same as 796. Rather worn.
	8.81g	R: ᶜ4 in field right above the crook.
		Catalogue Jameson, no. 1776 (ex Jameson coll.).
936-		Same as 796.
942.		R: ᶜ4 in field right above the crook.
		Elayi-Elayi, *Trésors*, p. 236, no. 145-151, not illustrated (Naplouse hoard TLI).

II.2.1.16. ᶜOzmilk's shekels with ᶜ5 on the reverse

943.	O16* - R23*	Same as 796.
	8.40g 21mm	O: guilloche border partly off the flan. Scratch.
	12h	R: ᶜ5 in field right above the crook.
		Jerusalem, RocMus, no. H1.32; Lambert, *QDAP* 1,

		1931, p. 16, no. 32 and pl. XIX; Elayi-Elayi, *Trésors*, pp. 174-175, no. 32 and pl. XXVIII (Tell Abu Hawam hoard TXXXV).
944.	O17* - R24* 8.60g 21mm 11h	Same as 796. O: head of the seahorse and guilloche border partly off the flan. R: ʿ5 in field right above the crook. Jerusalem, RocMus, no. H1.31; Lambert, *QDAP* 1, 1931, p. 16, no. 31 and pl. XIX; Elayi-Elayi, *Trésors*, p. 174, no. 31 and pl. XXVIII (Tell Abu Hawam hoard TXXXV).
945.	O18* - R25* 7.32g 19mm 11h	Same as 796. Rather crude style. O: guilloche border partly off the flan. R: ʿ5 in field right above the crook; guilloche border partly off the flan. Jerusalem, IM, no. 1102.
946.	O19* - R26* 8.80g 21mm 1h	Same as 796. O: guilloche border partly off the flan. R: ʿ5 in field right above the crook; guilloche border partly off the flan. Jerusalem, RocMus, no. H1.34; Lambert, *QDAP* 1, 1931, p. 16, no. 34 and pl. XIX; Elayi-Elayi, *Trésors*, p. 175, no. 34 and pl. XXIX (Tell Abu Hawam hoard TXXXV).
947.	O10 - R? 8.10g 21mm 12h	Same as 796. Slightly worn. O: guilloche border partly off the flan. R: ʿ5 in field right above the crook; guilloche border partly off the flan. Rome, VM, no. 203.
948.	O? - R173* 8.83g 21mm	Same as 796. Slightly worn. O: guilloche border partly off the flan. R: ʿ5 in field right above the crook. Tel Aviv, KNM, no. K1655.
949- 950.		Same as 796. R: ʿ5 in field right above the crook. Elayi-Elayi, *Trésors*, p. 187, no. 6-7, not illustrated (Safed hoard TXXXVII).
951- 957.		Same as 796. R: ʿ5 in field right above the crook. Elayi-Elayi, *Trésors*, p. 236, no. 152-158, not illustrated (Naplouse hoard TLI).

II.2.1.17. ʿOzmilk's shekels with ʿ6 on the reverse

958. O20* - R27* Same as 796.
     8.85g 20mm O: guilloche border partly off the flan.
     12h   R: ʿ6 in field right above the crook; guilloche border partly off the flan. Re-struck.
                   Jerusalem, RocMus, no. H1.35; Lambert, *QDAP* 1, 1931, p. 16, no. 30 and pl. XIX; Elayi-Elayi, *Trésors*, p. 175, no. 33 and pl. XXVIII (Tell Abu Hawam hoard TXXXV).

959. O20 - R28*   Same as 796.
     8.62g 21mm O: guilloche border partly off the flan.
     12h   R: ʿ6 in field right above the crook; guilloche border partly off the flan. Re-struck.
                   Jerusalem, RocMus, no. H1.36; Lambert, *QDAP* 1, 1931, p. 16, no. 36 and pl. XIX; Elayi-Elayi, *Trésors*, p. 175, no. 36 and pl. XXIX (Tell Abu Hawam hoard TXXXV).

960. O21* - R29* Same as 796.
     8.78g 21mm O: dolphin and guilloche border partly off the flan.
     1h   R: ʿ6 in field right above the crook; guilloche border partly off the flan.
                   Jerusalem, RocMus, no. H1.33; Lambert, *QDAP* 1, 1931, p. 16, no. 33 and pl. XIX; Elayi-Elayi, *Trésors*, p. 175, no. 35 and pl. XXIX (Tell Abu Hawam hoard TXXXV).

961. O105* - R?   Same as 796. Slightly worn.
     8.78g 21mm O: head of the seahorse obliterated, dolphin and guilloche border partly off the flan.
     12h   R: ʿ6̊ in field right above the crook; guilloche border partly off the flan.
                   Jerusalem, RocMus, no. H1.37; Lambert, *QDAP* 1, 1931, p. 16, no. 37 and pl. XIX; Elayi-Elayi, *Trésors*, p. 175, no. 37 and pl. XXIX (Tell Abu Hawam hoard TXXXV).

962. O? - R?   Same as 796. Rather worn.
     8.72g   O: seahorse and guilloche border partly off the flan.
                   R: ʿ6 in field right above the crook; guilloche border partly off the flan.
                   Empire Coins, Ormond Beach, 53, 1990, no. 57.

963. O? - R?   Same as 796. Rather worn.
     8.41g 21mm O: seahorse partly obliterated and guilloche border partly off the flan.
     1h   R: ʿ6̊ in field right above the crook; owl partly

		obliterated and guilloche border partly off the flan. Jerusalem, RocMus, no. H1.38; Lambert, *QDAP* 1, 1931, p. 16, no. 38 and pl. XIX; Elayi-Elayi, *Trésors*, p. 175, no. 38 and pl. XXIX (Tell Abu Hawam hoard TXXXV).
964- 965.		Same as 796. R: ʿ6 in field right above the crook. Elayi-Elayi, *Trésors*, p. 236, no. 159-160 (Naplouse hoard TLI).

II.2.1.18. ʿOzmilk's shekels with ʿ7 on the reverse

966.	O22* - R27'* 8.38g 20mm 2h	Same as 796. O: guilloche border partly off the flan. R: ʿ7 in field right above the crook; guilloche border partly off the flan, and crook partly obliterated. Jerusalem, RocMus, no. H1.54; Lambert, *QDAP* 1, 1931, p. 17, no. 54; Elayi-Elayi, *Trésors*, p. 176, no. 49 and pl. XXIX (Tell Abu Hawam hoard TXXXV).
967.	O22 - R30* 8.76g 20mm	Same as 796. O: guilloche border partly off the flan. R: ʿ7̊ in field right above the crook; guilloche border partly off the flan. Jerusalem, IM, no. 10683; Malloy, New York, 13, 8/12/1978, no. 98.
968.	O23 - R31* 8.16g	Same as 796. O: guilloche border partly off the flan. R: ʿ7 in field right above the crook. Elsen, Brussels, 86, 10/12/2005, no. 144.
969.	O23* - R32* 8.39g 22mm 11h	Same as 796. Split die. O: guilloche border partly off the flan. R: ʿ7 in field right above the crook; guilloche border partly off the flan. Jerusalem, RocMus, no. H1.43; Lambert, *QDAP* 1, 1931, p. 16, no. 43; Elayi-Elayi, *Trésors*, p. 176, no. 48 and pl. XXIX (Tell Abu Hawam hoard TXXXV).
970.	O23 - R32 8.67g 21mm 12h	Same as 796. O: guilloche border partly off the flan. R: ʿ7̊? in field right above the crook; guilloche border partly off the flan. Traces of gaze in field right. Jerusalem, RocMus, no. H1.47; Lambert, *QDAP* 1, 1931, p. 17, no. 47; Elayi-Elayi, *Trésors*, pp. 176-177, no. 54 and pl. XXIX (Tell Abu Hawam hoard

TXXXV).

971.	O23 - R33* 8.70g 20mm 12h	Same as 796. O: guilloche border partly off the flan. R: ʿ7 in field right above the crook; guilloche border partly off the flan. Shahaf coll., Haifa, no. 3 (bought in Akko).
972.	O24* - R34* 8.61g 21mm 1h	Same as 796. O: defect on the waves; guilloche border partly off the flan. R: $^{\ell}\!\!\not{7}$? in field right above the crook; guilloche border partly off the flan. Re-struck. Jerusalem, RocMus, no. H1.45; Lambert, *QDAP* 1, 1931, p. 17, no. 45; Elayi-Elayi, *Trésors*, p. 177, no. 55 and pl. XXX (Tell Abu Hawam hoard TXXXV).
973.	O24 - R35* 8.54g 20mm 1h	Same as 796. O: defect on the waves; guilloche border partly off the flan. R: $^{\ell}\!\!\not{7}$? in field right above the crook; guilloche border partly off the flan. Jerusalem, RocMus, no. H1.46; Lambert, *QDAP* 1, 1931, p. 17, no. 46; Elayi-Elayi, *Trésors*, p. 177, no. 56 and pl. XXX (Tell Abu Hawam hoard TXXXV).
974.	O24 - R36* 8.70g 20mm 1h	Same as 796. O: defect on the waves; guilloche border partly off the flan. R: $^{\ell}\!\!\not{7}$ in field right above the crook; border off the flan. Jerusalem, RocMus, no. H1.49; Lambert, *QDAP* 1, 1931, p. 17, no. 49; Elayi-Elayi, *Trésors*, p. 176, no. 53 and pl. XXIX (Tell Abu Hawam hoard TXXXV).
975.	O25* - R37* 8.58g 20mm 1h	Same as 796. O: guilloche border partly off the flan. R: ʿ7 in field right above the crook; dot above the head of the owl; guilloche border partly off the flan. Jerusalem, RocMus, no. H1.55; Lambert, *QDAP* 1, 1931, p. 17, no. 55; Elayi-Elayi, *Trésors*, p. 175, no. 42 and pl. XXIX (Tell Abu Hawam hoard TXXXV).
976.	O26* - R38* 8.86g 20mm 1h	Same as 796. O: guilloche border partly off the flan. R: ʿ7 in field right above the crook; guilloche border partly off the flan. Jerusalem, RocMus, no. H1.53; Lambert, *QDAP* 1, 1931, p. 17, no. 53; Elayi-Elayi, *Trésors*, p. 175, no.

		39 and pl. XXIX (Tell Abu Hawam hoard TXXXV).
977.	O27* - R39* 8.76g 21mm 12h	Same as 796. Pierced. O: dolphin and guilloche border partly off the flan. R: ʿ7 in field right above the crook; guilloche border partly off the flan. New York, ANS, no. N55 ; Betlyon, *Coinage of Phoenicia*, pl. 6, 1 (ex Newell coll.).
978.	O28* - R40* 8.82g 20mm 12h	Same as 796. O: guilloche border partly off the flan. R: ʿ7 in field right above the crook; guilloche border partly off the flan. Jerusalem, RocMus, no. H1.40; Lambert, *QDAP* 1, 1931, p. 16, no. 40; Elayi-Elayi, *Trésors*, p. 175, no. 40 and pl. XXIX (Tell Abu Hawam hoard TXXXV).
979.	O28 - R41* 8.26g 21mm 1h	Same as 796. O: dolphin and guilloche border partly off the flan. R: ʿ7 in field right above the crook; guilloche border partly off the flan. Jerusalem, RocMus, no. H1.57; Lambert, *QDAP* 1, 1931, p. 17, no. 57; Elayi-Elayi, *Trésors*, p. 176, no. 51 and pl. XXIX (Tell Abu Hawam hoard TXXXV).
980.	O28 - R42	Same as 796. O: guilloche border partly off the flan. R: ʿ7 in field right above the crook; guilloche border partly off the flan. Künker, Osnabrück, 11, 8-9/3/1988, no. 3615.
981.	O29* - R42* 8.55g 22mm 11h	Same as 796. Small cracks on the edge. R: ʿ7 in field right above the crook; guilloche border partly off the flan. Re-struck. Jerusalem, RocMus, no. H1.50; Lambert, *QDAP* 1, 1931, p. 17, no. 50; Elayi-Elayi, *Trésors*, pp. 175-176, no. 43 and pl. XXIX (Tell Abu Hawam hoard TXXXV).
982.	O? - R31 7.97g 21mm 1h	Same as 796. Small cracks on the edge and slightly worn. R: ʿ7 in field right above the crook; guilloche border partly off the flan. Re-struck. Jerusalem, RocMus, no. H1.42; Lambert, *QDAP* 1, 1931, p. 16, no. 42; Elayi-Elayi, *Trésors*, p. 176, no. 52 and pl. XXIX (Tell Abu Hawam hoard TXXXV).
983.	O? - R34 8.46g 23mm 1h	Same as 796. Slightly worn. O: guilloche border partly off the flan. R: ʿ7 in field right above the crook; guilloche border

		partly off the flan. Jerusalem, RocMus, no. H1.44; Lambert, *QDAP* 1, 1931, p. 17, no. 44; Elayi-Elayi, *Trésors*, p. 176, no. 45 and pl. XXIX (Tell Abu Hawam hoard TXXXV).
984.	O? - R37 8.73g 21mm 12h	Same as 796. Rather worn. O: dolphin and guilloche border partly off the flan. R: ʿ𐤆 in field right above the crook; guilloche border partly off the flan. Oxford, AM, no. 94 (from Keble College, Beirut).
985.	O? - R40 8.26g 21mm 12h	Same as 796. Slightly worn. O: head of the deity and guilloche border partly off the flan. R: ʿ7 in field right above the crook; guilloche border partly off the flan. Jerusalem, RocMus, no. H1.41; Lambert, *QDAP* 1, 1931, p. 16, no. 41; Elayi-Elayi, *Trésors*, p. 176, no. 50 and pl. XXIX (Tell Abu Hawam hoard TXXXV).
986.	O? - R174* 8.77g 20mm	Same as 796. Slightly worn. O: re-struck. R: ʿ𐤆 in field right above the crook; guilloche border partly off the flan. London, BM, no. 1947-4-6 486.
987.	O? - R175* 8.55g 21mm 1h	Same as 796. Slightly worn. O: guilloche border partly off the flan. R: ʿ7 in field right above the crook; guilloche border partly off the flan. Jerusalem, RocMus, no. H1.56; Lambert, *QDAP* 1, 1931, p. 17, no. 56; Elayi-Elayi, *Trésors*, p. 176, no. 44 and pl. XXIX (Tell Abu Hawam hoard TXXXV).
988.	O? - R176* 8.44g 21mm 11h	Same as 796. Slightly worn. O: guilloche border partly off the flan. R: ʿ7 in field right above the crook; guilloche border partly off the flan. Jerusalem, RocMus, no. H1.52; Lambert, *QDAP* 1, 1931, p. 17, no. 52; Elayi-Elayi, *Trésors*, p. 176, no. 46 and pl. XXIX (Tell Abu Hawam hoard TXXXV).
989.	O? - R176 8.25g 23mm 1h	Same as 796. Slightly worn. O: seahorse and guilloche border partly off the flan. R: ʿ𐤆? in field right above the crook; guilloche border partly off the flan. Jerusalem, RocMus, no. H1.48; Lambert, *QDAP* 1, 1931, p. 17, no. 48; Elayi-Elayi, *Trésors*, p. 177, no. 57 and pl. XXX (Tell Abu Hawam hoard TXXXV).

990.	O? - R176	Same as 796. Slightly worn. O: guilloche border partly off the flan. R: ʿ7 in field right above the crook; guilloche border partly off the flan. Schulman, Amsterdam, 6-7/4/1971, no. 338.
991.	O? - R177* 8.64g 21mm 10h	Same as 796. Slightly worn. O: head of the deity, seahorse and guilloche border partly off the flan. R: defect in field right and ʿ7 above the crook; guilloche border partly off the flan. Jerusalem, RocMus, no. H1.51; Lambert, *QDAP* 1, 1931, p. 17, no. 51; Elayi-Elayi, *Trésors*, p. 175, no. 41 and pl. XXIX (Tell Abu Hawam hoard TXXXV).
992.	O? - R? 8.43g 21mm 1h	Same as 796. Rather worn. O: heads of the deity and seahorse, dolphin and guilloche border partly off the flan. R: ʿ7 in field right above the crook; head of the owl obliterated and guilloche border partly off the flan. Jerusalem, RocMus, no. H1.39; Lambert, *QDAP* 1, 1931, p. 16, no. 39; Elayi-Elayi, *Trésors*, p. 176, no. 47 and pl. XXIX (Tell Abu Hawam hoard TXXXV).
993.	O? - R? 8.35g 21mm	Same as 796. Rather worn. O: seahorse and guilloche border partly off the flan. R: ʿ$\overset{o}{7}$ in field right above the crook; guilloche border partly off the flan. Haifa, NMN, no. 3.
994.	O? - R?	Same as 796. Rather worn. O: guilloche border partly off the flan. R: ʿ$\overset{o}{7}$ in field right above the crook; guilloche border partly off the flan. Superior Stamp and Coin, Beverly Hills, 17-23/6/1974, no. 324.
995- 997.		Same as 796. R: ʿ7 in field right above the crook. Elayi-Elayi, *Trésors*, p. 236, no. 162-163, not illustrated (Naplouse hoard TLI).
998- 1000.		Same as 796. R: ʿ7 in field right above the crook. Elayi-Elayi, *Trésors*, pp. 187-188, no. 8-10, not illustrated (Safed hoard TXXXVII).

II.2.1.19. ᶜOzmilk's shekels with ᶜ8 on the reverse

1001. O30* - R43*   Same as 796.
      8.90g 21mm   O: guilloche border partly off the flan.
                     R: ᶜ8 in field right above the crook; guilloche border partly off the flan.
                     Tel Aviv, KNM, no. K1656.

1002. O30 - R43   Same as 796.
      8.62g 20mm   O: guilloche border partly off the flan.
      1h   R: ᶜ8 in field right above the crook; guilloche border partly off the flan.
                     Jerusalem, RocMus, no. H1.62; Lambert, *QDAP* 1, 1931, p. 17, no. 62; Elayi-Elayi, *Trésors*, p. 177, no. 60 and pl. XXX (Tell Abu Hawam hoard TXXXV).

1003. O31* - R43   Same as 796.
      8.70g 21mm   O: dolphin and guilloche border partly off the flan.
      12h   R: ᶜ8? in field right above the crook.
                     Oxford, AM, no. 95 (ex Cunningham coll.).

1004. O31 - R44*   Same as 796.
      8.46g 21mm   O: dolphin and guilloche border partly off the flan.
      11h   R: ᶜ8 in field right above the crook; guilloche border partly off the flan. Slight scratches.
                     New York, ANS, no. N53 (ex Newell coll.).

1005. O32* - R45*   Same as 796.
      8.73g 20mm   O: dolphin and guilloche border partly off the flan.
      1h   R: ᶜ8 in field right above the crook; guilloche border partly off the flan.
                     Jerusalem, RocMus, no. H1.60; Lambert, *QDAP* 1, 1931, p. 17, no. 60; Elayi-Elayi, *Trésors*, p. 177, no. 58 and pl. XXX (Tell Abu Hawam hoard TXXXV).

1006. O32 - R45   Same as 796.
      8.72g 22mm   O: guilloche border partly off the flan.
      1h   R: ᶜ8 in field right above the crook; guilloche border partly off the flan.
                     Jerusalem, RocMus, no. H1.58; Lambert, *QDAP* 1, 1931, p. 17, no. 58; Elayi-Elayi, *Trésors*, p. 177, no. 59 and pl. XXX (Tell Abu Hawam hoard TXXXV).

1007. O32 - R45   Same as 796.
      8.60g 21mm   O: guilloche border partly off the flan.
      1h   R: ᶜ8 in field right above the crook; guilloche border partly off the flan.
                     Jerusalem, RocMus, no. H1.59; Lambert, *QDAP* 1, 1931, p. 17, no. 59; Elayi-Elayi, *Trésors*, p. 177, no. 61 and pl. XXX (Tell Abu Hawam hoard TXXXV).

1008. O33* - R46* Same as 796.
8.77g 22mm R: ʿ8 in field right above the crook; guilloche border
1h partly off the flan.
Spaer coll., Jerusalem (bought in Jerusalem).

1009. O34* - R47* Same as 796.
8.74g 21mm O: guilloche border partly off the flan.
12h R: ʿ8 in field right above the crook; guilloche border
partly off the flan.
Berlin, SM, no. 31 (ex Löbbecke coll.).

1010. O35* - R48* Same as 796.
8.57g 22mm O: guilloche border partly off the flan.
1h R: ʿ8 in field right above the crook; guilloche border
partly off the flan.
Jerusalem, RocMus, no. H1.61; Lambert, *QDAP* 1,
1931, p. 17, no. 61; Elayi-Elayi, *Trésors*, p. 177, no.
21 and pl. XXX (Tell Abu Hawam hoard TXXXV).

1011. O? - R43 Same as 796. Slightly worn.
8.81g 22mm O: seahorse, dolphin and guilloche border partly off
the flan.
R: ʿ8 in field right above the crook; guilloche border
partly off the flan.
Beirut, NM, no. 1327; Chéhab, *Monnaies*, no. 1327
and pl. LIV, 2 (AE [sic]).

1012. O? - R43 Same as 796. Slightly worn.
O: dolphin and guilloche border partly off the flan.
R: ʿ8 in field right above the crook; guilloche border
partly off the flan.
Schulman, New York, 6-9/5/1974, no. 2356.

1013. O? - R178* Same as 796. Slightly worn.
8.81g 22mm O: guilloche border partly off the flan.
R: ʿ8 in field right above the crook; guilloche border
partly off the flan.
London, BM, no. 1847-3-11 1; *BMC Phoenicia*, p.
232, no. 35, not illustrated.

1014. O? - R179* Same as 796. Slightly worn.
8.55g 20mm O: guilloche border partly off the flan. Small
1h scratches.
R: ʿ8 in field right above the crook; guilloche border
partly off the flan.
Jerusalem, RocMus, no. H1.63; Lambert, *QDAP* 1,
1931, p. 17, no. 63; Elayi-Elayi, *Trésors*, p. 177, no.
63 and pl. XXX (Tell Abu Hawam hoard TXXXV).

1015. O? - R180* Same as 796. Slightly worn.
R: ʿ8 in field right above the crook.

		Haifa, NMM; *Sefunim* 3, 1969-71, pp. 91-92 and pl. XVIII, 3 (obverse not illustrated); Elayi-Elayi, *Trésors*, p. 347 (found in the sea, near ʿAtlit).
1016.	O? - R? 8.42g	Same as 796. Rather worn. O: guilloche border partly off the flan. R: ʿ$\overset{8}{}$ in field right above the crook; guilloche border partly off the flan. Müller, Solingen, 53, 26-27/9/1986, no. 120.
1017.	O? - R? 8.25g	Same as 796. Rather worn. O: dolphin and guilloche border partly off the flan. R: ʿ$\overset{8}{}$? in field right above the crook; guilloche border partly off the flan. Albrecht-Hoffmann, Münz Zentrum, Köln, 50, 23/11/1983, no. 199.
1018.	8.81g	Same as 796. R: ʿ8 in field right above the crook. Elayi-Elayi, *Trésors*, p. 189, no. 1, not illustrated (Damascus hoard TXXXVIII).
1019-1026.		Same as 796. R: ʿ8 in field right above the crook. Elayi-Elayi, *Trésors*, p. 236, no. 164-171, not illustrated (Naplouse hoard TLI).

II.2.1.20. ʿOzmilk's shekels with ʿ9 on the reverse

1027.	O29 - R49* 8.82g 21mm 1h	Same as 796. Small crack on the edge. O: dolphin and guilloche border partly off the flan. R: ʿ$\overset{9}{}$ in field right above the crook; guilloche border partly off the flan. Jerusalem, RocMus, no. H1.85; Lambert, *QDAP* 1, 1931, p. 19, no. 85; Elayi-Elayi, *Trésors*, p. 179, no. 87 and pl. XXXI (Tell Abu Hawam hoard TXXXV).
1028.	O36* - R49 8.62g 22mm 12h	Same as 796. Slightly worn. O: guilloche border partly off the flan. R: defect on the leg of the owl; ʿ9 in field right above the crook; guilloche border partly off the flan. Jerusalem, RocMus, no. H1.87; Lambert, *QDAP* 1, 1931, p. 19, no. 87; Elayi-Elayi, *Trésors*, p. 179, no. 79 and pl. XXXI (Tell Abu Hawam hoard TXXXV).
1029.	O36 - R49 8.57g 22mm 12h	Same as 796. O: guilloche border partly off the flan. R: defect on the leg of the owl; ʿ9 in field right above the crook; guilloche border partly off the flan. Jerusalem, RocMus, no. H1.78; Lambert, *QDAP* 1,

1030. O36 - R49
8.28g 22mm
12h

1931, p. 18, no. 78; Elayi-Elayi, *Trésors*, p. 179, no. 80 and pl. XXXI (Tell Abu Hawam hoard TXXXV).
Same as 796.
O: guilloche border partly off the flan.
R: defect on the leg of the owl; ʿ9 in field right above the crook; guilloche border partly off the flan.
Jerusalem, RocMus, no. H1.79; Lambert, *QDAP* 1, 1931, p. 18, no. 79; Elayi-Elayi, *Trésors*, p. 180, no. 94 and pl. XXXI (Tell Abu Hawam hoard TXXXV).

1031. O36 - R50*
8.83g

Same as 796.
O: guilloche border partly off the flan.
R: defect on the leg of the owl; ʿ9 in field right above the crook; guilloche border partly off the flan.
Classical Numismatic Group, Lancaster-London, 42, 29-30/5/1997, no. 588.

1032. O37 - R51*
8.50g 20mm
12h

Same as 796. Split die.
O: guilloche border partly off the flan.
R: ʿ9 in field right above the crook; guilloche border partly off the flan.
Cambridge, FM, no. 1777:46; *SNG Cambridge*, no. 6085.

1033. O37 - R51
8.49g

Same as 796.
O: guilloche border partly off the flan.
R: ʿ9 in field right above the crook; guilloche border partly off the flan.
Lanz, Munich, 38, 24/11/1986, no. 414.

1034. O37* - R52
8.76g 20mm
12h

Same as 796. Chisel-cut.
O: head of the deity and guilloche border partly off the flan.
R: ʿ9 in field right above the crook; guilloche border partly off the flan.
Berlin, SM, no. 32.

1035. O38* - R52*
8.82g 20mm
1h

Same as 796. Small crack on the edge.
O: guilloche border partly off the flan.
R: ʿ9 in field right above the crook; guilloche border partly off the flan.
Jerusalem, RocMus, no. H1.91; Lambert, *QDAP* 1, 1931, p. 19, no. 91; Elayi-Elayi, *Trésors*, p. 178, no. 69 and pl. XXX (Tell Abu Hawam hoard TXXXV).

1036. O38 - R53*
8.74g 21mm

Same as 796.
O: guilloche border partly off the flan.
R: ʿ9 in field right above the crook; guilloche border partly off the flan.
Jerusalem, AI, no. 5549; Elayi-Elayi, *Trans* 11,

1996, p. 102, no. 6 and pl. IV, 16 (hoard TXXXVI).

1037. O38 - R54*
8.67g 20mm
12h

Same as 796. Small crack on the edge.
O: guilloche border partly off the flan.
R: ʿ9 in field right above the crook; guilloche border partly off the flan.
New York, ANS, no. N56 (ex Newell coll.).

1038. O38 - R55*
8.90g 20mm
11h

Same as 796.
O: guilloche border partly off the flan.
R: ʿ9 in field right above the crook; guilloche border partly off the flan.
Jerusalem, RocMus, no. H1.83; Lambert, *QDAP* 1, 1931, p. 18, no. 83; Elayi-Elayi, *Trésors*, p. 177, no. 65 and pl. XXX (Tell Abu Hawam hoard TXXXV).

1039. O38 - R55
8.82g

Same as 796.
O: guilloche border partly off the flan.
R: ʿ9 in field right above the crook; guilloche border partly off the flan.
Elayi-Elayi, *Trans* 11, 1996, p. 101, no. 3 and pl. IV, 13 (hoard TXXXVI).

1040. O38 - R55
8.50g 21mm
12h

Same as 796.
O: guilloche border partly off the flan.
R: ʿ9 in field right above the crook; guilloche border partly off the flan. Small scratches.
New York, ANS, no. N57 (ex Newell coll.).

1041. O39 - R53
8.24g 21mm
12h

Same as 796.
O: dolphin and guilloche border partly off the flan.
R: ʿ9 in field right above the crook; guilloche border partly off the flan.
Jerusalem, RocMus, no. H1.68; Lambert, *QDAP* 1, 1931, p. 18, no. 68; Elayi-Elayi, *Trésors*, p. 179, no. 84 and pl. XXXI (Tell Abu Hawam hoard TXXXV).

1042. O39 - R54
8.71g 20mm
12h

Same as 796.
O: heads of the deity and seahorse, and guilloche border partly off the flan.
R: ʿ9 in field right above the crook; guilloche border partly off the flan.
Jerusalem, RocMus, no. H1.89; Lambert, *QDAP* 1, 1931, p. 19, no. 89; Elayi-Elayi, *Trésors*, p. 178, no. 73 and pl. XXX (Tell Abu Hawam hoard TXXXV).

1043. O39 - R55
8.75g 21mm
12h

Same as 796.
O: guilloche border partly off the flan.
R: ʿ8 in field right above the crook; guilloche border partly off the flan.

1044. O39* - R55
8.66g 21mm
12h

1045. O39 - R56*
8.65g

1046. O39 - R56

1047. O39 - R57*
8.84g 21mm
1h

1048. O40* - R58*
8.78g

1049. O40 - R59*
8.82g 21mm

Jerusalem, RocMus, no. H1.64; Lambert, *QDAP* 1, 1931, p. 17, no. 64; Elayi-Elayi, *Trésors*, p. 179, no. 88 and pl. XXXI (Tell Abu Hawam hoard TXXXV).
Same as 796.
O: guilloche border partly off the flan.
R: ʿ9 in field right above the crook; guilloche border partly off the flan.
Jerusalem, RocMus, no. H1.65; Lambert, *QDAP* 1, 1931, p. 18, no. 65; Elayi-Elayi, *Trésors*, p. 178, no. 77 and pl. XXXI (Tell Abu Hawam hoard TXXXV).
Same as 796.
O: guilloche border partly off the flan.
R: ʿ9 in field right above the crook; guilloche border partly off the flan.
Classical Numismatic Group, Lancaster-London, 9-10/9/1994, no. 434.
Same as 796.
O: guilloche border partly off the flan.
R: ʿ9 in field right above the crook; guilloche border partly off the flan.
Berk, Chicago, 70, 16/3/1992, no. 224.
Same as 796.
O: heads of the deity and seahorse, and guilloche border partly off the flan.
R: ʿ9 in field right above the crook; guilloche border partly off the flan.
Jerusalem, RocMus, no. H1.67; Lambert, *QDAP* 1, 1931, p. 18, no. 67; Elayi-Elayi, *Trésors*, pp. 177-178, no. 66 and pl. XXX (Tell Abu Hawam hoard TXXXV).
Same as 796.
O: guilloche border partly off the flan.
R: ʿ9 in field right above the crook; guilloche border partly off the flan.
Elayi-Elayi, *Trans* 11, 1996, p. 102, no. 7 and pl. IV, 17 (hoard TXXXVI).
Same as 796.
O: guilloche border partly off the flan.
R: ʿ9 in field right above the crook; guilloche border partly off the flan. Graffito in field left of the head.
Elayi-Elayi, *Trésors*, p. 191, no. 1 and pl. XXXII (8.78g); *id.*, *Trans* 11, 1996, p. 102, no. 4 and pl. IV, 14 (hoard TXXXIX).

1050. O40 - R60* Same as 796.
8.10g 20mm   O: dolphin and guilloche border partly off the flan.
1h   R: ʿ9 in field right above the crook; guilloche border partly off the flan.
              Jerusalem, RocMus, no. H1.97; Lambert, *QDAP* 1, 1931, p. 19, no. 97; Elayi-Elayi, *Trésors*, p. 179, no. 85 and pl. XXXI (Tell Abu Hawam hoard TXXXV).

1051. O40 - R61* Same as 796.
8.88g   O: guilloche border partly off the flan.
              R: ʿ9 in field right above the crook; guilloche border partly off the flan.
              Elayi-Elayi, *Trans* 11, 1996, p. 101, no. 2 and pl. IV, 12 (hoard TXXXVI).

1052. O41* - R60 Same as 796.
8.74g 19mm   O: dolphin and guilloche border partly off the flan.
1h   R: ʿ9 in field right above the crook.
              Jerusalem, RocMus, no. H1.94; Lambert, *QDAP* 1, 1931, p. 19, no. 94; Elayi-Elayi, *Trésors*, p. 178, no. 71 and pl. XXX (Tell Abu Hawam hoard TXXXV).

1053. O41 - R61 Same as 796.
8.26g 21mm   O: dolphin and guilloche border partly off the flan.
1h   R: ʿ9? in field right above the crook.
              Jerusalem, RocMus, no. H1.80; Lambert, *QDAP* 1, 1931, p. 18, no. 80; Elayi-Elayi, *Trésors*, p. 180, no. 95 and pl. XXXI (Tell Abu Hawam hoard TXXXV).

1054. O41 - R61 Same as 796.
8.25g 21mm   O: guilloche border partly off the flan.
12h   R: ʿ9? in field right above the crook; guilloche border partly off the flan.
              Jerusalem, RocMus, no. H1.81; Lambert, *QDAP* 1, 1931, p. 18, no. 81; Elayi-Elayi, *Trésors*, p. 180, no. 96 and pl. XXXI (Tell Abu Hawam hoard TXXXV).

1055. O41 - R62* Same as 796.
8.80g 21mm   O: guilloche border partly off the flan.
12h   R: ʿ9 in field right above the crook; guilloche border partly off the flan.
              Paris, BNF, no. 1969/428 (from Byblos).

1056. O42 - R63 Same as 796.
8.78g 21mm   O: guilloche border partly off the flan.
11h   R: ʿ9 in field right above the crook; guilloche border partly off the flan.
              CGB, Paris, 19/6/2003, no. 137.

1057. O42* - R63* Same as 796.
8.71g 20mm   O: guilloche border partly off the flan.

	1h	R: ʿ9 in field right above the crook; guilloche border partly off the flan. Jerusalem, RocMus, no. H1.96; Lambert, *QDAP* 1, 1931, p. 19, no. 96; Elayi-Elayi, *Trésors*, p. 178, no. 75 and pl. XXX (Tell Abu Hawam hoard TXXXV).
1058.	O42 - R64* 8.73g 19mm 1h	Same as 796. O: guilloche border partly off the flan. R: ʿ9 in field right above the crook; guilloche border partly off the flan. Jerusalem, RocMus, no. H1.95; Lambert, *QDAP* 1, 1931, p. 19, no. 95; Elayi-Elayi, *Trésors*, p. 178, no. 72 and pl. XXX (Tell Abu Hawam hoard TXXXV).
1059.	O42 - R64 8.49g 19mm 1h	Same as 796. O: guilloche border partly off the flan. R: ʿ9 in field right above the crook; guilloche border partly off the flan. Jerusalem, RocMus, no. H1.93; Lambert, *QDAP* 1, 1931, p. 19, no. 93; Elayi-Elayi, *Trésors*, p. 180, no. 91 and pl. XXXI (Tell Abu Hawam hoard TXXXV).
1060.	O42 - R65* 8.91g	Same as 796. O: guilloche border partly off the flan. R: ʿ9 in field right above the crook; guilloche border partly off the flan. Elayi-Elayi, *Trans* 11, 1996, p. 101, no. 1 and pl. IV, 11; NFA, Beverly Hills, 18, 31/3/1987, no. 231 (hoard TXXXVI).
1061.	O43* - R65	Same as 796. R: ʿ9 in field right above the crook; guilloche border partly off the flan. Jidejian, *Lebanon*, p. 31.
1062.	O44* - R66* 8.70g 21mm	Same as 796. O: guilloche border partly off the flan. R: ʿ9 in field right above the crook; guilloche border partly off the flan. Tel Aviv, KNM, no. K1546.
1063.	O44 - R66 8.69g 20mm 11h	Same as 796. O: dolphin and guilloche border partly off the flan. R: ʿ9 in field right above the crook; guilloche border partly off the flan. New York, ANS, no. 48.19 (ex Gauthier coll.).
1064.	O44 - R67* 8.88g 22mm 1h	Same as 796. O: guilloche border partly off the flan. R: ʿ9 in field right above the crook; guilloche border partly off the flan.

1065. O44 - R67
8.42g 22mm
12h

Jerusalem, RocMus, no. H1.85; Lambert, *QDAP* 1, 1931, p. 18, no. 75; Elayi-Elayi, *Trésors*, p. 179, no. 86 and pl. XXXI (Tell Abu Hawam hoard TXXXV).
Same as 796. Small cracks on the edge.
O: guilloche border partly off the flan.
R: ᶜ9 in field right above the crook; guilloche border partly off the flan.
Jerusalem, RocMus, no. H1.76; Lambert, *QDAP* 1, 1931, p. 18, no. 76; Elayi-Elayi, *Trésors*, p. 179, no. 81 and pl. XXXI (Tell Abu Hawam hoard TXXXV).

1066. O45* - R68*
8.71g 21mm
10h

Same as 796.
O: guilloche border partly off the flan.
R: ᶜ9 in field right above the crook; guilloche border partly off the flan.
Jerusalem, RocMus, no. H1.70; Lambert, *QDAP* 1, 1931, p. 18, no. 70; Elayi-Elayi, *Trésors*, p. 178, no. 74 and pl. XXX (Tell Abu Hawam hoard TXXXV).

1067. O45 - R68
8.68g 20mm
11h

Same as 796.
O: guilloche border partly off the flan.
R: ᶜ9 in field right above the crook; guilloche border partly off the flan.
Jerusalem, RocMus, no. H1.90; Lambert, *QDAP* 1, 1931, p. 19, no. 90; Elayi-Elayi, *Trésors*, p. 179, no. 74 and pl. XXXI (Tell Abu Hawam hoard TXXXV).

1068. O45 - R68
8.34g 23mm
1h

Same as 796.
O: guilloche border partly off the flan.
R: ᶜ9 in field right above the crook; guilloche border partly off the flan.
Jerusalem, RocMus, no. H1.8; Lambert, *QDAP* 1, 1931, p. 18, no. 71; Elayi-Elayi, *Trésors*, p. 179, no. 83 and pl. XXXI (Tell Abu Hawam hoard TXXXV).

1069. O45 - R69*
8.58g 21mm
12h

Same as 796.
O: guilloche border partly off the flan.
R: ᶜ9? in field right above the crook; guilloche border partly off the flan. Scratches in field right.
Jerusalem, RocMus, no. H1.72; Lambert, *QDAP* 1, 1931, p. 18, no. 72; Elayi-Elayi, *Trésors*, p. 180, no. 90 and pl. XXXI (Tell Abu Hawam hoard TXXXV).

1070. O46* - R70*
8.93g 21mm
1h

Same as 796.
R: ᶜ9 in field right above the crook.
Jerusalem, RocMus, no. H1.77; Lambert, *QDAP* 1, 1931, p. 18, no. 77; Elayi-Elayi, *Trésors*, p. 177, no. 64 and pl. XXX (Tell Abu Hawam hoard TXXXV).

1071. O46 - R71* Same as 796.
8.75g 21mm O: guilloche border partly off the flan.
R: ʿ9 in field right above the crook; guilloche border partly off the flan.
Baramki, *Coins AUB*, p. 221, no. 11 and pl. XXVII, 8; id., *Coins 1866-1966*, p. 26, no. 88 and pl. III (reverse only illustrated).

1072. O47* - R72* Same as 796.
6.81g 19mm O: seahorse and guilloche border partly off the flan.
1h R: ʿ9? in field right above the crook; guilloche border partly off the flan.
Jerusalem, RocMus, no. 1268.1.

1073. O38 - R? Same as 796. Slightly worn.
8.57g O: guilloche border partly off the flan.
R: ʿ9 in field right above the crook; guilloche border partly off the flan.
Monetarium, Schweizerische Kreditanstalt, Zurich, 2, 27-28/4/1984, no. 279.

1074. O39 - R? Same as 796. Slightly worn.
8.75g 21mm O: dolphin and guilloche border partly off the flan.
R: ʿ9 in field right above the crook.
Haifa, NMM, no. 5.

1075. O42 - R? Same as 796. Slightly worn.
7.68g O: guilloche border partly off the flan.
R: ʿ9? in field right above the crook; guilloche border partly off the flan.
Vinchon, Paris, 9-10/12/1983, no. 172.

1076. O? - R49 Same as 796. Small crack on the edge. Slightly worn.
8.72g O: guilloche border partly off the flan.
R: defect on the leg of the owl; ʿ9 in field right above the crook; guilloche border partly off the flan.
Elayi-Elayi, *Trans* 11, 1996, p. 102, no. 9 and pl. IV, 19 (hoard TXXXVI).

1077. O? - R52 Same as 796. Slightly worn.
8.72g O: waves, dolphin and guilloche border partly off the flan.
R: ʿ9 in field right above the crook; guilloche border partly off the flan. Re-struck.
Hirsch, Munich, 168, 22-24/11/1990, no. 365.

1078. O? - R57 Same as 796. Slightly worn.
8.70g O: guilloche border partly off the flan.
R: ʿ9 in field right above the crook; guilloche border partly off the flan.

1079. O? - R58
8.83g 20mm
12h

1080. O? - R65
8.69g

1081. O? - R66
8.75g 22mm
12h

1082. O? - R66
8.73g

1083. O? - R66
8.70g 21mm
12h

1084. O? - R66
8.68g 22mm
1h

1085. O? - R66
8.45g 21mm
1h

Elayi-Elayi, *Trans* 11, 1996, p. 102, no. 10 and pl. IV, 20 (hoard TXXXVI).
Same as 796. Slightly worn.
O: part of the seahorse, deity and guilloche border, waves and dolphin off the flan.
R: ʿ𐤈 in field right above the crook; guilloche border partly off the flan.
Jerusalem, RocMus, no. H1.82; Lambert, *QDAP* 1, 1931, p. 18, no. 82; Elayi-Elayi, *Trésors*, p. 178, no. 68 and pl. XXX (Tell Abu Hawam hoard TXXXV).

Same as 796. Slightly worn.
O: guilloche border partly off the flan.
R: ʿ9 in field right above the crook; guilloche border partly off the flan.
Elayi-Elayi, *Trans* 11, 1996, p. 102, no. 11 and pl. V, 21 (hoard TXXXVI).

Same as 796. Slightly worn.
O: dolphin and guilloche border partly off the flan.
R: ʿ9 in field right above the crook; guilloche border partly off the flan.
Jerusalem, RocMus, no. H1.74; Lambert, *QDAP* 1, 1931, p. 19, no. 74; Elayi-Elayi, *Trésors*, p. 178, no. 70 and pl. XXX (Tell Abu Hawam hoard TXXXV).

Same as 796. Slightly worn.
O: dolphin and guilloche border partly off the flan.
R: ʿ9 in field right above the crook; guilloche border partly off the flan.
Elayi-Elayi, *Trans* 11, 1996, p. 102, no. 8 and pl. IV, 18 (hoard TXXXVI).

Same as 796. Slightly worn.
O: guilloche border partly off the flan.
R: ʿ𐤈? in field right above the crook; guilloche border partly off the flan.
Vienna, KHM, no. 34.070.

Same as 796. Slightly worn.
O: guilloche border partly off the flan.
R: ʿ9 in field right above the crook; guilloche border partly off the flan.
Toronto, ROM, no. 922.44.30; Elayi-Elayi, *Trésors*, p. 293, no. 26 and pl. XXXVI (Beni Hassan hoard TLXXV).

Same as 796. Slightly worn.
O: seahorse and guilloche border partly off the flan.
R: ʿ𐤈? in field right above the crook; guilloche

border partly off the flan.
Jerusalem, RocMus, no. H1.92; Lambert, *QDAP* 1, 1931, p. 19, no. 92; Elayi-Elayi, *Trésors*, p. 180, no. 92 and pl. XXXI (Tell Abu Hawam hoard TXXXV).

1086. O? - R181
8.67g 22mm
1h

Same as 796. Slightly worn.
O: seahorse and guilloche border partly off the flan.
R: ˁ9 in field right above the crook; guilloche border partly off the flan.
Jerusalem, RocMus, no. H1.84; Lambert, *QDAP* 1, 1931, p. 18, no. 84; Elayi-Elayi, *Trésors*, p. 178, no. 76 and pl. XXX (Tell Abu Hawam hoard TXXXV).

1087. O? - R181*
8.63g 20mm
1h

Same as 796. Small crack on the edge. Slightly worn.
O: guilloche border partly off the flan.
R: ˁ9 in field right above the crook; guilloche border partly off the flan.
Jerusalem, RocMus, no. H1.86; Lambert, *QDAP* 1, 1931, p. 19, no. 86; Elayi-Elayi, *Trésors*, pp. 178-179, no. 78 and pl. XXXI (Tell Abu Hawam hoard TXXXV).

1088. O? - R182*
8.20g 22mm
12h

Same as 796. Slightly worn.
O: seahorse, dolphin and guilloche border partly off the flan.
R: dot above the head of the owl; $^e9$? in field right above the crook; guilloche border partly off the flan.
Jerusalem, RocMus, no. H1.73; Lambert, *QDAP* 1, 1931, p. 18, no. 73; Elayi-Elayi, *Trésors*, p. 180, no. 97 and pl. XXXI (Tell Abu Hawam hoard TXXXV).

1089. O? - R183*
8.80g

Same as 796. Slightly worn.
O: dolphin and guilloche border partly off the flan.
R: ˁ9 in field right above the crook; guilloche border partly off the flan.
Elayi-Elayi, *Trans* 11, 1996, p. 102, no. 5 and pl. IV, 15 (hoard TXXXVI).

1090. O? - R?
8.53g 21mm
12h

Same as 796. Small crack on the edge. Rather worn.
O: guilloche border partly off the flan.
R: ˁ9? in field right above the crook; guilloche border partly off the flan.
New York, ANS, no. N54 (ex Newell coll.).

1091. O? - R?
8.39g 20mm
12h

Same as 796. Rather worn.
O: guilloche border partly off the flan.
R: ˁ9? in field right above the crook; guilloche border partly off the flan.
Comptoir général financier, Paris, 16/6/2000, no. 95.

1092. O? - R? Same as 796. Rather worn.
8.32g 23mm O: guilloche border partly off the flan.
12h R: ᶜ9? in field right above the crook; guilloche border partly off the flan.
Jerusalem, RocMus, no. H1.69; Lambert, *QDAP* 1, 1931, p. 18, no. 69; Elayi-Elayi, *Trésors*, p. 180, no. 93 and pl. XXXI (Tell Abu Hawam hoard TXXXV).

1093. 8.39g 19mm Same as 796.
1h R: ᶜ9 in field right above the crook.
Lambert, *QDAP* 1, 1931, p. 19, no. 88; Elayi-Elayi, *Trésors*, p. 179, no. 82, not illustrated (Tell Abu Hawam hoard TXXXV).

1094. Same as 796.
R: ᶜ9 in field right above the crook.
Elayi-Elayi, *Trésors*, p. 236, no. 204, not illustrated (Naplouse hoard TXXXV).

1095-
1099. Same as 796.
R: ᶜ9? in field right above the crook.
Elayi-Elayi, *Trésors*, p. 236, no. 172-176, not illustrated (Naplouse hoard TXXXV).

1100-
1126. Same as 796.
R: ᶜ9 in field right above the crook.
Elayi-Elayi, *Trésors*, p. 236, no. 177-203, not illustrated (Naplouse hoard TXXXV).

1127-
1136. Same as 796.
R: ᶜ9 in field right above the crook.
Elayi-Elayi, *Trésors*, p. 188, no. 11-20, not illustrated (Safed hoard TXXXVII).

II.2.1.21. ᶜOzmilk's shekels with ᶜ10 on the reverse

1137. O48* - R73* Same as 796.
8.84g 20mm O: dolphin and guilloche border partly off the flan.
R: ᶜ10 in field right above the crook.
Elayi-Elayi, *Trans* 11, 1996, p. 102, no. 12 and pl. V, 22 (hoard TXXXVI).

1138. O48 - R73 Same as 796.
8.87g 19mm R: ᶜ10 in field right above the crook.
Jerusalem, AI, no. 2564.

1139. O48 - R73 Same as 796.
8.86g 20mm O: head of the seahorse and guilloche border partly
1h off the flan.
R: ᶜ10 in field right above the crook; guilloche border partly off the flan.

The Coinage of Tyre in the Persian period   141

		Jerusalem, RocMus, no. H1.98; Lambert, *QDAP* 1, 1931, p. 19, no. 98; Elayi-Elayi, *Trésors*, p. 180, no. 98 and pl. XXXI (Tell Abu Hawam hoard TXXXV).
1140.	O48 - R73 8.85g	Same as 796. Yellowish. O: guilloche border partly off the flan. R: ʿ*10* in field right above the crook. Elayi-Elayi, *Trésors*, p. 191, no. 2 and pl. XXXII (8.69g); *id.*, *Trans* 11, 1996, p. 103, no. 14 and pl. IV, 24 (hoard TXXXIX).
1141.	O48 - R74* 8.52g 22mm 1h	Same as 796. O: guilloche border partly off the flan. R: ʿ*10* in field right above the crook. Jerusalem, RocMus, no. H1.102; Lambert, *QDAP* 1, 1931, p. 19, no. 103; Elayi-Elayi, *Trésors*, p. 181, no. 104 and pl. XXXII (Tell Abu Hawam hoard TXXXV).
1142.	O48 - R75 8.68g	Same as 796. O: dolphin and guilloche border partly off the flan. R: ʿ*10* in field right above the crook; guilloche border partly off the flan. Elayi-Elayi, *Trans* 11, 1996, p. 103, no. 15 and pl. V, 25 (hoard TXXXVI).
1143.	O49* - R75* 8.53g 20mm 12h	Same as 796. O: guilloche border partly off the flan. R: ʿ*10* in field right above the crook. Jerusalem, RocMus, no. H1.102; Lambert, *QDAP* 1, 1931, p. 19, no. 103; Elayi-Elayi, *Trésors*, p. 181, no. 103 and pl. XXXII (Tell Abu Hawam hoard TXXXV).
1144.	O49 - R76* 8.87g	Same as 796. O: guilloche border partly off the flan. R: ʿ*10* in field right above the crook; guilloche border partly off the flan. Graffito in field right of the head. Elayi-Elayi, *Trans* 11, 1996, p. 103, no. 13 and pl. V, 23 (hoard TXXXVI).
1145.	O49 - R77* 8.47g 20mm 12h	Same as 796. O: guilloche border partly off the flan. R: ʿ*10* in field right above the crook; guilloche border partly off the flan. New York, ANS, no. N59 (ex Newell coll.).
1146.	O50 - R75 8.72g	Same as 796. O: guilloche border partly off the flan. R: ʿ*10* in field right above the crook; guilloche bor-

1147. O50 - R77

der partly off the flan.
Dorotheum, Vienna, 22-23/9/1992, no. 107.
Same as 796.
O: dolphin and guilloche border partly off the flan.
R: ʿ*10* in field right above the crook; guilloche border partly off the flan.
Stack's, New York, 15-16/6/1972, no. 381.

1148. O50* - R78
8.71g 20mm
1h

Same as 796. Split die.
O: guilloche border partly off the flan.
R: ʿ*10* in field right above the crook; guilloche border partly off the flan.
Paris, BNF, no. 3222; *Catalogue De Luynes*, no. 3222 (ex De Luynes coll.).

1149. O51 - R79
8.65g 20mm
1h

Same as 796. Pierced.
O: guilloche border partly off the flan.
R: ʿ*10* in field right above the crook; guilloche border partly off the flan.
London, BM, no. 1905-10-6 2; *BMC Phoenicia*, p. 232, no. 36 and pl. XXIX, 14.

1150. O51* - R80*
8.71g 19mm
12h

Same as 796.
O: guilloche border partly off the flan.
R: ʿ*10* in field right above the crook; guilloche border partly off the flan.
Jerusalem, RocMus, no. H1.100; Lambert, *QDAP* 1, 1931, p. 19, no. 100; Elayi-Elayi, *Trésors*, p. 180, no. 100 and pl. XXXII (Tell Abu Hawam hoard TXXXV).

1151. O52* - R80
8.67g 21mm
1h

Same as 796. Split die.
O: guilloche border partly off the flan.
R: ʿ*10* in field right above the crook; guilloche border partly off the flan.
New York, ANS, no. N60; Newell, *Tyrus*, no. 15 (ex Newell coll.).

1152. O53* - R81
8.82g

Same as 796.
O: guilloche border partly off the flan.
R:]*10* in field right above the crook; guilloche border partly off the flan.
Classical Numismatic Group, Lancaster-London, 38, 6-7/6/1996, no. 435.

1153. O54 - R81
8.41g 20mm
12h

Same as 796.
O: guilloche border partly off the flan.
R: ʿ*10* in field right above the crook; guilloche border partly off the flan.
Paris, BNF, no. 3223; *Catalogue De Luynes*, no.

3223 (ex De Luynes coll.).

1154. O54* - R81*
8.18g 22mm
11h
Same as 796.
O: guilloche border partly off the flan.
R: ʿ*10* in field right above the crook; guilloche border partly off the flan.
Jerusalem, RocMus, no. H1.99; Lambert, *QDAP* 1, 1931, p. 19, no. 99; Elayi-Elayi, *Trésors*, p. 180, no. 106 and pl. XXXII (Tell Abu Hawam hoard TXXXV).

1155. O54 - R82*
8.83g
Same as 796.
O: seahorse and guilloche border partly off the flan.
R: ʿ*10* in field right above the crook; guilloche border partly off the flan.
Sternberg, Zurich, 12, 18-19/11/1982, no. 304.

1156. O55* - R83*
8.76g
Same as 796.
O: dolphin and guilloche border partly off the flan.
R: ʿ*10* in field right above the crook; guilloche border partly off the flan.
Hess, Lucerne, 249, 13/11/1979, no. 228.

1157. O56* - R84*
6.71g 20mm
9h
Same as 796. Plated.
O: dolphin and guilloche border partly off the flan.
R: ʿ*10* in field right above the crook.
Berlin, SM, no. 33 (ex Löbbecke coll.).

1158. O57* - R85*
8.63g
Same as 796.
O: dolphin and guilloche border partly off the flan.
R: ʿ*10* in field right above the crook.
Lanz, Munich, 60, 11/6/1992, no. 261.

1159. O58* - R86*
8.69g 19mm
12h
Same as 796.
O: head of the deity and guilloche border partly off the flan.
R: ʿ*10* in field right above the crook.
New York, ANS, no. 1978.64,224.

1160. O48 - R?
8,60g
Same as 796. Slightly worn.
R: ʿ*10* in field right above the crook.
Myers, Ariadne Galleries, New York, February 1976, no. 33 = Glendining, London, 27/9/1962, no. 145 = 12, 21-23/2/1961, no. 2677.

1161. O54 - R?
8.22g
Same as 796. Slightly worn.
O: guilloche border partly off the flan.
R: ʿ*10* in field right above the crook; guilloche border partly off the flan.
Agora, Tel Aviv, 21/5/1975, no. 267.

1162. O? - R77   Same as 796. Slightly worn.
      9.11g 21mm   O: guilloche border partly off the flan. Countermark
      12h   on the seahorse.
                        R: ʿ10 in field right above the crook; guilloche border partly off the flan.
                        Oxford, AM, no. 96; Elayi-Lemaire, *Graffiti*, p. 136, no. 180 and pl. XXV (from Keble College, Beirut).

1163. O? - R78*   Same as 796. Slightly worn.
      8.74g 21mm   O: deity, seahorse and guilloche border partly off the flan.
      11h
                        R: ʿ10 in field right above the crook; guilloche border partly off the flan.
                        Jerusalem, RocMus, no. H1.101; Lambert, *QDAP* 1, 1931, p. 19, no. 101; Elayi-Elayi, *Trésors*, p. 180, no. 99 and pl. XXXII (Tell Abu Hawam hoard TXXXV).

1164. O? - R79*   Same as 796. Slightly worn.
      8.58g 21mm   O: guilloche border partly off the flan.
      11h   R: ʿ10 in field right above the crook; guilloche border partly off the flan.
                        Jerusalem, RocMus, no. H1.105; Lambert, *QDAP* 1, 1931, p. 19, no. 105; Elayi-Elayi, *Trésors*, p. 181, no. 101 and pl. XXXII (Tell Abu Hawam hoard TXXXV).

1165. O? - R80   Same as 796. Slightly worn. Somewhat irregular die.
      8.47g 20mm   O: dolphin and guilloche border partly off the flan.
      11h   R: ʿ10 in field right above the crook; guilloche border partly off the flan.
                        Jerusalem, RocMus, no. H1.106; Lambert, *QDAP* 1, 1931, p. 19, no. 106; Elayi-Elayi, *Trésors*, p. 181, no. 105 and pl. XXXII (Tell Abu Hawam hoard TXXXV).

1166. O? - R86   Same as 796. Slightly worn.
      8.51g   O: waves, dolphin and guilloche border partly off the flan.
                        R: ʿ10 in field right above the crook; guilloche border partly off the flan.
                        Hirsch, Munich, 151, 24-27/9/1986, no. 169.

1167. O? - R184*   Same as 796. Slightly worn.
      8.55g 20mm   O: guilloche border partly off the flan.
      11h   R: ʿ10 in field right above the crook; guilloche border partly off the flan.
                        Jerusalem, RocMus, no. H1.104; Lambert, *QDAP* 1, 1931, p. 19, no. 104; Elayi-Elayi, *Trésors*, p. 181,

The Coinage of Tyre in the Persian period 145

		no. 102 and pl. XXXII (Tell Abu Hawam hoard TXXXV).
1168.	O? - R185*	Same as 796. Slightly worn. Chisel-cut.
	8.60g 21mm	O: guilloche border partly off the flan.
	12h	R: ʿ*10* in field right above the crook; guilloche border partly off the flan.
		Shahaf coll., Haifa, no. 1.
1169.	O? - R186*	Same as 796. Slightly worn.
	8.86g	O: guilloche border partly off the flan.
		R: ʿ*10* in field right above the crook; guilloche border partly off the flan.
		Künker, Osnabrück, 83, 17/6/2003, no. 427 = Hirsch, Munich, 84, 1973, no. 156.
1170.	O? - R187*	Same as 796. Slightly worn.
	8.80g	O: guilloche border partly off the flan.
		R: ʿ*10* in field right above the crook; guilloche border partly off the flan.
		Baramki, *Coins AUB*, p. 221, no. 10 and pl. XXVII, 7.
1171.	O? - R?	Same as 796. Rather worn.
		O: guilloche border partly off the flan.
		R: ʿ*10* in field right above the crook; guilloche border partly off the flan.
		Malloy, New York, 12, 25/4/1978, no. 520.
1172.	O? - R?	Same as 796. Rather worn. Chisel-cut.
		O: dolphin obliterated and guilloche border partly off the flan.
		R: ʿ*10* in field right above the crook; guilloche border partly off the flan.
		Kovacs, San Mateo, 6, 13/11/1985, no. 164.
1173.	8.75g	Same as 796.
		R: ʿ*10* in field right above the crook.
		Elayi-Elayi, *Trésors*, p. 189, no. 2, not illustrated (Damascus hoard TXXXVIII).
1174.	8.53g	Same as 796.
		R: ʿ*10* in field right above the crook.
		Elayi-Elayi, *Trésors*, p. 189, no. 3, not illustrated (Damascus hoard TXXXVIII).
1175.	8.47g	Same as 796.
		R: ʿ*10* in field right above the crook.
		Merzbacher, Munich, 15/11/1910, no. 841, not illustrated.
1176.	8.41g	Same as 796.

	R: ʿ10 in field right above the crook. Hirsch, Munich, 25, 29/11/1909, no. 3028, not illustrated (ex Philipsen coll.).
1177.	Same as 796. Chisel-cut. R: ʿ10 in field right above the crook. Elayi-Elayi, *Trésors*, p. 246; *id.*, *Trans* 11, 1996, p. 108, no. 2, not illustrated (Alep hoard TLV).
1178- 1186.	Same as 796. R: ʿ10 in field right above the crook. Elayi-Elayi, *Trésors*, p. 188, no. 21-29, not illustrated (Safed hoard TXXXVII).
1187- 1199.	Same as 796. R: ʿ10 in field right above the crook. Elayi-Elayi, *Trésors*, p. 236, no. 205-227, not illustrated (Naplouse hoard TLI).

II.2.1.22. ʿOzmilk's shekels with ʿ11 on the reverse

1200.	O59* - R86'* 8.78g	Same as 796. O: dolphin and guilloche border partly off the flan. R: ʿ11 in field right above the crook; guilloche border partly off the flan. Elsen, Brussels, 28, 20/2/1993, no. 299 = 147, October 1992, no. 57 = NFA, Encino, 12/10/1988, no. 568.
1201.	O60 - R86' 8.87g 20mm	Same as 796. O: dolphin and guilloche border partly off the flan. R: ʿ11 in field right above the crook; guilloche border partly off the flan. Monetarium, Schweizerische Kreditanstalt, Zurich, 30, December 1979, no. 89 = 24, December 1977, no. 92 = NFA, Beverly Hills, 4, 24-25/3/1977, no. 379 = Stack's, New York, 6/9/1973, no. 483.
1202.	O60* - R87* 8.82g 20mm 12h	Same as 796. O: guilloche border partly off the flan. R: ʿ11 in field right above the crook. Copenhagen, NatMus, no. 310; *SNG Copenhagen*, no. 310 and pl. 8; Forrer, *Weber Collection*, no. 8087 (ex Weber coll.).
1203.	O60 - R87	Same as 796. O: guilloche border partly off the flan. R: ʿ11 in field right above the crook; guilloche border partly off the flan. Sotheby's, London, 21-22/7/1981, no. 90.

1204. O61* - R88*   Same as 796.
      8.58g   O: guilloche border partly off the flan.
                     R: ⁽11 in field right above the crook; guilloche border partly off the flan.
                     Bourgey, Paris, 1-2/12/1999, no. 95.
1205. O61 - R88   Same as 796. Wrong weight (0.56g).
                     O: guilloche border partly off the flan.
                     R: ⁽11 in field right above the crook; guilloche border partly off the flan.
                     Künker, Osnabrück, 94, 27-28/9/2004, no. 1460.
1206. O62* - R89*   Same as 796.
                     O: guilloche border partly off the flan.
                     R: ⁽11 in field right above the crook; guilloche border partly off the flan.
                     Haifa, NMM, no. 6.
1207. O62 - R90   Same as 796.
                     O: guilloche border partly off the flan.
                     R: ⁽11 in field right above the crook; guilloche border partly off the flan.
                     Kurpfälzische Münzhandlung, Mannheim, 29, 11-13/12/1985, no. 54.
1208. O? - R89   Same as 796. Slightly worn.
                     R: ⁽11 in field right above the crook; guilloche border partly off the flan.
                     Haifa, NMM; *Sefunim* 3, 1969-71, pp. 91-92 and pl. XVIII, 3, obverse not illustrated; Elayi-Elayi, *Trésors*, p. 347 (found in the sea, near ⁽Atlit).
1209. O? - R?   Same as 796. Rather worn.
                     O: dolphin and guilloche border partly off the flan.
                     R: ⁽11 in field right above the crook; guilloche border partly off the flan.
                     Albrecht-Hoffmann, Münz Zentrum, Köln, 62, 4-6/11/1987, no. 442.

II.2.1.23. ⁽Ozmilk's shekels with ⁽12 on the reverse

1210. O63* - R90'*   Same as 796.
      8.61g 19mm   O: guilloche border partly off the flan.
                     R: ⁽12? in field right above the crook; guilloche border partly off the flan.
                     Jerusalem, IM, no. 392.
1211. O63 - R91*   Same as 796. Small cracks on the edge.
      8.88g   O: guilloche border partly off the flan.
                     R: ⁽12 in field right above the crook; guilloche bor-

1212. O63 - R91
8.83g

1213. O63 - R91

1214. O63 - R92*
8.65g 20mm
11h

1215. O63 - R93*
8.90g

1216. O63 - R94*
8.26g 19mm
11h

1217. O63 - R95
8.85g

1218. O64* - R95*
8.79g 22mm
11h

der partly off the flan.
Elayi-Elayi, *Trans* 11, 1996, p. 103, no. 17 and pl. V, 27 (hoard TXXXVI).
Same as 796.
O: guilloche border partly off the flan.
R: ʿ12 in field right above the crook; guilloche border partly off the flan.
Elayi-Elayi, *Trans* 11, 1996, p. 103, no. 18 and pl. V, 28; Monetarium, Schweizerische Kreditanstalt, Zurich, 5, 18-19/4/1986, no. 203 (hoard TXXXVI).
Same as 796.
O: guilloche border partly off the flan.
R: ʿ12 in field right above the crook; guilloche border partly off the flan.
Hesperia Art Bulletin, 10, no. 227.
Same as 796.
O: guilloche border partly off the flan.
R: ʿ12 in field right above the crook; guilloche border partly off the flan.
New York, ANS, no. 1978.64,225.
Same as 796.
O: guilloche border partly off the flan.
R: ʿ12 in field right above the crook; guilloche border partly off the flan.
Elayi-Elayi, *Trans* 11, 1996, p. 103, no. 16 and pl. V, 26; Berk, Chicago, 57, 29/3/1989, no. 163 = Pacific Coast Auction Galleries, Santa Barbara, 25-26/9/1986, no. 1628.
Same as 796.
O: guilloche border partly off the flan.
R: ʿ12 in field right above the crook; guilloche border partly off the flan.
New York, ANS, no. 48.19.
Same as 796.
O: guilloche border partly off the flan.
R: ʿ12 in field right above the crook.
Freeman & Sear, Chatsworth, 2, 31/1/1996, no. 61.
Same as 796.
O: guilloche border partly off the flan.
R: ʿ12 in field right above the crook; guilloche border partly off the flan.
Jerusalem, RocMus, no. H1.107; Lambert, *QDAP* 1, 1931, p. 19, no. 107; Elayi-Elayi, *Trésors*, p. 181, no. 107 and pl. XXXII (Tell Abu Hawam hoard

TXXXV).

1219. O64 - R96* Same as 796.
 8.74g 20mm O: head of the seahorse and guilloche border partly
 12h off the flan.
  R: ᶜ12 in field right above the crook; guilloche border partly off the flan.
  Oxford, AM, no. 97 (from Balliol College).

1220. O65* - R97* Same as 796.
 8.50g O: guilloche border partly off the flan.
  R: defect under the crook; ᶜ12 in field right above the crook; guilloche border partly off the flan.
  Elayi-Elayi, *Trans* 11, 1996, p. 103, no. 19 and pl. V, 28.

1221. O66* - R98* Same as 796.
 8.65g 21mm O: dolphin partly obliterated.
 12h R: ᶜ12 in field right above the crook.
  Spaer coll., Jerusalem (bought in Sebaste).

1222. O66 - R99* Same as 796.
 8.47g O: guilloche border partly off the flan.
  R: ᶜ12 in field right above the crook; guilloche border partly off the flan.
  Hirsch, Munich, 163, 27-30/9/1989, no. 525.

1223. O66 - R100* Same as 796.
 8.81g 20mm O: guilloche border partly off the flan.
  R: ᶜ12 in field right above the crook.
  Albrecht-Hoffmann, Münz Zentrum, Köln, 23, 12/11/1975, no. 195.

1224. O67* - R101* Same as 796.
 8.72g 19mm O: guilloche border partly off the flan. Crescent-shaped countermark on the edge.
  R: ᶜ12 in field right above the crook.
  London, BM, no. 1897-1-4 496; *BMC Phoenicia*, p. 232, no. 37 and pl. XXIX, 15; Sotheby's, London, 7/12/1866, no. 628 (ex Bunburry coll.).

1225. O67 - R102* Same as 796.
 8.57g O: guilloche border partly off the flan.
  R: ᶜ12 in field right above the crook.
  Schulman, Amsterdam, 6-8/3/1958, no. 3696.

1226. O67 - R103* Same as 796.
 8.92g 19mm O: guilloche border partly off the flan.
  R: ᶜ12 in field right above the crook. Unclear graffito.
  Sternberg, Zurich, 14, 24-25/5/1984, no. 171 =

		Münzen und Medaillen, Basel, January 1968, no. 19 = Vinchon, Paris, 17, 1967, no. 78.
1227.	O68 - R103 8.42g	Same as 796. O: guilloche border partly off the flan. R: ʿ12 in field right above the crook; guilloche border partly off the flan. Münzen und Medaillen, Basel, 194, 19-22/2/1997, no. 330.
1228.	O68* - R104* 8.20g 22mm 11h	Same as 796. O: guilloche border partly off the flan. R: defect in field right and ʿ12 above the crook. Paris, BNF, no. 2017; Babelon, *Perses*, no. 2017; id., *Traité*, pl. CXXII, 24.
1229.	O69* - R105* 7.94g 20mm 11h	Same as 796. Unusual style. O: guilloche border partly off the flan. R: ʿ12 in field right above the crook. New York, ANS, no. 1978.64,226.
1230.	O? - R91	Same as 796. Slightly worn. O: deity, seahorse and guilloche border partly off the flan. R: ʿ12 in field right above the crook; guilloche border partly off the flan. Ahlström, Stockholm, 35, 9-10/5/1987, no. 2107.
1231.	O? - R98 19mm 12h	Same as 796. Slightly worn. O: deity, seahorse and guilloche border partly off the flan. R: ʿ12 in field right above the crook. Paris, MBTS (ex Starcky coll.).
1232.	O? - R188* 8.36g 20mm	Same as 796. Slightly worn. O: seahorse and guilloche border partly off the flan. Crescent-shaped countermark. R: ʿ12 in field right above the crook; guilloche border partly off the flan. Tel Aviv, KNM, no. K9053.
1233.	O? - R189* 8.75g 20mm 12h	Same as 796. Slightly worn. O: dolphin and guilloche border partly off the flan. R: ʿ12 in field right above the crook; guilloche border partly off the flan. New York, ANS, no. N58; Ratto, Lugano, 4/4/1927, no. 2659 (ex Newell coll.).
1234.	O? - R190* 9.17g 21mm	Same as 796. Slightly worn. Chisel-cut. O: dolphin and guilloche border partly off the flan. R: ʿ12 in field right above the crook. Gorny, Munich, 42, 11/10/1988, no. 427 = Spink,

		Zurich, 20, 6/10/1986, no. 377 = Peus, Frankfurt/Main, 19, January 1971, no. 41.
1235.	O? - R191*	Same as 796. Slightly worn. Somewhat irregular die.
	8.45g 22mm	O: guilloche border partly off the flan.
		R: ʿ/2 in field right above the crook; guilloche border partly off the flan.
		Lanz, Munich, 22, 10/5/1982, no. 439 (who reads 11).
1236.	O? - R192*	Same as 796. Slightly worn.
	8.73g 20mm	O: head of the seahorse, dolphin and guilloche border partly off the flan.
	1h	R: ʿ/2 in field right above the crook.
		New York, ANS, no. N61 (ex Newell coll.).
1237.	O? - R?	Same as 796. Rather worn. Deep chisel-cut.
	8.49g	O: guilloche border partly off the flan.
		R: ʿ/2 in field right above the crook; guilloche border partly off the flan.
		Price, in *Essays Carson-Jenkins*, p. 34, 20 and pl. IX; Elayi-Elayi, *Trésors*, p. 246; *id.*, *Trans* 11, 1996, p. 108, no. 1 (Alep hoard TLVI).
1238.	O? - R?	Same as 796. Rather worn.
	8.40g 19mm	O: guilloche border partly off the flan.
	11h	R: ʿ/2 in field right above the crook; guilloche border partly off the flan.
		Jerusalem, RocMus, no. 1268.
1239.	O? - R?	Same as 796. Rather worn. Pierced.
	7.88g 22mm	O: guilloche border partly off the flan.
	12h	R: ʿ/2 in field right above the crook; guilloche border partly off the flan.
		Vienna, KHM, no. 22.288.
1240.		Same as 796.
		R: ʿ/2 in field right above the crook.
		Sotheby's, London, 4/5/1908, no. 713, not illustrated (ex Osborne O'Hagan coll.).
1241-		Same as 796.
1264.		R: ʿ/2 in field right above the crook.
		Elayi-Elayi, *Trésors*, p. 188, no. 30-53, not illustrated (Safed hoard TXXXVII).

II.2.1.24. ʿOzmilk's shekels with ʿ/3 on the reverse

1265.	O69 - R106*	Same as 796.
	8.65g 21mm	O: seahorse and guilloche border partly off the flan.
		R: ʿ/3 in field right above the crook; guilloche bor-

1266. O69 - R106
8.49g

Same as 796.
O: guilloche border partly off the flan.
R: *13* in field right above the crook; guilloche border partly off the flan.
Peus, Frankfurt/Main, 300, 3-4 and 9/11/1987, no. 1229.

1267. O69 - R106

Same as 796.
O: guilloche border partly off the flan.
R: *13?* in field right above the crook; guilloche border partly off the flan.
Superior Stamp and Coin, Beverly Hills, 15-18/10/1972, no. 253 = 14-15/10/1971, no. 435.

1268. O70* - R106
8.25g 21mm

Same as 796.
O: guilloche border partly off the flan.
R: *13* in field right above the crook.
Peus, Frankfurt/Main, 267, 12-13/10/1967, no. 40.

1269. O71 - R107
8.82g

Same as 796.
O: guilloche border partly off the flan.
R: *1̊3* in field right above the crook; guilloche border partly off the flan.
Elayi-Elayi, *Trans* 11, 1996, pp. 103-104, no. 20 and pl. V, 30 (hoard TXXXVI).

1270. O71* - R107*
8.34g 22mm
10h

Same as 796.
O: guilloche border partly off the flan.
R: *13* in field right above the crook; guilloche border partly off the flan.
Jerusalem, RocMus, no. H1.108; Lambert, *QDAP* 1, 1931, p. 19, no. 108; Elayi-Elayi, *Trésors*, p. 181, no. 108 and pl. XXXII (Tell Abu Hawam hoard TXXXV).

1271. O72* - R108
8.76g 21mm
12h

Same as 796.
O: guilloche border partly off the flan.
R: *13* in field right above the crook; guilloche border partly off the flan.
Paris, BNF, no. 2018; Babelon, *Perses*, no. 2018; id., *Traité*, pl. CXXII, 25.

1272. O73* - R108*
8.66g 20mm
12h

Same as 796.
O: defect on the waves; guilloche border partly off the flan.
R: *13* in field right above the crook; guilloche border partly off the flan.

1273. O73 - R108
8.66g

1274. O73 - R109*
8.84g

1275. O73 - R109
8.82g

1276. O73 - R109
8.61g

1277. O73 - R110
8.75g

1278. O73 - R110*

1279. O73 - R111*
8.88g 20mm

Paris, BNF, no. 3224; *Catalogue De Luynes*, no. 3224; Elayi-Elayi, *JNG* 37-38, 1987-88, pl. 4, 1 (ex De Luynes coll.).
Same as 796. Deep chisel-cut.
O: defect on the waves; dolphin obliterated and guilloche border partly off the flan.
R: ʿ*13* in field right above the crook; guilloche border partly off the flan.
Elayi-Elayi, *Trans* 11, 1996, p. 104, no. 22 and pl. V, 32; Kovacs, San Mateo, 6, 13/11/1985, no. 164 (hoard TXXXVI).
Same as 796.
O: defect on the waves; guilloche border partly off the flan.
R: ʿ*13* in field right above the crook.
Elayi-Elayi, *Trans* 11, 1996, p. 104, no. 23 and pl. V, 33 (hoard TXXXVI).
Same as 796.
O: defect on the waves; guilloche border partly off the flan.
R: ʿ*13* in field right above the crook; guilloche border partly off the flan.
Superior Stamp and Coin, Beverly Hills, 31/5-1/6/1988, no. 1554 (ex Moreira coll.).
Same as 796.
O: guilloche border partly off the flan.
R: ʿ*13* in field right above the crook; guilloche border partly off the flan.
NFA, Beverly Hills, 20, 9-10/3/1988, no. 812.
Same as 796.
O: guilloche border partly off the flan.
R: ʿ*13* in field right above the crook; guilloche border partly off the flan.
Coin Galleries, New York, 1965, no. C114 = 1964, no. E110.
Same as 796.
O: guilloche border partly off the flan.
R: ʿ*13* in field right above the crook; guilloche border partly off the flan.
Hirsch, Munich, 153, 18-20/2/1987, no. 174.
Same as 796.
O: seahorse and guilloche border partly off the flan.
R: ʿ*13* in field right above the crook.
Stockholm, RCC, no. 8.

1280. O73 - R111   Same as 796. Small cracks on the edge.
      8.45g   O: guilloche border partly off the flan.
                        R: ᶜ13 in field right above the crook; guilloche border partly off the flan.
                        Kunst und Münzen, Lugano, 17, June 1977, no. 150 = Ratto, Milan, 15, no. 253.
1281. O73 - R112*   Same as 796.
      8.71g   O: guilloche border partly off the flan.
                        R: ᶜ13 in field right above the crook; guilloche border partly off the flan.
                        London, BM, no. 1906-7-12 86; *BMC Phoenicia*, p. 232, no. 38, not illustrated.
1282. O74 - R112   Same as 796. Small cracks on the edge.
      8.79g   O: guilloche border partly off the flan.
                        R: ᶜ13 in field right above the crook; guilloche border partly off the flan.
                        Gorny, Munich, 100, 20/11/1999, no. 203 = Monetarium, Schweizerische Kreditanstalt, Zurich, 47, Spring 1987, no. 54 = 45, Spring 1986, no. 50.
1283. O74 - R113   Same as 796.
      8.82g 19mm   O: guilloche border partly off the flan.
      12h   R: ᶜ13 in field right above the crook; guilloche border partly off the flan.
                        NFA, Los Angeles, 29, 13/8/1992, no. 182 (who reads 'year 33') = Leu, Zurich, 53, 21-22/10/1991, no. 161 = Superior Galleries, Beverly Hills, 11-12/6/1986, no. 1418.
1284. O74 - R113*   Same as 796. Small crack on the edge.
      8.80g   O: guilloche border partly off the flan.
                        R: ᶜ1°3 in field right above the crook; guilloche border partly off the flan.
                        Elayi-Elayi, *Trans* 11, 1996, p. 104, no. 24 and pl. V, 34 (hoard TXXXVI).
1285. O74 - R114*   Same as 796.
      8.81g   O: guilloche border partly off the flan.
                        R: ᶜ13 in field right above the crook.
                        Elayi-Elayi, *Trans* 11, 1996, p. 104, no. 21 and pl. V, 31; England, Quarryville-London, 15, 5/6/1991, no. 257 (hoard TXXXVI).
1286. O74* - R115*   Same as 796.
      8.95g 20mm   O: guilloche border partly off the flan.
                        R: ᶜ13 in field right above the crook; guilloche border partly off the flan.

London, BM, no. 1906-7-12 5.

1287.	O75* - R116*	Same as 796.
	8.35g 23mm	O: guilloche border partly off the flan.

R: ʿ13 in field right above the crook. Graffito.
Jerusalem, MusRoc, no. 49467; Elayi-Elayi, *Trésors*, p. 345 and pl. XXXVII, 10; Elayi-Lemaire, *Graffiti*, p. 42, no. 18 and pl. I (from Kibboutz Ḥanita Museum).

1288.	O? - R106	Same as 796. Slightly worn.
	9.02g	O: seahorse and guilloche border partly off the flan.

R: ʿ13 in field right above the crook.
Peus, Frankfurt/Main, 329, 31/10-5/11/1990, no. 241.

1289.	O? - R?	Same as 796. Rather worn.
	8.60g	O: guilloche border partly off the flan.

R: ʿ1̊3 in field right above the crook.
Glendining, London, 12, 21-23/2/1961, no. 2677 (ex Lockett coll.).

1290.	8.55g	Same as 796. Plated.

R: ʿ13 in field right above the crook.
BMC Phoenicia, p. 232, no. 38 bis, not illustrated.

1291.	8.59g	Same as 796.

R: ʿ13 in field right above the crook.
Elayi-Elayi, *Trésors*, pp. 189-190, no. 4, not illustrated (Damascus hoard TXXXVIII).

1292-		Same as 796.
1302.		R: ʿ13 in field right above the crook.

Elayi-Elayi, *Trésors*, p. 188, no. 54-64, not illustrated (Safed hoard TXXXVII).

II.2.1.25. ʿOzmilk's shekels with ʿ14 on the reverse

1303.	O75 - R117	Same as 796.
	8.45g 21mm	R: ʿ14 in field right above the crook; guilloche border partly off the flan.

Kindler, *ErIs* 8, 1967, p. 323, no. 3 and pl. 46, 3; Barré, Saint Malo, April 1984, no. 31 = 30/6/1983, no. 84.

1304.	O76 - R111'	Same as 796. Wrong weight (398.70gr.).
		O: dolphin and guilloche border partly off the flan.
		R: ʿ14 in field right above the crook.

Schulman, Amsterdam, 205, June 1975, no. 80.

1305.	O76 - R118*	Same as 796. Small cracks on the edge.

	8.70g	O: guilloche border partly off the flan. R: ʿ14 in field right above the crook. Elayi-Elayi, *Trésors*, p. 104, no. 26 and pl. VI, 36 (hoard TXXXVI).
1306.	O76* - R119* 8.83g	Same as 796. Small dies. R: ʿ14 in field right above the crook. Overstruck. Elayi-Elayi, *Trésors*, p. 104, no. 25 and pl. V, 35; Ars Antiqua, London, 4, 11-12/12/2003, no. 311 = Superior Galleries, Beverly Hills, 12-14/12/1987, no. 548 (hoard TXXXVI).
1307.	O77 - R119 8.86g	Same as 796. O: dolphin and guilloche border partly off the flan. R: ʿ14 in field right above the crook. Vinchon, Paris, 14-15/11/1981, no. 42.
1308.	O77 - R120 8.81g	Same as 796. O: guilloche border partly off the flan. R: ʿ14 in field right above the crook. Empire Coins, Ormond Beach, 4, 9-10/11/1985, no. 127.
1309.	O77* - R120* 8.77g 20mm	Same as 796. O: guilloche border partly off the flan. R: ʿ14 in field right above the crook; guilloche border partly off the flan. London, BM, no. 1906-7-12 87; *BMC Phoenicia*, p. 232, no. 39 and pl. XXIX, 16.
1310.	O77 - R120	Same as 796. O: guilloche border partly off the flan. R: ʿ14 in field right above the crook. Glendining, London, 5/11/1977, no. 13.
1311.	O78* - R121* 8.06g 19mm	Same as 796. O: guilloche border partly off the flan. R: ʿ14 in field right above the crook. Tel Aviv, KNM, no. K1547.
1312.	O78 - R122* 8.93g 20mm	Same as 796. O: guilloche border partly off the flan. R: ʿ14 in field right above the crook. Leu, Zurich, 79, 31/10/2000, no. 768.
1313.	O78 - R122 8.77g	Same as 796. O: dolphin and guilloche border partly off the flan. R: ʿ14 in field right above the crook. Hirsch, Munich, 187, 19-23/9/1995, no. 692.
1314.	O78 - R123* 8.76g	Same as 796. O: guilloche border partly off the flan.

The Coinage of Tyre in the Persian period   157

		R: ʿ*14* in field right above the crook; guilloche border partly off the flan.
		Lanz, Munich, 125, 1-2/11/2005, no. 497.
1315.	O78 - R124* 8.76g 21mm 12h	Same as 796. Small cracks on the edge. O: guilloche border partly off the flan. R: ʿ*14* in field right above the crook; guilloche border partly off the flan. Berlin, SM, no. 35 (ex Löbbecke coll.).
1316.	O78 - R125* 8.63g 20mm 12h	Same as 796. Small cracks on the edge. O: guilloche border partly off the flan. R: ʿ*14* in field right above the crook; guilloche border partly off the flan. Berlin, SM, no. 34 (ex Prokesch-Osten coll.).
1317.	O78 - R126* 8.53g	Same as 796. Small dies. O: guilloche border partly off the flan. R: ʿ*14* in field right above the crook. NFA, Encino, 3, 27/3/1976, no. 8.
1318.	O79* - R127* 7.23g	Same as 796. Several cracks on the edge. R: ʿ*14* in field right above the crook. Sternberg, Zurich, 34, 22-23/10/1998, no. 142.
1319.	O80* - R128* 8.77g 20mm	Same as 796. O: guilloche border partly off the flan. R: ʿ*1̊4.* in field right above the crook; guilloche border partly off the flan. NFA, Beverly Hills, 15/1/1982, no. 261.
1320.	O77 - R? 8.68g 12h	Same as 796. Slightly worn. O: dolphin and guilloche border partly off the flan. R: ʿ*14* in field right above the crook; guilloche border partly off the flan. Troxell, *Davis Collection*, no. 286 (ex Davis coll.).
1321.	O106* - R?	Same as 796. Slightly worn. O: guilloche border partly off the flan. R: ʿ*14* in field right above the crook; guilloche border partly off the flan. Better Auction, Haifa, 4-6/7/1972, no. 41.
1322.	O107* - R? 8.59g	Same as 796. Slightly worn. O: guilloche border partly off the flan. R: ʿ*14* in field right above the crook; guilloche border partly off the flan. Coin Galleries, New York, 1968, no. A47.
1323.	O? - R117* 8.59g 22mm 1h	Same as 796. Small dies. Slightly worn. O: dolphin and guilloche border partly off the flan. R: ʿ*14* in field right above the crook.

		Paris, BNF, no. 3225; *Catalogue De Luynes*, no. 3225 (ex De Luynes coll.).
1324.	O? - R121 7.80g 22mm 12h	Same as 796. Slightly worn. O: head of the deity and guilloche border partly off the flan. R: ʿ*14* in field right above the crook. Shahaf coll., Haifa, no. 2.
1325.	O? - R124 8.77g	Same as 796. Slightly worn. O: guilloche border partly off the flan. R: ʿ*14* in field right above the crook. Schulman, Amsterdam, 237, October-November 1988, no. 116 = 286, 28-30/9/1987, no. 1558.
1326.	O? - R? 8.90g	Same as 796. Rather worn. O: guilloche border partly off the flan. R: ʿ*14* in field right above the crook. Kurpfälzische Münzhandlung, Mannheim, 46, June 1994, no. 139 = Coin Galleries, New York, 485, 28/3/1977, no. 485.
1327.	O? - R? 8.81g	Same as 796. Rather worn. R: ʿ*14* in field right above the crook. Peus, Frankfurt/Main, 279, 14-17/3/1972, no. 73.
1328.	O? - R? 8.72g	Same as 796. Rather worn. O: guilloche border partly off the flan. R: ʿ*1̊4* in field right above the crook. Peus, Frankfurt/Main, 323, 1-4/11/1988, no. 895.
1329.	O? - R? 8.33g	Same as 796. Rather worn. O: guilloche border partly off the flan. R: ʿ*1̊4* in field right above the crook; guilloche border partly off the flan. Müller, Solingen, 25, 16-17/2/1979, no. 82.
1330.	8.91g	Same as 796. R: ʿ*14* in field right above the crook. Elayi-Elayi, *Trésors*, p. 190, no. 9, not illustrated (Damascus hoard TXXXVIII).
1331.	8.77g	Same as 796. R: ʿ*14* in field right above the crook. Elayi-Elayi, *Trésors*, p. 190, no. 7, not illustrated (Damascus hoard TXXXVIII).
1332.	8.74g	Same as 796. R: ʿ*14* in field right above the crook. Elayi-Elayi, *Trésors*, p. 190, no. 5, not illustrated (Damascus hoard TXXXVIII).
1333.	8.73g	Same as 796.

		R: ꜥ14 in field right above the crook. Elayi-Elayi, *Trésors*, p. 190, no. 8, not illustrated (Damascus hoard TXXXVIII).
1334.	8.50g	Same as 796. R: ꜥ14 in field right above the crook. Elayi-Elayi, *Trésors*, p. 190, no. 6, not illustrated (Damascus hoard TXXXVIII).
1335- 1345.		Same as 796. R: ꜥ14 in field right above the crook. Elayi-Elayi, *Trésors*, p. 188, no. 65-75, not illustrated (Safed hoard TXXXVII).

II.2.1.26. ꜥOzmilk's shekels with ꜥ15 on the reverse

1346.	O81* - R129* 6.72g 21mm	Same as 796. Pierced. O: dolphin obliterated; border of dots. R: ꜥ1̊5? in field right above the crook; border of dots partly off the flan. New York, ANS, no. N68 (ex Newell coll.).
1347.	O82* - R130* 8.76g 20mm	Same as 796. O: border of dots partly off the flan. R: ꜥ15 in field right above the crook; border of dots partly off the flan. Münzen und Medaillen, Basel, 54, 26/10/1978, no. 375.
1348.	O83* - R131* 8.20g	Same as 796. O: border of dots partly off the flan. R: ꜥ15 in field right above the crook; border of dots partly off the flan. Münzen und Medaillen, Basel, January 1968, no. 20 (who reads 'year 35').
1349.	O84* - R132* 6.93g	Same as 796. O: border of dots partly off the flan. R: ꜥ15 in field right above the crook; border of dots partly off the flan. Freeman & Sear, Chatsworth, 1, 10/3/1995, no. 225.
1350.	O85* - R133* 8.03g	Same as 796. O: border of dots partly off the flan. R: defect on the legs of the owl; ꜥ15 in field right above the crook; border of dots partly off the flan. Bourgey, Paris, 7-8/11/1983, no. 95 = 10-11/6/1982, no. 155 = 13-14/11/1980, no. 86.
1351.	O85 - R133	Same as 796. O: border of dots partly off the flan.

1352. O86* - R134*
7.57g 19mm
12h

1353. O87* - R135*
7.30g 18mm
1h

1354. O88* - R136*
7.65g 20mm
11h

1355. O88 - R137*
8.78g 21mm
12h

1356. O89 - R138

1357. O89 - R139
8.75g

1358. O89* - R139*
8.70g 21mm
12h

R: defect on the legs of the owl; ʿ15 in field right above the crook; border of dots partly off the flan.
Berk, Chicago, 96, 18/6/1997, no. 157 = Myers, Ariadne Galleries, New York, 1971, no. 58.

Same as 796.
O: border of dots partly off the flan.
R: ʿ15 in field right above the crook; border of dots partly off the flan.
Leiden, RM, no. 8085.

Same as 796.
O: border of dots partly off the flan.
R: J15 in field right above the crook; border of dots partly off the flan.
New York, ANS, no. 47.97 (ex Petrie coll.).

Same as 796. Plated.
O: border of dots partly off the flan.
R: ʿ15 in field right above the crook; border of dots partly off the flan.
Paris, BNF, no. 2022; Babelon, *Perses*, no. 2022.

Same as 796.
O: border of dots partly off the flan.
R: ʿ15 in field right above the crook; border of dots partly off the flan.
Spaer coll., Jerusalem (bought in Jerusalem).

Same as 796.
O: dolphin and border of dots partly off the flan.
R: ʿ15 in field right above the crook; border of dots partly off the flan.
Harmer-Rooke, 19-20/3/1974, no. 941.

Same as 796. Slightly broken.
O: border of dots partly off the flan.
R: ʿ15 in field right above the crook; border of dots partly off the flan.
Malter, Encino, 1969, no. 152.

Same as 796. Small cracks on the edge.
O: border of dots partly off the flan.
R: ʿ15 in field right above the crook; border of dots partly off the flan.
Poinsignon Numismatique, Strasbourg, 19/11/1983, no. 114 = Monetarium, Schweizerische Kreditanstalt, Zurich, 40, May 1983, no. 106 = Bonhams, London, 7, 29-30/3/1982, no. 210 = Monetarium, Schweizerische Kreditanstalt, Zurich, 28, April 1979, no. 78.

1359. O90* - R140   Same as 796.
      8.88g   O: border of dots partly off the flan.
                    R: ʿ15 in field right above the crook.
                    Elayi-Elayi, *Trans* 11, 1996, p. 105, no. 31 and pl. VI, 41 (hoard TXXXVI).

1360. O90 - R141*   Same as 796. Small cracks on the edge.
      8.84g   O: border of dots partly off the flan.
                    R: ʿ15 in field right above the crook; border of dots partly off the flan.
                    Elayi-Elayi, *Trésors*, p. 192, no. 5 and pl. XXXII, 5; id., *Trans* 11, 1996, p. 105, no. 35 and pl. VI, 45; Superior Stamp and Coin, Beverly Hills, 1988 (hoard TXXXIX).

1361. O90 - R142*   Same as 796.
      8.38g 20mm   O: border of dots partly off the flan.
                    R: ʿ15 in field right above the crook; border of dots partly off the flan.
                    Hamburger, Frankfurt/Main, 12/6/1930, no. 857.

1362. O90 - R143*   Same as 796.
      8.72g   O: border of dots partly off the flan.
                    R: ʿ1̊5[in field right above the crook; border of dots partly off the flan.
                    Schulman, Amsterdam, 6-8/2/1969, no. 445.

1363. O90 - R144*   Same as 796.
      8.80g 20mm   O: border of dots partly off the flan.
                    R: ʿ15 in field right above the crook; border of dots partly off the flan.
                    England, Quarryville-London, 27, 29/9/1993, no. 749 = 25, 24/3/1993, no. 408 = Elsen, Brussels, 10, 27/6/1988, no. 121 = 7, 21/4/1987, no. 145.

1364. O91 - R145   Same as 796.
      8.78g   O: border of dots partly off the flan. Overstruck.
                    R: ʿ15 in field right above the crook; border of dots partly off the flan.
                    Elayi-Elayi, *Trans* 11, 1996, p. 106, no. 43 and pl. VII, 53 (hoard TXXXVI).

1365. O91 - R146   Same as 796.
      8.78g   O: border of dots partly off the flan.
                    R: ʿ15 in field right above the crook; border of dots partly off the flan.
                    Elayi-Elayi, *Trésors*, p. 106, no. 42 and pl. VII, 52 (hoard TXXXVI).

1366. O91* - R147* Same as 796.

	7.89g 19mm	O: border of dots partly off the flan. R: ʿ15 in field right above the crook; border of dots partly off the flan. Sternberg, Zurich, 12, 18-19/11/1982, no. 305.
1367.	O91 - R148* 8.77g	Same as 796. Small cracks on the edge. O: deity, seahorse and border of dots partly off the flan. R: ʿ15 in field right above the crook; border of dots partly off the flan. Elayi-Elayi, *Trans* 11, 1996, p. 106, no. 44 and pl. VII, 54 (hoard TXXXVI).
1368.	O91 - R148 8.73g	Same as 796. Small crack on the edge. O: deity, seahorse and border of dots partly off the flan. R: ʿ15 in field right above the crook; border of dots partly off the flan. Elayi-Elayi, *Trans* 11, 1996, p. 106, no. 45 and pl. VII, 55 (hoard TXXXVI).
1369.	O92* - R148 8.84g	Same as 796. O: dolphin, seahorse and border of dots partly off the flan. R: ʿ15 in field right above the crook; border of dots partly off the flan. Elayi-Elayi, *Trans* 11, 1996, p. 105, no. 34 and pl. VI, 44 (hoard TXXXVI).
1370.	O93 - R149* 8.87g	Same as 796. O: border of dots partly off the flan. R: ʿ15 in field right above the crook. Elayi-Elayi, *Trans* 11, 1996, p. 105, no. 32 and pl. VI, 42 (hoard TXXXVI).
1371.	O93 - R149 8.74g	Same as 796. O: border of dots partly off the flan. R: *15* in field right above the crook. Hirsch, Munich, 158, 4-6/5/1988, no. 157.
1372.	O93 - R149 8.59g	Same as 796. O: border of dots partly off the flan. R: ʿ15 in field right above the crook. Classical Numismatic Group, Lancaster-London, 46, 26/6/1998, no. 503 = Münzen und Medaillen, Basel, 26, 16-19/9/1996, no. 310 = Hirsch, Munich, 164, 29-30/11 and 1/12/1989, no. 397 = 160, 23-25/11/1988, no. 314 = 154, 13-16/5/1987, no. 271.
1373.	O93* - R149* 8.50g 19mm	Same as 796. O: border of dots partly off the flan.

The Coinage of Tyre in the Persian period

		R: ʿ15 in field right above the crook.
		Jerusalem, AI, no. 2697.
1374.	O93 - R149	Same as 796.
	8.01g 20mm	O: border of dots partly off the flan.
		R: ʿ15 in field right above the crook; border of dots partly off the flan.
		Tel Aviv, KNM, no. K1549.
1375.	O93 - R150	Same as 796.
	8.91g	O: dolphin and border of dots partly off the flan.
		R: ʿ15 in field right above the crook; border of dots partly off the flan.
		Elayi-Elayi, *Trans* 11, 1996, p. 105, no. 29 and pl. VI, 39 (hoard TXXXVI).
1376.	O93 - R150	Same as 796.
	8.72g 20mm	O: border of dots partly off the flan.
		R: ʿ15 in field right above the crook.
		Kroha, Kölner Münzkabinett, Köln, 66, 21-22/4/1997, no. 157 = Glendining, London, 12, 21-23/2/1961, no. 2678 = Sotheby's, London, July 1921, no. 328 (ex Lockett coll.).
1377.	O93 - R150*	Same as 796. Small cracks on the edge.
	8.67g 20mm	O: border of dots partly off the flan.
		R: ʿ15 in field right above the crook.
		Private coll.
1378.	O93 - R151*	Same as 796. Small crack on the edge.
	7.91g 20mm	O: border of dots partly off the flan. Overstruck.
	12h	R: defect under the letter; ʿ15 in field right above the crook; border of dots partly off the flan.
		Paris, BNF, no. 115 (ex De Vogüé coll.).
1379.	O93 - R152*	Same as 796.
	8.91g	O: border of dots partly off the flan.
		R: ʿ15 in field right above the crook; border of dots partly off the flan.
		Elayi-Elayi, *Trans* 11, 1996, p. 105, no. 30 and pl. VI, 40 (hoard TXXXVI).
1380.	O93 - R152	Same as 796.
	8.71g	O: border of dots partly off the flan.
		R: ʿ15 in field right above the crook; border of dots partly off the flan.
		Elayi-Elayi, *Trans* 11, 1996, p. 107, no. 47 and pl. VII, 57 (hoard TXXXVI).
1381.	O93 - R152	Same as 796.
	8.63g 21mm	O: border of dots partly off the flan.
	12h	

		R: ʿ15 in field right above the crook; border of dots partly off the flan.

1382. O93 - R152
8.57g 22mm

Paris, BNF, no. 2021; Babelon, *Perses*, no. 2021.
Same as 796.
O: border of dots partly off the flan.
R: ʿ15 in field right above the crook.
Beirut, NM, no. 1324; Chéhab, *Monnaies*, no. 1324 and pl. LIV, 3.

1383. O94 - R152
8.82g

Same as 796. Small crack on the edge.
O: border of dots partly off the flan.
R: ʿ15 in field right above the crook; border of dots partly off the flan.
Gorny, Munich, 55, 14/5/1991, no. 364.

1384. O94 - R153*
8.92g

Same as 796. Small dies.
O: tail of the seahorse and border of dots partly off the flan.
R: ʿ15 in field right above the crook.
Elayi-Elayi, *Trésors*, p. 191, no. 3, not illustrated; id., *Trans* 11, 1996, p. 104, no. 27 and pl. VI, 37; Superior Stamp and Coin, Beverly Hills, 12-14/12/1987, no. 547 (ex Pipito coll.) (hoard TXXXIX).

1385. O94 - R154*
7.80g

Same as 796.
O: border of dots partly off the flan.
R: ʿ15 in field right above the crook; border of dots partly off the flan.
Bourgey, Paris, 9-10/11/1976, no. 106.

1386. O94 - R160
8.80g

Same as 796. Unusual style.
O: border of dots partly off the flan.
R: ʿ15 in field right above the crook; border of dots partly off the flan.
Münzen und Medaillen, Basel, 495, January 1987, no. 28 = Gorny, Munich, 22, 25-26/5/1982, no. 147.

1387. O95* - R155*
8.52g 20mm
12h

Same as 796.
R: ʿ15 in field right above the crook; border of dots partly off the flan.
New York, ANS, no. N63 (ex Newell coll.).

1388. O95 - R155
8.45g

Same as 796.
O: border of dots partly off the flan.
R: ʿ15 in field right above the crook; border of dots partly off the flan.
Schulman, Amsterdam, 9-12/3/1959, no. 1365 = Glendining, London, 4/10/1957, no. 195.

1389. O95 - R155   Same as 796. Small dies.
      8.44g   O: border of dots partly off the flan.
                       R: ʿ15 in field right above the crook.
                       Albuquerque, Rouen, 49, 26/2/1995, no. 12 = Bourgey, Paris, 10-11/6/1982, no. 154 = Loudmer-Poulain, Paris, 15-16/6/1976, no. 112.
1390. O95 - R155   Same as 796.
      8.31g 20mm   O: tail of the seahorse and border of dots partly off
      12h   the flan.
                       R: ʿ15 in field right above the crook.
                       New York, ANS, no. N65 (ex Newell coll.).
1391. O95 - R156*   Same as 796. Small cracks on the edge.
      8.33g   O: border of dots partly off the flan.
                       R: ʿ15 in field right above the crook.
                       Classical Numismatic Group, Lancaster-London, 53, 15/3/2000, no. 659.
1392. O95 - R157*   Same as 796. Small cracks on the edge. Small dies.
      8.64g 21mm   R: ʿ15 in field right above the crook.
                       Bankhaus Aufhäuser, Munich, 13, 7-8/10/1997, no. 244 = Peus, Frankfurt/Main, 290, 5-7/10/1976, no. 140.
1393. O95 - R158   Same as 796.
      8.58g 22mm   R: ʿ15 in field right above the crook; border of dots
      12h   partly off the flan.
                       Spaer coll., Jerusalem (bought in Jerusalem).
1394. O96* - R158   Same as 796.
      8.66g   O: border of dots partly off the flan.
                       R: ʿ15 in field right above the crook; border of dots partly off the flan.
                       Lanz, Graz, 5, 1/12/1975, no. 256.
1395. O96 - R159*   Same as 796. Small cracks on the edge.
      7.70g 20mm   O: border of dots partly off the flan.
      11h   R: ʿ15 in field right above the crook; border of dots partly off the flan.
                       New York, ANS, no. 1977.158,756; Cahn, Frankfurt/Main, 60, 2/7/1928, no. 1069.
1396. O97* - R158*   Same as 796. Small dies.
      8.65g 21mm   R: ʿ15 in field right above the crook.
                       London, BM, no. 151 15; *BMC Phoenicia*, p. 232, no. 40, not illustrated; Rouvier, *JIAN* 6, 1903, p. 276, no. 1816 and pl. XVIII, 18.
1397. O97 - R160*   Same as 796.
      8.75g 19mm   O: border of dots partly off the flan.
      12h

R: ʿ1̊5? in field right above the crook; border of dots partly off the flan.
Elayi-Elayi, *La Monnaie*, p. 41 and pl. 1, 21.

1398. O97 - R161*
8.65g 19mm
12h
Same as 796.
O: border of dots partly off the flan.
R: ʿ15 in field right above the crook; border of dots partly off the flan.
New York, ANS, no. N66; Newell, *Tyrus*, no. 16 (ex Newell coll.).

1399. O97 - R162*
8.94g
Same as 796. Small cracks on the edge.
O: border of dots partly off the flan.
R: ʿ15 in field right above the crook; border of dots partly off the flan.
Elayi-Elayi, *Trans* 11, 1996, pp. 104-105, no. 28 and pl. VI, 38 (hoard TXXXVI).

1400. O97 - R163*
8.81g
Same as 796. Small cracks on the edge.
O: border of dots partly off the flan.
R: ʿ15 in field right above the crook; border of dots partly off the flan.
Elayi-Elayi, *Trans* 11, 1996, p. 106, no. 38 and pl. VI, 48 (hoard TXXXVI).

1401. O97 - R164*
8.80g
Same as 796.
O: border of dots partly off the flan.
R: ʿ15 in field right above the crook; border of dots partly off the flan.
Elayi-Elayi, *Trans* 11, 1996, p. 106, no. 40 and pl. VI, 50 (hoard TXXXVI).

1402. O97 - R164
8.71g 19mm
12h
Same as 796.
O: border of dots partly off the flan.
R: ʿ15 in field right above the crook; border of dots partly off the flan.
Brussels, NM, no. 15.

1403. O90 - R?
8.83g
Same as 796. Slightly worn.
O: border of dots partly off the flan.
R: ʿ1̊5 in field right above the crook; border of dots partly off the flan.
Elayi-Elayi, *Trans* 11, 1996, p. 107, no. 50 and pl. VII, 60 (hoard TXXXVI).

1404. O90 - R?
Same as 796. Slightly worn.
R: ʿ15 in field right above the crook; border of dots partly off the flan.
Hesperia Art Bulletin, 10, no. 228.

1405. O93 - R?
Same as 796. Slightly worn.

	8.77g	O: border of dots partly off the flan. R: ʿ15 in field right above the crook; border of dots partly off the flan. Hirsch, Munich, 173, 19-22/2/1992, no. 507 = 169, 20-22/2/1991, no. 552.
1406.	O93 - R? 8.64g	Same as 796. Slightly worn. O: border of dots partly off the flan. R: ʿ15 in field right above the crook; border of dots partly off the flan. Platt, Paris, March 1998, no. 308 = May 1997, no. 409.
1407.	O95 - R? 8.63g	Same as 796. Slightly worn. Small crack on the edge. Small dies. R: ʿI͂5 in field right above the crook. Kroha, Kölner Münzkabinett, Köln, 61, 17-18/11/1994, no. 143.
1408.	O108* - R? 8.70g 22mm	Same as 796. Slightly worn. O: border of dots partly off the flan. Overstruck. R: ʿI͂5 in field right above the crook; border of dots partly off the flan. Haifa, NMM, no. 1.
1409.	O? - R138* 8.80g	Same as 796. Slightly worn. Small dies. R: ʿ15 in field right above the crook; border of dots partly off the flan. Elayi-Elayi, *Trésors*, pp. 191-192, no. 4 and pl. XXXII, 4 (8.91g); *id.*, *Trans* 11, 1996, p. 106, no. 27 and pl. VI, 49; Superior Galleries, New York, 31/5/1989, no. 6104 = Superior Stamp and Coin, Beverly Hills, 5, Winter 1988/89, no. C43 (hoard TXXXIX).
1410.	O? - R140* 8.56g 20mm 12h	Same as 796. Slightly worn. O: border of dots partly off the flan. R: ʿ15 in field right above the crook; border of dots partly off the flan. New York, ANS, no. N64 (ex Newell coll.).
1411.	O? - R145* 8.64g 19mm 12h	Same as 796. Slightly worn. O: border of dots partly off the flan. R: ʿ15 in field right above the crook; border of dots partly off the flan. Jerusalem, RocMus, no. H12.118; Elayi-Elayi, *Trésors*, p. 145, no. 65 and pl. XXV, 65 (Khirbet el-Kerak hoard TXXVI).
1412.	O? - R146*	Same as 796. Slightly worn.

	8.68g	O: border of dots partly off the flan. R: ⸂15 in field right above the crook; border of dots partly off the flan. Elayi-Elayi, *Trans* 11, 1996, p. 107, no. 49 and pl. VII, 59 (hoard TXXXVI).
1413.	O? - R149 8.79g	Same as 796. Slightly worn. O: border of dots partly off the flan. R: ⸂15 in field right above the crook. Elayi-Elayi, *Trans* 11, 1996, p. 106, no. 41 and pl. VII, 51 (hoard TXXXVI).
1414.	O? - R158 8.82g	Same as 796. Slightly worn. Small cracks on the edge. R: ⸂15 in field right above the crook; border of dots partly off the flan. Elayi-Elayi, *Trésors*, p. 192, no. 6 and pl. XXXII, 6 (8.78g); *id.*, *Trans* 11, 1996, p. 106, no. 37 and pl. VI, 47; Hirsch, Munich, 176, 19-20/11/1992, no. 387 = 173, 19-22/2/1992, no. 506 = 169, 20-22/2/-1991, no. 551 = (hoard TXXXIX).
1415.	O? - R158 8.60g 12h	Same as 796. Slightly worn. O: dolphin, waves and border of dots partly off the flan. R: ⸂15 in field right above the crook; border of dots partly off the flan. *SNG Copenhagen* 1987, no. 467; Ratto, Lugano, 9/10/1934, no. 247.
1416.	O? - R196* 8.62g 19mm 12h	Same as 796. Slightly worn. Small cracks on the edge. Split die. Overstruck. O: border of dots partly off the flan. R: ⸂15 in field right above the crook. New York, ANS, no. N67 (ex Newell coll.).
1417.	O? - R197* 8.72g	Same as 796. Slightly worn. Small cracks on the edge. Small dies. O: border of dots partly off the flan. R: ⸂15 in field right above the crook. Elayi-Elayi, *Trans* 11, 1996, p. 107, no. 46 and pl. VII, 56 (hoard TXXXVI).
1418.	O? - R198* 8.83g	Same as 796. Slightly worn. Small cracks on the edge. Small dies. R: ⸂15 in field right above the crook. Elayi-Elayi, *Trans* 11, 1996, p. 105, no. 36 and pl. VI, 46 (hoard TXXXVI).
1419.	O? - R199* 8.84g	Same as 796. Slightly worn. O: border of dots partly off the flan. Overstruck.

The Coinage of Tyre in the Persian period

		R: ʿ15 in field right above the crook. Elayi-Elayi, *Trans* 11, 1996, p. 105, no. 33 and pl. VI, 43 (hoard TXXXVI).
1420.	O? - R200 8.24g	Same as 796. Slightly worn. O: border of dots partly off the flan. R: ʿ15 in field right above the crook. Berk, Chicago, 137, 31/3/2004, no. 204.
1421.	O? - R200*	Same as 796. Slightly worn. Chisel-cut. O: border of dots partly off the flan. R: ʿ15 in field right above the crook; border of dots partly off the flan. Graffito. Private coll.; Elayi-Lemaire, *Graffiti*, p. 54, no. 87 and pl. XV, 87.
1422.	O? - R201* 8.38g	Same as 796. Slightly worn. O: dolphin, waves and border of dots partly off the flan. R: ʿ15 in field right above the crook; border of dots partly off the flan. Hirsch, Munich, 242, 22-24/9/2005, no. 2259.
1423.	O? - R202* 8.85g	Same as 796. Slightly worn. O: border of dots partly off the flan. R: ʿ15 in field right above the crook; border of dots partly off the flan. Gorny, Munich, 40, 7/4/1988, no. 301 = Superior Stamp and Coin, Beverly Hills, 17-23/6/1974, no. 323 = 14-15/10/1971, no. 436.
1424.	O? - R203* 8.56g	Same as 796. Slightly worn. O: border of dots partly off the flan. R: ʿĩ5[in field right above the crook; border of dots partly off the flan. Numismatica, Vienna, 17, 22-23/6/1977, no. 104.
1425.	O? - R204* 8.56g	Same as 796. Slightly worn. O: border of dots partly off the flan. R: ʿ15 in field right above the crook. Classical Numismatic Group, Lancaster-London, 41, 19/3/1997, no. 704 (who reads 'year 35').
1426.	O? - R193* 8.99g	Same as 796. Rather worn. O: dolphin and border of dots partly off the flan. R: ʿ15 in field right above the crook; border of dots partly off the flan. Numismatica Ars Classica, Zurich, 1, 29-30/3/1989, no. 246 = Kricheldorf, Stuttgart, 29, 3-4/3/1975, no. 174.

1427. O? - R194* Same as 796. Rather worn.
8.82g 20mm R: ⁽15 in field right above the crook.
Art Gallery of South Australia, North Terrace, Adelaide, no. 731.

1428. O? - R195* Same as 796. Rather worn.
8.80g O: head of the seahorse and border of dots partly off the flan.
R: ⁽15 in field right above the crook; border of dots partly off the flan.
Barré, Saint Malo, December 1986, no. 56.

1429. O? - R? Same as 796. Rather worn.
8.74g R: ⁽15 in field right above the crook; border of dots partly off the flan.
Hirsch, Munich, 236, 23-25/9/2004, no. 2045 = 233, 12-14/2/2004, no. 1542.

1430. O? - R? Same as 796. Rather worn.
8.74g O: waves, dolphin and border of dots partly off the flan.
R: ⁽15 in field right above the crook; border of dots partly off the flan.
Lapp-Lapp, *Wâdi Ed-Daliyeh*, p. 59, no. 3 and pl. 80, 3; Elayi-Elayi, *Trésors*, p. 217, no. 3 (Wadi Daliyeh hoard TXLVIII).

1431. O? - R? Same as 796. Rather worn.
8.74g O: border of dots partly off the flan.
R: ⁽1°5 in field right above the crook.
Cross, *BA* 26, 1963, pp. 116-117 and fig. 4; Lapp-Lapp, *Wâdi Ed-Daliyeh*, p. 59, no. 4 and pl. 80, 4; Elayi-Elayi, *Trésors*, p. 217, no. 2 (Wadi Daliyeh hoard TXLVIII).

1432. O? - R? Same as 796. Rather worn.
8.71g 19mm O: border of dots partly off the flan.
R: ⁽15 in field right above the crook; border of dots partly off the flan.
Peus, Frankfurt/Main, 296, 31/10-2/11/1978, no. 147 = 290, 5-7/10/1976, no. 141 = 5, July 1968, no. 41.

1433. O? - R? Same as 796. Rather worn.
8.72g R: ⁽1°5[in field right above the crook; border of dots partly off the flan.
Baldwin, London, 34, 13/10/2003, no. 547.

1434. O? - R? Same as 796. Rather worn.
8.70g O: border of dots partly off the flan.

		R: ⟨15 in field right above the crook; border of dots partly off the flan.
		Elayi-Elayi, *Trans* 11, 1996, p. 107, no. 48 and pl. VII, 58 (hoard TXXXVI).
1435.	O? - R?	Same as 796. Rather worn.
	8.66g	O: deity and border of dots partly off the flan.
		R: ⟨15 in field right above the crook; border of dots partly off the flan.
		England, Quarryville-London, 14, 20/3/1991, no. 201.
1436.	O? - R?	Same as 796. Rather worn.
	8.44g	O: border of dots partly off the flan.
		R: ⟨15 in field right above the crook.
		Albuquerque, Rouen, 41, 16/3/1993, no. 53.
1437.	O? - R?	Same as 796. Rather worn. Small crack on the edge.
	8.39g	O: border of dots partly off the flan.
		R: ⟨15 in field right above the crook.
		Tel Aviv, KNM, no. K1548.
1438.	O? - R?	Same as 796. Rather worn.
	8.22g	O: border of dots partly off the flan.
		R: ⟨15 in field right above the crook; border of dots partly off the flan.
		Numismatica Ars Classica, Zurich, 27-28/2/1991, no. 1525.
1439.	O? - R?	Same as 796. Rather worn.
	8.20g	O: border of dots partly off the flan.
		R: ⟨15 in field right above the crook; border of dots partly off the flan.
		Deutsch, Tel Aviv, 11, 4/10/1993, no. 9.
1440.	O? - R?	Same as 796. Rather worn. Small dies.
	8.20g	R: ⟨15⟨ in field right above the crook.
		England, Quarryville-London, 25, 24/3/1993, no. 407.
1441.	O? - R?	Same as 796. Rather worn.
	7.95g	R: ⟨15 in field right above the crook; border of dots partly off the flan.
		Hirsch, Munich, 242, 22-24/9/2005, no. 2258.
1442.	O? - R?	Same as 796. Rather worn.
	7.89g	O: border of dots partly off the flan.
		R:]15[in field right above the crook; border of dots partly off the flan. Overstruck.
		Hirsch, Munich, 168, 22-24/11/1990, no. 364.
1443.	O? - R?	Same as 796. Rather worn. Plated.

	6.28g 19mm 12h	O: border of dots partly off the flan. R: ʿĪ͗5 in field right above the crook; border of dots partly off the flan. Berlin, SM, no. 17649.
1444.	O? - R?	Same as 796. Rather worn. O: border of dots partly off the flan. R: ʿ15 in field right above the crook; border of dots partly off the flan. Better Auction, Haifa, 4-6/7/1972, no. 42.
1445.	O? - R?	Same as 796. Rather worn. O: head of the seahorse, dolphin and border of dots partly off the flan. R: ʿĪ͗5? in field right above the crook; border of dots partly off the flan. Phoenix, Coincraft, London, P115, 1995, no. G577.
1446.	O? - R?	Same as 796. Rather worn. O: border of dots partly off the flan. R: ʿ15 in field right above the crook; border of dots partly off the flan. Myers-Adams, New York, 5, 15-16/5/1973, no. 268.
1447.	O? - R?	Same as 796. Rather worn. O: border of dots partly off the flan. R: ʿ15 in field right above the crook. Rauch, Vienna, 7, 4-5/6/1971, no. 87.
1448.	8.81g	Same as 796. R: ʿ15 in field right above the crook. Elayi-Elayi, *Trésors*, p. 190, no. 10, not illustrated (Damascus hoard TXXXVIII).
1449.	8.71g	Same as 796. R: ʿ15 in field right above the crook. Elayi-Elayi, *Trésors*, p. 190, no. 11, not illustrated (Damascus hoard TXXXVIII).
1450.	8.81g	Same as 796. R: ʿ15 in field right above the crook. Elayi-Elayi, *Trésors*, p. 190, no. 12, not illustrated (Damascus hoard TXXXVIII).
1451.	8.62g	Same as 796. R: ʿ15 in field right above the crook. Sotheby's, London, 19/1/1914, no. 295, not illustrated (ex Cumberland Clark coll.).
1452.	8.50g 21mm	Same as 796. R: ʿ15 in field right above the crook. Helbing, Munich, 8/11/1928, no. 4097, not illus-

		trated.
1453.		Same as 796.
		R: ⁽15 in field right above the crook.
		Numismatica Ars Classica, New York, Triton II, 1-2/12/1998, no. 1370, not illustrated.
1454-1456.		Same as 796.
		R: ⁽15 in field right above the crook.
		Lapp-Lapp, *Wâdi Ed-Daliyeh*, p. 57, n. 21, not illustrated; Elayi-Elayi, *Trésors*, p. 217, no. 4-6 (Wadi Daliyeh hoard TXLVIII).
1457-1510.		Same as 796.
		R: ⁽15 in field right above the crook.
		Elayi-Elayi, *Trésors*, p. 188, no. 76-128, not illustrated (Safed hoard TXXXVII).

II.2.1.27. ⁽Ozmilk's shekels with ⁽16 on the reverse

1511.	O97 - R165* 8.93g	Same as 796.
		O: border of dots partly off the flan.
		R: ⁽1̊6[in field right above the crook; border of dots partly off the flan.
		Peus, Frankfurt/Main, 300, 3-4 and 9/11/1987, no. 1230 (who reads 'year 15').
1512.	O98* - R152' 8.84g	Same as 796.
		O: border of dots partly off the flan.
		R: ⁽16 in field right above the crook.
		Burgan, Paris, 30/6/1987, no. 321.
1513.	O99* - R166* 8.50g	Same as 796.
		O: border of dots partly off the flan.
		R: ⁽16 in field right above the crook; border of dots partly off the flan.
		Haifa, NMM, no. 2; *Sefunim* 3, 1969-71, pp. 91-92 and pl. XVIII (obverse not illustrated); Elayi-Elayi, *Trésors*, p. 347 (found in the sea, near ⁽Atlit).
1514.	O99 - R167 8.75g	Same as 796.
		O: border of dots partly off the flan.
		R: ⁽1̊6 in field right above the crook; border of dots partly off the flan.
		Kölner Münzen, 9-10/4/1974, no. 55.
1515.	O100 - R167*	Same as 796.
		O: border of dots partly off the flan.
		R: ⁽1̊6 in field right above the crook; border of dots partly off the flan.

1516. O100* - R168*   Same as 796.
      7.15g   R: ⸢16 in field right above the crook; border of dots partly off the flan.
                     Hirsch, Munich, 170, 22-25/5/1991, no. 698.

1517. O101* - R169*   Same as 796.
      8.27g 19mm   O: border of dots partly off the flan.
                     R: ⸢16 in field right above the crook; border of dots partly off the flan.
                     Jerusalem, IM, no. 3878.

1518. O? - R?   Same as 796. Rather worn.
                     O: border of dots partly off the flan.
                     R: ⸢16 in field right above the crook; border of dots partly off the flan.
                     Schulman, Amsterdam, 18-21/3/1964, no. 62.

1519.   Same as 796.
                     R: ⸢16 in field right above the crook.
                     Numismatica Ars Classica, New York, Triton II, 1-2/12/1998, no. 1370.

1520-   Same as 796.
1521.   R: ⸢16 in field right above the crook.
                     Elayi-Elayi, *Trésors*, p. 188, no. 129-130, not illustrated (Safed hoard TXXXVII).

II.2.1.28. ⸢Ozmilk's shekels with ⸢17 on the reverse

1522. O102* - R170*   Same as 796. Plated.
      8.04g 19mm   O: border of dots partly off the flan.
      11h   R: ⸢17 in field right above the crook; border of dots partly off the flan.
                     London, BM, no. 151 15; *BMC Phoenicia*, p. 232, no. 41.

II.2.1.29. Shekels with inscription, if any, obliterated on the reverse

1523. 8.48g 21mm   Same as 796. Slightly worn.
      1h   O: border of dots partly off the flan.
                     R: inscription, if any, obliterated; border of dots partly off the flan.
                     Jerusalem, RocMus, no. H1.109; Lambert, *QDAP* 1, 1931, p. 19, no. 109; Elayi-Elayi, *Trésors*, p. 181, no. 109 and pl. XXXII (Tell Abu Hawam hoard TXXXV).

1524. 8.36g   Same as 796. Chisel-cut. Slightly worn.
                           R: inscription, if any, obliterated; border of dots partly off the flan.
                           Gorny-Mosch, Giessener Münzhandlung, Munich, 142, 10-11/10/2005, no. 1666.
1525. 8.21g 18mm   Same as 796. Slightly worn.
       4h   O: dolphin and border of dots partly off the flan.
                           R: inscription, if any, obliterated; border of dots partly off the flan.
                           London, BM, no. 1878-3-1 388; *BMC Phoenicia*, p. 232, no. 42, not illustrated.
1526. 7.59g   Same as 796. Worn and plated.
                           O: seahorse and border of dots partly off the flan.
                           R: inscription, if any, obliterated; border of dots partly off the flan.
                           Stern, *Dor Final Report*, p. 466, no. 9.
1527. 6.89g 19mm   Same as 796. Slightly worn and pierced.
                           O: border of dots partly off the flan.
                           R: inscription, if any, obliterated; border of dots partly off the flan.
                           Tel Aviv, KNM, no. K1796.
1528. 5.63g 19mm   Same as 796. Fragmentary and plated.
                           R: inscription, if any, out of the flan.
                           Tel Aviv, KNM, no. K1861.
1529.   Same as 796. Rather worn.
                           O: border of dots partly off the flan.
                           R: inscription unclear; border of dots partly off the flan.
                           Kurpfälzische Münzhandlung, Mannheim, 31, 18-19/12/1986, no. 113.
1530.   Same as 796.
                           O: dolphin and border of dots partly off the flan.
                           Haifa, NMM; *Sefunim* 3, 1969-71, pp. 91-92 and pl. XVIII (reverse not illustrated); Elayi-Elayi, *Trésors*, p. 347 (found in the sea, near ʿAtlit).
1531.   Same as 796. Rather worn.
                           O: dolphin and border of dots partly off the flan.
                           Haifa, NMM; *Sefunim* 3, 1969-71, pp. 91-92 and pl. XVIII, reverse not illustrated; Elayi-Elayi, *Trésors*, p. 347 (found in the sea, near ʿAtlit).
1532.   Same as 796?
                           UBS, Basel, 29-30/1/2004, no. 5933.
1533. 8.83g 21mm   Same as 796.
                           Peus, Frankfurt/Main, 15/3/1954, no. 572, not illus-

trated.

1534. 8.82g 20mm Same as 796.
Hirsch, Munich, 25, 29/11/1909, no. 3027, not illustrated (ex Philipsen coll.).
1535. 8.60g Same as 796.
Ball, Berlin, April 1937, no. 670, not illustrated.
1536. 8.40g 19mm Same as 796.
Hess, Frankfurt/Main, 224, 18/2/1936, no. 1726, not illustrated.
1537. 8.30g Same as 796.
Ball, Berlin, April 1937, no. 669, not illustrated.
1538. 7.95g Same as 796.
Ciani, Paris, 20-22/2/1935, no. 228, not illustrated (ex De Grandprey coll.).
1539. Same as 796.
Elayi-Elayi, *Trésors*, p. 273, not illustrated (Babylonian hoard TLXV).

3. Group III : Unclassified series

III.1. Silver series

III.1.1. Seahorse

III.1.1.a. With seahorse and owl to right

1540. O1* - R1* O: winged seahorse, to right, over dolphin; guilloche
0.72g 10mm border partly off the flan.
12h R: Owl standing to right, head facing; over its left shoulder, crook and flail; guilloche border.
New York, ANS, no. N37 (ex Newell coll.).
1541. O1 - R2* Same as 1540.
0.79g 10mm O and R: guilloche border partly off the flan.
Madrid, MAN, no. 21.69.4.
1542. O1 - R3* Same as 1540.
0.71g 10mm O and R: guilloche border partly off the flan.
6h London, BM, no. 1848-8-3 208; *BMC Phoenicia*, p. 230, no. 23, not illustrated.
1543. O2* - R4* Same as 1540.
0.69g 9mm O: guilloche border partly off the flan.
9h New York, ANS, no. N38 (ex Newell coll.).
1544. O2 - R5* Same as 1540.
0.76g 10mm O: guilloche border partly off the flan.
10h R: defect on the crook and flail; guilloche border

		partly off the flan.
		Jerusalem, RocMus, no. H7.40; Lambert, *QDAP* 2, 1933, p. 7, no. 40 and pl. I; Elayi-Elayi, *Trésors*, p. 214, no. 40 and pl. XXXIV (Abu Shusheh hoard TXLVII).
1545.	O2 - R6*	Same as 1540.
	0.64g	O and R: guilloche border partly off the flan. Jacquier, Kehl/Rhein, 25, Autumn 2000, no. 177 = 24, Spring 2000, no. 154 = 23, Autumn 1999, no. 205 = 22, Spring 1999, no. 191.
1546.	O2 - R7*	Same as 1540.
	0.52g	O: guilloche border partly off the flan. NFA, Encino, 12/10/1988, no. 567.
1547.	O3* - R8*	Same as 1540.
	0.64g	O: guilloche border partly off the flan. R: defects on the head and in front of the owl. Madrid, MAN, no. 21.69.6.
1548.	O3 - R9	Same as 1540.
	0.66g 10mm 12h	O: guilloche border partly off the flan. Berlin, SM, no. 254/1871.
1549.	O4* - R9*	Same as 1540.
	0.67g 10mm 11h	O and R: guilloche border partly off the flan. Paris, BNF, no. 3220; Babelon, *Traité*, pl. CXXII, 18; *Catalogue De Luynes*, no. 3220 (ex De Luynes coll.).
1550.	O5* - R10*	Same as 1540.
	0.60g 9mm 7h	O and R: guilloche border partly off the flan. Moussaïeff coll., London.
1551.	O5 - R11	Same as 1540. Unusual style.
	0.58g	O: guilloche border partly off the flan. Hirsch, Munich, 212, 22-24/11/2000, no. 418.
1552.	O6* - R11*	Same as 1540.
	0.64g 10mm 3h	O and R: guilloche border partly off the flan. Paris, BNF, no. 2005; Babelon, *Perses*, no. 2005.
1553.	O6 - R11	Same as 1540.
	0.62g 10mm 3h	Paris, BNF, no. 3219; Babelon, *Perses*, no. 2004; *Catalogue De Luynes*, no. 3219 (ex De Luynes coll.).
1554.	O7* - R12*	Same as 1540.
	0.68g 10mm 8h	O: guilloche border partly off the flan. Spaer coll., Jerusalem (bought in Akko).
1555.	O8* - R13*	Same as 1540.
	0.66g 10mm	R: dot above the head of the owl. Private coll.; Vinchon, Paris, 9-10/12/1983, no. 171.

1556. O9* - R14*   Same as 1540.
0.60g 9mm   O and R: guilloche border partly off the flan.
10h   Shahaf coll., Haifa, no. 26.

1557. O10* - R15*   Same as 1540.
0.65g 9mm   R: defect under the flail; guilloche border partly off
5h   the flan.
               Tel Aviv, KNM, no. K1322 (from Akko).

1558. O11* - R16*   Same as 1540.
0.60g 9mm   O and R: guilloche border partly off the flan.
6h   London, BM, no. 1902-2-6 166; *BMC Phoenicia*, p.
               230, no. 24 and pl. XXIX, 7.

1559. O12* - R17*   Same as 1540.
0.68g 10mm   O and R: guilloche border partly off the flan.
12h   Oxford, AM, no. 91.

1560. O13* - R18*   Same as 1540.
0.66g 9mm   O and R: guilloche border partly off the flan.
11h   Oxford, AM, no. 90 (ex Cunningham coll.).

1561. O2 - R?   Same as 1540. Slightly worn.
0.57g 10mm   Berlin, SM, no. 24.
12h

1562. O? - R1   Same as 1540. Slightly worn.
0.57g   O and R: guilloche border partly off the flan.
               Jerusalem, IM; Metcalf *et al.*, ʿ*Atiqot* 37, 1999, no.
               364, not illustrated (so-called 'didrachm') (ʿAtlit
               excavations).

1563. O? - R9   Same as 1540. Slightly worn.
0.56g 10mm   O: guilloche border partly off the flan.
12h   Nicosia, ArchM, no. o.c.434.

1564. O? - R19*   Same as 1540. Slightly worn.
0.53g   O: guilloche border partly off the flan.
               Madrid, MAN, no. 21.69.5.

1565. O? - R?   Same as 1540. Rather worn.
0.92g   O and R: guilloche border partly off the flan.
9h   *SNG Copenhagen*, no. 305 and pl. 8.

1566. O? - R?   Same as 1540. Rather worn.
0.82g   O and R: guilloche border partly off the flan.
               Vecchi, London, 2, 8/10/1984, no. 147 = Elsen,
               Brussels, 54, April 1983, no. 69.

1567. O? - R?   Same as 1540. Worn.
0.74g 9mm   O: guilloche border partly off the flan.
12h   Vienna, KHM, no. 33.284.

1568. O? - R?   Same as 1540. Rather worn.
0.72g 9mm   O and R: guilloche border partly off the flan.
               Albrecht-Hoffmann, Köln, 42, 10-13/11/1980, no.

131.

1569. O? - R?   Same as 1540. Rather worn.
       0.67g 9mm   O: guilloche border partly off the flan.
       3h   Spaer coll., Jerusalem (bought in Beirut).
1570. O? - R?   Same as 1540. Rather worn.
       0.62g 10mm   O and R: guilloche border partly off the flan.
                           Kindler, *ErIs* 8, 1967, p. 323, no. 10 and pl. 46, 10.
1571. O? - R?   Same as 1540. Rather worn.
       9mm   Haifa, NMM, no. 0937827.
1572. 0.61g 8mm   Same as 1540.
                           Hess, Frankfurt/Main, 224, 18/2/1936, no. 1727, not illustrated.
1573. 0.54g   Same as 1540.
                           Cahn, Frankfurt/Main, 60, 2/7/1928, no. 1068, not illustrated.

III.1.1.b. With seahorse to left and owl to right

1574. O1* - R1*   O: winged seahorse, to left, over two wavy lines; cable border partly off the flan.
       0.65g 11mm
       3h   R: owl standing to right, head facing; over its left shoulder, crook and flail; cable border partly off the flan.
                           Tel Aviv, KNM, no. K1331 (from Akko).
1575. O2* - R2   Same as 1574. Partly broken.
       0.28g 9mm   O and R: cable border partly off the flan.
                           Jerusalem, AI, no. 5361.
1576. O? - R?   Same as 1574. Rather worn.
       0.47g 9mm   O and R: cable border partly off the flan.
                           Kindler, *ErIs* 8, 1967, p. 323, no. 8 and pl. 46, 8.

III.1.1.c. With seahorse to right and owl to left

1577. O1* - R1*   O: winged seahorse, to right; border obliterated.
       0.50g 10mm   Overstruck.
       2h   R: Owl standing to left, head facing; over its right shoulder, crook and flail; border obliterated.
                           Shahaf coll., Haifa, no. 36.
1578.   Same as 1577.
                           Elayi-Elayi, *Trésors*, p. 237, no. 228, not illustrated (Naplouse hoard TLI).

III.1.1.d. With seahorse and ram's head to left

1579. O1* - R?
0.34g 9mm
2h
O: winged seahorse, to left, over two wavy lines; border obliterated.
R: ram's head to left; border of dots.
Tel Aviv, KNM, no. K1676; Kindler, *ErIs* 8, 1967, p. 323, no. 12 and pl. 46, 12 (from Akko).

1580. O2* - R?
0.44g 8mm
10h
Same as 1579.
O and R: border of dots partly off the flan.
Tel Aviv, KNM, no. K1675; Kindler, *ErIs* 8, 1967, p. 323, no. 11, not illustrated (from Akko).

III.1.1.e. With seahorse and dolphin to left

1581. O? - R?
0.43g 9mm
7h
O: winged seahorse, to left, over a wavy line; border obliterated.
R: dolphin to left; border of dots partly off the flan.
Tel Aviv, KNM, no. K1677 (from Akko).

1582. O? - R?
0.30g 6mm
Same as 1581.
O and R: border of dots partly off the flan.
Spaer coll., Jerusalem (bought in Jerusalem).

III.1.1.f. With seahorse and dolphin to right

1583. O1 - R1*
0.31g
Slightly broken.
O: winged seahorse, to right; border of dots, partly off the flan.
R: dolphin to right; border of dots.
Hirsch, Munich, 191, 24-28/9/1996, no. 719 = Hild, Karlsruhe, 64, 12-13/2/1993, no. 121.

1584. O1* - R2*
0.36g 8mm
Same as 1583.
O: border of dots partly off the flan.
Madrid, MAN, no. 21.69.2.

1585. O2* - R3*
0.23g 6mm
12h
Same as 1583.
O: border of dots partly off the flan.
Spaer coll., Jerusalem (bought in Akko).

1586. O2 - R3
0.23g 8mm
12h
Same as 1583.
O: border of dots partly off the flan.
Jerusalem, RocMus, no. 1269(1); O.R. Sellers, *The Citadel of Beth-Zur*, Philadelphia 1933, pp. 7, 72 and pl. XIV, 6; Elayi-Elayi, *Trésors*, p. 350 (Beth-Zur excavations).

1587. O2 - R4*
0.25g
Same as 1583. Broken.
Kibboutz Ḥanita Museum, no. 182; Elayi-Elayi, *Trésors*, p. 346 and pl. XXXVII, 12.

1588. O3* - R5*   Same as 1583.
      0.40g   O: border of dots partly off the flan.
      6h   R: defect under the dolphin.
                       Deutsch-Heltzer, *Trans* 13, 1997, p. 19 and pl. IV, 8
                       (from Eliachin).
1589. O4* - R6*   Same as 1583.
      0.30g   O and R: border of dots partly off the flan.
                       Jacquier, Kehl/Rhein, 22, Spring 1999, no. 192.
1590. O5* - R7*   Same as 1583. Small crack on the edge.
      0.24g   O: border of dots partly off the flan.
                       Klein, *Sammlung*, no. 727 (ex Klein coll.).
1591. O6* - R8*   Same as 1583.
      0.28g 8mm   Madrid, MAN, no. 21.69.1.
1592. O1 - R?   Same as 1583. Small crack on the edge. Slightly
      0.32g 9mm   worn.
      12h   O: border of dots partly off the flan.
                       Spaer coll., Jerusalem (bought in Jerusalem).
1593. O? - R9*   Same as 1583. Slightly worn.
      0.31g 8mm   Madrid, MAN, no. 21.69.3.
1594. O? - R?   Same as 1583. Rather worn.
      0.42g   Hirsch, Munich, 187, 19-23/9/1995, no. 169.
1595. O? - R?   Same as 1583. Rather worn.
      0.37g 8mm   O: seahorse almost completely out off the flan.
      5h   Tel Aviv, KNM, no. K1682; Elayi-Elayi, *Trésors*, p.
                       349 and pl. XXXVII, 16 (from Gaza area).
1596. O? - R?   Same as 1583. Rather worn.
      0.21g 7mm   O and R: border of dots partly off the flan.
                       Kindler, *ErIs* 8, 1967, p. 323, no. 14 and pl. 46, 14.
1597. O? - R?   Same as 1583. Partly broken.
      0.20g 7mm   Herzog, *Tel Michal*, no. 13 and pl. 72 (Tel Michal
                       excavations).
1598. O? - R?   Same as 1583. Partly broken.
      0.20g   Shahaf coll., Haifa, no. 42.

III.1.2. Dolphin

III.1.2.a. With dolphin/shell and owl to left

1599. O1* - R1*   O: dolphin to left, over a shell; border of dots partly
      0.62g 8mm   off the flan.
      12h   R: owl standing to left, head facing; over its right
                       shoulder, crook and flail; border of dots partly off
                       the flan.
                       New York, ANS, no. N24 (ex Newell coll.).
1600. O1 - R2   Same as 1599.

	0.77g	O and R: border of dots partly off the flan.
		Forrer, *Weber Collection*, no. 8084 (ex Weber coll.).
1601.	O2* - R2*	Same as 1599.
	0.77g	O: border of dots partly off the flan.
		SNG Copenhagen, no. 296 and pl. 8.
1602.	O2 - R3*	Same as 1599.
	0.74g	O: border of dots partly off the flan.
		R: defect on the owl.
		Greenwell, *NC*, 1890, pp. 6-7 and pl. II, 3; Forrer, *Weber Collection*, no. 8083; Elayi-Elayi, *Trésors*, p. 288, no. 1 (Delta hoard TLXXIII) (ex Weber coll.).
1603.	O2 - R4*	Same as 1599. Small cracks on the edge.
	0.73g 8mm	O: border of dots partly off the flan.
	8h	R: defect on the owl.
		Cambridge, FM, no. 01753.
1604.	O3 - R2	Same as 1599.
		O and R: border of dots partly off the flan.
		Kovacs, San Mateo, July 1979, no. 39.
1605.	O3 - R5*	Same as 1599.
	0.50g 9mm	Rouvier, *JIAN* 6, 1903, p. 271 and pl. XVIII, 8 (ex Rouvier coll.).
1606.	O3* - R6*	Same as 1599. Small cracks on the edge.
	0.76g 8mm	O: border of dots partly off the flan.
	9h	Leu, Zurich, 72, 12/5/1998, no. 316 = Sternberg, Zurich, 12, 18-19/11/1982, no. 302.
1607.	O3 - R6	Same as 1599.
	0.65g 9mm	O and R: border of dots partly off the flan.
	4h	Tel Aviv, KNM, no. K1326 (from Akko).
1608.	O4* - R6	Same as 1599. Slightly broken and plated.
	0.40g 8mm	O and R: border of dots partly off the flan.
	12h	Spaer coll., Jerusalem (bought in Jerusalem).
1609.	O5 - R7*	Same as 1599.
	0.52g 9mm	O and R: border of dots partly off the flan.
	12h	Berlin, SM, no. 6 (1-B).
1610.	O5* - R8*	Same as 1599.
	0.57g 9mm	O: border of dots partly off the flan.
	3h	R: defect on the crook.
		Paris, BNF, no. 1973.1.443 (ex Seyrig coll.).
1611.	O6* - R8	Same as 1599.
	0.43g 9mm	R: border of dots partly off the flan.
	3h	Tel Aviv, KNM, no. K1665 (from Akko).
1612.	O7* - R9*	Same as 1599.
	0.61g 8mm	R: defect on the owl (three legs).
	12h	London, BM, no. 1889-6-3 5; *BMC Phoenicia*, p.

1613. O8 - R9
0.74g 9mm

1614. O8* - R10*
0.64g 11mm
3h

1615. O9* - R11*
0.70g 11mm
9h

1616. O9 - R12*
0.56g 11mm
2h

1617. O10* - R13*
0.62g 11mm

1618. O11* - R14*
0.71g 10mm
4h

1619. O12* - R15*
0.33g 9mm
9h

1620. O13* - R16*
0.66g 8mm
6h

1621. O14* - R17*
0.85g 11mm
4h

1622. O5 - R?
0.69g 10mm
12h

1623. O7 - R?
0.52g 9mm
9h

1624. O15* - R?
0.50g 10mm
4h

228, no. 9 and pl. XXVIII, 14; Greenwell, *NC*, 1890, pp. 6-7 and pl. II, 4; Elayi-Elayi, *Trésors*, p. 288, no. 2 (Delta hoard TLXXIII) (ex Weber coll.).
Same as 1599.
Kindler, *ErIs* 8, 1967, p. 323, no. 21 and pl. 46.
Same as 1599.
O and R: border of dots partly off the flan.
Paris, BNF, no. 3210; *Catalogue De Luynes*, no. 3210 (ex De Luynes coll.).
Same as 1599. Plated.
O and R: border of dots partly off the flan.
Shahaf coll., Haifa, no. 66.
Same as 1599. Partly broken and plated.
O and R: border of dots partly off the flan.
New York, ANS, no. N25 (ex Newell coll.).
Same as 1599.
O and R: border of dots partly off the flan.
Kovacs, San Mateo, 1988.
Same as 1599.
O and R: border of dots partly off the flan.
London, BM, no. 1877-4-6 5; *BMC Phoenicia*, p. 228, no. 8, not illustrated.
Same as 1599.
O: border of dots partly off the flan.
R: dot in field right.
Paris, BNF, no. 1973-1-444 (ex Seyrig coll.).
Same as 1599. Some cracks on the edge.
O: border of dots partly off the flan.
R: border of dots partly off the flan; dot in field right.
Oxford, AM, no. 87.
Same as 1599.
O and R: border of dots partly off the flan.
New York, ANS, no. N26 (ex Newell coll.).
Same as 1599. Some cracks on the edge. Slightly worn.
O and R: border of dots partly off the flan.
Berlin, SM, no. 7 (ex Löbbecke coll.).
Same as 1599. Slightly worn.
O and R: border of dots partly off the flan.
New York, ANS, no. N25 (ex Newell coll.).
Same as 1599. Slightly worn and partly broken.
O and R: border of dots partly off the flan.
New York, ANS, no. N27 (ex Newell coll.).

1625. O16* - R?
0.61g 9mm
Same as 1599. Slightly worn.
O and R: border of dots partly off the flan.
Myers, Ariadne Galleries, New York, 9/12/1981, no. 297.

1626. O? - R18*
0.66g 9mm
5h
Same as 1599. Slightly worn and broken.
O: border of dots partly off the flan.
R: border of dots partly off the flan; defect in field right.
Paris, BNF, no. 1987; Babelon, *Perses*, no. 1987.

1627. O? - R19*
0.49g 10mm
6h
Same as 1599. Slightly worn and broken.
O: border of dots partly off the flan.
R: border of dots partly off the flan; defect in field left.
London, BM, no. 1894-5-4 14; *BMC Phoenicia*, p. 228, no. 10 and pl. XXVIII, 15 (bought in Istanbul).

1628. O? - R20*
0.74g 12mm
6h
Same as 1599. Slightly worn. Oval flan.
O and R: border of dots partly off the flan.
Paris, BNF, no. 1985; Babelon, *Perses*, no. 1985.

1629. O? - R21*
0.40g 9mm
3h
Same as 1599. Slightly worn. Plated.
O and R: border of dots partly off the flan.
Tel Aviv, KNM, no. K1325 (from Akko).

1630. O? - R22*
0.57g 11mm
4h
Same as 1599. Slightly worn. Small cracks on the edge.
Spaer coll., Jerusalem (bought in Jerusalem).

1631. O? - R23*
0.51g 11mm
3h
Same as 1599. Slightly worn.
O: border of dots partly off the flan.
R: border of dots partly off the flan; three dots in field left.
Berlin, SM, no. 5.

1632. O? - R24*
0.34g 10mm
2h
Same as 1599. Rather worn.
O and R: border of dots partly off the flan.
Paris, BNF, no. 1986; Babelon, *Perses*, no. 1986.

1633. O? - R25*
0.70g 12mm
Same as 1599. Slightly worn.
O: head of the dolphin and border of dots partly off the flan.
Paris, BNF, no. 3211; *Catalogue De Luynes*, no. 3211.

1634. O? - R?
0.82g
9h
Same as 1599. Rather worn.
O: border of dots partly off the flan.
R: defect in field right.
SNG Copenhagen, no. 297 and pl. 8.

1635. O? - R?
0.74g 9mm
10h
Same as 1599. Rather worn.
Tel Aviv, KNM, no. K1664 (from Akko).

1636. O? - R?   Same as 1599. Rather worn.
      0.60g   O and R: border of dots partly off the flan.
                    Peus, Frankfurt/Main, 300, 3-4 and 9/11/1987, no.
                    1225.
1637. O? - R?   Same as 1599. Rather worn.
      0.57g   *Catalogue Rosen*, no. 757 (ex Rosen coll.).
      1h
1638. O? - R?   Same as 1599. Worn.
      0.47g 8mm   O: border of dots partly off the flan.
      7h   New York, ANS, no. 1983.51.721 (ex Rosen coll.).
1639. O? - R?   Same as 1599. Worn.
      0.36g   O: border of dots partly off the flan.
                    Künker, Osnabrück, 24, 10-12/3/1993, no. 107.
1640. O? - R?   Same as 1599. Rather worn.
      9mm   O: border of dots partly off the flan.
                    Munich, SMS, no. 27.

III.1.2.b. With dolphin/shell and owl to right?

1641. O? - R?   O: dolphin to right, over a shell; guilloche border?
      0.57g 9mm   Worn.
                    R: owl standing to right, head facing; over its left
                    shoulder, crook and flail; guilloche border?
                    Kindler, *ErIs* 8, 1967, p. 323, no. 20 and pl. 46.
1642. O? - R?   Same as 1641. Rather worn.
      0.52g 9mm   O and R: guilloche border (?) partly off the flan.
      3h   Tel Aviv, KNM, no. K1672 (from Akko).

III.1.2.c. With dolphin and owl to left

1643. O1* - R1*   O: dolphin to left; guilloche border.
      0.50g 8mm   R: owl standing to left, head facing; over its right
      2h   shoulder, crook and flail; guilloche border?
                    Tel Aviv, KNM, no. K1681; Kindler, *ErIs* 8, 1967,
                    p. 323, no. 16 and pl. 46 (from Akko).
1644. O1 - R2*   Same as 1643.
      0.55g 8mm   O and R: guilloche border partly off the flan.
                    Jerusalem, IM, no. 3879.
1645. O2* - R3*   Same as 1643.
      0.35g 8mm   O and R: guilloche border partly off the flan.
      8h   Tel Aviv, KNM, no. K1324 (from Akko).
1646. O3* - R4*   Same as 1643.
      0.45g 9mm   O and R: guilloche border partly off the flan.
                    Kibboutz Ḥanita Museum, no. 210; Elayi-Elayi,
                    Trésors, p. 346 and pl. XXXVII, 11.

1647. O4 - R5* Same as 1643.
0.46g O and R: guilloche border partly off the flan.
Agora, Tel Aviv, 1, 14/5/1974, no. 35.
1648. O4* - R? Same as 1643. Slightly worn.
0.57g O and R: guilloche border partly off the flan.
Hirsch, Munich, 172, 27-29/11/1991, no. 356.
1649. O? - R6* Same as 1643. Slightly worn.
0.58g 9mm O and R: guilloche border partly off the flan.
Jerusalem, IM, no. 3882.
1650. O? - R7* Same as 1643. Slightly worn.
0.30g 10mm O and R: guilloche border partly off the flan.
Shahaf coll., Haifa, no. 48.
1651. O? - R? Same as 1643. Rather worn.
0.75g 11mm O and R: guilloche border partly off the flan.
Kindler, *ErIs* 8, 1967, p. 323, no. 17 and pl. 46.
1652. O? - R? Same as 1643. Worn.
0.52g 7mm O and R: guilloche border partly off the flan.
Beirut, AUB Museum, no. C1251; Baramki, *Coins AUB*, no. 1251.
1653. O? - R? Same as 1643. Worn.
Meyers, *Gush Ḥalav*, pp. 235-236 and fig. 235, 1 (Gush Ḥalav excavations).
1654. Same as 1643.
Baldwin, London, 34, 13/10/2003, no. 545, not illustrated.

III.1.2.d. With dolphin and owl to right

1655. O1* - R1* O: dolphin to right; guilloche border.
0.58g 8mm R: owl standing to right, head facing; over its left
4h shoulder, crook and flail; guilloche border.
New York, ANS, no. N40 (ex Newell coll.).
1656. O1 - R2* Same as 1655.
0.60g O: head of the dolphin and guilloche border partly
6h off the flan.
Deutsch-Heltzer, *Trans* 13, 1997, p. 19, no. 19 and pl. IV, 7 (from Eliachin).
1657. O1 - R3* Same as 1655.
0.67g Baldwin, London, 34, 13/10/2003, no. 537.
1658. O2 - R3 Same as 1655.
0.55g 9mm Shahaf coll., Haifa, no. 15.
7h
1659. O2* - R4* Same as 1655.
0.45g 7mm O and R: guilloche border partly off the flan.

The Coinage of Tyre in the Persian period

	8h	New York, ANS, no. N29 (ex Newell coll.).
1660.	O3* - R5*	Same as 1655. Split die.
	0.64g 8mm	London, BM, no. 1858-11-25 5; *BMC Phoenicia*, p.
	3h	228, no. 5 and pl. XXVIII, 12.
1661.	O3 - R6*	Same as 1655.
	0.66g 8mm	O: dolphin and guilloche border partly off the flan.
		New York, ANS, no. N30; Rouvier, *JIAN* 6, 1903, p. 270 and pl. XVIII, 6 (ex Newell coll. = ex Rouvier coll.).
1662.	O4* - R7*	Same as 1655.
	0.50g 8mm	O and R: guilloche border partly off the flan.
	2h	Shahaf coll., Haifa, no. 27.
1663.	O5* - R7	Same as 1655.
	0.66g	O and R: guilloche border partly off the flan.
		Classical Numismatic Group, Lancaster-London, 34, 6/5/1995, no. 196.
1664.	O6* - R8*	Same as 1655.
	0.42g	Hirsch, Munich, 205, 22-25/9/1999, no. 480.
1665.	O7* - R8	Same as 1655.
	0.46g	O and R: guilloche border partly off the flan.
		Klein, *Sammlung*, no. 726 (ex Klein coll.).
1666.	O8* - R9*	Same as 1655.
	0.66g 9mm	O and R: guilloche border partly off the flan.
	11h	New York, ANS, no. 55.54; Hess, Frankfurt/Main, 224, 18/2/1936, no. 1725.
1667.	O9* - R10*	Same as 1655. Small cracks on the edge.
	0.57g 9mm	R: guilloche border partly off the flan.
	12h	Tel Aviv, KNM, no. K1670; Kindler, *ErIs* 8, 1967, p. 323, no. 19 and pl. 46 (from Akko).
1668.	O10* - R11*	Same as 1655.
	0.72g 8mm	O and R: guilloche border partly off the flan.
	7h	Toronto, ROM, no. 949x15.449.
1669.	O11* - R12*	Same as 1655.
	0.47g 9mm	O: defect below; guilloche border partly off the flan.
	3h	R: guilloche border partly off the flan.
		London, BM, no. 1848-8-3 207; *BMC Phoenicia*, p. 228, no. 7 and pl. XXVIII, 13; Rouvier, *JIAN* 6, 1903, p. 270, no. 1780 and pl. XVIII, 5.
1670.	O12* - R13*	Same as 1655.
	0.61g	O and R: guilloche border partly off the flan.
	12h	London, BM, no. 1848-3-1 389; *BMC Phoenicia*, p. 228, no. 6, not illustrated.
1671.	O13* - R14*	Same as 1655.
	0.57g 8mm	O and R: guilloche border partly off the flan.

1672. O14* - R15*
0.75g

1673. O15* - R16*
0.56g

1674. O8 - R?
0.45g

1675. O9 - R?
0.62g

1676. O15 - R?
0.55g 8mm
12h

1677. O16* - R?
0.54g

1678. O? - R2
0.49g

1679. O? - R7
0.62g

1680. O? - R17*
0.82g 10mm

1681. O? - R18*
0.54g 8mm
6h

1682. O? - R?
1.02g 9mm

Münzen und Medaillen, Basel, 581, Nov./Dec. 1994, no. 113.
Same as 1655.
O and R: guilloche border partly off the flan.
Hirsch, Munich, 186, 10-12/5/1995, no. 560 = Sternberg, Zurich, 5, September 1993, no. 387.
Same as 1655.
R: guilloche border partly off the flan.
Elsen, Brussels, 83, 12/3/2005, no. 261 = Künker, Osnabrück, 94, 27-28/9/2004, no. 1459 = Numismatica, Vienna, 13, 9-11/11/1976, no. 366.
Same as 1655. Slightly worn.
O: guilloche border partly off the flan.
Malter, Encino, 29, 1990, no. 121.
Same as 1655. Slightly worn.
O and R: guilloche border partly off the flan.
Waddell, Gaithersburg, 60, Summer 1993, no. 81.
Same as 1655. Slightly worn.
Baramki, *Coins AUB*, p. 220, no. 1252 and pl. XXVII, 3.
Same as 1655. Slightly worn.
O: defect below; guilloche border partly off the flan.
R: guilloche border partly off the flan.
Spink Numismatic Circular, 10, December 1992, no. 7233.
Same as 1655. Slightly worn.
R: guilloche border partly off the flan.
Peus, Frankfurt/Main, 361, 6/11/1999, no. 250.
Same as 1655. Slightly worn.
O: guilloche border partly off the flan.
England, Quarryville-London, 15, 5/6/1991, no. 256 = 1, 1/5/1987, no. 89.
Same as 1655. Slightly worn.
O: head of the dolphin and guilloche border partly off the flan.
R: defect in field left.
Jerusalem, IM, no. 3881.
Same as 1655. Slightly worn.
O: head of the dolphin and guilloche border partly off the flan.
R: guilloche border partly off the flan.
Spaer coll., Jerusalem (bought in Jerusalem).
Same as 1655. Rather worn.
O: guilloche border partly off the flan.

	12h	Raynor-Meshorer, *Ancient Meiron*, p. 7, no. 1 (Meiron excavations).
1683.	O? - R?	Same as 1655. Rather worn.
	0.85g 9mm	O: guilloche border partly off the flan.
	1h	Tel Aviv, KNM, no. K1329 (from Akko).
1684.	O? - R?	Same as 1655. Rather worn.
	0.69g 7mm	O and R: guilloche border partly off the flan.
	6h	London, BM, no. 1863-12-20 2; *BMC Phoenicia*, p. 227, no. 4, not illustrated.
1685.	O? - R?	Same as 1655. Rather worn.
	0.62g 10mm	O: guilloche border partly off the flan.
	3h	Spaer coll., Jerusalem (bought in Jerusalem).
1686.	O? - R?	Same as 1655. Worn.
	0.60g 9mm	O: guilloche border partly off the flan.
	12h	Tel Aviv, KNM, no. K1327 (from Akko).
1687.	O? - R?	Same as 1655. Rather worn.
	0.60g 10mm	O and R: guilloche border partly off the flan.
	6h	Tel Aviv, KNM, no. K1328 (from Akko).
1688.	O? - R?	Same as 1655. Rather worn.
	0.55g 9mm	O and R: guilloche border partly off the flan.
	6h	Shahaf coll., Haifa, no. 22.
1689.	O? - R?	Same as 1655. Rather worn.
	0.55g 9mm	O and R: guilloche border partly off the flan.
	2h	Paris, BNF, no. H.S.1 (ex Seyrig coll.).
1690.	O? - R?	Same as 1655. Rather worn.
	0.55g 9mm	Warsaw, NM, no. 86631 (ex Semeran-Siemianowski coll.).
	9h	
1691.	O? - R?	Same as 1655. Worn.
	0.50g 9mm	Tel Aviv, KNM, no. K1673 (from Akko).
	12h	
1692.	O? - R?	Same as 1655. Worn. Small crack on the edge.
	0.48g 9mm	O and R: guilloche border partly off the flan. Briend-Humbert, *Tell Keisan*, p. 236, no. 4-1461, not illustrated (Tell Keisan excavations).
1693.	O? - R?	Same as 1655. Rather worn.
	0.47g 9mm	O and R: guilloche border partly off the flan.
	6h	Oxford, AM, no. 86 (from near Daphne).
1694.	O? - R?	Same as 1655. Rather worn.
	0.47g	R: guilloche border partly off the flan. Gorny, Munich, 36, 8/4/1987, no. 298.
1695.	O? - R?	Same as 1655. Rather worn.
	0.45g	Numismatic Art & Ancient Coins, Zurich, 4, 17/4/1986, no. 279.
1696.	O? - R?	Same as 1655. Rather worn.

	0.45g	R: guilloche border partly off the flan. Hirsch, Munich, 239, 17-18/2/2005, no. 1544.
1697.	O? - R? 0.45g 9mm 3h	Same as 1655. Rather worn and damaged. Tel Aviv, KNM, no. K1323 (from Akko).
1698.	O? - R? 0.44g 8mm	Same as 1655. Rather worn. Kindler, *ErIs* 8, 1967, p. 323, no. 11 and pl. 46.
1699.	O? - R? 0.41g 8mm 4h	Same as 1655. Rather worn. R: guilloche border partly off the flan. Spaer coll., Jerusalem (bought in Jerusalem).
1700.	O? - R? 0.38g	Same as 1655. Rather worn. O: guilloche border partly off the flan. Sheridan, *Numismatist* 8, 1971, p. 1130, no. 1 and pl.; Elayi-Elayi, *Trésors*, p. 203, no. 12 (Beirut hoard TXLIII).
1701.	O? - R? 0.35g 9mm 3h	Same as 1655. Worn. Tel Aviv, KNM, no. K1330 (from Akko).
1702.	O? - R? 0.30g 6mm	Same as 1655. Worn. Beirut, AUB Museum, no. 1253; Baramki, *Coins AUB*, p. 220, no. 1253.
1703.	O? - R?	Same as 1655. Rather worn. Peus, Frankfurt/Main, 10, September 1969, no. 49.
1704.	0.62g	Same as 1655. Elayi-Elayi, *Trésors*, p. 293, no. 25, not illustrated (Beni Hassan hoard TLXXV).
1705.	0.62g	Same as 1655. Plated. Sheridan, *Numismatist* 8, 1971, p. 1131, no. 11; Elayi-Elayi, *Trésors*, p. 203, no. 17, not illustrated (Beirut hoard TXLIII).
1706.	0.48g	Same as 1655. Sheridan, *Numismatist* 8, 1971, p. 1131, no. 4; Elayi-Elayi, *Trésors*, p. 203, no. 15, not illustrated (Beirut hoard TXLIII).
1707.	0.47g	Same as 1655. Baldwin, London, 34, 13/10/2003, no. 538, not illustrated.
1708.	0.48g	Same as 1655. Sheridan, *Numismatist* 8, 1971, p. 1130, no. 2; Elayi-Elayi, *Trésors*, p. 203, no. 14, not illustrated (Beirut hoard TXLIII).
1709-1710.	0.71g	Same as 1655. Milne, *RA*, 1905, p. 258, no. 1; Elayi-Elayi, *Trésors*, p. 293, no. 23-24, not illustrated (Beni Hassan hoard

TLXXV).

III.1.2.e. With dolphin to right and head of lion

1711. O1* - R1*   O: dolphin to right; border of dots.
      0.27g   R: head of lion *en face*; border of dots.
                     Jacquier, Kehl/Rhein, 22, Spring 1999, no. 193.
1712. O2* - R2*   Same as 1711. Small dies.
      0.23g 6mm   Jerusalem, RocMus, no. H7.42; Lambert, *QDAP* 2,
      5h   1933, p. 7, no. 42 and pl. I; Elayi-Elayi, *Trésors*, p.
                     214, no. 42 (Abu Shusheh hoard TXLVII).
1713. O3* - R?   Same as 1711. Slightly worn.
      0.18g 6mm   New York, ANS, no. N23 (ex Newell coll.).
      12h
1714. O? - R1   Same as 1711. Slightly worn.
      0.37g   Münzen und Medaillen, Basel, 484, January 1986,
                     no. 22.
1715. O? - R3*   Same as 1711. Slightly worn.
      0.25g 7mm   Kibboutz Ḥanita Museum, no. 183; Elayi-Elayi,
                     Trésors, p. 346 and pl. XXXVII, 13.
1716. O? - R?   Same as 1711. Worn.
      0.22g 6mm   Paris, BNF, no. 1987/464.
1717. O? - R?   Same as 1711. Rather worn.
      0.20g 6mm   R: border of dots partly off the flan.
                     Shahaf coll., Haifa, no. 35.
1718. O? - R?   Same as 1711. Rather worn.
      0.19g 6mm   Paris, BNF, no. 1965/829.28 (ex Seyrig coll.).
      1h   Found on the beach of Byblos.
1719. O? - R?   Same as 1711. Worn.
      0.18g 6mm   Paris, BNF, no. 1968/132 (ex Seyrig coll.).
1720. O? - R?   Same as 1711. Rather worn.
      0.23g   O: border of dots partly off the flan.
      5h   Classical Numismatic Group, Lancaster-London, 69,
                     8/6/2005, no. 638.
1721. O? - R?   Same as 1711. Rather worn.
      0.18g 6mm   O: border of dots partly off the flan.
                     Spaer coll., Jerusalem (bought in Jerusalem).

III.1.2.f. With dolphin and ram's head to left

1722. O1 - R1*   O: dolphin to left; border of dots.
      0.25g   R: ram's head to left; border of dots.
                     Münzen Auktion, Essen, 70, 6-8/12/1995, no. 110 =
                     69, 31/5-2/6/1995, no. 126.

1723. O1* - R2*   Same as 1722.
      0.33g 7mm   R: border of dots partly off the flan.
      6h   Paris, BNF, no. 1966/261 (from Gaza).
1724. O2* - R3*   Same as 1722. Small crack on the edge.
      0.28g 6mm   O: border of dots partly off the flan.
      12h   R: ram's head(?); border of dots partly off the flan.
                     Leu, Zurich, 86, 5-6/5/2003, no. 442.
1725. O3* - R4*   Same as 1722.
      0.32g 7mm   O and R: border of dots partly off the flan.
      12h   Oxford, AM, no. 100; Martin, London, 12/6/1990.
1726. O4* - R5*   Same as 1722.
      0.35g 7mm   O and R: border of dots partly off the flan.
      2h   Tel Aviv, KNM, no. K1333.
1727. O5* - R6*   O: ram's (or bull's?) head; border of dots partly off
      0.25g 7mm   the flan.
      4h   R: border of dots partly off the flan.
                     Shahaf coll., Haifa, no. 37.
1728. O6* - R7*   Same as 1722.
      0.25g 7mm   O and R: border of dots partly off the flan.
      2h   Tel Aviv, KNM, no. K1668; Kindler, *ErIs* 8, 1967,
                     p. 323, no. 15 and pl. 46 (from Akko).
1729. O7* - R8*   Same as 1722.
      0.33g   O and R: border of dots partly off the flan.
      7h   Classical Numismatic Group, Lancaster-London, 69,
                     8/6/2005, no. 637.
1730. O8* - R?   Same as 1722. Slightly worn.
      0.24g 7mm   O and R: border of dots partly off the flan.
      6h   Spaer coll., Jerusalem (bought in Jerusalem).
1731. O? - R2   Same as 1722. Slightly worn.
      0.23g 5mm   O and R: border of dots partly off the flan.
      9h   Paris, BNF, no. 1988; Babelon, *Perses*, no. 1988.
1732. O? - R9*   Same as 1722. Slightly worn.
      0.25g 7mm   O and R: border of dots partly off the flan.
      3h   Tel Aviv, KNM, no. K1667 (from Akko).
1733. O? - R?   Same as 1722. Rather worn.
      0.35g 8mm   O and R: border of dots partly off the flan.
      3h   Tel Aviv, KNM, no. K1332.

III.2. Bronze series

III.2.1. With seahorse to right and head of lion

1734. O1* - R1*   O: seahorse to right, over two lines of waves; border
      0.95g 11mm   of dots.
                     R: head of lion *en face*, with prey; border obscure.

		Kibboutz Ḥanita Museum, no. 205; Elayi-Elayi, *Trésors*, p. 346 and pl. XXXVII, 14.
1735.	O2* - R2*	Same as 1734.
		O: waves and border obscure.
		R: border obscure.
		Private coll.
1736.	O3* - R3*	Same as 1734.
	0.99g 10mm	O: border obscure.
	4h	R: dot above the head; border obscure.
		Tel Aviv, KNM, no. K1678 (from Akko).
1737.	O? - R4*	Same as 1734. Slightly worn.
	0.99g 10mm	O: waves, seahorse and border of dots partly off the flan.
	2h	R: border obscure.
		Tel Aviv, KNM, no. K1319; Kindler, *ErIs* 8, 1967, p. 323 and pl. 46, 13 (from Akko).

III.2.2. With dolphin to left and head of lion

1738.	O1* - R1*	O: dolphin to left; border of dots?
	1.06g 10mm	R: head of lion *en face*, with prey; border of dots?
	3h	Cambridge, Harvard University, no. 57.
1739.	O1 - R?	Same as 1738. Slightly worn.
	0.65g 9mm	O and R: border of dots?
	3h	Tel Aviv, KNM, no. K1336 (from Akko).
1740.	O1 - R?	Same as 1738. Slightly worn.
	0.57g 9mm	O and R: border of dots?
		Kindler, *ErIs* 8, 1967, p. 323, no. 18 and pl. 46.
1741.	O? - R2*	Same as 1738. Slightly worn.
	0.77g 11mm	O and R: border of dots?
		Cambridge, Harvard University, no. 58.

III.2.3. With shell and head of lion

1742.	O1* - R1*	O: shell; border of dots.
		R: head of lion *en face*, with prey; incuse square?
		Private coll. (from a hoard; information given by N. Vismara, 1993).
1743.	O2* - R2*	Same as 1742.
		O: border of dots partly off the flan.
		R: incuse square.
		Private coll.
1744.	O3 - R3	Same as 1742.
	0.90g	O: border of dots partly off the flan.
		Agora, Tel Aviv, 1, 14/5/1974, no. 37.

1745. O3* - R3*   Same as 1742.
                    O: border of dots partly off the flan.
                    Private coll.
1746. O3* - R4*   Same as 1742.
      0.90g 10mm   O: border of dots partly off the flan.
      3h   Tel Aviv, KNM, no. K1680; Kindler, *ErIs* 8, 1967,
                    p. 323, no. 25 and pl. 46 (from Akko).
1747. O3 - R5   Same as 1742.
                    O: shell and border of dots partly off the flan.
                    Private coll.
1748. O4* - R5*   Same as 1742.
                    O: shell and border of dots partly off the flan.
                    Private coll.
1749. O5* - R6*   Same as 1742.
      0.82g 9mm   O: border of dots partly off the flan.
      2h   R: incuse square.
                    Tel Aviv, KNM, no. K1679 (from Akko).
1750. O6* - R6   Same as 1742.
      0.65g 10mm   O: border of dots partly off the flan.
      12h   Spaer coll., Jerusalem (bought in Akko).
1751. O7* - R7*   Same as 1742.
      0.84g 9mm   O: border of dots off the flan.
                    R: incuse square.
                    New York, ANS, no. N71 (ex Newell coll.).
1752. O3 - R?   Same as 1742. Slightly worn.
      0.90g 9mm   O: border of dots partly off the flan.
                    Jerusalem, IM, no. 3890.
1753. O8 - R?   Same as 1742. Slightly worn.
      0.70g 8mm   O: shell and border of dots partly off the flan.
      7h   Shahaf coll., Haifa, no. 55.
1754. O8* - R?   Same as 1742. Slightly worn.
      0.59g 9mm   O: shell and border of dots partly off the flan.
      2h   R: incuse square.
                    New York, ANS, no. N69 (ex Newell coll.).
1755. O9* - R?   Same as 1742. Slightly worn.
      1.05g 9mm   O: shell and border of dots partly off the flan.
                    R: head of the lion partly off the flan.
                    Beirut, AUB Museum, no. C1260.
1756. O? - R8*   Same as 1742. Slightly worn.
      0.80g 9mm   O: border of dots partly off the flan.
      12h   Shahaf coll., Haifa, no. 58.
1757. O? - R8   Same as 1742. Slightly worn.
      0.70g 10mm   O: shell and border of dots partly off the flan.
      6h   R: head of the lion partly off the flan.

Shahaf coll., Haifa, no. 54.

1758. O? - R9
0.83g 9mm
Same as 1742. Slightly worn.
O: border of dots off the flan.
New York, ANS, no. N70 (ex Newell coll.).

1759. O? - R?
1.05g 10mm
1h
Same as 1742. Rather worn.
O: border of dots off the flan.
R: head of the lion partly off the flan.
Tel Aviv, KNM, no. K1320 (from Akko).

1760. O? - R?
0.72g 10mm
11h
Same as 1742. Rather worn.
O: border of dots off the flan.
R: incuse square.
Spaer coll., Jerusalem (bought in Jerusalem).

1761. O? - R?
0.71g 9mm
Same as 1742. Rather worn.
O: border of dots partly off the flan.
Jerusalem, IM, no. 869; Elayi-Elayi, *Trésors*, p. 170 (Akko hoard TXXXIV).

1762. O? - R?
0.70g 8mm
3h
Same as 1742. Rather worn.
O: shell and border of dots partly off the flan.
R: head of the lion partly off the flan.
Shahaf coll., Haifa, no. 59.

1763. O? - R?
0.55g 9mm
1h
Same as 1742. Rather worn.
O: shell and border of dots partly off the flan.
Shahaf coll., Haifa, no. 50.

1764. O? - R?
0.54g
Same as 1742. Rather worn.
O: border of dots partly off the flan.
Jerusalem, IM, no. 870; Elayi-Elayi, *Trésors*, p. 170 (Akko hoard TXXXIV).

1765. O? - R?
0.39g 9mm
Same as 1742. Rather worn.
O: shell and border of dots partly off the flan.
Jerusalem, IM, no. 849; Elayi-Elayi, *Trésors*, p. 169, no. 15 and pl. XXVII (Akko hoard TXXXIV).

1766. O? - R?
Same as 1742. Rather worn.
O: shell and border of dots partly off the flan.
Private coll.

III.2.4. With dolphin/shell to left and head of lion

1767. O1* - R1*
0.81g
12h
O: dolphin to left, over a shell; border of dots.
R: head of lion *en face*, with prey; no border.
Ariel, ʿ*Atiqot* 22, 1993, pp. 125-6, no. 5 and fig. 2; Elayi-Elayi, *NAC* 27, 1998, pp. 130, no. 2 and 139, pl. I (Tel Nahariya excavations).

1768. O2* - R2*
0.57g 9mm
Same as 1767. Small crack on the edge.
O: border of dots partly off the flan.

	6h	Jerusalem, IM, no. 834; Elayi-Elayi, *NAC* 27, 1998, pp. 132, no. 18 and 139, pl. I; *id.*, *Trésors*, p. 169, no. 7 and pl. XXVII (Akko hoard TXXXIV).
1769.	O3* - R3* 0.45g 9mm 6h	Same as 1767. O and R: no border. Jerusalem, IM, no. 831; Elayi-Elayi, *NAC* 27, 1998, pp. 133, no. 24 and 139, pl. I; *id.*, *Trésors*, p. 169, no. 12 and pl. XXVII (Akko hoard TXXXIV).
1770.	O4* - R4* 0.70g 10mm 5h	Same as 1767. O and R: no border. Shahaf coll., Haifa, no. 57; Elayi-Elayi, *NAC* 27, 1998, pp. 131, no. 7 and 139, pl. I.
1771.	O4 - R3 0.70g 9mm 6h	Same as 1767. O and R: no border. Shahaf coll., Haifa, no. 51; Elayi-Elayi, *NAC* 27, 1998, pp. 131, no. 8 and 139, pl. I.
1772.	O5* - R5* 0.75g 9mm 6h	Same as 1767. O and R: no border. Jerusalem, IM, no. 833; Elayi-Elayi, *NAC* 27, 1998, pp. 130, no. 4 and 139, pl. I; *id.*, *Trésors*, p. 168, no. 2 and pl. XXVII (Akko hoard TXXXIV).
1773.	O2 - R? 0.80g 9mm 9h	Same as 1767. Slightly worn. O: border of dots partly off the flan. R: no border. Shahaf coll., Haifa, no. 49; Elayi-Elayi, *NAC* 27, 1998, pp. 130, no. 3 and 139, pl. I.
1774.	O2 - R? 0.54g 9mm 6h	Same as 1767. Slightly worn. O and R: no border. Jerusalem, IM, no. 846; Elayi-Elayi, *NAC* 27, 1998, pp. 133, no. 22 and 139, pl. I; *id.*, *Trésors*, p. 169, no. 9 and pl. XXVII (Akko hoard TXXXIV).
1775.	O6* - R? 0.67g 9mm	Same as 1767. Slightly worn. O: dots in field; no border. New York, ANS, no. N72; Elayi-Elayi, *NAC* 27, 1998, p. 131, no. 13, not illustrated (ex Newell coll.).
1776.	O7* - R? 0.53g 9mm 6h	Same as 1767. Slightly worn. O: border partly off the flan. R: no border. Jerusalem, IM, no. 835; Elayi-Elayi, *NAC* 27, 1998, pp. 133, no. 23 and 139, pl. I; *id.*, *Trésors*, p. 169, no. 11 and pl. XXVII (Akko hoard TXXXIV).
1777.	O? - R3 0.88g 9mm	Same as 1767. Slightly worn. O and R: no border.

		Agora, Tel Aviv, 1, 14/5/1974, no. 36; Elayi-Elayi, *NAC* 27, 1998, p. 130, no. 1, not illustrated.
1778.	O? - R3*	Same as 1767. Slightly worn.
	0.60g 9mm	O: no border.
	6h	R: incuse square.
		Tel Aviv, KNM, no. K1334; Elayi-Elayi, *NAC* 27, 1998, pp. 132, no. 16 and 139, pl. I; Kindler, *ErIs* 8, 1967, p. 323, no. 22 and pl. 46 (from Akko).
1779.	O? - R6*	Same as 1767. Slightly worn.
	0.69g 9mm	O: border partly off the flan.
	12h	R: no border.
		Jerusalem, IM, no. 847; Elayi-Elayi, *NAC* 27, 1998, pp. 131, no. 11 and 139, pl. I; *id.*, *Trésors*, p. 168, no. 5 and pl. XXVII (Akko hoard TXXXIV).
1780.	O? - R6	Same as 1767. Slightly worn.
	0.69g 10mm	O and R: no border.
	6h	Jerusalem, IM, no. 848; Elayi-Elayi, *NAC* 27, 1998, pp. 131, no. 12 and 139, pl. I; *id.*, *Trésors*, p. 169, no. 13 and pl. XXVII, reverse to be turned (Akko hoard TXXXIV).
1781.	O? - R7	Same as 1767. Slightly worn.
	0.70g 10mm	Spaer coll., Jerusalem; Elayi-Elayi, *NAC* 27, 1998,
	6h	pp. 131, no. 9 and 139, pl. I (bought in Jerusalem).
1782.	O? - R7*	Same as 1767. Slightly worn.
	0.57g 9mm	Jerusalem, IM, no. 843; Elayi-Elayi, *NAC* 27, 1998,
	6h	pp. 132, no. 19 and 139, pl. I; *id.*, *Trésors*, p. 169, no. 8 and pl. XXVII (Akko hoard TXXXIV).
1783.	O? - R?	Same as 1767. Rather worn.
	0.72g 9mm	O and R: no border.
	5h	Jerusalem, IM, no. 840; Elayi-Elayi, *NAC* 27, 1998, pp. 130, no. 5 and 139, pl. I; *id.*, *Trésors*, p. 168, no. 3 and pl. XXVII (Akko hoard TXXXIV).
1784.	O? - R?	Same as 1767. Rather worn.
	0.72g 9mm	Spaer coll., Jerusalem; Elayi-Elayi, *NAC* 27, 1998,
	6h	p. 131, no. 6 and 139, pl. I (bought in Akko).
1785.	O? - R?	Same as 1767. Rather worn.
	0.70g 9mm	Tel Aviv, KNM, no. K1344.
	6h	
1786.	O? - R?	Same as 1767. Worn.
	0.69g 9mm	Jerusalem, IM, no. 845; Elayi-Elayi, *NAC* 27, 1998,
	6h	pp. 131, no. 10 and 139, pl. I; *id.*, *Trésors*, p. 168, no. 6 and pl. XXVII (Akko hoard TXXXIV).
1787.	O? - R?	Same as 1767. Rather worn.
	0.62g 9mm	Jerusalem, IM, no. 839; Elayi-Elayi, *NAC* 27, 1998,

	6h	pp. 132, no. 14 and 139, pl. I; *id.*, *Trésors*, pp. 169-170, no. 19 and pl. XXVII (Akko hoard TXXXIV).
1788.	O? - R?	Same as 1767. Rather worn.
	0.60g 9mm	O: border of dots partly off the flan.
	5h	Shahaf coll., Haifa, no. 56; Elayi-Elayi, *NAC* 27, 1998, pp. 132, no. 17 and 139, pl. I.
1789.	O? - R?	Same as 1767. Rather worn.
	0.60g 9mm	O and R: no border.
	5h	Jerusalem, IM, no. 837; Elayi-Elayi, *NAC* 27, 1998, pp. 132, no. 15 and 139, pl. I; *id.*, *Trésors*, p. 170, no. 20 and pl. XXVII (Akko hoard TXXXIV).
1790.	O? - R?	Same as 1767. Rather worn.
	0.55g 9mm	O: border of dots partly off the flan.
	6h	Shahaf coll., Haifa, no. 53; Elayi-Elayi, *NAC* 27, 1998, pp. 132, no. 20 and 139, pl. I.
1791.	O? - R?	Same as 1767. Rather worn.
	0.54g 9mm	Jerusalem, IM, no. 832; Elayi-Elayi, *NAC* 27, 1998, pp. 133, no. 21 and 139, pl. I; *id.*, *Trésors*, p. 169, no. 10 and pl. XXVII (Akko hoard TXXXIV).
	6h	
1792.	O? - R?	Same as 1767. Worn.
	0.24g 9mm	R: head of lion?
	6h	Jerusalem, IM, no. 868; Elayi-Elayi, *Trésors*, p. 170 (Akko hoard TXXXIV).
1793.	0.44g 9mm	Same as 1767.
		Kindler, *ErIs* 8, 1967, p. 324, no. 22, not illustrated; Elayi-Elayi, *NAC* 27, 1998, p. 133, no. 25.

III.2.5. With dolphin to right and head of lion

1794.	O1* - R1*	O: dolphin to right; border of dots.
		R: head of lion *en face*, with prey; border of dots.
		Spink Numismatic Circular, 7, September 1992, no. 4828.
1795.	O? - R2*	Same as 1794. Rather worn.
	0.57g 9mm	O: dolphin to right?; border obscure.
		R: defect in field left.
		Jerusalem, IM, no. 844; Elayi-Elayi, *Trésors*, p. 169, no. 14 and pl. XXVII (Akko hoard TXXXIV).
1796.	O? - R3*	Same as 1794. Rather worn. Small cracks on the edge.
	0.36g 9mm	
		O: dolphin to right?
		Jerusalem, IM, no. 841; Elayi-Elayi, *Trésors*, p. 169, no. 17 and pl. XXVII (Akko hoard TXXXIV).
1797.	O? - R4*	Same as 1794. Rather worn.
	0.38g 8mm	O: dolphin to right?; border of dots partly off the

flan.
Jerusalem, IM, no. 842; Elayi-Elayi, *Trésors*, p. 169, no. 16 and pl. XXVII (Akko hoard TXXXIV).

1798. O? - R5* Same as 1794. Rather worn.
0.78g 8mm O: dolphin to right?
Jerusalem, IM, no. 836; Elayi-Elayi, *Trésors*, p. 169, no. 18 and pl. XXVII (Akko hoard TXXXIV).

1799. O? - R6* Same as 1794. Rather worn.
0.71g 10mm O: dolphin to right?
Jerusalem, IM, no. 838; Elayi-Elayi, *Trésors*, p. 168, no. 4 and pl. XXVII (Akko hoard TXXXIV).

1800. O? - R? Same as 1794. Worn.
0.90g 8mm O: dolphin to right?
Shahaf coll., Haifa, no. 52.

1801. O? - R? Same as 1794. Worn.
0.88g 10mm R: head of lion?
Kibboutz Ḥanita Museum, no. 206; Elayi-Elayi, *Trésors*, p. 346 and pl. XXXVII, 15.

1802. O? - R? Same as 1794. Worn.
0.62g 9mm O: dolphin to right?
R: head of lion?
Jerusalem, IM, no. 853; Elayi-Elayi, *Trésors*, p. 170, no. 21 and pl. XXVII (Akko hoard TXXXIV).

III.2.6. Uncertain bronze coins

1803. O1* - R1* O: seahorse with curled wing, to left; border of dots.
0.50g 9mm R: owl standing to left, head facing; over its right
3h shoulder, crook and flail; *M* in field left.
Tel Aviv, KNM, no. K1318 (from Akko).

1804. O? - R1 Same as 1803. Rather worn.
0.75g 11mm R: *M?* in field left.
12h Tel Aviv, KNM, no. K1307 (from Akko).

1805. O? - R? Same as 1803. Worn.
0.75g 10mm O: seahorse to left?
1h R: owl to left?
Tel Aviv, KNM, no. K1674 (from Akko).

1806. O? - R? O: seahorse to left, over dolphin; guilloche border.
0.49g 9mm R: owl standing to left; guilloche border.
Sheridan, *Numismatist* 8, 1971, p. 1131, no. 8, not illustrated; Elayi-Elayi, *Trésors*, p. 204, no. 22 (Beirut hoard TXLIII).

1807. O? - R? O: dolphin to left, over a shell; border of dots.
0.83g 9mm R: owl standing to left; border of dots.
Sheridan, *Numismatist* 8, 1971, p. 1131, no. 7, not

		illustrated; Elayi-Elayi, *Trésors*, p. 204, no. 21 (Beirut hoard TXLIII).
1808.	O? - R?	Same as 1807.
	0.79g 11mm	Sheridan, *Numismatist* 8, 1971, p. 1131, no. 5, not illustrated; Elayi-Elayi, *Trésors*, p. 204, no. 20 (Beirut hoard TXLIII).
1809.	O? - R?	O: dolphin to right; guilloche border?
	0.59g 8mm	R: owl standing to right, head facing; over his left shoulder, crook and flail; guilloche border? Jerusalem, IM, no. 3880.
1810.	0.66g 8mm	Same as 1807. Sheridan, *Numismatist* 8, 1971, p. 1131, no. 3, not illustrated; Elayi-Elayi, *Trésors*, p. 204, no. 18 (Beirut hoard TXLIII).
1811.	0.35g 7mm	Same as 1807. Sheridan, *Numismatist* 8, 1971, p. 1131, no. 12, not illustrated; Elayi-Elayi, *Trésors*, p. 204, no. 23 (Beirut hoard TXLIII).

4. Mint of Tyre?

1812.	0.69g 10mm 6h	AR.
		O: seahorse with curled wing, to left; border of dots.
		R: owl standing to left, head facing; over its right shoulder, crook and flail; $\overset{o}{Y}$? in field left; border of dots.
		Copenhagen, NatMus, no. KP 2346,13; Elayi-Elayi, *Trésors*, p. 238, no. 302 (Naplouse hoard TLI).
1813-		AR. Same as 1812.
1814.		R: unattested letter.
		Elayi-Elayi, *Trésors*, p. 238, no. 301 (Naplouse hoard TLI).

CHAPTER II

STUDY OF DIES AND RELATIVE CHRONOLOGY

This chapter is concerned with the numismatic analysis of the catalogue of Chapter I. We shall comment the die analysis including die couples and die links, and explain the arrangement proposed in this corpus, based on a relative chronology, by groups and by series.

1. Group I: Dolphin

I.1. Without incuse impression on the reverse

The whole of Group I is characterised by the obverse motif which is always, whatever the denomination may be, a dolphin to right, over lines of waves. But the number of these lines varies depending on the denomination: a triple line on the shekels (I.1.1), a double line on the quarters of shekel (I.1.2), and a single line on the three other denominations - sixteenths (I.1.3), halves of sixteenth (I.1.4) and tenths of sixteenth (I.1.5). In most cases, the number of crests on the lines of waves also seems to vary depending on the denomination: 6 crests on the shekels, 5 on the fourths of shekel, 3 on the sixteenths, 2 on the halves of sixteenth and 1 on the tenths of sixteenth. Moreover, the obverse legend is different for these five denominations: *ŠLŠN* on shekels, *MḤṢ PR(S)* on quarters of shekel, *MR* on sixteenths, two (?) illegible letters on halves of sixteenth and *Š* on tenths of sixteenth. The reverse motif is not always the same in the five denominations used in this group. The shekels (I.1.1), quarters of shekel (I.1.2), sixteenths (I.1.3) and tenths of sixteenth (I.1.5) have the same motif: an owl standing to the right, head facing, with crook and flail over its left shoulder, in a shallow incuse impression. Only the halves of sixteenth (I.1.4) have a rosette with eight petals. The choice of iconography was probably intended to keep the unity of the group by using the same motif on the obverse and, at the same time, to differentiate the denominations by the number of wavy lines on the obverse, by the legend and by a different reverse motif in Series I.1.4. Such a differentiation was necessary for the very small denominations, having close weights. However, it was difficult to distinguish the types of the coins of Series I.1.4 and I.1.5, the diameter of which being comprised between 7 and 4mm. One should note that, at the very beginning of the Tyrian coinage, the system of denominations seems to be complete.

In order to form a corpus, the die sequence must first be established because it is the sole valid organisation principle. The die sequence is determined by the die comparison method, developed by numismatists from the end of the 19th century.[1] Our first die analysis of Tyrian shekels with dolphin in 1992[2] has now been complemented by new specimens, new observations and a re-examination of dies. The die analysis is not relevant to Group I.1 as the five series contain only 3 to 7 coins. The series of shekels (I.1.1) is only represented by 7 coins[3] and we have identified 7 couples of dies and 5 obverse dies. R1 is linked with O1 and O2; O3 with R2, R3 and R4; R4 with O3 and O4 (Fig. 2). The ratio n/o = 1.4, which means that this series is insufficiently known.[4] The series of quarters of shekel (I.1.2) is only represented by 6 coins (out of a total number of 7): 6 couples of dies and 6 obverses. R1 is linked with O1 and O2; R2 with O3 and O4 (Fig. 3). The ratio n/o is still smaller (1.16). The series of sixteenths (I.1.3) is represented by 3 coins (out of 5): 3 couples of dies and 3 obverses, with O1-R1, O2-R2, O3-R3;[5] there is no link. It is the same for Series I.1.4 (3 coins out of 5). Series I.1.5 is represented by 1 coin (out of 3): 1 couple of dies and 1 obverse. The volume of Group I.1 issues is relatively small: only 28 coins (total number) for the five series, 20 couples of dies and 18 obverse dies.

We now have to explain why we have put Group I.1 at the beginning of Tyrian coinage. Some authors do not differentiate between the Tyrian dolphin series with the owl surrounded by a shallow incuse impression and the one that is not surrounded.[6] Most authors put the series with the incuse impression first, before the series without it.[7] We have shown that the series without incuse

---

1. For the first die study, cf. F. Imhoof-Blumer, 'Die Münzen Akarnaniens', *NZ*, 1878, pp. 1-186.
2. J. Elayi, 'Les sicles de Tyr au dauphin', *NAC* 21, 1992, pp. 37-49.
3. Number of coins concerned by the die analysis, out of the whole number of coins preserved.
4. n = number of coins studied. o = number of obverse dies. For calculating the number of coins manufactured from the number of coins preserved, cf. *infra*, Chapter V.6.
5. O4 is isolated since the reverse is indistinct.
6. Head, *Historia Numorum*, p. 799; *Catalogue De Luynes*, p. 157.
7. J. Rouvier, 'Numismatique des villes de la Phénicie: Tyr', *JIAN* 6, 1903, pp. 269-270; Babelon, *Traité* II/2, pp. 611-612; *id., Perses*, pp. CXC-CXCI, 290-291 ('Classement fondé sur l'étude du style et des lettres ou dates'); *BMC Phoenicia*, pp. cxxvi-cxxvii, 227; P. Naster, 'La technique des revers partiellement incus des monnaies phéniciennes', in *Centennial Publication of the American Numismatic Society*, New York 1958, pp. 503-506 (= *Scripta Nummaria*.

impression was the first one for several reasons that we shall develop again.[8] The so-called Jordan hoard (TLIII)[9] contains a single Tyrian shekel, without incuse impression and perfectly preserved, which means that it had been recently minted and probably at the very beginning of the Tyrian coinage as there are no other Tyrian coins in the hoard, in an area where such coins would have been expected. On the other hand, for the Byblian and Aradian coinages it is clear that the series with the incuse impression on the reverse were not the first ones, because of the standards, the evolution of the types and their presence in the hoards.[10] The relatively small number of preserved coins belonging to Group I.1 (28 coins) compared with the number of preserved coins for Group I.2 (217 coins) confirms this relative chronology. The two overstruck examples in Group I.2 (no. 79 and 204) are not sufficiently clear to be able to establish that they have been overstruck on coins of Group I.1. But we have found one very clear case of overstriking: coin no. 50 belonging to Group I.2 was overstruck on a coin belonging to Group I.1. The type of the obverse is surrounded by the usual cable border, and the border of dots of the previous coin can be seen on the left edge of the flan. On the reverse, on the left of the incuse owl, it is possible to see the head, crook and flail of the previous owl without incusion. This coin definitively establishes that Group I.2 followed Group I.1. There is no indication either on the coins or in the available documentation for identifying the first Tyrian king who started minting coinage.[11]

I.2. With incuse impression on the reverse

Here, as in Group I.1, the dolphin is here the only obverse motif. The number of wavy lines also varies depending on the denomination: a triple line on the shekels (I.2.1), a double line on the quarters of shekel (I.2.2) and on the eighth (?) (I.2.3), and one line on the sixteenths (I.2.4) and halves of sixteenth of shekel (I.2.5). The legend of the obverse is different in each of these five denominations: ŠLŠN on shekels, MḤṢ PR(S) on quarters of shekel and on eighths (?), MR on sixteenths and ḤY/M on halves of sixteenth. The reverse motif is the same owl standing to the right, head facing, with crook and flail over its left shoulder, in a shallow incuse square, but with an incuse impression

---

Contributions à la méthodologie numismatique, Louvain-la-Neuve 1983, pp. 22-24); Betlyon, *Coinage of Phoenicia*, pp. 39-43, 65, n. 25.

8. Elayi, *Sidon*, p. 198; *id., loc. cit.* (n. 2), pp. 42-44; Elayi-Elayi, *Monnayage de Sidon*, pp. 618-619.

9. C.M. Kraay and P.R.S Moorey, 'Two Fifth Century Hoards from the Near East', *RN* 10, 1968, pp. 209-210; Elayi-Elayi, *Trésors*, pp. 240-241. For the absolute chronology, cf. *infra*, Chapter VII.

10. See, for example, J. Elayi, 'Les monnaies de Byblos au sphinx et au faucon', *RSF* 11, 1983, pp. 5-17; *id., Phénomène monétaire*, pp. 22-23.

11. Cf. *id.*, 'An Updated Chronology of the Reigns of Phoenician Kings during the Persian Period (539-333 BCE)', *Trans* 32, 2006, pp. 21-25, 36-37, Table 2.

surrounding type. Only the halves of sixteenth have a lion's head to the right. The number of denominations would appear to be the same, but there is in fact a difference: the tenths of sixteenth were no longer represented, possibly because they were too small to be used easily, and the eighth of shekel, represented only by one coin (no. 222), is possibly a quarter of shekel with an erroneous weight since it has exactly the same characteristics. The legend ḤY/M of the halves of sixteenth could be the same as the illegible legend of Series I.1.4.

The die analysis can be performed for three of the five series. The series of shekels (I.2.1) is represented by 44 coins (out of a total number of 153); we have identified 41 couples of dies and 17 obverses dies (Fig. 4). There are three groups of coins interlinked, presented here by decreasing number of size. In the first one, O1 is linked with R1, R2, R3 and R4; O2 with R4; O3 with R2, R4, R5, R6, R7 and R8; O4 with R8, R9 and R10; O5 with R3 and R11; O6 with R10, R11, R12 and R13; O7 with R13: therefore O1 to O7 are linked together and R1 to R13 are also linked together. In the second group, O8 is linked with R14 and R15; O9 with R15 and R16; O10 with R16, R17 and R18; O11 with R17 and R19; O12 with R19: therefore O8 to O12 are linked together and R14 to R19 are linked too. In the third group, O13 is linked with R20, R21, R22 and R23; O14 with R23, R24 and R25; O15 with R25: thus O13, O14 and O15 are linked together, and R20 to R25 the same. There are still two isolated pairs of dies: O16-R26 and O17-R27. It can be seen that some obverse dies have been used a lot: O3 with 6 reverse dies; O1, O6 and O13 with 4 reverse dies. The ratio n/o = 2.82, which means that this series is better known than Series I.1.1.

The series of quarters of shekel (I.2.2) is represented by 17 coins (out of 40), that is 16 couples of dies and 13 obverse dies (Fig. 5). O1 is linked with R1, R2 and R3; R4 with O2 and O3; O4 with R5 and R6: therefore R1, R2 and R3 are linked together; this is the same for O2 and O3, and for R5 and R6. The other pairs of dies are isolated: O5-R7, O6-R8, O7-R9, O8-R10, O9-R11, O10-R12, O11-R13, O12-R14, and O13-R15. The ratio n/o of this series, insufficiently known, is 1.30. The series of sixteenths of shekel (I.2.4) is represented by 8 coins (out of 16), with 8 couples of dies and 6 obverse dies (Fig. 6). O1 is linked with R1 and R2; O2 with R2 and R3, which means that R1 and R2 are linked together, and also R2 and R3. The other pairs of dies are isolated: O3-R3, O4-R4, O5-R5, and O6-R6. The ratio n/o = 1.33. The series of halves of sixteenth of shekel (I.2.5) is only represented by 4 coins (out of 7), with 4 couples of dies and 4 obverse dies (n/o = 1).

The volume of Group I.2 issues is not very abundant, albeit much more abundant than Group I.1: 217 coins (total number) for the five series (instead of 28), 73 couples of dies (instead of 20) and 41 obverse dies (instead of 18). J. Rouvier had attributed Group I.2, which he placed at the beginning of the Tyrian coinage, to a king 'Sirom' or 'Hiram' because of his misreading of the legend.[12] We have no idea as to the identity of the king who minted Group I.2;[13] he was possibly different from the king who started minting coinage; anyway, he probably belonged to the same dynasty because there was no change at all in the types.

2. Group II: Deity riding on seahorse

II.1. Phoenician standard

II.1.1. Anepigraphic coins

An important change occurred in the obverse types of Group II: instead of the dolphin as a main motif, there was a deity holding an arched bow and riding on seahorse, over two lines of waves and a small dolphin. We have classified three denominations in Group II: shekels, fourths of shekel and sixteenths. There were also other denominations but, in the present state of documentation, we have put them together in Group III (Unclassified series) because we do not have enough information to be able to classify them more precisely. The number of lines of waves and of crests is not so precisely linked to a particular denomination as in Group I; it depends more on the engravers' choice. Thus, we can find two lines both on the shekels and on the fourths and sixteenths of shekel; most of the time, there are two lines, with six to four crests. The sixteenths of shekel bear only the seahorse without the deity and the dolphin, probably because of the lack of space. On the other hand, the reverse motif was the same for the three denominations, as in Group I: an owl standing to right, head facing, with crook and flail over its left shoulder, with no more incuse impression surrounding type.

We have divided Group II into two parts depending on the standard: II.1 (Phoenician standard) and II.2 ('Attic' standard): this order is generally accepted. The main difficulty consisted in the arrangement of the series within each of these two parts. As far as coins following the Phoenician standard are concerned, J. Rouvier proposed 'Groups IV and V' for thick fabric anepigraphic series, 'Group VI' for flat fabric anepigraphic series, 'Groups VII to X' for all inscribed series.[14] B.V. Head only knew the flat fabric series.[15] E. Babelon proposed three groups: thick fabric inscribed or anepigraphic, thick fabric with numbers, flat fabric anepigraphic.[16] G.F. Hill and J. Babelon proposed two groups: thick fabric and flat fabric.[17] J.W. Betlyon proposed two series: Series

12. Rouvier, *loc. cit.* (n. 7), p. 269.
13. Cf. Elayi, *loc. cit.* (n. 11), *ibid.*
14. Rouvier, *loc. cit.* (n. 7), pp. 271-274.
15. Head, *Historia Numorum*, p. 799.
16. Babelon, *Perses*, pp. CXC-CXCI, 292-294.
17. *BMC Phoenicia*, pp. cxxvi-cxxix, 229 (no. 11-18), 230 (no. 19-24); Babelon, *op. cit.* (n. 6), pp. 158-159, no. 3212-3215 and 3216-3220.

3 including coins with letters *M* and *MB*, Series 4 including coins with thick and flat fabric, numbers and various uncertain denominations.[18]

Almost all the authors had placed the beautiful flat fabric series after the clumsy thick fabric series, interpreting the evolution as representative of technical progress. For example, E. Babelon wrote concerning the flat fabric series: 'le style des pièces est plus récent, le flan est plus large, plat et beaucoup moins épais; les bords sont réguliers. Ces pièces sont très abondantes; il n'y a dans le champ ni lettres ni dates'.[19] According to G.F. Hill, 'the thick lumpy fabric was discarded for a flatter make of coin, just as happened at Aradus'.[20] P. Naster, without classifying the flat fabric series, had made this interesting observation: 'cette série ... de gravure fine ..., dont la chouette se rapproche des toutes premières au contour creux, et dont les lignes des ondes de la mer sont triples comme sur ces mêmes pièces, doivent certainement être situées assez près de celles-là, pareillement sans chiffres'.[21]

The die analysis showed that O37 (thick fabric) is linked with O28 to O36 (flat fabric) by means of R37. This means that the thick fabric coins and the flat fabric coins followed each other but we ignore in which order. The flat fabric coins were minted first for the following reasons. Two arguments were already given by P. Naster: on the one hand, the delicacy of the engraving and the careful manufacturing of the series are similar to the previous two series with dolphin I.1.1 and I.2.1.[22] However, his third argument according to which there is an intermediate coin between Series I.2.1 and II.1.1.1 is not valid because this coin belongs to Series I.1.1 and not to Series I.2.1 (coin no. 1 of our catalogue). There are other arguments confirming that the flat fabric coins come immediately after Series I.2.1. First, the style of representation of the owl with a rather thick body, a large wing and short legs is the same as in the two previous series, mainly in Series I.1.1. It differs from the owl of the following series which is thinner and slender, with a narrower wing and longer legs. Another argument is given by a coin of Series II.1.1.1 (flat fabric), with the deity riding on seahorse on the obverse and the standing owl on the reverse, partly surrounded by an incuse impression (no. 294). This feature means that the engraver was in the habit of using this kind of technique, or in other words that this coin is chronologically very close to Series I.2.1. The new classification that we propose (Series I.1.1, Series I.2.1 and Series II.1.1.1) explains the content of the Tell

---

18. Betlyon, *Coinage of Phoenicia*, pp. 44-52.
19. Babelon, *Perses*, pp. CXC-CXCI; *id.*, *Traité*, pp. 610 sqq.
20. *BMC Phoenicia*, p. cxxviii. In a previous publication, we had followed him: Elayi-Elayi, *Trésors*, p. 183.
21. P. Naster, 'Le développement des monnayages phéniciens avant Alexandre, d'après les trésors', in A. Kindler ed., *The patterns of monetary development in Phoenicia and Palestine in Antiquity. International Numismatic Convention, Jerusalem, 27-31 December 1963*, Tel Aviv 1967, pp. 3-4 (= *Scripta Nummaria, Contributions à la méthodologie numismatique*, Louvain-la-Neuve 1983, p. 188).
22. *Ibid.*

Abu Hawam hoard TXXXV which was difficult to understand.[23] As a matter of fact, this hoard contains a sequence of all Tyrian series of Phoenician standard: one worn coin of thick fabric and anepigraphic, several coins with letters, numbers, letters and numbers, then series of 'Attic' standard until c. 337 (*13*). When the flat fabric series was expected after the thick fabric series, its absence had to be explained in the hoard, for example by selecting the most beautiful large fabric coins.[24] Now, the explanation is clear: the flat fabric coins were not represented in this hoard because they were older and the hoarding started with the thick fabric coins. The last argument is provided by the chronological markers of Sidonian coinage: some associations between Tyrian and Sidonian coins in hoards are meaningful in this respect. Thus a flat fabric Tyrian coin is associated in the hoard TLXI with a double shekel issued by King ʿAbdamon who reigned during the last quarter of the 5th century, just before Baʿana's reign (409/406-402).[25]

The degradation of the style of engraving and manufacturing was progressive and it was impossible to clearly distinguish thick fabric coins from large fabric coins because of several intermediate coins. That is why we have assembled all these coins in Series II.1.1.1 with the following order: II.1.1.1.a (flat fabric), II.1.1.1.b (thick fabric) and II.1.1.1.c (rather indistinct). This series of shekels (II.1.1.1) is represented by 92 coins (out of 153); we have identified 78 couples of dies and 53 obverses dies (Fig. 7). There are seven groups of couples of dies interlinked, six comprising flat fabric coins, and one comprising thick fabric coins. We have classified the first five groups by decreasing number of pairs of dies; then we have placed the isolated pairs of dies and then the sixth group, because it is linked with the thick fabric coins. In the first group of couples of dies, O1 is linked with R1; O2 with R1 and R2; O3 with R1; O4 with R1; O5 with R2; O6 with R2 and R3; O7 with R2 and R4; O8 with R4; O9 with R4: therefore O1 to O9 are linked together, and it is the same for R1 to R4. It can be seen that the reverse dies R1 and R2 have been much used (each of them with 4 obverse dies). In the second group, O10 is linked with R5 and R6; O11 with R6 and R8; O12 with R6 and R7; O13 with R9 and R10; O14 with R10: thus O10, O11 and O12 are linked together, just as R5 to R8. In the third group, O13 is linked with R9 and R10; O14 with R10: therefore O13 and O14 are linked together, just as R9 and R10. In the fourth group, O15 is linked with R11 and R12, linked together. In the fifth group, O16 and O17 are linked with R13, and therefore linked together. Then we have 10 isolated couples of dies: O18-R14, O19-R15, O20-R16, O21-R17, O22-R18, O23-R19, O24-R20, O25-R21, O26-R22, and O27-R23. In the sixth group, O28 is linked with R24, R25 and

---

23. Elayi-Elayi, *Trésors*, pp. 170-185. Cf. *id.*, 'Une série énigmatique de beaux sicles de Tyr', in *ACFP* VI, Lisbonne 2005 (in press).
24. *Id.*, *Trésors*, pp. 183-184.
25. *Ibid.*, pp. 265-266; *id.*, *Monnayage de Sidon*, p. 853. On absolute chronology, see below, Chapter VII. On the reasons of this manufacturing degradation, cf. Chapter V.

R26; O29 with R26 and R27; O30 with R28 and R29; O31 with 5 reverse dies: R25, R28, R30, R31 and R33; O32 with R31, R32 and R5; O33 with R32 and R33; O34 with R33 and R34; O35 with R35, R36 and R37; O36 and O37 with R37. This means that O28 to O37 are linked together, just as R24 to R37, and thus thick fabric coins are linked with large fabric coins. In the seventh group (thick fabric), O38 is linked with R38; O39 with R38 and R39; O40 with R39 and R40: therefore O38 to O40 on the one hand and R38 to R40 on the other hand are linked together. In the eighth group, O41 is linked with R41 and R42, linked consequently together. Then we have 12 isolated couples of dies: O42-R43, O43-R44, O44-R45, O45-R46, O46-R47, O47-R48, O48-R49, O49-R50, O50-R51, O51-R52, O52-R53, and O53-R54. The ratio n/o = 1.71, which means that this series is insufficiently known.

The series of quarters of shekel (II.1.1.2) is represented by 17 coins (out of 28), that is 16 couples of dies and 8 obverse dies (Fig. 8). O1 is linked with R1, R2 and R3; O2 with R3 and R4; O3 with 5 reverse dies: R4, R5, R6, R7 and R8; O4 with R8 and R9. Therefore O1 to O4 are linked together, and also R1 to R9. Four pairs of dies are isolated: O5-R10, O6-R11, O7-R12, and O8-R13. The ratio n/o = 2, that is little bit higher than the ratio of the previous series. Why can we consider the anepigraphic quarters of shekel of Series II.1.1.2 as a denomination of Series II.1.1.1? They are exactly identical in every respect except for their size and weight; moreover their weight follows the Phoenician standard and this denomination is not minted after that.

The series of sixteenths of shekel (II.1.1.3) is not similar to the shekels of Series II.1.1.1 and quarters of shekels of Series II.1.1.2, because the deity riding on seahorse to right is replaced by a seahorse alone to left, the guilloche border is replaced by a border of dots, and the owl of the reverse is standing to left and not to right. Why do we consider this series as a denomination of Series II? As will be shown later, the anepigraphic Series II.1.1.3 is linked with the inscribed Series II.1.2.2, which is a denomination of the shekel of Series II.1.2.1, which followed Series II.1.1.1. We first analyse the die sequence of the anepigraphic sixteenths of shekels (II.1.1.3); we shall analyse the continuation of the die sequence with a continuous numbering (II.1.2.2) after Series II.1.2.1, in order to follow the chronological order of our catalogue. The anepigraphic sixteenths taken into account for die analysis are 48 (out of 182); we have identified 52 couples of dies and 36 obverse dies (Fig. 9). We have identified four groups of couples of dies without links with Series II.1.2.1 and four groups linked with this series. In the first group, O1 is linked with R1 and R2; O2 with R2 and R3; O3 with R3; O4 with R3: therefore O1 to O4 are linked together, and also R1 to R3. In the second group, O5 is linked with R4, R5 and R6; O6 with R6 and R7; O7 with R8 and R9; O8 with R9: it means that O5 to O8 are linked together just as R4 to R9. In the third group, O9 is linked with R10 and R11; O10 with R11; O11 and O12 with R12: therefore O9 to O12 are linked together, and also R10 to R12. In the fourth group, O13 is linked with R13 and R14, consequently linked together. Then we have 17 isolated couples of dies: O14-R15, O15-R16, O16-R17, O17-R18, O18-R19, O19-R20, O20-R21, O21-R22, O22-R23, O23-R24, O24-R25, O25-R26, O26-R27, O27-R28, O28-R29, O29-R30, and O30-R31. In the last four groups, O31 is linked with R32 (anepigraphic) and R65 (inscribed), linked together. O32 is linked with R33 (anepigraphic) and R50 (inscribed), linked together. O34 is linked with R35 (anepigraphic); O35 with R35, R36 and R37 (anepigraphic); O36 with R37 (anepigraphic) and R39 (inscribed): therefore O34, O35 and O36 are linked together, just as R35, R36, R37 and R39. The ratio n/o = 1.44, this series being insufficiently known.

The volume of issues of Group II.1.1 (anepigraphic) is markedly more abundant than the previous Group I.2, based on the preserved coins: 367 coins (total number) for the three series (instead of 216), 140 couples of dies[26] (instead of 73), and 97 obverse dies (instead of 41). The increase in volume is all the more important as these results have to be broadened to encompass part of Group III (Unclassified series of denominations).

II.1.2. Inscribed coins

The inscribed Series II.1.2 is close to the anepigraphic Series II.1.1 (thick fabric) as far as the type, engraving and manufacturing are concerned; it followed (and not preceded) this series because the sixteenths of shekel of Series II.1.2.2 were minted after Series II.1.1.3 with which they are linked as we have seen. The main difficulty consisted in classifying the coins bearing different inscriptions. We have found no consistent argument in the bibliography and the coins of these series found in excavations and hoards provide no help on this subject. We tried to concentrate on die analysis and metrology, but the results were not very conclusive. The main difficulty consisted in classifying the series bearing letters (*M, MB, B, ṢR* and ʿ). We had tentatively placed these series at the end of the coins aligned on the Phoenician standard because of the occurrence of the letter *M* at the beginning of the following series II.2.1.1-5, and because the anepigraphic series and the series with numbers were linked together[27]. The consequence of this classification was, because of an interruption in the dating of issues, the attribution to Sidon of the inauguration of a regular yearly dating in 372 BCE. However, the analyses of the metallic composition of Tyrian coins now provide new information[28]. Series II.1.2.1.a (with *M*) takes place within a process of a progressive decrease in the percentage of silver:

---

26. In Series II.1.1.3, we do not consider the 6 pairs of dies formed with reverses of Series II.1.2.2.

27. Cf. J. Elayi, 'The Tyrian Monetary Inscriptions of the Persian Period', *Trans* 34, 2007, pp. 76-79.

28. Cf. A.G. Elayi, J.-N. Barrandon and J. Elayi, 'The Change of Standard of Tyrian Silver Coinage about 357 BCE as Determined by Fast Neutron Activation Analysis' (forthcoming).

from about 99-98% in Series I.2 to 96-94% in Series II.1, 84-66% in Series II.1.2.1.a, 70-68% in Series II.1.2.1.f-v, and finally coming back to 99-98% in Series II.2 at the same time as the change of standard. Therefore Series II.1.2.1.a (with *M*) follows the anepigraphic Series II.1.1 (thick fabric). Since coins with *MB* and *B* are linked together, we propose to place first coins with *M* according to our interpretation: king *M* reigning alone, then associating the crown-prince *B* to his power, then king *B* reigned alone. We have tentatively placed after them two series also bearing letters, represented only by three coins: Series II.1.2.1.d (with *ṢR*) and II.1.2.1.e (with ʿ). There is still a difficulty: the die links between the sixteenths of shekel of Series II.1.1.3 (anepigraphic) and Series II.1.2.2.b-i (with a number, and letter *Z* + number). Both of these series of sixteenths correspond, as we have seen, to the series of shekels (II.1.1.1.b and II.1.2.1.f-t). The results of the metallic analyses force us to place Series II.1.2.2.a (with *M*), which was probably a very short one as only two coins are preserved between the linked series of sixteenths. It may be that, besides this short series, the anepigraphic series of sixteenths (II.1.1.3) was still in use, at the same time as shekels inscribed *M*, *MB*, *B*, *ṢR* and ʿ, which were probably minted during a short period as only 48 coins are preserved. In the present state of documentation, this hypothesis for classifying these series seems to be the most likely.

The second problem consisted in interpreting the inscription *20* to *34* or *Z* to *Z14*: *Z* + number seems to be more likely as *Z* is separated from the number on the sixteenths of shekel (II.1.2.2) and because a sequence of *1* to *10*, and *20* to *34*, separated by a lack of 10 years, is somewhat difficult to explain. Since coins inscribed *1* are linked with coins inscribed *Z5* in Series II.1.2.2, the sequence is the following: *1* to *10*, then *Z* to *Z14*. Consequently, we have proposed the following classification, which needs to be confirmed: coins with *M* (II.1.2.1.a), coins with *MB* (II.1.2.1.b), coins with *B* (II.1.2.1.c), coins with *ṢR* (II.1.2.1.d), coins with ʿ (II.1.2.1.e), coins with *1* to *10* (II.1.2.1.f-k), coins with *Z* to *Z14* (II.1.2.1.l-t) and coins with *T4* and *T6* (II.2.1.1.u-v). In order to detect any possible interlinkage and because there is no information on the identity of the minting authority (kings? *M*, *B*, city of *ṢR*, kings? ʿ, *Z* and *T*), we were obliged to place the dies of all these coins together.

The series of shekels II.1.2.1 is represented by 55 coins (out of 101); we have identified 47 couples of dies and 33 obverse dies (Fig. 10).[29] 16 couples of dies have been identified for coins inscribed *M*: O1 is linked with R1, R2 and 3; O2 with R3, R4 and R5; therefore O1 and O2 are linked together, just as R1 to R5. O3 is linked with R6, R7 and R8; O4 with R8; thus O3 and O4 are linked together, just as R6, R7 and R8. O5 is linked with R9 and R10, linked also together. Then there are 4 isolated couples of dies: O6-R11, O7-R12, O8-R13, and O9-R14. O10 is linked with R15, inscribed *MB*, and O11 is also

---

29. We do not count re-cut dies as new dies.

linked with R15 and with R16, inscribed *B*: therefore O10 and O11 are linked together, just as R15 and R16, and the inscriptions *MB* and *B* are linked in one order or another. We have selected the sequence *M, MB, B* because of our interpretation.[30] For coins inscribed *ṢR*, there is one pair of dies: O12 linked with R17. For shekels bearing the number *1*, 4 isolated couples of dies have been preserved: O13 linked with R18, O14 with R19, O15 with R20 and O16 with R21. For coins inscribed *2*, there is only one pair of dies: O17 linked with R22. For coins inscribed *3*, 4 obverse dies have been preserved: O18 linked with R23, O19 and O20 with R24: therefore O19 and O20 are linked together. The obverse coin O21 is interesting because it is linked with R25' (R25 with number *2* re-cut by adding a vertical stroke for number *3*); R25 is not listed in fig. 10 because the corresponding obverse is rather indistinct. Moreover, O11 is linked with R26, R27 and R28 (inscribed *3*), and with R27' (R27 with number *3* re-cut for number *4*). Therefore R25, R25', R26, R27, R28 and R27' are linked together, that is coins bearing numbers *2, 3, 4* and *5*. There are 2 isolated pairs of coins: O22-R29 and O23-R30 (with number *4*). For coins inscribed *Z3*, there are 2 couples of dies: O24 linked with R31; O25 with R32 and also R33 (inscribed *Z4*): therefore R32 and R33 are linked together, just as coins inscribed *Z3* and *Z4*. The obverse coin O26 is also interesting since it is linked with R33 (*Z4*) and R34 (*Z5*), linking them together. O27 is linked with R35 (inscribed *Z10*); O28 with R36 (inscribed *Z11*); O29 is also linked with R36. Therefore O27, O28 and O29 are linked together, just as R35 and R36 and the inscriptions *Z10* and *Z11*. For coins inscribed *Z13*, we have identified only one couple of dies: O30 linked with R37, just as for coins inscribed *Z14*: O31 linked with R38. For coins inscribed *T6*, 2 isolated pairs of dies are preserved: O32 linked with R39, and O33 with R40. The ratio n/o = 1.42, which means that this series is insufficiently known: as a matter of fact, it covered several successive reigns and a long and difficult period as we shall see.

The inscribed sixteenths of shekel of Series II.1.2.2 present the same problems as the inscribed shekels of Series II.1.2.1. The analysis of dies follows the anepigraphic sixteenths of Series II.1.1.3 with which they are linked. The sixteenths taken into account for dies analysis are 38 (out of 80); we have identified 33 couples of dies and 28 obverses dies (Fig. 9). For coins inscribed *M*, there is one pair of dies: O37 linked with R38. For coins inscribed *1*, there are 9 couples of dies: R39 linked with O36 and anepigraphic coins; O38 linked with R40 and R41, linked together; O39 linked with R42; O40 with R43; O41 with R44; O42 linked with R45, R67 and R68 (inscribed *Z5*): therefore R45, R67 and R68 are linked together, just as coins inscribed *1* and coins inscribed *Z5*. For coins inscribed *2* above crook and flail, there are 7 couples of dies: O33 is linked with R44' (R44 with number *1* re-cut by adding a vertical stroke for number *2*) and R46, thus linked together and with the anepigraphic sixteenths;

---

30. Cf. *infra*, Chapter III.

O43 is linked with R44'; O44 is linked with R44' and R50 (inscribed *2* below crook and flail), therefore R44' and R50 are linked together, just as coins with *1, 2* above and *2* below; O45 is linked with R47; O46 with R48. For coins inscribed *2* below (linked with anepigraphic coins and coins with *2* above), there are 11 pairs of dies: O32 is linked with R49, and O33 with R50, thus linked together and with the anepigraphic sixteenths; 8 pairs are isolated: O47-R51, O48-R52, O49-R53, O50-R54, O51-R55, O52-R56, O53-R57, and O54-R58. For coins inscribed *10*, there are 7 couples of dies: O55 is linked with R59 and R60, thus linked together; O56 and O57 are linked with R61, and therefore linked together; O58 is linked with R62; O59 with R63; O60 with R64. For coins inscribed *Z4*, O61 and O62 are linked with R66, and therefore linked together. For coins inscribed *Z5* (linked with coins inscribed *1*), O63 is linked with R69; O64 with R70. The ratio n/o = 1.17 for this insufficiently known series. The volume of issues of Group II.1.2 (inscribed) has considerably decreased compared with the abundant Group II.1.1 (anepigraphic): 183 coins (instead of 367), 86 couples of dies (instead of 140), and 61 obverse dies (instead of 97); however, some unclassified denominations must be added to the shekels. This important decrease will be explained later in Chapter VII.

II.2. 'Attic' standard

II.2.1.1-13. Inscribed shekels

It is generally admitted that the Tyrian coinage conforming to the 'Attic' standard followed the coinage conforming to the Phoenician standard, the difference between scholars concerning only its dating.[31] We have divided these coins into two series: II.2.1.1-13, which includes all the coins bearing different letters and numbers, and II.2.1.14-29, attributed to the last king of Tyre, ʿOzmilk/Azemilkos.[32] We have only classified shekels as it was impossible to attribute any of the denominations series assembled in Group III with any confidence. The main difficulty consisted in classifying the coins bearing different inscriptions. There are roughly two groups of legends: with *M* and with *Ṣ*, that are linked together, but without knowing which one was the first. Therefore we have tentatively proposed placing the coins with *M* at the beginning of the series: *B1M* (II.2.1.1), *M2* (II.2.1.2), *M2ʾ* (II.2.1.3), *M3* (II.2.1.4), *M3ʾ* (II.2.1.5). Then, with the help of interlinkage, we place coins with *Ṣ*: *1Ṣ* (II.2.1.6), *2Ṣ* (II.2.1.7), *3Ṣ* (II.2.1.8), *ʿ3Ṣ* (II.2.1.9); *4Ṣ* (II.2.1.10). We were obliged to consider the dies of all these coins together in order to detect interlinkage and because there is no information on the minting authority (kings *M*, ʾ, ʿ, *Ṣ* or city of Tyre?). We placed coins with *Ṣ* and unclear figures apart,

---

31. Cf. *supra*, n. 7. The problem of dating will be examined in Chapter VII.
32. Cf. *infra*, Chapters III and VII.

likewise those that had the inscription obliterated, and with *4* and reverse type to left (II.2.1.11-13).

The series of shekels II.2.1.1-13 is represented by 48 coins (out of 91); we have identified 48 couples of dies and 31 obverse dies (Fig. 11). For shekels bearing *B1M*, 11 couples of dies have been preserved: O1 is linked with R1 to R5, therefore linked together; O2 is linked with R5, R6 and R7, linked together; O3 is linked with R7; O4 with R5 and R30 linked together just as O1, O2, O3, O4 and O22, and coins with *B1M* and *3Ṣ*. It is worth stating that O1 has been used with five reverse dies. For coins inscribed *M2*, there are 8 isolated pairs of dies: O5-R8, O6-R9, O7-R10, O8-R11, O9-R12, O10-R13, O11-R14, and O12-R15. We have identified 2 isolated pairs of dies for coins inscribed *M2'*: O13-R16, and O14-R17. For coins inscribed *M3*, there are 5 pairs of dies: O15-R18, O16-R19, O17-R20, and O18 linked with R21 and R22, linked together just as coins with *M3* and *M3Ṣ*. Besides this last link, O19 is linked with R23 (inscribed *M3Ṣ*) and R24 (inscribed *1Ṣ*), which means that these are also linked together. For coins inscribed *1Ṣ*, besides the previous link, we have O20 linked with R25. For coins inscribed *2Ṣ*, we have identified one obverse coin only: O21, linked with R26, R27 and R28 (inscribed *2Ṣ*), with R24' (R24 with *1Ṣ* recut by adding two vertical strokes for *3Ṣ*) and with R29 (inscribed *3Ṣ*), linked therefore together. For coins inscribed *3Ṣ*, besides the three mentioned links with coins inscribed *B1M*, *1Ṣ* and *2Ṣ*, O22 is linked with R30 (linked with O4 as mentioned above); O23 is linked with R31 and R32, linked together; O24 is linked with R33. For coins inscribed *4Ṣ*, there are 6 couples of dies: O25 is linked with R34 and R35, thus linked together; O26 and O27 are linked with R36, and also together; O28 is linked with R37; O29 with R38. For coins inscribed *4*, there are 2 isolated pairs: O30-R39 and O31-R40. The ratio n/o = 1.54 for this insufficiently known series. The volume of issues of Group II.2.1.1-13 has still decreased compared with the previous Group II.1.2: 91 coins (instead of 183), 48 couples of dies (instead of 86), and 31 obverse dies (instead of 61); however, some unclassified denominations have to be added to the shekels. We shall explain in Chapter VII why this decrease went on.

II.2.14-29. ʿOzmilk's shekels

The series of King Ozmilk's shekels (II.2.1.14-29) is represented by 268 coins (out of 653); we have identified 210 couples of dies and 102 obverse dies (Fig. 12). This series is regularly dated by the regnal years starting from year *3*. For year *3*, there are 10 obverse dies and 24 couples of dies: the first 3 are isolated (O1-R1, O2-R2, and O3-R3), then 21 are linked together and with coins of year 4. O4 is linked with R4 and R5; O5 with R5; O6 with R5 to R9; O7 with R5 and R16 (year *4*); O8 with R10; O9 with R10, R17 and R18 (year *4*); O10 with R9 to R15. Therefore, O4 to O10 are linked together, just as R4 to R11 (year *3*) and R12 to R18 (year *4*). The obverse coin O10 has been used with 7 reverse dies. For year *4*, 5 obverse dies have been preserved with 6 couples of dies (besides the 7 already mentioned): O11 is linked with R18; O12 with R18 and R19, thus linked together; O13 with R20; O14 with R21; O15 with R22. For year *5*, there are 4 obverse dies and 4 isolated pairs of dies: O16-R23, O17-R24, O18-R25, and O19-R26. For year *6*, there are only 2 obverse dies and 3 pairs of dies: O20 linked with R27 and R28, linked also together; O21 linked with R29. For year *7*, there are 8 obverse dies and 16 couples of dies: O22 is linked with R27' (R27 with *6* re-cut by adding a vertical stroke for *7*) and R30, linked together just as year *6* and year *7*; O23 is linked with R31, R32 and R33, linked together; O24 with R34, R35 and R36, linked together; O25 with R37; O26 with R38; O27 with R39; O28 with R40, R41 and R42, linked together; O29 is also linked with R42 (year *7*) and R49 (year *9*), linked therefore together. For year *8*, 6 obverse dies and 7 couples of dies have been preserved: O30 linked with R43; O31 with R43 and R44, thus linked together; O32 with R45; O34 with R47; O35 with R48. For year *9*, we have 12 obverse dies and 31 couples of dies (plus one linked with year *7*): O36 is linked with R49 and R50, linked together; O37 with R51 and R52; O38 with R52 to R55; O39 with R53 to R57; therefore O37, O38 and O39 are linked together and the same for R51 to R57. O40 is linked with R58 to R61; O41 with R58 to R61: therefore O40 and O41 are linked together, just as R58 to R62. O42 is linked with R63, R64 and R65, linked together; O43 is also linked with R65; O44 is linked with R66 and R67 (linked together); O45 with R68 and R69 (linked together); O46 with R70 and R71 (linked together); O47 with R72.

For year *10*, there are 11 obverse dies and 19 couples of dies: O48 linked with R73, R74 and R75; O49 with R75, R76 and R77; R50 with R75, R77 and R78; thus O48, O49 and O50 are linked together, just as R73 to R78. O51 is linked with R79 and R80; O52 with R80: thus O51 is linked with O52, and R79 with R80. O53 is linked with R81; O54 with R81 and R82: thus O53 and O54 are linked together, just as R81 and R82. Then O55 is linked with R83; O56 with R84; O57 with R85; O58 with R86. For year *11*, 4 obverse coins and 6 pairs of dies have been preserved: O59 linked with R86' (R86 with *10* re-cut by adding a vertical stroke for *11*), thus linking years *10* and *11*; O60 with R86' and R87, linked together, just as O59 and O60; O61 with R88; O62 with R89 and R90 (linked together). For year *12*, there are 7 obverse dies and 19 couples of dies preserved: O63 is linked with 6 reverse dies, R90' (R90 with *11* re-cut by adding a vertical stroke for *12*), R91, R92, R93, R94 and R95; O64 with R95 and R96; therefore O63 and O64 are linked together, just as R90' to R96. O65 is linked with R97; O66 with R98, R99 and R100 (linked together); O67 with R101, R102 and R103; O68 with R103 and R106: thus O67 and O68 are linked together, just as R101 to R104; O69 is linked with R105 (year *12*) and R106 (year *13*), linked therefore together. For year *13*, there are 6 obverse dies and 13 couples of dies (besides the one linked with year *12*): O70 is linked with

R106; O71 with R107; O72 with R108; O73 with R108 to R112; O74 with R112 to R115: thus O72, O73 and O74 are linked together just as R108 to R115; O75 is linked with R116 (year *13*) and R117 (year *14*), thus linked together. For year *14*, 5 obverse dies and 13 couples of dies have been preserved (plus one linked with year *13*): O76 is linked with R111' (R111 with *13* re-cut by adding a vertical stroke for *14*), R118 and R119; O77 with R119 and R120: thus O76 and O77 are linked together, just as R111', R118, R119 and R120. O78 is linked with 6 reverse dies (R121 to R126, linked together); O79 with R127; O80 with R128.

For year *15*, there are 17 obverse dies and 42 couples of dies: O81 to O87 are linked respectively with R129 to R135; O88 with R136 and R137 (linked together); O89 with R138 and R139 (linked together); O90 with R140 to R144 (linked together); O91 with R145 to R148; O92 also with R148: thus O91 and O92 are linked together, just as R145 to R148. O93 is linked with R149 to R152; O94 with R152, R153, R154 and R160; O95 with R155 to R158; O96 with R158 and R159; O97 with R158 to R164 (year *15*) and R165 (year *16*): therefore O93 to O97 are linked together, just as R149 to R165. For year *16*, there are 4 obverse dies and 6 pairs of dies (besides the one linked with year *15*): O98 is linked with R152' (R152 with *15* re-cut by adding a vertical stroke for *16*); O99 with R166 and R167; O100 with R167 and R168: thus O99 and O100 are linked together, just as R166 to R168; R101 is linked with R169. Only one obverse die and one pair of dies are preserved for year *17*: O102 linked with R170.

We would point out that five coins in this series are re-cut (R27', R86', R90', R111' and R152') and that O97 has been used with 7 reverse dies, O10, O63 and O78 with 6 reverse dies, and O6, O39, O73, O90 with 5 reverse dies. The ratio n/o = 2.05 for the whole series which is better known than the others. The ratio is higher for certain years: 2.71 (year 12), 2.60 (year 14), 2.58 (year 9), 2.47 (year 15), 2.40 (year 3). The volume of issues for the ʿOzmilk's shekels (II.2.1.14-29) is by far the most abundant of the whole of Tyrian coinage: 653 coins (instead of 91 for the previous series), 210 couples of dies (instead of 48), and 102 obverse dies (instead of 31); moreover this total does not include some unclassified series. We shall explain the reasons for this spectacular increase in Chapter VII.

3. Group III: Unclassified series

III.1. Silver series

As a precaution, we have assembled in Group III the series, all of them anepigraphic, which are difficult to insert in the catalogue based on a relative chronology, either because of the absence of any indication or because of the bad state of preservation of the coins. However we shall tentatively propose hypotheses for attributing some series, even though they need confirming. We have presented separately, in two groups, the silver series (III.1) and the bronze series (III.2). Inside each group, we have presented the series according to their main type, for example III.1.1. Seahorse, and III.1.2. Dolphin. It is important to stress that these denominations necessarily correspond to the series of shekels II.1.1, II.1.2 and II.2.1, especially to II.2.1 for which we have not identified any denomination fitting in with the shekels. The metallic composition of four of these coins was analysed, giving the following percentage of silver: 97.6% (no. 1614, Series III.1.2.a), 96.7% (no. 1731, Series III.1.2.f), 94.9% (no. 1718, Series III.1.2.e) and 87% (no. 1552, Series III.1.1.a). These results exclude the four coins from the first stage of Tyrian coins (with 99-98% of silver) and this is coherent with the fact that their types are very different from them. They can also be excluded from the last stage of Tyrian coins because the percentage of silver has been brought back to 99-98%. Therefore the four coins belong to the beginning of the intermediate stage with a decreasing percentage of silver, before the change of standard.

III.1.1. Seahorse

The anepigraphic series of sixteenths of shekel III.1.1.a bears on the obverse a winged seahorse to the right, over a dolphin, with a guilloche border, and on the reverse the usual owl standing to right, with a guilloche border; the engraving and manufacturing are carefully executed. All these features seem to be close to the type of Series II.1.1. These sixteenths of shekel of Series III.1.1.a could be related to the beautiful shekels of large fabric, then replaced by anepigraphic Series II.1.1.3 when the engraving and manufacturing were debased, related to the shekels of thick fabric. This is a hypothesis which needs to be confirmed by the analysis of coin no. 1552 (87% of silver). The coins of Series III.1.1.a taken into account for the die analysis are 21 (out of 33); we have identified 20 couples of dies and 13 obverse dies (Fig. 13). O1 is linked with R1, R2 and R3, thus linked together. O2 is linked with R4, R5, R6 and R7 (linked together). O3 is linked with R8 and R9; O4 with R9: therefore O3 and O4, R8 and R9 respectively are linked together. O5 is linked with R10 and R11; O6 with R11: therefore O5 and O6, R10 and R11 respectively are linked together. Then there are 7 isolated pairs of dies: O7-R12, O8-R13, O9-R14, O10-R15, O11-R16, O12-R17 and O13-R18. The ratio n/o = 1.53, which means that this series is insufficiently known.

Series III.1.1.b bears on the obverse a winged seahorse to the left, with two wavy lines below, instead of the dolphin, and the same owl standing to right; a cable border replaces the guilloche border. There are only three specimens which could be sixteenths of shekel. Series III.1.1.c, represented only by two specimens, is the reverse of the previous series: seahorse to right and owl to left; the border is obliterated. It is difficult to propose any classification for these two series.

The following three series with the winged seahorse on the obverse are smaller denominations: halves of sixteenth. Series III.1.1.d is represented by two coins only which are not well-preserved: it bears on the obverse a winged seahorse to left, and a ram's head to left on the reverse, with a border of dots. Series III.1.1.e is also represented by two coins which are not well-preserved: the obverse has the same winged seahorse to left and the reverse a dolphin to left, with a border of dots. On the obverse, Series III.1.1.f bears a winged seahorse to right and, on the reverse, a dolphin to right: in other words the same types as the previous series but reverted. This series is represented by 16 coins, 15 of which have been taken into account for the die analysis. We have identified 8 couples of dies and 6 obverse dies (Fig. 14). O1 is linked with R1 and R2, thus linked together. O2 is linked with R3 and R4 (linked together). Then there are 4 isolated pairs of dies: O3-R5, O4-R6, O5-R7 and O6-R8. The ratio n/o = 1.33, which means that this series is insufficiently known. It is difficult to classify, even approximately, these small denominations: their weight does not indicate whether they belong to the Phoenician or 'Attic' standard. If they could be situated in parallel with Sidonian coinage, we have shown that the thirty-seconds of shekel were no longer minted after the end of ʿAbdʿaštart I's rule (352 BCE).[33]

III.1.2. Dolphin

Six silver series have the dolphin on the obverse, the first four being sixteenths of shekel and the two others smaller denominations. Series III.1.2.a bears a dolphin to left, over a shell on the obverse, and an owl standing to left on the reverse; a border of dots surrounds both types. The coins of this series taken into account for the die analysis are 33 (out of 42); we have identified 22 couples of dies and 14 obverse dies (Fig. 15). O1 is linked with R1 and R2; O2 with R2, R3 and R4; O3 with R2, R5 and R6; O4 with R6: therefore O1, O2, O3 and O4 are linked together, just as R1, R2, R4, R5 and R6. O5 is linked with R7 and R8; O6 with R8: thus O5 and O6 are linked together, just as R7 and R8. O7 is linked with R9; O8 with R10: therefore O7 and O8 are linked together, and also R9 and R10. O9 is linked with R11 and R12 (linked together). Then there are 5 isolated pairs of dies: O10-R13, O11-R14, O12-R15, O13-R16 and O14-R17. The ratio n/o = 1.57, which means that this series is insufficiently known. Series III.1.2.b is represented by only 2 coins which are not well-preserved: it seems to bear the same types as the previous series, but turned to right, possibly with a guilloche border. Series III.1.2.c bears a dolphin to left on the obverse and an owl to left on the reverse, with a guilloche border.

---

33. Elayi-Elayi, *Monnayage de Sidon*, p. 416.

Only 5 coins (out of 12) can be used for the die analysis, with 5 couples of dies and 4 obverse dies (Fig. 16). O1 is linked with R1 and R2, thus linked together; there are also 3 isolated pairs of coins: O2-R3, O3-R4 and O4-R5. The ratio n/o = 1.25 is very small. Series III.1.2.d has the same types as the preceding series but reverted: dolphin and owl to right, with a guilloche border. The engraving and manufacturing are carefully executed as in Series III.1.1.a. These sixteenths of shekel are also possibly related to the beautiful shekels of large fabric (Series II.1.1). The coins taken into account for the die analysis are 19 (out of 56); we have identified 19 couples of dies and 15 obverse dies (Fig. 17). O1 is linked with R1, R2 and R3; O2 with R3 and R4: therefore O1 and O2 are linked together, just as R1, R2, R3 and R4. O3 is linked with R5 and R6 (linked together). O4 and O5 are linked with R7 and therefore linked together. O6 and O7 are linked with R8 and therefore linked together. Then there are 8 isolated couples of dies: O8-R9, O9-R10, O10-R11, O11-R12, O12-R13, O13-R14, O14-R15 and O15-R16. The ratio n/o = 1.26, which means that this series is insufficiently known.

Series III.1.2.e bears a dolphin to right on the obverse and a lion's head *en face* on the reverse, with a border of dots. Only 2 couples of dies have been identified for 2 coins (O1-R1 and O2-R2); the 9 other coins of the series are too badly preserved for a die analysis. Series III.1.2.f bears a dolphin to left on the obverse and a ram's head to left on the reverse, with a border of dots. Only 8 coins (out of 12) were taken into consideration for the die analysis: 8 couples of dies and 7 obverse coins have been identified (Fig. 18). O1 is linked with R1 and R2, therefore linked together. The other pairs of dies are isolated: O2-R3, O3-R4, O4-R5, O5-R6, O6-R7 and O7-R8. The ratio n/o = 1.14 (very small).

The type of the ram's head is only used for the small silver denominations of Series III.1.1.d. But the lion's head *en face* is used for the small silver denominations of Series III.1.2.e and also for the reverse of all the bronze series (III.2.1, III.2.2, III.2.3, III.2.4 and III.2.5). The bronze Series III.2.5 possibly replaced the small silver denominations of Series III.1.2.e, borrowing the same obverse and reverse types. Although the bronze coins of Series III.2.5 are not well-preserved, it does however seem that the lion only has a prey in its mouth on bronze coins; the border of the reverse is obscure.

III.2. Bronze series

78 bronze coins were assembled in this corpus, much less than Sidonian bronze coins (340).[34] Unlike the Sidonian coins, none of them can be classified and almost all of them are now kept in Israel, in private and public collections. We have identified five Tyrian series according to their types because their weights did not provide any help: Series III.2.1, III.2.2, III.2.3, III.2.4 and

---

34. *Ibid.*, no. 1466-1519, 2321-2608.

III.2.5; uncertain bronze coins are presented in Series III.2.6. All the coins, except two, are anepigraphic. On the obverse, Series III.2.1 bears a winged seahorse to right, with a border of dots, and a lion's head *en face* on the reverse, with border obscure. Only four coins have been preserved, with 3 couples of dies and no links: O1-R1, O2-R2 and O3-R3. Series III.2.2 bears a dolphin to left on the obverse and the same type as the previous series on the reverse; the border is uncertain (dots?). On the four preserved coins, we have only identified one pair of dies. Series III.2.3 bears a shell on the obverse, with a border of dots, and a lion's head, within an incuse square on the reverse (Fig. 19). 10 coins (out of 24) were taken into account for the die analysis: we have identified 9 couples of dies and 7 obverse dies. O1 is linked with R1, and O2 with R2. O3 is linked with R3, R4 and R5; O4 with R5: therefore, O3 and O4 are linked together, just as R3, R4 and R5. O6 and O7 are linked with R6, and also together; O7 is linked with R7. The ratio n/o = 1.27 (very small).

Series III.2.4 is similar to Series III.2.2 except for the shell below the dolphin (Fig. 20). Only 5 coins (out of 26) can be taken into consideration for the die analysis: 6 couples of dies and 5 obverse dies were identified. O1 is linked with R1; O2 with R2. O3 is linked with R3; O4 with R3 and R4: thus O3 and O4 are linked together, just as R3 and R4. O5 is linked with R5. The ratio n/o = 1.20 (very small). Series III.2.5 is similar to Series III.2.2, except for the dolphin turned to right. The 9 specimens are not well-preserved (a couple of dies only: O1-R1). 9 bronze coins were assembled in Series III.2.6: most of them are not well-preserved or not illustrated by a photograph in the publication of the Beirut hoard TXLIII. 2 bronze coins are interesting (no. 1803-1804): on the obverse they bear a winged seahorse to left, with a border of dots, and an owl standing to left, with the letter *M*, on the reverse. These bronze coins have the same types as the silver coins of Series II.1.2.2.i.[35] Because of letter *M*, they are possibly related with the shekels of Series II.1.2.1.a or II.2.1.1: however, the guilloche border is replaced by a border of dots.

As we have already stated, bronze, hence the bronze coins could have replaced the smallest silver denominations during the last stage of Tyrian coinage, just as in Sidonian coinage.[36]

4. Mint of Tyre?

False attributions to the mint of Tyre were proposed for several coins as well as false attributions of Tyrian coins to other mints. We have not taken these false attributions into account. However, the selection shown in our catalogue is sufficient for identifying all the coins that have been correctly attributed. However, we hesitate on some silver coins such as no. 1812, 1813 and

---

35. However, as we have not seen these coins, the two bronze coins could also be plated silver coins of Series II.1.2.2.a.
36. Elayi-Elayi, *Monnayage de Sidon*, pp. 416-419, 591.

1814, all of them belonging to the Naplouse hoard TLI. They followed usual Tyrian types: winged seahorse to left, with a border of dots, on the obverse, and owl standing to left, with the same border, on the reverse. They can be compared to the coins of Series II.1.1.3, but on the reverse they bear a letter which is unattested in this series (*Y*?).

CHAPTER III

ANALYSIS OF THE MONETARY INSCRIPTIONS

The presence of inscriptions on Tyrian coins dated from the Persian period was not systematic. As far as the shekels are concerned, in a first stage, they were all inscribed (Group I, Series I.1.1 and I.2.1). In a second stage, during a short period, they were anepigraphic (Group II, Series II.1.1.1). Then in a third stage, they again bore an inscription (Series II.1.2.1 and II.2.1). On the other hand, most of the small denominations were anepigraphic. It should be stressed that all the first series of coins minted by Tyre were inscribed, with no distinction between shekels and small denominations. With respect to the monetary inscriptions, the Tyrian mint was the first Phoenician mint to have issued inscribed coins as the first Byblian coins, prior to the Tyrian ones,[1] were anepigraphic. Arwad followed the example of the Tyrian mint on this point, but not Sidon who first issued anepigraphic coins.[2] The question is why the Tyrian minting authority had decided to inscribe legends on the first coins: we shall try to answer this question by analysing the inscriptions.

In this chapter, we take into account not only the monetary inscriptions, the written mark of the minting authority, but also the inscribed countermarks which can represent either official or private marks, and the graffiti which represent the free script of individuals.[3] From the combination of these three kinds of inscriptions, roughly contemporaneous and dated, made by individuals with different social origins, aims, script techniques and degrees of literacy, we get a triple viewpoint of Tyrian society, that is from about 450 to 332 BCE.

The Tyrian coinage, and more generally Phoenician coinages, have always been considered as Greek and studied by using two different approaches. Either the iconography was studied without taking into consideration the Phoenician

---
1. Cf. J. Elayi, 'L'ouverture du premier atelier monétaire phénicien', *BCEN* 32, 1995, pp. 73-78. This chapter is a developed version of the article of J. Elayi, 'The Tyrian Monetary Inscriptions of the Persian Period', *Trans* 34, 2007, pp. 65-101.
2. Cf. Elayi-Elayi, *Monnayage de Sidon*, pp. 437-441.
3. Cf. Elayi-Lemaire, *Graffiti*, pp. 210-211.

inscription (numismatists being ignorant of Semitic languages), or the inscription was studied alone without taking into account the numismatic aspect of the coin (specialists of West-Semitic scripts). However, even for them, monetary inscriptions have never been considered as real epigraphic documents which could be as significant as other categories of documents which alone were considered important.[4] We recognise as being the most scientific approach that which entails considering each coin as a whole, in all its aspects: iconographic, epigraphic (inscription, countermark and graffito if any), metrological and technical, before studying its meaning and function. The first study of Tyrian monetary inscriptions at the beginning of the 20th century was done by G.F. Hill who compiled in a table the different written forms found on the coins of the British Museum.[5] More recently, J.B. Peckham has studied them, based on Hill's table, as well as the old catalogue of E. Babelon and an incomplete publication of a Byblian hoard.[6] Several recent numismatic publications include the study of Semitic monetary inscriptions and other publications study some particular inscriptions.[7] After an initial preliminary study of the Phoenician monetary inscriptions, including the Tyrian ones,[8] we have made a basic study of the Sidonian inscriptions, taking into account a very large number of them, an updated chronology and the specific context of the script.[9]

Graffiti and inscribed countermarks are now better known. As early as the 19th century, the publications of J. Friedländer and F. Lenormant attracted the attention on to West-Semitic monetary graffiti.[10] Then during the first half of the 20th century, there was only one short article by C.C. Torrey on the graffiti

---

4. Cf., by example, V. Krings ed., *La civilisation phénicienne et punique. Manuel de recherche*, Leiden *et al.* 1990, pp. 205-214 (epigraphic category not considered); compare Elayi, *Sidon*, p. 49.

5. *BMC Phoenicia*, p. cxlvi.

6. J.B. Peckham, *The Development of the Late Phoenician Scripts*, Cambridge Ma. 1968, in particular pp. 47-50, 71-75; *BMC Phoenicia*; Babelon, *Perses*; Dunand, *Byblos I*, pp. 407-409.

7. For bibl., see J. Elayi and A. Lemaire, 'Numismatique', *Trans* 1, 1989, pp. 155-164; 4, 1991, pp. 119-132; 10, 1995, pp. 151-187; 17, 1999, pp. 117-153; 25, 2003, pp. 63-105; 33, 2007, pp. 23-55; A. Lemaire, in T. Hackens *et al.* eds, *A Survey of Numismatic Research 1985-1990*, Brussels 1991, pp. 151-187; H. Gitler, in A. Burnett *et al.* eds, *A Survey of Numismatic Research 1990-1995*, Berlin 1997, pp. 101-105; *id.*, in C. Alfaro and A. Burnett eds, *A Survey of Numismatic Research 1996-2001*, Madrid 2003, pp. 151-155; P. Naster, 'Toponymes en caractères araméens sur les monnaies anatoliennes', *RBN* 134, 1998, pp. 5-17.

8. J. Elayi, 'Etude paléographique des légendes monétaires phéniciennes d'époque perse', *Trans* 5, 1992, pp. 24-25; *id.*, 'Remarques méthodologiques sur l'étude paléographique des légendes monétaires phéniciennes', in C. Baurain *et al.* eds, *Phoinikeia Grammata. Lire et écrire en Méditerranée*, Namur 1991, pp. 187-200.

9. Elayi-Elayi, *Monnayage de Sidon*, pp. 437-470.

10. J. Friedländer, 'Münzen mit eingeritzen Aufschriften', *Berliner Blätter für Münz, Siegel- und Wappenkunde* 4, 1868, pp. 145-150; *id.*, 'Eingeritzen Inschriften auf Münzen', *ZN* 3, 1876, p. 44; F. Lenormant, 'Les graffiti monétaires de l'antiquité', *RN*, n.s. 15, 1874-77, pp. 325-346; *id.*, *La Monnaie dans l'Antiquité* I, Paris 1878, pp. 31-32; cf. also J.P. Six, 'Le satrape Mazaios', *NC*, 3rd ser. 4, 1884, p. 110.

of the Demanhur hoard.[11] From the Sixties, several publications have been devoted to the West-Semitic graffiti, namely those of L.Y. Rahmani and J. Naveh in 1966 regarding the graffiti of the Tel Tsippor hoard,[12] of A.H. Bivar concerning an Aramaic graffito,[13] of F. Vattioni about some graffiti[14] and of A. Kindler about the graffiti of the Tel Michal hoard.[15] A. Davesne, A. Lemaire and O. Masson studied the numerous graffiti of the Gülnar hoard.[16] J. Elayi and A.G. Elayi studied the graffiti of Phoenician coins.[17] J. Elayi and A. Lemaire studied the West-Semitic graffiti as a whole.[18] As far as the monetary inscribed countermarks are concerned, they are not listed in the corpora of Semitic inscriptions and are rarely mentioned in the catalogues of the so-called 'Greek' coins.[19] Countermarks are incidentally mentioned in some publications, namely those of F. Imhoof-Blumer, O. Mørkholm, S. Atlan and R.A. Moysey related to countermarks printed on coins of Asia Minor, those of G. Le Rider and H. Nicolet-Pierre, related to the countermarks printed on pseudo-Athenian coins,[20] and the study of J. Elayi and A.G. Elayi related to countermarks stamped on

11. C.C. Torrey, *Aramaic Graffiti on Coins of Demanhur*, NNM 77, New York 1937.
12. L.Y. Rahmani, 'A Hoard of Alexander Coins', in *L.A. Mayer Volume*, ErIs 7, Jerusalem 1964, pp. 33-38 and 168; *id.*, 'A Hoard of Alexander Coins from Tel Tsippor', *GNS* 16, 1966, p. 131; J. Naveh, *AION* 16, 1966, p. 33; *id.*, 'The Development of the Aramaic Script', *PIASH* 5, 1971-76, pp. 52-54.
13. A.H. Bivar, 'A Persian Monument at Athens and its Connections with the Achaemenid State Seals', in *W.B. Henning Memorial Volume*, London 1970, pp. 43-61.
14. F. Vattioni, 'I sigilli, le monete e gli avori aramaici', *Augustinianum* 11, 1971, pp. 80-81, no. 104-105 and 107-117.
15. A. Kindler, 'A Ptolemaic Coin Hoard from Tel Michal', *Tel Aviv* 5, 1978, pp. 159-169.
16. A. Davesne and O. Masson, 'A propos du trésor des monnaies de Gülnar en Cilicie: problèmes numismatiques et 'graffiti' monétaires', *RA*, 1985, p. 45; A. Lemaire, 'Notes d'épigraphie nord-ouest sémitique', *Syr.* 62, 1985, pp. 37-38; *id.*, in A. Davesne and G. Le Rider, *Gülnar II. Le Trésor de Meydancikkale*, Paris 1989, pp. 367-368.
17. J. Elayi and A.G. Elayi, 'A Treasure of Coins from Arados', *JANES* 18, 1986, pp. 11-12; *id.*, 'Le trésor monétaire aradien de Jéblé (Syrie)', in *ACFP* III, Tunis 1995, pp. 415-416; *id.*, *Trésors*, pp. 308-321; *id.*, 'Un nouveau trésor de tétradrachmes athéniens et pseudo-athéniens', *RN* 36, 1994, pp. 26-33.
18. Elayi-Lemaire, *Graffiti*, pp. 39-106 ; *id.*, 'Graffiti monétaires oust-sémitiques', in T. Hackens and G. Moucharte eds, *Numismatique et histoire économique phéniciennes et puniques*, Studia Phoenicia IX, Louvain-la-Neuve 1992, pp. 59-76.
19. See, for example, *BMC Lydia, Pamphylia, Pisidia*, p. 97, no. 26.
20. F. Imhoof-Blumer, *Kleinasiatische Münzen* II, Vienna 1902, pp. 312-314 ; O. Mørkholm, 'A South Anatolian Coin Hoard', *AArch* 30, 1959, p. 200 ; S. Atlan, *Untersuchungen über die Sidetischen Münzen des V. und IV. Jahrhunderts v. Chr.*, Ankara 1967, pp. 172-175 ; R.A. Moysey, 'The Silver Stater Issues of Pharnabazos and Datames from the Mint of Tarsus in Cilicia', *ANSMN* 31, 1986, pp. 37-58 ; G. Le Rider, 'Monnaies grecques récemment acquises par le Cabinet des Médailles', *RN* 3, 1961, pp. 13-14 ; *id.*, 'Contremarques et surfrappes dans l'Antiquité grecque', in *Numismatique antique. Problèmes et méthodes*, Annales de l'Est, Nancy-Louvain 1975, pp. 34-36 ; H. Nicolet-Pierre, 'L'oiseau d'Athéna, d'Égypte en Bactriane: quelques remarques sur l'usage d'un type monétaire à l'époque classique', in L. Kahil *et al.*, *Iconographie classique et identités régionales*, *BCH*, Suppl. XIV, Paris 1986, pp. 368-369 ; F. de Callataÿ, 'Les monnayages ciliciens du premier quart du IVe s. av. J.-C.', in O. Casabonne ed., *Mécanismes et innovations monétaires dans l'Anatolie achéménide*, Istanbul 2000, pp. 93-127.

Phoenician coins.[21] Let us mention finally the systematic study of West-Semitic monetary countermarks by J. Elayi and A. Lemaire.[22]

1. *The monetary inscriptions*

Although the specialists of West-Semitic epigraphy in general do not consider the monetary inscriptions, these inscriptions do however represent a necessary complement to the knowledge of Phoenician scripts in the Persian period and of the socio-cultural contexts. It is all the more necessary since the corpora of Phoenician inscriptions dated from this period are all limited to some extent. The Tyrian corpus for this period is particularly small, a few dozen at the most if we take into account the inscriptions discovered in all the Tyrian territory.[23] Compared with other kinds of inscriptions, a monetary inscription has the considerable advantage of existing in several, sometimes numerous specimens. By examining them, it is possible to carefully check the forms of letters and to identify their variants made by one single engraver or various contemporary engravers.

Firstly, we notice that the inscription appears on the obverse in Group I, while it is on the reverse in Group II coins. Why? Clearly this is not related to the dolphin as it is always represented on the obverse, either as the main design of the type or as a secondary symbol. Is it a question of space? There is more free space on the obverse of Group I, above the dolphin, than on the obverse of Group II where the divinity riding on seahorse occupies the entire field. However, in the first series of Group I, there was as much space on the obverse, above the dolphin, than on the reverse, to the right of the owl. There was possibly also a relation between the designs and the inscriptions: when the inscriptions became related to the king, they were more in their place on the reverse with the crook and flail, the symbols of kingship. As far as the arrangement of the inscription is concerned, it may depend on the space available, on the purpose of distinguishing two series or simply on the fancy of the engraver. It may happen that the long upper or lower shafts of some letters fall partly off the field when there is not enough space for them: this particularity must not be confused with the shape of the letters.

We shall present the epigraphic analysis of Tyrian monetary inscriptions (reading and interpretation) by following, as much as possible, the chronological order established in our corpus (Figs 21-26). From a methodological point of view, it is necessary to analyse the inscriptions, not for themselves but as

---

21. Elayi-Elayi, *Trésors*, pp. 54-57.
22. Elayi-Lemaire, *Graffiti*, pp. 107-205.
23. There is no corpus of Tyrian inscriptions dated from the Persian period. Cf. J. Elayi and J. Sapin, *Quinze ans de recherche (1985-2000) sur la Transeuphratène à l'époque perse*, Paris 2000, pp. 116-120 (with bibl.) ; A. Lemaire, 'Epigraphie', *Trans* 4, 1991, pp. 113-116; 10, 1995, pp. 143-147; 17, 1999, pp. 111-113; 24, 2002, pp. 137-139; 32, 2006, pp. 185-194.

being integrated in a specific context and a particular system. Even if some explanations seem to be interesting, they cannot be accepted if they do not fall within the logic of these Tyrian coins, even if we have not yet found the correct interpretation. We propose explaining first what can be said of the logic of the minting authority for the choice of monetary inscriptions. There are two different categories of inscriptions on Group I and Group II coins. The first part of Tyrian coinage (Group I) has been carefully organised in two stages, each one of them probably consisting of five denominations. From the inscription of the shekels, which is clearly an indication of weight, it is logical to think that all the Group I inscriptions were indications of weight intended for users who were able to read. At the beginning of its coinage, the minting authority thus followed the custom already in use for the weights.[24] It is not easy to interpret these inscriptions as they refer to a weighing system known by the users; therefore the references were not always explicit. They were clear for the users but they may be unclear for us. In the presentation of each inscription, after an epigraphic study, we examine first the different interpretations, and then we try to find the one which fits in with the Tyrian logic.

The first Tyrian inscription on the shekels (Series I.1.1) is easy to read, even if the first or last letters often fall off the field: ŠLŠN. J.P. Six was the first to read it in 1877; however, E. Babelon in 1893 and J. Rouvier in 1903 did not know how to read it (LŠLMN?, LŠLŠN?, ŠY?M?, 'Sitom or Sirom, Hiram').[25] The Š has a three-pronged form usual in the 5th century. The letter is generally more or less rounded on its right and left sides, with the same length for the two arms; the central line has the same length, it is well-centred, vertical and straight (no. 2 Obverse = O). But the three arms can be straight giving an angular shape to the letter (no. 60 O, 1st Š). The basis can be enlarged, straight (no. 80 O) and the three arms of different lengths (no. 69 O). The central line can be sometimes slightly tilted and moved rightwards or leftwards (no. 72 O). The L has a typical 5th century shape with the tendency to lengthen its shaft, to tilt it further to the right and to add a short drop-line (no. 7 O). The shaft is straight but sometimes slightly curved (no. 29 O). Sometimes it is still vertical (no. 83 O). The baseline is horizontal (no. 34 O) or oblique (no. 88 O), angular (no. 2 O) or rounded (no. 38 O). The drop-line is, in half of the cases, missing (no. 60 O). The N can be clearly distinguished from the L in this inscription by a much shorter upper shaft and a much longer lower shaft. The slant of the N is normally tilted right (no. 34 O) but this letter can be vertical (no. 81 O). The lower shaft is straight (no. 4 O) or slightly curved to the left (no. 7 O). As for the L, the baseline is horizontal (no. 2 O) or oblique (no. 7 O), angular (no. 72 O) or

---

24. Elayi-Elayi, *Poids phéniciens*, pp. 155-181.
25. J.P. Six, 'Observations sur les monnaies phéniciennes', *NC*, n.s. 17, 1877, p. 194, n. 82; Babelon, *Perses*, p. CXC; J. Rouvier, 'Numismatique des villes de la Phénicie: Tyr', *JIAN* 6, 1903, p. 269. E. Babelon read ŠLŠN only in 1909 (*Comptes Rendus du Congrès International d'Archéologie Classique, 2ᵉ Session*, Cairo 1909, p. 274).

rounded (no. 87 O). The lower shaft overlaps the baseline (no. 45 O). On coin no. 53 O, there is no lower shaft but the baseline ends on the right with a short vertical stroke. The interpretation of ŠLŠN is difficult. In 1877, J.P. Six had proposed 'thirty?', considering the shekel of 36.6g as a multiple of 30 denominations of 0.45g.[26] By analogy with the biblical word ʿŠRYN, 'tenth', in 1910, E. Babelon interpreted this word as 'schiloschon', 'one-thirtieth' of a mina.[27] This interpretation was generally accepted,[28] but nobody could find a satisfactory explanation from a metrological point of view. According to E. Babelon, it was a reference to a 'small mina of (13.68 x 30) 410gr.40'.[29] For G.F. Hill, 'the maximum of the pre-Alexandrine stater being 13.90 grammas, gives a Tyrian mina of 417.00 grammas'.[30] According to J.W. Betlyon, there is a problem because 'this weight x 30 is not a Phoenician mina; however, it does equal an Attic mina – that is, the weight of 50 Attic staters'.[31] For É. Puech, 'all the known ŠLŠN are equivalent to a heavy shekel'.[32] In 1992 we had accepted the traditional interpretation 'a thirtieth', which seems to be correct, but without knowing how to connect the weights of these shekels with a Phoenician (or non-Phoenician) mina.[33]

The Group I quarters of shekel (Series I.1.2 and I.2.2) do not bear the inscription ŠLŠN like the shekels do, but a different inscription of five letters which are difficult to read and interpret. It is also located above the dolphin, but in a different manner: entirely on the left of the fin in Series I.1.2 and with the first letter on the right of it in Series I.2.2, maybe as a typological variant between the two series. Several readings and interpretations have been proposed. J.P. Six understood MḤṢYT, 'half' of the unit, a 'drachm' of 6.80g.[34] J. Rouvier proposed to read ṢR, 'Tyre', without taking into account the other three letters.[35] E. Babelon and G.F. Hill proposed to read MḤṢ K(SP), 'half-(shekel) of silver' by comparison with mḥṣyt hšql in Ex 30:13,15.[36] In 1967, A. Kindler read on a coin found in Akko: MḤṢ ṢR, 'mint of Tyre', which was a tempting

26. Six, *ibid.*
27. Babelon, *loc. cit.* (n. 25), 1909, p. 274.
28. Z.S. Harris, *A Grammar of the Phoenician Language*, New Haven 1936, p. 151, *s.v.* 'ŠLŠ'; J. Hoftijzer and K. Jongeling, *Dictionary of the North-West Semitic Inscriptions*, Leiden et al. 1995, *s.v.* 'šlšn₂' (subst. sing. abs.).
29. Babelon, *Traité*, cols 612-613.
30. *BMC Phoenicia*, p. cxxvii.
31. Betlyon, *Coinage of Phoenicia*, pp. 41 and 64, n. 19.
32. É. Puech, in *RB* 92, 1985, p. 287.
33. J. Elayi and A.G. Elayi, 'Systems of Abbreviations Used by Byblos, Tyre and Arwad in their Pre-Alexandrine Coinages', *JNG* 37-38, 1987-88, pp. 14-18 (The systematic study of Tyrian coins has shown that all the shekels of Series I.1.1 and I.2.1 are inscribed) ; J. Elayi and A. Lemaire, 'Les petites monnaies de Tyr au dauphin avec inscription', *NAC* 19, 1990, p. 112, n. 33; J. Elayi, 'Les sicles de Tyr au dauphin', *NAC* 21, 1992, p. 41. See the metrological study, in Chapter VI.
34. Six, *loc. cit.* (n. 25), p. 194, n. 82.
35. Rouvier, *loc. cit.* (n. 25), p. 270, no. 1779.
36. *BMC Phoenicia*, p. cxxvii ; Babelon, *loc. cit.* (n. 25), p. 274 ; *id.*, *Traité*, col. 613.

meaning.[37] In 1982, J.W. Betlyon proposed to read MḤṢT, with a mistakenly reversed T: 'half of the šeqel', following the parallel of *Exodus*.[38] É. Puech proposed to read MḤṢT or MḤṢYT, 'half of half-shekel or drachma, or fraction – ¼ of shekel'.[39] Finally, L. Mildenberg proposed the same reading as G.F. Hill and E. Babelon, based on coin no. 182, where the fourth letter has a second stroke on its head, which however appears to be fortuitous.[40] In 1990, we proposed to read MḤṢ GR, and to tentatively understand 'striking of GR (hypocoristic)?'.[41] We are re-opening the file, integrating the new information provided by the systematic study of these coins and checking whether our reading and interpretation are consistent with the logic of the system.

As far as the reading is concerned, the first letter is clearly *M*. Most of the time it is vertical with a short straight shaft (no. 8 O), but it is sometimes slightly tilted right and curves leftwards throughout its length (no. 204 O). Its head can be a broad and relatively deep half-rectangle (no. 8 O), but the left shoulder may be curved and the baseline too (no. 9 O). Sometimes, the right shoulder is almost non-existent (no. 12 O). The central line, vertical or oblique, usually crosses the baseline with the exception of coin no. 182 O. The second letter is clearly a *Ḥ*. Its two shafts are in most cases parallel, vertical (no. 190 O) or tilted left (no. 9 O). Its right shaft tends to be longer below the cross-lines than its left (no. 9 O). The cross-lines slope down to the left (no. 11 O) or are horizontal (no. 190 O); they are parallel and hung or not to the shafts (no. 11 and 12 O). On coin no. 187 O, the *Ḥ* has a cursive form with all its lines curved. There is no problem for reading the third letter as a *Ṣ*. It has a rather short straight shaft, slightly tilted left, and a horizontal head with a *Zayin* form tilted into the shaft, generally at the angle of the contemporary *Z* (no. 11 O). There is a tendency for it to flatten and assume a more horizontal position, with less angularity in the lines (no. 193 O). Since the field above the dolphin is limited, the last letter or the last two letters are often partly off the flan, making them more difficult to read. However, they are complete and legible on several coins. The fourth letter seems to be a *G* rather than a *P* on some coins because of its angular form. Except on coin no. 13 O where it has the equilateral form, its right leg is longer and slightly tilted left (no. 12 O), but on coins no. 196 O and 198 O it is vertical (and very long). However, on the other coins, the letter is not angular and the right leg is more or less curved, just like its head (no. 10 O, 186 O, 187 O and 190 O). Therefore, *P* is also possible. The last letter is the

---

37. A. Kindler, 'The Mint of Tyre – the major Source of silver Coins in ancient Palestine', *ErIs* 8, 1967, p. 323, no. 2.
38. Betlyon, *Coinage of Phoenicia*, p. 64, n. 20.
39. Puech, *loc. cit.* (n. 32) ; *id.*, 'Les premières émissions byblites et les rois de Byblos à la fin du Ve siècle avant J.-C.', in *ACFP* II/1, Rome 1991, p. 295, n. 38.
40. Conference of 9-11-1988 in Cambridge (Mass.); then he has changed his mind and left the reading of *K*.
41. Elayi-Lemaire, *loc. cit.* (n. 33) 1990, pp. 109-112.

most difficult to read because most of the time its head is out of the field. However it is legible on some coins. Its shaft is fairly long, more reminiscent of a *R* rather than a *D*, and more or less tilted left. Its head is triangular with a curved upper line and the lower line is drawn flat into the shaft (no. 10 O), horizontal or sometimes oblique (no. 186 O). The head can be open on the top (no. 193 O) or on the left (no. 182 O). Therefore, we finally propose to remain cautious and to read *MḤṢ G/PR/D* instead of *MḤṢ GR*.

The interpretation of this inscription is difficult because we normally expect to find a relation with that of the shekel and this relation is problematic. Since *ŠLŠN* seems to give an indication as to the weight of the shekel, *MḤṢ G/PR/D* ought to give a similar indication as to the weight of the quarter of shekel, but this indication is not clear. Let us investigate systematically the possible interpretations of *MḤṢ G/PR/D*. An inscription of five letters does not normally represent abbreviations. Either it could be a single word, a personal name or two words *MḤ | ṢG/PR/D* or *MḤṢ | G/PR/D*. The word or personal name is unknown for the moment. *MḤ ṢG/PR/D* makes no more sense: *MḤ* is a Punic adjective meaning 'fat'[42] but *ṢGR*, *ṢGD* and *ṢPD* are unattested in West-Semitic inscriptions, and *ṢPR*, 'bird', has no place on a coin.[43] *MḤṢ* and *GR* are attested but their presence on coins is difficult to explain. *MḤṢ*, 'to strike', 'to kill (?)' (*ma-aḫ-zu-ú*) is an Old Canaanite root,[44] well-attested in biblical Hebrew.[45] It is tempting to apply this meaning to coins: 'to strike (coins)'. However another word exists, *MḤT* or *MḤTT* attested in Phoenician and Punic,[46] that has been connected with the root *MḤY*, 'to strike' and consequently 'to test', 'to control' (Syriac *MḤ*ʾ, 'to strike coins').[47] The second word *GR* is well-known in Phoenician with the meaning of 'client', 'follower', 'giver of hospitality',[48] but this does not fit with *MḤṢ*, 'to strike'. *GR* could be also connected with Hebrew *gērāh*, 'small weight, 1/20 shekel', or with Aramaic

---

42. *CIS* I, 166 A, l. 5.
43. Hoftijzer-Jongeling, *op. cit.* (n. 28), *s.v.* 'ṣpr₁'.
44. *DISO*, *s.v.* 'MḤṢ₁'; Hoftijzer-Jongeling, *ibid.*, *s.v.* 'mḥṣ₁'.
45. See, for example, *Nb* 24, 8; *Dt* 32, 39; 33, 11; *Jb* 26, 12; *Ps* 68, 22, etc.; L. Koehler and W. Baumgartner, *Hebräisches und Aramäisches Lexikon zum Alten Testament* II, Leiden 1974, p. 541.
46. Cf. A. Dupont-Sommer, 'Une nouvelle inscription punique de Carthage', *CRAI*, 1968, p. 128; J. Ferron, 'L'inscription urbanistique de la Carthage punique', *Muséon* 98, 1985, p. 59: *ŠQL MḤTT*, 'weigher of small coins', which seems to fit with the context. However, cf. M. Sznycer, 'L'inscription dite 'urbanistique' de Carthage', *Sem.* 51, 2003, pp. 47-48, who proposes 'weighers of damaged goods' from the root ḤTT, 'to damage', which is less suitable in the context. Anyway if we have this root, it would rather mean the broken pieces of silver weighed and used as money: cf. Hoftijzer-Jongeling, *op. cit.* (n. 28), *s.v.* 'mḥth'. Cf. also *RES* 1215; *KAI* 60, l. 3; M.F. Baslez and F. Briquel, 'Un exemple d'intégration phénicienne au monde grec: les Sidoniens du Pirée à la fin du IVe siècle', in *ACFP* II/1, Rome 1991, pp. 233-235; Tripolitaine 37, 11.6-7; etc.
47. *DISO*, *s.v.* 'MḤY'; Hoftijzer-Jongeling, *ibid.*, *s.v.* 'mḥt₁'.
48. Hoftijzer-Jongeling, *ibid.*, *s.v.* 'gr₁'.

'gr, 'wages', 'salary',[49] but it makes no sense here.[50] Therefore we had proposed to understand *GR* as a personal name, a hypocoristic of a name such as *GRʿŠTRT*, which could be the person in charge of the striking: *MḤṢ GR* could mean 'striking of GR'.[51] Even if this hypothesis is interesting, we no longer think this is likely because it does not fit with the logic of the system. We have to look for an indication of weight. As it has been proposed, *MḤṢ* can be understood as 'half', from the root *ḤṢY*, which seems to be attested in a Tyrian inscription.[52] But 'half' of what? Not of a shekel of course but of a half-shekel. Such a reference supposes that the half-shekel, which is represented in Sidonian coinage, not Tyrian,[53] was well-known in the city of Tyre as a weight. Normally, this weight was designated by the second word *G/PR/D*, very difficult to interpret. As a working hypothesis to be confirmed, we propose to read *PR* for *PR(S)*, 'portion', 'half a measure', here 'half a shekel'.[54] Therefore *MḤṢ PR(S)* would mean 'half of a half (-shekel)'. In this logic, the same indication of weight cannot be written on an eighth of shekel: coin no. 222 (Series I.2.3). Since this 1.55g coin is unique, it could be a quarter of shekel light in weight (plated or badly weighed).

The sixteenths of shekel of Series I.1.3 and I.2.4 bear an inscription of two letters: *MR/D*. The shape of the *M* is similar to that of this letter in the preceding inscription: it is vertical with a rather short rectilinear shaft, however oblique on coin no. 225 O. Its head is a half-rectangle (no. 15 O) but its left shoulder is often curved (no. 228 O). The central line crosses the baseline and is vertical (no. 15 O) or slightly oblique (no. 16 O). The second letter is tilted left with a more or less long shaft, pointing to a *R* rather than to a *D*, which is however not excluded. Its head is triangular, with the lower line oblique (no. 19 O) or with a curved upper line (no. 16 O). As far as the meaning of *MR/D* is concerned, we had proposed to interpret it as the abbreviation of *MḤṢ G/PR/D* by the first and last letters, following Phoenician parallels.[55] It was also usual that the inscription was complete on the shekels and abbreviated on the small denominations.[56] However, this hypothesis seems to be unlikely in the logic of an indication of weight on each denomination. The interpretation of *MR/D* is not easy. If it is a complete word, *MR* is attested in Semitic languages but not in

---

49. *Ibid.*, s.v. 'grh₁' and 'ʾgr₂'. Cf. *Ex* 30, 13; *Lv* 27, 25; *Nb* 3, 47; 18, 16; *Ez* 45, 12; *ʾᵃgōrat kesep*, 'payment', in 1 *S* 2, 36; cf. Koehler-Baumgartner, *op. cit.* (n. 45) I, Leiden 1967, p. 194.
50. Other hypotheses such as *MḤ(NT)* or *MḤ(ŠBM) Ṣ(R) GR(?)* (cf. Carthaginian coins) are no more likely: Elayi-Lemaire, *loc. cit.* (n. 33) 1990, p. 111, n. 28.
51. Elayi-Lemaire, *ibid.*, p. 112.
52. Hoftijzer-Jongeling, *op. cit.* (n. 28), s.v. 'mḥṣ₂', 'ḥṣy₂'; cf. *RÉS* 1204, 11.5-6 (Tyrian inscription possibly mentioning half of a basin).
53. Cf. Elayi-Elayi, *Monnayage de Sidon*, pp. 587-588.
54. Hoftijzer-Jongeling, *op. cit.* (n. 28), s.v. 'prs₂' (akk. *parāsu*).
55. Cf. for example, *GL* for *GBL* or *ʾK* for *ʾDRMLK*: Elayi-Elayi, *loc. cit.* (n. 33) 1987-88, p. 13.
56. Cf. *ibid.*, *ʿMG* for *ʿYN ʾL MLK GBL*.

Phoenician, and we cannot see which meaning could be connected with a coin: 'myrrh', '(a kind of) tool', 'vessel or measure?', 'spade'.[57] *MD* is attested with the meaning of 'garment' or 'measure',[58] which has no relevance to a coin. It follows that the inscription is abbreviated. We propose two alternative hypotheses that have to be improved. First, *MR* is inscribed on a 4th century Beer-Sheba Aramaic ostracon mentioning a list of payments, where it has been interpreted as *rbᶜ mᶜh*, 'quarter of a certain coin (obolos?)'.[59] Here it would be a quarter of the preceding denomination that is a quarter (of shekel). The second hypothesis would consist in considering *M* as the abbreviation of the preceding inscription *MḤṢ PR(Ṣ)*, thus *MR* would be understood as *M(ḤṢ PR) R(Bᶜ)* 'quarter of quarter (of shekel)'.

Apparently, according to their weights, the coins of Series I.1.4 and I.2.4 correspond to the same denomination, difficult to identify. Unfortunately, the inscription of two (?) letters is illegible on the coins of Series I.1.4. We may reasonably assume that it is the same as on the corresponding denomination of Series I.2.4. But even in this series, these two letters are difficult to read. É. Puech has proposed to read *ḤY*, Y. Meshorer and S. Qedar *ḤM*,[60] and we have proposed *ḤY/M*.[61] The first letter clearly reads as a *Ḥ*, with a shape similar to that of the inscription on quarters of shekel. Its two shafts are vertical, straight and parallel. Only the upper cross-line, which is oblique, is visible. The second letter, which has a vertical shaft and a head with two oblique strokes, could be *Y* or *M*. Until now, no interpretation has been proposed. Following the logic of these inscriptions, we have to look for an indication of weight. If it is a word, *ḤY*, 'life', 'living'[62] or *ḤM*, 'father-in-law', 'heat', 'straw' (unattested in Phoenician)[63] do not provide any suitable interpretation. Therefore, it is probably an abbreviation of one word (by the first two letters or by the first and last letters) or two words (by the first letters of each word). As a working hypothesis to be confirmed, we proposed to understand *ḤM(ŠM)*, 'fiftieth', since this denomination seems to represent approximately one fiftieth of shekel. However, as we shall see in Chapter VI, the reference was more likely the sixteenth of shekel, not the shekel; for the moment, we do not see the relation between 'half of sixteenth' and the inscription *ḤM*.

---

57. Hoftijzer-Jongeling, *op. cit.* (n. 28), *s.v.* 'mr₁', 'mr₅', 'mr₆'.
58. *DISO*, *s.v.* 'MD_{II}', 'MD_{III}'.
59. J. Naveh, 'The Aramaic Ostraca from Tel Beer-Sheba (Seasons 1971-1976)', *Tel Aviv* 6, 1979, p. 188, no. 37, l. 2; cf. Hoftijzer-Jongeling, *op. cit.* (n. 28), *s.v.* 'mᶜh₁' and 'rbᶜ₃'.
60. Puech, *loc. cit.* (n. 39), p. 295, n. 38 ; Meshorer-Qedar, *Samarian Coinage*, p. 125, no. IC3, IC4.
61. Elayi-Lemaire, *loc. cit.* (n. 33) 1990, p. 110.
62. Hoftijzer-Jongeling, *op. cit.* (n. 28), *s.v.* 'ḥy₁', 'ḥy₂'.
63. *Ibid.*, *s.v.* 'ḥm₁', 'ḥm₂', 'ḥm₃'.

The very small coins of Series I.1.5 bear a letter on the obverse, above the dolphin, only legible on coin no. 26. We have proposed to read it as a Š.[64] Its shape is similar to one Š of the legend ŠLŠN mentioned above: a three-pronged angular form with straight arms, the central one being shorter. Only one letter could fit into the very restricted field, therefore Š is an abbreviation, certainly not of ŠLŠN because of the meaning, but the interpretation is difficult. Still in the same logic of weight indication, there are several possibilities: maybe Š(T), 'fraction', without precision.[65] Š could also be the abbreviation of several ordinal numerals such as ŠNY, ŠLŠY, ŠŠY, ŠBʿY, ŠMNHY, ŠLŠM, etc. If the indication of weight is connected with the preceding denomination, ŠLŠY, 'third', seems to be too small and ŠŠY, 'sixth', too large. If the indication is connected with the shekel, it could be 'two hundredths' since this denomination represents approximately one two-hundredth of shekel, but we would have the dual form MʾTM and not ŠNM (MʾT). However, as we shall see in Chapter VI, the reference of this denomination was more likely the sixteenth of shekel, not the shekel. For the moment, we do not know the right interpretation of the letter Š. It is one thing to understand the logic of these inscriptions, quite another to understand all of them: we need further discoveries concerning the Tyrian system of weights in the Persian period.

In the Group II of Tyrian coinage, the logic of weight indication has been definitively abandoned. After an anepigraphic series (II.1.1), a new logic was developed, apparently for the first time in Phoenician coinages: indicating the date of issue from the years of reigns of Tyrian kings, accompanied or not by the abbreviated name of the king. Probably a little bit earlier, the abbreviation of the king's name was also inscribed on the coins of Sidon but the yearly dating started later, in 372 BCE.[66] The inscription is now always located on the reverse of the coins.

The shekels of Series II.1.2.1.a bear one letter in front of the owl, above the shafts of crook and flail. This letter reads M, vertical (no. 643 R) or slightly tilted right (no. 613 R). It has a moderate or long straight shaft, rarely curved (no. 633 R). Most of the time its head is a broad and relatively deep half-rectangle (no. 625 R), except on coin no. 643 R where the left shoulder is curved. The central line, always vertical, crosses the baseline (no. 628 R) or not (no. 636 R). This inscription can be better understood in connexion with the inscriptions of Series II.1.2.1.b and II.1.2.1.c. The shekels of Series II.1.2.1.b bear the letter M at the same place as in the preceding series, and the letter B behind the owl, between its tail and the extremities of crook and flail. The B may be vertical (no. 655 R) or slightly tilted to the right (no. 654 R). Its shaft is not very long; it breaks abruptly left from the head (no. 657 R) or it has a

---

64. Elayi-Lemaire, *loc. cit.* (n. 33) 1990, pp. 110-111.
65. Cf. Elayi-Elayi, *Poids phéniciens*, p. 209 (not 'half' because it has no sense here).
66. Cf. *id.*, *Monnayage de Sidon*, pp. 444-449.

rounded form (no. 652 R). Its head is not very large and it is triangular (no. 653 R), or with a curved upper line (no. 656 R). The letter *M* alone and *BM* were read by several authors, but without any interpretation.[67] E. Babelon has tentatively interpreted *BM* as the abbreviation of *B(ʿLMLK) M(LK)*.[68] This interpretation cannot be excluded, but there is another one which seems more likely: at the end of the reign of king *M* and before the reign of king *B*, there was possibly a period where king *M* associated *B*, the crown-prince, to the ruling power. We have parallels in the Sidonian kingship, for example Bodʿaštart/Yatonmilk, and Baʿalšillem II/ʿAbdʿaštart I.[69] There were several Tyrian kings prior to the Persian period, whose name begins with *M* or *B*: for example, Mattan, Merbaʿal, Baʿal, Balator, Balbacer.[70]

The shekels of Series II.1.2.1.d, represented only by two specimens, bear an inscription of two letters in front of the owl just as before, but this time below the shafts of crook and flail. The first letter is probably a *Ṣ*, with a rather short shaft, slightly tilted left. Its head is not very clear, with only two strokes instead of three, but a similar form appears in the inscriptions of Series I.2.2.[71] The second letter clearly reads as a *R*: it has a long, straight vertical shaft and a triangular head, with its upper line slightly curved.[72] *ṢR* has, for a long time, been understood as the name of the city, which seems very likely.[73] For a short time, the name of the city replaced the name of the king.[74] Series II.1.2.1.e, represented by only one specimen, has one letter placed behind the owl, between its tail and the extremities of crook and flail. This letter is a ʿ which has the usual circular form with, in addition, a dot inside.

The shekels of Series II.1.2.1.f-k have a numeral inscribed on the reverse, on the right, in front of the owl, above the joined shafts of flail and crook. As usual, the units are vertical strokes, most of the time they curve slightly to the left (no. 688 Reverse = R). They are regularly spaced and not assembled in groups of three, as is frequently the case in the Sidonian coinage.[75] The numerals *1* to *5* are represented, then probably *10* with a circular arc form (no. 691 R).

---

67. Babelon, *Traité*, cols 615-616, no. 993-995 (*M*); *id.*, *Perses*, p. 292, no. 1990 (*M*); Rouvier, *loc. cit.* (n. 25), p. 272, no. 1791 (*M*), 1792 (*BM*); *BMC Phoenicia*, p. 229, no. 11-12 (*M*), 13 (*MB*); *Catalogue De Luynes*, p. 158, no. 3213 (*M*).
68. Babelon, *Traité*, cols 617-618, no. 996; cf. E. Lipiński dir., *Dictionnaire de la civilisation phénicienne et punique*, Turnhout 1992, *s.v.* 'Baalmilk, Baalmalok'.
69. Cf. Elayi-Elayi, *Monnayage de Sidon*, pp. 599-600, 647.
70. Cf. Lipiński dir., *op. cit.* (n. 68), *s.v.*
71. See, for example, coins no. 188 and 190.
72. See, for example, coin no. 196.
73. Babelon, *Perses*, p. 292, no. 1989 ; *id.*, *Traité*, cols 617-618, no. 997 ; Rouvier, *loc. cit.* (n. 25), p. 270, no. 1779.
74. Cf., on this subject, Chapter VII.
75. Elayi-Elayi, *Monnayage de Sidon*, pp. 819-825.

E. Babelon, J. Rouvier, G.F. Hill and J.W. Betlyon read numerals *1* to *5*.[76] The shekels of Series II.1.2.1.l-t have, at the same place, a numeral from 1 to 14 (*1, 3, 4, 5, 10, 11, 13,* and *14*). The units are vertical (no. 697 R) and slightly curved to the left (no. 709 R) or to the right (no. 706 R). They are regularly spaced. The numeral *10* is a circular arc form, horizontal (no. 701 R) or oblique (no. 704 R); it is smaller than the units and placed to the right of them, either at the top, centre or bottom. The problem is the identification of the sign placed in front of the units or numeral *10*, sometimes at the same level (no. 709 R), sometimes not (no. 698 R). It may be of the same size (no. 704 R) or it may be smaller (no. 698 R). It has the characteristic form of the letter *Z* in the 5th century, with an angular shape and a more or less rotated stance to the left. The upper line is short, either straight (no. 698 R) or sometimes curved (no. 706 R); the join-line begins to move to a diagonal. The form of this letter could be confused with that of numeral *20* as on some lead weights,[77] but in the monetary inscriptions, Sidonian for example, the numeral has a different shape.[78] On the other hand, the separation of the letter from the numeral in Series II.1.2.2.f-i, as well as the gap of ten years from *10* (?) to *20* (if we were to accept this sign as a numeral), seem to confirm the reading *Zayn*. *Z10* is mentioned without interpretation by J. Rouvier; *Z4, Z11* and *Z13* are mentioned by G.F. Hill who suggests that the first sign 'represents 20, being made by duplicating the form 10, but turning the second portion upside down'.[79] H. Seyrig proposed reading *Z*, not to have a long gap in the sequence of dates, as did J.W. Betlyon.[80] We do not know the complete name of king *Z*, for example Z(akerbaʿal) known at Tyre.[81]

The shekels of Series II.1.2.1.u-v also have numerals and a letter on the reverse, but with a different arrangement: the numerals are in the same place as in the preceding series, that is in front of the owl, above the shafts of crook and flail. But the letter is behind the owl, between its tail and the extremities of crook and flail. The units, represented only by *4* and *6*, consist of vertical strokes, straight (no. 710 R) or slightly curving to the left (no. 713 R), regularly spaced. The shaft of the letter *T* tilts to the right. The crossbar and the drop-line have the same length. They are angular (no. 711 R) or drawn in a continuous curved stroke (no. 713 R). Unlike the previous inscription and other Tyrian monetary inscriptions, the reading is *4T*, which comes to the same thing: '4th

---

76. Babelon, *Perses*, pp. cxc, 292-293, no. 1991-1995; *id., Traité*, cols 610, 617-620, no. 998-1002; Rouvier, *loc. cit.* (n. 25), p. 273, no. 1793-1797; *BMC Phoenicia*, p. 229, no. 14-16; Betlyon, *Coinage of Phoenicia*, p. 48.
77. Cf. Elayi-Elayi, *Poids phéniciens*, pp. 174 and 373, fig. 5.
78. *Id., Monnayage de Sidon*, p. 827, fig. 41.
79. Rouvier, *loc. cit.* (n. 25), p. 272, no. 1790; *BMC Phoenicia*, pp. cxxviii, 230, no. 17-18.
80. H. Seyrig, 'Une prétendue ère tyrienne', *Syr*. 34, 1957, p. 97, n. 1; J.B. Peckham, *op. cit.* (n. 6), p. 72, hesitates between *Z* and *20*.
81. Lipiński dir., *op. cit.* (n. 68), *s.v.* 'Sic(h)arbas'; F.L. Benz, *Personal Names in the Phoenician and Punic Inscriptions*, Rome 1972, pp. 108-109; J. Elayi, 'An Updated Chronology of Phoenician Kings during the Persian Period (539-333 BCE)', *Trans* 32, 2006, pp. 13-43.

year of (king) *T*'s (reign)', instead of '(king) *T*'s 4th (year of reign)'. We do not know the complete name of king *T*, for example Tabnit known as king of Sidon.[82]

In Group II, unlike Group I, there are not many inscribed small denominations, only sixteenths of shekel. The inscriptions of the sixteenths correspond to the inscriptions of the shekels. Series II.1.2.2.a bears the letter *M* above the shafts of crook and flail, in the same place as on shekels. Its form is also similar, with a vertical shaft, straight (no. 715 R) or slightly curved (no. 716 R). Then, we have Series II.1.2.2.b-e inscribed with numerals alone: *1*, *2* and *10* are attested. They are also placed on the reverse, but since the type is turned to the left, numeral *1* is on the left, in front of the owl, above the shafts of crook and flail. The numeral *2* is alternately inscribed above the two shafts (II.1.2.2.c) and below them (II.1.2.2.d), maybe in order to distinguish between two issues of year 2. The numeral *10* is always below the shafts: it is a horizontal stroke, either straight (no. 768 R) or in a circular arc form (no. 752 R). Series II.1.2.2.f-i bears a letter and a numeral, which are separated: the letter is placed above the shafts of crook and flail and the numeral below them (no. 780 R), except on coin no. 779 where it is the reverse and on coin no. 776 where the letter is placed below the shafts and the numeral behind the owl. The numerals represented are *1*, *2*, *4* and *5*. The letter *Z* has the same form as on shekels. It is always separated from the numerals, and it is not a question of space for *1* and *2* (one and two strokes). This separation logically conduces to identify it as a letter and not as the numeral *20*.

After the change of standard, only the shekels were inscribed, always with a numeral and one or two letters on the reverse, in front of the owl, mainly above the shafts of crook and flail. But when there are two letters, the second one is inscribed below the shafts. There is an exception for one letter (*Ṣ*), placed not with the numeral but below the shafts. In Series II.2.1.1, we can read *B1* above the shafts and *M* below. The letter *B* may be slightly tilted to the left (no. 797 R), vertical (no. 798 R) or slightly tilted to the right (no. 808 R). Its shaft is never very long; it breaks abruptly left (no. 801 R), sometimes directly from the head (no. 798 R), or it has a rounded form (no. 808 R). Its head is triangular (no. 798 R) or with a curved upper line (no. 800 R), or square (no. 809 R). The letter *M* is in most cases vertical (no. 800 R) and sometimes slightly tilted to the right (no. 798 R). Its shaft is straight or slightly curved (no. 803 R), with a moderate length. Its head is a broad and relatively deep half-rectangle (no. 808 R), except on coin no. 803 R where it has a reverted bell shape. The central line, vertical (no. 797 R) or oblique (no. 801 R), crosses the baseline (no. 800 R) or not (no. 803 R). The letter *B* placed before numeral *1* has been interpreted

---

82. Benz, *ibid.*, pp. 185-186 ; Elayi, *ibid.*, pp. 25-29.

as a preposition, 'in', as in Mazday's coins minted in Sidon,[83] but this way of dating was in use in Aramaic, not in Phoenician. According to J.W. Betlyon, 'the ruler in 357, however, being a crony of the Persians, apparently felt obliged to use the system used by the satrapal government in dating his coins'.[84] This hypothesis is groundless since we know neither the date of the series nor its historical context. The letter *M* has been interpreted as *M(LK)*, 'king', or as the initial of a personal name, possibly the minting authority's name.[85] Another explanation seems to be more likely: in his first year of reign, king *B* would have associated the crown prince *M* to the ruling power.

Then we have alternately *M2* and *M2 ʾ*, *M3* and *M3 ʾ* (Series II.2.1.1-5). The numerals *2* and *3* are represented by straight strokes, vertical (no. 837 R) or slightly tilted right (no. 838 R). The letter *M* has a straight shaft, with different lengths: short (no. 822 R), moderate (no. 841 R) or long (no. 840 R). Its head is a broad and relatively deep half-rectangle (no. 839 R), with the left shoulder rounded (no. 828 R) and the baseline horizontal (no. 841 R) or oblique (no. 838 R). The central line is vertical (no. 834 R) or oblique (no. 818 R) and crosses the baseline (no. 820 R) or not (no. 821 R). The letter *ʾ* is vertical (no. 834 R) or slightly rotated to the left (no. 845 R). Its head is relatively large, with cross-lines converging to the left of the shaft (no. 845 R). The cross-lines are slightly curved (no. 836 R). J.P. Six first interpreted the *M* as the initial of *M(LK)* and the *ʾ* as the initial of Alexander's name, which is impossible as this series is much earlier than Alexander's conquest of Tyre; then he proposed understanding *ʾ(DN) M(LKM)*, 'Lord of the kings', which has no more sense here.[86] According to others, *M* would be a preposition before a numeral, similar to *B*.[87] This makes no sense since the preposition *M(N)* means 'from' and not 'in'. According to others, *M* could be the initial of *M(LK)*, 'king', of a personal name, or of a king's name.[88] In the same logic of associating the crown prince to the power by the preceding king, we propose to interpret *M2* as a first issue of king *M* in his second year of reign. *M2 ʾ* would be a second issue in the same year, associating the crown prince *ʾ* to the ruling power. There were several earlier kings in Tyre, whose name begins with *M* and *B* as we have said,[89] and also with *ʾ*: for example ʾAbimilk or ʾAbibaʿal.[90]

Series II.2.1.6-10 are somewhat different as far as the place of the letter is concerned: the numeral is always placed above the shafts of crook and flail but

---

83. Babelon, *Perses*, pp. cxci and 294; *id.*, *Traité*, cols 623-624; Rouvier, *loc. cit.* (n. 25), p. 274; *BMC Phoenicia*, pp. cxxix and 231; Betlyon, *Coinage of Phoenicia*, pp. 52, 55.
84. Betlyon, *ibid.*, p. 56.
85. *BMC Phoenicia*, p. cxxix; Betlyon, *ibid.*
86. Six, *loc. cit.* (n. 25), p. 191; *id.*, 'L'ère de Tyr', *NC*, 3rd series, 6, 1886, p. 106.
87. Babelon, *Traité*, cols 621-622; *Catalogue De Luynes*, p. 159.
88. *BMC Phoenicia*, p. cxxix; Betlyon, *Coinage of Phoenicia*, p. 56.
89. Cf. *supra*, n. 81.
90. Cf. Lipiński dir., *op. cit.* (n. 68), *s.v.*

the letter is below the shafts. Numerals *1* to *4* are attested. They are represented as usual by strokes, rarely straight (no. 846 R), most of the time curved to the left (no. 853 R). They have the same length (no. 844 R) or their length decreases from left to right (no. 860 R). They are sometimes assembled in groups of three strokes (no. 862 R). The letter Ṣ has a more or less long shaft that tilts leftwards, more so on coin no. 872 R. Its head is horizontal, with the shape of the contemporary angular Z (no. 847 R). It tends to flatten into a more continuous form (no. 872 R). This letter has been interpreted as the initial of Ṣ(R) or of a personal name.[91] The two hypotheses are plausible but the second one seems to be more likely. We could have the same logic as previously, namely two issues in year 3 of king Ṣ: *3*Ṣ and *3*Ṣ + ʿ, associating the crown prince ʿ to the ruling power. Since the abbreviation of the reigning king Ṣ is placed below the shafts in this series, the abbreviation ʿ has to be placed above. Names such as Ṣadiqmilk or Ṣadiqyaton for example are known Phoenician names.[92] According to G.F. Hill, this king Ṣ with numeral cannot be the same as king Ṣ with numeral plus ʿ because they were separated by 23 years:[93] he was mistaken as he erroneously interpreted ʿ as the numeral *20*. The letter ʿ is circular with a dot inside. It probably represents the first letter of King ʿ(ZMLK)'s name as in the last series. An alternative hypothesis would be that in the first year in which he minted coins (year 3 of his reign), King ʿ(ZMLK) associated the preceding king Ṣ to the ruling power by adding the initial of his name to his inscription: in this case, there would be two issues in year 3.

The most disputed inscriptions were those of the last Series (II.2.1.14-28). They are always located above the shafts of crook and flail. The numerals are continuous from *3* to *17*. The units are represented by strokes, more or less long (no. 1033 R) or short (no. 1356 R), more or less close together (no. 958 R) or spaced (no. 1322 R). They can be vertical (no. 1512 R) or oblique (no. 1394 R), straight (no. 1355 R) or slightly curving to the right (no. 1285 R). They can be regularly spaced (no. 1522 R) or assembled in groups of three strokes (no. 1039 R). The numeral *10* is horizontal (no. 1201 R) or oblique (no. 1342 R), like a circular arc (no. 1346 R), angular (no. 1376 R) or nearly straight (no. 1322 R). From *3* to *5*, the units are on the left of the letter, except for coin no. 945 R where they are below (Fig. 25). The numeral *6* is written with five units on the left of the letter and one below, the numeral *7* with two below. The numeral *8* is written with four units on the left of the letter and four below, the numeral *9* with five on the left of the letter and four below. Numerals *10* to *12* are written on the left of the letter. The numeral *13* is written either in the same manner or with ten on the left of the letter and three below. All the other numerals (from

---

91. Cf. Six, *loc. cit.* (n. 25), p. 191; *BMC Phoenicia*, p. cxxix (both hypotheses); Babelon, *Traité*, cols 623-624 (ṢR).
92. Cf. Benz, *op. cit.* (n. 68), s.v.
93. *BMC Phoenicia*, p. cxxix.

14 to *17*) are written in the same manner: ten on the left of the letter and the units below. The letter is clearly a ⁽, having varied shapes: most of the time circular (no. 1001 R), sometimes with a dot inside (no. 1270 R), it can be square (no. 979 R), oval (no. 917 R), irregular (no. 1212 R) or open (no. 890 R). In the first studies on Tyrian coinage, this letter was mistakenly interpreted, both by numismatists and by epigraphists as the sign for the numeral 20, which calculated as 37 years.[94] In 1932, C. Lambert first proposed to read letter ⁽ and others followed him.[95] The main arguments are that the sign always represents the letter Z and that there are different signs for representing the numeral *20*.[96] Inscriptions ⁽*16* and ⁽*17* are mentioned erroneously as 36 and 37 by some authors.[97]

Even when the letter ⁽ has been read, it has been mistakenly interpreted as the abbreviation of ⁽*(KW)*, 'Akko', and attributed to the mint of Akko.[98] In 1957, H. Seyrig preferred to interpret this letter as the abbreviation of a Tyrian king and in 1963, F.M. Cross proposed to understand ⁽*(ZMLK)*.[99] This interpretation needed a long time to be accepted, but it is now generally admitted.[100] ⁽ZMLK, "⁽Ozmilk/⁽Uz(z)imilk/⁽Az(z)imilk' means 'strength (is) Milk' or

---

94. Babelon, *Perses*, p. 295; *id.*, *Traité*, cols 625-627; Rouvier, *loc. cit.* (n. 25), p. 275; *BMC Phoenicia*, pp. cxxx-cxxxi and 232; *Catalogue De Luynes*, pp. 159-160; Newell, *Tyrus*, pp. 15-23; M. Lidzbarski, *Handbuch der nordsemitischen Epigraphik*, Weimar 1898, Schrifttafel III; G.A. Cooke, *A Text-Book of North-Semitic Inscriptions*, Oxford 1903, p. 351.

95. C. Lambert, 'A Hoard of Phoenician Coins', *QDAP* 1, 1932, p. 13; S. Ronzevalle, 'Les monnaies de la dynastie de ⁽Abd-Hadad et les cultes de Hiérapolis-Bambycé', *MUSJ* 23, 1940, pp. 5-7; Seyrig, *loc. cit.* (n. 72), pp. 94-95; the date is therefore not 'lowered' of twenty years; we do not know any coin inscribed Z on the obverse and ⁽*4* on the reverse. Peckham, *op. cit.* (n. 6), p. 72; Betlyon, *Coinage of Phoenicia*, pp. 58, 75, etc.

96. Cf. Elayi-Elayi, *Poids phéniciens*, pp. 167-169; *id.*, *Monnayage de Sidon*, p. 452.

97. J. Brandis, *Das Münz-Mass- und Gewichtswesen in Vorderasien bis auf Alexander den Grossen*, Berlin 1866, p. 514; Babelon, *Traité*, cols 625-628; Rouvier, *loc. cit.* (n. 25), p. 276; *BMC Phoenicia*, p. 232.

98. Since Series II.2.1.14-28 were dated from the Hellenistic period, they were mixed with the Alexander Tyrian coinage: cf., for example, E.T. Newell, *The Dated Alexander Coinage of Sidon and Ake*, New Haven 1916, p. 39; Lambert, *loc. cit.* (n. 95), pp. 13-14; Kindler, *loc. cit.* (n. 37), pp. 318-324; O. Mørkholm, 'The Hellenistic Period', in R. Carson *et al.*, *A Survey of Numismatic Literature 1972-1977*, Bern 1979, p. 66; M.J. Price, 'On Attributing Alexanders – Some Cautionary Tales', in *Greek Numismatics and Archaeology, Essays in Honor of M. Thompson*, Wetteren 1979, pp. 241-246.

99. Seyrig, *loc. cit.* (n. 80), pp. 94-97; F.M. Cross, 'The Discovery of the Samaria Papyri', *BA* 26, 1963, pp. 116-118; *id.*, 'Papyri of the Fourth Century B.C. from Dâliyeh', in D.N. Freedman and J.C. Greenfield eds, *New Directions in Biblical Archaeology*, New York 1969, p. 51; M. Narkiss, *Coins of Palestine*, Vol. 2, Jerusalem 1938, p. 47 (*non vidi*).

100. See, for example, A. Lemaire, 'Le monnayage de Tyr et celui dit d'Akko dans la deuxième moitié du IVᵉ siècle av. J.-C.', *RN* 18, 1976, pp. 11-24; *id.*, 'Le royaume de Tyr dans la seconde moitié du IVᵉ siècle av. J.-C.', in *ACFP* II/1, Rome 1991, pp. 131-154; Elayi-Elayi, *loc. cit.* (n. 33), pp. 15-16; J. Teixidor, *Bulletin d'Épigraphie Sémitique (1964-1980)*, Paris 1986, p. 433, no. 78; Betlyon, *Coinage of Phoenicia*, pp. 53-59.

'(my) strength (is) Milk'.[101] We know from classical sources that the king who was on the throne of Tyre when Alexander besieged the city was Ἀζέμιλκος, 'Azemilkos'.[102] He was probably allowed on to the throne and the Phoenician letters ʿ and possibly ʿK on Alexander tetradrachms could be abbreviations of his name.[103] The attribution of the series with ʿ and a numeral to ʿOz-milk/Azemilkos, the last king of Tyre in the Persian period is very likely. The attribution to Akko has been refuted by several good arguments.[104] And now, the systematic study of Tyrian coinage confirms that these coins have Tyrian pre-Alexandrine types, that there is no gap in Tyrian coinage in the last part of the Persian period, and that their attribution to the mint of Tyre fits perfectly with the historical context of this period.[105]

As far as the numerals of Series II.2.1.14-28 are concerned, they are clearly attested continuously from *3* to *17*. The numeral *16* is inscribed on eleven coins (no. 1512-1522); it is particularly clear on coin no. 1513. The numeral *17* is only attested on coin no. 1524; several scholars have read this, the only mistake being that they interpreted the letter ʿ as the numeral *20*.[106] We have carefully examined this coin in the British Museum with a magnifying glass and we can say that the reading is definitely confirmed. It is not excluded that, on some coins bearing the inscription ʿ*15*, one or two strokes representing units are out of the flan and than they have been issued in year 16 or 17.[107]

2. *The monetary graffiti*

There are very few graffiti on Tyrian coins and they are more difficult to read than monetary legends because, in general, they are not incised very carefully. We have collected only 7 out of the 1,814 coins of our catalogue: 4 Phoenician, 2 Aramaic and 1 illegible (Fig. 26). All of them are inscribed on the reverse of the coins, around the owl, which is where there is most free space in the field. The shekel no. 288 (Series II.1.1.1.a) has on the reverse, in front of the owl, above the shafts of crook and flail, an incised Phoenician ʾ to be read in the same sense as the type. It has a straight shaft rotated in an anti-clockwise

---

101. Benz, *op. cit.* (n. 68), *s.v.*; Lipiński dir., *op. cit.* (n. 68), *s.v.* (with bibl.); Betlyon, *ibid.*, p. 74, n. 100. See the parallel of ʿZBʿL/ʿZYBʿL: *KAI* 11, p. 16; J. Friedrich and W. Röllig, *Phönizisch-Punische Grammatik*, Rome 1999, § 96 bis a.
102. Arr., *An.* II 15, 6-7; 24, 5; Curt. IV 2, 2.
103. Newell, *op. cit.* (n. 98), pp. 39-40; *id., Alexander Hoards, Demanhur 1905*, New York 1923, pp. 134-139; A.R. Bellinger, 'An Alexander Hoard from Byblos', *Ber.* 10, 1950-51, pp. 37-49, no. 57-80; A. Spaer, 'A Hoard of Alexander Tetradrachms from Galilee', *INJ* 111, 1965-66, pp. 1-7, no. 9, 11-23; Rahmani, *loc. cit.* (n. 12) 1966, pp. 129-139, no. 19-26; A. Kindler, 'Silver Coins bearing the Name of Judea from the Early Hellenistic Period', *IEJ* 24, 1974, p. 75, pl. 11, M-N.
104. See at last A. Lemaire, *loc. cit.* (n. 100) 1991 (with previous bibl.).
105. Cf. Chapter VII.
106. Rouvier, *loc. cit.* (n. 25), p. 276, no. 1817-1818; Babelon, *Traité*, cols 625-626, no. 1016; *BMC Phoenicia*, p. 232, no. 41; Betlyon, *Coinage of Phoenicia*, p. 58, no. 37.
107. For example, no. 1424, 1433, 1440, etc.

direction to the left. Its head is large, with cross-lines converging to the left of the shaft. This form is similar to that of monetary inscriptions of Series II.2.1.5 which is almost contemporary. The same Phoenician letter can be read on the reverse of the shekel no. 1049 (Series II.2.1.20), behind the owl, between the head and the crook. It can be read by turning the coin in an anti-clockwise direction to 11h. Its shaft is shorter because of the lack of space and its head more opened.[108] The letter *N* can be read on the reverse of the shekel no. 1144 (Series II.2.1.21), in front of the head of the owl, in the same direction as the type. According to the most likely hypothesis, the graffiti of just one letter could represent the initial of a personal name. The shekel no. 1421 (Series II.2.1.26) bears two letters incised on the obverse, on each side of the crook and flail. They can be read by turning the coin to 4h.[109] The first letter is *Z*, with an angular form, not rotated leftwards. The second letter seems to be ', having a very short shaft and a large head with cross-lines converging to the left of the shaft. It could be the abbreviation of a Semitic name such as *Z(BD)', Z(BYN)', Z(BN)', Z(KRY)'* (Aramaic ostraca) or *Z(W)'* (Ammonite seal).[110] The shekel no. 921 bears a graffito of three letters on the reverse in front of the owl, incised with a hard point. It is to be read at 3h, in Aramaic *NḤB*. The foot of the *N* is longer than the upper shaft; the baseline is horizontal. The letter *Ḥ* has a cursive form with two cross-lines, the second one joining the right shaft in a continuous curve. The *B* has a square open head and its shaft breaks abruptly left with a slightly curved tip. It is probably a personal name meaning 'timorous', mentioned in a Phoenician graffito inscribed on a Ras Shamra vase dated from the 5th-4th centuries.[111] It can be compared to *nḥby* in Biblical Hebrew.[112]

The shekel no. 1287 (Series II.2.1.24) bears on the reverse, down behind the owl, a graffito of four letters, which reads in Aramaic *LRYŠ* (at 7h).[113] The shaft of the *L* is straight and slightly tilted to the right. Its baseline is straight, horizontal and relatively long. The *R* is vertical, with a small open head. The *Y* is vertical and the headlines are parallel. Its tail is a short straight line jutting upwards. The *Š* is half-triangular, with the central line moving up the left arm.

---

108. The reading of the Greek letter *A* is less likely because of the lenght of the cross-line.

109. Elayi-Lemaire, *Graffiti*, pp. 54, no. 87, 71: a reverted reading *'Z* could give the abbreviation of a personal name such as *'Z(YBW)* or *'Z(NYH)*, attested in Egyptian Aramaic.

110. Cf. I. Ephʿal and J. Naveh, *Aramaic Ostraca of the fourth Century BC from Idumaea*, Jerusalem 1996, no. 157:2; A. Lemaire, *Nouvelles inscriptions araméennes d'Idumée* II, Paris 2002, *s.v.*; W.E. Aufrecht, *A Corpus of Ammonite Inscriptions*, Lewiston et al. 1989, p. 135, no. 52.

111. Elayi-Lemaire, *Graffiti*, p. 45, no. 32; A. Lemaire and J. Elayi, 'Graffiti monétaires ouest-sémitiques', in T. Hackens and G. Moucharte eds, *Numismatique et histoire économique phéniciennes et puniques*, Studia Phoenicia IX, Louvain-la-Neuve 1992, p. 72, no. 45; R.A. Stucky, *Ras Shamra, Leukos Limen. Die Nach-ugaritische Besiedlung von Ras Shamra*, Paris 1983, p. 27.

112. *Nb* 13,14; cf. M. Noth, *Die Israelitischen Personennamen im Rahmen der Gemeintsemitischen Namengebung*, Hildesheim 1966, p. 229.

113. Elayi-Lemaire, *Graffiti*, pp. 42, no. 18, 76.

The meaning of *LRYŠ* is not totally clear. If we understand *L-RYŠ*, 'to RYŠ', we do not know any parallel in Aramaic. It can be compared with *RYŠW* in Nabataean,[114] and possibly *RŠ* in north Arabic or *RYS* in Qatabanite.[115] The graffito on the reverse of coin no. 1226 (Series II.2.1.23) is illegible based on the photograph of the sale catalogue.

3. *The monetary countermarks*

The monetary countermarks are also very few, only 7 out of the 1,814 coins in our catalogue: 1 Phoenician, 1 Aramaic, 2 illegible and 3 anepigraphic (Fig. 26). Unlike the graffiti, the countermarks are located on the obverse of five coins and on the reverse of two coins. A countermark can be stamped anywhere on the coin because it obliterates the previous impression and is always legible. The first countermark is stamped on the obverse of the shekel no. 1162 (Series II.2.1.21), on the central part of the seahorse.[116] It has a half-circular shape, with one Phoenician letter: *D* or *R*. Its shaft is of an average length and its head is somewhat rounded as on some earlier monetary inscriptions (coins no. 228 and 230). The shekel no. 329 (Series II.1.1.1.b) bears a countermark exactly at the same place as the previous one.[117] It has an approximate square form, with its angles lightly rounded. Two Aramaic letters can be read in the same direction as the type: *ỸD/R*. The letter *Y* has a vertical stance, with its shaft slightly tilted right and rounded. Its central line and its foot are horizontal. Rather than the word *YD*, 'hand', it is probably the abbreviation of a personal name, such as *YD(ʾL)*, *YD(Wʿ)*, *YD(Yʿ)*, *YD(NYH)*, *YD(ʾL)*[118] or, if *YR* has to be read, *YR(BN)*, *YR(MY)*, *YR(PʾL)*, *YR(ḤW)*, *YR(PYH)* or *YR(ʾ)*.[119] The shekel no. 656 (Series II.1.2.1.c) bears exactly in the same place an approximate square countermark with rounded angles containing two letters which are unfortunately illegible. We would conclude that this countermark is the same as the previous one, but the outline of the square is somewhat different. The shekel no. 703 (Series II.1.2.1.q) bears on the reverse, below the owl, one or maybe two countermarks, which are somewhat indistinct. The first one could be a

---

114. A. Negev, *Personal Names in the Nabataean Realm*, Jerusalem 1991, p. 60, no. 1071.
115. G.L. Harding, *An Index and Concordance of Pre-Islamic Arabian Names and Inscriptions*, Toronto 1971, pp. 278, 292.
116. Elayi-Lemaire, *Graffiti*, pp. 136, no. 180, and 177.
117. *Ibid.*, pp. 129, no. 138, and 172.
118. M. Maraqten, *Die semitischen Personennamen in der alt- und reichsaramäischen Inschriften aus Vorderasien*, Hildesheim 1988, p. 82, *s.v.* 'YDʿL'; W. Kornfeld, *Onomastica aramaica aus Ägypten*, Vienna 1978, p. 52, *s.v.* 'YDNYH'; P. Grelot, *Documents araméens d'Égypte*, Paris 1972, p. 498; B. Porten, *The Elephantine Papyri in English*, Leiden *et al.* 1996, B43, B44, B25, B26, B22, B48; A. Lemaire, *Nouvelles inscriptions araméennes d'Idumée au Musée d'Israël*, Paris 1996, p. 164, *s.v.* 'YDYʿ'; *id., op. cit.* (n. 110), p. 272, *s.v.* 'YDW', 'YDWʾL'.
119. Maraqten, *ibid., s.v.* 'YRBN', 'YRMY', 'YRPʾL'; Kornfeld, *ibid.*, p. 54, *s.v.* 'YRḤW', 'YRPYH'; Lemaire, *ibid., s.v.* 'YRʾ'; *id., op. cit.* (n. 110), *s.v.* 'YRMʾ', 'YRPʾL'.

hollow circle with one letter inside, and the second a hollow crescent. The shekel no. 639 (Series II.1.2.1.a) bears a hollow countermark on the reverse, in front of the owl, below the shafts of crook and flail. It has a crescent-shape, frequent in countermarks.[120] The same countermark is found on the obverse of the shekel no. 1224 (Series II.2.1.23), on the left, outside the guilloche border. It is also found on the obverse of the shekel no. 1232 (same series), on the right above the dolphin.

4. *Palaeographical analysis of the Tyrian monetary inscriptions*

Before proceding to a palaeographical analysis of the Tyrian monetary inscriptions, it is necessary to try to understand the material reasons that may have modified the script. The forms of letters are explained first by the kind of the inscribed object and of the tool that has been used. The engraving of the die was made using a burin, by incision and in reverse order. We shall study in Chapter V in detail the technical aspects of this kind of engraving. Let us only say here that the engraver came up against the particular hardness of the die made of iron, sometimes hardened, or of bronze, and against the difficulty in drawing curved lines with a burin. This could explain at least partly some triangular or square heads and angular shafts, for example those of *B*, *M* and ʿ. The need to engrave in reverse order could explain why some letters are tilted in the wrong direction, or even completely reversed (which is very rare in the Tyrian inscriptions). There were two other difficulties for the engraver, namely the die was small, and even very small for the denominations. Secondly, the free space in the field was very restricted. This could explain why the inscription was sometimes cut in several parts as in Series I.1.2. The letters were quite small and the upper and lower shafts were sometimes shorter and slanting, as in Series I.1.1 for *L* and *N*. We would also like to point out that vertical letters take less space than tilted letters. The limited space on Tyrian coins may be one of the reasons why the letters of the monetary inscriptions are often vertical. In other words, these particularities due to material reasons must not be confused with the local characteristics of the script. The above-mentioned difficulties encountered by an engraver of coin dies were the same for an engraver of countermark dies.[121] On the contrary, a graffito was easier to write since it was inscribed directly on the coin, which was not as hard as the die. It was probably incised with any hard point rather than with a professional engraving tool.[122] The differences encountered in the monetary scripts also came from the different hands: either an experienced engraver, using appropriate tools in the case of monetary legends and countermarks, or just anybody, inexperienced and using any kind of tool in the case of graffiti. These three kinds of scripts (legends,

---

120. See, for example, Davesne-Le Rider, *op. cit.* (n. 16), pp. 351-368.
121. Cf. Elayi-Lemaire, *Graffiti*, pp. 157-159.
122. *Ibid.*, pp. 16-17.

countermarks and graffiti) are therefore quite different. Another important difference is the fact that a graffito was a unique inscription whereas legends and countermarks were duplicated several times. This is underscored by the study of similar dies used for striking coins or stamping countermarks. However, the duplication was limited in Phoenician monetary workshops by the fact that in the Persian period they probably did not use complete punches in order to obtain a large number of identical dies.[123]

The constraints encountered by the engravers could also come from the minting authority. Even if we have no information on this point, it is likely that the mint's die engravers had models at their disposal. This has been much discussed, mainly for Greek and Latin inscriptions, in order to know whether there was always a minute and an *ordinator*.[124] As far as the Phoenician and Punic inscriptions are concerned, this problem was mainly discussed from the El-Hofra inscription that ends as follows: WKTBT MSPRM ʾRBʿM WŠLŠ, 'and you will write 43 letters'.[125] The engraver was probably illiterate since he has copied out a minute bearing the text of the inscription to be engraved (43 letters), adding the line of comment without noticing that it did not belong to the inscription. In this case, the minute was necessarily written by the person who had ordered the inscription and not by the person in charge of the workshop. Since the latter knew that his engraver was illiterate, he would certainly not have written a comment for him. This inscription attests to the use of minutes by engravers and the possible employment of illiterate engravers. However this issue belongs to another period and another area. In the case of Tyrian monetary inscriptions, they represented an official order, highly symbolic since the civic coinage conveyed, among others, the symbols of the minting authority, which is of the city of Tyre. The engravers of Tyrian dies were probably given minutes and they had to conform to them as much as possible. For example they were informed about the respective importance and place of the different inscriptions (names of the king, of the city, dates, etc.) and about the abbreviations to be used. The place of letters or numerals could also change in order to distinguish some issues.

Although the rules in the Tyrian mint seem to be particularly strict, the engravers possibly kept some freedom in the arrangement of the space on the dies. They were probably not obliged to reproduce exactly the forms of the

---

123. Cf. already Elayi, *loc. cit.* (n. 8) 1991, pp. 192-193.
124. Cf. L. Robert, 'Épigraphie et paléographie', *CRAI*, 1995, pp. 195-222 (with bibl.).
125. *RES* 1543; J.G. Février, 'Remarques sur l'épigraphie néopunique', *OA* 2, 1963, pp. 257-267; P. Mazza, 'Note sul problema dell'*ordinatio* nell'epigrafia punica', *RSF* 6, 1978, pp. 19-26; H. Benichou-Safar, *Les tombes puniques de Carthage*, Paris 1982, pp. 187-205; M.G. Amadasi Guzzo, *Scavi a Mozia – Le inscrizioni*, Rome 1986, p. 93; C. Bonnet, 'La terminologie phénico-punique relative au métier de lapicide et à la gravure des textes', *SEL* 7, 1990, pp. 111-112; *id.*, 'Les scribes phénico-puniques', in Baurain *et al.* eds, *op. cit.* (n. 8), pp. 147-172; Hoftijzer-Jongeling, *op. cit.* (n. 28), *s.v.* 'mrsp'. Cf. Elayi-Elayi, *Poids phéniciens*, pp. 256-258.

letters inscribed on the minute (unless they were illiterate engravers who drew the letters without any personal initiative). They themselves chose the kind of script, archaistic, semi-cursive or cursive, taking into account however the tradition of monetary script in the local workshop, being more or less conservative.[126] They could also change the size of the letters, when they had enough space: in general, Tyrian monetary inscriptions were smaller than Sidonian ones when it was not a matter of space. Of course the graphic variants in a same inscription depended on the engraver, for example the two Š in the inscription of Series I.1.1 often have different forms. This observation is important because it shows that a letter did not have just one form at a given moment and place, but several. The engravers could choose their tools: letters were sometimes engraved by two burins of different sizes, which produced a combination of thin and thick strokes as in ink writing.[127] Finally, the style of writing was particular to each engraver, either careful or careless. The analysis of monetary scripts reveals different hands, for example in the issue of year 15 of ʿOzmilk (Series II.2.1.26), the inscriptions of coins no. 1346 and 1359 were made by different engravers. Even more so than the script of monetary inscriptions, the script of graffiti reflects the state of the standard non-official script in Tyre, at the time when they were inscribed. But their small number, the fact that they are unique and the uncertainty as to the origin of their authors represent a drawback for interpreting them. There is only a confirmation of the form of the Tyrian letter ʾ in the 4th century since it is similar in the graffiti of no. 288, 1049 and 1421 and in the legends of Series II.2.1.3 and II.2.1.5.

Therefore the monetary inscriptions provide important complementary information for the study of Tyrian script. Until now, most epigraphists, mainly interested in monumental inscriptions, have ignored them. However, the Phoenician inscriptions can only be used for drawing conclusions on the script if there are many occurrences of the same letters as in the ʾEšmunʿazor's inscription, or if they are duplicated several times as in the Bodʿaštart's inscriptions.[128] Unfortunately this is not the case for the Tyrian inscriptions of the Persian period. Epigraphists must be very cautious when they theorise about the characteristics of a given letter when they have only a few occurrences (or even only one) of this letter.[129] As far as Tyre is concerned, the monetary inscriptions are very precious because they offer several occurrences of letters, therefore providing a serious basis for an epigraphic study.

It is now possible to describe the characteristics of the Tyrian script from about 450 to 332 BCE by using monetary inscriptions, to show its evolution, to place it in the corpus of Tyrian inscriptions, and to compare the tradition of

---

126. Cf. Elayi, *loc. cit.* (n. 8) 1991, p. 196.
127. Compare, for example, coin no. 1387 (thin strokes) and coin no. 1373 (thick strokes).
128. Elayi-Elayi, *Sidon*, pp. 38-45, no. II, VI-XXIX.
129. Elayi, *loc. cit.* (n. 8) 1991, pp. 187-200.

script in the Tyrian mint with other Phoenician mints.[130] In the Tyrian monetary inscriptions as in the Byblian, thirteen different letters have been used, as opposed to the Sidonian inscriptions where only six letters were used.[131] Our preliminary study of Tyrian monetary inscriptions[132] can now be completed thanks to the large number of coins systematically analysed in this corpus. We have distributed the forms of letters into three periods: Group I (3rd quarter of the 5th century), Group II.1 (1st third of the 4th century) and Group II.2 (2nd third of the 4th century), in order to show the possible evolution (Figs 27-28).

The letter ʾ is only represented in Series II.2.1.3 and II.2.1.5. It is vertical or slightly rotated to the left. Its head is relatively large, with convergent cross-lines just left of the shaft in a narrow angle, the upper one sometimes being longer. The letter *B* presents a large variety of forms. It is vertical or slightly tilted right on the coins of Group II.1. Its shaft is not very long: it had a curved form or breaks abruptly left from the head. Its head is not very large and it is triangular, or with a curved upper line. On the coins of Group II.2, *B* is almost always vertical. Its shaft is sometimes curved but it mainly breaks left, forming an open angle. Its head is mostly triangular, rarely curved or square. Therefore, there was an evolution in the stance of the letter, and in the form of its shaft and head.

The following letter is problematic since it is not clear whether it is *G* or *P*, *P* being preferred for the meaning, based on a hypothesis to be confirmed. The equilateral form is exceptional and sometimes it has unequal legs like *G*. But other forms relating to *P* are also represented: a short line drawn to the top of the shaft, a curved right leg, or a rounded head. There is a similar problem for the letter *Z*, which could also be numeral *20*, *Z* being preferred because of the meaning and close parallels. It has the characteristic 5th century form: angular with a stance more or less rotated to the left. The upper line is in general short, either straight or more or less curved. The lower line is longer, also straight or more or less curved. Exceptionally, the upper and lower lines are vertical. The join-line begins to move towards a diagonal. The letter *Ḥ* is in general vertical, sometimes slightly tilted left. Its two shafts are mostly parallel and straight, except for some rare cases where they are divergent or sinuous. The three cross-lines (rarely two or one) are horizontal in most cases and rarely slope down to the left or to the right. They hang to the shafts except in a few cases. There are several varieties of *L*. It has a vertical stance or, most of the time, is more or less slanted to the right. Its shaft is long, straight or slightly curved. The foot is horizontal or oblique, angular or rounded. There is a short drop-line in half of the cases.

---

130. The analysis of monetary inscriptions by J.B. Peckham (*op. cit.* [n. 6], pp. 71-72) is useless because it is based on a small number of coins and a mostly outdated bibliography.
131. Elayi-Elayi, *Monnayage de Sidon*, pp. 459-461.
132. Elayi, *loc. cit.* (n. 8) 1992, pp. 24-25.

The letter which is most frequently represented throughout the Tyrian coinage is M. In Group I, it is mostly vertical with a short straight shaft, slightly tilted right in a few cases or curved leftward. Its head is in general a broad and relatively deep half-rectangle, but the left shoulder and the baseline are sometimes curved. The vertical or oblique central line is usually long and crosses the baseline. On the coins of Group II.1, the slightly tilted left stance predominates. The shaft is longer, straight or slightly curved. There are more square shoulders than curved ones. The central line rarely crosses the baseline. On the coins of Group II.2, the same evolution as the previously described is confirmed.

The N cannot be confused with the L in these inscriptions since the lower shaft is much longer than the upper. Rarely vertical, it is in general more or less tilted to the right. The lower shaft is straight, sometimes only slightly curved leftwards; it sometimes protrudes above the baseline. The ʿ presents several different forms. On the coins of Group II.1, it has the usual circular form, with a dot inside. On those of Group II.2, we find the same form as well as many others, with or without a dot inside, square, oval, irregular or open.

It is possible to follow the evolution of $\c{S}$, represented in the three periods selected. On the coins of Group I, it has a rather short straight shaft, slightly tilted left, and a horizontal head with a *zayin* form tilted into the shaft, generally at the angle of the contemporary Z. There is a tendency for it to flatten and assume a more horizontal position, with less angularity in the lines. This tendency seems to continue on the coins of Group II.1, not well represented. However, on the coins of Group II.2, the angular *zayin*-shaped head seems to predominate. The evolution concerns the lengthening of the shaft and a more leftward stance of the letter. On the coins of Group I, R is to be read instead of D despite some examples with short shafts, the shortening of the shaft apparently being due to the lack of space. The letter is rarely vertical, most of the time it is slightly tilted to the left. Its head has various forms: triangular, rounded, open on the top, open on the left side, with a horizontal or oblique baseline. On the coins of Group II.1, the shaft is long and its head is triangular with a curved upper line.

The $Š$ is only attested on the coins of Group I, but twice in each inscription. It has the three-pronged basic form common to the 5th century, with many variants. It is mostly rounded, the central line dropping into the middle of the curved, or at times flat, baseline. It is sometimes more squat and even rectangular, or rounded like the Greek letter ω. Its arms and central line can be straight or slightly curved right. There also exists the half-triangular form, with the central line dropping into the apex of the angle. The central line sometimes moves up on the right or left arm. The T is only represented on a few coins of Group II.1. Its shaft is not very long, being straight and tilted right. The crossbar and the drop-line have the same length. They are angular or drawn in a continuous curved stroke.

The figures of units are represented by parallel strokes. On the coins of Group II.1, they have the same length, they are regularly spaced, vertical or tilted left or right, straight or slightly curved. On the coins of Group II.2, they are still more various: besides the preceding forms, the strokes can be more or less long or short (sometimes like dots), with different lengths in the same numeral. They can be close or spaced, and rarely gathered by groups of three. The numeral *10* is represented by a stroke, which has several forms and stances. On the coins of Group II.1, it is horizontal, rarely oblique. It has a more or less deep half-circular form. Exceptionally, it is almost a straight stroke. On the coins of Group II.2, the oblique stance becomes more frequent. The half-circular form flattens more and more until becoming almost a straight stroke. Exceptionally it forms an open angle.

The Tyrian monetary inscriptions represent a significant addition to the Tyrian epigraphic corpus prior to the Hellenistic period, which is particularly small. Although outside Tyre, the geographic distribution of the Tyrian script is unknown,[133] we can use several parallels to Tyrian monetary inscriptions. However, they have no relation with a recently published votive inscription in the name of a Tyrian: this inscription has been related with ʾEšmunʿazor's and Bodʿaštart's inscriptions and erroneously dated from the mid-second half of the 5th century; moreover it is quite dubious.[134] The letter ʾ has the old formal shape, already attested in a Rachidieh inscription dated from the 8th century and in graffiti from Tell Keisan (Stratum 4a, 600-580 BCE).[135] The same formal shape was still in use during the Persian period, for example in a votive inscription dated from the last third of the 6th century and in a graffito found at Achzib (5th-4th centuries).[136] This form of ʾ continued during the Hellenistic period since it is attested in the Umm el-ʿAmed inscriptions and in the jar stamps of Tyre el-Bass.[137] The *B* that is vertical or with a slightly leftward tilt, already attested from the beginning of the 6th century at Tell Keisan, continues in the Persian period. It is found for example on a Tyrian amulet probably dat-

---

133. It did not necessarily coincide with the civic Tyrian territory.

134. P. Bordreuil, 'Nouvelle inscription phénicienne dédiée à Milqart', in *ACFP* V/1, Palermo 2005, pp. 135-137; cf. J. Elayi, 'Bibliographie', *Trans* 32, 2006, pp. 122-123; A. Lemaire, 'Epigraphie', *Trans* 32, 2006, p. 191.

135. P. Bordreuil, 'Deux épigraphes phéniciennes provenant des fouilles de Tell Rachidieh', *Annales d'Histoire et d'Archéologie* 1, 1982, pp. 137-140, no. 1; Briend-Humbert, *Tell Keisan*, pl. 91, 1-3 (Stratum 4a = 600-580).

136. A. Lemaire, 'Inscription royale phénicienne sur bateau votif', in M. Heltzer and M. Malul, *Tᵉshûrôt LaAvishur, Studies in the Bible and the Ancient Near East, in Hebrew and Semitic Languages, Festschrift Y. Avishur*, Tel Aviv-Jaffa 2004, p. 126*; B. Delavault and A. Lemaire, 'Les inscriptions phéniciennes de Palestine', *RSF* 7, 1979, pp. 4 and pl. III, 5 (7th century), 5 and pl. III, 6 (5th-4th centuries).

137. Peckham, *op. cit.* (n. 6), pl. VI, 4-8; I. Kawkabani, 'Les estampilles phéniciennes de Tyr', *AHL* 21, 2005, p. 12, no. J-B 5, l. 2 (The facsimile does not always match the photograph).

ing from the 5th century rather than the 6th,[138] and in the inscriptions of Umm el-ʿAmed and the jar stamps of Tyre el-Bass.[139] Considering the parallels, since they have the same confusing forms, does not solve the problematic reading of G or P.[140] A similar problem occurs for letter Z and numeral 20. By example, in the so-called tithe seals, this sign has two possible interpretations: in the seal of Bit Zitti (BT ZT), the first sign is clearly Z, the second (similar) could be Z (ʿZ 13 Ṣ) or 20 (ʿ33 Ṣ), ʿZ or ʿ being possibly the abbreviation of ʿZ(MLK), king of Tyre.[141] In Phoenician weights, this sign is to be read 20 because of the meaning of the inscriptions, while in the Umm el-ʿAmed inscriptions it has to be read Z.[142] However, in the jar stamps of Tyre el-Bass, when the sign must be read 20, it is rotated to the right, with its top line horizontal, but where it must be read Z, the form is different and it is rotated to the left.[143] The different forms of Ḥ are paralleled for example in the above mentioned votive inscription and Tyrian amulet for the Persian period, and later on in the Umm el-ʿAmed inscriptions and jar stamps of Tyre el-Bass.[144] The different forms of L are attested in the same votive inscription and Tyrian amulet, in an Akko inscription dated from the 5th century and in an Achzib graffito.[145] The forms of M and N slightly tilted right with a curved shaft are attested for example in the votive inscription and Tyrian amulet.[146] The angular form of N is attested in the jar stamps of Tyre el-Bass.[147] The circular form of ʿ is very well attested and the square form in the seal of Bit Zitti and the jar stamps of Tyre el-Bass.[148] The forms of Ṣ with an angular head have parallels in the votive inscription already mentioned, the Akko and Umm el-ʿAmed inscrip-

---

138. Briend-Humbert, *Tell Keisan*, pl. 91, 5; P. Bordreuil, 'Attestations inédites de Melqart, Baal Ḥamon et Baal Ṣaphon à Tyr', in C. Bonnet *et al.* eds, *Religio Phoenicia*, Studia Phoenicia IV, Namur 1986, pp. 82-83, fig. 4A-B, l. 1 (square head).

139. Peckham, *op. cit.* (n. 6), *ibid.*; Kawkabani, *loc. cit.* (n. 137), pp. 14, no. J-B 10, l. 2; 36, no. J-B 64, l. 1.

140. Cf., for example, Peckham, *ibid.*, pp. 66-69, pls V-VI; Kawkabani, *ibid.*, p. 21, no. J-B 26, l. 2, no. J-B 28, l. 2.

141. J.C. Greenfield, 'A Group of Phoenician City Seals', *IEJ* 35, 1985, p. 130, fig. 1; Lemaire, *loc. cit.* (n. 100) 1991, pp. 135, fig. 2e, and 142. The seal of Akshaf (ʾKŠP) also can be read ʿZ 16 or ʿ36.

142. Elayi-Elayi, *Poids phéniciens*, p. 380, fig. 12; Peckham, *op. cit.* (n. 6), p. 69, pl. VI, 4-8.

143. Kawkabani, *loc. cit.* (n. 137), pp. 10, no. J-B 1 (20); 26, no. J-B 37, l. 2 (Z).

144. Lemaire, *loc. cit.* (n. 136), p. 126; Bordreuil, *loc. cit.* (n. 138), p. 82, fig. 4A, l. 1; Peckham, *op. cit.* (n. 6), p. 69, pl. VI, 4-8; Kawkabani, *ibid.*, pp. 16, no. J-B 16, l. 1; 18, no. J-B 20, l. 1; 26, no. J-B 37, l. 2 (with only two cross-lines).

145. Lemaire, *ibid.*, p. 126; Bordreuil, *ibid.*, p. 82, fig. 4A, l. 1; M. Dothan, 'A Phoenician inscription from ʿAkko', *IEJ* 35, 1985, pl. 13, A, ll. 1-2; Delavault-Lemaire, *loc. cit.* (n. 136), p. 5 and pl. III, 6.

146. Lemaire, *ibid.*; Bordreuil, *ibid.*, l. 2.

147. Kawkabani, *loc. cit.* (n. 137), p. 26, no. J-B 38, l. 2.

148. Lemaire, *loc. cit.* (n. 100) 1991, p. 135, fig. 2e; Kawkabani, *ibid.*, p. 15, no. J-B 13, l. 2.

tions and the jar stamps of Tyre el-Bass.[149] The *R* has hardly evolved from an Achzib graffito dated from the 7th century to the seal of Bit Zitti, the Tyrian amulet, the jar stamps of Tyre el-Bass and Umm el-ᶜAmed inscriptions of the 3rd-2nd centuries.[150] The form with an open head on the left is found on the Tyrian amulet.[151] The different forms of *Š*, characteristic of the Persian period, are attested in the Akko inscription and the seal of Bit Zitti.[152] The *T* is attested in the jar stamps of Tyre el-Bass.[153] There are parallels for the units assembled in groups of three and for the numeral *10*, half-circular or angular, in the Akko inscription, the seal of Bit Zitti and the above-mentioned jar stamps.[154]

If we now compare the script of the Tyrian monetary inscriptions with that of the three other Phoenician mints, it will be possible to characterise the particularities of each of them. It is necessary to take into account the letters and numerals attested and the date of the coins. Only nine of the thirteen Tyrian letters are represented in the Byblian monetary inscriptions, seven in the Aradian and three in the Sidonian, and numerals from 1 to 17 are represented in the Aradian and Sidonian inscriptions. The Tyrian ʾ is very different from the Byblian and Aradian and seems close to the Sidonian ʾ, rarely attested. The Tyrian *B* is comparable with the Byblian *B* but different from the Sidonian and Aradian letter (rarely attested). The Tyrian *P* (if our reading is correct) is close to the Byblian and Aradian *P*. Letter *Z* (if our interpretation is correct) is similar to the Byblian *Z*; it cannot be compared with the Sidonian letter in Mazday's monetary inscriptions because of the Aramaic influence on this script. The *L* is only attested on Byblian coins: the forms with vertical stance are similar, but the tendency of the shaft to tilt to the right appears in the mid-5th century in Tyre and only in the first half of the 4th century in Byblos. Letter *M*, attested in the four mints, has some similar characteristics during the second half of the 5th century: the vertical stance, the short straight shaft, the rather long central line crossing the baseline. But the shoulder is different: mostly square in Arwad and Sidon, rounded in Byblos, with both forms represented in Tyre. In the 4th century, this letter follows a completely different evolution: in Tyre, the shaft is longer, the shoulders are mostly square and the central line rarely crosses the baseline. In Byblos, the central line lengthens while in Arwad, the letter tilts to the right, the shaft becomes longer and curved. It is not attested in Sidon during

---

149. Lemaire, *loc. cit.* (n. 136), p. 126; Dothan, *loc. cit.* (n. 145), pl. 13B, l. 3; Peckham, *op. cit.* (n. 6), p. 69, pl. VI, 4-8; Kawkabani, *ibid.*, pp. 12, no. J-B 5, l. 1; 14, no. J-B 10, l. 1.

150. Delavault-Lemaire, *loc. cit.* (n. 136), p. 4 and pl. 5; Lemaire, *loc. cit.* (n. 100) 1991, p. 135, fig. 2e; Bordreuil, *loc. cit.* (n. 138), p. 82, fig. 4A, l. 3; Kawkabani, *ibid.*, pp. 12, no. J-B 5, l. 1; 14, no. J-B 10, l. 2; Peckham, *ibid.*

151. Bordreuil, *ibid.*, fig. 4B, l. 1.

152. Dothan, *loc. cit.* (n. 145), pl. 13A, ll. 1-2; Lemaire, *loc. cit.* (n. 100) 1991, p. 135, fig. 2e, l. 1.

153. Kawkabani, *loc. cit.* (n. 137), pp. 11, no. J-B 3, l. 1; 15, no. J-B 13, l. 1.

154. Lemaire, *loc. cit.* (n. 100) 1991, pl. 135, fig. 2e, l. 3; Dothan, *loc. cit.* (n. 145), pl. 13A, l. 3, B, l. 2; Kawkabani, *ibid.*, pp. 16, no. J-B 14, l. 4; 26, no. J-B 37, l. 2, J-B 38, l. 3.

this period. The Tyrian *N* of the 5th century is closer to the Byblian *N* of the 4th century and different from the Aradian. The ʿ, represented in the four mints, is mostly circular but the other forms are also attested, the open form being more frequent in Byblos. The *R*, only represented in Byblos, is close to the different forms of the Tyrian letter, except that its shaft always seems to be vertical. The Tyrian *T*, represented on few specimens, is similar to some forms of the Sidonian letter. Letters *Ḥ*, *Ṣ* and *Š* are not attested in the monetary inscriptions of the other mints. The Tyrian numerals are close to the Sidonian ones, but in Tyre, the units are rarely assembled in groups of three, which predominates in Sidon, and they are more often straight and vertical in Sidon. The sign for *10* is different from that of Arwad where it is always a straight stroke.

The comparison between the monetary scripts of the four mints is difficult and somewhat biased due to the fact that a only small number of letters are attested for Sidon and that our conclusions are only based on a systematic analysis for Sidon and Tyre. However, each mint seems to have its own characteristics in the monetary scripts. There is some similarity between the Tyrian, Sidonian and Byblian monetary scripts, much less with the Aradian.[155] However, the monetary scripts seem to be more formal and conservative in their development in Tyre and Sidon than in Byblos and Arwad. When a letter is attested at different periods and it is possible to compare them (*M* and *Ṣ*), the evolution seems to be very slow. The lack of cursive contemporary scripts for Tyre but also for the other Phoenician cities makes the study of the cursive influence on the monetary scripts difficult. Only for a few Tyrian forms of *Ḥ*, *M* and ʿ, it is possible to detect a cursive influence. This influence seems to be more present in the Byblian and mainly Aradian inscriptions.

5. Sociocultural aspects of the Tyrian monetary script

In general, the epigraphists are not interested in the sociocultural aspects of scripts, such as the different points of view of those who ordered, wrote and read the inscription.[156] Did the engravers of Tyrian dies know how to write or not?[157] In theory, it was not necessary since they had to reproduce a model and the example of the above mentioned El-Hofra inscription shows that there were illiterate engravers.[158] However, two arguments tend to prove that they were usually literate. The first argument is the graphical variants that it is possible to observe on the dies made by the same engravers, or in the re-engraved dies (more difficult to observe): there is no doubt that they mastered the writing,

---

155. The comparison between the Tyrian and Sidonian scripts by J.B. Peckham is not enough argumented as far as the monetary inscriptions are concerned: *op. cit.* (n. 6), pp. 71-75.

156. Cf. Elayi, *loc. cit.* (n. 8) 1992, pp. 32-34; *id.*, *loc. cit.* (n. 8) 1991, pp. 190-191.

157. We have studied this question for the dies engravers and the moulds makers of weights: Elayi-Elayi, *Poids phéniciens*, pp. 258-260.

158. Cf., above, n. 125.

since illiterate engravers would not have risked graphical variants. The second argument is the phenomenon of the letters which are partly or totally reversed: this came from the fact that they possessed the automatism of writing from right to left and that they used it sometimes by error in the reversed inscriptions of the dies. However, we do not know whether they were just literate or really educated. Compared with the contemporary Greek engravers, the Tyrian as well as the Sidonian, Aradian and Byblian engravers never signed their dies in the present state of documentation. If this was the case, this would mean that the first engravers performed a personal work and the latter performed a public work. We shall see in Chapter V the technical aspects of engraving dies.

For whom were the monetary inscriptions intended? Their function was similar to that of the designs on the coins: to represent the minting authority but with supplementary precision such as the value of the coin, the name of the king or the date of issue. However, the Tyrian shekels exported as merchandise coins as far as Mesopotamia or Iran[159] were certainly not intended to be read because, in this function, only the metallic value was considered. In their local circulation within the territory of Tyre, Tyrian coins could not be read by several people such as the inhabitants who were illiterate, the other Phoenicians who were illiterate, the foreigners staying or just passing by the city and who were ignorant of Phoenician script. If these people had to use Tyrian coins, they probably identified them by the typology, weight or denomination. Currently, some scholars consider that the first series of coinages were not intended to be read or, if so, only by coins specialists such as money-changers. However, some elements seem to indicate that literate local users also read the first monetary inscriptions. Not only were the indications of values on Group I coins useful for money-changers but probably for users too. In the successive series having the same typology such as II.2.1.4 (*M3*) and II.2.1.6 (*1Š*), the change of abbreviation had a sense if it was read by the Tyrian users. When king *M* probably associated the crown prince ʾ (*M2ʾ*) to the reigning power, the purpose of propaganda is obvious.

As a matter of fact, there is a tendency to underestimate the degree of literacy of the Phoenician society, in particular the Tyrian, probably because of the small epigraphical corpus, which has been preserved by comparison with the neighbouring societies. One of the main reasons of this deficiency is the use of perishable material for writing.[160] The use of papyrus by Phoenicians, already attested about 1100 BCE in the report of Wen-amon, is confirmed for the 1st

---

159. Cf. Elayi-Elayi, *Trésors*, figs 25-26.
160. Cf., for example, W. Culican, 'The iconography of some Phoenician Seals and Seal Impressions', *AJBA* 1, 1968, pp. 57-58; A.R. Millard, 'The Uses of the Early Alphabets', in Baurain *et al.* eds, *op. cit.* (n. 8), pp. 101-114. For comparison with other societies, see, for example, C. Pébarthe, *Cité, démocratie et écriture. Histoire de l'alphabétisation d'Athènes à l'époque classique*, Paris 2006.

millennium by the discovery of bullae, which served to seal such documents.[161] The large diffusion of writing is well-documented in the Persian period, and even earlier, by the use of *ostraca*, various marks of manufacturers, monetary countermarks, inscribed weights and seals, and various graffiti on pottery, then on coins. These different kinds of scripts show that the writing was not limited to the palace or temple and not only in the hands of professional scribes, since the alphabetic script was much more accessible than the syllabic cuneiform script for example.[162] The development of the cursive script, well-attested for example in the monetary inscriptions of Arwad and Byblos in the 4th century, shows the large diffusion of writing in the popular levels of society.[163] In Tyre however, the influence of cursive script in the monetary inscriptions is not important. But the fact that the first Tyrian series was inscribed means that the writing was largely diffused in this city. The use of abbreviations in the third quarter of the 5th century in Sidon seems to be new in Phoenicia, maybe on the model of Greek monetary abbreviations. Tyre followed this use about the end of the 5th century in her coinage (Series II.1.2.1). There are several other indications of the large diffusion of writing, for example the maledictions in Sidonian and Byblian funeral inscriptions addressed, among others, to everybody (*KL 'DM*).[164] It is interesting to remark that the Aḥiram inscription was only addressed to kings, governors and commanders, but that a graffito was added on the wall of the grave: 'Beware! Behold, there is disaster for you under this!' *LD'T HN YPD LK TḤT ZN*.[165] More than for a magical purpose, such inscriptions were logically addressed to possible ordinary robbers who were able to read them. It is impossible to know the degree of literacy of the Tyrian society, but certainly many users of the coins were literate, if not educated. Therefore, despite other possible reasons, the minting authority probably intended the monetary inscriptions, from the beginning of the coinage, to be read by a part of the local users.

Finally we shall wonder as to the function of graffiti and countermarks in Tyrian coinage. This phenomenon has to be evaluated by comparison with other coinages: only 7 graffiti and 7 countermarks on Tyrian coins. It is more than in Byblian coinage where as yet we have seen neither countermarks nor graffiti.[166] But it is less than in Sidonian coinage (15 graffiti and 4 counter-

---

161. Culican, *ibid.*, pp. 57-61; N. Avigad, 'Seals and Sealings', *IEJ* 14, 1964, p. 194; E. Gubel, 'Cinq bulles inédites des archives tyriennes de l'époque achéménide', *Sem.* 47, 1998, pp. 59-64. A.R. Millard, *ibid.*, considers that Phoenicians possibly used, like their neighbours, other perishable material such as leather rolls, wood and wax tablets for writing. Cf. also A. Lemaire, 'Vom Ostrakon zur Schriftrolle', *ZDMG*, Suppl. VI, 1985, pp. 112-116.
162. Cf. Millard, *ibid.*
163. Cf. Elayi, *loc. cit.* (n. 8) 1992, pp. 28-32; Elayi-Elayi, *Trésors*, pp. 310-311.
164. *KAI* 13, 1.3; 14, II.4, 6-7, 11, 20, 22; 10, 1.11; 1, 1.2; 2.
165. *KAI* 2.
166. Our observation is provisional as we have not yet finished our corpus of Byblian coinage.

marks),[167] in Aradian coinage (8 graffiti and 11 countermarks),[168] and in the Meydancikkale hoard for example (hundreds of graffiti and countermarks).[169] As we have already written, 'in a context that could be described as 'monetary anarchy' because of the various contemporary systems of exchange (barter, weighed metal, merchandise coins used in monetary economy), a coin could still be considered by some people as a personal, valuable object among others. Its owner of the moment could have marked it in order to recognize it eventually in the potential event of loss or theft or in a shared deposit out of a banking context'.[170] The beginning of monetary graffiti in Transeuphratene, probably parallel to the graffiti of owners on vases and other objects, could be related with the development of the cursive script and indicate the diffusion of literacy during this period in the coastal cities. The Tyrian monetary countermarks were not official but private, and probably stamped by people who dealt with money (testers, bankers and changers) as marks of control and guarantee. Each of them probably used the punch that he had made for this purpose. There is a relation between the phenomenon of the small countermarks and that of the monetary graffiti. Thus, both seem to be linked to the circulation of coins out of their minting area. This can be seen, for example, from the fact that they are absent on the Byblian coins, which were not exported out of the city, and that they are usually found on worn coins, that is having circulated a lot. These two phenomena seem to have begun in the 6th century in Asia Minor at the same time as the beginning of coinage. Then they seem to have expanded during the 4th century to the entire Levantine coast, from the south of Asia Minor to Egypt, peaking in the last third of the 4th century and the first half of the third. The small, private countermarks seem to have been diffused from the area of circulation of Persian shekels, towards the Phoenician cities and Egypt, maybe through Arwad, who had possessions as far as Al-Mina, was trading with Cilicia and aligned her coinage on the Persian standard.[171]

---

167. Elayi-Elayi, *Monnayage de Sidon*, pp. 453-456.
168. Cf., provisionally, Elayi-Lemaire, *Graffiti*, pp. 43, no. 24; 46, no. 36; 47, no. 48; 52, no. 79; 55, no. 92; 58, no. 116; 61, no. 135; 63, no. 149; 130, no. 142; 133, no. 160, 163; 134, no. 164, 167, 169; 136, no. 178; 150, no. 268-271.
169. Davesne-Le Rider, *op. cit.* (n. 16).
170. Elayi-Elayi, *Trésors*, p. 310; Elayi-Lemaire, *Graffiti*, p. 209, n. 1.
171. Elayi-Elayi, *ibid.*, pp. 310-317; Elayi-Lemaire, *ibid.*, pp. 209-210.

CHAPITRE IV

ANALYSIS OF ICONOGRAPHY

The Tyrian monetary iconography of the Persian period was as conservative as the Sidonian[1] because the Tyrian coins had only eight different motives represented either as main or secondary motives or both. The owl, the deity, the head of lion, the head of ram and the rosette were only used as main designs. The dolphin, the seahorse and the shell were alternately used as main and secondary motifs. The sea, symbolised by lines of waves, is most of the time represented below the dolphin, the deity riding on seahorse and the seahorse alone. Some types are complex such as the deity riding on seahorse above waves and dolphin. In these cases, it is difficult to see all the details as most of the coins are more or less worn or damaged. As for the monetary inscriptions, it is first necessary to give as accurate a description as possible of the motifs that are represented before moving on to their interpretation. We shall study them by order of frequency and importance: main or secondary use, obverse or reverse, shekels or small denominations. It is important to consider also their possible evolutions (or absence of evolution), their relation with the monetary inscriptions and the relation between obverse and reverse types. We shall study the representations of these motifs on shekels because the details are easier to observe, but we shall also consider their representations on small denominations when necessary.

1. The owl

The owl is the most frequent motif used in the Tyrian coinage. It is always represented on the reverse of the coins, in all the silver series of the Persian period, except in Series III.1.1.d, III.1.1.e, III.1.1.f and III.1.2.e. The owl is completely absent from the bronze series.

---

1. Cf. Elayi-Elayi, *Monnayage de Sidon*, pp. 471-539.

Although it is stated in most publications, the Tyrian owl has nothing to do with the owl represented on Athenian silver tetradrachms, the so-called 'owls'.[2] Some scholars have noticed that the Tyrian owl bore a closer resemblance to the Egyptian model of the reliefs and statuary, but for them it was only a matter of style: the Tyrian owl was depicted as a copy of the Athenian owl, but 'in the Syro-Phoenician style, after that of the Egyptians'.[3] Other scholars consider that the Tyrian owl imitated the Egyptian owl used in the M hieroglyph, and that it could be a linguistic borrowing.[4] As a matter of fact, the Tyrian owl is also different from the Egyptian engraved or painted hieroglyph since it is represented with the crook and flail.[5]

We first have to identify the exact species of owl represented on the Tyrian coins. Then we shall question whether the Tyrian engravers had the opportunity to observe such birds in the territory of Tyre and whether their representations are realistic. Both Athenian and Tyrian owls belong to the family of *Strigidae*, nocturnal or crepuscular birds hunting for prey, which are true predators by the shape of their beak and clawed feet. But the Athenian owl is a small owl (*Athene noctua*) while the Tyrian is an 'eared' owl. From its representation, it could be either the *Asio otus* (long-eared owl) or the *Otus scops* or *Otus brucei* (scops owl) characterised in particular by the two egrets (tufts of feathers above the eyes), vertically erect most of the time.[6] The *Asio otus*, common in Europe, also lives in Asia Minor and southwards to Lebanon. In size, it is about 35cm long; it lives in woods, copses of conifers and broad-leaved trees that were then plentiful on the western side of the Lebanon coastal range. It feeds on insects, birds, micro-mammals and sometimes attacks relatively large preys.[7] The *Otus scops* and *Otus brucei* are smaller (19cm), mainly insects-eaters, and live in the trees of orchards and gardens. They are common on Eastern Mediterranean shores.[8] It is impossible to confuse these three last birds (*Asio otus*, *Otus scops* or *brucei*) with the *Athene noctua* because of their important typological differ-

---

2. For example *BMC Phoenicia*, p. cxxvii; Babelon, *Perses*, p. CLXXXIX.
3. Betlyon, *Coinage of Phoenicia*, p. 41.
4. P. Grierson, in P. Naster, 'Le développement des monnaies phéniciennes avant Alexandre, d'après les trésors', in *Proceedings of the International Numismatic Convention*, Tel Aviv 1967, pp. 21-22; P. Naster, 'La technique des revers partiellement incus des monnaies phéniciennes', in *id.*, *Scripta Nummaria, Contributions à la méthodologie numismatique*, Louvain-la-Neuve 1983, pp. 22-23.
5. The hieroglyphic hawk is alone or with a flail only (without crook): cf. J. Elayi, 'Les monnaies de Byblos au sphinx et au faucon', *RSF* 11, 1983, p. 14; *id.*, 'Le monnayage de Byblos avant Alexandre: problèmes et perspectives', *Trans* 1, 1989, pp. 13-14.
6. Cf. for example, F. Hüe and R.D. Etchécopar, *Les oiseaux du Proche et du Moyen Orient*, Paris 1970, pp. 405-407; R.H. Voous, *Owls of the Northern Hemisphere*, London 1988, p. 42. We thank J.-F. Voisin (Laboratoire des Mammifères et oiseaux, Muséum d'Histoire Naturelle, Paris) for his help. According to him, the *Bubo bubo* (eagle owl) seems to be excluded, in particular because the orientation of its subocular tufts of feathers is rather horizontal than vertical. Another factor has also to be considered, namely the variations in the distribution of species from Antiquity.
7. Hüe-Etchécopar, *ibid.*, pp. 416-417.
8. *Ibid.*, pp. 405-407.

ences. It is clear that the Tyrian engravers did not imitate the Athenian model, although the *Athene noctua* was also known in the Eastern Mediterranean and that they could see it represented on the numerous imported Athenian tetradrachms.

However, the tail and wings of the Tyrian owl are often surprisingly long, and the body thin. That is why G.F. Hill has considered it as a hybrid bird, with an owl's head (Athenian) and a hawk's body (Egyptian).[9] But the realistic details are sufficient to show that the engravers started from a direct observation of a species known in the city of Tyre: either *Asio otus* or *Otus scops* or *Otus brucei*. Of course, it cannot be excluded that the somewhat hawk-shaped aspect of this owl was inspired by the Egyptian model. As a matter of fact, the appearance of this bird changes considerably depending on its position. For example, when the *Otus scops* is discovered, it stands up and stresses, making it appear much thinner than it really is, and its egrets become particularly apparent.[10] It is probably this position which was reproduced by the Tyrian engravers. On the other hand, we must take into account a rather forceful stylization, especially on the coins of Series I.2.1 where the use of the semi-incuse method of engraving (the whole type is in relief surrounded by the characteristic incuse impression) has made the body of the owl thinner or at least has given this illusion.

The differences in the representations of the owl on Tyrian coins also depend on the different styles of the engravers. These differences are expressed over and above two permanent features: firstly, the reverse type owl with crook and flail remains unchanged throughout all the coinage in order to be more easily recognisable inside and outside the minting city. Secondly, the engravers were continuously anxious to produce a realistic representation of this species of the owl that they could observe in the territory of Tyre.[11] Some engraving details, such as the large egrets, could not have been borrowed either from an Athenian model where they do not exist, nor an Egyptian one where they are very small or totally absent. We shall study the representations of the owl on shekels as it is easier to observe them because in general they have been more carefully engraved and are larger in size. Moreover, the representations of the owl on small denominations are not, as a general rule, different from those of shekels since they would have been executed by the same engravers at the same time. There are approximately three stages in the representations of owls: a careful and accurate representation (Series I.1.1, I.2.1 and II.1.1.1.a), a more or less careless representation (Series II.1.1.1.b-c, 1.2.1) and a more and more

---

9. *BMC Phoenicia*, p. cxxxiv.
10. Hüe-Etchécopar, *op. cit.* (n. 6), p. 405.
11. We do not agree with the groundless comment of L. Sole, 'Le emissioni monetali della Fenicia prima di Alessandro-II', *SEAP* 18, 1998, p. 85.

stylised and hasty representation (Series II.2.1). This general trend does vary however, depending on the skill of engravers.

In Series I.1.1, the volumes are favoured with respect to the lines. The owl is made in high relief so that the representation seems to be realistic and lively. Its body and head are relatively large and full. Its legs, apart, are covered with feathers looking like 'pants', with oblique edges, which exist on the Egyptian owl, but not on the Athenian. The feathers are represented in different manners, depending on where they are on the body: dots on the breast and legs, three rows of short parallel strokes on the wing, ending in one long feather, separated from the seven long strokes representing the tail feathers (no. 1, 4, 8). These rows go lengthwards, unlike the hieroglyph and the Athenian owl where they go widthwards.[12] The claws are correctly represented on both sides of the two legs as on the Athenian owl and unlike the Egyptian where they are on one side only. The head is rounded, with globular eyes, some kind of eyebrows, beard and two dots representing the egrets. This head is very different from the Athenian with larger eyes and longer bill, and from the Egyptian with smaller eyes and longer bill, both of them without long egrets.[13] The different dots were possibly made by different sized punches. The crook and flail are similar to the Egyptian symbols of power worn by the god Osiris and the pharaohs.[14] The crook ends with a hook turned upwards, more or less large and open, sometimes with its tip curved to the left (no. 4). The hanging part of the flail is decorated by transverse, then lengthway strokes. Both shafts of the crook and flail remain undecorated.

In Series I.2.1, the engraving of the owl was complicated by the techniques of semi-incusion, that is an incuse impression fitting an outline of type, but the engraving is still very careful and accurate. The owl looks thinner but it is perhaps only an impression because of the surrounding line. Its legs are close together and the feather 'pants' are tightened (no. 50). There is a line of dots along the left part of the wing (no. 38). The feathers of the extremity of the wing and of the tail are joined together (six long strokes on no. 66). The beard is more protruding and the egrets look like long ears (no. 38, 51). The flail is decorated by transverse chevrons on coin no. 38, by alternate transverse and lengthway strokes on coin no. 66.

In Series II.1.1.1.a, the engraving is particularly careful, accurate and lively, without the constraint of the incuse impression. The representation of the owl is well-balanced, neither too thin nor too fat, with a good reproduction of volume and details, and location within the field. The legs are parallel and slightly apart, the feather 'pants' are slightly tightened. The extremity of the wing and

---

12. See, for example, C. Aldred et al., *L'Égypte du crépuscule*, Paris 1980, p. 77, fig. 57 (Petosiris' sarcophagus made of wood inlaid with polychrom glasses); Kraay, *Greek Coins*, p. 287.
13. Aldred et al., *ibid.*; Kraay, *ibid.*
14. Aldred et al., *ibid.*, p. 118, fig. 104 (wood painted stela from Deir el-Bahari, representing a singer of Amon and Osiris).

the tail are assembled in five long strokes. The feathers on the body and legs are represented by lines of dots, probably made by a punch. The wing is made of five curved dotted lines (no. 283) or partly with cable lines (no. 299). The head is more or less rounded with a beard, globular circled eyes, eyebrows continued by a small nose, and rounded ears for egrets. The hook of the crook is almost closed. The hanging part of the flail is alternately made by transverse and lengthway strokes. Both shafts are represented by thin lines.

When the style begins to be debased (Series II.1.1.b), the representation of the owl becomes careless and clumsy: for example, the owl is bent forward too much, its legs are distorted, its tail is too short and raised, and the shafts of crook and flail are not straight (coin no. 342). In Series II.1.2.1, there is less volume: the owl begins to become flat, the strokes are thick and quite clumsy, and the tail is made of four thick lines (no. 666). Sometimes the owl looks to be humped, which results from observing the bird in a certain position (no. 627). The hook of the crook ends with a reverse curved tip (no. 698).

After the change of standard, the owl becomes stylised and more or less rigid and flat (Series II.2.1). Its body is thinner, its head is smaller and its tail and legs are longer, the 'pants' on its legs become larger (no. 807). The different feathers are represented in various manners, which bear no resemblance to the Athenian and Egyptian owls: on the breast and legs, they are semicircles with a dot inside; on the wing, there is a first row on the top with small strokes, surrounded by a semicircular row with longer fan-shaped strokes, then below, a triangle with parallel strokes and the wing ends in a very long feather joined to the three or four tail feathers (no. 807, 854). The claws are composed of dots. The head is flattened at the bottom and is surrounded by short strokes, the ears and eyes are made of dots and the nose is represented by a vertical stroke between them (no. 854). Sometimes, the nose continues into the eyebrows (no. 807). The shafts of crook and flail are less oblique than before the change of standard, they are rarely straight and parallel. The hook of the crook has an upward tip. The hanging part of the flail is made of two long thin strokes intersected by two short transverse strokes in the middle and at the bottom (no. 859). However, in Series II.2.1.2 and II.2.1.4, the triangle of the wing is missing, the tail is shorter and the body of the owl slightly plump (no. 822, 837). In the last series of King ʿOzmilk (II.2.1.14-28), the style of representation was the same as it was earlier, from year 3 to year 9, but with a progressive debasement (no. 887 and 1061 for example). The left leg of the owl moves forward. From the issues of year 10 to year 17, the leg and breast feathers are made of dots. The style is sometimes particularly clumsy, with the tail made of two feathers and curved upwards and the crook and flail almost horizontal (no. 1229, 1234), the leg and body joints indicated by dots (no. 1346), the feet represented by three slightly oblique strokes (no. 1393). Most of the issues of years 15, 16 and 17 seem to be particularly clumsy (no. 1346, 1393). However, we do not exclude the possibility that some coins, which we have not seen, are ancient imitations or modern counterfeits.

The symbolic meaning of the Tyrian owl is difficult to understand because this animal is not mentioned in any Phoenician inscription; however, it is well-attested in the Old Testament.[15] It does not belong to the usual Phoenician iconography, like the hawk for instance,[16] and it is rarely represented, one example being a glass owl of the Persian period found in Tyre, but without crook and flail.[17] Instead of being held respectively in left and right hands as usual, they are carried over the left shoulder of El, on a Phoenician stele from Egypt.[18] The owl, symbol of Athena on Athenian tetradrachms, is presented in ancient Near Eastern cultures, depending on its species, as preying on small rodents and birds, living in ruined cities, as an awe-inspiring creature, thought to give omens, etc.[19] As far as the Tyrians of the 5th century are concerned, we do not know the meaning that this species of owl being, an essential symbol of their coins, had for them. However, this owl is represented with the symbols of Tyrian royal power – Osirian crook and flail – in the Egyptian manner, as on Byblian coins.[20] Therefore, the meaning of the owl is necessarily related to the idea of power and domination. The idea of aggressiveness which characterises this predator (if it is the *Asio otus*) could point to the military power of the city, particularly of the king when his name is associated with the owl on the reverse type. This military power also seems to be related to the divine warrior of the obverse in the series of Group II. The owl could also generate an idea of speed as this kind of owl is a fast-flying bird: this idea would correspond exactly to that expressed by the fast-swimming dolphin and the winged seahorse represented on the obverse.

2. The dolphin

The dolphin is also a very frequently used motif in the Tyrian coinage. It is almost always represented on the obverse, hence highlighting its importance, often as the main design, but most of time as a secondary symbol. It is repre-

---

15. Cf. G.R. Driver, 'Birds in the Old Testament', *PEQ* 87, 1955, pp. 13-15, 135-136 (with bibl.).
16. E. Gubel, 'The iconography of inscribed Phoenician glyptic', in B. Sass and C. Uehlinger, *Studies in the Iconography of Northwest Semitic Inscribed Seals*, Fribourg-Göttingen 1993, p. 120, no. 60 (seal of YḤZBʿL).
17. E. Gubel ed., *Les Phéniciens et le monde méditerranéen*, Catalogue de l'Exposition de Bruxelles, 21/5-6/7/1986, p. 243, no. 278.
18. Cf. R. Dussaud, *L'art phénicien du IIe millénaire*, Paris 1949, p. 52, fig. 17.
19. Cf. Driver, *loc. cit.* (n. 15), *ibid.*; T.E. Homerin, 'Echoes of a Thirsty Owl: Death and Afterlife in Pre-Islamic Arabic Poetry', *JNES* 44, 1985, pp. 165-184, espec. 166, n. 6 (with bibl.); *Encyclopedia of Religion and Ethics* I, Edinburgh 1908, pp. 523-524. Cf. the tablet of the deity Kilili standing on two lions between two facing owls: E. Von der Osten-Sacken, 'Überlegungen zur Göttin auf dem Burneyrelief', in *XLVIInd RAI*, Helsinki 2002, pp. 479-487, espec. 480 and pl. 1.
20. Cf. Elayi, *loc. cit.* (n. 5) 1983, pp. 5-17.

sented on the reverse in Series III.1.1.e and III.1.1.f. It is lacking only in silver Series II.1.1.3, II.1.2.3 and III.1.1.a-d, and in bronze Series III.2.1 and III.2.3.

The dolphin represented on the obverse of the coins from the beginning of the Tyrian coinage, belongs to the well-known species of the *Delphinus delphis*. This kind of dolphin, about 2m/2.50m long, is used to living in warm temperate seas and is particularly frequent in the Mediterranean and Black Sea.[21] Our first question is to ask whether its representation on Tyrian coins is realistic. Tyrian seafarers certainly knew the dolphins since they often swam zigzagging in front of their ships travelling at between 15 and 30 knots, because their body is perfectly adapted to swimming rapidly. The fact that they have lungs obliges them to frequently swim back to the surface in order to breathe. That is why they jump out of the water, and then immediately dive back in, head first with the curved movement that is represented on the coins of Group I. This movement is reproduced in a real-life situation by the Tyrian engravers who had no doubt observed them from the seashore as dolphins are not at all scared and probably came in very close to the island of Tyre. Likewise, some realistic details can only be explained by a direct observation of dolphins. First the head, seen in profile, is easily recognisable by its long and narrow nose, clearly separated from the receding forehead by a deep groove. The length of the beak, which is from 13 to 15cm, has been respected in proportion to the length of the body. However, the field on the coin is very cramped with the result that it often falls out of the flan or is interrupted by the dotted circle. The lump of the forehead, enlarging with age, is very marked here, which means that it is fully-grown. The eye of the dolphin is relatively large and surrounded by a black circle. The engravers have enlarged it more than it is in reality, probably in a perspective of stylisation.

The dorsal fin, represented by horizontal grooves, is in the correct position on most coins, but is a little too far forward on some coins. The shape of the caudal fin, which is long, forked and grooved, is correct but it is seen from above or from three-quarters, not in profile. For example, on the Syracuse silver decadrachms, the four dolphins represented on the obverse are in profile, which is less decorative. It is difficult to say whether the Tyrian engravers did not know how to represent a dolphin laterally[22] or whether they preferred the decorative rather than the realistic effect. Below the dolphin is represented one of the two paws: it is represented with horizontal grooves because, at first sight, it looks like the ventral fin of a fish, but it contains the skeleton which is typical of a land mammal's limb. When the dolphin is seen in profile, only one paw can be seen, smaller than the dorsal fin and located further forward. On most of

---

21. Cf., for example, J.R. Norman and F.C. Fraser, *Les géants de la mer. Requins. Baleines. Dauphins*, Paris 1938, pp. 401-403; *Traité de zoologie* XIII/3, Paris 1958, p. 2385.
22. It can be seen from the Phoenician iconography of the Persian period that this aspect of representation was not always mastered.

the coins, the paw is not pushed forward and its size is not reduced. Rather than an error of representation, it could be an attempt to obtain a degree of symmetry in a perspective of stylisation.

However, there is one particular feature of this dolphin, which never seems to have been noticed: it is the small lateral wing with horizontal strokes, fixed a little bit in front of the paw by a tie made of four vertical grooves. This cannot be a defect of the die[23] because it can be seen on several coins with different obverse dies (no. 1, 2, 3, 4, 7, 8, 12, 38, 50, 66, 190). It is often partly obliterated because it is located on the most protruding part of the obverse which is the first to get worn. However, this wing is very clear on some well-preserved coins such as no. 3 or 7. The identification of a wing is quite certain for the following reasons: its shape differs from those of the fins and paws, the Tyrian engravers were too familiar with dolphins to confuse a wing with fins and paw, and this wing is similar to the small stylised wing of the seahorse represented on the later small denominations (no. 719).

Therefore the representation of the dolphin on Tyrian coins is a mixture of styles: it is both realistic reflecting a direct and accurate observation, stylised in line with coin engraving requirements and imaginary due to the addition of a wing, transforming the dolphin into a mythical animal, the winged dolphin.[24] When the dolphin becomes a secondary symbol on the following series, it is not clear whether the wing was still represented because of the small size of the animal and the more stylised or clumsy representation. When the engraving is very precise and detailed, the wing could be invisible: it is possibly represented on the dolphins of coins no. 271, 302, 313, and 1283 for example, but this needs further confirmation.

Just as when the owl figured on the reverse, the representation of the dolphin on the obverse depends on the different styles of the engravers. The dolphin is easier to observe on the shekels because of the larger size of the coins, but it seems to be similar on the small denominations except for a more stylised representation on the smallest coins. In Series I.1.1, the dolphin is represented, as we have said, diving head first into water immediately after having jumped out. Its body is formed in high relief so that its head and body are relatively large and full (no. 3). There is a dot between the end of the body and the caudal fin. The eye is a large dot surrounded by a circle (no. 7). We have already analysed above the other details of this representation. In Series I.2.1, the only difference is that the dolphin's body is generally thinner seeming therefore to be longer. In Group I, the sea is represented below the dolphin by wavy lines. The number of lines and crests depends on the denominations: three lines with

---

23. As it has been groundless stated by L. Sole, *loc. cit.* (n. 11), p. 93.
24. On the different registers of coin iconography, cf. J. Elayi, 'Remarques méthodologiques sur l'étude iconographique des monnaies phéniciennes', *MUSJ* 60, 2007 (*Mélanges J.-P. Rey-Coquais*), pp. 47-54.

six crests on shekels, two lines with five crests on quarters of shekel, two lines with three crests on sixteenths of shekel and one line with one crest on the smallest denomination.

In Series II.1.1.1 and II.1.2.1, the dolphin has become a secondary symbol, placed below the lines of waves, which themselves are below the deity riding on seahorse. Its size is much smaller and it is relatively detailed. However, the main difference is in the movement: its body is slightly curved and it is now swimming and not jumping because it is under the surface of the sea, below the lines of waves (no. 271). In Series II.2.1, the representation of the dolphin is more or less stylised, or clumsy, and with no detail, and its body is no longer curved but straight. In the small denominations where the dolphin is the main obverse or reverse symbol the sea is never represented. It can be jumping with its body curved (no. 1588) or swimming with its body straight (no. 1767). Its tail can be turned upwards in Series III.1.2.c (no. 1643) where it is similar to the dolphins represented on a Punic stele.[25] Its body can be large (no. 1589) or more or less thin (no. 1767).

Even if there are no Phoenician written sources mentioning dolphins, the animal is very common, unlike the owl, both in Phoenician iconography as in other coinages. It appears in Aradian coinage, held by the tail in each hand of the ichthyomorphic deity or represented below the war-galley.[26] The dolphin is also a motif encountered in Phoenician and Punic iconography such as on seals, clay pellets, weights or steles for instance.[27] It is most frequently found in Greek coinages such as those of Syracuse, Tarentum, Nesos, Pyrgos, Peparethos, Methymna, Iasos, etc.[28] In the Graeco-Roman world, the dolphin is associated with several myths and stories from Pindar to Plutarch. It was regarded as the king of sea animals, presented as a socialising animal guiding and rescuing people, displaying intelligent care and forethought that likened it to humans (even able to commit suicide).[29] Associated with Poseidon, Dionysus and Aph-

---

25. E. Lipiński dir., *Dictionnaire de la civilisation phénicienne et punique*, Turnhout 1992, pl. XVd.
26. *BMC Phoenicia*, pl. I, 1-10; cf. J. Elayi and A.G. Elayi, 'La divinité marine des monnaies préalexandrines d'Arwad', *Trans* 21, 2001, pp. 133-148; *id.*, 'Baʿal Arwad', in *ACFP* V/1, Palermo 2005, pp. 129-132; cf. also, later, the winged genius riding on dolphin in the coinage of Berytus: *BMC Phoenicia*, pl. X, 5.
27. Gubel, *loc. cit.* (n. 16), pp. 115-116, no. 27-28; P. Bordreuil, 'Tanit du Liban (Nouveaux documents religieux phéniciens III)', in E. Lipiński ed. *Phoenicia and the East Mediterranean in the first Millennium B.C.*, Studia Phoenicia V, Leuven 1987, p. 83, fig. 1; P. Bordreuil and E. Gubel eds, 'BAALIM VI', *Syr.* 67, 1990, p. 511, fig. 30AB; S. Moscati dir., *I Fenici*, Milan 1988, pp. 22, 306.
28. Cf., for example, F.E. Zeuner, 'Dolphins on coins of the Classical Period', *BICS* 10, 1963, pp. 97-103 (with bibl.).
29. J. Wiesner, *s.v.* 'Delphin', in *Lexikon der Alten Welt*, Stuttgart 1965, p. 706; L. Van der Stockt, 'Plutarch and Dolphins: Love is all you need', in J. Boulogne ed., *Les Grecs de l'Antiquité et les animaux. Le cas remarquable de Plutarque*, Lille 2005, pp. 13-21 (with bibl.).

rodite, dolphins were presented as instruments of the gods.[30] Pindar believed them to be music-lovers:
'Like a dolphin of the sea
Who on the waveless ocean deep,
Is moved by the lovely sound of flutes'.[31]

The symbolic meaning attached to the dolphin in the Tyrian coinage is far from clear. According to a Greek myth, a dolphin rescued Ino and Melicerte and brought them back to Corinth; Melicerte was named Palemon and became the protector of seafarers.[32] But the identification of Melicerte/Palemon with the Tyrian god Milqart, which has been proposed, seems to be unlikely especially as Milqart is never represented riding on a dolphin.[33] Although we do not know the Tyrian mythology of the Persian period, the meaning of the winged dolphin is probably related to that of the winged seahorse. As we have said, the idea of speed could be present (as in the case of the owl on the reverse) as the dolphin is a fast-swimming animal. It could represent, as well as the seahorse, a good mount for riding across the seas, an idea developed in several myths, in the same way as the war-galley of the three other Phoenician coinages but with an additional divine component. The reduction in the size of the dolphin in the Group II Series, from the last quarter of the 5th century, undoubtedly signifies a lessening of its importance. It could also mean an evolution in the attributes of the Tyrian deity and perhaps too a development of human representation in Tyrian monetary iconography at the expense of animal representation.

3. The seahorse

The seahorse is, after the owl and dolphin, the most frequently used motif in Tyrian coinage. Completely absent from Group I, it was thereafter almost continuously represented on the Tyrian coins, always on the obverse. However, it cannot be said that it replaced the dolphin, which never disappeared from the Tyrian coinage. The seahorse was used as a main motif on several small denominations: silver Series II.1.1.3, II.1.2.2, II.2.1, III.1.1 and bronze Series III.2.1. It was a secondary symbol on the shekels and quarters of shekel: Series II.1.1.1, II.1.1.2 and II.1.2.1.

The seahorse of the Tyrian coinage is an entirely mythical animal, contrary to the owl, which was a realistic representation and to the dolphin which, except for the addition of a wing, was also a realistic representation. Even if the

---

30. Van der Stockt, *ibid.*, p. 16.
31. Pindar, Frg. 125, lines 69-71.
32. Cf. E. Will, *Korinthiaka*, Paris 1955 (with bibl.).
33. Cf. M. Fantar, 'Le cavalier marin de Kerkouane', *Africa*, 1966, pp. 19-32; *id.*, *Le dieu de la mer chez les Phéniciens et les Puniques*, Rome 1977, p. 105; C. Bonnet, 'Le culte de Leucothéa et de Mélicerte, en Grèce, au Proche-Orient et en Italie', *SMSR* 52, 1986, p. 53; *id.*, *Melqart. Cultes et mythes de l'Héraclès tyrien en Méditerranée*, Leuven 1988, pp. 388-390.

starting point for the representation was the marine animal known as the seahorse (*syngnathus hippocampus*, Linné), which the engravers probably knew, the mythical Tyrian seahorse is quite different. It has the head, forelock and forelegs of a horse, harnessed and galloping, and is similar to the Sidonian horses of Series III.1, dated from the last quarter of the 5th century and contemporary.[34] The seahorse has the same tail and fins as the dolphin of the Tyrian previous series of Group I. The wing is reminiscent of that of the owl of the reverse but it is spread, like the wing of the sphinx, vultur and seahorse of the more or less contemporary Byblian coinage.[35] Since it is a mythical animal, the representations rely partly on a conventional stereotype and partly on the imagination of each engraver.

In the carefully worked representations of Series II.1.1.1, where the seahorse is a secondary motif, the forehead of the horse is realistic, even expressing the effort of the galloping animal with the curved neck and open mouth. All the details of the head with the short mane, the prominent neck, cheek, eye, nose, chin, together with the jointed legs with hoofs are indicated (no. 266). The tail of the seahorse is curved upwards, ending with a dot and a bifurcate caudal fin just like the dolphin below. But it has in addition two ventral fins, grooved by several short oblique strokes (eight to ten on coin no. 266). The wing is curled and is generally composed of three parts: four or five lines of dots on the body, then a set of long parallel curled feathers, covering a second identical set of feathers which are much longer and curled upwards. The differences of detail, thickness, number of lines of dots, of feathers, orientation of the wing, care or clumsiness, depend on the style of each engraver. The same thing can be said for the quarters of shekel. For example, in spite of the smaller field, the representation of the seahorse of the quarter of shekel no. 402 can be compared to that of shekel no. 283. In Series II.1.2.1 where the seahorse is also a secondary motif, the representation follows the same model as in the previous series, but with less care (no. 698). In Series II.2.1, the wing is thinner and the representation of the feathers more or less stylised: two lines of dots, then a row of short transverse strokes and then a set of long curled feathers (no. 837). The style can be more or less clumsy (no. 846, 1234, 1393). On coin no. 859, there is only one line of dots. There are no more lines of dots on the coins minted after year 12 (no. 1272). The head of the seahorse becomes more and more stylised with the mane represented by dots (no. 1036). Its legs too become formed by dots (no. 1234). The tail becomes more sinuous, the ventral fins are

---

34. Elayi-Elayi, *Monnayage de Sidon*, pp. 54-68 and pls V-X; on the forelocks of the horses, see N. Vismara, 'Particolari dell' iconografia del cavallo nelle terre di confine dell'Asia Minore: elemento decorativo od indice culturale? Alcuni spunti per una riflessione', in *VIIe Colloque International. La Transeuphratène à l'époque perse: Frontières et courants d'échanges culturels*, Paris 22-24 March 2007 (to be published in *Trans*).

35. *BMC Phoenicia*, pl. I, 1-6.

reduced to one spine (no. 887), and then they are no longer represented (coin no. 1283).

When the seahorse is the only motif on the obverse of small denominations, it can be facing either to the right, as on the shekels, or to the left. In Series II.1.1.3, II.1.2.2 and III.1.1, it is represented with the same details as on the shekels of Series II.1.1.1 with the two ventral fins, but without the harness as there is no rider. The differences depend on the engravers' individual style and skill: with dots for mane and legs represented downwards (no. 430), with legs and tail horizontal (no. 745), with a short thick tail (no. 1588). In the bronze Series III.2.1, the representation of the seahorse is stylised and clumsy, with a large head and fins, and a small wing and tail (no. 1734).

The seahorse is represented in Phoenician iconography and more frequently in Graeco-Roman iconography. For example, in the Aradian coinage, there is a seahorse under the war-galley of the more or less contemporary second Aradian series, but with a thinner and small wing and a more sinuous tail, and it is represented together with a dolphin on a Phoenician seal dated from the 6th or 5th century[36]. It is frequent in Byblian coinage, in the series with the war-galley, which started in the last quarter of the 5th century. The type of Byblian seahorse is stylised, with a long sinuous tail and a small vertical wing. The seahorse is represented with a rider, probably a marine deity, on a clay tablet found in the Punic city of Kerkouane.[37] This seahorse also has the head and forelegs of a horse, the tail of a fish with a three-pronged caudal fin and two ventral fins, but it has no wing. The same type of seahorse with rider is encountered on a clay disk found at Tamuda, a Punic establishment in Morocco.[38] The Tyrian seahorse has been compared with the Cherub of Ezechiel's prophecy in the Bible.[39] There is no precise description of the Cherub, but it is presented as a hybrid winged animal used as a divine mount, which effectively could be related to the Tyrian seahorse. Regarding the circulation of the Tyrian coins with seahorse, the writer, at the draft stage, has possibly mentioned the Cherub evoking the Tyrian seahorse, especially as the only word in Hebrew for designating the seahorse would have been $k^e r\bar{u}b$. This hypothesis does not seem unlikely but needs to be confirmed because of the very difficult textual context. The obverse type of Tyrian shekels with the deity riding on seahorse has been borrowed by the mint of Tarsus for a series represented in the Celenderis hoard.[40]

36. *Ibid.*, pls. XI, 9-15; XII, 1-4; Gubel ed., *op. cit.* (n. 17), no. 256.
37. Fantar, *op. cit.* (n. 33), pp. 43-94 and pl. IV, 1.
38. Found by M. Tarradell: cf. Fantar, *ibid.*, p. 77.
39. Ez 28, 16.16; cf. P.-M. Bogaert, 'Le Chérub de Tyr (Ez 28, 14.16) et l'hippocampe de ses monnaies', in R. Liwak and S. Wagner, *Prophetie und geschichtliche Wirklichkeit in alter Israel, Festschrift für S. Herrmann*, Stuttgart *et al.* 1991, pp. 29-38; P. Bordreuil, '*parōket* et *kappōret*. À propos du saint des saints en Canaan et en Judée', in P. Butterlin *et al.* eds, *Les espaces syro-mésopotamiens, Volume d'hommage offert à Jean-Claude Margueron*, Subartu XVII, Turnhout 2000, pp. 164-165.
40. Cf. C.M. Kraay, 'The Celenderis Hoard', *NC*, 1962, pp. 1-15, esp. 9, no. 5-6.

The reverse bears a deity with trident and an ear of corn. The traditional interpretation of this series is that it was intended to pay Phoenician seafarers.[41] Another series from Tarsus bears the protome of an animal with the head and forelegs of a horse and a wing on the obverse. This could be either the seahorse or the winged horse Pegasus, another type from the same mint.[42] In Delos, the Berytians and Ascalonites worshipped the god Poseidon, carried on a chariot driven by seahorses, which are also represented on the Hellenistic coins of Berytus.[43] The same scene is also attested in the Punic world, for example in a mosaic of Sousse, now in the Bardo Museum, in Tunis.[44] The seahorse alone or as a divine mount driven mostly by Poseidon/Neptune is frequently found in the Greek world.[45] However, most of the time, the seahorse is not winged as on the Tyrian coins.

The symbolic meaning of the seahorse is difficult to interpret, as Tyrian mythology is not well-known and the minting authority's purpose in using this symbol not clearly understood. However, what can be said is that the seahorse was an excellent mount for travelling, even better than the dolphin since it represented a combination of three animals, each of them living in a different element: the horse on earth, the bird in the air and the dolphin in the sea. Moreover, all these animals are renowned for their speed. Therefore, the seahorse represented the divine mount *par excellence*, and at the same time, a substitute for the powerful Tyrian war-galley, as we shall now see.

4. *The deity*

We now have to study the deity represented on Tyrian coins within the obverse scene where he is the central motif. He cannot be studied separately because he is never represented alone like the dolphin or seahorse. It is a complex scene, similar to some of those that are represented on the obverse and reverse of the Sidonian double shekels.[46]

This scene is the most precise and skilfully engraved in the first series where it appears: Series II.1.1.1.a. The shekels belong to the so-called 'flat fabric' category, with the largest diameter of all the Tyrian coins (25-28mm). The different elements (deity, seahorse, waves, and dolphin) are positioned so

41. Cf. *ibid*. Cf. our comment in Chapter VII.
42. Cf. Kraay, *op. cit.* (n. 12), no. 1034; Babelon, *Traité* II/2, no. 522, 524, 525, 530; P. Chuvin, 'Apollon au trident et les dieux de Tarse', *JSav*, 1981, pp. 305-326; Bonnet, *op. cit.* (n. 33), pp. 153-155.
43. P. Roussel and M. Launey, *Inscriptions de Délos (N°s 1497-2879)*, Paris 1937, 1519, 37-39; 1720; 2325; *BMC Phoenicia*, pl. VII, 1-12.
44. Cf. Fantar, *op. cit.* (n. 33), pp. 31-42, pl. I, 2 (with bibl.)
45. *DAGR*, s.v. 'hippocampus'; G.M.A. Richter, *Engraved Gems of the Greeks and the Etruscans*, London 1968, no. 332; P. Gauckler, *Inventaire des mosaïques de la Gaule et de l'Afrique. III. Afrique Proconsulaire*, Paris 1910, no. 421, 433; E. Lipiński, *Itineraria Phoenicia*, Leuven *et al.* 2004, pp. 428-429.
46. Elayi-Elayi, *Monnayage de Sidon*, pp. 471-524.

as to cover all the free space of the field, thereby making the scene well-balanced without being overcrowded. Since we have already analysed the dolphin and the seahorse, we shall now consider just the deity and the waves. The position of the deity on the seahorse and the proportions are not exact, mainly for two reasons: his mount is unusual and he is unable to look like a rider on a horse, and the engravers are still influenced by the Egyptian representation of the chest seen face on and with the head in profile. The head of the deity is too big compared to his torso and to the body of the seahorse. His chest is only represented down to waist level and he has one foot emerging by the side of the right leg of the seahorse. If he rides side-saddle, his right leg passes between the wing and the body of the seahorse. If he rides side-saddle, his two legs are on the left side of the seahorse. On some coins, the foot is under the stomach of the seahorse, which would mean an astride position (no. 277). On others, it is below the wing and on the stomach, which would mean a side-saddle position (no. 283). The deity has a long beard and moustache. It is uncertain whether he is wearing a flat headdress on the top of the head with swollen hair or a bun on the nape (no. 277) or whether he has only a headband (no. 313). Sometimes, there is a dot on the top of his forehead, which is difficult to interpret (no. 295). Anyway, even if the face sometimes resembles that of the deity of the Sidonian double shekels[47], the headdress does not appear to be a crown.[48] His arms are naked and muscular. He is wearing a pleated dress on the chest with a v-neck, partly covered by the beard (no. 295). The dress has been compared with that of the deity on Sidonian double shekels,[49] but it is different here because it is sleeveless. The foot of the deity is long and pointed because he is probably wearing a poulaine (no. 271, 283), similar to that of the king of Sidon represented on the Sidonian double shekels.[50] Sometimes, the extremity of the foot is a line of five dots (no. 266). With his right hand the deity holds the reins of the harnessed head of the seahorse. Only one rein is represented (no. 313), unlike the Sidonian coins where the charioteer holds one rein in his left hand and five to seven gathered reins in his right hand.[51] With his left arm stretched forward he is holding a bow and quiver (no. 298). In fact, part of the bow and quiver and three feathered arrows can be seen. They are similar to those of the bowman on the Sidonian half-shekels.[52] But here the bow is not bent. It seems to be the usual Phoenician type, the composite strongly reflex bow with 'si-

---

47. J. Elayi and A.G. Elayi, 'La scène du char sur les monnaies de Sidon d'époque perse', *Trans* 27, 2004, pp. 89-108.
48. Betlyon, *Coinage of Phoenicia*, p. 46.
49. Said erroneously to be Persian: *ibid.*; cf. Elayi-Elayi, *loc. cit.* (n. 47), pp. 89-94.
50. Cf., for example, Elayi-Elayi, *Monnayage de Sidon*, pl. LVI, 17.
51. Cf. *ibid.*, p. 496 and pls XV, 471 (5), XVIII, 528 (6) and XXII, 602 (7).
52. Cf. *ibid.*, pl. IV, 71.

yahs' that is rigid extremities.[53] The quiver seems to be used for arrows only and is not of the 'gorytos' type for holding the bow as well.[54] The seahorse is represented galloping and flying over the sea represented by wavy lines; it is not swimming although with its dolphin-shaped tail it is capable of swimming. The sea is represented by the three thin wavy lines with seven crests (no. 313). However, there is sometimes only one thick line (no. 246). The number of lines seems to be left to the choice of the engraver. The number of crests also appears to be left to the engraver, but it is reduced on the small denominations in an irregular fashion, unlike Group I where the number of crests varied exactly according to the different denominations.

The scene represented on the obverse of Series II.1.1.1.a is identical on the quarters of shekel of Series II.1.1.2, except for the number of wavy lines, which is reduced to two. The engraving is always very carefully worked and is as precise as possible, but as the coin is smaller (only about 1.5cm in diameter), fewer details are represented by the engravers.

The scene of Series II.1.1.b is identical to that of Series II.1.1.a, but the conditions are completely different. The shekels of this series belong to the so-called 'thick fabric' category. Since the flans are smaller (21-22mm in diameter) and the size of the dies always the same (about 22mm), part of the type falls off the flan (no. 335). Moreover, the engraving is less accurate and skilful, and becomes stylised (no. 342). Most coins in this series are quite worn, unlike those of Series II.1.1.a. They may have been hoarded less often because of their bad workmanship, hence provoking their poorer state of preservation. The following inscribed Phoenician standard series (Series II.1.2.1.a-v) present similar difficulties in representing the obverse scene. Moreover, the representation of the sea has changed, becoming more stylised: two lines with four crests on the shekels.

After the change of standard, the same scene is represented on the obverse of the shekels. The diameter of the coins is the same as in the previous series, with less thickness. But the engravers made new dies, smaller in diameter (18-19mm) so that the scene fits into the field. The coins of Series II.2.1 are not in general as carelessly worked as in the previous series, but they are never as neatly engraved as in the first Tyrian series and they are stylised as if they were made for a kind of mass production. In Series II.2.1.1-13, the sea was repre-

---

53. Cf., for example, G. Ransing, *The Bow: Some Notes on its Origin and Development*, Acta Archaeologica Ludensia, Lund 1967; Y. Yadin, *The Art of Warfare in Biblical Lands in the Light of Archaeological Study*, London 1963; H.W. Müller, *Der 'Armreif' des Königs Ahmose und der Handgelenkschutz des Bogenschützen in Alten Ägypten und Vorderasien*, Mainz 1989, pp. 41-49; R.H. Wilkinson, 'The Representation of the Bow in the Art of Egypt and the Ancient Near East', *JANES* 20, 1991, pp. 83-99.

54. On Phoenician arrows, bows and quivers, cf. J. Elayi and A. Planas Palau, *Les pointes de flèches en bronze d'Ibiza dans le cadre de la colonisation phénico-punique*, Paris 1995, pp. 227-228 (with bibl.).

sented by two wavy lines with five or six crests. The foot of the deity, the quiver and the ventral fin of the seahorse were so stylised (no. 798) that they eventually disappeared (no. 850). In Series II.2.1.14-28, the two wavy lines have four or five crests. The details (foot, quiver, ventral, and fin) have disappeared except on some rare coins (no. 1272). The head of the deity is very stylised, with dots for eye and nose, with some kind of headdress or hat (no. 925, 926, 1002, and 1036). From Series II.2.1.19 onwards, the guilloche circle is replaced by a circle of dots, much easier to engrave.

What was the symbolic meaning of the scene with the deity riding on seahorse? We do not know any parallel representations. Several interpretations have been proposed, relating this scene to other divine riders. The Tyrian deity has been compared with Baʿal Hadad of the Ugaritic texts who was presented as a rider of his cloudy entourage:[55] 'Here we seem to have the old Canaanite Rider of the Clouds in a seagoing version as Rider of the Waves'.[56] According to other authors, the Tyrian scene is similar to that of the Tarentine didrachms, representing the mythical hero Taras, riding on dolphin.[57] Since these coins were issued from about 510 BCE onwards, they could have inspired the Tyrian engravers. However, since the dolphin was the main motif of Tyrian Group I, there would not have been any reason to replace it by a winged seahorse as a mount for the deity. The scene of Poseidon on a chariot drawn by seahorses, common in the Greek world and used in the Hellenistic coins of Berytus, has also been proposed as a parallel,[58] Poseidon being assimilated to Milqart in Larnaka for example.[59] Other authors have centred their reasoning on the identification of Milqart and Herakles and on the association which Herakles had with aquatic monsters.[60] It has also been stressed that the Tyrian scene was the result of a syncretism inspired by different sources, which could only 'explain the apparent problems of a deity riding on winged seahorse, over the sea, with a bow in one hand'.[61]

---

55. *CTA* 5.5.6-8; F.M. Cross, *Canaanite Myth and Hebrew Epic*, Harvard 1973, p. 17; M. Weinfeld, 'Ugaritic 'Rider of the Clouds' and ' Gatherer of the Clouds'', *JANES* 5, 1973, pp. 421-426; Betlyon, *Coinage of Phoenicia*, pp. 46, 67-70; *id.*, 'Canaanite Myth and the Early Coinage of the Phoenician City-States', in M. Silver ed., *Ancient Economy in Mythology: East and West*, Savage/Maryland 1991, p. 148.

56. R.S. Hanson, *Tyrian Influence in the Upper Galilee*, Cambridge Ma. 1980, p. 20.

57. Head, *Historia Numorum*, pp. 54-55, figs 23-25; W. Fischer-Bossert, *Chronologie der Didrachmenprägung von Tarent 510-280 v. Chr.*, Berlin 1999.

58. Lipiński, *op. cit.* (n. 45), pp. 428-429; Fantar, *op. cit.* (n. 33), pp. 27-42; *BMC Phoenicia*, p. xlvii and pls VII, 1-3, 5, 12; X, 3.

59. Cf. E. Lipiński, *Dieux et déesses de l'univers phénicien et punique*, Leuven 1995, p. 233 (with bibl.).

60. Cf. R. Dussaud, 'Melqart', *Syr.* 25, 1946-48, pp. 205-206; R. Flacelière and P. Devambez, *Héraclès: images et récits*, Paris 1966, pp. 105-109; M.C. Astour, *Hellenosemitica*, Leiden 1965, pp. 208-211.

61. Cf. Betlyon, *Coinage of Phoenicia*, p. 46.

This last proposition seems to be the most reasonable one. However, we now have to ask whether the borrowings from different sources were due to the engravers, the minting authority, popular Tyrian 5th century beliefs, or whether this image had been elaborated earlier in the Tyrian mythology and had progressively changed. Since this scene is known nowhere else in the present state of our documentation and since it was suddenly chosen by the minting authority to represent the city instead of the dolphin, it could be a new emerging image, corresponding to an evolution or a change in Tyrian mythology which occurred in the late 5th century BCE. This syncretistic scene appears to be very rich in meaning. In our opinion, what is put forward is the maritime vocation of the city (dolphin-like tail of the seahorse, small dolphin, wavy lines), the religious protection of the city and/or the king (deity in action), and its military power over the sea, earth and air (the triple aspect of the seahorse, speed, mobility, a fighting deity stretching his bow forward). As a matter of fact, this scene corresponds to the representation of the war-galley on the coinages of Sidon, Arwad and Byblos, but with much more power: not only on the sea with the powerful fleet of Tyre, but also on the earth with her army. Power in the air did not have any realistic sense in Antiquity, but possibly indirectly through storms. The wing of the seahorse undoubtedly had a relation with the owl of the reverse, holding the symbols of kingship, but the meaning of this relation is not clear for us.

The last question is the following: who was this Tyrian divine rider? He was certainly an important Tyrian deity if not the main deity. There is a related question which is still much debated: who was the main Tyrian deity at that time, known as $B^cL\ \c{S}R$, 'lord of Tyre'?[62] It is difficult to answer this question, first because there were several deities in the Tyrian pantheon throughout the length of the city's history: Athirat, Milqart, Bethel, Ba'al Šamim, Ba'al Malage, Ba'al Ṣaphon, Ba'al Ḥamon, Ba'al Kur, Šamaš, ʾEšmun, ʿAštart, Milk-ʿaštart (at Ḥamon/Umm el-ʿAmed), etc.[63] Moreover, it is not always easy to identify those who were especially worshipped in Tyre at the end of the 5th and in the 4th centuries. Finally, we do not have at our disposal clear representations of all these deities for comparison. The study is even further complicated by the fact that each of these deities is often considered as a combination or fusion of others: for example, Milqart and Rašap, Milqart and Nergal, Milqart and Herakles, etc.[64] Several proposals have been made for identifying the Ba'al

---

62. *CIS* I, 122 and 122 bis.
63. Cf. N. Naʾaman, 'Esarhaddon's Treaty with Baal and Assyrian Provinces along the Phoenician Coast', *RSF* 22, 1994, pp. 3-8. Lipiński, *op. cit.* (n. 59), pp. 219-276 (with bibl.). However, we do not agree with his interpretation of Baʾliraʾsi: cf. J. Elayi, 'Baʾliraʾsi, Rêsha, Reshbaʿl. Étude de toponymie historique', *Syr.* 58, 1981, pp. 331-341; *id.*, in *Trans* 13, 1997, pp. 210-214.
64. Cf., for example, W.F. Albright, *Yahweh and the Gods of Canaan*, Doubleday 1968, pp. 145-146; F.M. Cross, 'The Papyri and Their Historical Implications', in Lapp-Lapp, *Wâdi Ed-*

Ṣur: namely Baʿal Šamim, Bethel and Milqart. Most authors have proposed Milqart,[65] mainly because of the bilingual inscription of Malta, dated from the 2nd century BCE, clearly devoted to *MLQRT BʿL ṢR*, 'Milqart lord of Tyre', being Ἡρακλῆς Ἀρχηγέτης, 'Herakles Archegetes' in the Greek version.[66] However this proposal has been called into question by the following arguments: there were several Tyrian gods and no inscription found in Phoenicia mentions Milqart as a Tyrian god.[67] As a matter of fact, there are some inscriptions found in Phoenicia mentioning Milqart[68] and more explicitly the Tyrian Milqart, such as bronze tesserae dated from the 2nd century (*LMLQRT BṢR*, 'to Milqart in Tyre'), and a lead weight dated from 290/289 BCE (*LMLQRT/ŠT 10/BṢR*, 'to Milqart/year 10/in Tyre').[69] The reading of a seal is not certain: *MLQRT BṢR* or *MLQRT RŠP*.[70] Finally, after assembling all the attestations of Milqart in Phoenician inscriptions and classical sources, it appears that Milqart was probably the main Tyrian god at that time, 'lord of Tyre' (*BʿL ṢR*) and also 'protector of Tyre' (*ʿL ḤṢR*).[71] Neither Baʿal Šamim nor Bethel are good candidates to be the main deity of Tyre. Even though Baʿal Šamim is mentioned before Milqart in the 7th century treaty concluded between Baʿalu king of Tyre and Assarhaddon king of Assyria,[72] the classification followed a func-

---

Daliyeh, p. 59; J.M. Solá Solé, 'Miscellánea púnico-hispana I.3. HGD ʾRŠF y el Panteon Fenicio Púnico de España', *Sefarad* 16, 1956, pp. 341-355; H. Seyrig, 'Antiquités syriennes. Héraclès-Nergal', *Syr.* 24, 1947, pp. 62-80; Dussaud, *loc. cit.* (n. 60), pp. 205-206; M. Dunand, 'Stèle araméenne dédiée à Melqart', *BMB* 3, 1939, pp. 65-76; Betlyon, *Coinage of Phoenicia*, pp. 67-70; Bonnet, *op. cit.* (n. 33), pp. 27-114 (with bibl.).

65. From the beginning with the deciphering of Phoenician by J.-J. Barthélémy in 1758: cf. M. Delcor, 'L'alphabet phénicien: son origine et sa diffusion de Samuel Bochart à Emmanuel Rougé. Trois siècles de recherches, XVIIᵉ-XIXᵉ siècles', in C. Baurain et al. eds, *Phoinikeia Grammata. Lire et écrire en Méditerranée*, Liège-Namur 1991, pp. 21-32; Bonnet, *op. cit.* (n. 33); id., 'Melqart est-il vraiment le Baal de Tyr?', *UF* 27, 1995, pp. 695-701 (with bibl.). Cf. aussi J. Dus, 'Melek ṣōr-Melqart? (Zur Interpretation von Ez 28.11-19)', *ArOr* 26, 1958, pp. 79-185.

66. *CIS* I, 122 and 122bis; *KAI* 47; M.G. Guzzo Amadasi, *Le iscrizione fenicie e puniche delle colonie in Occidente*, Rome 1967, Malta no. 1-1bis.

67. B. Peckham, 'Phoenicia and the Religion of Israel', in P.D. Miller et al. eds, *Ancient Israelite Religion, Essays in Honor of F.M. Cross*, Philadelphia 1987, pp. 79-99, espec. 91; M.S. Smith, in *JAOS* 110, 1990, pp. 590-592.

68. *IGLS* VII, no. 4001, pp. 25-26; J.-P. Rey-Coquais, *Arados et sa Pérée*, Paris 1974, p. 25; F. Briquel-Chatonnet, 'Les derniers témoignages sur la langue phénicienne en Orient', *RSF* 19, 1991, pp. 6-7; cf. also the Aramean inscription of Bredj: *KAI* 210.

69. P. Bordreuil, 'Attestations inédites de Melqart, Baal Hammon et Baal Saphon à Tyr', in *Religio Phoenicia*, Studia Phoenicia IV, Namur 1986, p. 81, fig. 3 (tessera); id. and E. Gubel, 'Baalim', *Syr.* 65, 1988, pp. 438, II.4, 439, fig. 3; Elayi-Elayi, *Poids phéniciens*, pp. 125, no. 333, 176-177.

70. Bordreuil, *ibid.*, p. 78, fig. 1; Bonnet, *op. cit.* (n. 33), p. 54; Lipiński, *op. cit.* (n. 59), p. 230; N. Avigad and B. Sass, *Corpus of West Semitic Stamp Seals*, Jerusalem 1997, no. 719.

71. M.G. Amadasi Guzzo, 'Cultes et épithètes de Milqart', *Trans* 30, 2005, pp. 9-18 (with bibl.).

72. R. Borger, *TUAT* 1/2, Gütersloh 1983, pp. 158-159; G. Pettinato, 'I rapporti politici di Tiro con l'Assiria alla luce del 'Trattato tra Asarhaddon e Baal', *RSF* 3, 1975, pp. 145-160; N.

tional and not a hierarchic order.[73] Other proposals such as Apollo or Poseidon[74] are unlikely as these Greek deities could not have been introduced into the Tyrian pantheon as early as the 5th century.

The interpretation of the deity on the coins as a syncretistic deity[75] is interesting but has not been clearly explained. Without focusing on the difficult problem of his identification, we would make some important remarks. Since the seahorse, thanks to its triple form (horse, bird, dolphin), masters the three elements (earth, sky, sea), it could be reminiscent of the three Tyrian deities invoked at the beginning of the treaty concluded between kings Baʿal and Assarhaddon: Baʿal Šamim, Baʿal Malage and Baʿal Ṣaphon.[76] These three deities are asked, in the event of a violation of the treaty, to provoke a storm capable of destroying all the ships, of breaking the cables, of matching the moorings, of swallowing them up in the sea. Thus in the 7th century Tyre three types of Baʿal were ruling the natural forces: Baʿal Šamim in the sky,[77] Baʿal Malage on the earth[78] and Baʿal Ṣaphon on the sea.[79] The seahorse representing the three previous deities would be therefore mounted by an important Tyrian god at that time, one who was a bowman and later related to Heracles.[80] We now have to conclude, considering the two main proposals: an unidentified deity[81] or Milqart.[82] Milqart seems to be an interesting hypothesis, but one which needs to be confirmed.

Naʾaman, 'Esarhaddon's Treaty with Baal and Assyrian Provinces along the Phoenician Coast', *RSF* 22, 1994, pp. 3-8.

73. Cf. Bonnet, *loc. cit.* (n. 65), pp. 700-701.
74. Betlyon, *Coinage of Phoenicia*, p. 147 (with bibl.).
75. *Ibid.*, p. 46.
76. Cf. Pettinato, *loc. cit.* (n. 72), pp. 152-154, IV, l. 10'.
77. Cf. Lipiński dir., *op. cit.* (n. 25), *s.v.* 'Baal Shamêm' (with bibl.); H. Niehr, *Der Höchste Gott*, Berlin-New york 1990.
78. Cf. Lipiński dir., *ibid.*, *s.v.* 'Baal Malagê'; F.O. Hvidberg-Hansen, 'Baʿal-malagê dans le traité entre Asarhaddon et le roi de Tyr', *AcOr* 35, 1973, pp. 57-81 (related as Dagan to harbours or vegetation).
79. Cf. *ibid.*, *s.v.* 'Baal Saphon' (with bibl.).
80. Cf. Bonnet, *op. cit.* (n. 33), pp. 428-430.
81. It was our previous position: Elayi-Elayi, *Trésors*, pp. 145, 171. Cf. also Betlyon, *Coinage of Phoenicia*, p. 46 ('marine deity'); Bonnet, *op. cit.*, p. 85 ('On ne peut donc se prononcer sur l'identification du dieu en question'); Bogaert, *loc. cit.* (n. 39), p. 35; E. Acquaro, 'Iconografie monetali fenicie', *Byrsa* 1, 2003, pp. 1-6.
82. Cf. for example, Babelon, *Perses*, p. CXC; *BMC Phoenicia*, pp. cxxvi-cxxvii; P. Naster, 'Hoofdkenmerken van de munten van Tyrus in de vroege Vᵉ en IVᵉ eeuwen v. C.', in E. Gubel *et al.* eds, *I Redt Tyrus/Sauvons Tyr*, Studia Phoenicia I-II, Leuven 1983, pp. 91-95; Bonnet, *loc. cit.* (n. 33), p. 59 ('A vrai dire, l'identification de Melqart reste hypothétique: on ne voit guère qui d'autre pourrait être cette divinité tyrienne digne de figurer sur le monnayage'); Gubel, *op. cit.* (n. 17), *s.v.* 'monnaies'; Sole, *loc. cit.* (n. 11), p. 94; Lipiński, *op. cit.* (n. 45), pp. 427-429. R.S. Hanson's argument according to which *BM* and *M* would mean respectively (B)aʿal (M)ilqart and (M)ilqart (*op. cit.* [n. 56], p. 19) is not reliable: for the meaning of these inscriptions, cf. above, Chapter III.

5. The shell

The shell is a less important motif than the previous one, but it is quite frequent, appearing in nine series: on the obverse of the shekels of Series I.2.1 and the divisionary series I.2.2, I.2.3 (?), I.2.4 and I.2.5, always below the wavy lines. In the silver Series III.1.2.a and III.1.2.b (1/16 of shekel), it is represented below the dolphin. In the bronze Series III.2.4, it also appears below the dolphin and in Series III.2.3, it is the only motif on the obverse. It was a permanent motif in Tyrian coinage.

This shell had been misinterpreted as a murex, representing Tyre's role in the production of purple dye, until our article of 1991 in which, based on scientific arguments, we showed that it was definitely not a murex.[83] However, the ancient misinterpretation has not totally disappeared.[84] We shall demonstrate again why this shell cannot be a murex and what it is precisely. M. Dunand had already questioned the fact that the shell represented on Byblian coins was a murex, and identified it as a conch; P. Naster cautiously called it a shell.[85] Later imperial Tyrian coins have the murex, sometimes with the representation of the legend of the dog finding a murex.[86] The shell discovered by the dog is clearly a *Murex brandaris*, having a spiral body with spikes and an elongated siphon-shaped canal; the dot on the opening could represent the hypobranchial purple-producing gland.[87] On the other hand, the shell represented on Tyrian pre-Alexandrine coins is not a muricid, but a *Charonia variegata* (Lamarck 1816) (*Charonia seguenza* is a junior synonym), a marine gastropod of the Ranellidae family, commonly known as the Atlantic Trumpet Triton and widespread in the Eastern Mediterranean.[88] The shape of the shell is characterised by a long spiral which is more or less smooth (no. 1742) or patterned (no. 1751, 1758); its opening is rather wide, with a siphon-shaped canal turned downwards. It can be seen that this canal is erroneously turned upwards: the engrav-

---

83. J. Elayi, 'Etude typologique des sicles de Tyr au dauphin', *Cahiers Numismatiques* 108, 1991, pp. 13-17 (with bibl.).
84. Sole, *loc. cit.* (n. 11), pp. 93-94; C. Mazzucato, 'Il murice nelle monete fenicie e puniche', *Byrsa* 2, 2003, pp. 121-130.
85. Dunand, *Byblos I*, pp. 407-408; P. Naster, 'Trésors de monnaies de Byblos du IVᵉ s. av. J.-C. trouvés à Byblos', in T. Hackens and G. Moucharte eds, *Numismatique et histoire économique phéniciennes et puniques*, Studia Phoenicia IX, Louvain-la-Neuve 1992, p. 42.
86. *BMC Phoenicia*, p. 291, no. 473; P. Naster, 'Le chien et le murex des monnaies impériales de Tyr', *NAC* 14, 1985, pp. 257-260.
87. *Traité de zoologie* V/3, Paris 1968, pp. 59, 306. Cf. A. Gruvel, *Les Etats de Syrie – Richesses marines et fluviales – Exploitation actuelle – Avenir*, Paris 1931, p. 441; L.B. Jensen, 'Royal Purple of Tyre', *JNES* 22, 1963, pp. 104-118; Lipiński dir., *op. cit.* (n. 25), s.v. 'pourpre' (with bibl.). A *Murex brandaris* is also represented on the Sidonian coins of Severus Alexander: Babelon, *Perses*, p. 269, no. 1849.
88. Cf., for example, G. d'Angelo and S. Gargiullo, *Guida alle Conchiglie Mediterranee*, Milano 1979, p. 132. We would thank B. Métivier, Department 'Milieux et Peuplements Aquatiques', Muséum National d'Histoire Naturelle, Paris, for helping us to identify this shell and giving his comments.

ers probably forgot to make a reverted representation on the die in order to produce a correct one on the coin. This kind of mistake occurred sometimes, particularly in monetary inscriptions. Therefore a stylised murex, distorted and unrecognisable, is excluded as the representation of a conch is quite clear and realistic, except for the reverted canal. In Series I.2.1, I.2.2, I.2.3, I.2.4 and I.2.5, the shell is turned to the right and the siphon-shaped canal is represented upwards, that is reverted (no. 48, 50). In the bronze Series III.2.3, the shell is turned to the left and the canal is represented downwards, that is also reverted (no. 1745, 1750, 1758). In the silver Series III.1.2.a, the shell under the dolphin is also turned to the left but the canal is represented upwards, which is correct (no. 1599, 1608, 1620). The Atlantic Trumpet Triton was a well-known shell in Antiquity, used for example as a trumpet once the end had been broken off; it was used in a funeral context in several Near Eastern cultures.[89] Several of them were found by M. Dunand in Byblos, near deposits of offerings, and could have been used as drinking vases.[90] The meaning of this shell on Tyrian coins is not clear but it was definitely not economic as in the case of the murex, and it was probably a religious marine motif, related to the dolphin. It was used in a Tyrian ritual from around 450 to 333 BCE because it is represented from the beginning right through to the end of the Tyrian coinage of the Persian period.

6. *The head of lion*

The head of lion appears in three different aspects: in profile, full face and full face with a prey in its mouth. The head of lion in profile appears in the silver Series I.2.5 as the only motif on the reverse. The very carefully worked engraving on these small denominations (no. 241, 242) shows all the details of the head. The attitude of the lion is threatening with an opened roaring mouth and showing its fangs, facing towards the right. The eye is represented by a dot, the ear by a crescent-shape and the mane by lines of dots on the forehead and the back of the head. The muscle structure of the head is also represented. The full face head of lion appears in the silver Series III.1.2.e, also as the only motif on the reverse. The engraving is done with care, showing the muscle structure of the head (no. 1711, 1712, 1720). The eyes are two dots inside a hollow circle, the nose is long, the ears are clearly drawn on each side; neither the mane nor the mouth are visible. Therefore it could be a lion or a lioness. This head has sometimes been confused with a bull's head because the ears had been interpreted as horns.[91]

The third representation of the full face head of lion holding a prey appears in four bronze Series (III.2.1, III.2.2, III.2.3, III.2.4), always on the reverse. At

89. Cf. Dunand, *Byblos I*, pp. 407-408 (with bibl.).
90. *Ibid.*
91. Betlyon, *Coinage of Phoenicia*, pp. 43, 27 (Babelon, *Traité*, II, 2, no. 992).

first we wondered whether it was a scalp, the head of a lioness or the head of a lion.[92] According to A. Kindler,[93] it is a scalp but it does appear to be either a scalp or a mask as the animal's jaws are not distended and it holds a prey in its mouth. According to D.T. Ariel, it is a lioness' head because it has no mane:[94] in fact, the mane is represented in a stylised manner by a line of vertical strokes (no. 1734, 1737, and 1749) or dots (no. 1772, 1778). The comparison with the motif of the head of lion in profile mentioned above confirms that the bronze series represent a lion too. However, it is impossible to know whether it was a lion with a short mane covering only the top of the shoulders as on Sidonian coins or with a long mane covering the shoulders, flanks and part of the stomach as in Assyrian and Persian representations.[95] The lion with a long mane was attested in Syria-Phoenicia as early as the 4th millennium BCE: it is the so-called Indian or Asian lion (Family: *Panthera*. Species: *leo*. Gender: *Persicus*).[96] It is impossible to check the length of the mane because only bones are found in the excavations, of course, and because there are no longer any lions today in the whole of the Near East. However, one can still note the same difference between the lions of North Africa which have a long and abundant mane, and those of the Indian reserve of the Gir forest which have a short mane. Such a difference in representation between Sidonian (and Tyrian?) lions, and Assyrian and Persian lions could correspond to a geographical distribution of short and long mane lions, something which unfortunately cannot be checked;[97] or it could be explained by different artistic representations. In addition, it can be noticed that the lion of the bronze series also has a somewhat human appearance due to the shape of its forehead and its eyes with eyebrows: this could have been the engraver's choice or based on some mythical aspect of the lion.

---

92. J. Elayi and A.G. Elayi, 'La dernière série tyrienne en bronze aux types civiques', *NAC* 27, 1998, pp. 129-139.

93. A. Kindler, 'The Mint of Tyre – The Major Source of Silver Coins in Ancient Palestine', *ErIs* 8, 1967, pp. 318-324.

94. D.T. Ariel, 'Coins from Excavations at Tel Nahariya, 1982', *ʿAtiqot* 22, 1993, pp. 125-127.

95. Elayi-Elayi, *Monnayage de Sidon*, pp. 484-485. For Persian lions, cf. for example A. Farkas, *Achaemenid Sculpture*, Istanbul 1974, pl. XV, fig. 32; pl. XIX, fig. 36; M.C. Root, *The King and Kingship in Achaemenid Art*, Leiden 1979, pl. XVI, fig. 16b; pl. XXVIII, fig. 28a-b (with bibl.). For neo-Assyrian lions, cf. for example P. Albenda, 'Lions on Assyrian Wall Reliefs', *JANES* 2, 1974, pp. 9 and 24, fig. 19; C.E. Watanabe, 'Symbolism of the Royal Lion Hunt in Assyria', in J. Prosecky ed., *Intellectual Life of the Ancient Near East*, Prague 1998, pp. 439-450.

96. Cf. for example J.-O. Gransard-Desmond, 'Le lion dans la Syrie antique: confrontation des textes au matériel archéologique', *Orient-Express*, 2001/1, pp. 16-18. We thank F. Petter, Prof. at the Muséum National d'Histoire Naturelle of Paris, Department 'Mammifères et Oiseaux' who gave us informations on this subject.

97. According to F. Petter, Indian lions would be differentiated by a smaller brain and a more elongated head. This observation ought to be taken into account in the analysis of ancient lions bones' discoveries.

The last characteristics of this lion are the two elements falling from both sides of the mouth, and which are not found on the head of lion in the silver series. It has nothing to do with the usual type of lion's head or scalp holding a ring in its mouth, as when used as door knockers or door pulls.[98] Nor can they be interpreted as the lower extremities of the lion's mask on both sides as on some Samian coins,[99] because it is not a mask. According to D.T. Ariel, these elements are drool, coming from the mouth, expressing the ferocity of the animal.[100] If it was meant to be drool, why does it only fall from the sides of the mouth and not from the middle, on the skin? We have proposed another hypothesis which seems more likely: it could be a prey since the lion striking down another animal is a well-known Phoenician motif, for example on Byblian coins.[101] Identification of the prey is difficult: the elongated aspect of these two elements could indicate a snake or parts of a prey, partially devoured. But the details of elements which are visible on some coins - head or legs? (no. 1767, 1743, 1745, 1746, 1748, 1749, 1772 and 1778) - seem to suggest that it is more like a four-legged animal, stylised due to the lack of space.[102] Tyrian mythology is not sufficiently well-known in providing us with help to identify this animal.

The Tyrian lion's head in profile is quite similar to the lion's head in Sidonian coinage, in the scene of the man (Sidonian deity) slaying the lion standing in front of him on its hind legs.[103] The lion motif is quite common in Phoenician iconography, for example in the maʿabed and in the so-called 'meghazil' of Amrit, on the so-called 'stele of Amrit', on the stele of Qadbun, on the Aḥiram sarcophagus, on low reliefs from Byblos and Umm el-ʿAmed, on two Sidonian sculptures and on a late Tyrian sarcophagus.[104] The main function of lions was to protect doors, palaces, temples or tombs, expressed by a powerful, aggressive and impressive image.[105] This function is well-illustrated by the inscriptions of two lions, door guards in Til-Barsip: the eastern lion was called 'the impetuous hurricane, powerful attacker, which fells the rebels, which provides the heart with satisfaction' and the western lion: 'the one which charges at rebels and devastates enemy country, which ejects the good and welcomes

---

98. Cf. for example O. Kurz, 'Lion-masks with rings in the West and in the East', in M. Barasch ed., *Studies in Art*, Scripta Hierosolymitana 25, Jerusalem 1972, pp. 22-41.
99. Cf. J.P. Barron, *The Silver Coins of Samos*, London 1966, pl. VIII, 8, 13.
100. Ariel, *loc. cit.* (n. 94), p. 127.
101. Cf., for example, Babelon, *Perses*, pl. XXVI, 23; *BMC Phoenicia*, p. 96, no. 10.
102. Elayi-Elayi, *loc. cit.* (n. 92), pp. 135-136.
103. *Id., Monnayage de Sidon*, pl. XII, no. 320.
104. Cf., for example, E. Renan, *Mission de Phénicie*, Paris 1864, pls XII, XIII, LV; E. Gubel, *Art phénicien. La Sculpture de tradition phénicienne*, Paris 2002, p. 18, fig. XVII; p. 51, no. 38; p. 53, fig. 9; p. 71, no. 59; p. 87, no. 79; Lipiński dir., *op. cit.* (n. 25), pp. 10-11 and fig. 7, *s.v.* 'Ahiram/Ahirôm' (with bibl.); N. Jidejian, *Tyre through the Ages*, Beirut 1969, fig. 74; M. Dunand and N. Saliby, *Le temple d'Amrit dans la pérée d'Aradus*, Paris 1985, pp. 20-21, figs 6-7.
105. Cf., for example, Gransard-Desmond, *loc. cit.* (n. 96), pp. 16-18; I. Cornelius, 'The lion in the art of the ancient Near East: a study of selected motifs', *JNSL* 15, 1989, p. 63.

the bad people'.[106] In Tyre, particularly on coins, the lion was probably connected with the Herakles myth involving the Tyrian deity Milqart,[107] who was possibly the deity riding on seahorse on the shekels. The Milqart-Heracles assimilation, attested by Herodotus in the middle of the 5th century, could have been earlier, but it clearly existed at the beginning of Tyrian coinage. The Heraclean type wearing the *leonte* had been known in Phoenicia since the 6th century BCE; it also inherited Near Eastern traditions such as the function of master of lions, which symbolised domination over evil forces.[108] The motif of the lion can therefore be understood as being connected with the deity riding on seahorse, possibly Milqart.

7. The head of ram

This motif is still less important than the previous one as it only appears on the reverse of two divisionary silver series: Series III.1.1.d and III.1.2.f (halves of sixteenth). The first series bears the seahorse to left on the obverse, and appears to have a head of ram to left on the reverse. All four preserved specimens (no. 1579, 1580, 1581 and 1582) are corroded and not very clear. The second series, represented by 12 coins, bears on the obverse a dolphin to left and on the reverse a head of ram to left. The identification of the ram is quite clear on some coins (no. 1722, 1725, 1726 and 1729), with the characteristic head shape in profile and the dotted semicircular horn, turned leftwards. The horn is a little less clear on coin no. 1724 where the motif is interpreted as the head of a sheep. The head represented on coin no. 1727 has been interpreted as the head of a bull:[109] however engraving such minute coins is not easy and appears particularly unskilful in this instance.

This domestic sheep (male ram) was widespread in Syria-Phoenicia at that time (Family: *Bovidae*. Subfamily: *Caprinae*. Genus: *Ovis*. Species: *Aries*, Linné 1758).[110] The motif of the ram is well-attested in Phoenician iconography, although not as common as the lion motif: for example on Byblian, Sidonian and Salaminian coins, on steles, bowls, amulet cases and sceptres. On Sidonian coins, the king represented in a religious function following the deity carried on a chariot, holds a sceptre with a ram's head surmounted by the Hathoric symbol: this royal sceptre has its origin in the liturgical Egyptian

---

106. F. Thureau-Dangin and M. Dunand, *Til-Barsib*, Paris 1936, pp. 148-150.
107. *BMC Phoenicia*, pp. cxxiv-cxxvii, n. 2; cf. C. Bonnet, *Melqart. Cultes et mythes de l'Héraclès tyrien en Méditerranée*, Leuven-Namur 1988, pp. 399-415.
108. Cf. Bonnet, *ibid*., pp. 409-415 (with bibl.).
109. See J.W. Betlyon, *Coinage of Phoenicia*, pp. 43 and 65, n. 27, quoting Babelon, *Traité*, II, no. 992.
110. We would thank F. Poplin, Department 'Anatomie comparée', Muséum National d'Histoire Naturelle, Paris, for his comments.

sceptre of Khnum, borrowed by the Phoenicians, via Ugarit.[111] The Egyptian origin of the general motif of the ram is the representation of Amon with a ram's head for expressing the idea of protection.[112] The head of this animal is also represented on a silver rhyton bearing a neo-Elamite inscription under the chin.[113] The Tyrian coins motif seems to be indicative of a non-marine animal (like the owl), especially revered within the Tyrian cult, possibly expressing the religious protection of the city, but we cannot interpret its meaning precisely because of the lack of documentation.

8. *The rosette*

The rosette was the least important motif in Tyrian coinage as it only appeared in Series I.1.4, on very small coins (halves of sixteenths) and on the reverse. The Tyrian rosette has a central dot and eight petals, regularly arranged around it. This motif was extremely common in Near Eastern cultures, with a varied number of petals however.[114] The rosette motif appeared in Ugarit/Ras Shamra in the 15th-13th centuries, and in Ras Ibn Hani in the 13th century on luxurious objects, in religious and royal contexts (axes, gold cups, ivories).[115] The winged rosette also appeared as a religious/royal symbol on seal impressions bearing the names of Hittite kings and queens of the 14th and 13th centuries BCE (King Suppiluliuma I and Queen Tawananna, King Hattusili III and Queen Puduhepa, King Tudhaliya IV).[116] From the Hittite Empire, the rosette motif, winged or not, moved in to the Neo-Hittite kingdoms of Northern Syria: in Zincirli (relief depicting King Kilamuwa, funeral stela), Tell Halaf (architectural motif of the temple-palace), and Malatya (statue, possibly of a king).[117] The rosette motif (not winged) was also probably used as a symbol of power

---

111. *BMC Phoenicia*, p. 94, no. 1 and pl. XI, 9; L. Mildenberg, *Vestigia Leonis*, Freiburg-Göttingen 1998, pl. VI, 56; E. Gubel, *Phoenician Furniture*, Studia Phoenicia VII, Leuven 1987, pl. X, 29; Moscati dir., *op. cit.* (n. 27), pp. 311, 388, 437; P. Naster, *Scripta Nummaria, Contributions à la méthodologie numismatique*, Louvain-la-Neuve 1983, pl. X, 5a-b.

112. Cf., for example, C. Aldred *et al.*, *L'Egypte du crépuscule*, Paris 1980, pp. 179, fig. 158; 229, fig. 223; 252-253, figs 249-250.

113. F. Vallat, 'Une inscription élamite sur un rhyton en argent à tête de bélier', *Akkadica* 116, Jan.-Feb. 2000, pp. 585-539.

114. Cf., for example, J.M. Cahill, 'Royal Rosettes fit for a King', *BAR* 23/5, 1993, pp. 48-57, 68-69 (with bibl.). It was also known elsewhere, for example in Egypt on a coffin of the tomb of Tutankhamon: P. Xella, *La terra di Baal*, Rome 1984, p. 160.

115. Xella, *ibid.*, pp. 64, 85-86; M. Yon, *La cité d'Ougarit sur le tell de Ras Shamra*, Paris 1997, pp. 174, no. 56; 176-177, no. 60; A. Bounni *et al.*, *Ras Ibn Hani, I. Le palais nord du Bronze Récent. Fouilles 1979-1995, Synthèse préliminaire*, Beirut 1998, pp. 17 and 164, fig. 125.

116. Cf. E. Akurgal, *The Art of the Hittites*, London 1962, p. 61.

117. *Ibid.*, p. 138, pls 129-130 and 106-107; S. Mazzoni, 'Réflexion sur l'espace architectural de la période syro-hittite', in P. Butterlin *et al.* eds, *Les espaces syro-mésopotamiens, Volume d'hommage offert à J.-C. Margueron*, Subartu XVII, Paris 2006, p. 243, fig. 10 (the rosette is associated with the merlon and guilloche); cf. also a Syrian statuette wearing a headband with rosette: I. Benda-Weber, *Zwei autochthone Ethnien Kleinasiens zwischen Orient und Okzident*, Bonn 2005, pl. 45, 12-13.

and sovereignty from the 9th century in Assyria: relieves of the Northwest palace in Nimrud portrayed King Ashurnasirpal II (883-859 BCE) wearing rosette bracelets.[118] Then, almost every Assyrian king was portrayed wearing a rosette ornament: Shalmaneser III, Shamshi-Adad V, Tiglath-Pileser III, Esarhaddon and Ashurbanipal (668-631 BCE).[119] The rosette motif was also used for royal officials and objects belonging to the king[120] and for representing foreign kings.[121] This motif possibly appeared too in the Transjordanian kingdom of Ammon in the 9th/8th centuries (diadem of a statue).[122] Kings of Judah could have borrowed the motif from the Assyrian model: it was used mainly for stamp/seal impressions on ceramic jar handles in the 7th-6th centuries, possibly replacing the four-winged scarab and the two-winged disk, and more rarely on seals.[123] The rosette motif, already attested in Iran (Kirmanshah) in the 8th century (bronze cup with rosette and rams),[124] was common in the Achaemenid Empire, for example in Persepolis, in architecture and different types of objects; it is difficult to know whether it was a divine or royal symbol or purely a decorative motif.[125] The rosette motif was also well-attested in the Greek world in the classical and Hellenistic periods, later than the Tyrian series, for example on black stamped Greek and East Greek pottery, coins of

---

118. Cf. R.D. Barnett, *Assyrian Palace Reliefs and their Influence on the Sculptures of Babylonia and Persia*, London 1960, pls 25-29; P. Amiet, *Art of the Ancient Near East*, New York 1980, pp. 283, pls 119, 121, and p. 404, pl. 603.

119. Cf. Amiet, *ibid.*, pp. 293, pl. 122; 413-415, 418, pls 126, 129; 618, 623, 634; Barnett, *ibid.*, pp. 29-30, pls 61, 63, 65, 83-84, 105; J.B. Pritchard, *Ancient Near East in Pictures Relating to the Old Testament*, Princeton 1954, pp. 153-154, 300, pls 442, 445, 447.

120. Cf. D. Ussihkin, *The Conquest of Lachish by Sennacherib*, Tel Aviv 1982, pp. 88-89, fig. 71; 90-91, fig. 72; 115, fig. 65; Amiet, *ibid.*, pp. 283, pl. 119; 406, pl. 603; Barnett, *ibid.*, pp. 27-30, pls 26-27, 31, 43, 64, 76, 82, 84, 99; R.D. Barnett and M. Falkner, *The Sculptures of Assur-nasirapli II (883-859 B.C.), Tiglath-Pileser III (745-727 B.C.) Esarhaddon (681-669 B.C.) from the Central and South-West Palaces at Nimrud*, London 1962, pp. 55, pl. 6; 72, pl. 23; U. Magen, *Assyrische Königsdarstellungen – Aspekte der Herrschaft*, Mainz-am-Rhein 1986, pls 1, 1; 2, 9-10, 12; 3, 3, 5 (reliefs); 8, 8 (stele); 8, 4 and 12, 4 (seals); 12, 2 (ivory); 13, 1, 5; 15, 1; 16, 1-2 (jewels represented on reliefs); D. Harden, *The Phoenicians*, Baltimore 1971, p. 285, pl. 69 (ivory panelled box from Nimrud).

121. Barnett, *ibid.*, p. 121.

122. T. Ornan, 'The Dayan Collection', *IMJ* 2, 1983, pp. 14-16, 18; Cahill, *loc. cit.* (n. 114), p. 68.

123. Cahill, *ibid.*, pp. 48-57; *id.*, 'Rosette Stamp Seal Impressions from Ancient Judah', *IEJ* 45, 1995, pp. 231-252 (with typology); *id.*, 'Rosette stamp seal impressions', in I. Beit-Arieh ed., *Tel ʿIra: A Stronghold in the Biblical Negev*, Jerusalem 1999, pp. 360-364; A.D. Tushingham, 'New Evidence Bearing on the Two-Winged LMLK Stamp', *BASOR* 239, 1980, pp. 61-65; O. Keel and C. Uehlinger, *Göttinen, Götter und Gottessymbole. Neue Erkenntnisse zur Religionsgeschichte Kanaans und Israels aufgrund unerschlossener ikonographischer Quellen*, Freiburg et al. 1992, § 204; B. Sass and C. Uehlinger, *Studies in the Iconography of Northwest Semitic Inscribed Seals*, Fribourg-Göttingen 1993, pp. 210, figs 66-67; 248, pl. II, 13.

124. Moscati dir., *op. cit.* (n. 27), p. 437.

125. Cf., for example, E.F. Schmidt, *Persepolis I*, Chicago 1953, pls 20, 22-23, 24, 27-52 (friezes on reliefs); *id.*, *Persepolis II*, Chicago 1957, pp. 40, 60 (a divine symbol), 72-76, 78, 89, 91; *id.*, *Persepolis III*, Chicago 1970, pp. 39, 74, 84, 100, 105, 127; cf. also A.D.H. Bivar, 'A Rosette Phiale inscribed in Aramaic', *BSOAS* 24, 1961, pp. 189-199.

Erythrae (Ionia), stamp impressions on the archives of Seleucia on Tigris.[126] The rosette motif is rarely attested in the Neo-Babylonian and Persian periods in the present state of documentation; its use could have originated in Ugarit, North-Syria or the Persian Empire. However, it was better attested later or outside Phoenicia: a sarcophagus from Tyre, a weight from Arwad (Roman period), a bilingual stele (Phoenician/Greek) from Athens (350-300 BCE), a silver bowl from Athienou or Golgoi, and a stele with a Hathoric scene from Zawiya.[127] The rosette motif was also well-attested in Carthage: a gold hair ring (6th-5th centuries), a stele with four rosettes and two dolphins just like the Tyrian series (4th century), a golden breastplate (3rd-2nd centuries); in Sicily and Sardinia: a gold ring from Tharros (6th-5th centuries), two steles from Sulcis (3rd-2nd centuries); and in Ibiza: several terracotta figurines from the necropolis of Puig des Molins (5th- 3rd centuries).[128]

How can we interpret the rosette motif on Tyrian coins? We can say that it was known in Phoenician iconography, but not frequent. It was not widespread in Tyre as it was only used on one series, on very small coins and on the reverse. Purely decorative use is a possibility.[129] But other meanings are also possible: a religious symbol, in connection with the dolphin on the obverse, or a royal symbol, corresponding to the owl with flail and crook on shekels. We have no answer for the moment.

9. *The crescent-shaped countermark*

The crescent-shaped countermark appears only on two Tyrian shekels (no. 1224 and 1232). This small hollow countermark has to be classified in the so-called private countermarks, unlike the official ones.[130] These kinds of countermarks were intended to guarantee the standard or the weight of the silver, or both; they were made by coin controllers or changers with small dies. The crescent motif is one of the most common in the ancient Near East and in

---

126. Cf. B.A. Sparkes and L. Talcott, *Black and Plain Pottery*, The Athenian Agora XII, Princeton 1970, *passim* (from c. 420 BCE); *BMC Ionia*, p. 121, 37; A. Invernizzi, 'Stelle e rosette tra le impronte di sigilli degli archivi di Seleucia al Tigri', in E. Acquaro ed., *Alle soglia della classicità. Il Mediterraneo tra tradizione e innovazione*, Pisa-Rome 1996, pp. 801-811.
127. Jidejian, *op. cit.* (n. 104), pl. 101; Gubel, *op. cit.* (n. 104), pp. 35, no. 14; 157, no. 177; *id., op. cit.* (n. 111), pp. 47-48, pl. X, 29; 212, pls XLI-XLII.
128. M.-L. Buhl, *A Hundred Masterpieces from the Ancient Near East*, Copenhagen 1974, p. 65, no. 54; Moscati dir., *op. cit.* (n. 27), pp. 306, 373 (Carthage). *Ibid.*, pp. 321, 325, 387 (Tharros, Sulcis). *Ibid.*, pp. 241, 348-349 (Puig des Molins).
129. As stated by J.W. Betlyon, *Coinage of Phoenicia*, p. 66, n. 32.
130. Babelon, *Traité* I/1, col. 642; G. Le Rider, 'Contremarques et surfrappes dans l'Antiquité grecque', in *Numismatique antique. Problèmes et méthodes*, Nancy-Louvain 1975, pp. 30, 56; Elayi-Lemaire, *Graffiti*, pp. 202-205.

particular in Phoenician iconography, as the moon and is often associated with a disk representing the sun.[131]

In conclusion, it appears that the Tyrian coins reveal the symbols chosen by the minting authority to represent the city: that is why the selected motifs are very few in number and therefore very meaningful. They are firmly organised into a hierarchy: the dolphin and the owl are represented in most series and in most denominations; then comes the deity riding on seahorse and the seahorse alone. The other motifs (shell, lion's head, ram's head, rosette) are relatively restricted and consequently much less meaningful. The relation between the obverse and reverse motifs is worth analysing because it provides a better understanding of the message conveyed by the minting authority. The first key idea was the religious protection of the city symbolised by the Tyrian deity (possibly Milqart) and the protecting animals (seahorse, dolphin, owl, lion, ram). The second idea, expressed through the religious symbols and connected with them, was that of the city's sovereignty and power, expressed through the crook and flail on the owl's shoulder, the dolphin and seahorse possibly representing the war-galley, the bow of the deity and maybe the rosette. Even if the representation of the animals and the shell is based on observation, the mythical aspect is the most important unlike the engravings on Sidonian coins.[132] Consequently, Tyrian monetary iconography provides less concrete information (bow, dress and headdress, species of animals) than on Tyrian mythology (principal Tyrian deity, his triple function on sea, earth and air, his animal symbols, the symbol of the shell).

---

131. Cf., for example, Moscati dir., *op. cit.* (n. 27), p. 306; F. Cumont, 'Deux autels de Phénicie', *Syr.* 8, 1927, pp. 163-168, pl. XXXVIII; Gubel, *op. cit.* (n. 104), p. 455, no. 40; Lipiński dir., *op. cit.* (n. 25), p. 431, *s.v.* 'symboles'; H. Sader, *Iron Age Funerary Stelae from Lebanon*, Cuadernos de Arqueología Mediterránea 11, Barcelone 2005, pp. 117-120 (with bibl.).

132. Elayi-Elayi, *Monnayage de Sidon*, pp. 471-539.

CHAPTER V

THE TYRIAN MONETARY WORKSHOP

The techniques used for manufacturing coins and the functioning of the monetary workshop are rarely studied. As regards the Tyrian coinage of the Persian period, only P. Naster,[1] J. Elayi and A.G. Elayi[2] have taken this aspect of research into account. However, from a scientific point of view, a coin must be studied as a whole: besides the inscription, the iconography, the weight and the style, that are usually considered, it is also necessary to investigate the metal used, the manufacturing techniques, the possible alterations and thence to envisage how the workshop functioned, to think about the craftsmen involved, how the manufacturing process was organised, the volume of production and the different methods of counterfeiting. For lack of explicit Phoenician and non-Phoenician inscriptions related to coin manufacturing and of discoveries of a workshop or monetary tools, valuable information is provided by the technical details and defects of the coins, by what we know from other mints, from the engraving of seals and stones in the Phoenico-Punic, Greek and Roman world (better known) and from the experience of modern engravers.

1. The monetary metals

Getting to the root of coin manufacturing, we shall investigate the nature and origin of the metals used for the coins; unfortunately we have no information concerning the dies, punches, moulds and tools because none have been preserved. As far as we know, in the Persian period, the Tyrian workshop only

---

1. P. Naster, 'La technique des revers partiellement incus des monnaies phéniciennes', in *Centennial Publication of the American Numismatic Society*, New York 1958, pp. 503-511 (= *Scripta Nummaria. Contributions à la méthodologie numismatique*, Louvain-la-Neuve 1983, pp. 22-29).
2. J. Elayi, 'Remarques méthodologiques sur l'étude paléographique des légendes monétaires phéniciennes', in C. Baurain *et al.* eds, *Phoinikeia Grammata. Lire et écrire en Méditerranée*, Namur 1991, pp. 187-198; Elayi-Elayi, *Poids phéniciens*, pp. 207-263 (concerning both weights and coins).

used silver for coins and, later and less often, bronze, just like the neighbouring mints of Sidon[3] and Arwad and most of the Greek mints in the same period.[4] However, the mint of Byblos did not use bronze before the late Hellenistic period.

Where did the Tyrian workshop get its silver and bronze supplies from? The Phoenician cities did not possess within their territories either silver-mines (*KSP*),[5] copper-mines (in Hebrew *n^eḥōšet*)[6] or tin-mines (in Hebrew *bādil*),[7] both metals, copper and tin, being used for bronze alloy (*NḤŠT*).[8] As a matter of fact, copper and tin are very scarce in the Lebanese mountains and, even if these unproductive lodes were exploited in Antiquity, this was only occasional and on a small scale.[9] No doubt that the Phoenicians got their supplies of metals from elsewhere: copper probably came first from neighbouring Cyprus and maybe too from Sardinia, tin from the Cassiterides islands (Cornwall), French Brittany through Gaul, or from Galicia skirting round Iberia, and silver mainly from Iberia which had numerous lodes of silver-bearing lead (areas of Huelva, Upper Andalusia and Ibiza).[10] Another important supply for the silver of Tyrian coins was probably the import of Greek merchandise coins, in particular

---

3. For Sidon, cf. Elayi-Elayi, *Monnayage de Sidon*, pp. 589-591.
4. Cf., for example, Kraay, *Greek Coins*.
5. *KAI* 13, l. 4 ; cf. *DISO*, s.v. 'KSP'; J. Hoftijzer and K. Jongeling, *Dictionary of the North-West Semitic Inscriptions*, Leiden et al. 1995, s.v. 'ksp₂'.
6. *Dt* 8,9; cf. L. Koehler and W. Baumgartner, *Lexicon in Veteris Testamenti Libros*, Leiden 1953, s.v. Cf. Elayi-Elayi, *Poids phéniciens*, p. 239: read *NḤŠT* instead of *BRZL*.
7. *Ez* 27, 12; cf. Koehler-Baumgartner, *ibid.*, s.v.
8. *KAI* 10, l. 4; Hoftijzer-Jongeling, *op. cit.* (n. 5), s.v. 'nḥšt'.
9. Cf. J.P. Brown, *The Lebanon and Phoenicia I*, Beirut 1969, pp. 87-104; J.D. Muhly, *Copper and Tin. The Distribution of Mineral Resources and the Nature of the Metal Trade in the Bronze Age*, Hamden 1973; M. Mackay, 'The Problem of Tin from Byblos', *Ber.* 31, 1983, pp. 143-146; R. Khawlie, 'The Problem of Tin from Byblos', *ibid.*, pp. 147-149; J.D. Muhly, 'Sources of the Tin and the Beginnings of Bronze Metallurgy', *AJA* 89, 1985, pp. 275-291; T. Schneider, 'Looking for the Source of Tin in the Ancient Near East', *Qad.* 15, 1985, pp. 98-102; Elayi, *Économie*, pp. 46-47. Cf. also R.J. Forbes, *Metallurgy in Antiquity*, Leiden 1950, espec. p. 298 (copper); H. Limet, *Le travail du métal au pays de Sumer au temps de la IIIe dynastie d'Ur*, Paris 1960, pp. 85-98 (with bibl.).
10. For Cyprus, cf. for example J.D. Muhly et al. eds, *Early Metallurgy in Cyprus, 4000-500 B.C.*, Nicosia 1982. For Sardinia, cf. M.S. Balmuth and R.J. Rowland eds, *Studies in Sardinian Archaeology*, Ann Arbor 1984-86, I, pp. 114-162; II, pp. 229-271; C. Tronchetti, *I Sardi. Traffici, relazioni, ideologie nella Sardegna arcaica*, Milan 1988; S.F. Bondi, 'La colonizzazione fenicia', in *Storia dei Sardi e della Sardegna* I, Rome 1988, pp. 147-171, 440-444 (with bibl.); P. Bernardini, 'La Sardegna e i Fenici. Appunti sulla colonizzazione', *RSF* 21, 1993, pp. 29-81. For Iberia, cf. A. Blanco Freijeiro et al., *Excavaciones arqueológicas en el Cerro Salomón (Riotinto, Huelva)*, Seville 1970; id., *Ancient Mining and Metallurgy in South-West Spain*, London 1982 ; D. Ruiz Mata and J. Fernández Jurado, *El yacimiento metalúrgico tartésico de San Bartolomé de Almonte*, Huelva Arqueológica 8, Huelva 1986; C. Domergue, *Les mines de la Péninsule Ibérique dans l'Antiquité romaine*, Rome 1989, pp. 141-154; J. Elayi and A. Planas Palau, *Les pointes de flèches en bronze d'Ibiza dans le cadre de la colonisation phénico-punique*, Paris 1995, pp. 223-260 (with bibl.).

Athenian tetradrachms which were found in large quantities in the Near East.[11] They were probably melted rather than overstruck as their weight was different. Indeed we have discovered no trace of overstriking on tetradrachms. But we have noticed some traces of overstriking on Tyrian coins of previous series of the same weight and diameter, probably because it was easier and more economic. However the phenomenon of overstriking seems to be more restricted in Tyre (about ten cases) than in Sidon (about one hundred cases).[12] After having analysed the metallic composition of Sidonian coins,[13] we have also analysed a sample of Tyrian coins.[14]

When the Tyrians started their monetary workshop, they drew on a long Phoenician tradition of metal working, mainly developed during the first half of the first millennium. This tradition is attested, for example in the Assyrian *Annals*, by several mentions of gold, silver and bronze objects paid as a tribute to Assyrian kings by Tyre and the other Phoenician cities, and also in the Bible: 'A worker in bronze Ḥiram (of Tyre) was a man of great skill and ingenuity, versed in every kind of craftsmanship in bronze'.[15] The Phoenicians knew the process of producing silver from lead ores by smelting these ores, especially galena, and by cupellation. But it seems unlikely that raw ore was sent directly to goldsmiths and monetary craftsmen. The discovery of metallurgical workshops in several mining districts where Phoenicians came for supplies seems to indicate that ore was processed on the spot.[16] The Phoenicians also knew the

---

11. Cf. Elayi, *Phénomène monétaire*, p. 26; J. Elayi and J. Sapin, *Quinze ans de recherche (1985-2000) sur la Transeuphratène à l'époque perse*, Paris 2000, pp. 175-178 (with bibl.).

12. No. 52, 79, 204, 387, 841, 1306.

13. Cf., in general, J.-N. Barrandon and M.F. Guerra, 'Méthodes d'analyse appliquées à la numismatique', in C. Morrisson and B. Kluge eds, *A Survey of Numismatic Research 1990-1995*, Berlin 1997, pp. 825-830 (with bibl.); B. Bouyon et al., *Systèmes et technologie des monnaies de bronze (4ᵉ s. avant J.-C. – 3ᵉ s. après J.-C.)*, Wetteren 2000, pp. 92-197 (with bibl.); M.R. Cowell, 'A short Review of the Application of Scientific Analysis Techniques to Coinage', in C. Alfaro and A. Burnett eds, *A Survey of Numismatic Research 1996-2001*, Madrid 2003, pp. 929-933 (with bibl.). For Sidon, cf. A.G. Elayi, J.N. Barrandon and J. Elayi, 'The Devaluation of Sidonian Coins in 365 B.C.E. as Determined by Fast Neutron Activation Analysis and first Bronze Issues' *AJN* 17, 2007, pp. 1-8.

14. Cf. A.G. Elayi, J.N. Barrandon and J. Elayi, 'The Change of Standard of Tyrian Silver Coinage about 357 BCE as Determined by Fast Neutron Activation Analysis' (forthcoming).

15. Cf., for example, J. Elayi, 'Les cités phéniciennes et l'Empire assyrien à l'époque d'Assurbanipal', *RA* 77, 1983, pp. 47-48; G. Bunnens, 'Le luxe phénicien d'après les inscriptions royales assyriennes', in *Phoenicia and its Neighbours*, Studia Phoenicia III, Leuven 1985, pp. 125-128; 1 R 7, 13-4; 2 Ch 2, 13. Cf. G. Falsone, 'La Fenicia come centro di lavorazione del bronzo nell'età del Ferro', *DArch* 3, ser. 6, 1988, pp. 79-110; id., in V. Krings ed., *La civilisation phénicienne et punique, Manuel de recherche*, Leiden et al. 1995, pp. 426-439 (with bibl.). On bronze weights manufacturing, cf. Elayi-Elayi, *Poids phéniciens*, pp. 243-245 (with bibl.).

16. Cf., for example, D. Ruíz Mata, 'El poblado metalúrgico de época tartésica de San Bartolomé (Almonte, Huelva)', *MM* 22, 1981, pp. 150-170; J. Ramón, 'El yacimiento fenicio de Sa Caleta', in *I-IV Jornadas de Arqueología Fenicio-Púnica (Ibiza, 1986-1989)*, Ibiza 1991, pp. 177-196; id., 'La colonización arcaica de Ibiza: Mecánica y proceso', in *La Prehistòria de les Illes de la Mediterrània Occidental*, X Jornades d'Estudis Històrics Locals, Palma de Mallorca 1992, pp. 456-460. For cupellation, cf. R.J. Forbes, *Studies in Ancient Technology VIII*, Leiden 1964, pp. 172-177;

process of forced draught, able to increase the temperature inside the furnaces to more than 1200° C, so that copper ore could be melted. Copper metallurgy is attested for example in the mining district of Tel Batash/Timnah in the 12th-11th centuries by the discovery of metallurgical workshops with furnaces, ores, slags and tools, in the Northern palace of Ras Ibn Hani in the 13th century by the discovery of a limestone crucible for copper oxide-shaped ingots, and in Cyprus (Athienou, Enkomi, Kition, Idalion) by the discovery of metallurgical remains dated from the 14th to the 3rd centuries.[17] The copper, refined and alloyed with tin in various percentages, and with lead, a less expansive metal,[18] produced bronze used for manufacturing different kinds of objects, among others, coins.

2. The flans

The Tyrian monetary workshop, having got the silver and bronze, either by refining it itself or (more probably) by buying refined metals, started manufacturing the flans. Since no Tyrian flan has been discovered, the only information available on this manufacturing process is provided by observing the coins themselves. If we disregard alterations produced later by the striking, such as flattening, increasing of the thickness at the periphery, distortions, cracks, splits, etc., we can obtain some precise information on the flans. The shapes of the flans vary from very irregular ones to almost perfectly circular ones. The very irregular forms occurred mainly in the first phase of the Tyrian coinage (Phoenician standard) and the circular forms in the second phase ('Attic' standard). Some flans are more or less oval (no. 19, 33, 38, 84, 190, 199, 287 and 820), rarely triangular (no. 408) or square (no. 313); most of them have no special shape (no. 36, 57, 60, 77, 83, 357, 374, 378, 389 and 730). Some flans are only slightly irregular (no. 1, 3, 5, 6, 12, 44, 262, 824, 1235 and 1554); several are roughly circular (no. 2, 7, 10, 39, 50, 246, 259, 315, 376, 778, 800 and 944) or almost perfectly circular (no. 796, 797, 804, 887, 1396, 1552 and 1553). Some irregular flans bear one sprue (no. 37, 83, 85, 385, 776, and 1235) or two opposite sprues (no. 283). Several flans, that have a rather circular form,

---

P. Craddock et al., 'The refining of gold in the Classical world', in D. Williams ed., *The art of the Greek goldsmith*, Edinburgh 1999, espec. pp. 111-112 (with bibl.); W.A. Oddy, 'Gilding: an Outline of the technological History of the Plating of Gold on to Silver or Copper in the Old World', *Endeavour* 15, 1991, p. 30, fig. 2.

17. Cf., for example, H.G. Conrad and B. Rothenberg, *Antikes Kupfer im Timna-Tal*, Bochum 1980; J. Lagarce et al., 'Les fouilles à Ras Ibn Hani en Syrie (Campagnes de 1980, 1981 et 1982). Contribution à l'étude de quelques aspects de la civilisation ugaritique', *CRAI*, 1983, pp. 274-279 ; 1984, pp. 401-408 ; 1987, pp. 282-288 (copper was refined in Ras Ibn Hani by liquation); T. Dothan and A. Ben-Tor eds, *Excavations at Athienou, Cyprus: 1971-1972*, Jerusalem 1983, pp. 132-138; Muhly et al. eds, *op. cit.* (n. 10).

18. For the origin and use of lead, cf. Elayi-Elayi, *Poids phéniciens*, pp. 240 and 245-254. The analyses of Tyrian coins have shown that their metallic composition included lead: Elayi et al., *loc. cit.* (n. 14).

bear one sprue (no. 1215, 1280, 1372, 1388, 1426 and 1446) or two opposite sprues (no. 895, 1003, 1050, 1286, 1400, 1511, 1514, 1515, 1524 and 1783). Some flans are more or less thick (no. 79, 335, 338, 340 and 355), some others, mainly circular, are thin (no. 796, 797, 887, 1552 and 1553). Some flans were possibly re-cut (no. 507 and 713). How can these observations be interpreted?

The more or less irregular shaped flans were probably not made by a mould with circular alveoli. We have no information on the process used, but we could for example propose the following hypothesis: small silver ingots of no particular shape were poured on to a stone slab, taken from the melted metal using a measure (kind of spoon?) in order to always have the same weight. It was the same problem for manufacturing the irregular flans of croeseids, Persian shekels and darics, and pseudo-Athenian tetradrachms.[19] It is difficult to know how the flans that have a kind of geometric shape (oval, square or triangular) were made. The two flans that may have been re-cut (no. 507 and 713) were probably neither made by cutting a silver slab nor by cutting a metallic bar into sections because they are only partly re-cut. Their weight is normal (0.66g and 13.10g respectively): therefore some metal was removed, not fraudulently, but weights which were too high after the flans had been struck were quite possibly adjusted. The process of manufacturing irregular flans with one or two casting sprues is difficult to explain.[20] During manufacturing, a small bit of metal possibly flowed between two flans, similar to a casting sprue. If the flans were weighed before the striking, this small quantity of metal was kept in place if it was necessary to adjust the weight afterwards.[21] On the other hand, the almost circular coins with one or two opposite casting sprues clearly show the technique used for making the flans: they were made using monovalve or bivalve moulds, containing circular alveoli arranged in strings. The sprues could have been forgotten by the workers making the flans. But this hypothesis seems unlikely because the weights of the coins with sprues are correct.[22] Therefore it is more likely to conclude that the flans were weighed before being struck, and that one or two sprues were kept in order to make up for any weight shortage. There can be also one sprue for the flans placed on the lower side of the mould. The flans are rarely perfectly circular, which could be explained either by the

---

19. Cf., for example, E.T. Hall and D.M. Metcalf, *Methods of chemical and metallurgical Investigation of ancient Coinage*, London 1970; D.M. Metcalf and W.A. Oddy, *Metallurgy in Numismatics*, London 1980; D.R. Cooper, *The Art and Craft of Coinmaking, A History of Minting Technology*, London 1988, p. 9 (with bibl.).
20. Cf. for example, M. Thirion, 'Le trésor de Fraire', *RBN* 108, 1962, p. 72, n. 24.
21. The weights of irregular coins with sprues seem to be normal (no. 37 : 13.57g ; no. 83 : 13.24g ; no. 85 : 13.64g ; no. 283 : 13.71g ; no. 776 : 0.46g ; no. 1235 : 8.45g).
22. Coins with one sprue : no. 37, no. 83, no. 85, no. 385, no. 1215 (8.90g), no. 1280 (8.45g), no. 1388 (8.45g) and no. 1426 (8.99g), no. 1446. Coins with two sprues : no. 895 (8.80g), no. 1003 (8.70g), no. 1050 (8.10g), no. 1286 (8.95g), no. 1400 (8.81g), no. 1511 (8.93g), no. 1514 (8.75g), no. 1515, no. 1524 (8.36g) and no. 1783 (0.72g).

unequal cooling of the metal poured,[23] or by the deformations produced by the striking, even today for example as on medals not surrounded with a protective collar.[24]

As is well-known, in Antiquity, mainly in the Near East, the monetary flans were made by casting metal into moulds and they were then struck.[25] This casting technique was used in this area for flans, not for coins,[26] but it was used at that time for making other metallic objects, such as jewels, figurines, arrowheads and weights, mainly with stone moulds (especially limestone), more rarely metal or clay moulds.[27] Monetary moulds were rarely discovered, possibly because the minting authorities kept them in safe places just like the dies and destroyed them when they were out of use in order to prevent forgers from holding them. As for clay moulds, they cannot be preserved as they had to be broken in order to recover the flans. Some moulds used for making flans in strings were discovered in the Near East, all of them fragmentary and undated or dated later than from the Persian period: the mould of Paphos dated from the Ptolemaic period,[28] the one found in the Jordan valley dated between 100 and 90 BCE,[29] the one found in the citadel of Jerusalem dated from the late Hasmonean period,[30] the one of Khirbet Rafi' dated from the 1rst century BCE or the 1rst century A.D.,[31] and the two Samaria moulds, both unstratified.[32] The limestone mould of the Jordan valley, preserved together with some strings of flans and bronze coins of Alexander Jannaeus (Group C of Y. Meshorer), pro-

---

23. Bouyon *et al.*, *op. cit.* (n. 13), p. 7.
24. We thank D. Gedalje, engraver at the Monnaie de Paris, for his explanations.
25. Cf. G.F. Hill, 'Ancient Methods of Coining', *NC* 5, 1922, pp. 7-8; Le Rider, *Fouilles de Suse*, p. 11 and fig. 1. On the improvement of the flans making in the Ptolemaic monetary workshop of Alexandria, cf. Bouyon *et al.*, *op. cit.* (n. 13), pp. 14-28.
26. As it was used for example in the Chinese monetary workshops and, from time to time, in the Greek, Indian and Roman workshops. Cf. J. Cribb ed., *Money from cowrie shells to credit cards*, London 1966, pp. 96-97.
27. On the moulds for jewels, figurines and weapons, cf., for example, Dunand, *Byblos I*, pls CVI-CVIII; on the moulds for arrowheads, see Elayi-Planas Palau, *op. cit.* (n. 10), pp. 223-225 and fig. 41 (with bibl.). On the moulds for weights, cf. Elayi-Elayi, *Poids phéniciens*, pp. 247-256 and pl. XLIV, 18-19 (with bibl.). The monetary moulds of the Roman empire were different and consisted of clay disks: cf., for example, Hill, *loc. cit.* (n. 25), pp. 3-5; R. Turcan, 'Les moules monétaires de Verbe-Incarné (Lyon)', *TM* IV, 1982, pp. 10-22, espec. 19, fig. ; Bouyon *et al.*, *op. cit.* (n. 13), pp. 7 and 24.
28. K. Nicolaou, 'Découverte d'un hôtel des Monnaies de l'époque ptolémaïque à Paphos (Chypre)', *BSFN* 27, 1972, pp. 310-315.
29. J. Elayi and A.G. Elayi, 'Un moule monétaire de l'époque d'Alexandre Jannée', *BSFN* 50/9, 1995, pp. 1084-1088 and fig. 2 (these objects, from the J. Starcky collection, now in the Musée Bible et Terre Sainte of the Institut Catholique de Paris, are said to come from the Jordan valley).
30. R. Amiran and A. Eitan, 'Excavations in the Citadel', *IEJ* 20, 1970, p. 11 and pl. 7D.
31. A. Kloner, 'Flan mould from Kh. Rafi'', *'Atiqot* 11, 1976, pp. 112-113, fig. 1 and pl. XXXII, 1-4; Y. Meshorer, *Ancient Jewish Coinage* I, New York 1982, p. 55 and pl. 56, 8-11.
32. J.W. Crowfoot *et al.*, *The Objects from Samaria*, London 1957, p. 467, fig. 118, 2-3 (presented, as it seems, as moulds for jewels). See also a fragment of mould from the Aegean sea, dated from the 1rst century BCE, in the British Museum (no. 7, Case 7, Room 68).

duced a large number of flans, at least 45 on three strings, 15 alveoli being preserved for the central string.[33] The mould from Khirbet Rafi‛, also of limestone, was made of three superposed slabs, with two sets of 12 rows, each row having 12 alveoli, so that 288 flans could be produced at the same time.[34] The Jerusalem mould had at least 5 rows of 7 alveoli giving at least 35 in total.[35] In general, the flans made by one mould seem to have the same size. However, one of the two Samaria moulds had 7 alternate rows of small and large alveoli.[36] The second mould had at least 4 rows of alveoli of the same size on each side, which means that it included 3 slabs.[37] In all these moulds, each alveolus has a hole in its centre and which appears in relief on the unstruck flans. This hole could be a mark for hollowing out the alveolus or it could be intended for a better contact with the flans.[38]

There is no evidence for saying whether the Tyrian moulds used for flans in strings were made of one, two or three slabs. The obverse of an unstruck Sidonian coin shows some shrinkage, which means that the surface of the metal contained in the alveolus was cooled in the open air and that the mould was made of one slab.[39] The mould from the Jordan valley was also made of one slab as is shown by the fact that the alveoli were juxtaposed without a small channel between them as in the Khirbet Rafi‛, Jerusalem and Samaria moulds. In this case, there was also no need to have a funnel to pour through at one extremity of the mould. Our observations regarding the edge of the Tyrian coins are interesting but cannot be extended from the coins that we have examined to the whole coinage. The edge has different forms, irregular, rounded or straight. The rounded forms are the most frequent (no. 69, 296, 680): even if the flans were made in alveoli with straight edges, the rounded forms are probably due to the striking. The straight forms are not numerous (no. 862, 889, 1148, 1272): they could be explained by the use of a kind of collar during the striking in order to avoid distorted edges or by polishing the edges afterwards. The unequal thickness of some flans (no. 818, 889, 1153, 1272) is maybe due to the use of a mould made of one slab, which was slightly sloping so that the metal poured into the alveoli was horizontal, with an unequal thickness. We have noticed some traces of re-cutting (no. 862), polishing (no. 49, 296, 1228) and sprue removal (no. 848).[40]

One of the most delicate steps in the manufacture of the flans was adjusting the weights. Firstly, the quantity of metal had to be measured out as carefully as

---

33. Elayi-Elayi, *loc. cit.* (n. 29), pp. 1084-1088.
34. Kloner, *loc. cit.* (n. 31), p. 113, fig. 1 and pl. XXXII, 1-4.
35. Amiran-Eitan, *loc. cit.* (n. 30), pl. 7D.
36. Crowfoot *et al.*, *op. cit.* (n. 32), p. 467, fig. 118, 3.
37. *Ibid.*, fig. 118, 2.
38. According to Y. Meshorer, *op. cit.* (n. 31), pp. 55-56.
39. Elayi-Elayi, *Monnayage de Sidon*, p. 548, no. 2195.
40. Cf. Bouyon *et al.*, *op. cit.* (n. 13), pp. 24-25.

possible before making the flans. According to D.R. Cooper, the molten metal was poured directly into the alveoli of the moulds using small crucibles: some twenty of them were found in a Celtic workshop in Bratislava dated from 150 BCE; they were conical (7x4cm) and could contain about 500g of silver.[41] The alveoli had to be carefully hollowed out in order to contain a volume of metal corresponding to the exact weight of the flans. With moulds made of only one slab, it was even more difficult to fill all the opened alveoli in the same way and, in addition, the uneven cooling of the metal probably resulted in differences from one alveolus to another. When the flans were made without moulds, a measure (spoon?) was probably used for measuring the flan-ingot metal out of the crucible. In principle, the use of moulds with alveoli ought to have made it easier to adjust the weights, thereby minimising the need to weigh the flans. In reality, the observation of several re-cut edges shows that weighing was still in use. On the other hand, the use of overstriking saved a lot of time because it put an end to the weighing of flans and even their manufacture: however, in this case, the accuracy of the weight depended on the weight and composition of the previous reused coin. The erroneous weights of some Tyrian coins bearing no visible alteration[42] are difficult to explain: an error in adjusting the weight in Antiquity or an error of modern weighing?

Some coins reveal errors at the metal preparation stage. For example, the edges of several coins have cracks or splits:[43] according to D.R. Cooper, they were caused by the metal cooling more rapidly towards the exterior than in the centre but, as we shall see later on, most of them are probably explained by the phenomenon of striction during the striking.[44] Some coins have their surface more or less riddled with small holes (no. 248, 267, 361, 363, 383, 391, 499 and 840). If this can be explained by bubbles produced by humidity inside the alveoli, the bubbles have been crushed by the striking: unfortunately we did not check this interpretation because we were unable to examine any of the coins displaying these small holes.

The flan manufacturing process in the Tyrian workshop went through several stages and evolved during the Persian period, just as it did in the Sidonian workshop.[45] In the early days of coinage (Groups I.1 and I.2), the flans were more or less circular, meaning that moulds with alveoli were already being used for different denominations. But at the same time, irregular flans were also made without moulds. In Groups II.1.1 and II.1.2, both techniques were also

---

41. Cf. Cooper, *op. cit.* (n. 19), pp. 11-12 and figs 8-9.
42. No. 247, 1072, 1205 and 1304.
43. For example, flans with cracks : no. 31, 32, 47, 53, 55, 72, 91, 248, 253, 272, 276, 278, 288, 301, 408, 851, 1076, 1316, 1360, 1407. Flans with splits : no. 280, 888, 969, 1032, 1148, 1151, 1416, 1660.
44. Cooper, *op. cit.* (n. 19), p. 9, fig. 4. We thank P. Andrieux for his explanations on this subject.
45. Elayi-Elayi, *Monnayage de Sidon*, pp. 550-551.

used simultaneously. An important change occurred from the beginning of Group II.2, together with the change of standard: the flans were made using moulds with circular alveoli. It should be stressed that this change occurred in the Sidonian coinage at the beginning of ʿAbdʿaštart I's reign, in 365 BCE.[46] However, the other technique, without the mould, had never completely disappeared (no. 824). The diameter of the flans corresponds in principle to the diameter of the coins, except for some minor differences due to the crushing of the striking for example.[47] Just as in Sidonian coinage,[48] the flan diameter evolved during the Persian period but differently, depending on the denomination. If we consider the diameter of the shekels, to begin with it was (Group I.1.1) of about 20mm, with a small variation between 19-21mm (Fig. 29). It increased to about 24mm in Groups I.2.1 and II.1.1.1, with an increased variation (respectively 20-26 and 18-28mm). Then the diameter decreased to about 20-21mm and remained unchanged for all the groups. At the same time, the variation did not change in Group II.1.2.1 (16-27mm), and then decreased: 17-23mm in Group II.2.1.1-13 and 18-23mm in Group II.2.1.14-29. When moulds were in regular use, the variations in diameter naturally became much smaller. The diameter was also naturally reduced from 24mm to 20-21mm with the change of standard, and consequently the loss of weight, but curiously this reduction in diameter started in the last group with the Phoenician standard (II.1.2.1); in fact, the following coins, having the same diameter, where thinner. The quarters of shekel, only of the Phoenician standard, followed a similar evolution as regards the diameter (Fig. 30): about 13mm in Group I.1.2, 14mm in Group I.2.2 and 16mm in Group II.1.1.2. But the variations in diameter have a different evolution: 8-14mm in Group I.1.2, 13-15mm in Group I.2.2 and 14-19mm in Group II.1.1.2. The sixteenths of shekel, only of the Phoenician standard, followed a similar evolution as regards the diameter (Fig. 31), but with different variations in diameter: about 8mm (Group I.1.3), 8mm with a variation of 7-9mm (Group I.2.4), 9mm with a variation of 7-11mm (Group II.1.1.3) and 9mm with a variation of 7-10mm (Group II.1.2.2). Unclassified Group III.1.1 has a diameter of about 10mm with a variation of 8-11mm; unclassified Group III.1.2 is different because the diameter is about 9mm with a variation of 6-12mm.

3. *The dies*

Another Tyrian workshop operation was making the dies. To our knowledge, no Tyrian or Phoenician dies have been found to date. However, we have an indirect knowledge of their shape by observing their impression on the coins, and of what they were made of from the Greek or Celtic dies of the same

---

46. *Ibid.*
47. The diameters are not known for all the coins and more or less according to the series.
48. Elayi-Elayi, *Monnayage de Sidon*, pp. 550-551.

period, that have been preserved.[49] The engraving in high relief needed a very hard metal capable of withstanding strong and frequent striking. The dies were sometimes made of bronze like the two pairs of obverse and reverse dies of Athenian (or pseudo-Athenian?) tetradrachms found in Egypt and seemingly dating from the 4th century, and the reverse die of another Athenian tetradrachm of unknown provenance.[50] The dies could also be made of iron as was a reverse die of Berenice II Queen of Egypt,[51] or of 'steel' like a reverse die of Philip II King of Macedonia.[52] The obverse die, probably securely fixed in an anvil, was much larger than the coin to be struck. The reverse die was cylindrical and engraved on the whole surface of its section, much smaller than the section of the obverse die. The shape of the Tyrian dies was probably similar to that of the tetradrachms found in Egypt.[53] A lead Phoenician weight has an unusual motif on its base: a kind of vertical cylinder, slightly rounded at its upper end and slightly enlarged at its lower end, is placed above a horizontal element, rather thick, with two parallel sides, the upper side being slightly dented.[54] It could be a reverse die or stamp, and an obverse die or an object (coin or weight) intended to be struck. The monetary interpretation cannot be totally excluded although it is somewhat surprising on a weight.

The observation of the Tyrian coins gives an idea of the diameter and shape of the dies that have been used. For example, the substantial decentring of the obverse motif on some coins indicates the minimum diameter of the dies. Even if the obverse die was securely fixed in the anvil, it ought to be possible, with a strong magnifying glass, to distinguish the trace of separation between them: on the coins that we could examine, we have noticed no trace of the edge of the

---

49. On the ancient dies in general, cf. C.C. Vermeule, 'Some Notes on Ancient Dies and Coining Methods', *Numismatic Circular* 61, 1953, cols 399-402; R. Tylecote, *The Prehistory of Metallurgy in the British Isles*, London 1986, p. 118; W. Malkmus, 'Addenda to Vermeule's Catalog of Ancient Coin Dies', *SAN* 17/4, 1989, pp. 80-81; 18/4, 1993, pp. 99-101; F. de Callataÿ, 'La dimension des coins monétaires de tétradrachmes hellénistiques d'après l'étude des monnaies décentrées', in B. Kluge and B. Weisser eds, *XII. Internationaler Numismatischer Kongress, Berlin 1997, Akten I*, Berlin 2000, p. 244; M. Manov, 'Two New Coin Dies Found in Bulgaria', *Annotazioni Numismatiche* 48, 2002, pp. 1118-1121.

50. E.S.G. Robinson, 'Athenian Coin Dies from Egypt', *NC* 6th series 10, 1950, pp. 298-299; J.N. Svoronos, 'ΣΦΡΑΓΙΣ ΑΘΗΝΑΙΟΥ ΤΕΤΡΑΔΡΑΧΜΟΥ', in *Corolla Numismatica B.V. Head*, Oxford 1906, pp. 285-295. Cf. also C. Boehringer and O. Pennisi di Floristella, 'Syrakusanischer Münztempel der Epoche des Agathokles', in *Festschrift für Leo Mildenberg*, Wetteren 1984, pls 4, no. 2 and 5, no. 4 (reverse die of Syracuse); Cooper, *op. cit.* (n. 19), p. 8 and fig. 2, 1-4 (with bibl.); M.-L. Berdeaux-Le Brazidec et al., 'Un coin de monnaie à la croix découvert à Villevieille (Gard)', *Cahiers Numismatiques* 171, 2007, pp. 13-29 (with bibl.).

51. Babelon, *Traité* I/1, col. 907, fig. 25.

52. *Ibid.*, col. 906, fig. 24. On the hardening of iron, cf. *ibid.*, pp. 915-920; R.J. Forbes, *Studies in Ancient Technology* IX, Leiden 1972, pp. 204, 218-222, 250-253 and 282; T. Hackens, 'Terminologie et techniques de fabrication', in *Numismatique antique. Problèmes et méthodes*, Annales de l'Est, Nancy-Louvain 1975, pp. 10-12 (with bibl.).

53. Robinson, *loc. cit.* (n. 50), p. 299.

54. Elayi-Elayi, *Poids phéniciens*, pp. 86, no. 169, 193, 246 and pl. XI.

obverse die. The shekels are rarely very decentred, but some examples of decentring do give an idea of the minimum diameter of the obverse dies. For example, the obverse die of coin no. 1163 had a diameter of at least 34mm (8mm visible because of a decentring x2, +18mm for the diameter of the circular border). The obverse die of coin no. 870 had a diameter of at least 31mm (7mm x2, +17mm). The width of the diameter visible outside the border is of 9mm for coin no. 1079, 7mm for coin no. 933, and 6mm for coins no. 992 and 1047, but the diameter of the border is difficult to calculate. Similar observations were made on small denominations: the obverse die of coin no. 187 (quarter of shekel) had a diameter of at least 20mm (4mm x2, +12mm), of coin no. 12 16mm (2mm x2, +12), of coin no. 195 15mm (2mm x2, +11). The obverse die of coin no. 17 (sixteenth of shekel) had a diameter of at least 11mm (2mm x2, +7). The reverse die had a much smaller diameter than the obverse die, which hardly goes beyond the border (1 or 2mm): therefore, in contrast with the obverse dies, it is easier to know the precise diameter of the reverse dies. Two kinds of reverse dies have been used: square section dies for incuse squares and circular section dies for circular reverse types. The square reverse die of the shekel no. 56 had 18mm on one side. The reverse die of coin no. 345 (shekel) had a diameter of 23mm (2mm x2, +19), of coin no. 870 20mm (1mm x2, +18), of coins no. 820 and 933 19mm (1mm x2, +17). The reverse die of coin no. 408 (quarter of shekel) had a diameter of 13mm (1mm x2, +11mm). The reverse dies used for making incuse squares were not entirely square like no. 15 and 22: their angles were sometimes slightly rounded, maybe by wear (no. 2, 8, 42, 51).

The technique of engraving the dies, based on metalworking skills, was similar to the older technique of engraving seals,[55] for example because of the combination of motif and inscription, the exiguous and rounded field (except for incuse squares) and the reverted engraving. However, the material and tools were different. Moreover the difference of style between the motif and the inscription on some seals probably means that the motif was prepared in advance and the inscription added later at the buyer's request.[56] The situation was different for the Tyrian coins since we have not seen any coin where the motif and inscription on the same side were made by two different engravers. It would appear that the same engraver engraved the motif and the inscription, which is logical since both represented the symbol chosen by the minting au-

---

55. Cf., for example, Elayi, *Phénomène monétaire*, p. 21; E. Gubel, 'La glyptique et la genèse de l'iconographie monétaire phénicienne', in T. Hackens and G. Moucharte eds, *Numismatique et histoire économique phéniciennes et puniques*, Louvain-la-Neuve 1992, pp. 1-11; E. Porada, 'Of Professional Seal Cutters and Nonprofessionally Made Seals', in M. Gibson and R.D. Biggs eds, *Seals and Sealing in the Ancient Near East*, Malibu 1977, pp. 7-14; D. Gerin, 'Techniques of Die-engraving: Some Reflections on Obols of the Arcadian Ligue in the 3rd Century B.C.', in M.M. Archibald and M.R. Cowell, *Metallurgy in Numismatics*, London 1993, pp. 20-25.

56. Cf., for example, P. Bordreuil, *Catalogue des sceaux ouest-sémitiques inscrits de la Bibliothèque Nationale et du musée biblique Bible et Terre sainte*, Paris 1986, p. 3.

thority for the issue.[57] However it occasionally happened that the engraver of the obverse die was different from the engraver of the reverse die, which can be explained by a different duration for the two dies:[58] the reverse die wore out more quickly because of its movement. While the obverse die was still in use, a new reverse die could have been made by another engraver. Another difference between the engraving of seals and dies is the following: on the seals combining a motif and an inscription, the inscription was usually placed in the lower part of the field;[59] on the dies, the inscription was often placed in the upper part.

Some Tyrian coins have retained traces of the preliminary work performed by the engraver on the die before the engraving. The use of a compass for tracing a circle is attested by several details: traces of the circle in relief on the coins, visible between the dots of the border (no. 80 O, 182 O, 439 O, 470 R, 747 O and R, 1368 O, 1384 O and R, 1387 O and 1548 R), circle not closed (no. 53), dot in the centre of the circle produced by the hole of the point of the compass in the die (no. 186 O and 432 O).[60] This dot is much more frequently observed on Sidonian coins.[61] On Tyrian coins, either it is not visible because of the high relief of the motif at this position or, less probably, because it has been carefully rubbed away on the coins. The use of compasses is as well attested on shekels as on small denominations. However it became difficult on very small coins such as no. 26 where the well drawn circle was probably done without a compass. Several borders were also drawn without compasses, for example no. 430 O which reveals no traces of a circle between the spaced dots, no. 446 R and 462 R with no traces of a circle when the border is interrupted, and several coins with an irregular (no. 21 O, 461 O, 489 O, 750 O, 781 O and 1670 R) or jutting out border (no. 717 O).

The method of the so-called incuse square was used on the reverse of several Tyrian coins during the Persian period. These incuse squares have nothing to do with the 'primitive incuse squares' frequently used on the reverse of ar-

---

57. Elayi, *loc. cit.* (n. 1), p. 192.
58. Cf., for example, L. Robert, 'Monnaies dans les inscriptions grecques', *RN* 6, 1962, pp. 18-24; *ID*, no. 1450, side A, l. 198 and no. 1430, l. 30 (5 obverse and 18 reverse dies) ; Bouyon *et al.*, *op. cit.* (n. 13), p. 61 (on average, in the Hellenistic period, one obverse die was used with 3.6 reverse dies).
59. Cf., for example, B. Buchanan and P.R.S. Moorey, *Catalogue of Ancient Near Eastern Seals in the Ashmolean Museum* III, Oxford 1988, pl. X, no. 291, 292, 295 and 300.
60. The interpretation of this central dot is accepted in other coinages such as ancient Greek coinages : Hill, *loc. cit.* (n. 25), p. 23; G. Le Rider, 'Sur la fabrication des coins monétaires dans l'antiquité grecque', *Schweizer Münzblätter* 29, 1958, pp. 4-5 (with bibl.); M. Dhénin, 'Quelques remarques sur le travail des graveurs de coins', in G. Depeyrot *et al.* eds, *Rythmes de la production monétaire, de l'Antiquité à nos jours*, Louvain-la-Neuve 1987, pp. 453-457.
61. Cf. Elayi-Elayi, *Monnayage de Sidon*, pp. 554-555.

chaic Greek and Persian coins, but they are 'evolved type squares'.[62] For a long time, at least until the middle of the 4th century, important Greek cities used an incuse square on the reverse die which was always smaller than the obverse die and the flan. The preservation of the incuse square, in some workshops such as Cyzicus, is explained by the fact that these mints wanted to maintain confidence in their coinages which had been in existence for several generations.[63] The case of Tyre seems to be different because the incuse square was not systematically used on the reverse, but only from time to time in a few silver series, never in bronze series; it can be found on all denominations: for example no. 29 (shekel), no. 182 (quarter of shekel), no. 222 (eight), no. 223 (sixteenth), no. 239 (half of sixteenth). We do not see any particular explanation for the use of these square reverse dies; it is seemingly random and in parallel to the use of circular reverse dies. On the reverse of coin no. 62, the outline of the square is underlined by an incuse line like the outline of the owl; it is also partly the same for coin no. 80.

The incuse method involving partly in relief and partly in hollow, was used on the reverse dies of Aradian, Sidonian and Byblian coinages just like the incuse square method, but less frequently and only during a limited period. It was only used for the various denominations bearing an owl: I.2.1, I.2.2, I.2.3 and I.2.4, not for I.2.5 with the profile head of a lion. However, it is different here from other Phoenician coinages: the owl is outlined by a shallow incuse impression, giving the illusion that it is in relief in a shallow surface. In fact, the field and owl were engraved on the die in hollow while the outline was in relief. This method of engraving was misunderstood by E. Babelon who wrote for example for Byblos 'ram engraved in hollow' and for Sidon 'goat engraved in hollow',[64] whereas they were actually engraved in relief on the dies. J.P. Six also misunderstood the method, using the term 'countermark'.[65] P. Naster wondered whether the hollow elements were not added using punches after the striking.[66] He showed that several reasons prove that punches were not used, such as the absence of deformation on the other side of the coins, and the analysis of the process: the engraver first prepared the field level, keeping the elements that were to be in hollow on the coin in relief, then he engraved these elements in hollow, and finally the details of the remaining surface. This incuse method was very difficult to execute: for example, the relief of the body of the owl and the details of the feathers were rarely well-represented, and most of the time in a hasty and clumsy way (no. 40, 49, 59, 62). The field around the owl

62. P. Naster, 'Le carré creux en numismatique grecque', in *Numismatique antique. Problèmes et méthodes*, Annales de l'Est, Nancy-Louvain 1975, p. 20 (= *id., Scripta Nummaria. Contributions à la méthodologie numismatique*, Louvain-la-Neuve 1983, pp. 45-50).
63. *Ibid.*, p. 20.
64. Babelon, *Perses*, p. 192, no. 1342; p. 229, no. 1565.
65. J.P. Six, 'Observations sur les monnaies phéniciennes', *NC* 17, 1877, pp. 177-241.
66. Naster, *loc. cit.* (n. 62), pp. 25-28.

has rarely the same regular level. In fact, there was more work to do on Tyrian coins because more metal had to be taken off: all the field surface except for the outline of the owl. The Tyrian engravers were accustomed to doing a hollow engraving, used for seals, but not relief engraving, used later for cameos.[67] According to P. Naster, the semi-incuse method 'used by the cities of Tyre, Arados and Byblos was in fact always the same and is a simple variant of the usual method or, in a way, it is the sum of the usual hollow engraving and the incuse engraving of coins as it was practised in Magna Graecia'.[68] He means the method of engraving the motif on both sides of the coin, in relief on the obverse and in hollow on the reverse, which was in use at the end of the 6th century in some mints in Magna Graecia (Tarentum, Poseidonia, Caulonia, Sybaris, Sirinos, Metapontum and Croton).[69]

In fact, the Phoenician incuse method seems to have another origin, other than these coinages: the engravers of the incuse Tyrian coins, who probably inaugurated this method before Sidon, Byblos and at last Arwad, were possibly inspired by a method of sculpture used in Egyptian low reliefs. It is the so-called 'relief in hollow', obtained by surrounding all the low reliefs motifs with an incuse impression. The incuse impression surrounding the owl of the Tyrian coins could be a derivative of the Egyptian method, frequently used over several centuries.[70] We also have to mention the possible influence of the earlier coins of Kalymna of Caria, minted in about 520: they depict a lyre surrounded by an incuse impression, unique among all the Greek coinages and that could itself have been borrowed from Egypt low-reliefs.[71] Following Tyre, the other Phoenician monetary workshops used the same incuse method, but each of them in a different and original way: an incuse ram and a head of bull on the Byblian coins, heads of Bes and goat on the Sidonian coins and a crescent on the Aradian coins. In conclusion, the incuse method was a Tyrian innovation, used in the second stage of the Tyrian coinage and followed by the other Phoenician mints. It was only in use for a short time, probably because it was a difficult method and perhaps also because it was not very attractive. As in the Sidonian coinage, it was used during the last third of the 5th century.

The Tyrian engravers used to surround the types of obverse and reverse coins with a border: a guilloche border or, which were easier to engrave, a

---

67. The earliest cameos are not earlier than Alexander: cf. Naster, *ibid.*, p. 27 and n. 3 (with bibl.).
68. *Ibid.*, p. 28.
69. *Id.*, 'La technique des monnaies incuses de Grande-Grèce', *RBN* 93, 1947, pp. 5-17 (= *id.*, *op. cit.* [n. 1], pp. 8-17).
70. Cf., for example, E. Naville, *The XIth Dynasty Temple at Deir el-Bahari* I, London 1907, pl. XVIII; II, London 1910, pl. IX G and (4b) (XXIrst century); C. Aldred *et al.*, *L'Egypte du crépuscule*, Paris 1980, p. 81, fig. 62 and p. 82, fig. 63; J. Elayi, 'Les sicles de Tyr au dauphin', *NAC* 21, 1992, p. 42; *id.*, 'La place de l'Egypte dans la recherche sur les Phéniciens', *Trans* 9, 1995, p. 22.
71. Cf., for example, G.K. Jenkins, *Monnaies grecques*, Fribourg 1972, pls 30-31.

cable border or a border of dots. The same type of border was used for both obverse and reverse. Chronologically, the border of dots and the cable border were generally used in the first and last phases of Tyrian coinage; in between, the guilloche border was used, but sometimes in parallel with the two other kinds of border. The reverse dies of silver coins with square shapes had no borders, nor did the reverse dies of bronze coins (Series III.2.4).

It sometimes happened that the size of the dies was not adapted to the size of the flans. For example several dies are too small: no. 42 R, 52 O, 186 O, 193 O, 196 O, 222 O, 282 O and R, 404 O and R, 875 R, 889 O, 900 O, 901 O, 1583 R, 1585 R, 1586 R and 1614 O; they are less often too large: no. 486 O and 1397 R.[72] This could be explained by a lack of synchronisation between the person making the flans and the die engraver, or by a mistake on the part of the hammerer using dies of smaller or larger denominations.

On about 100 coins, we have observed one or several defects which are more or less visible, but the damaged dies continued to be used (for example no. 182 R, 378 R, 618 O, 826 O, 973 O, 1029 R, 1274 O and 1603 R). It was the same for dies that were cracked (for example no. 888, 969, 1032, 1148, 1151, 1416 and 1660), as they were probably used until they were totally broken. When dies were worn, especially reverse dies which wore out more quickly, the engravers could re-engrave them as can be seen from other coinages,[73] but re-engraving of this nature is difficult to detect (no. 713 R), except when the date is changed by the additional stroke of a unit in the next issue (R27' of no. 966, R86' of no. 1200, R90' of no. 1210, R111' of no. 1304 and R152' of no. 1512). Therefore, just like the Sidonian mint,[74] the Tyrian mint made significant savings in its workload, during the whole of this period, particularly as regards Group II.

None of the tools used by the Tyrian engravers have been discovered, however it is possible to infer some of them from their indirect traces on the coins, by means of the dies. The engravers had compasses, probably of different sizes for the different denominations, because it would not have been easy to draw circles of 28 and 6mm for example with the same tool; at least their point was probably thinner. They also had at their disposal different sized burins for motifs and inscriptions, and hammers adapted to the burins. In addition, they needed a kind of vice in which the dies were held during the engraving process. We still do not know whether a magnifying process was used for engraving the

---

72. Sometimes one die, sometimes the pair of dies has an inadequate size.
73. Cf., for example, G. Le Rider, *Antioche de Syrie sous les Séleucides. Corpus des monnaies d'or et d'argent I. De Séleucos I à Antiochos V c. 300-161*, Paris 1999, p. 61, no. 15; p. 64, no. 54-55; p. 65, no. 76; p. 77, no. 3; pp. 97-98, no. 13; p. 100, no. 79, etc.; cf. F. de Callataÿ, 'Étude de technique monétaire: le rapport 'nombre de coins de revers/nombre de coins de droit' à l'époque hellénistique', *RAHAL* 32, 1999, pp. 91-102.
74. Cf. Elayi-Elayi, *Monnayage de Sidon*, pp. 558-560.

dies of minute coins, since no tool ressembling to a magnifying glass has been discovered up to date, even though this is quite conceivable.

Concerning the much-debated question of the existence of standard punches for Greek dies,[75] according to our observations, neither Tyre nor any other Phoenician workshop seems to have used a complete punch to make dies in the Persian period. If the engraver had a punch at his disposal to facilitate making a substantial number of identical dies, it would not have been necessary to make so many different dies for each series, especially complex motifs, nor to keep using worn and even damaged dies over a long period.[76] The existence of such punches is also refuted by the traces of the compass point used by the engraver in his preliminary work: the dot is in relief on the coin, corresponding to the hollow made on the die. If a punch had been used for the die, the dot, in hollow on the punch and in relief on the die, would be in hollow on the coin. In the same way, where a circle in relief is visible on the coins between the dots of the border, it is the trace of the compass point on the die and not on a punch. Therefore the Tyrian engravers worked directly on the dies. However, the hypothesis of summary punches for giving a rough shape to the die, even if it cannot be proved, remains possible.

On the other hand, the use of partial punches seems to be likely, but probably limited to the dot-shaped element, of different sizes, used for the border and sometimes for other motifs such as the mane and legs of the seahorse and owl (no. 473 and 477). The more extensive use of these dot-shaped punches in some series (II.1.1.3 and II.2.1.26) is probably due to hurried, clumsy or careless engravers. When such a punch was used for the border of dots, if its position was not always vertical but sometimes oblique, the circular shape of the dots became oval (no. 222 O, 1370 R, and 1374 R). The tools still used today by the traditional engravers of the 'Monnaie de Paris', as they correspond to the same needs, probably differ very little from those of the Tyrian engravers:[77] compasses, burins, gravers and hammers, all of them coming in different sizes for specific uses, often made by the engravers themselves in order to best suit their precise needs. For example, they often use partial punches that they make: some of them bear a double or triple motif (one, two or three juxtaposed dots) in order to save time. They need magnifying glasses, for engraving letters of 2/3mm for example, using very thin burins. As we have seen in Chapter III, the engravers probably followed a pattern provided by the minting authority, but

---

75. The theory of complete punches was mainly supported by G.F. Hill, O. Ravel, C. Seltman and W. Schwabacher, but fighted by L. Naville, S.P. Noe and G. Le Rider; H.A. Cahn and G.K. Jenkins found no traces of punches in the coinages that they have examined: see bibl. in Le Rider, *loc. cit.* (n. 60), pp. 1-5 and Hackens, *loc. cit.* (n. 52), pp. 11-12 ; Elayi, *loc. cit.* (n. 57), pp. 192-194.

76. For example, no. 192, 197, 665, 693, 616-621 (with different defects).

77. All these informations were provided by D. Gedalje.

they could organise the field to be engraved depending on material restraints as well as their own fancy.

4. Striking

After the monetary flans and dies had been made came the striking. This process has been studied in several publications, mainly from late documents, Roman and especially Medieval.[78] The Tyrian workshop is only known from its coinage. At first the obverse die had to be fixed in the anvil, the flan was then placed over this die and the reverse die over the flan before it was struck with a hammer (or by another means?). The reverse Tyrian die had a maximum diameter of about 20mm for the shekels: it was therefore possible to hold it firmly in the hand, putting the thumb on the index and second finger.[79] For convenience' sake, the person in charge of the striking has been named 'the hammerer' (Roman *malleator*). The Tyrian shekels of Phoenician standard were large coins (not as large as the Sidonian double shekels however). The engraving was in high-relief, especially in the case of an incuse impression where the thickness of the motif in hollow was added to that of the motif in relief.[80] The strength required for striking was such that it was probably impossible to hold the reverse die at the same time with one hand and the hammer with the other hand. There were probably two people: one person who held the die, maybe with tongs for safety, and one who struck with the hammer.[81] However, according to some authors, it was impossible to strike the large Ptolemaic bronze coins weighing about 40g by hand and that is why they proposed different hypotheses of machines of the type mechanical hammer or rammer, depending on the state of technical know-how at the time.[82] A machine may not have been necessary for the Tyrian shekels (about one third of the weight of Ptolemaic bronze coins). However, the first question concerning the tempera-

---

78. A monetary workshop is possibly represented in a painting of Pompei: E.J. Seltman, 'The Picture of a Roman Mint in the House of the Vettii', *NC*, 1898, pp. 294-303. On the striking process, cf., for example, Babelon, *Traité* I, pp. 844-846; Hill, *loc. cit.* (n. 25), pp. 1-43; Vermeule, *loc. cit.* (n. 49); P. Balog, 'Notes on ancient and medieval Techniques', *NC* 6th ser. 15, 1955, pp. 195-202; D.B. Sellwood, 'Some Experiments in Greek minting Technique', *NC* 7th ser. 3, 1963, pp. 217-231; F. Delamare *et al.*, 'A Mechanical Approach to Coin Striking: Application to the Study of Byzantine Gold Solidi', in W.A. Oddy ed., *Metallurgy in Numismatics* 2, London 1988, pp. 41-52; Elayi-Elayi, *La monnaie*, pp. 195-204 (with bibl.); G. Le Rider, *La naissance de la monnaie. Pratiques monétaires de l'Orient ancien*, Paris 2001, p. 18, fig. 2 (representation of the position of dies). Cf. however K. Konuk, 'A Coin Minting Scene on an Attic Ceramic Fragment of c. 480 BC', in *XIII Congreso Internacional de Numismática*, Madrid 15-19 Sept. 2003.
79. According to F. de Callataÿ (*loc. cit.* [n. 49], p. 250), the limit is a diameter of 35mm.
80. Some authors questioned that the human strenght was sufficient for striking the largest denominations such as Syracusan decadrachms : cf., for example, L. Mildenberg, *The Coinage of the Bar Kokhba War*, Aarau *et al.* 1984, p. 18 and n. 28.
81. The use of tongs for holding the dies is attested for the Roman period.
82. Bouyon *et al.*, *op. cit.* (n. 13), pp. 52-73.

ture of the striking remains unsolved.[83] There was no lesser difficulty, albeit different, for the striking of small denominations: it was not easy to position the small flan correctly, or the small reverse die over the flan; then the striking power had to be adapted to the size of the coin. The phenomenon of striction, for example, shows that the striking power was too great as it produced cracks on the edge of the coins.[84]

The decentring of the motifs on the coins provides us with indirect information about the striking process. Our observations of Tyrian coins are almost identical to our observations of Sidonian coins.[85] Firstly, the decentring occurred much more often on the reverse than on the obverse.[86] Decentring on the reverse implies that the reverse die was not correctly placed over the flan. Decentring on the obverse can also be explained by the fact that the flan was not correctly placed over the fixed obverse die, but it could also mean that the hammerer did not hold his reverse die in an axis which was perpendicular to the plane of striking. In this case, the reverse die was pushed to the side by the stroke of the hammer, producing a decentring of the flan on the obverse.[87] In most cases, the instances of decentring appear to follow the same direction: between 12h and 13h depending on the nomenclature used for die axes. This observation has already been made by F. de Callataÿ for the Seleucid tetradrachms.[88] According to him, it is normal since it confirms a clear preponderance, both in Antiquity as well as today, of right-handed people in the population: as a matter of fact, the hammer stroke made by the right hand pushes the metal in the 9-12h direction with respect to the obverse die which appears as 12-3 h on the coin. This means too that the obverse die fixed in the anvil was positioned vertically in relation to the hammerer, which was logical. It can also be noticed that decentring generally occurred more often on small denominations than on shekels (about 1/7), possibly because the shekels were struck more easily and more carefully than the small denominations. Decentring becomes less frequent in Series II.2.1, that is with the generalisation of circular flans: either it was easier to place the dies over circular flans or the quality of production improved.

The question of the orientation of die axes was first approached at the beginning of the 20th century by G. MacDonald and G.F. Hill,[89] but it was only

---

83. *Ibid.*, pp. 16-21.
84. See, above, n. 43.
85. Cf. Elayi-Elayi, *Monnayage de Sidon*, pp. 562-563.
86. We only take into consideration the strongly marked decentrings.
87. Cf. de Callataÿ, *loc. cit.* (n. 49), p. 246.
88. *Ibid.*, p. 247 (with bibl.).
89. G. MacDonald, 'Fixed and Loose Dies in Ancient Coinage', in *Corolla Numismatica. Essays in Honour of B.V. Head*, Oxford 1906, pp. 178-188; *BMC Phoenicia*, p. v: 'Special attention has been paid to the identification of dies, and also to the position in which obverse and reverse dies were placed relatively to each other in striking'.

studied in the 1960s,[90] however it was always considered as a minor question: 'In my view, the importance of this revolutionary innovation is not adequately appreciated even today', according to L. Mildenberg.[91] Still now, sale catalogues rarely indicate the axis orientation,[92] so it is difficult to make a comprehensive study of this question. G.F. Hill was the first in 1910 to notice the orientation of most of the Sidonian coins at 12h: 'Throughout the series of Sidon the coins are struck from dies fixed, unless otherwise stated'.[93] F. de Callataÿ has recently studied the axis orientation of Greek coins and concluded that the Sidonian coinage represented 'the oldest example of strict adjusting of dies with swivelling iconographic types at 12h'.[94] His conclusion was exact, but it was based on a small number of coins and on the erroneous chronology of J.W. Betlyon. We have dealt with this question in our corpus of the Sidonian coinage;[95] our conclusion was the following: the axis orientation at 12h was mainly followed on the double shekels; it was less often followed on the small silver denominations and on bronze coins.[96]

Did the adjusting of axes need a special tool for holding the dies in position? Some authors think such tool was necessary,[97] similar for example to the tongs of Beaumont-sur-Oise bearing the dies of a Constantin aureus minted in Antioch, or to the nested dies of Faustina the Young.[98] Other authors consider that the adjusting was not done by any mechanical means but by guide markers for example, which were put on the dies.[99] Other authors hesitate between these

90. For Greek coins, cf. L. Mildenberg, "Those ridiculous arrows'. On the meaning of the die position', *Nomismatika Chronika* 8, 1989, pp. 23-27 (= U. Hübner and E.A. Knauf eds, *Leo Mildenberg. Vestigia Leonis. Studien zur antiken Numismatik Israels, Palästinas und der östlichen Mittelmeerwelt*, Freiburg-Göttingen 1998, pp. 263-264); F. de Callataÿ, *Les monnaies grecques et l'orientation des axes*, Milan 1996. For Roman coins, cf. E. Milliau, 'Quelques monnaies romaines d'Antioche; étude de la direction des revers', *RBN* 106, 1960, pp. 317-319; J. Guey and C. Carcassonne, 'Coins de droit et de revers. Étude descriptive d'un échantillon', *RN* 6, 1970, pp. 7-32; P. Bastien and H. Huvelin, 'Orientation des axes de coins dans le monnayage impérial romain', *BSFN* 26, 1971, pp. 130-135; C. Brenot, 'Observations sur les orientations d'axes d'un groupe d'antoniniani de Victorin issus des mêmes coins de droit et de revers', *BSFN* 28, 1971, pp. 135-139.

91. Mildenberg, *ibid.*, p. 23.

92. Lanz and Leu Numismatik use to indicate the axes orientation, others only episodically (for example, Burgan, Glendining, Sternberg and Waddell).

93. *BMC Phoenicia*, p. 139, n. 1.

94. De Callataÿ, *op. cit.* (n. 90), p. 83.

95. Elayi-Elayi, *Monnayage de Sidon*, pp. 563-568.

96. It was the same for the cities following later the Sidonian innovation: cf. de Callataÿ, *op. cit.* (n. 90), p. 99.

97. Cf., for example, Seltman, *loc. cit.* (n. 78), pp. 299-302; MacDonald, *loc. cit.* (n. 89), p. 178; *id.*, *The Evolution of Coinage*, Cambridge 1916, pp. 65-66; J.G. Milne, *Greek Coins and the Study of History*, London 1939, p. 46; P. Naster, 'La trouvaille d'antoniniani de Grotenberge et le monnayage de Postume', *RBN* 97, 1951, pp. 25-88 (= *id.*, *op. cit.* [n. 62], pp. 229-232).

98. Babelon, *Traité* I/1, cols 911-913 (Cabinet des Médailles, BNF, Paris); Vermeule, *loc. cit.* (n. 49), p. 398 (Fogg Art Museum, Harvard).

99. Cf., for example, M. von Bahrfeldt, 'Antike Münztechnik', *Berliner Münzblätter* 35, 1904, p. 439; Le Rider, *Fouilles de Suse*, p. 21; O. Mørkholm, *Early Hellenistic Coinage from the*

two systems.[100] Our study of the Sidonian coinage showed that no mechanical method was used because, in most of the series, there is a slight deviation at 11h or at 1h: if the dies had been fixed in position, the orientation at 12h would have been more regular, and the decentring would have been identical on the obverse and reverse of the same coin.[101] Our documentation on the operation of striking (monetary dies, representations), which is late, indicates that the reverse die was held by the hand.[102] If a suitable tool were to have existed for adjusting the axes, it would have spread quickly, which was not the case at all.[103] Therefore, it seems likely that guide markers were put on each of the two dies so that the reverse die was correctly positioned for striking, similar perhaps to the marks that are visible on a die of Berenice and on a Syracusan die.[104]

Why did the Sidonian workshop decide to orientate its die axes at 12h? According to F. de Callataÿ, it was 'to prevent the image of the king [that is the attendant following the chariot] from falling off the flan', as on Persian darics and shekels where the image (of the Great King) had to be complete.[105] This hypothesis is impossible because, when axis orientation at 12h started (Groups I and II), the chariot was not yet followed by the king of Sidon.[106] Another hypothesis was proposed, by which this process was intended to combat counterfeits; this is impossible for two reasons:[107] this process could not have been kept secret as there were probably forgers inside the workshop[108] (moreover this process could easily be detected just by observing the coins) and it would have needed to be more rigorous to identify forgers. The other hypotheses that have been proposed are possible: it was easier to always put the reverse die in the same position in order to identify more rapidly whether the striking was well-done.[109] This process would have been useful for striking the incuse coins of Magna Graecia where the identical motifs of obverse and reverse had to

---

Accession of Alexander to the Peace of Apamea (336-188 B.C.), Cambridge 1991, pp. 15-16; de Callataÿ, *op. cit.* (n. 90), pp. 90-95.

100. Milne, *op. cit.* (n. 97), p. 44; O. Mørkholm first hesitated between the two systems: 'The Autonomous Tetradrachms of Laodicea ad Mare', *ANSMN* 28, 1983, p. 96; J. Melville Jones, *A Dictionary of Ancient Coins*, London 1983, pp. 76-77; Mildenberg, *op. cit.* (n. 80), pp. 24-25.

101. Cf. L. Naville, *Les monnaies d'or de la Cyrénaïque de 450 à 250 avant J.-C.*, Geneva 1951, p. 11.

102. Cf. de Callataÿ, *op. cit.* (n. 90), p. 94 (with bibl.).

103. Cf. Le Rider, *Fouilles de Suse*, p. 21.

104. Different kinds of marks could have been used for the die of Berenice, cf. Babelon, *Traité* I/1, col. 907, and for that of Syracuse, cf. Boehringer-Pennisi di Floristella, *loc. cit.* (n. 50), pls 4, no. 2 and 5, no. 4.

105. De Callataÿ, *op. cit.* (n. 90), pp. 83 and 97.

106. The examples given *ibid.*, p. 83, n. 384, where the charriot is represented alone, are not relevant.

107. Given by F. de Callataÿ, *ibid.*, p. 100.

108. See for example the case of Dyme in Achaia, where six persons in charge of the workshop, accused to have minted plated coins, were put to death: *Syll.* ³530.

109. Le Rider, *Fouilles de Suse*, p. 21.

coincide exactly.[110] This new process was perhaps intended for the quality of the mint from the beginning of the Sidonian coinage.

The orientation of die axes had already been used, at the end of the 6th century, by several cities of Magna Graecia for their incuse series, but it was a technical necessity during a short period because the obverse motif had to fit in exactly with the identical incuse motif of the reverse. The systematisation of this process in all Sidonian coinage, shortly after 450, was understood as being a technical innovation and was progressively followed. The other Phoenician cities only adopted die orientation in the 4th century: Tyre, then Arwad, then Byblos.[111] In the Tyrian Group I (I.1 and I.2), there is no fixed choice of the orientation at 12h, but perhaps only a tendency: 14 coins at 12h, 1 (1h), 4 (2h), 11 (3h), 5 (4h), 6 (5h), 9 (6h), 6 (7h), 0 (8h), 7 (9h), 2 (10h) and 7 (11h). In Group II.1, the situation has not changed: 53 coins at 12h, 20 (1h), 18 (2h), 35 (3h), 22 (4h), 23 (5h), 33 (6h), 18 (7h), 4 (8h), 27 (9h), 12 (10h) and 19 (11h). A clear change did occurred at the time of the change in standard from the Phoenician to the 'Attic' (Group II.2.1): 104 coins at 12h, 59 (1h), 4 (2h), 1 (3h), 1 (4h), 0 (5h), 0 (6h), 0 (7h), 1 (9h), 3 (10h) and 34 (11h).[112] Unclassified series of Group III are similar to Group I and Group II.1, without a selected orientation, but maybe a tendency at 12h: 23 coins at 12h, 2 (1h), 9 (2h), 17 (3h), 8 (4h), 4 (5h), 13 (6h), 5 (7h), 4 (8h), 9 (9h), 4 (10h) and 3 (11h). The bronze series (III.2) have different axis orientations, but mainly at 6h: 18 coins at 6h, 1 (7h), 0 (8h), 1 (9h), 0 (10h), 1 (11h), 5 (12h), 3 (1h), 3 (2h), 5 (3h), 1 (4h) and 4 (5h). By about 400, the mints of Rhodes, Samos and Sardis had followed the Sidonian innovation, before the three Phoenician cities of Tyre, Arwad and Byblos; Athens did the same, but with an original adjustment at 9h.[113] The spread of the adjustment at 12h first reached the Oriental part of the Mediterranean, then the whole Mediterranean world in the 1rst century BCE.[114]

Some defects noticed on the coins also provide indirect information on the process of striking. The question of the temperature of the flan when it was struck remains unsolved: however the traces of overstriking on several coins could possibly mean that the flan was not hot.[115] Overstriking on previous series which were no longer in circulation, was used in the Tyrian workshop: no. 52, 79, and 204 (Group I.2), 387 (II.1.1), 839, 841 (II.2.1.3), 1306

---

110. Cf. Naster, *loc. cit.* (n. 69), p. 15 : 'les monnayeurs devaient connaître un dispositif, probablement à coulisseau, qui fixait le coin mobile par rapport au coin dormant'.
111. Cf. de Callataÿ, *op. cit.* (n. 90), pp. 83-85 (with bibl.). See our corpus of Aradian and Byblian coinages in preparation.
112. For Group II.2.1.1-13, we have: 23 coins at 12h, 9 (1h), 3 (2h), 1 (3h), 0 (4, 5, 6, 7, 8, 9 and 10h) and 6 (11h). For Group II.2.14-29, we have: 81 coins at 12h, 50 (1h), 1 (2h), 0 (3h), 1 (4h), 0 (5, 6, 7 and 8h), 1 (9h), 3 (10h) and 28 (11h).
113. *Ibid.*, pp. 118-119.
114. Cf. the maps showing this spreading: *ibid.*, pp. 102-119.
115. No. 85 R, 91 R, 402 O, 406 O, 672 R, 841 O, 908 O, 918 O, 934 O, 958 R, 959 R, 981 R and 982 R.

(II.2.1.25), 1364, 1378, 1408, 1416, 1419, and 1442 (II.2.1.26) and 1577 (III.1.1). This process was only in frequent use in year 15 of King ʿOzmilk. Either it was not in current use as in the Sidonian workshop, or the traces of overstriking were deleted (by heating the flan before striking?). Finally we have observed traces of poor striking (no. 480 R), and traces of re-striking when the outline of the motif was double, due to a second hammer stroke, more numerous in Group II.2.1. This second stroke could be an error or intended to correct a first badly aimed stroke.

5. Alterations not related to the manufacturing process

Coins defects related to the manufacturing process must not be confused with the alterations of various origins related to the circulation of the coins from the time they were minted until they were discovered. These alterations can be classified into two categories: casual and deliberate. As casual alterations, we shall mention for example the flaws, scratches (no. 297 O, 339 O, 917 R and 943 O), the traces of gazes and scrapes mainly caused by cleaning (no. 185 R, 254 R, 278 O and R, 303 R, 309 O and R, 317 R, 334 O, 366 O and R, 379 O and R, 400 O and R, 425 O and R, 476 O and R, 970 R, 1001 R, 1004 R, 1008 R, 1014 O, 1040 R, 1069 R, 1624 O and R, 1659 O), the traces of corrosion (no. 7, 25, 325, 781 and 1162) due to a long stay in a damaging environment, and the frequent breaks of the edges, mainly due to the brittleness of the metal (for example no. 65, 257, 280, 290, 313, 343, 379, 449, 473, 531, 538, 539, 1357, 1575, 1583, 1587, 1597, 1598, 1608, 1616 and 1626). The most frequent casual alterations are, by far, the traces of wear because most of the coins listed in the catalogue of our corpus came from the mass coinage in circulation, and are consequently more or less worn.[116] Among the hoards of Tyrian coins, that we have listed (Appendix I), most of the coins hoarded are more or less worn because they were taken from the monetary mass in circulation (for example TXIII-XIV-XV, TXXXIV and TLXIX).[117] The Khirbet el-Kerak hoard (TXXVI) and the Tell Abu Hawam hoard (TXXXV) were probably hoarded all at the same time since the earliest coins are more or less worn and the latest well-preserved.[118] Interesting research has been conducted to calculate the wear of coins, more particularly per year, but it is not relevant for dated Tyrian coins as no single issue is represented by a sufficient number of samples.

Deliberate alterations are quite numerous and of different kinds in the Tyrian coinage of the Persian period. We have recorded seven countermarks

---

116. The different stages of wear are indicated in the Catalogue in Chapter I.
117. Elayi-Elayi, *Trésors*, pp. 92-114 (TXIII-XIV-XV); 168-170 (TXXXIV) and 279-281 (TLXIX).
118. *Ibid.*, pp. 139-147 (TXXVI) and 170-185 (TXXXV). For the different interpretations of the nature of the hoards, see *ibid.*; many of them are difficult to interpret.

made with a punch (no. 329 O, 703 R, 639 R, 656 O, 1162 O, 1224 O and 1232 O) and six graffiti incised with a hard point (no. 288 R, 912 R, 1049 R, 1226 R, 1287 R and 1421 O).[119] 5 coins are in fragments, four of them dating from the 5th century (no. 65, 89, 90, 382 and 1528); 56 coins have one chisel-cut, most of them (33) dating also from the 5th century;[120] they have sometimes two chisel-cuts (no. 255, 351 and 680) or even three (no. 323 and 628). The fragments of coins are explained in a context of weighed metal: in order to obtain a certain weight of silver, the coins were divided, when necessary, into fragments, just like ingots, jewels or other silver fragments. The cutting of coins could be also intended to reveal plated coins. Even if it partly obliterated the type when it was very deep (no. 628), it was frequently used for checking whether the coin was genuine.[121] This explains why all the fragments of coins and cut coins are always silver coins, never bronze ones. Among the other deliberate alterations, we also have to mention as well two cases of edges clipping (no. 806 and 1230), which could be interpreted as a fraudulent theft of metal, and seven pierced coins (no. 379, 823, 977, 1149, 1239, 1346 and 1527), which could have been used as items of jewellery.

6. Workshop operations

How did the Tyrian monetary workshop operate? No doubt it was under the direct control of the minting authority since it printed the symbols of the city. It was therefore absolutely necessary for the minting authority to control the quality, weight and function of the official coinage. As we have shown above, several craftsmen, specialised in different fields, were involved in the coins manufacturing: metal-founders (*NSK*) for metal processing and making the flans, craftsmen in charge of the control adjustment of the weights, stone-cutters for making stone moulds for flans, metal-founders for making dies and punches, die 'engravers' (*ḤRṢ*), 'coins weighers' (*ŠQL MḤTT*)[122] and strong and precise hammerers.[123] At all events there was probably also a person in charge of the coin issues. All these craftsmen were not necessarily official craftsmen: the Tyrian monetary workshop was probably similar to the Greek workshops, which were informal in the sense that the coin production was not entirely

---

119. See above, Chapter III.2 and 3.
120. No. 10, 51, 53, 55, 60, 86, 186, 202, 207, 222, 248, 267, 274, 284, 288, 294, 325, 326, 331, 335, 338, 339, 355, 356, 370, 374, 381, 403, 406, 408, 409, 416, 523, 615, 626, 630, 633, 665, 668, 670, 672, 675, 676, 678, 703, 713, 841, 842, 911, 1034, 1168, 1172, 1177, 1234, 1421 and 1524.
121. Cf. Elayi, *loc. cit.* (n. 2), p. 189.
122. Hoftijzer-Jongeling, *op. cit.* (n. 5), s.v. 'nsk₁', 'ḥrṣ₄' and 'ḥrṣ₅', 'mḥt₁'; E. Lipiński dir., *Dictionnaire de la civilisation phénicienne et punique*, Turnhout 1992, s.v. 'corporations' (with bibl.).
123. Cf. de Callataÿ, *loc. cit.* (n. 49), p. 247 : '... la frappe était une activité fatiguante et ... plusieurs ouvriers devaient très probablement se relayer dans cet exercice au cours de la même journée'.

carried out in this workshop and that other specialised workshops could be commissioned to do part of the work.[124] For example, the metal processing could be done directly *in situ* in the mining districts or in a bronze-founder's workshop, likewise the stone processing in a stone-cutter's workshop. The engraving of dies represented an important step in the minting process: as the style of some engravers is sometimes reminiscent of seal-engraving, they could previously have been, or still be seal-engravers at the same time, fulfilling orders in their workshop for the Tyrian monetary workshop. And it is possible too that official seals engravers worked in the same workshop as the dies engravers. At all events, the control of the weights and conformity of the coins to the official order, the organisation of the issue and the storage of the dies were part of the Tyrian monetary workshop functions. The terminology used to designate these different craftsmen is still not well-known in spite of some preliminary studies into this question.[125] In Phoenician, $HR\d{S}$ could mean either 'gold' or 'engraving' or 'chiselling',[126] but we do not know whether the die-engraver had the same name as the stone-engraver of moulds or monumental inscriptions.[127] $\check{S}QL$ meaning 'weigher' is attested in a Carthaginian inscription,[128] and the 'weigher of coins' is possibly called $\check{S}QL\ M\d{H}TT$ in the so-called Carthaginian urbanistic inscription.[129]

As regards the equipment in the workshop, we have already mentioned some of the tools indirectly attested by the coins themselves and by parallel sources: crucibles and measures for molten metal, moulds for flans, vices, burins and compasses of different sizes, partial punches, obverse and reverse dies, anvils for fixing the reverse dies, scales and weights. It is interesting to compare this list of tools with the later representation of tools in Roman or Medie-

---

124. Cf., for example, Babelon, *Traité* I/1, cols 844-846 (with bibl.).
125. Cf., for example, F. Mazza, 'Note sul problema dell'ordinatio nell'epigrafia punica', *RSF* 6, 1978, pp. 19-26; H. Benichou-Safar, *Les tombes puniques de Carthage*, Paris 1982, pp. 187-205; M.G. Amadasi Guzzo, *Scavi a Mozia – Le iscrizioni*, Roma 1986, p. 93; C. Bonnet, 'La terminologie phénico-punique relative au métier de lapicide et à la gravure des textes', *SEL* 7, 1990, pp. 111-122; *id.*, 'Les scribes phénico-puniques', in Baurain *et al.* eds, *op. cit.* (n. 2), pp. 147-172.
126. Hoftijzer-Jongeling, *op. cit.* (n. 5), *s.v.* 'ḥrṣ₄' and 'ḥrṣ₅'.
127. Cf. Elayi-Elayi, *Poids phéniciens*, pp. 259-260 (with bibl.). Cf. also D. Bodi, 'Néhémie ch. 3 et la charte des bâtisseurs d'une tablette néo-babylonienne de l'époque perse', in *7th international Conference: La Syrie-Palestine à l'époque perse: frontières et courants d'échanges culturels*, Paris 22-24/3/2007 (to be published in *Trans*).
128. *RÉS* 15.
129. According to A. Dupont-Sommer, 'Une nouvelle inscription punique de Carthage', *CRAI*, 1968, p. 128; A. Mahjoubi and M.H. Fantar, 'Une nouvelle inscription carthaginoise', in *RANL*, ser. VIII, 21, fasc. 7-12, July-December 1966, pp. 201-209; M. Sznycer, 'Sur une nouvelle inscription punique de Carthage', *GLECS* 12, 1967-68, pp. 5-6; G. Garbini, 'Note di epigrafia punica – III. 10. Su una nuova iscrizione Cartaginese', *RSO* 43, 1968, pp. 11-13; J. Ferron, 'L'inscription urbanistique de la Carthage punique', *Muséon* 98, 1985, pp. 46-78; Elayi-Elayi, *Poids phéniciens*, p. 215.

val monetary workshops.[130] In fact, we say 'the Tyrian monetary workshop' for convenience, but it is not excluded that this workshop comprised more than one workshop within the territory of the Tyrian city. Several engravers worked for the Tyrian mint at the same time as can be seen from the different styles of engraving in each issue. As it has been stressed above, the Tyrian engravers were literate and quite possibly cultivated individuals.[131]

Besides the official workshop, there were other workshops, probably secret, belonging to forgers as evidenced by the counterfeit coins.[132] The first forgers appeared right at the beginning of the Tyrian and other Phoenician coinages. This phenomenon was probably worrying enough for the minting authority to try to put a stop to it, for example by making the flans after Series II.1.1.1.b thinner, because they were extremely thick and easy to hollow out in order to remove some of the silver.[133] At least 34 Tyrian coins in our catalogue are plated, which is considerably more than in the catalogue of Sidonian coins (5).[134] Some small weight coins (no. 257 and 290) could also be forgeries; two coins (no. 806 and 1230?) were clipped in order to remove some of the silver. We did wonder whether the few Sidonian coins with reverted types were genuine[135] but the question is quite different for the Tyrian coinage where type reversion was frequent, the intention probably being to distinguish between different series (for example Series III.1.2.c with dolphin and owl to left, and Series III.1.2.d with dolphin and owl to right). As for the category of coins with a somewhat crude style which exists in most ancient coinages, it is always difficult to give a satisfactory explanation: 'provincial', 'barbarous imitation (or style)', 'unusual'.[136] It is difficult to know whether these coins were made by clumsy engravers, a 'provincial' workshop seeking to imitate Tyrian coins, or clumsy forgers, indeed, different explanations could exist for each and every one of these coins.

Finally, we shall consider the Tyrian workshop's production from the point of view of quality and quantity. Even if the capacity for innovation is less pre-

---

130. Cf., for example, Cribb ed., *op. cit.* (n. 26), pp. 90-91; A. Mutz, *Römische Waagen und Gewichte aus Augst und Kaiseraugst*, Augst 1983, pp. 10-11 and figs 2-3.
131. See above, Chapter III.5.
132. For the modern fakes, cf. Appendix II.
133. Elayi-Elayi, *Trésors*, pp. 313-315 (but the order of the series is somewhat different). On the forgers of weights, cf. Elayi-Elayi, *Poids phéniciens*, pp. 260-263, and more recently J.-R. Kupper, 'De l'usage frauduleux des poids et mesures', *Akkadica* 121, 2001, pp. 1-4.
134. No. 14, 247?, 342, 354, 374, 378, 380, 427, 428, 429?, 460?, 633, 634?, 643, 645?, 706, 728, 771, 824, 825?, 867, 888, 929?, 1140 (yellowish), 1157, 1290, 1443, 1522, 1526, 1528, 1608, 1615, 1616 and 1629. Cf. Elayi-Elayi, *Monnayage de Sidon*, p. 573. None of the plated coins bears a chisel-cut because it would have revealed the forgery and such coins would have been taken off the circulation: cf. M. Jungfleisch, 'Les tétradrachmes fourrés du trésor de Pithom (Tell el Maskhouta, 1948)', *Numismatic Circular*, dec. 1949, cols 608-610.
135. Elayi-Elayi, *ibid.*, p. 574.
136. No. 828, 885, 886, 945, 1229, 1386 and 1551. Cf. *BMC Phoenicia*, pp. 154, 231; Mildenberg, *op. cit.* (n. 80), p. 22.

sent here than in the Sidonian workshop,[137] Tyre did start a yearly dating on her coinage before Sidon (Series II.1.2.1.a); she also inaugurated the technique of incusion, later followed by Sidon, Byblos and Arwad. The orientation of axes at 12h and the generalisation of circular flans occurred around the change of standard, probably following the Sidonian initiative. The date of inauguration of bronze series is unknown but seems to be later than the first Sidonian bronze series in 356 BCE. The Tyrian types were less complex than the Sidonian ones, but at the beginning of her coinage Tyre used skilful die engravers just like Sidon. The Tyrians also displayed a concern for quality in the first stage of their coinage, less intent than Sidon it would seem on performing technical feats. The Tyrian workshop had worked economically, at least at some periods, like the Sidonian one, which lowered the quality of its production: some use of overstriking (less than Sidon), re-engraving of worn dies or the addition of a unit in the following issue, the use of damaged coins over long periods, putting into circulation re-struck and off-centre coins or coins with various defects, the recruitment of some clumsy dies engravers. Some series are less carefully worked, in particular Series II.1.1.1.b, and in general most of the series minted after that. The Tyrian workshop craftsmen might have been obliged to work in climate of emergency as it was a difficult period. However the Tyrian coins are original, namely by their types, their legends, their different denominations, the particular treatment of incusion, and borrowings mainly from Egypt.

We shall now examine the Tyrian production of coins from a quantitative point of view and try to understand its evolution. We shall first considerer the number of coins that have been preserved (Fig. 32). The 1,811 silver and bronze coins are broken down as follows: 28 coins (Group I.1), 217 coins (Group I.2), 550 coins (Group II.1) and 744 coins (Group II.2). Unclassified Group III contains 272 coins. The most abundant series by far is Series II.2.1.14-29, with 653 coins, minted by ʿOzmilk over a 17 year period. It is clear that the number has increased significantly from one group to another from around 450 to 333 BCE. By far the most numerous silver denominations are the shekels (1,161 coins, that is 64.10% of the total amount), followed by the sixteenths of shekel (398, that is 21.98%) (Fig. 33). The other denominations are far less numerous: the quarters of shekel (157, that is 8.67%), then the halves of sixteenth (13, that is 0.72%), then the tenths of sixteenth (3 coins) and the eighth (?) of shekel (one coin). In reality, the small number of minute denominations preserved is probably biased by the difficulty in finding them. The quarters of shekel were minted in Group I and Group II.1, then they have disappeared (Fig. 32). The tenths of sixteenth only appear to be linked with Group I.1. As for the sixteenths and halves of sixteenth, it is difficult to say whether they were minted up to the end of the Persian period because several series

---

137. Cf. Elayi-Elayi, *Monnayage de Sidon*, p. 574.

belong to unclassified series of Group III. The bronze coins are much less numerous than the silver coins (78 instead of 1,733 that is 4.31%): apparently there was only one denomination.

The preceding remarks can approximately be applied to the number of obverse dies (Fig. 34). The 414 obverse dies of the silver coins that we have identified[138] are distributed as follows: 18 obverse dies (Group I.1), 41 (Group I.2), 158 (Group II.1) and 133 (Group II.2), plus 64 obverse dies for unclassified Group III. The highest number is in Series II.2.1.14-29 minted by King ʿOzmilk, with 102 obverse dies. The proportion of obverse dies by denomination (silver and bronze) is the following: for the silver denominations, the most numerous by far are the shekels (241 obverse dies, that is 55.79% of the total amount), followed by the sixteenths of shekel (122 O, that is 28.24%) (Fig. 35). The number of obverse dies for the other denominations is much less numerous: the quarters of shekel (27 O, that is 6.25%), then the halves of sixteenth (22 O, that is 5.09%), the eight of shekel (?) and tenths of sixteenth (1 O for each one). Concerning the sole bronze denomination, we have identified 18 obverse dies for all the series (4.17%). Considering now the reverse dies (Fig. 36),[139] they are in general more numerous than obverse dies (529 instead of 414 for silver denominations). They are distributed as follows: 16 reverse dies (Group I.1), that is less than obverse dies, 53 (Group I.2), 177 (Group II.1), 206 (Group II.2) and 77 (Group III), plus 18 for the bronze denominations. The highest number is in Series II.2.1.14-29, minted by ʿOzmilk, with 170 reverse dies. The proportion of reverse dies by denomination (silver and bronze) is the following: for the silver denominations, the most numerous by far is for the shekels (332 reverse dies, that is 60.69% of the total amount), followed by the sixteenths of shekel (138 R, that is 25.23%) (Fig. 37). Then we have the quarters of shekel (32 R, that is 5.85%), the halves of sixteenth (25 R, that is 4.57%), the eight of shekel (?) and tenths of sixteenth (1 R for each of them). We have identified 18 reverse dies for the bronze denominations, all series included.

The yearly dated series of ʿOzmilk gives an idea of the number of obverse dies used per year; this information is only available for shekels as it was impossible to relate other denominations to this king with certainty (Fig. 38). 102 obverse dies were used at least during the 17 years of his reign, in reality for 15 years because he started minting his coinage in the third year of his reign.[140] On average, almost 7 obverse dies (at least) were manufactured per year. If we go into the details of the yearly production, we have the following results: 10 obverse dies for year 3 (that is 347 BCE), 5 O for year 4 (346), 4 O for year 5

---

138. We have considered only the obverse dies related with reverse dies, not isolated ones. 36 other obverse dies are isolated because the reverse was damaged and therefore unidentifiable.
139. In the same way, we have not taken into account the 92 isolated reverse dies.
140. We do not take into account here the dies of the previous year re-used with the addition of a unit.

(345), 2 O for year 6 (344), 8 O for year 7 (343), 6 O for year 8 (342), 12 O for year 9 (341), 11 O for year 10 (340), 4 O for year 11 (339), 7 O for year 12 (338), 6 O for year 13 (337), 5 O for year 14 (336), 17 O for year 15 (335), 4 O for year 16 (334) and 1 O for year 17 (333). Thus the main years for die manufacture were 347, 341-340 and mainly 335, with the smallest number of dies being produced in 344 and 333.[141] It is interesting to compare this yearly production of obverse dies over the 15 years for example with the corresponding production over the 14 years of the Sidonian king ʿAbdʿaštart I (365-352 BCE).[142] Even if we include the parallel obverse dies of Mazday's coins (353-352 BCE), the total comes to 45 (against 102 for ʿOzmilk); on average, ʿAbdʿaštart I produced 3 obverse dies per year (instead of almost 7 for ʿOzmilk); the maximum yearly production was 8 in 352 BCE (instead of 17 in 335 for ʿOzmilk). From 347 to 333, the peak production for Sidon (10 O in 346 and 13 in 342) did not quite reach that of Tyre (10 O in 347, 12 in 341, 11 in 342, and 17 in 335).

Numerous publications continue to be devoted to an evaluation of the volume of issues.[143] The quantification of the number of minted coins must be performed following two steps: firstly to estimate the original number of obverse dies produced by using a statistical method; secondly to multiply this estimation by the average number of coins that each coin was able to strike. This number is estimated by using written sources, results of numismatic studies and experimental simulations. It is very tempting, for economic history, to know the volume of issues. What results can reasonably be reached for the Tyrian monetary workshop during the Persian period? The ratio (Fig. 39) is

---

141. See Chapter VII.6 for the reasons of these differences in production.
142. Elayi-Elayi, *Monnayage de Sidon*, pp. 577 and 837, fig. 51.
143. Cf., for example, F.J. Mora Màs, 'El coeficiente entre al número de ejemplares y al número de cuños; alcance de su contenido de información estadística', in *Symposium numismático de Barcelona, 27-28 febrero de 1979* I, Barcelona 1980, p. 514; F. de Callataÿ, 'A propos du volume des émissions monétaires dans l'Antiquité', *RBN* 130, 1984, pp. 37-48; W.W. Esty, 'Estimating the Size of a Coinage', *NC* 144, 1984, pp. 180-183; *id.*, 'Estimation of the Size of a Coinage: a Survey and Comparison of Methods', *NC* 146, 1986, pp. 185-215; L. Villaronga, 'De nuevo la estimación del número original de cuños de una emisión monetaria', *Gacetta Numismática* 85, 1987, pp. 31-36; T.V. Buttrey, 'Calculating Ancient Coin Production: Facts and Fantasies', *NC* 153, 1993, pp. 335-351; F. de Callataÿ, G. Depeyrot and L. Villaronga, *L'argent monnayé d'Alexandre le Grand à Auguste*, Brussels 1993 (with bibl.); F. de Callataÿ, 'L'estimation du nombre originel de coins: en augmentant l'échantillon', in M. Crusafont *et al.* eds, *Homenatge al Dr. Leandre Villaronga*, *Acta Numismatica* 21-23, Barcelona 1991-93, pp. 31-48; *id.*, 'Calculating ancient coin production: Seeking a balance', *NC* 155, 1995, pp. 289-311; *id.*, 'Le volume des émissions monétaires dans l'antiquité', *AIIN* 44, 1997, pp. 53-62; *id.*, 'Les taux de survie des émissions monétaires antiques, médiévales et modernes. Essai de mise en perspective et conséquences quant à la productivité des coins dans l'Antiquité', *RN*, 2000, pp. 87-109; S. Buttrey and T. Buttrey, 'Calculating ancient coin production, again', *AJN* 9, 1997, pp. 113-135; A. Savio, 'La numismatica e i problemi quantitativi: Intorno al calcolo del volume delle emissioni', *RIN* 98, 1997, pp. 11-48; *id.*, 'Ancora sulla numismatica e i problemi quantitativi', *AIIN*, 1997, pp. 45-52; K. Lockyear, 'Hoard structure and coin production in antiquity – an empirical investigation', *NC* 159, 1999, pp. 215-243.

relatively good for the three series that are represented by a sufficient number of coins: n/o^{144} = 2.82 for Series I.2.1 (shekels), n/o = 2.05 for Series II.2.1.14-29 of ʿOzmilk (shekels) and n/o = 2 for Series II.1.1.2 (quarters of shekel). The ratio is much less good for the four following series: n/o = 1.71 for Series II.1.1.1 (shekels), n/o = 1.57 for Series III.1.2.a (sixteenths of shekel), n/o = 1.54 for Series II.2.1.1-13 (shekels) and n/o = 1.53 for Series III.1.1.a (sixteenths of shekel). We shall apply the so-called 'Carter method'[145] to the series for which the ratio n/o is relatively good and the number of preserved coins sufficient. In this way it will be possible to derive an approximate comparison of the volume of issues of three reigns, for shekels only: those of the two anonymous kings of Group I.2.1 and Group II.1.1.1, and King ʿOzmilk.

As far as the average number of coins struck with a single obverse die is concerned, several divergent hypotheses have been proposed (between 4,000 and 50,000).[146] In fact, all the coinages and periods must not be confused. It is also important to take into account the specific conditions of each issue, in particular the workshop's policy regarding the useful life of dies. As we have shown, in the Tyrian workshop, a high tolerance level was set in relation to die defects, just as in the Sidonian workshop. It is possible to use the estimation for an obverse die engraved in Delphi by the Amphictionic league in the 4th century BCE: based on the written sources and on numismatic analysis, P. Kinns concluded that this die was used for striking between 23,333 and 47,250 coins.[147] According to F. de Callataÿ, in this case, the real figure would have been closer to 47,250.[148] All things considered, we shall use the lower limit of around 20,000 which had been agreed by F. de Callataÿ, G. Depeyrot and L. Villaronga in 1993.[149] What results can be obtained in this way? We shall only consider the three best-documented cases. The anonymous king of Group I.2.1 minted during an unknown lapse of time 340,000 shekels (of around 14g), that is around 4.76 tons of silver, plus the series of small denominations. The other anonymous king of Group II.1.1.1 minted during an unknown lapse of time, 1,060,000 shekels, that is around 14.84 tons of silver, plus the series of small denominations (among them 0.56 ton of silver for the 160,000 quarters of shekel of Group II.1.1.2). The volume of production for the shekels of the second anonymous king was three times greater than the first, but the comparison

144. n = number of coins studied. o = number of obverse dies.
145. G.F. Carter, 'Simplified Method for Calculating the Original Number of Dies from Die-Link Statistics', *ANSMN* 28, 1983, pp. 195-206; on the other methods, cf., for example, de Callataÿ, *loc. cit.* (n. 143) 1984, pp. 37-48; *id.*, 'L'utilisation des statistiques en numismatique (métrologie, estimation du nombre de monnaies émises)', *Les nouvelles de l'archéologie* 39, 1988, pp. 8-10 (with bibl.).
146. Cf., for example, de Callataÿ, *loc. cit.* (n. 143) 1991-93, pp. 46-48; Buttrey, *loc. cit.* (n. 143), pp. 335-351; de Callataÿ *et al.*, *op. cit.* (n. 143), pp. 8-11 (with bibl.).
147. P. Kinns, 'The Amphictionic Coinage reconsidered', *NC* 143, 1983, p. 19.
148. De Callataÿ, *loc. cit.* (n. 143) 1991-93, p. 47, n. 10.
149. De Callataÿ *et al.*, *op. cit.* (n. 143).

is biased by the fact that the lengths of the two reigns are unknown. Over a 15 year period, King ʿOzmilk minted 2,040,000 shekels (of around 8g), that is 16.32 tons of silver; per year, he minted on average 136,000 shekels, that is 1.08 ton of silver, plus the series of small denominations. It is interesting to note that the 16.32 tons of silver used by ʿOzmilk for minting shekels can be compared with the 14.84 tons used by the anonymous king of Group II.1.1.1. While the total number of shekels was double: 2,040,000 instead of 1,060,000, it must be remembered that the standard was different (around 8g instead of 14g). It is also interesting to compare the estimated yearly production of ʿOzmilk (1.08 tons of silver for shekels) with the yearly estimated production of the Sidonian kings (for double shekels): 1.53 tons for ʿAbdʿaštart I, 1.7 tons for Tennes, 2.7 tons for Evagoras (?) and 1.5 tons for ʿAbdʿaštart II. The weight of silver used by Sidon per year for the double shekels was higher than that used by Tyre, but not by much. In any case, none of these figures can be used with any degree of precision because they have no value by themselves, yet they do provide a relative rough estimate of the volume of coinage issued by the monetary workshop of Tyre.[150]

---

150. Cf. J. Elayi, in *Cahiers Numismatiques* 119, 1994, p. 67 (concerning the book mentioned in the preceding note).

CHAPTER VI

METROLOGICAL STUDY

This chapter is based on our two previous metrological studies written in French: the first one is our book on Phoenician weights[1] and the second one is Chapter VI of our corpus of Sidonian coinage.[2] We refer to these two studies in particular for the analysis of the difficulties encountered in studying the metrology of ancient weights and coins in general and more precisely Phoenician ones, and to the limited number of studies published nowadays in this field of research.[3]

In order to make this chapter self-consistent, we shall recall the main points of our metrological method which are needed to understand it before applying this method to the study of the metrology of Tyrian coinage. New information concerning the metrology of Phoenician coinages has been brought to light by the analysis of the metallic composition of two sets of coins from the Sidonian[4] and Tyrian coinages.[5] Their important conclusions will help us to resolve the main difficulties remaining in the interpretation of the statistical results of these coinages.

---

1. Elayi-Elayi, *Poids phéniciens*.
2. *Id.*, *Monnayage de Sidon*.
3. Cf. Elayi-Elayi, *Poids phéniciens*, pp. 287-292, with bibliography ; cf. also W.W. Esty, 'Statistics in Numismatics', in C. Morrison *et al.* eds, *A Survey of Numismatic Research 1990-1995*, Berlin 1997, pp. 817-823 ; *id.*, 'Statistics in Numismatics', in C. Alfaro and A. Burnett eds, *A Survey of Numismatic Research 1996-2001*, Madrid 2003, pp. 921-927; F. de Callataÿ, *Quantifications et Numismatique antique. Choix d'articles (1984-2004)*, Wetteren 2006.
4. A.G. Elayi, J.-N. Barrandon and J. Elayi, 'The Devaluation of Sidonian Silver Coinage in 365 BCE and the First Bronze Issues', *AJN* Second Series 19, 2007, pp. 1-8.
5. *Id.*, 'The Change of Standard of Tyrian Silver Coinage about 357 BCE as Determined by Fast Neutron Activation Analysis' (forthcoming).

1. Terminology and methodology

We have defined a terminology for the metrological analysis of Phoenician weights, and adapted it to the analyses of ancient coins in general and those of Sidon in particular, in order to better analyse the difficulties, to better select the aims and to elaborate a methodology.[6] We only define here the terminology needed for the coins of Tyre by using the terminology elaborated for the previous studies.

a. The theoretical monetary standard

We define the theoretical monetary standard as the theoretical weight reference (legal weight) decided at some moment by the minting power. Numerous researches have been conducted in order to retrieve this standard, but it cannot be known with precision in Antiquity. Even when it is mentioned in texts and regardless of the precision of the information available (for example equivalencies of systems[7] or equivalencies with vegetal elements), it is impossible to know the exact relation with our present weight system.[8] As far as the Phoenician coins are concerned, neither text nor inscription gives any indication regarding the theoretical standards used by each city. We know from the inscribed Phoenician weights that the shekel (*ŠQL*) was a Phoenician weighing standard,[9] more specifically Sidonian as two weights bear the inscription *ŠQL ṢDN*, 'shekel of Sidon': a tortoise-shaped weight of 11.70g[10] and a calf's head-shaped weight of 6.15g (inscribed *ŠT*, which could mean 'half'),[11] both dating from the 8th century BCE. The average weight obtained from these two specimens is 12g, but an average based on just two weights needs to be taken very cautiously.[12] There is also a lead square weight of 197.70g, dated from the first third of the 3nd century, inscribed *LMLQRT / ŠT 10 / BṢR*, 'To Milqart / year 10 / in Tyre'.[13] Due to the significant amount of wear undergone by lead weights in general and to the lack of information concerning this later isolated example, it is difficult to ascertain any relation between its weight and the

---

6. Elayi-Elayi, *Poids phéniciens*, pp. 292-295; id., *Monnayage de Sidon*, pp. 581-584.
7. Cf., for example, some textual information concerning the equivalencies in N. Parise, 'Unità ponderali e circolazione metallica nell'Oriente mediterraneo', in T. Hackens et al. eds, *A Survey of Numismatic Research 1985-1990*, Brussels 1991, p. 28 ; C. Zaccagnini, 'Notes on the Weight System at Alalah VII', *Or.* 48, 1979, p. 472, nn. 2-3 ; A. Ben-David, 'The Philistine Talent from Ashdod, the Ugarit Talent from Ras Shamra, the ' PYM' and the 'N-S-P', *UF* 11, 1979, p. 30.
8. Several researchers tried to find the theoretical unity of weight: cf., for example, P. Naster, 'La méthode en métrologie numismatique', in *Numismatique antique. Problèmes et méthodes*, Annales de l'Est, Nancy-Leuven 1975, pp. 64 et 69 (with bibl.).
9. Elayi-Elayi, *Poids phéniciens*, pp. 156-161.
10. *Ibid.*, pp. 47 and 157-159, no. 3.
11. *Ibid.*, pp. 47-48 and 159, no. 5.
12. *Ibid.*, pp. 296-297.
13. *Ibid.*, pp. 125 and 274-275, no. 333.

modified 8.77g standard of the Tyrian shekels dated from the 4th century, before 332 BCE.

b. The manufactured monetary standard (primary standard)

From the agreed theoretical weight, the next stage is the manufacturing of a standard. The precision of the weight of this standard is a function of the technical capacities that existed at the time of manufacturing, concerning, in short, the accuracy of the scales and the precision of the weights. Even today, it is not technically possible to manufacture an exact weight, decided theoretically, because of the two types of well-known error: Type A and Type B. The primary and secondary standard weights were probably made and kept in secure places as is suggested by other indications : for example the discoveries of these weights in Mesopotamian temples. The only Phoenician weight, which could have been a standard weight, is a hematite weight found in the Milkʿaštart temple at Umm el-ʿAmed.[14] The weight given by M. Dunand is 438.50g: it has a reverted flattened cone shape and seems to be in a good state of preservation, except for some insignificant scratches. As we have already stated, it was probably a Phoenician mina of 50 shekels, with a shekel of about 8.77g, corresponding to the modified Tyrian monetary standard (see definition below).[15]

c. The problem of manufacturing the monetary flans and the coins

Whatever the method of manufacturing the flans (measure or mould), the flans obtained were not equal. There are also two types of deviations between the theoretical weight of the primary or secondary standards and the weights of the manufactured flans, which are again deviations of types A and B. If the deviations of Type B are practically impossible to calculate, the deviations of Type A probably result in a standard deviation of a normal distribution, due to the dispersion of the volumes of the moulds and to the dispersion between the weights of the flans obtained from the same mould. The mean value of the normal distribution (representing the function of distribution of the manufactured weights according to the normal law) is what we have called 'the ancient average weight' or the most probable weight of the flans manufactured. When the weight of the flans has been adjusted by weighing, the dispersion of the weights is due to the adjustment of the weight of the flans. Neither the normal

---

14. *Ibid.*, pp. 151, no. 453, and 316.
15. *Ibid.*, pp. 278-279. It is difficult to say whether the square bronze weights inscribed with the letter *H*, found mainly in the territory of Tyre and Southern Phoenicia, and in use from the 8th to the 4th centuries, correspond to the Tyrian monetary modified standard because of their relative small number and important dispersion of their weights.

distribution representing the manufactured weights nor their mean value is directly attainable.

d. The contribution provided by the texts

Since the average weight of the manufactured specimens, when they come out of the workshop, is not attainable for the moment, scholars try to find a model using statistical numismatics for estimating the legal weight and the upper and lower tolerance limits. The result of this method is compared with a sample for which, thanks to the texts, the weight and tolerance limits are known. This is the case, for example, in a text relating to gold coins of Henri VI, minted in 1423 of our era.[16] As far as the Phoenician coins are concerned, and the Tyrian coins in particular, no such information and no satisfactory model are available.

e. The modified standard of the shekel, its multiples and fractions

The Gaussian distribution which represents the function of distribution of the weights manufactured in Antiquity is modified by wear, corrosion, various alterations, the type and length of circulation, the nature of the monetary metal, cleaning, the conditions of preservation, as well as errors in modern coin-weighing operations, etc. These weight modifications also modify the distribution function and result in a new Gaussian distribution with a trail towards low-weight coins (see hereafter, § 2). The apex of the Gaussian curve obtained from the well-preserved specimens, namely the Gaussian curve minus the trail therefore defines the modified standard. If these well-preserved specimens were fleur-de-coin, the modified standard, that is the apex of the Gaussian curve, would coincide with the ancient average weight of the coins manufactured. Thus the modified standard is the most probable present weight deduced from the greatest possible number of relatively 'well-preserved' specimens of a module, in their present state. We place this weight in a confidence level and we call it the 'modified standard of the denomination considered'.

Insofar as the number of specimens is sufficient in order to treat the Gaussian curve and its trail towards the small weights correctly, the method we

---

16. F.G. Skinner, *Weights and Measures*, London 1967, pp. 33 and 39 ; J. Guey and C. Carcassonne, 'Le poids de la livre romaine d'après le système de l'as libral (échantillons Haeberlin)', *BSFN* 29, 1974, p. 597 ; M. A. Powell, 'Ancient Mesopotamian Weights Metrology : Methods, Problems and Perspectives', in M.A. Powell and R.H. Sack eds, *Studies in Honor of Tom B. Jones*, Neukirchen-Vluyn 1979, p. 83 ; R. Kletter, 'The Inscribed Weights of the Kingdom of Judah', *Tel Aviv* 18, 1991, p. 131 ; C. Carcassonne *et al.*, 'Recherche du poids légal à partir des poids réels – I. Monnaies médiévales – II. Solidi du Bas Empire', *BSFN* 29, 1974, pp. 616-621.

use does not need any other parameter (such as the global average weight, the modal weight, the median weight, the interquartile space, etc.).[17]

Why is the modified standard the best parameter that we can measure today?

1) Because its value does not include the trail, which is much more affected by wear than the coins mathematically selected and fitted by the Gaussian curve. This will produce a first limitation of the effect of wear on this parameter. Wear efficiently contributes to the mean value of the weights, for example.

2) The value of the theoretical monetary standard has been transformed into the apex of the normal distribution of the struck coins that we called the manufactured monetary standard in Antiquity. The best image of this apex that we are able to calculate today is the modified standard, which is the apex of the original Gaussian curve after it has been deformed over time (wear).

3) The fact that the major contribution to the present Gaussian curve is due to the right-hand part of the curve containing the weight of the most well-preserved coins, limits even more the shift between the manufactured monetary standard and the modified standard. In conclusion, this is the best parameter that we can measure today.

It now has to be pointed out that the modified standard of the denomination considered depends, by definition, on wear and other alterations.[18] Therefore, it is not impossible that, when calculating the modified standard of the shekel from the modified standard of the different denominations, slightly different values are obtained. For example, the modified standard of the shekel calculated from the shekel denomination (in the case of the Tyrian coins) and the one calculated from a small denomination can give different values if the wear of shekels is on average different from that of the small denominations. For a given coinage and denomination, the modified standard becomes more precise when considering a larger and larger sample, until it becomes stabilised when the number of coins is relatively substantial (for example when the value is taken out of a monetary corpus). What would be interesting and delicate would be to find, from the data and wear, the theoretical monetary standard, always within a selected confidence level. At present, we cannot obtain a better parameter than the modified standard that we extract from the available weights of the coins.

In practice, we have created histograms with steps which exceed a certain limit imposed by the available data in every case. In principle we would like to have small steps to get the best resolution. However if the number of coins is too small within the steps of the histograms, this would lead to insignificant

---

17. On these terms, cf. Elayi-Elayi, *Poids phéniciens*, pp. 294-295, with bibl.
18. On wear's studies, see in particular F. Delamare, 'Modeling the Wear of Coins', in *Actes Congr. Num. Bruxelles 1991* IV, Brussels 1993, pp. 349-360 ; id., *Le Frai et ses Lois*, Cahiers Ernest Babelon 5, Paris 1994.

fluctuations that in some cases mask the phenomenon or create insignificant structures due to weights being rounded up or down for example. The steps of the histograms considered in each figure take the preceding considerations into account. Sometimes we have preferred to lose in resolution in favour of the statistical meaning of the results, namely optimising a combination of χ^2, standard deviation σ, the shape of the Gaussian curve and the need to compare results one with another. However, it has to be pointed out that, if the standard deviation depends on the chosen width of the step (h), the modified standard almost does not depend on it, provided that we choose a step that does not bias the results (avoiding abnormal ones). As regards the shekels after the change of standard for example, a variation of the step of the histogram between 0.05 and 0.11g changes the value of the modified standard of 0.02g while the standard deviation varies from 0.30 to 0.39g (Figs 40 and 41). On the contrary, when the number of coins studied is small, the enlargement of the step of the histogram can change the weight of the modified standard more significantly.

2. Illustration of the method determining the modified standard

So far, we have only dealt with the modified standard and presented the main features that characterise the Gaussian curve and its trail. Increased wear of the coinage for a specified module results:
1. in a smaller value for the modified standard,
2. in a larger resolution for the Gaussian curve,
3. in an increase in the importance of the Gaussian trail.

In our metrological analysis, we handle data that contain some erroneous results (incorrectly-weighed coins, false coins, etc.) and some results which are less accurate than others (less accurate weighing or roughly rounded weights). We have been able to filter some of the erroneous results, but we cannot rectify the inaccurate weighing. These few biased results increase the dispersion and therefore the resolution of the Gaussian curve, that is its FWHM (full width at half-maximum) or, equivalently, its standard deviation.

We are going to demonstrate the changes in the shape of the Gaussian curve by giving some practical examples selected from real coins. The first example shows the degradation of the coins due to the effect of cleaning. When looking at the Tell Abu Hawam hoard TXXXV,[19] the first fourteen coins, dated from just before the change of standard 'had an outer coating of green corrosion, under which thin layers of red cuprous oxide adhered to the silver surfaces, indicating a large proportion of copper in the alloy'.[20] Fig. 42 indicates the weight of the coins before they were cleaned while fig. 43 shows the same hoard after cleaning. The first remark concerns the standard deviation of the

---

19. Cf. Elayi-Elayi, *Trésors*, pp. 170-185.
20. C. Lambert, 'A Hoard of Phoenician Coins', *QDAP* 1, 1931, p. 11.

curve: 0.38g before cleaning and 0.43g after cleaning. We have to stress the fact that the shape of the fitted Gaussian curve is mainly a function of the right hand side of the weights of the histogram in order to avoid trail effects in general. Resolution would have been better before cleaning if we consider all the points. The second remark concerns the decrease in the value of the modified standard due to cleaning: 8.68g instead of 8.92g. If we compare the average weights before and after cleaning, it would have been larger. The third remark concerns the trail that increases very obviously between fig. 42 and fig. 43.

In the second example, we compare the modified standard and the FWHM of a coinage with the ones extracted from a well-preserved hoard of this coinage: the Sidonian Beithir hoard TXXI.[21] The modified standard and standard deviation of the double shekels of Sidon before devaluation (Fig. 44) are 28.02g and 0.32g, and that of the Beithir hoard are 28.26g and 0.24g (Fig. 45). The conclusion, as expected, is simple: the modified standard decreases and the standard deviation increases with wear: the wear of the coinage is bigger than that of this well-preserved hoard.

In a third example, we compare the modified standard and the standard deviation of a coinage with those of a very corroded hoard: the Khirbet el-Kerak hoard TXXVI.[22] The modified standard and standard deviation of the double shekels of Sidon after devaluation (Fig. 46) are 25.67g and 0.20g, and those of the Khirbet el-Kerak hoard are 25.06g and 0.46g (Fig. 47). The difference is obvious both in the figures and in the results: the wear of the hoard is bigger than that of the coinage. Since the double shekels before devaluation have a decreasing silver percentage, this results in a lighter weight for coins with less silver which results themselves in a bigger standard deviation.

In a fourth example, we compare the very well-preserved TXXXVI hoard[23] with the Tyrian coinage of the same period. In this hoard, the modified standard is bigger: 8.82g instead of 8.77g for the whole coinage and the standard deviation is better: 0.29g instead of 0.34g for the whole coinage (Figs 48 and 40).

3. The problem of the addition of copper

If the general statements concerning the shape of the Gaussian curve were in line with our expectation, the results concerning the trail sometimes gave unexpected shapes. Our main concern in the corpus of the Sidonian coinage being to determine the modified standard, we have not dealt with this problem specifically but it was obvious that something unexpected blurred the trails of

---

21. Elayi-Elayi, *Trésors*, pp. 128-133.
22. *Ibid.*, pp. 139-147.
23. J. Elayi and A.G. Elayi, 'Nouveaux trésors de monnaies phéniciennes (*CH* VIII)', *Trans* 11, 1996, pp. 101-108.

some of the histograms, making them much more significant than others and producing an obviously unexpected phenomenon, which proved to be even more evident in the Tyrian coinage. In any case, we lacked information to handle this problem. In order to understand this phenomenon, we launched a series of analyses of the composition of some selected representative set of coins from Sidonian and then Tyrian coinages. A significant breakthrough has been obtained from these analyses.

The interpretation of results such as those of fig. 49 representing all the shekels before the change of standard, became possible after the analysis of the metallic composition of Sidonian coins and then of Tyrian coins. From these analyses we learned that some time after the beginning of the coinage, the percentage of silver, which originally was of about 99-98%, slowly felt to about 75% and even lower just before the Sidonian devaluation, and to about 68% and possibly lower before the Tyrian change of standard. Even if, while the composition changed, the volume of the flan did not change much because the flans were probably still prepared in the same manner, part of the volume of silver was replaced by copper in these coins. This change of metal reduced the weight of the coins, the density of copper (8.94) being lower than that of silver (10.5). In fig. 41 we have sketched the expected change in weight, as a function of the proportion of silver in the coins.

In the trail of the coins before the change of standard, we have interferences from:
    a) the change of the silver content,
    b) the normal wear of the coins,
    c) the abnormal corrosion related to the copper in the coin resulting in a larger loss of weight due to cleaning as we have seen above in the Tell Abu Hawam hoard,
    d) a possible change of weight decided by the minting authority for a new series.

All these factors explain the abnormal form of the trail of the Gaussian curve on the one hand and the increase of its resolution on the other. The devaluation in the Sidonian case, and the change of standard in the Tyrian case, put an end to this phenomenon because we found that the coins again had a fixed amount of silver, about 98% of the total weight for all the coins and the Gaussian curve regained a normal shape.

4. *Metrological analysis of the Tyrian silver coinage*

In Phoenician coinages, two categories of denominations were struck: one category contained an amount of silver used for important transactions, for hoarding or for exporting silver,[24] while the other category was used for daily

---
24. Cf. Elayi-Elayi, *Monnayage de Sidon*, pp. 586-589.

transactions. For example, Sidonian double shekels or Tyrian, Byblian and Aradian shekels belonged to the first category. Their use by the Phoenicians in transactions was quite limited compared with the second category of coins. As for the fractions such as halves or quarters of shekel, they complemented the sizeable transactions, and were therefore rare. The highest denomination of the second category, used for daily transactions, was a large one gram fraction which can be found in all Phoenician coinages (sixteenth of shekel or similar): around 0.76g before devaluation and 0.72g after devaluation for Sidon, around 0.63g before the change of standard and 0.53g after the change of standard for Tyre. It was probably the denomination equivalent, as far as its trade function was concerned, of the approximately 0.72g obol in Greek coinages.[25] The sixteenth of shekel was generally complemented by smaller denominations down to some hundredths of a gram of silver, or bronze denominations which appeared in Tyrian, Aradian and mainly Sidonian coinages.

a. The shekels

Even though the Tyrian shekel did not have the same value as the double shekel of Sidon, it had, albeit not exactly the same, at least a similar evolution. The first shekels struck (Series I.1, I.2 and II.1.1.1.a) were quite regular, relatively flat, with fine engraving and they display a good striking technique. Fig. 50 shows the distribution curve of this type of shekel and fig. 49 shows that of all the shekels before the change of standard. The modified standard of the shekel is 13.56g. While fig. 50 corresponds to our expectations, namely the weights of the coins are represented by a Gaussian curve with a trail towards the small weight values, fig. 49 has a completely different shape. The Gaussian curve corresponding to that of fig. 50 is still present but the trail has an unexpected shape. Fig. 49 recalls the result that we obtained for the Sidonian double shekels before devaluation (Fig. 44).[26] After the change of standard, the modified standard is equal to 8.77g. Fig. 40 represents all the Tyrian shekels with the new standard and again has a normal shape, namely a Gaussian curve with a trail, just like that of the Sidonian double shekels after devaluation.[27] As stated, it is the change in the composition of the coins that is primarily responsible for these blurred form of the trail in the case of Tyrian shekels before the change of standard and of Sidonian double shekels before devaluation. This phenomenon disappeared after the change of standard and the normal Gaussian shape with a trail reappeared. Because of its proximity with the Attic standard (didrachms of 8.66g at the time of King Philip II of

---

25. On the Greek obol, cf., for example, S. Psoma, 'Le nombre de chalques dans l'obole dans le monde grec', *RN* 154, 1998, pp. 12-24.
26. Elayi-Elayi, *Monnayage de Sidon*, p. 841, fig. 55.
27. *Ibid.*, p. 842, fig. 56.

Macedonia),[28] the new Tyrian standard has for a long time been referred to as 'Attic'. Having no more information on the Tyrian standard, we propose keeping 'Attic' in reverted commas. However, its proximity with the Attic standard could possibly facilitate equivalencies between the two standards and trade between Tyre and Greek cities following this standard. Moreover, this could have help to re-establish confidence in the export of Tyrian shekels as merchandise coins as everybody knew the Athenian tetradrachms which had been imported into the Near East for more than a century. However, another conclusion can be drawn from the analyses of the Tyrian silver coinage: the amount of silver in the coins after the change of standard corresponds approximately to the amount of silver in the coins before the change of standard (the complement in weight being essentially copper). We had the same result for the coinage of Sidon. This raises the following question: is this a devaluation or a change of standard? It is in any case a progressive devaluation with respect to the original 13.56g silver coin together with a very probable alignment on the Attic standard.

b. The quarters of shekel

The quarters of shekel are quite difficult to study because they were only struck before the change of standard; some of these coins contain a mixture of silver and copper with a variable amount of copper. That is why we do not expect to have a good Gaussian curve with a normal trail. Fig. 51 shows the results of the 63 known specimens of quarters of shekel and gives 3.16g for the modified standard. Obviously the right part of the Gaussian curve does not contain enough coins to give as good results as for the shekels.

c. The sixteenths of shekel

The Tyrian sixteenths of shekel are much more difficult to study than the Sidonian sixteenths of shekel because the dating is missing and their iconography is not so helpful in the present case. We shall use all the available information in order to separate the coins struck before and after the change of standard. However, in some series, the iconography is not clearly related to the

---

28. Cf. G. Le Rider, *Le monnayage d'argent et d'or de Philippe II frappé en Macédoine de 359 à 294 avant J.-C.*, Paris 1977, p. 408; id., *Monnayage et finances de Philippe II. Un état de la question*, Athens 1996, p. 50: the Attic standard chosen by Philippus II was retained by Alexander for gold coinage. The value of this standard decreased in silver tetradrachms for Aradian mint after c. 320 and for Tyrian mint after c. 320: cf. F. Duyrat, *Arados hellénistique. Etude historique et monétaire*, Beirut 2005, p. 127; O. Mørkholm, 'The Attic Coin Standard in the Levant during the Hellenistic Period', in S. Scheers ed., *Studia Paulo Naster Oblata I. Numismatique antique*, Leuven 1982, pp. 143, 146; C. Flament, *Le monnayage en argent d'Athènes. De l'époque archaïque à l'époque hellénistique (c. 550-c. 40 av. J.-C.)*, Louvain-la-Neuve 2007.

group before or after the change of standard or is not clear enough because of the wear. If we consider all the sixteenths of shekel, it was impossible to separate them based on their weight because of the small difference in weight following the change of standard, the addition of copper before this change, the difficulty in identifying the iconography of some coins, and the very large weight dispersion in each series. However, two groups, one obviously issued before the change of standard (Fig. 52) and the other (Fig. 53) after, give a modified standard of 0.63g and 0.53g respectively. The total of the sixteenths of shekel gives 0.57g for the modified standard (Fig. 54).

d. The smallest denominations

If the reference for the smallest denominations is not the shekel but the sixteenth of shekel as for the Greek divisions of the obol for example, there would be the half of the sixteenth, an equivalent of the Sidonian thirty-second of shekel. Since we do not know the name of this denomination in Phoenician, for the moment we shall refer to it as the 'half of sixteenth'. The total number of halves of sixteenth is too small to make a detailed study. The modified standard extracted from all the preserved specimens is 0.27g, which is about half the value of the sixteenths of shekel after the change of standard (Fig. 55). This denomination had a modified standard of 0.32g in Sidonian coinage.[29] However, we have to be very cautious because of the small total number of coins of this denomination.

The smallest denomination, represented by only three coins (no. 26-28), is around 0.06g, equal to approximately one tenth of the sixteenth. As a provisional name we propose the 'tenth of sixteenth'.

5. *Metrological analysis of the Tyrian bronze coinage*

For only one denomination of bronze, a total number of 70 specimens have been listed, sufficient to be taken into consideration here. The modified standard is 0.67g (Fig. 56). However, the dispersion of the results is quite large as this applies to bronze coins generally: this does not exclude some modifications from one issue to another that appear if we reduce the step of the histograms. In contrast with Sidon who struck a real system of bronze denominations,[30] Tyre struck a denomination which very probably corresponds to the smallest Sidonian silver denomination. We do not have enough specimens (only three) to make a serious statistical study.

---

29. On the value of Greek bronze coins, see, for example, O. Picard, 'La valeur des monnaies grecques en bronze', *RN* 154, 1998, pp. 5-6; Psoma, *loc. cit.* (n. 25), pp. 12-24; C. Grandjean, 'La valeur des monnaies de bronze du Péloponnèse à l'époque classique et hellénistique', *ibid.*, pp. 31-40.
30. Elayi-Elayi, *Monnayage de Sidon*, pp. 382-384.

CHAPTER VII

THE COINAGE OF TYRE
AND THE HISTORY OF THE CITY

The first aim of this chapter is to propose the historical and socio-economical interpretation of the Tyrian coinage dated from the Persian period, which is possible through its context and all other available sources. The history of Tyre during this period was closely linked to the history of Sidon,[1] which is now relatively well-known and provides substantial help for the present chapter, as does the general context of Transeuphratene in the Persian period. None of the historical studies published until now on this area use the numismatic sources correctly, either because they were unaware of their interest or because they did not know them sufficiently or because they did not know how to use them, for example by using unfounded or obsolete publications, that ought to be abandoned even if they contribute to the historian's theory. We shall follow the chronological order of the different Tyrian monetary groups for underscoring their particular contexts and the light that they can bring.

1. *Tyre before the inauguration of her coinage*

It is important to understand how the Tyrian economy operated before the inauguration of coins. The Phoenicians, in particular the Tyrians, had no cause to be jealous of the Greeks as far as trading activities are concerned;[2] even so, their coinages appeared at least one and a half centuries later than Greek coinages.[3] Yet they knew them very well since numerous imported coins were

---

1. Cf. Elayi-Elayi, *Monnayage de Sidon*, pp. 593-687.
2. Cf. Elayi, *Phénomène monétaire*, pp. 21-31.
3. The date of the first coins gave rise to numerous hypotheses, ranging from the beginning and end of the 7th century: see, for example, O. Picard, 'Les origines du monnayage en Grèce', *L'Histoire* 6, 1978, pp. 13-20; D. Kagan, 'The Dates of the Earliest Coins', *AJA* 86, 1982, pp. 343-360; M. Vickers, 'Early Greek Coinage. A Reassessment', *NC* 145, 1985, pp. 1-44; G. Le Rider, *La naissance de la monnaie. Pratiques monétaires de l'Orient ancien*, Paris 2001, pp. 41-122.

discovered in the Near East: Athenian tetradrachms which represented the bulk of importations, but also Cypriot coins and coins from other Greek cities.[4] Moreover, all the material conditions giving access to the stage of minted coins seemed to be in place since several centuries: a good supply of metals, a sound knowledge of metalwork, the technique of engraving seals which made it easier for engravers to move on to engraving dies, the rich iconography of seals where several motifs originate, and the use of metal (weighed and probably counted too) in trade. So what is the explanation for such a late inauguration of Phoenician coinages? What was the economic context of Tyre at that time? Our documentation regarding these questions is very limited and similar information in relation to the context surrounding the inauguration of the first Greek coins is not very useful because the period was quite different.

Because of Persian dominion, the Tyrian economy was necessarily integrated into the Persian economy. Tyre was subjected to a series of constraints such as the payment of tribute and various taxes, compulsory conscription, the disposal of her fleet, her dockyards, her specialised labourers, and part of her territory as a base of operations, the alienation of some lands, likewise a compliant foreign policy, the acceptance of Persian control, etc.[5]. But the Persians relied on the support of Phoenicians for supplying faraway goods and as a base of their maritime power. In return, Phoenician cities were allowed to retain their political and economic autonomy. The sources provide more information on Sidon than on Tyre, and moreover the kings of Sidon had established privileged relations with the Persian kings. At that time Tyre was the second Phoenician city in order of importance so we expect it was in a more or less similar situation with respect to the Persians. A later source, difficult to understand, also suggests some kind of privileged relations between Tyre and the Persians: 'Tyre which had bought her entire autonomy from the Persian kings, kept it even under the Romans' dominion, since, thanks to some gifts, she had obtained confirmation of ancient royal decrees'(οὐχ ὑπὸ τῶν βασιλέων δ' ἐκρίθησαν αὐτόνομοι μόνον μικρὰ ἀναλώσαντες, ἀλλὰ καὶ ὑπὸ τῶν Ῥωμαίων βεβαιωσάντων τὴν ἐκείνων)[6]. The Persian control was relatively limited: from the available documentation, there was no Persian populating colony in the Tyrian territory and probably less Persian residents than in Sidon. Yet, Persians also used the Tyrian territory, in particular Akko, as a military base for preparing their campaigns against Egypt. After the Sidonian revolts of the 4th century, Persians probably gave to Tyre the lands of Dor and Jaffa, previously granted to Sidon as we know from the inscription of 'Ešmunᶜazor.[7]

---

4. *IGCH*, no. 1478, 1479 and 1483; *CH* VIII, no. 45; cf. also Elayi-Elayi, *Trésors*, pp. 369-370.

5. Cf. J. Elayi, 'La domination perse sur les cités phéniciennes', in *ACFP* II, Rome 1991, pp. 77-85; id., *Sidon*, pp. 137-159.

6. Str. XVI, 2.23.

7. *KAI* 14, ll. 18-20. Cf. Elayi-Elayi, *Monnayage de Sidon*, pp. 612-613.

The evolution from a palatial economy to a civic economy was underscored for Tyre, with an intermediate stage of mixed economy at the beginning of the 7th century. The first step was represented by the biblical text where King Ḥiram of Tyre asked King Salomon for food for his palace in return for cedar and cypress wood to build the temple of Jerusalem.[8] The second step is illustrated by the Assyrian treaty concluded between King Baʿal (*Ba-a-lu*) of Tyre and King Esarhaddon.[9] Although the text is slightly lacunary, the treaty clearly distinguished the ships of Baʿal and those of the Tyrians: ^{GIŠ}MÁ *šá* ^{M}*ba-a-lu lu šá* UN^{MEŠ} KUR *ṣur-ri*, 'a ship of Baʿal or of the people of the country of Tyre'.[10] Together with the reduction of the palatial economy, emerged another type of economy, of a civic nature, accompanied by a reduction in royal power and a political emergence of the city, all the more so since this evolution is clearly attested for the Persian period.[11] The third step was, in the Persian period, the disappearance of the palatial economy as illustrated in the Bible: in return for cedar wood for the temple of Jerusalem, Jehoshua and Zerubbabel gave food, drink and oil to the Sidonians and Tyrians, no more to their kings.[12] The existence of economic networks outside the official framework is well-attested in the Near East from the Old Babylonian period.[13] In the Persian period, trading activities were probably exerted by private individuals, as it is attested for Sidon: 'her private citizens had amassed great riches from her shipping' (τῶν ἰδιωτῶν διὰ τὰς ἐμπορίας μεγάλους περιπεποιημένων πλούτους).[14] If the Tyrian authorities played a part in import trade, no doubt it was only for providing basic foods essential to them or for helping them to pay the taxes imposed by the Persians; or they could have favoured trading activities by some measures even if these measures were taken for a political purpose.[15]

How were payments made in Tyre before the inauguration of coinage? They were probably of different kinds, depending on the trading partners, the goods

---

8. 1 *R* 5, 23-24. Cf. Elayi, *Economie*, pp. 2-6.

9. It is dated from around 677-676 BCE by E. Weidner, *Der Staatsvertrag Assurnirâris VI von Assyrien mit Matiʾilu von Bit-Agusi*, *AfO.B* 8, Graz 1932-33, p. 33; around 670 by H.J. Katzenstein, *The History of Tyre*, Jerusalem 1973, pp. 268-269; G. Pettinato, 'I rapporti politici di Tiro con l'Assiria alla luce del 'trattato tra Asarhaddon e Baal'', *RSF* 3, 1975, p. 159; S.F. Bondì, 'Note sull' economia fenicia – I. Impresa privata e ruolo dello Stato', *EVO* 1, 1978, p. 143.

10. For the details of analysis of this text, see Elayi, *Économie*, pp. 4-6.

11. S.F. Bondì, *loc. cit.* (n. 9), pp. 141-143, related the decrease of the palatial economy to the strong Assyrian pressure during the reign of Tiglath-Pileser III, to the colonization and to the development of the commercial private venture; cf. Elayi, *ibid.*, pp. 5-6.

12. *Esd* 3, 7.

13. Cf., for example, A. Archi ed., *Circulation of Goods in non-palatial Context in the Ancient Near East*, Rome 1984; E. Lipiński, 'Deux marchands de blé phéniciens à Ninive', *RSF* 3, 1975, pp. 1-6.

14. DS. XVI, 41.4.

15. For all the Tyrian economical questions, see Elayi, *Économie*, pp. 56-76, and *id.*, *Sidon*, pp. 137-159; for a study of Sidonian trade in the same period, see Elayi-Sayegh, *Beyrouth II*, pp. 285-320. For Bronze Age and Iron Age, see L. Sole, 'Le emissione monetali della Fenicia prima di Alessandro-I', *SEAP* 16, 1997, pp. 76-82 and 92-96 (with bibl.).

and the period concerned: barter, weighed metal and counted metal were systems of exchange, that had been working well for a long time. Barter was probably used on a local scale, for example by countrymen going to Tyre to sell agricultural produce and exchanging it against the products they needed. This system persisted long after the inauguration of minted coins as is shown by a passage of Aristophanes. The Athenian Diceopolis asked a merchant coming from Thebes to sell agricultural products which system of payment he used, in coins or in kind: 'Let's see now, how much do you sell it for? Or do you want to take with you other goods from here?'.[16] The system of barter was also used on a larger scale, for example in maritime trade when the ships sold their freight or part of it in the harbours of the Tyrian territory and left their holds filled with new goods, that they went and sold in another harbour, with the real mediation of weighed or counted metal (even if the goods exchanged were evaluated in a unit of account).

Payments in weighed metal were probably the most frequently used in Tyrian trade because it was the common system throughout Near East before the commercial use of coins and it was still in use even after the diffusion of Greek and Persian coinages, for example in Babylonia where it was the only currency until the Seleucid period.[17] In a customs register from Elephantine, taxes imposed on the freight of ships were paid in gold or silver,[18] but the use of gold for payments was particular to Egypt: in Phoenician cities, only silver was in use.[19] What kind of shape was the weighed silver? In Akkadian texts from Babylon, the material aspect of silver was designated by the term *šibirtu*, 'lump': this kind of silver was used for buying estate like lands, houses or slaves.[20] The silver which was classified according to its purity was stamped 'with the g.-mark' (*ša ginnu*).[21] The non-monetary hoards discovered in the Near East, Mesopotamia, Iran and Egypt, give an idea of the different shapes of weighed metal: bar-shaped ingots, intact or cut into various fragments, rings, jewels, plates, both intact and fragmented, pieces of Greek silver coins, and various silver fragments melted or hacked. Therefore, weighed silver consisted

---

16. Ar., *Ach.*, vv. 898-899; see also vv. 813-814, 830-832 and 900-904.

17. See, for example, F. Joannès, 'Métaux précieux et moyens de paiement en Babylonie achéménide et hellénistique', *Trans* 8, 1994, pp. 137-144; P. Vargyas, 'Silver and Money in Achaemenid and Hellenistic Babylonia', in *Assyrologia et Semitica, Festschrift für J. Oelsner*, AOAT 252, Neukirchen-Vluyn 2000, pp. 513-521: even during the Seleucid period, when coins were in currency, silver was still weighed, at least in strictly 'Babylonian' milieus.

18. P. Briant and R. Descat, 'Un registre douanier de la satrapie d'Egypte à l'époque achéménide (*TAD* C3, 7)', in N. Grimal and B. Menu eds, *Le commerce en Egypte ancienne*, Cairo 1996, pp. 75-78.

19. With certain exceptions: cf. Elayi-Elayi, *Trésors*, pp. 88-89 (Byblos hoard TX).

20. Joannès, *loc. cit.* (n. 17), pp. 142-143.

21. H. Pognon, 'Notes assyriologiques. Contrat d'association (ou de commandite) du 5 Marhechwan de l'an 4 de Darius', *JA*, 1921, pp. 30-53; Joannès, *ibid.*, pp. 137-142; according to P. Vargyas, '*Kaspu ginnu* and the monetary reform of Darius I', *ZA* 89, 1999, pp. 263-284, the *ginnu* silver would be legal silver: for a different view, see G. Le Rider, *op. cit.* (n. 3), pp. 30-35.

of basic forms (bars, rings or rounds),[22] completed by objects or various fragments in order to obtain complex totals; in such hoards, coins, if any, were considered as any fragment of silver. Some thirty or so non-monetary hoards dated from different periods, were found in the Near East: the hoards of Ras Shamra (525-520 BCE) with some fragmented Greek coins,[23] of Zinjirli (8th century), Tel Batash/Timnah (Late Bronze-Iron Age I), the four hoards of Beth-Shean (Iron Age I), the three hoards of Megiddo (Iron Age I), the hoards from a cave in the desert of Judaea (Iron Age I or II), of Tell Keisan (second half of the 11th century), of Dor (end of the 11th-beginning of the 10th centuries), of En-Hofez and Arad (10th-9th centuries), of Tawilan (10th-9th centuries?), of Eshtemo'a (8th century?), the five hoards of Ekron (end of the 7th century), the hoards of En-Gedi (7th century-beginning of the 6th), of Samaria (late 4th century), and of Sheshem and Gezer.[24] The Athenian silver tetradrachms, imported in great quantities into Transeuphratene during the Persian period, were possibly used too in a system of counted metal. They were appreciated insofar as they were reputed for warranting a good percentage of silver; many of them have received one or several chisel-cuts in order to check that they were not plated. When the content was warranted, it was no longer necessary to weigh these coins because their weight was known and constant: counting them was sufficient. Yet it was necessary to weigh silver when the silver amount was less than a tetradrachm. Weighing silver and counting coins necessitated jobs such as weigher and assayer; both roles were possibly performed by the same person. There is no attestation of them for Tyre, but for example in texts from Larsa dated from the 18th century, which mention Sin-uselli who was at the same time responsible for the authentification of silver and assayer.[25] Some touchstones were also discovered, used for testing gold and silver.[26]

---

22. For the rounds, cf. the non-monetary hoard of Dor and other hoards in the Tel Aviv Museum: P. Vargyas, 'Money in the ancient Near East before and after coinage', *ASOR Newsletter* 49/3, 1999, p. 15; Le Rider, *ibid.*, p. 36 and n. 2. Cf. also M. Dunand, *Fouilles de Byblos II*, Paris 1954-58, p. 386, no. 10725-10741 and pl. LXXVI.

23. *IGCH*, no. 1478.

24. M.S. Balmuth, 'The monetary Forerunners of Coinage in Phoenicia and Palestine', in *The Patterns of Monetary Development in Phoenicia and Palestine in Antiquity*, Tel Aviv-Jerusalem 1967, pp. 25-32; Sole, *loc. cit.* (n. 15), pp. 80-82; Vargyas, *loc. cit.* (n. 22), p. 15; *id.*, *loc. cit.* (n. 21), p. 266. For mixed hoards containing Phoenician coins, cf. Elayi-Elayi, *Trésors*, pp. 35-43 and 370-371; R. Kletter, 'Iron Age Hoards of Precious Metals in Palestine – an 'Underground Economy'?', *Levant* 35, 2003, pp. 139-152 (with bibl.); H. Gitler, 'A *Hacksilber* and Cut Athenian Tetradrachm Hoard from the Environs of Samaria: Late Fourth Century BCE', *INR* 1, 2006, pp. 5-14 (with bibl.).

25. M. Stol, 'State and private business in the land of Larsa', *JCS* 34, 1982, pp. 150-151. The function of weigher (ŠQL and PLS in Phoenician, ταλαντοῦχος in Greek, *libripens* in Latin) was always symbolically present in sales, even in the stage of coins: cf. Elayi-Elayi, *Poids phéniciens*, pp. 214-217 (with bibl.).

26. P. Bordreuil, 'Contrôleurs, peseurs et faussaires: trois épigraphes phéniciennes énigmatiques', in T. Hackens and G. Moucharte eds, *Numismatique et histoire phéniciennes et puniques*, Louvain-la-Neuve 1992, pp. 13-15 and pl. V, 1 (touchstone from the Amanus); J.-L. Huot, 'Ilšu-

Just like the Assyrians, Babylonians and Egyptians among others, the Phoenicians used a system of exchange mainly based on weighed silver, completed by counted silver and barter, which worked perfectly and was suitable for all kinds of operations, even the most complex ones. This system which could be called 'pre-monetary' in the sense that minted coins were not used as such, worked in fact as a monetary system since it used the four functions of currency: evaluation by means of a unit of account (*ŠQL?*),[27] deferred payment (for example repayment of a loan or payment of a rent), exchange (purchasing and sale of goods and various services) and reserve (hoarding).[28] Greek coins imported into the Near East, all of them staters, were only considered for their metallic value and were integrated into the system of weighed or counted metal. As G. Le Rider has quite rightly pointed out, the fact that the system of weighed silver was still in use during the Hellenistic period, in spite of Greek coins circulating, shows that it gave complete satisfaction to everybody.[29]

2. *The inauguration of Group I.1 of Tyrian coinage (around 450 BCE)*

The question of the inauguration of Group I of Tyrian coinage must be considered in comparison with that of other Phoenician coinages since they were closely connected. In terms of relative chronology, the order of inauguration of these coinages seems to have been the following: Byblos, Tyre, Sidon and Arwad, as we have shown.[30] Several proposals have been made for dating this inauguration: between the beginning of the 5th century and the beginning of the 4th, with groundless argumentations.[31] As a matter of fact, the dates of inauguration cannot be established in an absolute chronology, but only approximately in the present state of our documentation. By way of preliminary remark, the

---

ibnišu l'orfèvre de l'E.babbar de Larsa; la jarre L. 76.77 et son contenu', *Syr.* 56, 1979, pp. 20-21 (touchstone from Larsa); cf. R. Bogaert, 'L'essai des monnaies dans l'Antiquité', *RBN* 122, 1976, pp. 8-12.

27. Cf., for example, *KAI* 69, l. 7, and mainly G.A. Cooke, *A Text-book of North-Semitic Inscriptions*, Oxford 1903, no. 62, l. 6; A. Lemaire, *Nouvelles inscriptions araméennes d'Idumée* II, Paris 2002, *s.v.* 'ŠQL' and 'Š'.

28. Cf. the study of Egyptian system by B. Menu, 'La monnaie des Egyptiens de l'époque pharaonique (de l'Ancien Empire à la Ière domination perse)', in A. Testart dir., *Aux origines de la monnaie*, Paris 2001, pp. 80-88; A. Testart, 'Moyen d'échange/moyen de paiement. Des monnaies en général et plus particulièrement des primitives', *ibid.*, pp. 21-33.

29. Le Rider, *op. cit.* (n. 3), p. 17. Cf. G. Perrot and C. Chipiez, *Histoire de l'art dans l'Antiquité. III Phénicie-Chypre*, Paris 1885, pp. 893-894 ('Peuple utilitaire, sans cesse préoccupés d'atteindre le but avec aussi peu de frais que possible, les Phéniciens n'ont pas inventé la monnaie parce qu'ils pouvaient s'en passer ... ').

30. Cf. Elayi, *loc. cit.* (n. 2), pp. 22-24; *id.*, *Sidon*, pp. 197-198.

31. Cf., for example, E.T. Newell, *Some Unpublished Coins of Eastern Dynasts*, NNM 30, New York 1926, p. 9; G.K. Jenkins, 'Recent Acquisitions of Greek Coins by the British Museum', *NC* 19, 1959, p. 41 (beginning of the 5th century); *BMC Phoenicia*, p. 94 (beginning of the 4th century). J.W. Betlyon, *Coinage of Phoenicia*, gave the following dates without any justification: c. 450 for Sidon (p. 3), 435 for Tyre (p. 39), 430 for Arwad (p. 78) and 425 for Byblos (p. 111).

total absence of Phoenician coins in the hoards dated from the second half of the 5th century gives a *terminus post quem*. The coins of Byblos with the crouching sphinx and stylized double lotus, many of them discovered on the beach, seem to be the oldest coins of this city since they conform neither to the weight system nor to the motifs of the following Byblian coins and since their production technique is similar to the first Tyrian and Sidonian coins.[32] Some indications seem to show that they were slightly previous to Tyrian coins: the use of non-Phoenician standard in the first series, the composition of the Syrian hoard TXVII containing only Byblian coins from the first series, and of the Byblian hoard TX containing ten similar Byblian coins and only one Tyrian coin from the first series, very well-preserved. The city of Tyre seems to have inaugurated her coinage slightly after Byblos, around 450: there was indeed a Tyrian shekel from Series I.1.1, almost *fleur-de-coin*, in the Jordan hoard TLIII.[33] If, as it seems, this hoard is near enough complete, its chronological study is reliable: starting from the latest coins (Athenian tetradrachms from Group V of C.G. Starr, coins of Baʿalmilk I of Kition and a Lycian coin), the different authors agreed in dating the burial around the middle of the 5th century. C.M. Kraay and P.R.S. Moorey proposed 'around 445', C.G. Starr '450 or slightly after' and H. Mattingly proposed linking the burial of the hoard with the attack of Kition by Cimon in 450/449, and recently dated it from 454.[34] Since the Tyrian coin of the hoard is almost *fleur-de-coin*, it was probably hoarded slightly after having been struck and it means that the date of hoarding probably took place a very short time after the inauguration of Tyrian coinage. Therefore this hoard is very important since it provides a chronological marker, relatively reliable, for the inauguration of the Tyrian coinage. The absence of Sidonian coins, which normally ought to be represented in the hoard because of the location of its discovery and of its composition, gives an indication as to the posteriority of the Sidonian coinage; it was not expected to find either Aradian or Byblian coins in this area. Other hoards, buried around the middle of the 5th century, contain Byblian and/or Tyrian coins, not Sidonian (hoards TX, TXVII and TLIII),[35] which means that the city of Sidon had no mint at that time. Sidonian coins of Group II are represented in hoard TXXIX, buried around the middle of the second half of the 5th century, in hoard TLXVIII, possibly buried

32. Cf. J. Elayi, 'Les monnaies de Byblos au sphinx et au faucon', *RSF* 11, 1983, pp. 6-12; *id.*, 'Les monnaies préalexandrines de Byblos', *BSFN* 41, 1986, p. 14; A. Lemaire and J. Elayi, 'Les monnaies de Byblos au sphinx et au faucon: nouveaux documents et essai de classement', *RBN* 137, 1991, pp. 29-36.

33. Elayi-Elayi, *Trésors*, pp. 87-90 and 115-116.

34. *Ibid.*, pp. 240-241; C.M. Kraay and P.R.S. Moorey, 'Two Fifth Century Hoards from the Near East', *RN* 10, 1968, pp. 209-210; C.G. Starr, *Athenian Coinage 480-449 B.C.*, Oxford 1970, p. 63; H.B. Mattingly, 'The Jordan Hoard (IGCH 1482) and Kimon's last Expedition', in *Proceedings of the 10th International Congress of Numismatics*, London 1986, pp. 59-64; *id.*, 'A new light on the early coinage of Teos', *SNR* 73, 1994, p. 8.

35. Elayi-Elayi, *Trésors*, pp. 87-90, 115-116 and 240-241.

at the same time, and in hoard TLIV, buried during the last quarter of the 5th century.[36] It can be deduced that the Sidonian coinage was inaugurated quite some time before 425, during the third quarter of the 5th century, probably a short time after that of Tyre, inaugurated around 450.[37] The Aradian coinage was the last of the four Phoenician coinages because Aradian coins are still later represented than Sidonian coins in hoards: it was probably inaugurated around the end of the third quarter of the 5th century.[38]

The first issues of the four Phoenician cities do not seem to have been concerted since they were not simultaneous, but there is not much of a time difference between them, covering at the most only the small time span of the second third of the 5th century, but this span is still probably more limited around the middle of this century. It seems that, after the initiative of Byblos, the other three cities had successively followed her example. What was the new context of the area in the second third of the 5th century that made it favourable to the inauguration of struck coins? Was the context the same for the four Phoenician cities? How is it possible that Byblos, who was then the least powerful city since she apparently had no fleet,[39] started her coinage before Sidon, the first Phoenician city in the Persian period? One of the reasons explaining why Byblos was imitated by the other cities was possibly mimesis. Another reason could be the following: the Cypriot cities of Kition/*KT(Y)* and Lapethus/*LPŠ* started minting coins in the first half of the 5th century, the first being an ancient colony of Tyre and the second seemingly being linked to Byblos as regards language and religion.[40] The role played by Cyprus as a cultural intermediary between the Phoenician and Greek cities must always be kept in mind. If the Phoenician cities at that time had a greater quantity of silver available, it was possibly too another reason for inaugurating coinages. Since they had no silver deposits in their territories, they probably used the imported Greek tetradrachms (mainly Athenian) by re-melting.[41] The Athenian production was then considerably increasing and reached its peak during the third quarter of the 5th

---

36. *Ibid.*, pp. 133-137, 149-151, 241-245 and 277-279.
37. L. Sole has proposed 'intorno al 435 a.C.', a date probably too late: *loc. cit.* (n. 15), p. 88.
38. Cf. Elayi, *loc. cit.* (n. 2), pp. 23-24.
39. *Id.*, 'Byblos et la domination assyrienne', *BaghM* 16, 1985, pp. 393-397; *id.*, 'Les symboles de la puissance militaire sur les monnaies de Byblos', *RN* 26, 1984, pp. 40-47.
40. *BMC Cyprus*, pp. xxix and liii. For Kition, cf., for example, M. Yon ed., *Kition-Bamboula* I-III, Paris 1982-85. For Lapethos, see in particular some pronominal suffixes: W.R. Lane, 'The Phoenician Dialect of Larnax tès Lapethou', *BASOR* 194, 1969, pp. 39-45, whose conclusions are yet excessive; cf. also the Byblian gods mentioned in an inscription from Lapethus: A.M. Honeyman, 'Larnax tès Lapethou. A Third Phoenician Inscription', *Le Muséon* 51, 1938, pp. 195-298 (l. 9).
41. See here above, Chapter V.1.

century;[42] there was also an upward trend in the importation of both isolated and hoarded Athenian tetradrachms.[43]

But the main point is the political context of the second third of the 5th century: in spite of deficient documentation, the situation of Byblos seems to have been very different from that of Sidon, Tyre and Arwad. The local context was largely determined by the evolution of Persian dominion, and Persian maritime power was mainly based on the Phoenician fleets, first of all the Sidonian, which represented substantial difficulties.[44] Now Byblos had no fleet at that time and therefore cannot have shared these difficulties: on the contrary, it was apparently going through a peaceful period, as is shown for example by the inscription of King Yeḥawmilk, probably contemporary with the first Byblian monetary series, related to prestigious works conducted under his reign in the temple of *B'LT GBL*, 'the Mistress of Byblos'.[45]

In contrast, the cities of Tyre, Sidon and Arwad were led into naval actions conducted by Persians during this period. Classical texts and Greek inscriptions, that are our only sources of information on these events, do not describe in detail the precise role of each Phoenician fleet in the different battles; however, the Sidonian fleet probably always had a preponderant place and the Tyrian fleet probably also had an important place. Xerxes was murdered in 465 and replaced by Artaxerxes I: the end of Xerxes' reign and the beginning of his successor's reign were marked by various disturbances in the western part of the Persian Empire. After the defeats of Salamis (480) and Mycale (September 479), the Phoenician fleets in Persian service did not achieve the successes of the preceding period but were defeated several times by the Athenians and their allies:[46] at the Eurymedon in 466 (where they would have lost 200 ships),[47] in Egypt in 460 or 459, and at Salamis of Cyprus in 450 (where they would have

---

42. Starr, *op. cit.* (n. 34), pp. 81-83.
43. C.M. Kraay and P.R.S. Moorey, *loc. cit.* (n. 34), pp. 181-235, had underlined the fact that the beginning of some Phoenician coinages coincided with the scarcity of Athenian coins in the hoards of this area; however, they had not taken into account all the discoveries and C.M. Kraay seems to have changed his mind when he mentioned in contrast the abundance of imports in the 5th century and their decreasing in the 4th (*Greek Coins*, p. 76).
44. Cf. J. Elayi, 'Byblos et Sidon, deux modèles de cités phéniciennes à l'époque perse', in *7ᵉ Colloque sur la Transeuphratène à l'époque perse: frontières et courants d'échanges culturels*, Paris 22-24 mars 2007 (to be published in *Trans* 35, 2008).
45. *KAI* 10.
46. After the second Persian war, the first mention of Phoenician fleets in Persian service occurred in DS. XI,60.5, related with the new Persian threat and Cimon's first campaigns, that is around 470: cf. Elayi, *Sidon*, p. 168.
47. Thc. I, 100.1. Cf. J. de Romilly, *Thucydide I*, p. L; G. Pavano, *Dionisio d'Alicarnasso, Saggio su Thucydide*, Palermo 1968, p. 48, XIII, 41. Lycurgus (*Leocr., Fragments*, p. 55, 72) mentions the capture of 100 ships but seems to have confused the battle of the Eurymedon with that of Salamis in 450; cf. Elayi, *ibid.*, pp. 168-169.

lost 100 ships).⁴⁸ Lycurgus also mentioned the 'plundering of the whole of Asia' (ἅπασαν δὲ τὴν 'Ασίαν κακῶς ποιοῦντες), that could correspond to the passage of Diodorus relating the pursuing of Phoenician ships as far as Phoenicia after the Athenian victory of Salamis.⁴⁹ He finally mentioned the 'devastation of Phoenicia and Cilicia' (Φοινίκην δὲ καὶ Κιλικίαν ἐπόρθησαν), that he placed before the battle of the Eurymedon, but according to B.D. Meritt, the period of 460-454 would be more suitable for an Athenian military feat of this kind.⁵⁰ Moreover, for the first time, the Phoenician cities were directly threatened by the Athenian fleet as is shown by the list of men killed in the war (in Greece, Cyprus, Phoenicia and Egypt) from the Erectheides tribe of Athens, dated from 459 or 458,⁵¹ following the Athenian support of Pharaoh Inaros' revolt. A fragment of inscription discovered in the Heraion of Samos mentions the capture of 17 Phoenician ships by the Samians. R. Meiggs and D. Lewis follow the datation (460-456) and argumentation of W. Peek, according to whom the only possibility for a Samian victory over Phoenician ships was probably at Memphis, during the Egypt campaign; the restoration of [Μέμ]φιος on line 2 seems to be likely and fits with what we know from classical sources.⁵² A passage of Plutarch is probably related to the second campaign of Egypt, when the Athenian fleet lead by Cimon supported Inaros' revolt and defeated at Memphis the Persian fleet, consisting of Phoenician and Cilician ships.⁵³ The only Phoenician victory known from the available documentation occurred at the end of the Egypt campaign in 454 or slightly later: however, maybe it was not all the Phoenician ships since Thucydides wrote: 'a Phoenician fleet' (Φοινίκον ναυτικόν).⁵⁴ According to Ctesias, then the Megabyxus' revolt took place in Syria but his account is difficult to interpret.⁵⁵ In conclu-

---

48. DS. XII, 3.3; Thc. I, 100.4; Lycurg. *ibid.*; R. Meiggs and D. Lewis, *A Selection of Greek Historical Inscriptions to the End of the Fifth Century B.C.*, Oxford 1969, no. 34; DS. XI, 62.3; XII, 3.3. On the possible reasons of these defeats, cf. Elayi, *ibid.*, pp. 170-171.

49. Lycurg., *ibid.*; DS. *Ibid.*; cf. Elayi, *ibid.*, pp. 168-169.

50. Lycurg., *ibid.*; cf. B.D. Meritt *et al.*, *The Athenian Tribute Lists* III, Princeton 1953, p. 11, n. 23; Elayi, *ibid.*, p. 169.

51. *IG* I², 929; Meiggs-Lewis, *op. cit.* (n. 48), no. 33 (460-459); see in particular P. Salmon, *La politique égyptienne d'Athènes, VIᵉ et Vᵉ siècles av. J.-C.*, Brussels 1965, p. 156; C.W. Clairmont, *Patrios nomos. Public Burial in Athens during the Fifth and Fourth Centuries B.C.*, Oxford 1983, pp. 130-135, 298-300 (459-458); Meritt *et al.*, *ibid.*, p. 174. Cf. Elayi, *ibid.*, pp. 169-171.

52. Thc. I, 104.2; Ctes. 63; cf. Meiggs-Lewis, *ibid.*, no. 34; W. Peck, 'Ein Seegefecht aus den Perserkriegen', *Klio* 32, 1939, pp. 289-306.

53. Plut., *Cim.* XVIII, 4-5; cf. Meritt *et al.*, *op. cit.* (n. 50) III, p. 147. On the value of Plutarch's testimony, see lastly T. Duff, *Plutarch's Lives. Exploring Virtue and Vice*, Oxford 1999; C. Pelling, *Plutarch and History*, Swansea-London 2002.

54. Thc. I, 110.4; cf. A.W. Gomme, *A historical Commentary on Thucydides* I, Oxford 1945, p. 323.

55. Cf. J.M. Bigwood, 'Ctesias' account of the revolt of Inarus', *Phoenix* 30, 1976, pp. 1-25; G. Seibt, *Griechische Söldner im Achaimenidenreich*, Bonn 1977, pp. 35-39; P.A. Rahe, 'The military Situation in Western Asia on the eve of Cunaxa', *AJPh* 101, 1980, pp. 88-90; T.S. Brown,

sion, the first monetary series of Tyre, Sidon and Arwad were issued in a troubled period and in a context of successive naval defeats in Persian service.

Is it possible to estimate the number of Phoenician ships destroyed in these defeats? According to classical sources, the number of Phoenician ships involved in the Persian fleet was given as 300 in the second Persian War and also as 300 in the events of 412-409.[56] In 480, in the battle of Salamis, the Persian fleet would have had 200 ships destroyed, not including the captured ships; in 479, in the battle of Mycale, 200 Phoenician and Cypriot ships are reported to have been burnt; in 466, in the battle of the Eurymedon, 200 Phoenician ships are reported to have been destroyed; in 450, in the battle of Salamis of Cyprus, the Phoenicians would have lost around 100 ships.[57] Even if these figures must not be taken literally, they still express reality: the very heavy losses of Phoenician fleets and probably the destruction of most of their naval power, mainly the Sidonian fleet, which was ranked top, but also that of Tyre, the second most powerful one. Around the end of the third quarter of the 5th century, the Phoenician fleets were supplemented by a contingent from Byblos when this city acquired naval power.[58] However the Byblian fleet was probably too small to compensate for Phoenician losses,[59] since in 333 both Byblian and Aradian fleets totalled only 80 ships.[60] It was very costly to maintain a large fleet, particularly during a long period as was the case for the Tyrian, Sidonian and Aradian fleets which were in Persian service from the time of the Ionian revolt. In addition to these expenses there was the rebuilding of the war-galleys destroyed in the successive defeats of the first half of the 5th century: the rate of rebuilding probably experienced difficulties in the wake of the destructions. This heavy work would be enough to explain the inauguration of the Tyrian, Sidonian and Aradian coinages: these cities possibly tried to take fiscal advantage of

'Megabysus son of Zopyrus', *AW* 15, 1987, pp. 65-74; T. Petit, *Satrapes et satrapies dans l'Empire achéménide de Cyrus le Grand à Xerxès Ier*, Paris 1990, pp. 194-195; K.G. Hoglund, *Achaemenid Imperial Administration in Syria-Palestine and the Missions of Ezra and Nehemiah*, Atlanta 1992, pp. 150-151 (who does not accept the reality of Megabyxus' revolt). P. Briant, *From Cyrus to Alexander. A History of the Persian Empire*, Eisenbrauns, Winona Lake 2002; English translation of *Histoire de l'Empire perse. De Cyrus à Alexandre*, Fayard, Paris 1996, pp. 577-578 and 582, admits the existence of this revolt but neither explains the function of Megabyxus nor the enrolment of Greek mercenaries.

56. Hdt VII, 89; DS. XI, 3.7 (beginning of the second Persian War); XIII, 36.5, 38.4, 42.4, 46.6 (events of 412-409); there would have been at Aspendus only 147 ships (Thc. VIII, 38).

57. DS. XI, 19 (Salamis); Hdt IX, 104 (Mycale); Thc. I.100, 1 (Eurymedon); DS. XI, 62.3, XI, 3.3; Lycurg., *Leocr.*, *Fragments*, pp. 55, 72 (Salamis of Cyprus).

58. Elayi, *loc. cit.* (n. 39) 1984, pp. 40-47.

59. Arr., *An.* II, 20.1-2.

60. Cf. O. Casabonne, 'Notes ciliciennes', *Anatolia Antiqua* 4, 1996, p. 116. However, minting coins is not always related to war as is shown from the example of Polycrates of Samos who had a powerful fleet but minted few coins.

the difference between the value of raw silver and the official rate of exchange of their currency.[61]

On the other hand, the creation of a coinage was at that time the best way for a city to declare her independence or autonomy. For the Phoenician cities it was probably of the utmost importance since they were under the Persian dominion. However they did not feel the need for money at the beginning of the Persian Empire, possibly because the Persians respected local institutions and traditions. But after 480, their relations with them seem to have deteriorated, something that could be explained by their repeated defeats (except for Byblos) and therefore the tarnishing of their image. No doubt they appreciated the authorisation to mint coins given by the Persians, in recognition of their autonomy and because coinage was one of the best, if not the best, communication media and means of propaganda in the ancient world.[62]

In addition to the fiscal and political aspects of the money, did the commercial aspect play a role in the inauguration of Phoenician coinages? In other words, did the Phoenicians understand how useful Greek coins were as a mean of payment in trade? The traditional hypothesis concerning the commercial function of money put forward as the explanation for the first Greek coinages, is now much questioned and with solid arguments.[63] Yet in the middle of the 5th century, the situation was different since Greek coins were in current use for trade, although the other means of payment had not completely disappeared.[64] In fact, from the moment very small denominations were issued, they were probably intended, at least partly, to be used in everyday life. In the next stage, the use of bronze coins instead of the minute silver coins probably made payments still easier. One should point out that the electrum coinage of the Lydian kings already comprised very small denominations of the stater (slightly more than 14g): twenty-fourths, forty-eighths and ninety-sixths. Very early too, at the end of the 6th century or beginning of the 5th, very small denominations of the drachma were issued (hemiobols, trihemitetartemorions, tetartemorions

---

61. Cf. P. Grierson, in Balmuth, *loc. cit.* (n. 24), p. 32; G. Le Rider, *op. cit.* (n. 3), pp. 239-266, estimates at 5% the benefit of the Athenians for themselves and for the manufacturing of coins in the 5th century: in other words, the face value of currency was 5% higher than its intrinsic value as a metal.

62. According to G. Le Rider, *ibid.*, pp. 256-257, both fiscal and political aspects were essential in the new coinage inaugurated in Asia Minor in the 6th century.

63. See, for example, C.M. Kraay, 'Hoards, Small Change and the Origin of Coinage', *JHS* 84, 1964, pp. 76-91; O. Picard, *Les Grecs devant la menace perse*, Paris 1980, p. 77; J.-M. Servet, *Nomismata: État et origines de la monnaie*, Lyon 1984, pp. 41-74; Le Rider, *ibid.*, pp. 260-266.

64. See, for example, E. Will, 'Fonctions de la monnaie dans les cités grecques de l'époque classique', in *Numismatique antique. Problèmes et méthodes*, Annales de l'Est, Nancy-Louvain 1975, pp. 233-246; coins were already linked to trade in Hdt I, 94; D.M. Schaps, 'The Invention of Coinage in Lydia, in India, and in China (part I)', *BCEN* 44, 2007, pp. 281-300; '(part II)', *ibid.*, pp. 313-322 (with bibl.).

and hemitetartemorions), for example by the mint of Thebes.[65] In contrast, small bronze denominations appeared in Aegean Greece only at the very end of the 5th century and beginning of the 4th.[66] It would appear, then, that the Phoenicians had enough time, in the Greek harbours where they used to go, to understand just how useful coins could be in trade. If this is right, the question we must look closely at now is whether they were able to create an operational monetary system straight away and to use their first series in trade.

When Tyre started minting her Group I.1, she issued the highest Phoenician denomination as her shekel weighed around 14g while the earlier Byblian shekel only weighed around 9.60g.[67] It was also different from Sidon who apparently started her coinage a short time later than Tyre, with a smaller denomination: the half-shekel of around 7g.[68] The Sidonian Group I mainly would appear to be a coinage-test, all the more so in that Sidon was the number one Phoenician city at that time; she clearly did not intend to compete in this field with Tyre, her neighbouring city. Tyre seems to have had a slightly different purpose when she started her coinage: on the one hand, she chose a relatively heavy standard and her coinage comprised five different denominations: shekel, quarter of shekel, sixteenth of shekel, half of sixteenth and tenth of sixteenth of shekel, which meant a prestigious and flexible monetary system. Moreover, the legends inscribed on each denomination were apparently intended to identify each of them.[69] But on the other hand, the total amount of coins of Group I.1 which have come down to us (28), small in comparison with later groups, points to a limited volume of issues. This could mean too that Tyre also wanted to make a test at the beginning, like Sidon. However, she has immediatly selected her main political and religious symbols (dolphin and owl bearing crook and flail), assigned to represent the image that the city wanted to give of herself, but without providing any indication for identifying the king who was responsible for the issue. This purpose is confirmed by the fact that the first Tyrian monetary production was carefully executed in terms of engraving and manufacturing. Even if it was probably rather costly to open a monetary workshop, the expenses incurred in making the coins of Group I.1, with a restricted volume, were not very significant. What functions did these first coins have? As we have shown, their political function is almost certain. Their fiscal function is likely, although restricted by the relatively small volume pro-

---

65. *BMC Lydia*, pp. 4, 21, 24 and 26; cf., for example, Le Rider, *op. cit.* (n. 3), pp. 96-100; D. Bérend, 'Réflexions sur les fractions du monnayage grec', in A. Houghton *et al.* eds, *Studies in Honor of Leo Mildenberg*, Wetteren 1984, pp. 7-30 (with bibl.).
66. Cf., for example, M. Amandry, 'Manipulations, innovations monétaires et techniques financières dans le monde grec', *Revue de la BN* 44, 1992, p. 61 (with bibl.).
67. J. Elayi, 'L'ouverture du premier atelier monétaire phénicien', *BCEN* 32, 1995, pp. 73-78.
68. Elayi-Elayi, *Monnayage de Sidon*, pp. 624-625 (unless no double shekel of Group I had been preserved, that seems to be rather unlikely since large coins are usually the best preserved).
69. For the meaning of the legends, see here above, Chapter III.

duced. Their commercial function is possible because of the flexibility of the system with its five denominations; yet it was also restricted by the small volume of production, and in any case the coins could not be used for all types of payment. From its limitation, it follows that Group I.1, inaugurated around 450 BCE, did not last for long (beginning of the third quarter of the 5th century).

3. Group I.2 (last part of the third quarter of the 5th century)

Group I.2 seems to follow the same logic as Group I.1, with the same types, same inscriptions and also five (or maybe only four) denominations. Nor too can it be attributed to a precise king, because the genealogy of Tyrian kings is unknown at that time.[70] We know from Herodotus that king Ματτήν was on the throne of Tyre in 480, because he was in command of the Tyrian fleet at the battle of Salamis.[71] This king can be named Mattan III, according to our knowledge of the previous kings bearing this name: Mattan I (c. 829-821) and Mattan II (c. 730).[72] We have no information stating that Mattan III and his father Hiram (IV if he reigned) belonged to the same dynasty as Hiram III and Ittobaal IV (?).[73] An absolute datation of Group I.2 is difficult. On the one hand, coins of this Group were represented in the hoard TLIV, buried during the last quarter of the 5th century, but that gives only a *terminus ante quem*, and in the hoard TLXVIII, that was buried either in the middle of the second half of the 5th century or in the time of Alexander,[74] which provides no help in dating them. On the other hand, Group I.2 followed Group I.1, securely dated around 450 and which probably did not last for long as stated above. Therefore we propose dating Group I.2 from the last part of the third quarter of the 5th century.

In what political context did the Group I.2 issues take place? Our documentation is very deficient, exclusively non-Phoenician (Thucydides and Diodorus) and does not specify the precise role of each Phoenician fleet just as in the previous period. However, in contrast with the previous events, the so-called Phoenician fleet, that is the Sidonian, Tyrian, Aradian (and Byblian?) fleets in Persian service, never intervene militarily. But strangely enough, it did play a major role in Persian policy in the Eastern Mediterranean, sometimes brandished as a threat, sometimes promised as an unexpected assistance. H. Wallinga's hypothesis, followed by R. Descat, according to which, after Sala-

---

70. J. Elayi, 'An Updated Chronology of the Reigns of Phoenician Kings during the Persian Period (539-333 BCE)', *Trans* 32, 2006, pp. 21-25 and 36-37, Table 2.

71. Hdt VII, 98. Cf. J. Elayi, 'The Role of the Phoenician Kings at the Battle of Salamis (480 BCE)', *JAOS* (forthcoming).

72. According to the datation of H.J. Katzenstein, *The History of Tyre*, Jerusalem 1973, p. 349. For other proposals of dating, see, for example, G. Garbini, *Storia a ideologia nell'Israele antico*, Brescia 1986, pp. 67-71.

73. Cf. Elayi, *loc. cit.* (n. 70), pp. 22-23.

74. Cf. Elayi-Elayi, *Trésors*, pp. 243-245 and 277-279.

mis and Mycale, 'the Achaemenids had no more permanent navy',[75] seems unfounded. It is clear from the Sidonian coinage where the continuous representation of the city's war-galley means that this fleet was always at Artaxerxes I's disposal. It was probably the same for the Tyrian fleet. In spite of the purported agreement known as 'Peace of Callias',[76] Miletus came into conflict with Samos in 441 over a border issue. The Milesians were defeated and appealed to Athens to establish a democratic government in Samos. The Samian exiles took refuge with Pissouthnes', satrap of Sardis who entered into an alliance (συμμαχία) with them for helping them to re-conquer Samos; after they had expelled the Athenians, Pericles sailed towards Samos. According to classical sources, Pissouthnes intended to send the Phoenician fleet to support the Samians against Athens.[77] However, the role of this fleet is far from clear: everybody was talking about it but it was never seen. It was said to have sailed towards Caria and Caunus, in violation of the second clause of the 'Peace of Callias', with the intention of providing assistance to the Samians against the Athenian fleet of Pericles. However both Athenians and Samians looked for it, for opposing reasons, but could not find it. One may well wonder why in the end it did not intervene: it could be that false news were spread by the Persians as an attempt to brainwash, but the most likely would be that the Samos affair, a major incident for the Athenians, was probably quite minor for the Persians.[78] In any case, what needs to be said is that during this period Tyre apparently did not suffer any naval defeats and therefore did not incur any expenses for rebuilding her fleet, unlike the previous period.

Group I.2 seems to have been more important than Group I.1 since 217 shekels have been preserved compared with 28 for the previous group, that is to

---

75. H. Wallinga, 'The Ancient Persian navy and its predecessors', in H. Sancisi-Weerdenburg ed., *Achaemenid History I. Sources, Structures and Synthesis*, Leiden 1987, pp. 47-78; *id., Ships and Sea-Power before the great Persian War. The Ancestry of the ancient Trireme*, Leiden *et al.* 1993, p. 30: 'Accordingly, the current belief that the Phoenician cities possessed large standing navies, which in the event they had to put at the disposal of the Persian king, is no more than adventurous speculation'. This assertion is based on insufficient information, especially in numismatics, and cannot be accepted: see the comments of J. Elayi, in *Trans* 8, 1994, pp. 177-180; see also R. Descat, 'Remarques sur les rapports entre les Perses et la mer Noire à l'époque achéménide', in *Ikinci Tarih Boyunca Karadeniz Kongresi Bildileri*, Samsun 1990, p. 544; Briant, *op. cit.* (n. 55), pp. 974-975.

76. On the 'Peace of Callias', see in particular E. Badian, 'The Peace of Callias', *JHS* 107, 1987, pp. 1-39 (with bibl.); *id.*, 'The King's Peace', in *Georgica. Greek Studies in Honor of G. Cawkwell*, *BICS* Suppl. 58, London 1991, pp. 25-48; A.B. Bosworth, 'Plutarch, Callisthenes and the peace of Callias', *JHS* 110, 1990, pp. 1-13; V.M. Strogetsky, 'The problem of Callias' peace and its significance for the evolution of the Delian League', *VDI*, 1991, pp. 158-168; E. Bloedow, 'The peaces of Callias', *SO* 67, 1992, pp. 41-68; G. Shrimpton, *EMC* 13, 1994, pp. 415-418.

77. Thc. I, 116.1,3; DS. XII, 27.4; cf. Elayi, *Sidon*, p. 171; Briant, *op. cit.* (n. 55), p. 581.

78. E. Will, *Le monde grec et l'Orient* I, Paris 1980 (1rst ed.: 1972), pp. 282-284; A.W. Gomme, *op. cit.* (n. 54), p. 353, pointed out, without explaining it, to the absence of article before Φοινίσσα νῆες (§3, contrary to §1): it could be a simple omission or it could mean that the Persians would not have used, if the case arised, the whole Phoenician fleet, in the affair of Samos.

say with a much larger volume of production assuming that the present number of coins constitutes, in relative terms, a representative sample. The decision to increase the volume of production could possibly have been taken because of the success of the test-coinage of Group I.1. However, there were no major changes between the two groups as in the Sidonian coinage.[79] The obverse and reverse types remained unchanged, except for the addition of the shell and the introduction of incuse impressions on the reverse. The legends were the same without any reference to the political authority, king or city, and the style was always carefully worked. The number of denominations was still five, although the existence of eighths of a shekel is not certain and the tenths of sixteenth were perhaps no longer minted. Were the functions of the coins of Group I.2 the same as those of Group I.1? Their political function is almost certain and their fiscal function was probably increased by the much larger quantity of minted coins, even if their manufacture was more costly. As for their commercial function, it is always possible: besides the flexibility of the system, it was facilitated by the fact that a much larger number of coins was in circulation. We have proposed to ascribe Group I.2 to the last part of the third quarter of the 5th century but we do not know how long it lasted.

4. Group II.1.1 (around 425-394 BCE)

It is difficult to establish an absolute chronology of the following Tyrian groups until c. 349 BCE, the first year of ʿOzmilk's reign and whose coinage minted during the Persian period was yearly dated until 333/2. For several reasons as we shall see, we propose to date Group II.1.1 from around 425 to around 394: this period approximately corresponds to the Sidonian Group III (around 425 until 402) and to the beginning of the coinage of King Baʿalšillem II of Sidon (401-366).[80] There is an association of a Tyrian shekel of large fabric and a Sidonian double shekel of King ʿAbdamon in the hoard TLXI; this king reigned during the last quarter of the 5th century just before Baʿana's reign (409/406-402).[81] Therefore we tentatively propose to ascribe Group II.1.1 to the period around 425-394 (battle of Cnidus).

The political context of the Tyrian Group II.1.1 seems at first not to have been very different from the preceding one, with documentation being deficient as far as the Phoenicians are concerned and without any differentiation between the Tyrians and other Phoenicians. Persian history during this period is also difficult to interpret, especially as the available documentation is almost exclusively limited to Asia Minor and Egypt. After the death of Artaxerxes I (465-

---

79. Cf. Elayi-Elayi, *Monnayage de Sidon*, pp. 617-627.
80. *Ibid.*, pp. 627-650.
81. Cf. Elayi-Elayi, *Trésors*, pp. 265-266: therefore a date in the 5th century as O. Mørkholm proposed seems to be the most likely and is confirmed by the Syracusan tetradrachm and the six Athenian tetradrachms with eye full.

424) and of his wife Damaspia (the same day), their legitimate son Xerxes II ascended the throne but was murdered, forty-five days later, by his half-brother Sogdianos who became king. A short time later, another half-brother seized power under the name of Darius II (423-404); he was then succeeded by Artaxerxes II (404-359). During the new events of Samos in 412-409, the main actors were Darius II, not directly but through his satraps (Tissaphernes and Pharnabazus), and the Greek cities (particularly Athens and Sparta). As before and even more so, the Phoenician fleet played an enigmatic role, that of a 'ghost-fleet', keenly expected by some and feared by others (not always the same ones). Firstly, it can be observed that Thucydides and Diodorus diverge on one important point relating to the Persian strategy:[82] the former attributes the main role to Tissaphernes,[83] the latter to Pharnabazus. Because of Thucydides' qualities as a historian and the fact that he was contemporary with the Peloponnesian War, his testimony seems to be more reliable. The first passage of Diodorus is concerned with the summer of 412, this being the period of the first treaty of alliance concluded between Sparta and Darius II:[84] according to him, the Phoenician fleet was sent to bring help to the Spartans. Yet it never reached its destination since, in the winter of 412-411 or at least after the summer, Alcibiades then adviser to the satrap Tissarphernes, advised him to send back the Phoenician fleet, thinking this would make his return to Athens easier. The arguments given by Thucydides and Diodorus are more or less similar: for example it would not be to the Persian king's advantage to make either of the two cities, Sparta or Athens, too powerful. Thucydides was embarrassed for explaining the role played by the Phoenician fleet and showed how Tissaphernes followed Alcibiades' advice.[85] The second passage of Diodorus is related to the third treaty concluded between the Spartans and the Persians in the summer of 411, with an issue at stake: the arrival of the Phoenician fleet as promised. Tissaphernes again promised but intended to follow Alcibiades' advice. The reciprocity expressed in the terms of the treaties between the Spartans and the Persians was in reality only apparent since the Spartans had to give up Ionia in return for a Persian grant and naval support which they never received. Thucydides (or his source) was deceived by the diplomatic language and did not understand that the Spartans had made a fool's deal.

The events of the summer of 411 are related by Thucydides.[86] In Athens, the democracy had been replaced by the Four Hundred; the Peloponnesians of Miletus began to have dissensions since they started to have doubts about the

---

82. DS. XIII, 36.5, 37.5; Thc. VIII, 41.1, 5; 59. On Thucydides' sources, cf. E. Lévy, 'Les trois traités entre Sparte et le Roi', *BHC* 107, 1983, pp. 221-223.
83. He mentions only later (VIII, 109) the agreement between Pharnabazus and the Spartans; cf. Gomme, *op. cit.* (n. 54), p. 146.
84. DS. XIII, 36.5 and 38.4; on these treaties, cf. Lévy, *loc. cit.* (n. 82), pp. 221-237.
85. Thc. VIII, 46.5.
86. *Ibid.*, 78; 81.3; 87.1, 3, 6; 88.1; 99.

arrival of the Phoenician fleet promised by Tissaphernes. Alcibiades changed his speech in the Athenian assembly of Samos,[87] namely Tissaphernes had promised him that the Phoenician fleet would support the Athenians. According to Thucydides, Alcibiades invented this story in order to be appointed strategus and probably because he also wanted to discredit Tissaphernes in the eyes of the Spartans and to compel him as a result to support the Athenians. For the first time, this passage provides information about the position of the Phoenician fleet: Aspendus, located close to the Eurymedon which was indeed a halting-place on the road to Ionia. Thucydides even specified the number of Phoenician triremes (147) while Diodorus mentioned this number twice (300), the same number as that given by Herodotus for the battle of Salamis.[88] The lying speech of Alcibiades did not exactly fulfil his aim: Tissaphernes was completely discredited in the eyes of the Spartans, but he tried to make up for it by sending (or pretending to send once more) the Phoenician fleet to their aid. On hearing that, Alcibiades also hastened towards Aspendus in order to bring the Phoenician fleet or, at least, to prevent it from helping the Spartans. Thucydides found it abnormal that this fleet never sailed further than Aspendus and proposed several explanations without retaining any of them.[89]

Then the events subsequent to the establishment of the Five Thousand at Athens are also related by Thucydides and Diodorus.[90] At that time the Spartans had more confidence that the Phoenician fleet would arrive[91] because they were sure that it was at Aspendus and that Tissaphernes had fetched it. But their hopes were yet again dashed by the Athenian victory against Tissaphernes at Cynossema: the fleet was once more sent back home. Then Thucydides and Diodorus related the events of the autumn of 411:[92] triumphal return to Samos of Alcibiades who claimed that he had contributed to the departure of the fleet[93] and Tissaphernes' attempted explanation to the Spartans, especially concerning the promise from support of the fleet.[94] From the sparse information on the Phoenician cities at that time, it is impossible to check whether they were threatened by the king of the Arabs and by the Egyptians.[95] However it would be reasonable to assume that Darius II did not want the Phoenician fleet to neglect its surveillance mission of Egypt for a long period: the Egypt and Judaea troubles were probably more worrying than the conflict between Athe-

---

87. *Ibid.*, 81.3.
88. *Ibid.*, 87.1, 3; DS. XIII, 42.4; 46.6. Cf. Hdt VII, 89; however this number represented both Phoenician fleets and those of the 'Syrians of Palestine'; cf. Gomme, *op. cit.* (n. 54), pp. 341-342.
89. Thc. VIII, 87.1, 3, 6; 88.1; 99; cf. Lévy, *loc. cit.* (n. 82), p. 237.
90. DS. XIII, 38.4-5, 42.4, 46.6; Thc. VIII, 108.1, 109.1.
91. DS. XIII, 38.4-5: this passage is parallel to that of Thc. VIII, 99.
92. Thc. VIII, 108.1, 109.1; DS. XIII, 42.4, 46.6.
93. Thc. VIII, 108.1.
94. *Ibid.*, 109.1; DS. XIII, 42.4; 46.6.
95. DS. XIII, 46.6; cf. D.M. Lewis, 'The Phoenician fleet in 411', *Historia* 7, 1958, pp. 392-397; Briant, *op. cit.* (n. 55), pp. 596-597 (with bibl.).

nians and Spartans which was quite minor for the Persian Empire. It would hardly be an exaggeration to say that the Persian king waited for the Greeks to tire themselves out fighting together.

Some of the coins minted in Tarsus in the last third of the 5th century are very interesting: on the reverse they have the usual local types (standing deity with trident or standing man, and *TRZ* in Aramaic), but their obverse bears the Tyrian type with the deity riding right on a seahorse, above a triple line of waves.[96] The representation of the type corresponds to that of the Tyrian Group II.1.1, but without the dolphin, either not represented or out of the field. According to C.M. Kraay, these issues were probably minted by Tissaphernes and intended to pay the Phoenician fleet.[97] O. Casabonne interpreted it as a simple borrowing of a Tyrian motif.[98] Because of the important role played by the Phoenician fleet in Asia Minor under Tissaphernes, these coins were more probably minted in Tarsus by this satrap in order to pay the Phoenicians. The choice of a Tyrian type, and not a Sidonian although at that time Sidon had then the most powerful fleet, could be explained firstly by this reason: the Tyrian fleet had a more important role in the fleet sent to Asia Minor. But there could also be another explanation: the motif on the obverse of the contemporary Sidonian double shekels - a war-galley in front of fortress - was not suitable because of the representation of the walls of a city other than Tarsus and because of the complexity of the scene that would hardly have fitted in the restricted field of shekels. Moreover the Tyrian motif of the deity riding on a seahorse was more suitable in this case since, as we have shown,[99] it was the symbol of Tyrian power over the sea (seahorse symbolizing war-galley), land (strung bow) and air (wings). Therefore, these coins were quite connected with the contemporary events of Samos. One may well wonder why Tissaphernes always promised to send the Phoenician fleet, initially to the Spartans, then to the Athenians, but in fact never sent it. It is possible that he followed Alcibiades' advice stating that it would not be to the advantage of the Persian king to make Athens or Sparta too powerful. In spite of the role played by Tissaphernes, then by Pharnabazus, one cannot talk about the weakening of the Persian Empire simply on the grounds that the Persian king did not personally intervene in these events, since he had no reason to do so. On the other hand, the increasing embarrassment of Tissaphernes, according to the Greek sources, could show that he was not really able to send the Phoenician fleet. In all probability, since the Phoenicians were still loyal to the Persian king, they probably took orders from him and not from a satrap. The only occurrence when they possibly

---

96. Kraay, *Greek Coins*, no. 1049-1050.
97. *Ibid.*, pp. 280-281; *id.*, 'The Celenderis Hoard', *NC*, 1962, p. 15.
98. O. Casabonne, 'Présence et influence perses en Cilicie à l'époque achéménide – Iconographie et représentations –', *Anatolia Antiqua* 4, 1996, p. 134 and n. 98; *id.*, *La Cilicie à l'époque achéménide*, Paris 2004, pp. 70, 124 and 252, pls 2, 6-7.
99. See here above, Chapter IV.

obeyed a direct order from the king was when they assembled their ships in Cilicia.[100] However the aim of Darius II's strategy in Asia Minor is far from being clear, Persian inefficiency being especially obvious at sea. Possibly he thought the satraps could gain out of the alliance with the Spartans, that the military operations would be financed by the re-establishment of the tribute in the Greek cities, and that competition between satraps was the best way to prevent one of them from becoming too powerful.[101] In all events, Persian policy became much more drastic from 407 onwards, when Darius sent his son Cyrus as κάρανος to Asia Minor, with full powers and enough money, which meant that Pharnabazus and Tissaphernes were henceforth subordinated to him.[102] After Darius II's death in 404, his eldest son ascended the throne under the name Artaxerxes II: then started a fratricidal struggle with Cyrus the Young that ended in the latter's death at the battle of Cunaxa in 401. The role of the Phoenicians in these events is not well-documented: we only know that Artaxerxes II assembled an army in Phoenicia (no precision) under the command of the general Abrocomas, probably slightly after his accession in 404, in order to prepare a campaign against Amyrtaeus who had proclaimed himself pharaoh in 404 and had seized the Delta whereas Upper Egypt was still under Persian dominion.[103] The evolution of relations between the Persians and the Phoenicians is not documented during the second half of the 5th century, but we know that they were in contact with the satraps more than with the Persian kings. However, some events in Cyprus indirectly inform us about some troubles which occurred in Tyre at that time. According to classical sources,[104] in Salamis, a first Phoenician dynasty (around 449-430) had been overthrown by the Eacid dynasty, this dynasty then being overthrown by Abdemon, a Tyrian exile (ἐκ Φοινίκης ἀνὴρ φυγάς) who had been welcome at the Salaminian court. This Abdemon would have been, unlike the previous Phoenician king, a friend of the Persians imposed by them on the throne of Salamis around 415.[105] If the accounts given by Isocrates and Diodorus are reliable, the pro-Persian party in Tyre would have been dismissed and some Tyrians, such as Abdemon, exiled. He was then driven out by Evagoras in 411, himself previously banished.

Artaxerxes II's reign was relatively long (404-358) and his vigorous attitude contrasted to the passive attitude of Darius II. First it was urgent to restore order in Asia Minor and to undertake a campaign against Egypt since, in 400,

---

100. Thc. VIII, 88.5.
101. Cf. Briant, *op. cit.* (n. 55), pp. 593-597.
102. In Lycia in particular, there would have been a strengthening of the Persian authority at the end of the 5th century: cf. W.A.P. Childs, 'Lycian Relations with Persians and Greeks in the fifth and fourth Centuries reexamined', *AS* 31, 1981, p. 69.
103. Isocr., *Phil.* 101; Hdt III, 15; DS. XI, 71.3; Xen., *An.* I, 4.5.
104. Isocr., *Ev.* IX, 19-20, 26; DS. XIV, 98.1; Thpp., FHG 111.
105. See E. Lipiński dir., *Dictionnaire de la civilisation grecque et punique*, Turnhout 1992, *s.v.* 'Abdémon'; Elayi-Elayi, *Monnayage de Sidon*, p. 634.

Amyrtaeus had been proclaimed pharaoh in Elephantine and, in 398, Nepherites founded the XXIXth Dynasty. As a matter of fact, there was no campaign against Egypt, which is difficult to understand.[106] Artaxerxes put Pharnabazus in charge of preparing the Persian fleet, and gave him the necessary funds. The satrap sailed across to Cyprus and ordered the Cypriot kings to prepare a fleet of some hundred triremes: he appointed as its admiral Conon, who had taken refuge at the court of Evagoras after the Athenian defeats of 405. Then Conon sailed across to Cilicia, where he began preparations for the war against the Spartans.[107] They were informed of the preparation of a Persian naval force by a Syracusan trader returning from Phoenicia: 'He noticed the presence of Phoenician triremes, some of them coming from elsewhere, others already fitted with crews recruited on the spot, finally others that were fitting out; moreover he learnt that their number must be increased up to 300 ... To his mind, the Persian king and Tissaphernes were preparing this expedition; as for their aim, he ignored it'.[108] In the spring of 396, the Spartan king Agesilaus arrived in Ephesus with 12,000 soldiers intent on ensuring the autonomy of the Greek cities of Asia Minor. Tissaphernes was obliged to call a truce in order to gain time since, on one hand he had to wait until the royal Persian army had rejoined him and, on the other hand, until the Phoenician shipyards had finished building the war-galleys promised to Conon.[109] According to Diodorus, probably after 396, his fleet was rejoined by a Cilician contingent of 10 triremes and by a Phoenician fleet of 80 triremes led by the king of Sidon (ὁ Σιδωνίων δυνάστης).[110] It is clear that the Phoenician fleet still existed at that time, even though it may not have fought during the preceding half-century, and because the king of Sidon still played a pre-eminent role in the eyes of the Persians since he was in command of the whole Phoenician fleet, not only the Sidonian one. Because of his presence and his function, it can be assumed that most of the ships were Sidonian but there were probably Tyrian and Aradian ships too.[111] According to the Syracusan trader, there were in the Phoenician harbour (possibly Sidon) three categories of Phoenician war-galleys: those already fitted out (probably Sidonian), those being fitted out (probably Sidonian too) and those coming from other Phoenician cities, probably from Tyre and Arwad. In 396, Conon urged the Rhodians to rise up against the Spartans and to welcome his fleet.[112] When Tissaphernes was put to death in 395 by order of Artax-

---

106. P. Grelot, *Documents araméens d'Égypte*, Paris 1972, no. 7 and 105; cf. Briant, *op. cit.* (n. 55), pp. 634-635.
107. DS. XIV, 39.1-4.
108. Xen., *Hell.* III, 4.1.
109. *Ibid.*, III, 4.1-6; Nep., *Ages.* 2.4; DS. XIV, 79.4-8; *Hell. Oxyr.* IX, 2-3.
110. DS. XIX, 79.7-8; *Hell. Oxyr.* 4.2.
111. As for the Byblian ships, we have no information. There were also 10 'Phoenician' ships from Cilicia, maybe from the Phoenician harbour of Myriand(r)us.
112. DS. XIV, 79.5-6.

erxes,[113] Conon and Pharnabazus lead the Persian fleet to the Cnidian Chersonese where they met the Spartan fleet, lead by Peisander.

The battle of Cnidus was brilliantly won by the Persian fleet in 394. Besides the accounts of Diodorus and Xenophon,[114] there is a lacunary passage in the *Oxyrhyncus Papyri* probably related to the same event, that can be partly restored from Diodorus: κατὰ δὲ αὐ]τὸν χρόνον Φοινίκων [παρεγενήθησαν ἐνενήκοντ]α νῆες εἰς Καῦνον, ὧν [δέκα μὲν ἔπλευσαν ἀπὸ Κιλι]κίας, αἱ δὲ λείπουσαι [προσῆλθον ἀπὸ Φοινίκης], 'Around the same time, [90] Phoenician ships [reached] Caunus, among which [10 came from Cili]cia and the others [came from Phoenicia]'.[115] After that the text is more difficult to restore:]ασακτων ὁ Σιδώνιος[... Βασ]ιλεῖ τοῖς ταύτης τῆς[... πε]ρὶ τὴ[ν] ναυαρχίαν Φαρ[ναβάζ ...]ντων αὐτὸν τῶν παρά[....[116] If we use the parallel passage of Diodorus, it is about the leader of the Phoenician fleet who was the king of Sidon. We have proposed to read ...]α Σάκτων ὁ Σιδώνιος[..., the Greek name of Baʿalšillem II, king of Sidon in 394, something like 'The Shipowner'.[117] It is well worth noting that the Phoenician fleet was relatively small at Cnidus (only 80 ships): Artaxerxes had probably kept the main part of it for keeping an eye on Egypt. The battle of Cnidus was important for the Athenians as it stimulated Athenian imperialism: they welcomed Conon and his fleet and erected a statue for him. Apparently, the Phoenicians and in particular the king of Sidon Baʿalšillem II, the leader of the fleet, were always loyal to Artaxerxes II and represented his main naval support. However, the situation was very different from the time of the Persian Wars because they were no longer under the command of the Persian king but of the satrap Pharnabazus and they fought by the side of the Athenian Conon.

Groups II.1.1 took place initially in a context without sea-battles just as in the preceding period, if we can have confidence in the lacunary documentation. However, the Tyrian fleet always represented an important part of the Phoenician fleet in the service of the Persians and Tyre had to provide for its maintenance. The second stage of this period seems to have been different: after some internal troubles leading to the exile of some Tyrians, the Tyrians may have taken part in the army assembled by Abrocomas after 404 in Phoenicia (in Sidon or Tyre?). They probably participated in the fleet fitted out by Tissaphernes in Phoenicia (in Sidon?) and to the battle of Cnidus. All this meant a significant increase in expenses for Tyre. Group II.1.1 had an increasing volume of production according to the coins preserved: 367 instead of 217 for the pre-

---

113. *Ibid.*, 80.1-5; Xen, *Hell.* III, 4.21-24; *Hell. Oxyr.* 11.2-12.4, 19.3.

114. DS. XIV, 83.4-7; Xen., *Hell.* IV, 3.11-12.

115. B.P. Grenfell and A.S. Hunt, *The Oxyrhyncus Papyri* V, London 1908, p. 149, col. III, 1.26; *Hellenica Oxyrhynchia*, ed. E. Kalinka (Teubner), Lipsiae 1927, A IV, 2.

116. The restorations proposed in the Teubner edition are groundless, just as those proposed by F. Mazza *et al.*, *Fonti classiche per la civiltà fenicia e punica* I, Rome 1988, p. 131, T1.

117. See our analysis in Elayi-Elayi, *Monnayage de Sidon*, pp. 638-640.

ceding group. However, we must probably add to this group one or several denominations of Group III (unclassified series). Major changes were introduced into the Tyrian coinage at that time, namely around 425 BCE. The obverse motif was changed: the dolphin was relegated to the field below and replaced by the deity riding a seahorse.[118] The reverse motif was always the owl with crook and flail, but the incuse impression fitting outline of type disappeared. The inscription was also suppressed so that we do not know to what king this anepigraphic group is to be ascribed. Four denominations have been kept, probably those which seemed to be the most functional when they were used: shekels, fourths of shekel, sixteenths and probably halves of sixteenth of shekel too. The making of Group II.1.1 coins was still more carefully worked than previously, with skilful engraving, a larger diameter and less thick.[119] These beautiful coins probably correspond to a change of king and maybe even of dynasty: they expressed the fact that the Tyrian coinage had come to maturity in its different aspects, in contrast with the more or less contemporary Sidonian Group III, with the continuation of incuse motif on the reverse, some hesitations and an apparently more restricted volume of production (266 instead of more than 367).[120] The progressive and substantial degradation of the coins of this group that we have analysed in detail is probably connected with the difficulties of Tyre in the second stage of this period, which as we have shown is only partly known. Because these difficulties were reflected in the coinage, it seems that Tyre was confronted with more difficulties than Sidon during this period. The function of the coins of Group II.1.1 was always political, fiscal in order to try to overcome the economic and possibly commercial difficulties due to the flexibility of the system and the increasing number of coins in circulation.

5. *Group II.1.2 (around 393-358 BCE)*

Group II.1.2 is the last before the change in standard from the Phoenician to the 'Attic'. An absolute chronology is very difficult to establish. Yet we have tentatively proposed to ascribe it to the period of around 393-358 BCE for the following reason: from this group, all the coins bear letters and/or numbers, that we have interpreted as abbreviations of the king's or city's names and yearly dating: by adding all these inscriptions to those of the following groups, in retrospect we obtained approximate dates.

The political context of Group II.1.2 was much more troubled than the preceding period. The documentation is more abundant but it concerns mainly

---

118. On the meaning of this change, see here above, Chapter IV.
119. Cf. J. Elayi and A.G. Elayi, 'Une série énigmatique de beaux sicles de Tyr', in *6° Congresso Internacional de Estudos Fenício Púnicos, Lisboa 25 de Setembro a 1 de Outubro 2005* (to be published) and above, Chapter V.
120. Cf. Elayi-Elayi, *Monnayage de Sidon*, pp. 627-635.

Sidon and the Phoenicians without being precise. After the sea-battle of Cnidus, Pharnabazus and Conon took advantage of that to expel the Spartans from the Ionian cities and the islands, except for Abydus.[121] In the spring of 393, the Persian fleet went back to sea; it liberated the Cyclades, seized Cythera and landed in the Isthmus of Corinth. Then Pharnabazus left to Conon a part of the fleet (80 triremes) and money for rebuilding the walls of Athens and Piraeus.[122] The composition of the fleet left to Conon is unknown but as the number was the same as the fleet of Cnidus, we can assume that it was the same Phoenician fleet.

Besides the events of Asia Minor, Artaxerxes II was mainly concerned about the troubles of Cyprus and Egypt, but the re-conquest of Egypt, which was his main purpose, could not be achieved without first having re-conquerred Cyprus. In spite of his collaboration with the Persians against the Spartans up until 394, Evagoras I of Salamis pursued a precise plan, namely that of extending his rule over the other Cypriot cities. According to an inscription dated from his year 2 (392?), Milkyaton, king of Kition, had achieved a victory against his 'enemies and their Paphian auxiliaries', that is probably Evagoras and his allies.[123] We know from Diodorus and Isocrates how Evagoras rebelled against the Persians, took the major part of the island and tried to extend his dominion to Asia. Diodorus insists on the conquest of Tyre, without saying anything precise about the other Phoenician cities (τινων ἑτέρων, 'some others').[124] These events are presented in the same manner by Isocrates,[125] but with the usual pomposity of a panegyric, with even a borrowing from the *Persians* of Aeschylus, probably because of the parallel of the two Salamis.[126]

This insistence on Tyre is unexplained when the most powerful city at that time was Sidon. It is possible that only Tyre was 'seized' by Evagoras: if that was the case, why? In fact, he would have had good reasons to focus on this city: first, Tyre was the mother-city of Kition, the rival city of Salamis that he had just subjugated; second, he could remember that he had expelled Abdemon, a Tyrian exile, who had seized power in Salamis. However it is difficult to understand how he could succeed in taking Tyre so easily, a city that had resisted in the face of several sieges by Assyrian and Babylonian kings; it even took the powerful strength of Alexander some seven months to seize the city. The possibility that the Tyrians had spontaneously submitted to Evagoras does not seem likely since they were always conscious of the strength of being on an

---

121. DS. XIV, 84.3.
122. *Ibid.*, 84.5.
123. M. Yon and M. Sznycer, 'Une inscription phénicienne royale de Kition (Chypre)', *CRAI*, 1991, pp. 791-821; *id.*, 'A Phoenician victory trophy at Kition', *RDAC*, 1992, pp. 157-165.
124. DS. XV, 2.4.
125. Isocr., *Pan.* 161; *Ev.* 62; see also Thpp., *FHG* 115, F 103; cf. F.W. König, *Die Persika des Ktesias von Knidos*, Graz 1972, p. 26, § 63.
126. Eschl., *Pers.* 284-285.

island and were eager for their independence. With him they adopted the same attitude as they did later towards Alexander: a warm reception and submission in Palaetyrus (Ushu in the Akkadian texts) on the mainland, not on the island of Tyre. It was possibly a subterfuge of the Tyrians to escape Persian domination without falling under that of Evagoras. In 333, Alexander did not accept the subterfuge of the Tyrians because, before going inland, he wanted to rally all the Phoenician fleets so as not to be attacked in the rear. Evagoras did not have the same concern because he did not intend to go inland and he did not have a fleet capable of seizing the island: therefore, since for him the real seizure of Tyre was neither possible nor necessary, he could content himself with a partial and symbolic occupation of the territory of Tyre. But why did Isocrates and Diodorus join in this game? It is not surprising because both of them were interested in relating fair deeds and 'unexpected' results (παραδόξως or ἀνελπίστως):[127] there is no doubt that the account of the seizure of Tyre made a better impression than the seizure of Palaetyrus. However a geographical error on the part of Diodorus cannot be completely excluded since Book XV, mainly based on Ephorus, contains many confusions of this type: for example, he has confused Histiaea, a city of the northern coast of Euboea, with Histiaeotis in Thessaly.[128] Isocrates exaggerated when he wrote that the whole of Phoenicia was devastated by Evagoras: for sure, he did not try to seize the powerful city of Sidon where there was moreover a Persian garrison and it is uncertain whether, with the exception of Tyre, other Phoenician cities supported his action. In any case, he had searched for all possible foreign supports: at first he had dispatched an embassy to Athens who sent him 10 triremes in 390-389 (seized by the Spartans), then 10 triremes and 800 peltasts ordered by Chabrias in 388-387; he had also sent an embassy to Pharaoh Achoris who gave him an insufficient amount of money (in 388, he had helped to restore this pharaoh in place of Psammuthis I).[129] Xenophon draws attention to the inconsistency of these alliances: Athens, an ally of Artaxerxes, supported Evagoras to fight against him, while the Spartans, at war against Artaxerxes, stopped the Athenian triremes sailing to fight against him.[130] What is reported by Isocrates to be the conquest of Cilicia by Evagoras was probably only an alliance: Cypriot

127. DS. XV, 1.2 and 5.
128. *Ibid.*, 30.3 (written 'Hestiaea').
129. Lys., *Arist.* XIX, 21-23, 43; Xen., *Hell.* VI, 8.24; DS. XV, 4.3, 8.2; cf. A. Destrooper-Georgiades, 'Chypre et l'Egypte à l'époque achéménide à la lumière des témoignages numismatiques', *Trans* 9, 1995, pp. 152-154. On the dating of the reign of Psammouthis I, see D. Devauchelle, 'Notes sur les inscriptions démotiques des carrières de Tourah et de Mâsarah', *ASAE* 69, 1983, pp. 169-180; J.-Y. Carrez-Maratray, 'Psammétique le tyran. Pouvoir, usurpation et alliances en Méditerranée orientale au IVᵉ s. av. J.-C.', *Trans* 30, 2005, pp. 39-40: according to this author, the alliance concluded between Athens and Egypt in 389, just before the performance of the *Ploutos* of Aristophanes, was not anti-Persian, but connected to the situation, Athens needing corn and money.
130. Xen., *ibid.*

colonies were founded in Cilicia Pedias in the 8th century,[131] which could perhaps explain why some support was given to the Cypriot king. The date of Evagoras' campaign in Phoenicia is difficult to establish. The summer of 380 represents a *terminus ante quem*: it is the date of publication, on the occasion of an olympic festival, of the *Panegyric* of Isocrates, which was probably written during the ten or fifteen preceding years.[132] According to Diodorus, the extension of the Evagoras uprising towards Asia started in 386/385, but most authors prefer a later date (382/381) because the 'seizure' could only have occurred when the Persians were in Egypt (around 385-383?) and because they thought he already 'possessed' Tyre when he started his military operations in Cyprus.[133] Yet dating the 'seizure' of Tyre around 385-383 is a frail hypothesis as it too is based itself on hypotheses.

Evagoras' campaign in Phoenicia is far from clear. From the battle of Cnidus, there was a reversal of alliances: Artaxerxes, worried by the reawakening of Athenian imperialism and advised by the satrap Tiribazus, had promulgated the so-called 'peace of Antalcidas', favourable to the Spartans, in 386. Evagoras was supported by Athenian commanders who also supported Pharaoh Achoris, himself supported by Pharnabazus. It is not clear whether the Phoenicians, in particular the Sidonians and Tyrians who probably took part in the first expedition against Egypt, interrupted their relations with Athens and Pharnabazus at that time in order to stay loyal to the Persians. Classical sources are rather ambiguous concerning the attitude of the Phoenician cities towards the expedition of Evagoras to Phoenicia: neither favourable nor hostile, they seem to have stayed cautiously on the reserve. A question arises concerning the 20 Tyrian triremes at the disposal of Evagoras.[134] Did he seize them or did they join him of their own free will? What did such a small number of ships represent: the ships of Palaetyrus, a small part of the Tyrian fleet, which was then engaged in Egypt, a symbolic contribution or support provided by an anti-Persian faction? In the present state of documentation, it is impossible to answer these questions. It is uncertain whether an enigmatic passage of Diodorus is related to the small amount of Tyrian support; after having mentioned the support provided to Evagoras by the king of the Arabs, he added: 'and by some others (kings?) whom the king of the Persians mistrusted' (καὶ ἄλλοι τινὲς οἱ ἐν ὑποψίαις ὄντες τῷ τῶν Περσῶν Βασιλεῖ).[135]

Artaxerxes seems to have reacted against the revolt of Evagoras as early as 391/390 and given the command of his fleet to Hecatomnus, 'dynast of Caria', and that of the army to Autophradates, satrap of Lydia. There was possibly a

---

131. Cf. J. Elayi and A. Cavigneaux, 'Sargon II et les Ioniens', *OA* 18, 1979, pp. 59-75.
132. G. Mathieu and E. Brémond, *Isocrate, Panégyrique*, pp. 5-6.
133. C. Vial, *Diodore* XV, p. 121 (with bibl.).
134. *Ibid.*, XV, 2.4.
135. *Ibid.*

first unsuccessful campaign but we have no information about it.[136] In fact, Persian military preparations probably went on until 387/386: a fleet of 300 triremes was assembled at Phocaea and Cyme under the command of the satrap Tiribazus, and an army was assembled in Cilicia under the command of the satrap Orontes. In spite of the large number of triremes, the Phoenician and Cilician fleets do not seem to have taken part in this campaign because the fleet was equipped in Ionia (Phocaea and Cyme) and the army was composed of Greek mercenaries recruited in these areas, and of Cypriots.[137] What was the reason for this surprising decision? It was certainly not strategic since the Cilician and especially Phoenician harbours were much closer from Cyprus than Ionian harbours: in fact, the fleet was obliged to secure operational bases in Cilicia as is shown by the monetary issues of Tiribazus in Issus, Mallus and Tarsus.[138] Possibly Artaxerxes did not use the Cilician fleets because, according to Isocrates, Cilicia had been separated from the Persian Empire since Evagoras' expedition: 'Most of the Cilician cities had fallen into the hands of our allies (οἱ μεθ' ἡμῶν ὄντες) and the others are easy to conquer'.[139] But why did Artaxerxes not use any of the Phoenician fleets, that had probably already made up the main part of the Persian fleet in the first campaign of Egypt? Perhaps it was because he reserved them for this mission. Isocrates wrote with his usual rhetorical exaggeration: 'Did not Egypt and Cyprus revolt against him (the Persian king), are not Phoenicia and Syria devastated by war, is not Tyre, the object of his pride, occupied by his enemies?'.[140] If the *Panegyric* was published during the summer of 380, it would mean that, at this date, Tyre still 'belonged' to Evagoras. After the failure of the first Egypt campaign, the Phoenician fleets and the Persian army, probably raised for a large part in Transeuphratene, had possibly suffered heavy losses, so they could not be used in the Persian expedition against Cyprus.

The Persian fleet won a naval battle at Kition while the army besieged Salamis in 383/381.[141] Afterwards Tyre probably came back under Persian control, just like the other Phoenician cities that had eventually supported Evagoras,[142] but we do not know whether there was a repression against them. Maybe not since the Cypriot king himself was allowed to stay on the throne of

136. DS., XIV, 98.4; Thpp., *FGH*, 115, F 103; Isocr., *Ev.* 60-62.
137. Isocr., *Pan.* 135, 153; Polyaenus, *Les stratagèmes* VII, 20; DS. XV, 2.1-2.
138. G. Hill, *A History of Cyprus* I, Cambridge 1940, p. 137 and n. 3; A. Davesne, 'La circulation monétaire en Cilicie à l'époque achéménide', *REG*, 1988, pp. 505-508; C.M. Harrison, *Coins of the Persian Satraps*, Ann Arbor 1992, pp. 346-377.
139. Isocr., *Pan.* 161.
140. *Ibid.*, 160.
141. DS., XV, 3.4-6; 4.1; A.J. Sachs and H. Hunger, *Astronomical diaries and related texts from Babylonia, I: Diaries from 652 B.C. to 262 B.C.*, Vienna 1988, no. 441; M. Heltzer, 'The Persian invasion to Cyprus and the date of the submission of Evagoras', in *Acts of the third International Congress of Cypriot Studies*, Nicosia 2000, pp. 717-719.
142. DS., *ibid.*, 8.2-3; 9.2.

Salamis, provided that he paid tribute and obeyed the Persian king. The peace of Antalcidas and the end of Evagoras' upraising meant that the energetic policy of Artaxerxes was fruitful: the cities of Asia Minor were reintegrated into the Persian Empire, the Greek cities of Europe had undertaken not to intervene any more and Cyprus was again under Persian control.

The situation of Egypt was completely different. As we have said, the first campaign against Egypt probably occurred at the same time as the uprising of Evagoras, around 385-383: it was a failure. Isocrates, our only source on this campaign, gives us no information regarding its organization or progress:[143] it is reasonable to assume that the Phoenician fleets, at least the Sidonian and Tyrian ones, took part in it and that the Persians used the logistic usual bases in the campaigns against Egypt, such as Sidon and Akko, a town in the territory of Tyre located about 40km from the island as the crow flies. The independence of Egypt represented a genuine danger for the Persians, all the more so since Pharaoh Achoris was preparing an offensive against them and was enrolling a large number of Greek mercenaries, among others the Athenian Chabrias. However it cannot be said that Achoris held Palestine and Southern Phoenicia while Evagoras held Northern Phoenicia and Cilicia.[144]

In 373, date of the second Persian campaign against Egypt, alliances have changed again: there was a momentary reconciliation between Athens and Artaxerxes. This time, preparations for the campaign took place in the territory of Tyre, in the city of Akko, therefore with the participation of the Tyrians and maybe of other Phoenicians. One reason for this participation could be the fact that from 383, they had enough time to rebuild their fleets; yet we do not know whether they took part in this expedition of their own free will. The Persian king had obtained that Athens should recall Chabrias who had been put in charge of the Egyptian defence by the new Pharaoh Nectanebo I, and sent Iphicrates to Asia in order to prepare a new expedition against Egypt.[145] The preparations for this campaign took place in Akko: according to Diodorus, 20,000 mercenaries were enrolled, only 12,000 according to Nepos.[146] A passage from Polyaenus is related to the same event but this author was only interested in the anecdotal aspect and we do not know whether his account is exact. Moreover his language is rather vague and the interpretation of his text is still problematic: for example, the critical apparatus gives for ἐναιτίους, that is

---

143. Isocr., *Pan.* 140.
144. DS., XV, 29.1-2; cf. R.A. Moysey, *Greek Relations with the Persian Satraps: 371-343 B.C.*, Princeton 1974, p. 15; see the critiques of T.T.B. Ryder, 'Spartan Relations with Persia after the King's Peace: a Strange Story in Diodorus 15.9', *CQ* 13, 1963, pp. 105-109.
145. DS., XV, 41.3; Polyaenus, *Les stratagèmes* III, 9.56.
146. Nep., *Iph.* II, 4; on the value of his testimony, see, among others, T. McCarthy, 'The Content of Cornelius Nepos' *De Viris illustribus*', *CIW* 67, 1974, pp. 383-391; J. Geiger, *Cornelius Nepos and ancient political biography*, Wiesbaden 1985.

incomprehensible, ἐναντίους, αἰτίους or ὑπαιτίους.[147] A second passage from Polyaenus[148] is also included in the part devoted to Iphicrates, at the end, after an episode located in Thrace: he has not connected it with the episode located in Akko and it does not seem to bear any relation to it. According to Polyaenus, Iphicrates was in command of a Persian fleet of one hundred war-galleys, a figure different from that given for the fleet in Akko.[149] Since the Persian fleet was mainly composed of Phoenician ships, it would not be very likely that he had attacked a Phoenician town (?) with Phoenician ships; moreover Iphicrates, who was in the service of the Persians, was on the same side as the Phoenicians in 374, so such an attack is unlikely and Polyaenus would not have designated the Phoenicians using the term οἱ πολέμιοι, 'the enemies'. Therefore one has to exclude the years 374/373 when Iphicrates was in the service of Artaxerxes. When did his expedition occur then? The fact that he could succeed his attack without being disturbed and safely install his camp on this Phoenician shore proves that it was a period when the Persians were much less vigilant. It could be after 385-383 (?), when Evagoras possibly 'seized' Tyre, and before the re-establishment of Persian authority over the Western satrapies that revolted (Iphicrates was dead in 354). The use of the term οἱ πολέμιοι would mean that this event took place at a time when Athens had broken her relations with the Persians and when the Phoenicians (at least those mentioned here) were not revolting against the Persians. The expedition of Iphicrates is not presented by Polyaenus as being well-organised but more as a raid that he used to undertake (relatively small fleet, improvised aspect of the operation). The topographic indication 'marshy shore' is not sufficient for locating the site of the expedition but could for example point to southern Phoenicia where this kind of shore was not rare. Of course, our preceding comments are valid provided the details given by Polyaenus are exact.

The second Persian attempt to re-conquer Egypt in 373 was a failure, just like the first, although Pharaoh Nectanebo was then deprived of the support of Chabrias. These repeated failures of the Phoenician fleets in the face of the Egyptian fleet alone are quite surprising but we have no explanation. Some authors consider the second Persian failure in Egypt as the event which launched, from about 369, the first satrap revolts,[150] the main two figures being Datames (Tarkumuwa?), satrap of Cappadocia, and Ariobarzanes, satrap of

---

147. F. Schindler, 'Die Überlieferung der Stratagemata des Polyainos', *SÖAW. PII* 284/1, 1973; O. Seel, 'Trogus, Caesar und Livius bei Polyainos', *RhM* 103, 1960, pp. 230-271; R.J. Phillips, 'The Sources and Methods of Polyaenus', *CP* 76, 1972, pp. 297-298; S. Lasso de la Vega, 'Un nuevo manuscrito de Polieno', *CFC* 12, 1977, pp. 9-45.
148. Polyaenus, *Les stratagèmes* III, 9, 63.
149. DS. XV, 41.3.
150. E. Will *et al.*, *Le monde grec et l'Orient* II, Paris 1975, pp. 67-68; Childs, *loc. cit.* (n. 102), pp. 72-77; Moysey, *op. cit.* (n. 144), pp. 93-164.

Phrygia or Dascylium.[151] However Diodorus mentioned the Datames' revolt separately from the so-called 'great satraps' revolt'.[152] According to Nepos,[153] Datames was sent to Akko together with Pharnabazus and Tithraustes in order to prepare the second campaign against Egypt; after his failure, he was put in command of the Persian army and ordered to stop the troubles provoked by Aspis of Cataonia. Then he came back to Akko, broke his relations with the Persian king and became allied with Ariobarzanes. The chronology and the precise development of Datames' revolt are slightly uncertain but it occurred certainly much earlier than 361.[154] As we have shown, the countermark with the bull and B^cL was stamped on the coins circulating at Tarsus, during the period of issue of Group I of Datames between 374/3 and 369/8: it can be explained either by an urgent need for money or for a particular type of payment, at all events in relation with the preparation of the revolt.[155] Ariobarzanes was the first ally of Datames: according to Demosthenes, he revolted in 366, supported by the Athenian Timotheus and the Spartan Agesilas.[156] Artaxerxes sent a fleet against him commanded by Mausolus and an army led by Autophradates, having returned from his expedition against Datames; he would have been put to death in 364 (?).[157] There is no information about the Phoenician cities at that time; they were probably still loyal to the Persian king and their fleets, at least the Sidonian and Tyrian ones, took part in the Persian operations against the rebels, presumably without being affected very much by these revolts located in Asia Minor.

In short, the period of the first third of the 4th century was a period of troubles. All the classical authors tried to show that Artaxerxes had to face up to numerous revolts, which were not only concomitant but also linked by networks of alliances between rebels. For example, according to them, during Evagoras' revolt, the whole Transeuphratene would have seceded, just like Egypt. We agree with P. Briant when he writes: 'While the existence of unrest is established, there is nothing to suggest that it constituted a vast common

---

151. On the name of Datames, cf. A. Lemaire, 'Recherche d'épigraphie araméenne en Asie Mineure et en Egypte et le problème de l'acculturation', in H. Sancisi-Weerdenburg and A. Kuhrt eds, *Achaemenid History VI, Asia Minor and Egypt: old cultures in a new Empire*, Leiden 1991, pp. 203-205; Briant, *op. cit.* (n. 55), pp. 666-667; O. Casabonne, 'Notes ciliciennes', *Anatolia Antiqua* 5, 1997, pp. 35-38; G. Le Rider, 'Le monnayage perse en Cilicie au IVe siècle', *NAC* 26, 1997, pp. 157-159; Elayi-Lemaire, *Graffiti*, pp. 188-189; J. Wiesehöfer, 'Tarkumuwa und das Farnah', in W. Henkelman and A. Kuhrt eds, *A Persian Perspective. Essays in Memory of Heleen Sancisi-Weerdenburg*, Leiden 2003, pp. 173-187.
152. DS. XV, 91.1.
153. Nep., *Dat.* § 1-3, 1-4, 3-5, 4-5.1.
154. Cf. Briant, *op. cit.* (n. 55), pp. 659-662.
155. Cf. Elayi-Lemaire, *Graffiti*, pp. 188-199.
156. Dem., *Rhod.* 9-10.
157. On the political context in Asia Minor, see Briant, *op. cit.* (n. 55), pp. 660-663. P. Debord, *L'Asie Mineure au VIe siècle (412-323 a.c.). Pouvoirs et jeux politiques*, Bordeaux 1999, p. 346, proposed a later date for the death of Ariobarzanes (363/362 or later).

front formed at the instigation of Achoris and/or Evagoras'.[158] The biased accounts of classical authors can be explained by the following reasons: Isocrates intended to demonstrate how weak the Persian army was and to convince the Greeks that they should launch a new offensive in Asia Minor. Other authors such as Diodorus for example, strove to capture spectacular events and therefore gave dramatised interpretations.[159] Concerning the Phoenician cities, a network of alliance probably existed between Tyre and Evagoras, but we lack information on other cities. If the quinquereme was truly invented in Salamis of Cyprus and introduced into Sidon during the reign of Baʿalšillem II,[160] this would imply that there were also relations between the king of Sidon and Evagoras. The two fragments of altars inscribed with the name of Achoris, which were found in Sidon (temple of ʾEšmun) and in the Tyrian town of Akko, attest to relations between the pharaoh and the kings of Sidon and Tyre; however, nothing permits the conclusion that there was a συμμαχία between them.[161] At all events, the Tyrian and Sidonian fleets were still probably part of the Persian fleet in the two campaigns against Egypt and, since they both failed, they had to face heavy losses.

During the second third of the 4th century, the troubles increased further. The end of the long reign of Artaxerxes II (until 359 BCE) seems to have been difficult for him. The question of the connection between the Western revolts against the Persian king also arises for this period, with even more acuteness. This is always much disputed, all the more so since the sources are often lacunary and questionable. The two main theories are conflicting: the first one that could be called 'maximalist', considers that all the Western revolts against the Persian king were in line with a large coalition aiming to put an end to Persian domination.[162] The second one that could be called 'minimalist', more recently elaborated, aims to reduce the revolts to localised conflicts which never seri-

---

158. Briant, *ibid.*, p. 651.
159. For example, Isocr., *Pan.* 161-162; DS. XV, 90, 2-4.
160. Cf. Elayi-Elayi, *Monnayage de Sidon*, pp. 487-490.
161. J. Leclant, 'Relations entre l'Egypte et la Phénicie', in *The Role of the Phoenicians in the Interaction of Mediterranean Civilizations, Archaeological Symposium at the American University of Beirut*, Beirut 1968, p. 20; G. Scandone, 'Testimonianze egiziane in Fenicia dal XII al IV sec. a.c.', *RSF* 12, 1984, pp. 149-151; P. Salmon, 'Les relations entre la Perse et l'Egypte du VIe au IVe siècle av. J.-C.', in E. Lipiński ed., *The Land of Israel: Cross-Road of Civilizations*, Leuven 1985, pp. 147-168; J.D. Ray, 'Egypt: Depedence and Independence (425-343 B.C.)', in *Achaemenid History I, Sources, Structures and Synthesis*, Leiden 1987, pp. 79-95; J. Elayi, 'La place de l'Égypte dans la recherche sur les Phéniciens', *Trans* 9, 1995, pp. 12-13 and n. 6 (with bibl.); E. Gubel, *Art phénicien. La Sculpture de tradition phénicienne*, Paris 2002, p. 81, no. 70.
162. See mainly Moysey, *op. cit.* (n. 144); *id.*, 'IG II² and the great satrap's revolt', *ZPE* 67, 1987, pp. 93-100; *id.*, 'Observations on the Numismatic Evidence relating to the Great Satrapal Revolt of 362/1 B.C.', *REA* 91, 1989, pp. 107-139; *id.*, 'Diodorus, the satraps and the decline of the Persian Empire', *AHB* 5, 1991, pp. 113-122; *id.*, 'Plutarch, Nepos and the Satrapal Revolt of 362/1 B.C.', *Historia* 41, 1992, pp. 158-166.

ously threatened the Persian Empire.[163] These two theories are probably both excessive and each revolt ought to be analysed with more objectivity: however, such a sizeable study goes beyond the scope of the present Tyrian corpus. We shall focus here on the participation in the revolts of the Phoenicians, more particularly the Tyrians, and try to verify whether the city of Tyre came within possible networks of alliances. By analysing the Athenian decree *IG* II² 141 in honour of ʿAbdʿaštart I, the king of Sidon, called Straton by the Greeks, we have shown that he had initiated an alliance with Athens on political, diplomatic and economic levels.[164] This decree took place in the first part of his reign, between 365 and 359, possibly in 364.[165] Should the king of Sidon have decided to take part in a revolt against Artaxerxes II, Athens would appear as a valuable ally because she was fighting against the Thebans, the new allies of the Persians, because she had supported Ariobarzanes' revolt against Artax-

---

163. M. Weiskopf, *Achaemenid System of Governing in Anatolia*, Berkeley 1982 (PhD.); *id.*, *The So-Called 'Great Satraps' Revolt', 366-360 B.C.*, Wiesbaden 1989; P. Briant, *op. cit.* (n. 55), in partic. pp. 659, 993 and 994, follows M. Weiskopf but with several reserves; *id.*, 'Histoire et idéologie: les Grecs et la "décadence perse"', in *Mélanges P. Lévêque* II, Paris 1989, pp. 33-47; J. Elayi, *Sidon* (1989), pp. 179-184, followed R.A. Moysey, since the typed version of M. Weiskopf's PhD. was then not yet distributed.

164. *CIG* 87; *IG* II 86; C. Michel, *Recueil d'inscriptions grecques*, Brussels 1897-1900, suppl. 1-2, Paris-Brussels 1912-27, no. 93; E.L. Hicks and G.F. Hill, *A Manual of Greek Historical Inscriptions*, Oxford 1901², no. 111; *Syll.*³, 185; M.N. Tod, *A Selection of Greek Historical Inscriptions* II, Oxford 1948, no. 139; cf. J.S. Schubert, *De proxenia attica*, Lipsiae 1881, p. 61; A.C. Johnson, 'Notes on Attic Inscriptions', *CPh* 9, 1914, p. 423; R.P. Austin, 'Athens and the Satraps' Revolt', *JHS* 64, 1944, pp. 98-100; A. Lambrechts, *Teksten Uitsicht von de Athense Proxeniedekreten tot 323 v.c.*, Brussels 1958, p. 154, no. 73; R.A. de Laix, *Probouleusis at Athens. A Study of Political Decision Making*, Berkeley et al. 1973, p. 132; D. Knoepfler, 'Une paix de cent ans et un conflit en permanence: étude sur les relations diplomatiques d'Athènes avec Erétrie et les autres cités de l'Eubée au IVᵉ siècle av. J.-C.', in E. Frézouls and A. Jacquemin eds, *Les relations internationales, Actes du Colloque de Strasbourg 15-17/6/1993*, Paris 1995, pp. 329-330; C. Veligianni Terzi, *Wertbegriffe in den attischen Ehrendekreten der Klassicher Zeit*, Stuttgart 1997, A1 83; W.T. Loomis, *Wages, Welfare Costs and Inflation in Classical Athens*, Ann Arbor 1998, p. 125, no. 27, 299; *SEG* XII, 85; XXVI, 73; XXXII, 347; XLV, 53, 1210; E. Culasso Gastaldi, *Le prossenie ateniesi des IV secolo a.c. onorati asiatici*, Alexandria 2003; Elayi-Elayi, *Monnayage de Sidon*, pp. 651-655; Elayi, *ʿAbdʿaštart Iᵉʳ*, pp. 99-105.

165. See the abundant bibliography on the datation of this decree: Jonhson, *ibid.*, pp. 417-423 (378/377); Boeckh, in *CIG* 87 (376/364); *Syll.*³, 185 (376-360); Knoepfler, *ibid.*, pp. 329-330 (end of years 370); Hicks-Hill, *ibid.*, 111 (370-362); A. Schaefer, *Demosthenes und seine Zeit*, Leipzig 1885², I, 94; W. Judeich, *Kleinasiatische Studien*, Marburg 1892, p. 198; J.S. Traill, *Persons of Ancient Athens*, Toronto 1994 (368/367); G. Glotz and R. Cohen, *Histoire grecque* III, Paris 1941 (367/366); Michel, *ibid.*, no. 93; Tod, *ibid.*, no. 139; P.J. Rhodes, *The Athenian Boule*, Oxford 1972, pp. 260 and 278; A.S. Henry, 'Polis/Acropolis, Paymasters and the Ten Talents Fund', *Chiron* 12, 1982, pp. 109, 111 and 118; *id.*, *Honour and Privileges in Athenian Decree. The Principal Formulae of Athenian Honorary Decrees*, Hildesheim et al. 1983, p. 337; M.H. Hansen, '*Rhetores* and *Strategoi* in Fourth-Century Athens', *GRBS* 24, 1983, p. 170; R. Develin, *Athenian Officials 684-321 B.C.*, Cambridge 1989, pp. 262-263; Briant, *op. cit.* (n. 55), p. 368; Austin, *ibid.*, pp. 98-100; *PRE*, *s.v.* 'Straton'; R.A. Moysey, 'The date of the Straton of Sidon decree (IG II² 141)', *AJAH* 1, 1976, pp. 182-189; Culasso Gastaldi, *ibid.*, following Elayi, *ibid.*, p. 248; see now Elayi, *ʿAbdʿaštart Iᵉʳ*, pp. 99-105.

erxes and because she was allied with Pharaoh Tachos who intended to rebel against the Persians.

According to Diodorus, the so-called 'great satraps' revolt' started from 362/361, the rebels 'having made an agreement for a concerted action' (συντεθειμένους δὲ κοινοπραγίαν).[166] Among them were Ariobarzanes, satrap of Phrygia, Mausolus, dynast of Caria, Orontes, satrap of Mysia, Autophradates, satrap of Lydia, and also Lycians, Pisidians, Pamphylians, Cilicians, Syrians, 'Phoenicians and almost all the coastland peoples' (Φοίνικες καὶ σχεδὸν πάντες οἱ παραθαλάσσοι).[167] If all the peoples mentioned above were to have taken part in the revolt, this would mean that the Persian Empire had lost its maritime power, which was not the case. As a matter of fact, since Artaxerxes III possessed 300 ships in 356/355 when he threatened Chares and Artabazus with the intervention of his fleet,[168] and since he succeeded in straightening out the situation in a masterly way, it is unthinkable that he had neither Phoenician nor Cilician fleets. Therefore the reservation of Diodorus ('almost all the coastland people') probably meant that all their fleets had not withdrawn their support. It is clear that the spectacular presentation of Diodorus cannot be understood literally. Thus he has amalgamated revolts which did not occur at the same time, for example the one of Ariobarzanes which was earlier. The federative role of Orontes was probably exaggerated; there was seemingly not a single concerted action, the rebels had probably various purposes and not only the purpose of destabilising or overthrowing the Persian king. However, as P. Debord asserted: 'The 'Great satraps' revolt' corresponds indeed to reality'.[169] During the years 360 and probably slightly later, several revolts did take place, some of them being concerted, and they provoked a degree of destabilisation in the Western part of the Persian Empire.

Is Diodorus reliable when he writes that the Phoenicians took part in this concerted action? It seems unlikely that the entire Phoenicians rose up since the Persian fleet remained powerful as mentioned above, the restriction of Diodorus probably concerning part of them. The spread of Tachos' revolt towards Syria in about 359 probably provided the most appropriate period for Phoenician revolts: however it is uncertain whether the Egyptian army intended to link up with that of the satrap Orontes.[170] By order of Tachos, his son Nectanebo is said to have besieged 'cities in Syria' (τὰς ἐν τῇ Συρίᾳ πόλεις), maybe inland since Tachos was then 'nearby Phoenicia' (περὶ Φοινίκην).[171] At all events, under the command of Ochus, the Persians launched a counter-offensive

---

166. DS. XV, 90.3.
167. *Ibid.*, 90.3-4.
168. *Ibid.*, XVI, 22.2.
169. Debord, *op. cit.* (n. 157), pp. 302-366, in particular 366. See the different points of view here above, nn. 162-163.
170. Briant, *op. cit.* (n. 55), pp. 663-665 and 674.
171. DS. XV, 92.4; cf. Briant, *ibid.*, pp. 663-665.

against the pharaoh, seemingly in 359 when Artaxerxes II was still on the throne.[172] According to the sources, Tachos' expedition failed because of internal Egyptian problems since Nectanebo, probably supported by the Persians, seized the throne. Tachos took refuge in Sidon before reaching Susa.[173] Both the traditional links between the Phoenician cities and Egypt, and the escape of Tachos to Sidon could mean that this city had participated in the revolt. It was probably also around 359 that the king of Sidon ʿAbdʿaštart I revolted against the Persians.[174]

Group II.1.2 belonged to this period of troubled political context, with increasing difficulties around the end of it. Just like Sidon, Tyre had probably to face an increase in expenditure to refit and reconstruct her fleet. Little care was devoted to the production of the coins of this group, just like the coins of the last stage of Group II.1.1: this degradation could also be related to the difficulties experienced by Tyre during this period. For periods of a roughly similar length, the decrease in the volume of production and in the number of obverse dies according to the coins preserved could also be linked to these difficulties. However, we must probably add one or several denominations of Group III (Unclassified series). The number of denominations has decreased as there are only shekels, sixteenths of shekel and maybe tenths of sixteenth (Unclassified series of Group III) but no more quarters of shekel. The types have not changed but the coins again bear an inscription on the reverse while in Group I, it was on the obverse. For the first time in all ancient coinages, from around 388, Tyre has dated the issues of her coins, probably by the regnal years: first with numbers alone, then with a letter and a number. The classification of Tyrian coins, corrected by the analyses of their metallic composition, now shows that the first regular dating system has to be attributed to an anonymous Tyrian king around 388; this system was followed by Baʿalšillem II of Sidon, in 372.[175] The next dated coinage was that of king Pumiathon of Kition from around 359 BCE, probably imitating Tyre and/or Sidon; this system was then followed, from 312, by the Seleucid coinage dated with Greek letters according to the Seleucid era, then by the Ptolemaic coinage, dated by the regnal years.[176] This Tyrian innovation was very important since our modern coins still bear the date of issue, most of the time yearly. We have tentatively proposed the following classifica-

172. The sources are not quite clear on this point: DS. XVI, 40.2-5; Just., *Prol.* X; cf. Briant, *ibid.*, p. 666.
173. Xen., *Ages.* II, 30; Athenaeus IV, 150b-c; cf. G. Zecchini, *La cultura storica di Ateneo*, Milan 1989; P. Braund and J. Wilkins eds, *Athenaeus and his world. Reading Greek Culture in the Roman Empire*, Exeter 2000.
174. Elayi-Elayi, *Monnayage de Sidon*, pp. 656-667; Elayi, *ʿAbdʿaštart I*ᵉʳ, pp. 125-138.
175. Elayi-Elayi, *ibid.*, pp. 635-637.
176. *BMC Cyprus*, pp. 21, no. 2 and 75, no. 81 (Pumiathon reigned from around 361 to 312 and his coins are dated from 3 to 47). The Chinese coins began to be dated, by the inscription, from around 200 BCE and, by the regnal year, from the 4th century A.D. We thank F. Thierry for this information.

tion of Group II.1.2 coins: undated coins with *M* (king *M*), *MB* (king *M* associating the crown-prince *B* to his power), and *B* (king *B*), *ŞR* (name of the city) and ʿ (king ʿ); then a dated sequence of *1* to *10*, without any letter for identifying the king; then a dated sequence from Z^{177} to *Z 14*, with an abbreviation (king *Z*); and finally a dated sequence with *T 1* to *T 6* (king *T*).

We now have to examine Justin's account concerning a revolt of slaves who seized power in the city of Tyre, taking advantage of their masters' exhaustion as a result of long battles against the Persians; only one master was spared together with his young son and was settled on the throne by the slaves; his name was Straton, in Phoenician ʿAbdʿaštart. The article on this revolt published in 1981 must now be updated.[178] The only source for this event is Justin, a Roman historian of the IInd or IIIrd century A.D., who abbreviated the *Historiae Philippicae* of Trogus Pompeius, probably contemporary with Livy.[179] The revolt is explicitly dated by Justin in the Persian period; F.K. Movers had already questioned this date in 1849, his argument being that this account follows immediately after the foundation of Carthage.[180] In fact, there is a logic: Justin wants to show that the establishment of a colonial empire by Tyre (in particular the foundation of Carthage and Utica) was possible when the city was prosperous, which she no longer was at the time of the slaves' revolt: 'Before the slaughter of their masters when they abounded in wealth and people, they sent settlers to Africa and founded Utica' (*Ante cladem dominorum cum et opibus et multitudine abundarent, missa in Africam juventute Uticam condidere*).[181] Then the short mention of Alexander's conquest was presented as the outcome of the bad situation provoked by the slaves' revolt and as restoring the prosperity of Tyre. No other serious arguments were given against a datation in the Persian period.[182] How reliable is Justin's account? It presents several defects such as the author's interest more for anecdotes and moral stories than for important events: the theme of the competition organised for choosing

---

177. Coins with *Z* could mean that the accession year was counted as year 0, contrary to the Sidonian dating. This kind of dating was also attested in the Near East: see, for example, *ARAB* II, § 55 ('From my accession year to my fifteenth year of reign'); L. Depuydt, 'Evidence for Accession Dating under the Achaemenids', *JAOS* 115, 1995, pp. 193-204; T. Boig, 'The 'Accession Year' in the Late Achaemenid and Early Hellenistic Period', in C. Wunsch ed., *Mining the Archives. Festschrift for Christopher Walker on the Occasion of His 60th Birthday*, Dresden 2002, pp. 25-34.
178. Cf. J. Elayi, 'La révolte des esclaves de Tyr relatée par Justin', *BaghM* 12, 1981, pp. 139-150.
179. Just., *Epitoma historiarum Philippicarum Pompei Trogui* XVIII, 3-4.
180. F.K. Movers, *Die Phönizier* II/1, Bonn 1849, p. 343.
181. Just. XVIII, 4. The translation of *clades dominorum* into 'the slaughter of their masters (by Alexander)' is invalidated by the context: G. Bunnens, *L'expansion phénicienne en Méditerranée: essai d'interprétation fondé sur une analyse des traditions littéraires*, Brussels-Rome 1979, p. 174.
182. See, for example, W.B. Fleming, *History of Tyre*, New York 1915, p. 49; N. Jidejian, *Tyre through the Ages*, Beirut 1969, p. 61.

a king, the trick used to win and the role of the slave were literary known themes in Antiquity.[183] Justin wanted to illustrate the following moral: '... slaves can be superior by trickery not by wisdom' (... *malitiaque servos, non sapientia vincere*). Another defect is that he did not situate the event in its context, but viewed it through his conception and interest, just like all the ancient authors. Finally Justin's account is rather short, but it seems to be an accurate summary of the book of Trogus Pompeius. Obviously expressions such as *lares dominorum occupant* or *rem publicam invadunt* are typically Latin and did not correspond to the Tyrian reality in the Persian period. However, some accurate details tend to prove the authenticity of the account. The indications on the topography of Tyre at that time are quite exact: the special height of the houses (*editissimisque culminibus urbis*) is confirmed by Assyrian reliefs and ancient authors. The existence of the island of Tyre (*insula*) was anterior to the building of a mole by Alexander. The large square (*campus*) seems to correspond to the εὐρυχωρία mentioned by Josephus, built by Ḥiram I in the east of the city in order to be used as a market for the harbour.[184] The *campus* of Justin, where all the slaves went in order to see the sun rise was necessarily located in the Eastern part of the city; after the building of the mole by Alexander, this area was completely changed and either the *campus* did not exist anymore or it was not located in the east since the city extended over the mole in the Roman period. These old topographical details, previous to Alexander's conquest, probably come from authentic sources. Therefore, even if an older date cannot totally be excluded,[185] the date indicated by Justin can almost certainly be believed.

As a matter of fact, the context of time seems to be as authentic as the topographical context. The revolt is situated after the long battles between Tyrians and Persians and possibly when the Tyrians were in Persian service (*Ibi Persarum bellis diu varieque fatigati victores quidem fuere*) and before Alexander's conquest (*Itaque Alexander Magnus, cum interjecto tempore in Oriente bellum gereret*). The lapse of time between the two events could not be too long otherwise Alexander would not have decided to suppress the consequences of the revolt had they not still been very visible. In the first stage of the Persian period, there was no problem between the Tyrians and the Persians since the Tyrian king Mattan (Μάττην) had good relations with Xerxes, being ranked

---

183. For example Herodotus' account (III, 84-85) on the choice of Darius: the Persians decided to choose as a king the man whose horse would neigh the first at the sunrise and Darius won thanks to his attendant. On the reliability of Justin's account, cf. B.M. Schanz, *Geschichte der Römischen Literatur bis zum Gesetzgebungenswerk des Kaisers Justinian* II/4, Munich 1959, pp. 319-327.

184. Jos., *A.J.* VIII, 145; *C. Ap.* I, 113, 118; cf. Movers, *op. cit.* (n. 180), p. 195; K. Lehman-Hartleben, *Hafenanlagen: Die antiken Hafenanlagen des Mittlemeeres*, Leipzig 1963², p. 245; H.J. Katzenstein, *The History of Tyre*, New York 1973, pp. 16 and 93.

185. A date in the 9th century proposed by F.K. Movers, *ibid.*, p. 343, is not relevant because ʿAbdʿaštart has not his place in the list of Tyrian kings. If need, it could take place under the last Assyrian kings (Sargon II, Sennacherib, Esarhaddon): cf. Elayi, *loc. cit.* (n. 178), p. 141, n. 11.

second in the war council before the battle of Salamis, after the king of Sidon.[186] If this event had already occurred when Herodotus went to Tyre around the middle of the 5th century, he would probably have related such an interesting anecdote.[187] As we have shown above, there is no information on serious difficulties in Tyre before the very end of the 5th century. According to Strabo, the city was so wealthy that she always succeeded in recovering from the destructions caused by wars or earthquakes 'thanks to the seafaring knowledge of her inhabitants, in which the Phoenicians were always superior to everybody, and thanks to her purple dyeing, since the Tyrian purple was the best'.[188] However, the situation of Tyre was particular and difficult as the Tyrians wanted to keep their island free from foreign occupation, as much as possible. As a consequence, the island was isolated in front of the Tyrian mainland territory, successively occupied by Assyrians, Babylonians and Persians. However this mainland territory was essential as it furnished agricultural supplies, water and woods for trade for the numerous inhabitants of the island. The asphyxiation of Tyre began in the 7th century, under the last Assyrian kings Sennacherib, Esarhaddon and Ashurbanipal who tried to seize the island several times by blockading it, without success.[189] Because of these failures, the inhabitants of the island who needed to keep in contact with the Tyrians of the mainland were certainly concerned in many ways, as can be seen from the letters of Qurdi-aššur-lamur, the Assyrian governor based in Ushu (facing the island) who allowed the trade of cedar wood on certain conditions.[190] While Sidon could develop her trade and become prosperous under the protection of the occupying authorities, Tyre was to progressively lose her power and prosperity.

We have analysed here above the continuous troubles which affected Tyre from the end of the 5th century until the middle of the 4th.[191] The difficulties of the city during this period are reflected by the progressive degradation of her coinage from Series II.1.1.1.b and possibly by traces of destruction in some sites belonging to Tyre, such as Akko and Sycaminon (Tell es-Samak).[192] Other reasons could explain the slaves' revolt at that time, besides the difficulties of the Tyrians: their large number (... *servis suis multitudine abundan-*

186. Hdt VIII, 67; cf. Elayi, *loc. cit.* (n. 71).
187. Hdt II, 44. On Herodotus' travels see, for example, J. Lacarrière, *Hérodote et la découverte de la terre*, Paris 1968; D. Gondicas and J. Boëldieu-Trévet, *Lire Hérodote*, Rosny-sous-Bois 2005 (with bibl.).
188. Str. XVI, 2.23; cf. also Curt. IV, 4.19-21.
189. Cf. J. Elayi, 'Les cités phéniciennes et l'Empire assyrien à l'époque d'Assurbanipal', *RA* 77, 1983, pp. 45-58; *id.*, 'Les relations entre les cités phéniciennes et l'Empire assyrien sous le règne de Sennachérib', *Sem.* 35, 1985, pp. 24-26; *id.*, *Cités phéniciennes*, p. 20; M. Botto, *Studi storici sulla Fenicia. L'VIII e il VII secolo a.c.*, Pisa 1990 (with bibl.).
190. H.W. Saggs, 'The Nimrud Letters, 1952-Part II', *Iraq* 17, 1955, pp. 127-130 (letters XII-XIII).
191. Cf., *supra*, Chapter VII, 4-5.
192. For example, M. Dothan, 'Tel Akko', *RB* 82, 1975, pp. 84-86; Y. Elgavish, 'Shiqmona', *RB* 77, 1970, pp. 386-387.

tibus), the fact that they were possibly armed and trained for fighting if they had to fight with their masters, and maybe the fact that they had been forbidden to marry as it was the first thing they did when they seized power (*conjuges ducunt*). Our information on the condition of slaves in Phoenicia is very scarce and does not cover the Persian period (enslavement for debts and after being defeated).[193] However, it is possible to compare with neighbouring peoples: in Palestine, slaves could marry and have children and those 'born in the house' seemed to have military obligations, just as in Carthage.[194] It is possible that the Tyrian slaves had particular demands for having contributed to their masters' victory[195] and that these demands were refused. This could be supported by the fact that their revolt was not spontaneous but concerted (*conspiratione facta*). Justin explained that it was a major event since it was a genuine danger for all ancient societies based on slavery: 'this crime of the slaves caused much agitation and represented a fearful example for the whole world' (*Celebre hoc servorum facinus metuendumque exemplum toto orbe terrarum fuit*); he was aware of the danger since slaves' revolts grew in number around the end of the first millennium.

The Tyrian slaves decided to choose the king by a kind of divine designation, the first of them to see the sunrise (*servis ... de statu rei publicae deliberantibus placuisset regem ex corpore suo creari eumque potissimum quasi acceptissimum diis, qui solem orientem primus vidisset ...*). They had not expected the trick of Straton's slave who had spared and hidden his master. We have to correct a misunderstanding of the text:[196] it was the slave, not Straton, who saw the sun lighting the top of the houses. The text is quite clear: 'he (the slave) told his master Straton the news. Thanks to the idea given by him (Straton) ... he (the slave) was the only one to look westwards' (*rem ad Stratonem ... dominum ... detulit. Ab eo formatus ... solus occidentis regionem intuebatur*). Obviously the master who was timorously hiding (*occulte latentem*) would not have dared to be seen by the slaves. The next moralising sentence confirms this interpretation (*Tunc intellectum est, quantum ingenua servilibus ingenia praestarent; malitiaque servos, non sapientia vincere*). Justin does not say

---

193. Elayi, *Cités phéniciennes*, pp. 63-67; A. Lemaire, 'L'esclave', in J.A. Zamora ed., *El hombre fenicio. Estudios y materiales*, Rome 2003, pp. 219-222 (with bibl.).

194. For Palestine, see *Gn* 14, 14; *Ex* 21, 2-11; *Dt* 15, 12-18; see recently J. Van Seters, 'The Law of Hebrew Slave', *ZAW* 108, 1996, pp. 534-546; R. Westbrook, 'The Female Slave', in V.H. Matthews *et al.* eds, *Gender and Law in the Hebrew Bible and the Ancient Near East*, Sheffield 1998, pp. 214-238 (with bibl.). For Carthage, see App., *Lib.* 59, 260; *Hann.* 9, 35; DS. XIV, 77.3; Pol., *fr.h.* XXX, VIII, 8.4; Oros., *Hist.*, IV, 6, 18. See, for example, I. Mendelsohn, *Slavery in the Ancient Near East*, New York 1949; P. Brulé and J. Oulhen eds, *Esclavage, guerre, économie en Grèce ancienne*, Hommages à Y. Garlan, Paris 1997; J. Andreau and R. Descat, *Esclavage en Grèce et à Rome*, Paris 2006.

195. For example, after military deeds, the Spartan Helots could be liberated: cf. I.M. Diakonoff, 'Slaves, Helots and serfs in early antiquity', *AAH* 22, 1974, pp. 45-78.

196. Fleming, *op. cit.* (n. 182), p. 49; Jidejian, *op. cit.* (n. 182), p. 61.

whether the slave intended to use the trick for himself or for his master. At all events, the other slaves were impressed by this outstanding idea and interpreted the survival of Straton and of his son as an expression of divine will (*velut numine quodam reservatos arbitrantes*). The main purpose of this revolt (to kill all the masters) had failed, yet it completely changed the political and social status of the city. Firstly, the accession of Straton to the throne inaugurated a new dynasty. Then he had to take the slaves into account since the preceding royal family, aristocracy and free Tyrian population had been decimated, at least partly; obviously Justin was exaggerating when he asserted that they murdered all the free people including the masters (*omnem liberum populum cum dominis*) as he later mentioned the free people present in Tyre in the time of Alexander (*innoxiis ... incolis insulae*): it was only the island population that was concerned. Anyway Straton remained on good terms with the slaves since his family remained in power after his death, his son then his nephews (*Post cujus mortem regnum ad filium ac deinde ad nepotes transiit*).[197] The social status of the slaves had completely changed: they were free, they could marry, they took possession of their masters houses and estates (that later Alexander returned to the free inhabitants of the island: *ingenuis et innoxiis incolis insulae adtributi*).[198] Provided with new rights, privileges and wealth, with a king chosen by them, no doubt they played a major role in the government of their city; this role was only limited by their respect towards their king whom they believed to have been invested by the gods.

This political change seems to be reflected by classical sources as we have shown.[199] We have compared the account of Arrian concerning the attitudes of Tyre and Arwad with respect to the same situation in 333/2 BCE: the kings were far from their cities with their fleets commanded by the Persian satrap Autophradates and the two cities had to send a delegation to welcome Alexander.[200] The Aradian delegation was led by Straton (ʿAbdʿaštart), son of king Gerostratus (Gerʿaštart), who decided to crown Alexander and to offer him the city of Arwad and her territory. In contrast, the son of the king was a member of the Tyrian delegation among other prominent men (καὶ γὰρ ἦσαν τῶν ἐπιφανῶν ἐν Τύρῳ οἵ τε ἄλλοι καὶ ὁ τοῦ Βασιλέως τῶν Τυρίων παῖς).[201] The Tyrian representatives were sent by the will of the 'people' (πρέσβεις Τυρίων ἀπὸ τοῦ κοινοῦ ἐσταλμένοι). Τὸ κοινόν had several meanings: 'state', 'government', 'senate', 'public authority', 'common will'. It is difficult to select the exact meaning since we do not know whether Tyre had a popular representative

---

197. We do not know why Justin used the plural form *nepotes* (Successive rules? Joined rule?).
198. We wonder who were then the new slaves since the ancient societies could not work without them.
199. Elayi, *loc. cit.* (n. 178), pp. 145-146; *id.*, *Cités phéniciennes*, pp. 47-50, 75.
200. Arr., *An.* II, 13-24.
201. *Ibid.*, 15. His name is even not mentioned.

body.[202] However this text seems to attest to the existence of a popular authority which decided how to welcome Alexander (ἐγνωκότων Τυρίων, 'the Tyrians having decided'). Moreover the Macedonian king understood this since he answered to the Tyrians, not to the son of the king (ἐκέλευσεν ἐπανελθόντας φράσαι Τυρίοις). It could be objected that this son was still a child but, if so, he would have had no place in the delegation. If he was a young man, he could have replaced his father during his absence, as Alexander was only sixteen years old when Philip entrusted him with his kingdom during his campaign against Byzantium. On the other hand, the fact that Alexander forgave King Azemilcus ('Ozmilk) and the most prominent Tyrians, after the seizure of Tyre (τε τῶν Τυρίων οἱ μάλιστα ἐν τέλει καὶ ὁ Βασιλεὺς 'Αζέμιλκος) seems to indicate that he did not hold them responsible for the resistance offered by Tyre. Diodorus' account is similar to that of Arrian in that he mentions neither the king nor his son, but only the Tyrians (Οἱ δὲ Τύριοι ... διεκώλυσαν αὐτὸν τῆς εἰς τὴν πόλιν εἰσόδου).[203] None of the decisions concerning the organisation of the city's resistance was led by the king or his son, always by a vote of the Tyrians (ἐψηφίσαντο).[204] Therefore the Tyrian kingship was very different at that time from the Aradian one: while in the latter, the king had a strong executive power and his son replaced him during his absence, in the Tyrian kingship, the executive power was held, not by the king but by the people, in a form it is impossible to specify and the king's son had no power when his father was absent. That is the sense in which we understand a difficult passage from Justin's account: 'he (Alexander) only spared the family of Straton and strengthened the power of his dynasty' (*genus tantum Stratonis inviolatum servavit regnumque stirpi ejus restituit*). That is to say the power of the king was very weak following the slaves' revolt and necessitated reinforcing.

Justin gives an original interpretation of Alexander's action in Tyre in 332 BCE. He presents him as the 'champion of public safety' (*ultor publicae securitatis*) and explains his fierceness against the defeated Tyrians by the desire to punish the ancient slaves for their crime (*ob memoriam veteris sceleris crucibus adfixit*) and to suppress the consequences of their revolt. According to this author, Alexander destroyed the race of the slaves and preserved the family of Straton and the free surviving inhabitants of the island, to whom he returned their estates and prerogatives (*ingenius et innoxiis*[205] *incolis insulae adtributis*). In this way he would have allowed the city of Tyre to recover her prosperity as

---

202. Cf. Elayi, *loc. cit.* (n. 178), pp. 145-146; *id.*, *Cités phéniciennes*, pp. 48-49.
203. DS. XVII, 40.
204. *Ibid.* It is uncertain who were the ἄρχοντες mentioned by Diodorus.
205. *Innoxius* means here 'intact', 'having not suffer any harm' and designates the free surviving Tyrians. The interpretation of H. Seyrig 'la ville semble avoir été repeuplée à l'aide de gens amenés d'alentour' is not convincing ('Antiquités syriennes. 64 – Sur une prétendue ère tyrienne', *Syr.* 34, 1957, p. 97): *incolis insulae* clearly designates the 'inhabitants of the island' (the postpositive genitive is usual in Justin's account).

it was prior to the revolt (*Tyrii Alexandri auspiciis conditi ... cito convaluere*). Justin did not intend to summarise the seizure of Tyre but to present what, in this event, had a relation with the revolt. One of Alexander's aims was possibly to suppress the consequences of the revolt but his action was probably not as developed as Justin says because, from this event, there was such a population-mix that it was not easy to distinguish between ancient slaves and people who were free. The other classical sources do not confirm Justin's interpretation neither do they invalidate it; they also describe Alexander's fierceness against the defeated Tyrians, giving the same details concerning crucifixion, and mentioning how, contrary to expectations, he forgave the king and the most prominent inhabitants.[206] By mistake, Diodorus locates an episode in Tyre which actually occurred in Sidon, namely the replacement of Straton by Abdalonymus:[207] he had probably confused King Straton, established on the throne of Tyre by the slaves and the Sidonian king Straton (ʿAbdʿaštart II) dethroned by Alexander.

Justin's account, other classical sources and inscriptions enable an approximate dating of the Straton dynasty to be made. The name Straton/ʿAbdʿaštart is well-attested in the Phoenician dynasties of the 4th century BCE: two Sidonian kings ʿAbdʿaštart I and ʿAbdʿaštart II, and the son of the Aradian king Gerostratus/Gerʿaštart. When the slaves' revolt started in Tyre, Straton was middle-aged (*senex*) and his unnamed son was still a child (*parvulus*); the age difference between father and son was probably not very great.[208] Straton had reigned a few years until his young son was old enough to accede to the throne. The descendant of Straton who was on the throne in 332 was Azemilcus/ʿOzmilk. This king had a son old enough to participate in the Tyrian delegation that welcomed Alexander, which was seventeen years after his accession to the throne. It is uncertain whether this unnamed son succeeded his father on the throne in the Hellenistic period.[209] Therefore, ʿOzmilk who ascended to the throne in c. 349 BCE could either be the son of Straton or a nephew of his son if we adhere to Justin's account.

We now have to examine the bilingual inscription of Delos *CIS* I, 114 that possibly mentions this Tyrian king Straton. The Greek text is clear: 'the Tyrian Hieronautai' (οἱ ἐκ Τύρου ἱερoναῦται) dedicated from Tyre and Sidon to Apollo offerings.[210] The Phoenician text is very damaged: *BŠT ... [L] MLK[Y]*

---

206. Arr., *An.* II, 24; DS. XVII, 47; Curt. IV, 2.
207. DS. *ibid*. Justin did not mistake because he knew well the circumstances of Straton's accession to the throne.
208. In fact, the meaning of *senex* was different from the modern 'old man'. By example, according to the constitution of Servius Tullius, in the electoral comices, men were classified after 45 years in the centuries of 'seniores': Cic., *Rep.* 2, 39.
209. A. Lemaire, 'Le royaume de Tyr dans la seconde moitié du IVᵉ siècle av. J.-C.', in *ACFP* II/1, Rome 1991, p. 148.
210. Cf. J. Elayi, 'L'inscription bilingue de Délos *CIS* I, 114', *BaghM* 19, 1998, pp. 549-555; *id.*, *ʿAbdʿaštart Iᵉʳ*, p. 95.

MLK ʿBD[ ] MLK [ṢDNM ...] L[...] L..., 'In the year [x of the] reign of king ʿAbd[ ] king of the [...'. The reading of *ʿBDʿ[* by E. Renan, allowing ʿAbdʿaštart to be restored, is uncertain as far as the *ʿayin* is concerned.[211] Since the ἱεροναῦται are Tyrian, the inscription is probably dated by the Tyrian regnal years. The palaeographical analysis gives an approximate datation in the second part of the 4th century. Therefore this Tyrian king could be Straton/ʿAbdʿaštart of the revolt, maybe in the last part of his reign, or Abdalonymus/ʿAbdalonym. Another document is possibly related to the Tyrian slaves' revolt, namely a Greek oracle:

Αὐτὰρ ἐπεὶ σκήπτροισι Μακεδόνες αὐχήσουσι
Κᾶρες δ'οἰκήσουσι Τύρον, Τύριοι ἀπολοῦνται,

that we propose to translate:

'When Macedonians will glory in their sceptres,
Rascals will settle in Tyre, Tyrians will be murdered'.[212]

Although the style of oracles is always allusive and difficult to understand when the context is unknown, this oracle seems to correspond to the slaves' revolt described by Justin. The first line contains a date in an enigmatic form: it probably alludes to the Macedonian hegemony starting with Philip II, Alexander's father, who ascended to the throne in 360. The second line is clear except for the first word Κᾶρες, 'Carians'. Obviously Carians had nothing to do with Tyre in this period, but in a proverbial meaning, κᾶρ meant 'worthless man', 'rascal'.[213] Now the oracle can be understood: by this term it designated the slaves who revolted and murdered the Tyrians and we would have a date in 360 BCE or in the following years.

We now have to examine whether this likely event is reflected in the Tyrian coinage. As it appears, there are two possible sequences which could be related to the slaves' revolt: 1. coins with *ṢR* ('Tyre') and *ʿ* (*ʿ[BDʿŠTRT]*) (Series II.1.2.1.d and II.1.2.1.e) possibly around 390; 2. coins with *1Ṣ* to *4Ṣ* (*Ṣ[R]*, 'Tyre') and *ʿ3Ṣ* (*ʿ[BDʿŠTRT] Ṣ[R]*, '3rd year of ʿAbdʿaštart, Tyre') (Series II.2.1.6-11), after the changing of standard of c. 357, possibly around 354/350. These dates are approximate but anyway the first year of ʿOzmilk's reign – c. 349 BCE – represents a *terminus ante quem*, and the period covering the slaves' revolt seems to be around 390-350. During the whole of this period, the volume of production of Tyrian coins decreased significantly: 183 coins preserved in Series II.1.2 (instead of 367 in the preceding series) and 91 in Series II.2.1.1-13 (instead of 653 in the following series of ʿOzmilk). If this revolt is reflected in the Tyrian coinage, an argument in favour of the second hypothesis (around 354/350) could be that the context of the period is more favourable since the Persians were particularly troubled on several different sides: Persian,

---

211. *Ibid.* for the bibliography and interpretations.
212. *Or. Syb.* IV, 88. Cf. Elayi, *loc. cit.* (n. 178), pp. 148-149.
213. This meaning is well-attested: Pol. X, 32.11; Eur., *Cycl.* 650; Arstd. I, 163.

Sidonian and Tyrian; this would fit with the Greek oracle. However, we shall remain cautious without choosing one of these two hypotheses, within the likely period of around 390-350 BCE.

6. Group II.2 (around 357-333/2 BCE)

This group is clearly distinguished from the preceding group, not by the types which have not altered but by the change of standard from the Phoenician to the 'Attic'. It is also relatively well-dated in absolute chronology because, in retrospect from 332, we date the 17 years of the reign of ʿOzmilk (c. 349-333/2) and before that, around eight yearly dated coins (c. 357-350): Series II.2.1.1-5 and II.2.1.6-11.

The political context of Group II.2 was troubled as in the previous period. The change of standard including a substantial loss of weight (from 13.56g to 8.77g) was without any doubt at least partly due to economic difficulties, following on from a significant decrease in the percentage of silver in the preceding period and there was an increase in silver after the change.[214] It is interesting to note that this occurred around 357, that is some eight years after the devaluation of the Sidonian coinage decided by ʿAbdʿaštart I in 365 BCE. The economic difficulties of Tyre were in fact accumulated since the very end of the 5th century as shown by the progressive degradation of the Tyrian coinage: the difficulties came mainly from the participation in the campaigns of the Persians, most of them being failures, and from internal difficulties such as the slaves' revolt which occurred around 390-350, maybe 354/350. The situation was always troubled in the Western part of the Persian Empire. The succession of Artaxerxes II in 359 was difficult because Artaxerxes III Ochus had dismissed from the throne his two older brothers: Darius and Ariaspes. As P. Briant notes, 'it appears that the new Great King found himself beset with troubles in Asia Minor shortly after his accession – or perhaps the troubles had always been there in latent form'.[215] For example, between around 357 and 355, the Athenian commander Chares, during his war against his revolted allies, concluded an agreement with Artabazus, satrap of Hellespontic Phrygia who had revolted against the Persian king; with the help of Chares, this satrap won over the Persian army.[216] Due to Persian pressure, Athens stopped supporting Artabazus who allied with the Thebans and succeeded, thanks to the support of Pammenes, in twice winning over the satraps sent by the Persian king. Then,

---

214. See the analyses of the metallic composition of Tyrian coins: A.G. Elayi, J.-N. Barrandon and J. Elayi, 'The Change of Standard of Tyrian Silver Coinage about 357 BCE as Determined by Fast Neutron Activation Analysis' (forthcoming).

215. Briant, *op. cit.* (n. 55), p. 681.

216. DS. XVI, 7.3-4; 21-22.1-2; *FGH* 105 F4. R.A. Moysey, *op. cit.* (n. 144), p. 165, considered that there was, from 357 to 343, a 'second satraps' revolt', different from the first one as, in addition of the satraps, there were the local rulers.

forsaken by the Thebans, maybe in 352, he fled to Macedonia.[217] According to Diodorus, during the period 361-351, Artaxerxes sent his generals several times in order to try, in vain, to re-conquer Egypt,[218] failing again in 351.[219]

We have shown[220] that the king of Sidon ʿAbdʿaštart I had probably revolted against the Persians around 360/359 and was repressed in about 355 because of the Babylonian tablet mentioning the sending of Sidonian prisoners by Artaxerxes III to Babylon and Susa, dated from year 4 (355) rather than year 14 (345).[221] Since Sidon seems to have been loyal to the Persians until the beginning of ʿAbdʿaštart I's reign, what were the reasons for his revolt? The weight of expenses linked to the fleet in Persian service was heavier for Sidon since this city was the main support of the Persian fleet. If she was the capital of Transeuphratene, she had additional charges due to the presence of Persian residents and satrapic administration. The revolt of Egypt with which Sidon was traditionally linked probably played a major role, just as the relations of ʿAbdʿaštart I with Athens and Nicocles of Salamis did.[222] After the suppression of ʿAbdʿaštart's revolt, Artaxerxes III did however let him on the throne, just as Evagoras was allowed on to the throne of Salamis by Artaxerxes II after his revolt. In spite of the assertion of Diodorus concerning the participation of the Phoenicians in a revolt around 362/1,[223] there is no confirmation of the participation of Tyre.

We shall examine the role of Mazday/Mazaios in Transeuphratene again in order to update our previous study and to include recent literature and new coins.[224] There are three main old hypotheses of datation which no longer sit comfortably with the present state of documentation. The complexity of the question involving both history, classical sources and numismatics, explains why some authors still follow outdated hypotheses. That is why we shall analyse the question in detail. The first hypothesis is based on a computation of 21 years, following the regnal years of Artaxerxes III (years 1-4 = beginning of his reign; years 16-21 = end of his reign): it goes back to E. Babelon.[225] The sec-

217. Cf. Debord, *op. cit.* (n. 157), p. 396 (with bibl.).
218. DS. XVI, 40.3-5; P. Briant, *op. cit.* (n. 55), p. 682, considered this passage as 'highly suspect' whereas it is in reality somewhat confused because of the flashbacks.
219. Isocr., *Phil.* 101; Dem., *Rhod.* 11-12.
220. Cf. Elayi-Elayi, *Monnayage de Sidon*, pp. 658-660.
221. J.N. Strassmaier, 'Einige kleinere babylonische Keilschrifttexte aus dem Britischen Museum', in *Actes du Huitième Congrès International des Orientalistes*, Stockholm 1889, Sec. I, Sémitique B, no. 28; S. Smith, *Babylonian Historical Texts Relating to the Capture and Downfall of Babylon*, London 1924, pp. 148-149; A.K. Grayson, *Assyrian and Babylonian Chronicles*, New York 1975, p. 114, no. 9.
222. Cf. Elayi, *ʿAbdʿaštart Ier*, pp. 125-138.
223. DS. XV, 90.
224. Cf. Elayi-Elayi, *Monnayage de Sidon*, pp. 660-664; *id.*, 'Le monnayage sidonien de Mazday', *Trans* 27, 2004, pp. 155-162.
225. Babelon, *Traité* II, 2, pp. 581-582; *id.*, *Perses*, p. XLVIII: 'les pièces que Mazaios fit frapper à l'imitation des monnaies des rois de Sidon, depuis l'an 353 jusqu'à l'an 332, dans un des

ond hypothesis is based on a computation of 10 years (years 16-21 = end of Artaxerxes III's reign; years 1-4 = beginning of Darius III's reign): it goes back to J. Rouvier and G.F. Hill.[226] The third hypothesis involves considering that the coins bore the dates of his reign as satrap over Cilicia and Transeuphratene.[227] Mazday would have minted his coinage before and after the Sidonian king Tennes, from 362/361 to 558 and from 347/346 to 342/341 BCE. A few authors still adhere to the second hypothesis, with some variants: for example, A. Lemaire attributes the dates 16-21 to Artaxerxes III, 1-2 to Arses/Artaxerxes IV or to Darius III, and 3 to Darius III.[228] He forgets year 4, which is however taken into consideration in this hypothesis and clearly attested for example on the sixteenth of shekel no. 2040, because he relies on the double shekels rather than on the fractions;[229] however, some kings issued only fractions, such as in the first Sidonian and Aradian series. The wish to follow the second hypothesis leads him to unexplained computations: either 343-336 and 333, or 343-338 and 333, which do not correspond with anything in the context, the revolt of Tennes having been suppressed in 347.[230] He does not take into account the reign of king ᶜᶜ, possibly Evagoras (346-343), who was in any case a king favourable to Artaxerxes III, appointed just after the suppression of Tennes' revolt in 347: therefore the Persian king retook Sidon in 346, not in 343 when the pro-Persian king ᶜAbdᶜaštart II ascended to the throne; P. Briant follows the second hypothesis as an established fact, without giving any reasons.[231] The last argument is that there is a Sidonian 'obol' dated from year 20 in an unpublished Naplouse hoard supposedly buried in 338/7 BCE.[232]

---

ports de la Cilicie'. See however A. Lemaire, in T. Hackens et al., *A Survey of Numismatic Research 1985-1990*, Brussels 1991, p. 98, n. 19, who still follows a no longer valid hypothesis.

226. J. Rouvier, 'Les rois phéniciens de Sidon, d'après leurs monnaies, sous la dynastie des Achéménides', *RN* 6, 1902, pp. 250-260; *BMC Phoenicia*, pp. xcviii-xcix.

227. Betlyon, *Coinage of Phoenicia*, pp. 14-20, 35. This hypothesis is rejected by C.M. Harrison, *op. cit.* (n. 138), p. 374.

228. A. Lemaire, 'La Transeuphratène en transition', in P. Briant and F. Joannès eds, *La transition entre l'empire achéménide et les royaumes hellénistiques (vers 350-300 av. J.-C.)*, Paris 2006, pp. 405-410, 420-422, 426; concerning the Persian period, the reference to J.D. Grainger, whose book treated of the Hellenistic period, is not relevant.

229. *Ibid.*, p. 408, n. 28: '... les dates des seizièmes de sicle ... posent souvent de difficiles problèmes de lecture'. The reference to the remarks of T. Boiy is not relevant because this author treats only of the Sidonian chronology after 333 BCE.

230. *Ibid.*, pp. 421, 426: c. 351, 349 or 346 are wrong dates. There is no accession year in the chronology of the Sidonian kings: similarly year 1 of Mazday corresponds to 353 and not 354. We take into account 333 (year 21) since Sidon surrendered to Alexander at the end of this year or at the beginning of the following year.

231. As suggested by A. Lemaire, *ibid.*, p. 421: 'La reprise en mains perse se manifesta par le fait que Mazday y frappa monnaie à côté du monnayage local du roi ᶜAbdᶜaštart/Straton, probablement un roi sidonien persophile ...'. Briant, *op. cit.* (n. 55), pp. 713-714, and 1015-1016: 'We also know that Mazaeus struck coins at Sidon and his coins continue without interruption between 343 and 333'.

232. Cf. J. Dušek, *Les manuscrits araméens du Wadi Daliyeh et la Samarie vers 450-332 av. J.-C.*, Leiden-Boston 2007 (thesis under the direction of A. Lemaire), pp. 533-534 (with bibl.). The

When this hoard will be published, the following points will need to be checked: the authenticity of the coin, the reading of number 20, the burial date of the hoard and the possibility of intrusion of the Sidonian coin, because such an interpretation seems to be impossible as we show hereafter.

Our hypothesis, first presented in 1989, was confirmed and improved in our Sidonian corpus in 2004: Mazday issued his coinage in Sidon over a 21 years period, between 353 and 333.[233] The sequence of dates attested on Mazday's coins in the present state of documentation is as follows: 1, 2, 3, 4, 5, 6, 9, 10 (possible), 11 (possible), 12 (possible), 14 (possible), 16, 17, 18, 19, 20 and 21;[234] there is a new clear attestation of 9 on a fraction published in 2006.[235] The fact that Mazday did not issue coins in certain years (7, 8, 13 and 15) does not mean an interruption of his coinage: just as with ʿAbdʿaštart II during years 4 and 8, he did not need to mint money during these years, maybe because he had enough coins from previous issues. Since years 4, 5, 6 and 9 are clearly attested, none of the preceding hypotheses can fit any longer with the sequence that we have highlighted. On the one hand, there is no place in the continuous computation of the civic Sidonian coinage between 401 and 333 for an interruption containing the 21 years of Mazday's coinage. On the other hand, the identification of some common engravers confirms that the Mazday' coinage was contemporary with the end of the ʿAbdʿaštart I's coinage, Tennes, Evagoras and ʿAbdʿaštart II's coinages from 353 to 333 BCE: the engraver no. 12 worked for the Tennes' issues of years 3 and 4 (349-348) and for the Mazday's issue of year 10 (344); the engraver no. 16 worked for the Evagoras' issues of years 1, 2, 3 and 4 (346-343) and for the Mazday's issues of years 11, 16, 17, 19 and 20 (343, 338, 337, 335, 334); the engraver no. 19 worked for the Evagoras' issue of year 4 (343) and for the Mazday's issue of year 14 (340).[236] Moreover, the die links observed on double shekels between coins with year 10 (?) and 16, years 11 (?), 16, 17 and 19, and on sixteenths of shekel inscribed 5, 9, 17 and 18 reinforce the interpretation of a continuous sequence of 21 years.[237]

It appears clearly now that the coinage of Mazday was not dated by the regnal years of the Persian kings but by the years of his government over Transeuphratene. Just as he did in his coinage issued at Tarsus, Mazday has adopted in

comments on coinage and the chronology based on it are not reliable since they are not based on the last scientific developments.

233. Elayi, *Sidon*, p. 218; Elayi-Elayi, *loc. cit.* (n. 224), pp. 155-162; *ibid.*, *Monnayage de Sidon*, pp. 660-667. Our hypothesis was followed by several authors: for example, L. Sole, 'Le emissioni monetali della Fenicia prima di Alessandro-II', *SEAP* 18, 1998, p. 115; Debord, *op. cit.* (n. 157), pp. 415-416; Le Rider, *loc. cit.* (n. 151), pp. 159-160.

234. As often as possible, we have directly examined the coins, for example no. 2040 (year 4), 2045 (year 5), 2048 (year 9).

235. Elsen, Brussels, List 236, 2006, no. 74; cf. Elayi, *loc. cit.* (n. 70), pp. 20-21.

236. Elayi-Elayi, *Monnayage de Sidon*, pp. 504-540.

237. *Ibid.*, pp. 426-429, 808-809.

Sidon the monetary uses of the local mint for civic coinage: types, standard, denominations, system of dating, and even Sidonian engravers. The only differences were the name *MZDY* written in full and not abbreviated, the *B-* before the date, the Aramaic writing of the legend (including however some features of Sidonian writing) and the use of some engravers not known from the preserved Sidonian coins. As P. Debord noticed, 'il n'y a pas d'obstacle à supposer que Mazaios a pu faire battre monnaie pour son compte à Sidon, profitant des infrastructures préexistantes, en même temps que d'autres séries étaient frappées pour les autorités locales'.[238] The objection has been raised that the dating in the Persian period followed the regnal years of the local dynasts or of the Persian kings, and that Mazday did not use a dating based on his years of government in his other monetary issues of Tarsus and Babylon. Besides the fact that the years attested on Mazday's Sidonian coins are inconsistent with any Persian computations as we have shown, dating a coinage by regnal years was unparallel at that time as Sidon had followed a Tyrian innovation. Therefore the objection is unacceptable since Mazday's dated coinage was an unprecedented situation. This Persian official, relatively well-known from classical sources and coins, was appointed by Artaxerxes III in 353 to be in charge of Transeuphratene, mainly of the city of Sidon which had revolted under ʿAbdʿaštart I. This function is known by the title inscribed on some coins of his Tarsian coinage: *MZDY ZY ʿL ʿBRNHR' WḤLK*, 'Mazday who (is) over (= in charge of) Transeuphratene and Cilicia'.[239] Brochubelus, one of his sons, was 'praetor of Syria' (*Syriae praetor*), a function impossible to be specific about but he was probably one of his father's collaborators.[240] It may be asked why Mazday had minted his coinage in Sidon. There are at least two possible reasons: he had to keep a close watchful eye on this powerful rebel city and which was possibly the capital of Transeuphratene. Mazday who was appointed to Cilicia around 360[241] was probably responsible for restoring public order in Transeuphratene,

238. Debord, *op. cit.* (n. 157), p. 416.
239. Cf. L. Mildenberg, 'Notes on the Coins Issues of Mazday', *INJ* 11, 1990-91, pp. 9-23 (= U. Hübner and E.-A. Knauf eds, *Leo Mildenberg. Vestigia Leonis. Studien zur antiken Numismatik Israels, Palästinas und der östlichen Mittelmeerwelt*, Freiburg-Göttingen 1998, p. 46); A. Lemaire, 'Remarques sur certaines légendes monétaires ciliciennes (Vᵉ-IVᵉ s. av. J.-C.)', in O. Casabonne ed., *Mécanismes et innovations monétaires dans l'Anatolie achéménide. Numismatique et Histoire*, Paris 2000, pp. 134-136; P. Briant, 'Numismatique, frappes monétaires et histoire en Asie Mineure achéménide (quelques remarques de conclusion)', *ibid.*, pp. 268-269 (who compares this title with the Egyptian title of Pherendates in his correspondence in Demotic with the authorities of the Khnûm's sanctuary in Elephantine). We do not refer to the Mazday's coin of Menbig/Hierapolis bearing the inscription *MZDY ZY ʿL ʿBR NHR'*, 'Mazday who (is) over Transeuphratene' since we have doubts about its authenticity: see J. Elayi and J. Sapin, *Quinze ans de recherche (1985-2000) sur la Transeuphratène à l'époque perse*, Paris 2000, pp. 172-175 (with bibl.); P. Briant, *Darius dans l'ombre d'Alexandre*, Paris 2003, p. 76.
240. Curt. V, 13, 11; Arr. III, 21, 1; VII, 6, 4; cf. Briant, *op. cit.* (n. 55), pp. 744, 802, 868, 1039 and 1073.
241. Cf. Harrison, *op. cit.* (n. 138), p. 351 and n. 17 (with bibl.); Debord, *op. cit.* (n. 157), p. 415; Le Rider, *loc. cit.* (n. 151), pp. 163-167.

especially after ʿAbdʿaštart I' revolt: it is possible that he first minted in Tarsus in order to prepare military operations for suppressing this revolt.[242] The identification of the capital of the satrapy of Transeuphratene is a difficult question: as we have shown, mainly Sidon but also Damascus are good candidates and possibly the capital was not always at the same place during the whole Persian period.[243]

The official title of Mazday has been much discussed, but as it has evolved, it could help to establish the chronology of his activities. As far as Phoenicia is concerned, there is an apparent problem in the account given by Diodorus: according to him, there was a first unsuccessful military expedition against the Sidonian king Tennes in revolt, led by 'Belesys, the satrap of Syria, and Mazaeus, the governor of Cilicia' (βέλεσυς ὁ τῆς Συρίας σατράπης καὶ Μαζαῖος ὁ τῆς Κιλικίας ἄρχων).[244] A.F. Rainey and C.M. Harrison literally took the title given to Mazday by Diodorus; O. Casabonne considered that the nature of his power was similar to that of his predecessors, namely that he was not satrap of Cilicia at that time; according to G. Le Rider, Mazday's power was more restricted than that of Belesys, he was appointed for a limited mission in Sidon in 354, then succeeded Belesys in Syria as the 'grand maître de la Transeuphratene et de la Cilicie'; P. Debord considered that Mazday was endowed, besides his title of satrap, with a command like Tiribazus, Pharnabazus and Datames; as for J.W. Betlyon, he wrote that perhaps Belesys ruled inland regions, and Phoenicia was attached to Cyprus and Cilicia, and that Diodorus was confusing two revolts, those of ʿAbdʿaštart I and Tennes.[245] As a matter of fact, the information given by Diodorus on the titles of Belesys and Mazday is quite questionable since, two lines later, he gave them other titles: 'the above-named satraps' (τοῖς προειρημένοις σατράπαις).[246] It can be seen from numerous examples that Greek authors had a vague idea of Persian civilian and military titles[247] and we have to say that our present knowledge concerning Maz-

---

242. According to a hypothesis of E.T. Newell, 'Myriandros-Alexandria Kat'Isson', *AJN* 53, 1919, pp. 4-5.
243. Cf. Elayi, *Sidon*, pp. 144-146; *id., Trans* 13, 1997, p. 204 (with bibl.).
244. DS. XVI, 42.1.
245. J.P. Six, 'Le satrape Mazaios', *NC* 4, 1884, pp. 97-159; A.F. Rainey, 'The Satrapy 'beyond the River'', *AJBA* 1, 1968-71, pp. 70-71; Harrison, *op. cit.* (n. 138), p. 350; O. Casabonne, 'Le syennésis cilicien et Cyrus: l'apport des sources numismatiques', in P. Briant ed., *Dans les pas des Dix-mille. Peuples et pays du Proche-Orient vus par un Grec*, Toulouse 1995, p. 165; Le Rider, *loc. cit.* (n. 151), pp. 159-160; Debord, *op. cit.* (n. 157), p. 416; Betlyon, *Coinage of Phoenicia*, pp. 14, 15, 33, n. 49 (however with a wrong dating). Cf. also O. Leuze, *Die Satrapieneinteilung in Syrien und im Zweistromlande von 520-320*, Halle 1935, pp. 234-235: according to this author, Belesys disappeared after the revolt and Mazday took in charge Transeuphratene and Cilicia. P. Desideri and A.M. Jasink, *Cilicia. Dall' età di Kizzuwatna alla conquista macedone*, Turin 1990, p. 198; J.D. Bing, 'Datames and Mazaeus: the Iconography of Revolt and Restoration in Cilicia', *Historia* 47, 1998, p. 65 and n. 72; Wiesehöfer, *loc. cit.* (n. 151), pp. 184-185 and n. 68.
246. DS. XVI, 42.2.
247. Cf., for example, Briant, *op. cit.* (n. 55), pp. 340-341 (with bibl.).

day still remains insufficient. If Mazday already controlled Sidon and Transeuphratene, as is shown from his coinage, his intervention against a revolt in this area was logically the most justified; he probably called on Belesys to help him suppress the revolt. In our opinion, Belesys, mentioned nowhere else in the ancient sources, was probably not satrap of Transeuphratene, maybe for example hyparch of 'Syria', but we do not know his exact function and his precise responsibility. However, as the chronology of Diodorus is especially fluctuating in his book XVI, as he had a tendency to compress certain events and used flashbacks to the preceding paragraph, we are inclined to think that the expedition of Belesys and Mazday was in fact an earlier expedition, launched during the revolt of ʿAbdʿaštart I around 358-356, when Mazday did not yet govern Transeuphratene.[248]

Finally, since from 355 onwards Transeuphratene was clearly under the control of Mazday, appointed by the energetic king Artaxerxes III, even if Tyre had not participated in the revolt of ʿAbdʿaštart I, she was still probably closely monitored because of her earlier troubles, as mentioned above: consequently we wonder whether the slaves' revolt could have occurred in such conditions, and whether a somewhat earlier date is not more suitable. We shall cautiously leave this question unsolved.

As we have seen above, the coinage of Group II.2 reflects an accumulation of Tyrian economic difficulties, starting with a change of standard and followed by a significant decrease in the percentage of silver in the preceding series. In similar circumstances, Sidon had chosen to devaluate her coinage of around 1.20g for the shekel,[249] while Tyre had changed the standard, which corresponds to a devaluation of around 6.50g, a much bigger change, probably because the situation of Tyre was even worse than that of Sidon at that time. The important decrease in the volume of production, still more significant than in the preceding period (91 preserved coins instead of 183 in Series II.1.2), confirms this point. Other reasons for the Tyrian change of standard could have been to facilitate trade with the areas using Attic standard, and for making the exported Tyrian shekels more attractive with a similar standard to the exported Athenian tetradrachms. The change of standard in the Tyrian coinage has been much debated for a very long while. Because the new Tyrian standard was Attic or close to the Attic, for a long time this part of the Tyrian coinage was attributed to the period following the conquest of Alexander in 332, with a very abundant literature.[250] The last series of ʿOzmilk was even attributed to Akko

---

248. Elayi, *Sidon*, p. 232, n. 163; *id.*, *ʿAbdʿaštart Iᵉʳ*, p. 137; on the fluctuating chronology of Diodorus, see, for example, P. Goukowsky, *Diodore de Sicile, Bibliothèque historique, Livre XVII*, Paris 1976, pp. XLIV-XLVIII and p. 58, n. 1.
249. Elayi-Elayi, *Monnayage de Sidon*, pp. 586-587.
250. See, for example, J.-P. Six, 'L'ère de Tyr', *NC* 3rd series VI, 1886, pp. 102-103; Babelon, *Perses*, pp. CXC-CXCI, 294-295; *id.*, *Traité* II/2, pp. 622-628; *BMC Phoenicia*, pp. cxxix-cxxxi, 231; E.T. Newell, *The Dated Alexander Coinage of Sidon and Ake*, New Haven 1916;

instead of Tyre since the letter ʿ was understood as the initial of Akko.[251] But the discovery of several hoards in Palestine containing Tyrian coins has progressively begun to lend credence that Tyre has changed her standard before the conquest of Alexander in 332. The most difficult aspect to understand was that a defeated city was still allowed to mint her own civic types under the authority of the new Macedonian ruler. The first correction to the wrong attribution of these Tyrian coins was suggested in 1939, and then developed by F.M. Cross after the discovery of the papyri of the Wadi Daliyeh, together with a hoard (TXLVIII) including two Tyrian shekels and a Sidonian fraction.[252] He refused H. Seyrig's argument founded on the supposition that the Attic standard was introduced to Phoenicia and Palestine by Alexander, because he could see pre-Alexandrine Palestinian coinage following the Attic standard. This was not the case for some Palestinian mints, for example Jerusalem, Gaza and Ashdod, which used Attic standard. Without referring to the Wadi Daliyeh discovery, P. Naster had proposed, as early as 1963, to place Group II.2 coins until year 17 of ʿOzmilk before the coming of Alexander; however, one of his arguments was wrong: he put in parallel ʿ17 (year 17 of ʿOzmilk) and G7 on Aradian coins (that he misread 17).[253] In 1975, C.M. Kraay also placed all the civic Tyrian coinage in the Persian period.[254] A. Lemaire, in 1976, re-examined this proposition and published a clear presentation of it, completed in 1991 with dated inscriptions on pottery, stamped handles and seals.[255] However, his dating of ʿOzmilk's coinage from 347/46 to 309/08, that is 15 years before the coming of Alexander and 24 years after is not totally exact and has to be updated and corrected as we shall see later on.[256]

id., *Tyrus*, pp. 15-23; Seyrig, *loc. cit.* (n. 205), pp. 93-98; and more recently O. Mørkholm, 'The Hellenistic Period', in R. Carson *et al.* eds, *A Survey of Numismatic Literature 1972-1977*, Bern 1979, p. 66; M.J. Price, 'On Attributing Alexanders – Some Cautionary Tales', in *Greek Numismatics and Archaeology, Essays in Honour of M. Thompson*, Wetteren 1979, pp. 241-246.

251. See above, Chapter III.

252. M. Narkiss, *The Coins of Palestine II. Non-Jewish Coins*, Jerusalem 1939, p. 47; F.M. Cross, 'The Discovery of the Samaria Papyri', *BA* 26, 1963, pp. 110-121; id., 'Papyri from the Fourth Century B.C. from Dâliyeh', in D.N. Freedman and J.C. Greenfield eds, Garden City, NY 1969, pp. 53-54; id., 'Coins', in Lapp-Lapp, *Wâdī ed-Dâliyeh*, pp. 53-59, followed, for example, by E. Stern, 'The Dating of Stratum II at Tell Abu Hawam', *IEJ* 18, 1968, pp. 216-217; cf. Elayi-Elayi, *Trésors*, pp. 216-218 (with bibl.).

253. P. Naster, 'Le développement des monnayages phéniciens avant Alexandre, d'après les trésors', in A. Kindler ed., *The patterns of the monetary development in Phoenicia and Palestine in Antiquity, International Numismatic Convention, Jerusalem 1963*, Jerusalem 1967, pp. 16-17, in particular 17, n. 40 (= P. Naster, *Scripta Nummaria. Contributions à la méthodologie numismatique*, Louvain-la-Neuve 1983, pp. 191-192, in particular 191, n. 2); see, for example, Elayi-Elayi, *Trésors*, pp. 24-35.

254. Kraay, *Greek Coins*, p. 290, etc.

255. A. Lemaire, 'Le monnayage de Tyr et celui dit d'Akko dans la deuxième moitié du IVᵉ siècle av. J.-C.', *RN* 18, 1976, pp. 11-24; id., *loc. cit.* (n. 209), pp. 131-150; cf. also id., *loc. cit.* (n. 228).

256. See already all our publications on Tyrian coinage, for example, Elayi-Elayi, *Trésors*, pp. 185, 216-218; id., *loc. cit.* (n. 70), pp. 24-25.

First we have to study the conclusions drawn by our numismatic analysis of Series II.2.1.14-29. These coins are dated from year 3 to year 17 of ʿOzmilk, that is from around 347 to 333/2, as we shall show. However, there were some difficulties. Since we lack evidence regarding the Tyrian system, we supposed that, as in Mesopotamia or Egypt for example, the regnal years were the same as the years of the calendar, that is each regnal year began with the new year's day. But the Phoenician (lunar) calendar is not well-known and it is uncertain whether the year began in the Spring (March/April) or in the Autumn (ʾTNM, September/October), as in the so-called 'Gezer calendar'.[257] Another question arises as to how to treat portions of years: for example, when a preceding king died with some portion of his last calendar year unfinished and a new king acceded to the throne at some point prior to the next new year's day. It was possible to count either two years (last year of the preceding king and first year of the new) or only one year as later in the case of Ptolemy XII Auletes and his daughter Cleopatra VII: 'the thirtieth year which is also the first'.[258] For the Sidonian coinage, without knowing exactly the beginning of the year and the system of transition between two reigns, we have considered that the shorter regnal years were all in all compensated by longer regnal years during this period of five reigns.[259] Another difficulty consisted in determining whether the Tyrian reckoning of regnal years followed the so-called accession-year system, mainly used for example in Assyria and Persia, in which the portion of a year from the accession of the king to the end of the then current calendar year was only named 'accession year'.[260] As we have shown,[261] the Sidonians followed the so-called non accession-year system, in which the portion of a calendar year remaining from the accession of the king to the end of the calendar year was already treated as year 1 of the new king, whether it was long or short. In the Tyrian coinage, it is less clear since in one case, the accession-year could have been represented by a letter without a number: in Series II.1.2.1.1, the inscription is first letter Z alone (name of the king?), then Z + 1 to 14. However, later, ʿOzmilk in particular may have followed the well-established Sidonian system without taking into account the accession-year. There is no way of checking this as ʿOzmilk started his coinage from year 3 but the preceding series has 1Ṣ to 4Ṣ, not Ṣ alone, which seems to be significant. Another problem is the dating of the last dated series in the Persian period as the siege of

---

257. *KAI* 182; E. Koffmahn, 'Sind die altisraelitischen Monatsbezeichnungen mit den kanaanäisch-phönikischen identisch?', *BZ* 10/2, 1966, pp. 197-219; M. Dahood, 'Some Eblaite and Phoenician Months Names', in *ACFP* I/2, Rome 1983, pp. 595-598; cf. J. Elayi, 'On Dating the Reigns of Phoenician Kings in the Persian Period', in C. Sagona ed., *Beyond the Homeland: Markers in Phoenician Chronology*, ANES, Louvain (forthcoming).
258. T.C. Sheat, 'Notes on Ptolemaic Chronology', *JEA* 46, 1960, p. 91.
259. Elayi-Elayi, *Monnayage de Sidon*, pp. 635-637.
260. Depuydt, *loc. cit.* (n. 177), pp. 193-204; Boig, *op. cit.* (n. 177), pp. 25-34.
261. Elayi-Elayi, *Monnayage de Sidon*, pp. 635-637.

Tyre lasted around seven months and ended in July/August 332 BCE.[262] It is possible that during this dramatic siege, there was no issue of coins or just a very limited issue with ʿ17. This plated coin indicated difficulties of silver supply and a mobilisation of all the metal workers to make weapons. This was true also for the year(s) preceding the siege during the Tyrians' military preparation. Consequently, taking into account the preceding observations, the exact computation of 17 years of ʿOzmilk's coinage was from 349/348 to 333/332, or in other words from around 349 to around 333.

Compared with all other Tyrian series and taking into account the length of the period of issue, Series II.2.1.14-29 is by far the most abundant: 653 shekels preserved, to which some unclassified divisionary series must be added (only 91 shekels in Series II.2.1.1-13; 102 shekels in Series II.1.2.1). In the 262 coins studied, we have identified 210 couples of dies and 102 obverse dies without counting the re-cut dies (only 48 couples of dies and 31 obverse dies in Series II.2.1.1-13). Since it was possible to know how many dies were made every year, it can be noticed that certain years were very productive: year 3 = 346 BCE (10 obverse dies), year 9 = 341 (12), year 10 = 340 (11) and mainly year 15 = 335 (17). These results are more reliable, because of the ratio, for years 3, 9 and 15. The less productive years were years 17 = 333 (1 obverse die) and 6 = 344 (2). The increase and decrease in the volume of issues are significant and connected with special events, as we shall see. The style is not skilful but less neglected than in the preceding series; however, from year 15, some kind of degradation can be observed (border of dots replacing border of guilloche, several reverse dies re-cut ...).[263] In contrast with Sidon where the exports of Sidonian coins as merchandise coins seem to have stopped from the reign of Tennes (351-348),[264] the Tyrian exports had considerably increase, mainly during the reign of ʿOzmilk. His shekels are represented in 9 hoards: TXXVI (Khirbet el-Kerak), TXXXV (Tell Abu Hawam), TXXXVI (area of Gaza), TXXXVII (Safed), TXXXVIII (Damascus), TXLVIII (Wadi Daliyeh), TLI (Naplouse), TLII (Moshav Dalton), and TLVI (area of Aleppo).[265] All these numismatic conclusions show that, during the reign of ʿOzmilk, Tyre was much more prosperous that previously. They have now to be examined in the light of the events of this period.

---

262. See, for example, F. Verkinderen, 'Les cités phéniciennes dans l'Empire d'Alexandre le Grand', in E. Lipiński ed., *Phoenicia and the East Mediterranean in the First Millennium B.C.*, Studia Phoenicia V, Leuven 1987, pp. 287-295; J.D. Grainger, *Hellenistic Phoenicia*, Oxford 1991, pp. 37-38.

263. Cf. above, Chapter V.

264. Elayi, *ʿAbdʿaštart Iᵉʳ*, p. 145; Elayi-Elayi, *Monnayage de Sidon*, p. 657.

265. Elayi-Elayi, *Trésors*, pp. 139-147, 170-191, 216-218, 231-240 and 246; for other Tyrian hoards, see also *id.*, 'Nouveaux trésors de monnaies phéniciennes (*CH* VIII)', *Trans* 11, 1996, pp. 101-112; *id.*, 'Nouveaux trésors de monnaies phéniciennes (*CH* IX)', *Trans* 26, 2003, pp. 105-117; H. Gitler and O. Tal, *The Coinage of Philistia of the Fifth and Fourth centuries BC*, Milan-New York 2006, p. 51. Cf. here below, Appendix I.

The reign of ʿOzmilk during the Persian period (about 349-332) corresponds to the reigns of three successive Persian kings: years 10 to 21 of the reign of Artaxerxes III who was murdered (349-338), the reign of Arses/Artaxerxes IV who was poisoned (August-September 338-336) and part of the reign of Darius III (336-332) who was murdered in 330. While this period was difficult for the Persian Empire because of dynastic crises, it was better for Tyre after 347, when the city was favoured by Persia as we shall see. According to some questionable Greek accounts, Artaxerxes III did not take part in military campaigns because of his cowardice but finally decided to lead the military expedition against Egypt in 351.[266] In fact, he succeeded in putting an end to the various revolts of satraps who were obliged to dismiss their mercenaries, yet Egypt was still independent. A second group of revolts arose against the Persians, initiated by Sidon according to Diodorus, who gave us a detailed but unique account of this event, so we have to remain cautious.[267] In contrast with the previous period, the revolts were no more led by Persian satraps, but by local dynasts: Phoenician cities, Cypriot cities and Egypt, the best known being the so-called revolt of Tennes. The dating of this revolt has been much debated, with propositions varying between 355 and 345.[268] Thanks to the yearly dated Sidonian coinage in addition to all other sources, the chronology of this revolt is now relatively well-established. We shall focus on the aspects of this event connected with Tyre.[269]

According to Diodorus, the starting point of the revolt was a Phoenician common council in Tripolis/ ʾTR, a city with quite a special status, in particular since it was formed by three fortified cities belonging to Sidon, Tyre and Arwad.[270] The Sidonians (or only an anti-Persian Sidonian faction) took advantage of the hegemony of their city in persuading the rest of the Phoenicians to make a bid for their independence, with at least Tyrians and Aradians being mentioned. The Cypriot kings also joined the revolt 'in imitation of the Phoenicians' (μιμησάμενοι τοὺς Φοίνικας ἀπέστησαν);[271] the Pharaoh Nectanebo

---

266. DS. XVI, 40.3-5; Isocr., *Phil.* 101; Dem., *Rhod.* 11-12.
267. DS. XVI, 40.5, 42.5, 40.33; Orose, *Histoires* III, 7.8.
268. Cf., for example, Babelon, *Traité* II/2, cols 575-578 (355-351); *PRE, s.v.* (354-350); Hill, *op. cit.* (n. 138), p. 146 (351); A.T. Olmstead, *History of the Persian Empire*, Chicago 1948, p. 435 (346); D. Barag, 'The effects of the Tennes rebellion on Palestine', *BASOR* 183, 1966, pp. 7-8 (350-345); H. Bengtson, *Griechische Geschichte von den Anfängen bis in die römische Kaiserzeit*, Munich 1969, p. 407 (before 345); J.W. Betlyon, 'A new Chronology for the Pre-Alexandrine Coinage of Sidon', *ANSMN* 21, 1976, pp. 27-30 (351-348/7 ou 345/4); *id., Coinage of Phoenicia*, pp. 16-17 (348/347); Briant, *op. cit.* (n. 55), pp. 682-684 ('It does not seem that the revolt lasted as long as from 351 to 346 ...'); Debord, *op. cit.* (n. 157), p. 416 (355); etc. The approximate date 'vers 350' given by J. Elayi, *Sidon*, pp. 182-184, has now to be corrected.
269. For a detailed comment, cf. Elayi-Elayi, *Monnayage de Sidon*, pp. 668-673.
270. DS. XVI, 41.1-3; cf. Elayi, *Cités phéniciennes*, pp. 77-81; *id.*, 'Tripoli (Liban) à l'époque perse', *Trans* 2, 1990, pp. 59-71; J. Elayi and A.G. Elayi, 'La première monnaie de ʾTR/Tripolis (Tripoli, Liban)?', *Trans* 5, 1992, pp. 143-151.
271. DS. XVI, 42.5.

who had defeated the Persians in 351 made an agreement of συμμαχία with the Sidonians.[272] Diodorus described then the important preparations for the war of the Sidonians: many war-galleys, mercenaries, weapons, etc.[273] They probably took advantage of the preparations made for the next Persian campaign against Egypt.[274] Even if the Tyrians and Aradians were not mentioned, we can assume that they also participated, even if to a lesser extent, in these preparations as this was usually the case in the service of the Persians. The first act of revolt occurred in Sidon[275] but the Tyrians and Aradians were probably implicated as Artaxerxes 'being apprised of the rash acts of the insurgents, issued threatening warnings to all the Phoenicians and in particular to the people of Sidon'.[276] The *Philip* of Isocrates, written in 347, mentioned the revolts in progress in Cyprus, Phoenicia and Cilicia: 'either they have abandoned (the Persian king) or they are overcome by such misfortunes that he could not get anything from these peoples' (νῦν δὲ τὰ ἀφέστηκεν τὰ δ'ἐν πολέμῳ καὶ κακοῖς τοσούτοις ἐστὶν ὥστ' ἐκείνῳ μὲν μηδὲν εἶναι τούτων τῶν ἐθνῶν χρήσιμον).[277] The first reason for this revolt was, according to Diodorus, the failure of the Persian campaign against Egypt in 351: 'the Phoenicians and the kings of Cyprus had imitated the Egyptians' (τῶν Φοινίκων καὶ τῶν ἐν Κύπρῳ βασιλέων μιμησαμένων τοὺς Αἰγυπτίους).[278] Another reason was the unbearably presence for him of the Persian satraps and generals residing in Sidon.[279] However, this reason is also true for Tyre because the Tyrian territory was used for establishing Persian bases like Akko against Egypt, very close to Tyre. We have analysed in detail the course of the revolt of Sidon, the role of Tennes, the role of other representative organisms, the burning of the fleet by the Sidonians themselves and the seizure of the city after Tennes' betrayal.[280]

Diodorus gave only a few indications about other Phoenician cities involved in the revolt. According to his presentation, it seems that Artaxerxes III decided to concentrate his action against Sidon from the beginning, since 'he encamped not far from Sidon'.[281] Then 'his aim was to overwhelm the Sidonians with a merciless disaster and to strike terror into the other cities by their punishment'.[282] He achieved his aim: 'so the disasters which had overtaken Sidon had

272. *Ibid.*, 41.3.
273. *Ibid.* 41.4-5; 42.2; 44.6.
274. Briant, *op. cit.* (n. 55), p. 487; Elayi-Elayi, *Monnayage de Sidon*, pp. 667-676.
275. C. Clermont-Ganneau, 'Le paradeisos royal achéménide de Sidon', *RB* 30, 1921, pp. 107-108.
276. DS. XVI, 41.6.
277. Isocr., *Phil.* V, 102 and pp. 7-8: it was written in 347 and completed in the spring or at the beginning of the summer of 346; cf. S. Perlman, 'Isocrates, Philippus: a Reinterpretation', *Hist.* 6, 1957, p. 306, n. 1.
278. DS. XVI, 40.5. Cf. also C. Mossé, in Will *et al.*, *op. cit.* (n. 150), p. 68.
279. DS. XVI, 41.2.
280. Cf. Elayi-Elayi, *Monnayage de Sidon*, pp. 670-673 (with bibl.).
281. DS. XVI, 44.4-5.
282. *Ibid.*, 45.2.

such an ending, and the rest of the cities, panic-stricken, went over to the Persians'.[283] Based on Diodorus' account which is our only source, Tyre surrendered to Artaxerxes III immediately after the suppression of the Sidonian revolt. Since we know from the Sidonian yearly dated coinage that the revolt was suppressed and Tennes put to death in his year 5, his last year which is 347, we can assume that Tyre also surrendered around 347.[284] The date of 345 for the suppression of the revolt comes from a wrong datation of the Babylonian tablet mentioning Sidonian prisoners.[285] But since this date does not fit with his computation of the reign of ʿOzmilk, A. Lemaire had changed Diodorus' account,[286] supposing that the Tyrians surrendered before Sidon in 347/346;[287] he had yet to find another place for years 16 and 17 of ʿOzmilk, which do not sit within the remaining Persian period. In consequence, he dated year 16 from 332/31 and year 17 from 331/30, giving the following explanations: ʿ16 is only attested by the misreading of one coin by J. Rouvier and the coin with ʿ17 is plated, 'small' civic coins were still issued in parallel with Alexander's tetradrachms, and the same phenomenon can be observed in Tarsus, Arwad and Byblos.[288] All these explanations are groundless: as we have shown, the Babylonian tablet dates from 355 and not 345; there is no need to correct Diodorus' account as we shall see; year 16 is clearly attested by 11 coins; the plated coin with year 17 is explained by the very difficult context; Tyrian shekels were important denominations since during this period they were largely exported as merchandise coins; as far as we know, the civic Sidonian, Aradian and Byblian coinages did not continue after the coming of Alexander.[289] Based on the discoveries of the Wadi Daliyeh where the last two papyri are dated from 18 March 335 (WDSP 1) and from between 355 and 332 (WDSP 36, frg. 1,1), and

---

283. *Ibid.*, 45.6. Artaxerxes probably also wanted to put down the Sidonian political system that he considered responsible for the revolt (execution of the 'hundred', then of the 'five hundreds' representative citizens). He did not intend to destroy his best naval base, but to change the institutions of Sidon in order to obtain her complete submission. Cf. D. Agut-Labordère, 'Les frontières intérieures de la société militaire égyptienne: l'invasion de l'Egypte par Artaxerxès III à travers Diodore XVI, 46-45', in *VIIe Colloque International, La Transeuphratène à l'époque perse: Frontières et courants d'échanges culturels*, Paris 22-24 mars 2007 (to be published in *Trans* 35, 2007).

284. Concerning the relation of the revolt of Cypriot cities with the Sidonian revolt, cf. Elayi-Elayi, *Monnayage de Sidon*, pp. 674-675 (with bibl.). This revolt was probably suppressed just after the Sidonian one, that is in 346.

285. See here above, in this chapter. A wrong datation is given by A. Lemaire, *loc. cit.* (n. 209), p. 255, and P. Briant, *op. cit.* (n. 55), pp. 683-685.

286. DS. XV, 44-45 (351/0).

287. Lemaire, *loc. cit.* (n. 209), p. 145.

288. *Id.*, *loc. cit.* (n. 255), pp. 22-23.

289. Cf. Elayi-Elayi, *Monnayage de Sidon*, p. 687; J. Elayi, 'Gerashtart, King of the Phoenician City of Arwad in the 4th cent. BC', *NC* (in press); J. Elayi and A.G. Elayi, *The Coinage of the Phoenician City of Byblos in the Persian Period (Vth-IVth cent. BCE)* (in preparation). For a different view, cf. G. Le Rider, 'Histoire économique de l'Orient hellénistique', *Annuaire du Collège de France*, 1995-1996, pp. 841-844.

since the siege of Tyre ended in 332, F.M. Cross reasonably proposed to date the Tyrian coins with ʿ15 from around 334,[290] which A. Lemaire does not accept.[291]

In our computation, it is important to point out that year 3 of ʿOzmilk corresponds to 347 (or 346), that is to say the end of the Sidonian revolt, and that this king inaugurated his coinage with quite a large volume of production. On the other hand, even if Tyre had taken part in this revolt to some extent, she surrendered immediately in 347, there is no information concerning Persian reprisals against her, and her king ʿOzmilk who ascended to the throne around 349 was not deposed. Moreover classical sources seem to suggest that Tyre had recuperated some lands taken from Sidon. Curtius mentions that Alexander granted a favour to the new king of Sidon ʿAbdalonym/Abdalonymus: 'he also added to his authority the area adjacent to the city' (*regionem quoque urbi adpositum dicioni eius adiecit*).[292] This area was probably not Dor and Jaffa, which were separated from the main Sidonian agglomeration by the territory of Tyre.[293] But it could be Sarepta/Sarafand, a town situated about 14km from Sidon and 25km from Tyre. This town successively belonged to the two cities: in the Persian period, it seems to have belonged to Sidon. But Sidon lost her because the *Periplus* of Pseudo-Scylax, dated from 338-335/4, mentioned that she belonged to Tyre, which is confirmed by the seal inscribed ʿŠR/ṢRPT/ʿ12, 'tithe (of) Sarepta, (year) 12 of ʿO(zmilk)', probably dated from year 12 of ʿOzmilk, that is 338/7, and by a difficult verse of Obadiah.[294] It was usual, in the neo-Assyrian and neo-Babylonian empires just as in the Persian Empire, that the rivalry between Tyre and Sidon was used as a mean of control over the two cities: when one of them became too powerful, the central power favoured the other one and vice versa.[295] The entire context could explain why ʿOzmilk

290. F.M. Cross, in Lapp-Lapp, *Wâdi Ed-Daliyeh*, p. 58; cf. D.M. Gropp, *Wadi Daliyeh II. The Samaria Papyri from Wadi Daliyeh*, DJD 28, Oxford 2001, pp. 1-116.

291. Lemaire, *loc. cit.* (n. 255), p. 21; J. Dušek, *op. cit.* (n. 232), p. 445, does not take up a position on it ('the period between 335 and 332').

292. Curt. IV, 1.26. Cf. Barag, *loc. cit.* (n. 268), p. 8, n. 8; E. Stern, 'The Dor Province in the Persian Period in the Light of the Recent Excavations at Dor', *Trans* 2, 1990, p. 154; A. Lemaire, 'Populations et territoires de la Palestine à l'époque perse', *Trans* 3, 1990, pp. 58-59. On the value of Curtius' testimony, cf., for example, J.E. Atkinson, *A Commentary on Q. Curtius Rufus' Historiae Alexandri Magni, Books 3 and 4*, Amsterdam 1980; P. Moore, *Quintus Curtius Rufus' 'Historia Alexandri Magni': A Study in Rhetorical historiography*, Oxford 1995; D. Spencer, *The Roman of Alexander: Studies in Curtius Rufus*, Cambridge 1997; E. Baynham, *Alexander the Great. The unique history of Quintus Curtius*, Ann Arbor 1998.

293. Cf. F. Verkinderen, *loc. cit.* (n. 262), pp. 306-307, who does not take up a position. According to the Lemaire's interpretation of an unpublished tithe seal, Sippori/Sephoris in Western Galilee belonged to Tyre at that time: *loc. cit.* (n. 228), pp. 423-424.

294. Ps.-Scyl., *Periplus* 104; J.B. Pritchard, *Sarepta. A preliminary Report on the Iron Age*, Philadelphia 1975, pp. 97-98; Lemaire *loc. cit.* (n. 255) 1991, pp. 140-141; *Ab* 20; J.D. Watts, *Obadiah. A critic exegetical Commentary*, Grand Rapids 1969, p. 19. Cf. Elayi, *Sidon*, pp. 88-92.

295. Cf. J. Elayi, 'Les cités phéniciennes entre liberté et sujétion', *DHA* 16, 1990, pp. 93-113; *id.*, 'La domination perse sur les cités phéniciennes', in *ACFP* II/1, Rome 1991, pp. 77-85.

started to mint a very abundant coinage, relatively speaking, and significantly increased the exports of coins: Tyre recovered her prosperity to the detriment of her rival Sidon.[296] ʿOzmilk did not mint coins in his years 1 and 2, maybe not because he was not allowed to do so by the Persian king,[297] but because there was sufficient currency in circulation.

After having violently suppressed the Sidonian revolt around 347, Artaxerxes III ordered Idrieus, satrap of Caria, to send against the Cypriots a fleet of 40 war-galleys carrying infantry troops, led by the Athenian Phocion and Evagoras II, the previous king of Salamis. The Persian troops concentrated in front of Salamis in order to frighten the Cypriot kings who probably surrendered in 347 or 346: while Tennes had been put to death, Pnytagoras of Salamis was allowed on to the throne.[298] It is possible that the king ʿʿ placed on the throne of Sidon in 346 was Evagoras II, a friend of the Persian king.[299] During his reign (346-343), the coinage issued by Mazday in Sidon was very limited, which could mean that Mazday was still in place but that Artaxerxes III controlled the situation directly through Evagoras II. It is uncertain whether the Tyrians took part in this Cypriot expedition since they had just surrendered to Artaxerxes.

Diodorus put the re-conquest of Egypt in his account together with the suppression of the Sidonian and Cypriot revolts. However, the Egypt campaign occurred later even if military preparation possibly started as from 346. According to Diodorus, the Sidonians expelled Evagoras II in 343, probably because he was a foreign pro-Persian king who 'misgoverned their city' (κακῶς δὲ τὰ κατὰ τὴν ἀρχὴνδιοικησάς),[300] possibly taking advantage of the fact that the Persians were engaged in the campaign of Egypt. Evagoras II was obliged to rush to Cyprus again where he was 'arrested and paid the penalty', probably because the anti-Persian movement had increased in the island. It is surprising that Artaxerxes waited four years after the suppression of the Sidonian and Cypriot revolts. He had probably decided this time to succeed and to take the necessary time to assemble a sufficient number of troops. Even if the overwhelming superiority of the number of Persian troops was a *topos* in Diodorus' account, it was probably partly true: Nectanebo had 20,000 Greek mercenaries, 20,000 Libyans, 60,000 Egyptian 'warriors' (μαχίμοι) and an incredible number of 'river-boats' (πλοῖα ποτάμια).[301] Artaxerxes had gathered 300,000 foot soldiers (among them a contingent of 4,000 soldiers commanded by Mentor, previously in the service of Tennes), 30,000 horsemen, 300 war-galleys and

---

296. *Id.*, *ʿAbdʿaštart I*ʳ, pp. 125-147.
297. As stated by J.W. Betlyon, *Coinage of Phoenicia*, p. 58.
298. DS. XV, 42.6-9, 45.6; cf. Debord, *op. cit.* (n. 157), p. 401; Elayi-Elayi, *Monnayage de Sidon*, pp. 674-675.
299. Elayi-Elayi, *ibid.*, pp. 677-679.
300. DS. XVI, 43.3.
301. *Ibid.*, 47.6.

500 additional transport ships.[302] The Tyrian and Aradian fleets probably took part in this expedition but to obtain such a total of 300 war-galleys (compared with the 40 ships sent to Cyprus in 346),[303] the Sidonian fleet was surely included. It means that the Persian king had to wait until the Sidonians had repaired and rebuilt their fleet which had been destroyed in 347. Even if the chronology of Diodorus is not exact, he did point out to the length of the military preparations, which was true.[304] Part of them probably took place in the territory of Tyre, in particular in Akko, the nearest important harbour to Egypt. The last campaign of Egypt started before the end of 343 and Artaxerxes seized Memphis in the Summer of 342, not in 345/4.[305] With the conquest of Egypt after several failures, Artaxerxes had attained all his objectives and reinforced his power and prestige. According to Diodorus, there were only a few limited troubles in Asia Minor, and Mentor was appointed in order to suppress them, for example the revolt of Hermeias, tyrant of Atarneus.[306] However, it is uncertain whether Phoenician fleets, in particular Tyrian, were used for maintaining order among local rulers. From this period began the first diplomatic and military reports between Artaxerxes and Philip II, with in particular the exile of Artabazus by Philip, then his return to Persia and the Perinthus affair.[307]

Sources are lacunary concerning the short reign of Arses/Artaxerxes IV (338-336). On the Greek side, the main events were the victory of Chaeronea carried off by Philip against the Thebans in 338 and the foundation of the Corinthian confederacy, of which he was the leader (ἡγεμών). We have to mention here the mysterious episode of Khabbabash, related in Egyptian hieroglyphs on the so-called 'Satrap stela', dated from 312/311. According to some authors, the mention of 'Xerxes' designated Artaxerxes III or Artaxerxes IV so that Khabbabash would have reigned as a pharaoh between about 342-338; according to others, 'Xerxes' designated any of the Persian kings so that Khabbabash would have reigned between 338 and 336.[308] It is related that Khabbabash went

302. *Ibid.*, 40.6, 42.2, 47.4.
303. *Ibid.*, 42.7.
304. *Ibid.*, 46.7.
305. Cf. G.L. Cawkwell, 'Demosthenes' policy after peace of Philocrates I', *CQ* 13, 1963, pp. 136-138; E.J. Bickerman, 'Notes sur la chronologie de la XXXe dynastie', in *Mélanges Maspéro* I, Cairo 1934, pp. 77-82; A.B. Lloyd, 'Manetho and the thirty-first dynasty', in J. Baines *et al.* eds, *Pyramid Studies and Essays presented to I.E.S. Edwards*, London 1988, pp. 154-160; *contra* M. Sordi, *Kokalos* 5, 1959, p. 107.
306. DS. XVI, 52.3-52-8; cf. S. Ruzicka, *Politics of a Persian Dynasty: the Hecatomnids in the Fourth Century*, London 1992, pp. 120-122.
307. Cf. Briant, *op. cit.* (n. 55), pp. 688-690 (with bibl.); M. Brosius, 'Why Persia became the enemy of Macedon', in Henkelman-Kuhrt eds, *op. cit.* (n. 151), p. 237.
308. Cf. A. Spalinger, 'The Reign of King Chabbash: An Interpretation', *ZÄS* 105, 1978, pp. 142-154; R.K. Ritner, 'Khabbabash and the Satrap stela: a grammatical rejoinder', *ZÄS* 107, 1980, pp. 135-137; H. Goedicke, 'Comments of the Satrap Stela', *BES* 6, 1985, pp. 33-54; W. Huss, 'Der Rätselhäfte Pharao Chababasch', *SEL* 11, 1994, pp. 97-112; Briant, *op. cit.* (n. 55), pp. 717-718 and 1017-1018 (with bibl.); D. Devauchelle, 'Réflexions sur les documents égyptiens datés de la deuxième domination perse', *Trans* 10, 1995, pp. 35-43; S. Burstein, 'Prelude to Alexander: the

to the marshes of the Delta, 'inspecting all the branches of the Nile flowing into the Mediterranean in order to repel the *kbnt*-ships of Asian people out of Egypt'.[309] This means threat or attack by a Persian fleet coming from the Syro-Phoenician coast. However, we have no information about this Persian expedition sent towards Egypt in order to suppress the revolt of this pharaoh who is not mentioned elsewhere. Anyway, this event possibly occurred during the reign of ʿOzmilk. After the participation of Tyre in the Persian conquest of Egypt in 342, she possibly also took part in this expedition against Khabbabash due to her proximity from the Delta.

What we do know of Tyre during the short reign of Darius III[310] is her place in the Persian military preparations against Alexander and the conquest of the city by the Macedonian king. In 336, the Macedonians carried out the first offensive by sending an expedition to Asia Minor lead by Parmenion, Attalus and Amyntas, in order to prepare the landing for the royal army:[311] although we lack information about this expedition, it seems to have been disadvantageous for the Persians. Alexander then acceded to the throne after Philip II's murder and sent a new expedition to Asia Minor, lead by Hecataeus. According to Diodorus, Darius understood how dangerous Alexander was and reacted 'by fitting out a large number of ships of war and assembling numerous strong armies, choosing at the same time his best commanders, among whom was Memnon of Rhodes' (τριήρεις τε πολλὰς κατασκευαζόμενος καὶ πολλὰς δυνάμεις ἀξιολόγους συνιστάμενος, ἡγεμόνας τε τοὺς ἀρίστους προκρίνων, ἐν οἷς ὑπῆρχε καὶ Μέμνων ὁ Ῥόδιος).[312] It is very likely that the Phoenician fleets were part of the fleet fitted out by Darius. At that time Phoenician cities still occupied an exceptional place in the strategic Persian system as the prime location for recruiting seamen, having dockyards and a reserve of wood in the neighbouring Mount Lebanon, as Arrian wrote: 'the fleet which was the best and the most powerful in the Persian fleet was that of the Phoenicians' (τὸ ναυτικὸν ὅπερ πλεῖστόν τε καὶ κράτιστον τοῦ Περσικοῦ, τὸ Φοινίκων).[313]

---

reign of Khababash', *AHB* 14, 2000, pp. 149-154; E. Badian, 'Darius III', *HSCIPh* 100, 2000, pp. 241-268; Briant, *op. cit.* (n. 239), pp. 67-69 and 563; D. Schäfer, 'Persian foes, Ptolemaic friends? The Persians on the Satrap Stela and in contemporary texts', in *Organisation des pouvoirs et contacts culturels dans les pays de l'empire achéménide*, Colloque Collège de France, Paris, 9-10 Nov. 2007.

309. On the *kbnt*-ships; cf. A.B. Lloyd, 'Triremes and the Saite navy', *JEA* 58, 1972, pp. 268-279; *id.*, 'Were Necho's Triremes Phoenician?', *JHS* 95, 1975, pp. 45-61; Spalinger, *ibid.*, p. 149 and n. 42; J.C. Darnell, 'The *Kbnt.wt* ships of the late period', in J.H. Johnson ed., *Life in a Multicultural Society. Egypt from Cambyses to Constantine and beyond*, Chicago 1992, pp. 67-89.

310. For the historiography of this reign, cf. Briant, *op. cit.* (n. 239); cf. also R.J. van der Spek, 'Darius III, Alexander the Great and Babylonian Scholarship', in Henkelman-Kuhrt eds, *op. cit.* (n. 151), pp. 289-346.

311. DS. XVI, 91.2; Just. IX.

312. *Ibid.*, XVII, 7.2.

313. Arr., *An.* II, 17.3; on the value of Arrian's testimony see, for example, P.A. Stadter, *Arrian of Nicomedia*, Chapel Hill 1980; A.B. Bosworth, *From Arrian to Alexander. Studies in*

Therefore, the substantial preparations of the Persian fleet and army by Darius III from 335 could explain the large volume of Tyrian shekels dated from year 15 of ʿOzmilk (335/4) for paying expenses and having to face up to financial difficulties, resulting in a small decrease in the silver content and plated coins, noticeable in some coins of year 15 and 17, the last one probably minted during the siege (333 or 332). At the beginning of the Spring of 334, Alexander departed with his army toward Hellespont and crossed it without the Persians trying to prevent the Macedonian landing. The reasons why the Persians did not intervene have been much questioned: Diodorus gave the usual explanations such as the slowness of Persian army, the absence of strategy (they would not have imagined a Macedonian landing);[314] the surprise effect has also been given as an explanation.[315] Such an absence of the Persian fleet is not easy to understand because, a few weeks later when Alexander was in Miletus, this fleet arrived, comprising 400 war-galleys, equipped with well-trained crews, coming in particular from Phoenicia and Cyprus, in contrast with the Alexander's fleet which at that time consisted of only 100 triremes and transport ships.[316] This surprising absence has also been explained by the fact that it was occupied at that time by the revolt of Khabbabash in Egypt: however this hypothesis has to be confirmed from a chronological point of view.[317] The Persian defeat at the Granicus in 334 was followed by a series of impressive victories carried off by Alexander in Asia Minor, for example the seizure of Miletus by the Macedonian fleet under the command of Nikanor before the coming of the Persian fleet,[318] and finally the seizure of Sardis.

However, Darius kept the hegemony at sea by far, all the more so Alexander had dismissed his fleet in Miletus except for the Athenian squadron and some transport ships. In the Summer of 334 BCE, Darius appointed Memnon as 'commander of Lower Asia (coastal area) and of the whole fleet' (τῆς τε κάτω Ἀσίας καὶ τοῦ ναυτικοῦ παντὸς ἡγεμών).[319] According to Arrian, Alexander knew that he was inferior at sea, but he had no more money and 'on the other hand he considered that from then on Asia was in his power thanks to his army, that he no longer needed a fleet and that by seizing the coastal cities, he would get rid of the Persian fleet, having no further need to recruit its crews nor to carry out a landing in Asia' (ἄλλως τε ἐπενόει, κατέχων ἤδη τῷ πεζῷ τὴν Ἀσίαν, ὅτι οὔτε ναυτικοῦ ἔτι δέοιτο, τάς τε παραλίους πόλεις λαβὼν

---

historical interpretation, Oxford 1988; H. Tonnet, *Recherches sur Arrien, sa personnalité et ses écrits atticistes* I-II, Amsterdam 1988; F. Sisti, *Arriano, Anabasi di Alessandro* I, Florence 2001.

314. DS. XVII, 18.2, 4.

315. E. Grzybek, *Du calendrier macédonien au calendrier ptolémaïque. Problèmes de chronologie hellénistique*, Basel 1990, pp. 61-66. Cf. bibl. on different hypotheses in Briant, *op. cit.* (n. 55), p. 1043.

316. Arr., *An.* I, 11.6, 18.5-8; II, 13.7, 18.4.

317. E.A. Anson, 'The Persian fleet in 334', *CP* 84, 1989, pp. 44-49.

318. Arr., *An.* I, 18.3-9, 19; DS. XVII, 22.2-4.

319. Arr., *ibid.*, 20.3; II, 1.1; DS. *ibid.*, 23.5-6.

καταλύσει τὸ Περσῶν ναυτικόν, οὔτε ὁπόθεν τὰς ὑπηρεσίας συμπληρώσουσιν οὔτε ὅποι τῆς Ἀσίας προσέξουσιν ἔχοντας).[320] Such a plan was very risky as it could be countered in Asia Minor where the Persians controlled several Lycian and Carian harbours, the island of Kos from where Memnon had set sail, etc.: Alexander realised the situation in 333 and decided to assemble a new military fleet.[321] In the Summer of 333, Darius had left Babylon at the head of the royal army and was in Syria when he heard about the death of Memnon in Mytilene. According to Diodorus, Memnon had planned to send the Persian fleet and army to Macedonia in order to transfer the war to Europe and his death was very damaging to the Persian forces. But his point of view was partial and he used to attribute the Persian deeds to the Greek commanders in their service.[322] Darius replaced Memnon with Pharnabazus and Autophradates who recaptured Mytilene. In spite of some failures, the Persian fleet retained its superiority. It seems that Darius, fully conscious of how dangerous the Macedonian offensive was, had developed a double strategy, both on sea and on land: while Pharnabazus and Autophradates would re-conquer the coastland of Asia Minor, he himself would confront the Macedonian army. As for Alexander, he continued to move southwards with the intention of seizing the Phoenician cities before penetrating inland: he could realise his project after his victory gained in Issos in November 333.

If we can trust classical sources, which are our only sources on the subject, the various reactions of the Phoenician cities facing Alexander are very informative. All the authors have contrasted the resistance of Tyre with the submission of the other Phoenician cities, Plutarch mentioning their spontaneous submission[323] and Diodorus their warm welcome: 'as he came into Phoenicia, he received the submission of all the other cities, for their inhabitants accepted him willingly' (καταντήσας εἰς τὴν Φοινίκην τὰς μὲν ἄλλας πόλεις παρέλαβεν, ἑτοίμως τῶν ἐγχωρίων προσδεξαμένων αὐτόν).[324] Arrian's account is more precise that those of the authors of the 'Vulgate': he mentioned the spontaneous submission of Byblos but no more than that, and the enthusiastic welcome of Arwad and Sidon ('the Sidonians having themselves invited him as they loathed the Persians and Darius' (αὐτῶν Σιδωνίων ἐπικαλεσαμένων κατὰ ἔχθος τῶν Περσῶν καὶ Δαρείου).[325] According to Curtius, Straton 'had surrendered more at the desire of the people than on his own accord' (*deditionem magis popularium quam sua sponte fecerat*); it is not known whether there was a pro-Greek faction in Sidon at that time but at all events the hostility of the

---

320. Arr., *ibid.*, 20.1; cf. also I, 18.6-8; DS. XVII, 23.1-3.
321. Curt. III, 1.19-20.
322. DS. XVII, 18.2-4; cf. Briant, *op. cit.* (n. 55), pp. 817-818 (with bibl.); in fact, Memnon's first aim was probably to recapture the Macedonian conquests in Achaemenid territories.
323. Plut., *Alex.* XXIV, 4.
324. DS. XVII, 40.2; Curt. IV, 2.1, who does not give any precision.
325. Arr., *An.* II, 13.7; 15.6

Sidonians towards the Persians was so great that it was sufficient to explain their attitude.[326]

Three classical authors have written full accounts of Alexander's siege of Tyre. The account of Arrian, a Greek born in Nicomedia in A.D. 96, is the most detailed and consistent; he based it on two authorities, contemporaries of Alexander whom they served as generals: Aristobulus and Ptolemaeus (later Ptolemaeus I). According to Arrian, 'since Alexander was dead when they both wrote their histories, there lay on them neither any constraint nor any hope of gain in writing other than plain fact'.[327] Diodorus is less reliable because he is less rigorous and used mainly the *History of Alexander* by Cleitarchus of Alexandria, whose aim was to glorify Alexander in his own fashion, with a rich Greek tradition which is lacking in Arrian's account.[328] Plutarch, in his *Life of Alexander*, used every kind of material, good and bad;[329] however, his testimony can be accepted when it corroborates those of Arrian and Diodorus. According to classical sources, while the king of Tyre was at sea with the Persian fleet, the city was prepared to make a nominal submission and sent out from Tyre a delegation of the king's son and noblemen to meet Alexander.[330] The Macedonian king bade the envoys to tell the Tyrians that he proposed to come to Tyre and offer a sacrifice to Heracles (Milqart). The Tyrians understood that Alexander intended to occupy their city and they answered him saying that there was a temple of Heracles on the mainland in Palaetyrus and he could properly offer a sacrifice to the god there. Alexander got angry and said:

---

326. Curt. IV, 1. Cf. Elayi, *Sidon*, pp. 185-186.

327. Arr., *An.* I, Preface 1-2. On this author, cf., for example, A.B. Bosworth, *A historian commentary on Arrian's history of Alexander* I, Oxford 1980, pp. 226-256. On Aristobulus, cf. Stadter, *op. cit.* (n. 113), pp. 695 sqq. On Ptolemaeus, cf. P.A. Brunt, 'Persian accounts of Alexander's campaigns', *CQ* 12, 1962, p. 153 and n. 3; A.B. Bosworth, 'Arrian and the Alexander Vulgate', in *Alexandre le Grand: image et réalité, Entretiens Hardt* 22, Geneva 1976, pp. 16-23 (Omissions and exaggerations would come from Ptolemaeus); P.A. Brunt, *Arrian, Anabasis Alexandri, Books I-IV*, London 1976, pp. XVI-XXXIV; P. Vidal-Naquet, 'Flavius Arrien entre deux mondes', in P. Savinel, *Arrien. Histoire d'Alexandre, L'anabase d'Alexandre le Grand*, Paris 1984, pp. 311-394.

328. W.W. Tarn, *Alexander the Great II, Sources and Studies*, Cambridge 1950, p. 78 (Diodorus would have used late technical books); L. Pearson, *The lost histories of Alexander the Great*, New York 1960, pp. 238 sqq.; P. Goukowsky, *Diodore de Sicile, Livre XVII*, Paris 1976, pp. XIV-XXXI; Bosworth, *op. cit.* (n. 327), p. 251; N.G.L. Hammond, *Three historians of Alexander the Great*, Cambridge 1983, pp. 42-82 (on p. 3, he refuses the term 'Vulgate' because Diodorus and Curtius used several sources).

329. On the value of Plutarch's testimony, see more recently Duff, *op. cit.* (n. 53); Pelling, *op. cit.* (n. 53). On other sources, see H. Bardon, *Quinte-Curce, Histoires I*, Paris 1947, pp. VII-X; Pearson, *ibid.*, pp. 56, 238; Hammond, *ibid.*, pp. 42-43, 49, 51, 53, 79, 98-99, 113, 118-127; L. Santi Amantini, *Storie Filippiche, Epitome da Pompeo Trogo*, Milan 1981, pp. 39-49; W. Rutz, 'Zur Erzählungskunst des Quintus Rufus, die Belagerung von Tyrus', *Hermes* 93, 1965, p. 382.

330. On the various Tyrian institutions mentioned in these accounts, cf. Elayi, *Cités phéniciennes*, pp. 48-50.

'Therefore I want you to know that either I will enter your city or besiege it' (*proinde sciatis licet, aut intraturum me urbem, aut oppugnaturum*).[331]

Tyre's resistance to Alexander has been explained by several reasons. One of them given by classical authors was the desire for independence: 'Tyre, famous among all the cities of Syria and Phoenicia because of her extent and fame, seemed to be more prepared to consider Alexander as an ally rather than a master' (*Tyrus, et claritate et magnitudine ante omnes urbes Syriae Phoenicesque memorabilis, facilius societatem Alexandri acceptura videbatur, quam imperium*).[332] Tyre refused the sacrifice of Alexander inside the island as a symbol of vassalage, since she wanted to keep a kind of neutrality for the island following tradition.[333] The Tyrians were confident in their strength as Arrian stressed: 'The city was an island, and strengthened all around with high walls; moreover, any movements from the seaward side were in the Tyrian's favour, as the Persians were still supreme at sea and the Tyrians had plenty of ships left'.[334] Moreover they were encouraged to endure the siege by the presence of a Carthaginian delegation which arrived in Tyre to celebrate the annual festival, since they relied on the possible help of the strong Carthaginian fleet.[335] Caution could be another reason to refuse access to the city: it seemed to be the safest course due to the uncertain outcome of Alexander's war with Darius.[336] According to Diodorus, the Tyrians wanted to remain loyal to the Persian king: they would draw Alexander into a long and difficult siege in order to give Darius time to make military preparations.[337] Darius himself had possibly encouraged the Tyrians to resist against Alexander.[338] As a matter of fact, it was in the interest of the Tyrians to remain on the side of the Persians because, from 347 onwards, they had been ranked by the Persians as the prime city ahead of Sidon as we have shown. If the Persians were defeated by Alexander, Tyre would fall back to become a second rank Phoenician city, behind Sidon. Therefore the Tyrian pro-Persian position, in contrast to Sidon and the other Phoenician cities, can easily be understood. Some authors even state that Tyre could obtain, in the event of a Persian victory, even higher status from Darius such as full independence.[339] The usual rivalry between Tyre and Sidon is expressed here by the fact that the Sidonian fleet helped Alexander to seize Tyre; however, according to Curtius, the Sidonians then remembered their

---

331. Curt. IV, 2.5.
332. *Ibid.*, 2.2.
333. Cf. Verkinderen, *loc. cit.* (n. 262), p. 296 and n. 50.
334. Arr., *An.* II, 18.1-2; Curt. IV, 2.7-8.
335. DS. XX, 14.1-2; cf. J. Elayi, 'The relations between Tyre and Carthage during the Persian Period', *JANES* 13, 1981, pp. 15-29. The way Carthage had abandonned Tyre was probably explained by a crisis between the two cities at that time.
336. See, for example, Jidejian, *op. cit.* (n. 182), p. 70.
337. DS. XVII, 40.3.
338. Cf. Briant, *op. cit.* (n. 239), p. 76.
339. Cf. Verkinderen, *loc. cit.* (n. 262), p. 295 (with bibl.).

bonds with the Tyrians and secretly rescued 15,000 of them.[340] Two other reasons are given by some authors: the first one is the wish to save the democratic revolution established by the slaves' revolt as according to Justin, Alexander would have suppressed the consequences of this revolt.[341] The second one, unlikely, is that Tyre was not so Hellenized as Sidon at that time and therefore not favourable to Greek dominion.[342]

The aim of Alexander in the siege of Tyre was to maintain his reputation as an undefeated conqueror and above all to assemble all the Phoenician fleets before penetrating far inland so that the Persians meanwhile could not transfer the war into Greece.[343] It is interesting to examine the different movements of the Phoenician fleets after Alexander's arrival. According to Arrian, 'at that time, Gerostratus king of Aradus and Enylus king of Byblos, when they heard that Alexander had seized their cities, left Autophradates and his fleet and joined Alexander with their fleets and the triremes of the Sidonians (αἱ τῶν Σιδωνίων τριήρεις) so that about 80 Phoenician war-galleys had sailed towards him'.[344] Alexander would have welcomed these fleets because he knew they were not in the service of the Persians of their own free will,[345] but in reality he needed them. There is a problem concerning the Sidonian fleet: as only part of the fleet joined Alexander because of the small number of ships, where was the rest of the fleet and King ʿAbdʿaštart II? If Arrian's chronology is correct on this point, the above-mentioned passage takes place during the siege of Tyre and after that Alexander had established his naval base at Sidon: 'he sailed towards Sidon taking with him the hypaspistai and Agrianes in order to assemble all the war-galleys which had already joined him' (αὐτὸς τούς τε ὑπασπιστὰς ἀναλαβὼν καὶ τοὺς Ἀγριᾶνας ἐπὶ Σιδῶνος ἐστάλη, ὡς ἀθροίσων ἐκεῖ ὅσαι ἤδη ἦσαν αὐτῷ τριήρεις).[346] Which war-galleys were these? Was the rest of the Sidonian fleet there? According to some authors, ʿAbdʿaštart had remained in Sidon on the orders of the Persians in order to resist Alexander and prevent a new revolt of the Sidonians, with the rest of the fleet.[347] This hypothesis is based on a passage of Curtius, which seems to mean that the king was in his city when he surrendered.[348] This is not convincing since it is

---

340. Curt. IV, 4.15.
341. Just., *Epitoma historiarum Philippicarum Pompei Trogui* XVIII, 3; cf. Verkinderen, *loc. cit.* (n. 262), p. 296.
342. Verkinderen, *ibid.* (with bibl.). Anyway it is impossible to compare the relatively abundant information on Sidon and the scarce information on Tyre at that time.
343. Arr., *An.* II.17.1-4.
344. *Ibid.*, II, 20.1.
345. *Ibid.*, 20.3.
346. *Ibid.*, 19.6.
347. Cf. H. Hauben, 'The king of the Sidonians and the Persian imperial fleet', *AncSoc* 1, 1970, p. 7 (with bibl.), followed by S.F. Bondì, 'Istituzioni e politica a Sidone dal 351 al 332 av. Cr.', *RSF* 2, 1974, p. 157; Elayi, *Sidon*, p. 194, n. 156: 'il avait dû déjà regagner Sidon'.
348. Curt. IV, 1.16.

unlikely that Darius did not have his main support, namely the Sidonian fleet, with him in this difficult situation, and that ʿAbdʿaštart was not himself in command of his fleet; on the other hand, Curtius' testimony arouses suspicion since his aim was to relate how Abdalonymus was designated king.[349] We have proposed a more likely hypothesis: ʿAbdʿaštart was by the side of Darius with his entire fleet; some war-galleys 'of the Sidonians' deserted, following the Aradian and Byblian fleets, which could be explained by their hostility towards the Persians and their exclusion from power. Since ʿAbdʿaštart was attached to the Persian king, he probably remained with him until the Persian fleet did not exist any more, when all the Phoenician fleets had joined Alexander. Anyway when Alexander reached Tyre after the rendition of Sidon, Arrian wrote that 'the Persians still had the supremacy over the sea' (τῶν τε Περσῶν ἔτι θαλασσοκρατούντων).[350] This means that the Tyrian and Sidonian fleets (except for some Sidonian ships), two major fleets, were always loyal to Darius. However, when Alexander occupied Sidon, where was the Sidonian fleet based? Possibly in a harbour of the Sidonian territory which had not yet been occupied by the Greeks. When did ʿAbdʿaštart surrender to Alexander? Possibly when the Macedonian king assembled a powerful fleet during the siege of Tyre. What was going to happen to the Tyrian fleet? At the beginning of the siege, all the Tyrian fleet, under the command of its king, probably left Darius in order to defend the city; this fleet was powerful enough to impress Alexander.[351] The Tyrians sailed up to the mole and mocked him. When they saw the work advancing with unexpected rapidity, they transported their children, women and old men to Carthage; the remaining fleet still consisted of eighty triremes, which were made ready for a naval engagement. In spite of some differences between the various accounts, there were three phases concerning the action of the Tyrian fleet: first it sailed freely around Tyre as long as Alexander did not yet have a substantial fleet, trying to stop the advance of the mole. In the second phase, when Alexander had succeeded in assembling a fleet of 190 triremes, having received Cypriot and Greek war-galleys,[352] the Tyrian fleet was obliged to remain safe in the shelter of the Tyrian harbours and king ʿOzmilk probably came back to his palace; the three ships moored for defence in the mouth of the Sidonian harbour were sunk by Alexander.[353] In the third phase, the fleet inside the harbour probably looked on powerlessly during the seizure of the city, and was mostly sunk or seized (*naves autem omnes fere aut demer-*

---

349. The other accounts of Diodorus, Justin and Plutarch on this episode contain some confusions: cf. I.L. Merker, 'Notes on Abdalonymos and the Dated Alexander Coinage of Sidon and Ake', *ANSMN* 11, 1964, pp. 13-20; Elayi, *Cités phéniciennes*, pp. 50-51.
350. Arr., *An.* II, 18.2.
351. DS. XVII, 40.4.
352. *Ibid.*, 42.1-5; Curt. IV, 3.
353. DS. XVII, 43.3.

sit, aut cepit).[354] The whole Sidonian fleet probably took part in the last stage of the siege, and was maybe used to secretly rescue 15,000 Tyrians from their ships.

King ʿOzmilk, the 'chief magistrates' (οἱ μάλιστα ἐν τέλει) and the members of the Carthaginian delegation had taken refuge in Heracles' temple: to these Alexander granted complete pardon.[355] Arrian completed his narrative in this way: 'The Tyrian sacred ship, consecrated to Heracles, which he (Alexander) captured during the attack, he hallowed to Heracles with an inscription either of his own composition or of someone else which was not worth recording; that is why I did not trouble to copy it. Tyre was then captured during the archonship of Anicetus in Athens in the month of Hecatombaeon'.[356] In contrast with ʿAbdʿaštart II, the last pro-Persian king of Sidon, who was deposed by Alexander, ʿOzmilk was allowed to retain the throne. It is surprising since the Tyrian king seemed to have remained loyal to Darius and had resisted Alexander. Probably the fact that the power of this king was weak had alleviated his responsibility with regard to Alexander who considered only the people of Tyre as being responsible for the city's resistance: the king was not in the Tyrian delegation sent to Alexander to refuse access to the island.[357] Although this goes beyond the scope of the present book, we shall examine the computation proposed by A. Lemaire for the whole ʿOzmilk's reign during the Persian and Hellenistic periods – 39 years from 347/46 to 309/08[358] – which for several reasons is not quite exact. Firstly, as we have shown above, ʿOzmilk acceded to the throne in about 349 BCE (and not 347/46). The silver denominations dated from year *26*[359] are not relevant here as they are much earlier than ʿOzmilk's reign; they correspond to our Series II.1.2.2.b-i with *1* to *10* and *Z1* to *Z5* (rather than *21* to *25*). The bronze denominations inscribed TY, ʿK and *26* (or *Z6*), if they are related to the same reign, have to be dated from about 324 and not 322/21.[360] The tetradrachms and gold staters, possibly minted in Tyre by Alexander and inscribed ʿK and a date from *20* (or *Z*) to *29* (or *Z9*), if they are related to the same reign, have to be dated from about 330 to 321, and not from 328/27 to 319/18.[361] The conclusion that the tetradrachms with ʿK and a num-

---

354. Curt. IV.4; Arr., *An.*, II, 24-25.
355. Arr., *An.* II, 24.5; cf. Elayi, *Cités phéniciennes*, p. 49. DS. XVII, 47.1-6, had placed by error this Sidonian episode in Tyre: this is now confirmed by the bilingual inscription of Cos: C. Kantzia, '... timos Abdalônymou [Sid]ônos basileôs', *AD* 35, 1980, pp. 1-15; M. Sznycer, 'La partie phénicienne de l'inscription bilingue gréco-phénicienne de Cos', *ibid.*, pp. 17-30.
356. Arr., *An.* II, 24.6.
357. On the compared Phoenician institutions, cf. Elayi, *Cités phéniciennes*, pp. 39-53.
358. Lemaire, *loc. cit.* (n. 209), p. 150. Cf. Elayi, *loc. cit.* (n. 70), pp. 24-25.
359. Lemaire, *ibid.*, pp. 136 and 150; *id.*, *loc. cit.* (n. 255), pp. 14, n. 2 and 22.
360. *Id.*, *loc. cit.* (n. 209), pp. 136 and 150; cf. E.T. Newell, *The Dated Alexander Coinage of Sidon and Ake*, New Haven 1916, pp. 60-61; *id.*, *op. cit.* (n. 250), p. 1.
361. Lemaire, *ibid.*, pp. 133 and 150; cf. Newell, *ibid.* 1916. According to M.J. Price, *The Coinage in the Name of Alexander the Great and Philip Arrhidaeus* I-II, Zurich-London 1991, pp. 405-414, the dating is still different and groundless: year 1 (346/5), year 14 (333/2), year 32

ber from 1 to 8 were minted from year 32 to year 39 of ʿOzmilk is unsupported: the hypothesis of a co-regency between ʿOzmilk and his son bearing the same name, not mentioned in the sources, is unlikely.[362] In fact, this hypothesis was proposed in order to fit in with several inscriptions that A. Lemaire had dated from the reign of King ʿOzmilk. Three inscriptions on wine jars excavated at Shiqmona are dated from year 25 of an unnamed king:[363] provided that this date genuinely did refer first to a Phoenician king, then to a Tyrian king (and not Sidonian), and then to ʿOzmilk (rather than to another Tyrian king), it would correspond to about 325 and not 323/22. Several stamps on jars excavated at Tell Balata (Sheshem) bear the inscription *Ṭ26*, that the author interpreted as *Ṭ(B)*, 'go(od wine year) 26' and were ascribed to the same king in year 322/21:[364] provided that this is a date and that the attribution to ʿOzmilk's reign is correct (which has to be confirmed), it would correspond to about 324. The other documents also ascribed to ʿOzmilk's reign are four tithe seals: the seal of Sarepta inscribed *ʿ12*, that of Akshaph inscribed *ʿ36* (or *ʿẒ̊ 16*), that of Bêt-Zêt/Bit-Zitti inscribed *ʿ33Ṣ* (or *ʿZ 13 Ṣ*) and that of Bet-Beṭen inscribed *ʿ19*.[365] If these seals were really dated by the regnal years of a Tyrian king and if this king was ʿOzmilk, they have to be dated from about 338 BCE (and not 336/35), 314 or 334 (and not 312/11), 317 or 337 (and not 315/14), 331 respectively (and not 329/28). The last two documents ascribed to ʿOzmilk's reign are a Phoenician ostracon from Khirbet el-Qôm/Maqqedah dated from year 35 of an unnamed king, and a jar from the Gaza area possibly dated from year 11:[366] both datings have to be confirmed. Therefore the chronology of ʿOzmilk's reign as proposed by A. Lemaire has to be updated. If his reign continued during the beginning of the Hellenistic period, as it seems, its length cannot be established: since years 33 and 36 are not securely attested and if the tetradrachms dated from 20 to 29 were minted by ʿOzmilk, he could have reigned at least until about 321. If the ostracon from Khirbet el-Qôm inscribed 35 is dated from his reign, he could have reigned until about 315: however all this has to be confirmed.

(315/4), the new dating being year 1 (315/4) to year 11 (305/4). He has listed all the Tyrian silver, gold and bronze coins dated from this period (no. 3242-3302).

362. Lemaire, *ibid.*
363. *Ibid.*, pp. 137-139 (with bibl.).
364. *Ibid.*, pp. 139-140 (with bibl.).
365. *Ibid.*, pp. 140-150 (with bibl.); A. Lemaire ascribed the seal *ʿŠR/LBT/B1* to a Tyrian king preceding ʿOzmilk (pp. 143-144), but it could be too a Sidonian king.
366. Id., *Nouvelles inscriptions araméennes d'Idumée au Musée d'Israël*, Paris 1996, pp. 121-123, no. 203; *id., loc. cit.* (n. 228), pp. 423-424 (with bibl.); J. Naveh, 'Unpublished Phoenician Inscriptions from Palestine', *IEJ* 37, 1987, pp. 27-30.

CONCLUSION

E. Renan was extremely disappointed with his excavations in Tyre in 1861: 'The excavations of Sour present many more difficulties than those of Saida. I do not think that any great city which has played such an important role during centuries has left less traces than Tyre'.[1] The systematic excavations started in 1947 by M. Chéhab had provided numerous and important results but only for the remains of the Hellenistic and mainly Roman and Byzantine periods. The levels of the Persian period remain almost unknown.[2] However an important discovery regarding this period was made in 2007: Alexander's engineers cleverly exploited a sublittoral sand spit to build a causeway and seize the offshore island of Tyre in 333-332 BCE.[3] Because of the lack of archaeological information on the Persian period, this book is particularly important because significant historical conclusions were reached regarding this period, based on the Tyrian monetary corpus and on all the other available data: Phoenician and other inscriptions, Hebrew, Greek and Latin texts, and archaeological finds.

Firstly, we have established a chronological catalogue of 1,814 coins, classified by series and denominations, with as complete as possible descriptions and references, facsimiles of inscriptions and photographs of the different coins. This catalogue can be used equally as well by scholars searching accurate information as by numismatists or collectors simply wishing to identify coins. It is followed by a study of the dies and a classification of the coins based on a relative chronology.

The study of the monetary inscriptions provides a substantial complement to the corpus of Tyrian inscriptions dated from the Persian period, which is quite scanty. The paleographic study was particularly fruitful because it was based on multiple duplications of the same letters by the same engravers or by different engravers, contemporary or successive: this enabled us to assess the constraints and the degree of liberty enjoyed by each engraver, just as the evolution of writing. The use of dates provided information on the Tyrian system of dating and on the signs used for numbers. Three levels of writing were analysed: the official monetary inscriptions, the countermarks of moneychangers or controllers and the private graffiti. It was also possible to study the engraving tech-

---

1. E. Renan, *Mission de Phénicie*, Paris 1864, pp. 528-529.
2. See here above, Introduction (with bibl.).
3. N. Marriner *et al.*, 'Holocene Morphogenesis of Alexander the Great's Isthmus at Tyre in Lebanon', *Proceedings of the National Academy of Sciences* 104/22, May 2007, pp. 9218-9223.

niques and the tools used by professional engravers and ordinary individuals. Lastly, we have considered the different functions of monetary writing and what it reveals regarding the degree of alphabetisation within the Tyrian society.

The iconographical study of the motifs represented on the coins has also provided a variety of information, albeit less technical and realistic than that of the Sidonian coins: only the deity gives an indication of the Tyrian garment and headdress, and of one weapon (the bow with quiver and arrowheads). The Tyrian monetary iconography furnishes more information on religion: the smiting deity, protector of the city, probably Milqart, riding on a winged seahorse which was a rapid mount both at sea, on earth and in the air; the animals which were probably attributes or symbols of this deity – dolphin, lion and ram – and the decreasing importance of the dolphin. The owl bearing crook and flail on its shoulder represented kingship. In this way, the symbols chosen by the Tyrian minting authority clearly expressed on the obverse the power of the city (mainly maritime) and her protection, and kingship on the reverse.

By observing the material particularities of these coins, it was possible to learn about the manufacturing techniques and processes. We have gleaned information about how the coins were produced, about the supply of metals, the work of the metallurgists preparing the metals, the flans and dies, that of the stone-workers making flan moulds, that of the controllers adjusting the weights, the work of the engravers engraving the dies, that of the workers in charge of striking and the persons responsible for production. We have obtained quite a precise insight into the Tyrian monetary workshop, controlled by the minting authority but probably functioning in an informal fashion. Just like the Sidonian monetary workshop, the Tyrian workshop functioned on the cheap (using coins with defects, re-engraving of coins, numerous decentred coins). However, from the beginning of its coinage through to the end of the 5th century, it was striving for quality; then followed the comparatively debased production of the 4th century. The Tyrian monetary workshop was innovative, just like the Sidonian; it used the semi-incusion technique in a particular way, and inaugurated a yearly dating system for the first time at the beginning of the 4th century (around 388 BCE). The Tyrian workshop followed the Sidonian example in using circular moulds from around 357, in reducing flan diameter and in minting bronze coins (only one denomination compared to the three for Sidon). We have also tried to evaluate the volume of Tyrian coins issued and to show how the production evolved. In addition, we have studied the problem of forged coins and intentional alterations (fragmentation of coins by using them as metal, chisel-cuts for checking content).

The metrological study focused firstly on defining a relevant terminology and on developing a statistical method to identify with precision the modified standard of the shekel and its fractions, without needing to resort to any other method (such as average weight, modal weight, interquartile space, etc.). The first standard used in Tyrian coinage until around 358 BCE was the Phoenician standard (modified standard: 13.56g). Afterwards, Tyre used the so-called 'Attic' standard (modified standard: 8.77g). This important change followed a period when the silver percentage in the coins decreased (falling to about 68%). The percentage of silver went back to the initial percentage of Tyrian coins (about 99-98%). This study also reached some conclusions regarding the most used denominations, the relation between the inauguration of bronze coins and the disappearance of certain silver denominations, the equivalence between silver and bronze, and the effects of wear on coins.

The numismatic analysis, combined with all the available sources, led to significant historical conclusions. As regards the inauguration date of Tyrian coinage, Tyre opened her monetary workshop after Byblos, around 450 BCE. Without being either concerted or simultaneous, it seems that Tyre followed the initiative of Byblos a few years later. Among the possible reasons for this decision was mimicry, consisting in imitating Byblos and the Cypriot city of Kition, an ancient colony of Tyre. There could also have been at that time a larger quantity of silver available because of the increasing imports of Athenian tetradrachms, used for melting. During the first half of the 5th century, the Tyrians had suffered repeated naval defeats in Persian service and had to face substantial war expenses. Minting coins was also the best way to restore their image, tarnished by the defeats. Group I.1 of the Tyrian coinage, with five inscribed denominations, probably had a very limited volume of issues and lasted for only a short period, possibly partly as a trial.

Group I.2 seems to follow the same logic as Group I.1, also inscribed, with five denominations and minted during a short period (last part of the third quarter of the 5th century), however with a much larger volume of production than the preceding group. The decision to increase the production could possibly have been taken because of the success of the Group I.1 coinage trial. In contrast with the previous period, Tyre appears not to have been directly involved in any battle; however our documentation is lacking in this respect and in any case it was costly to maintain a large fleet over a long period.

It is difficult to establish an absolute chronology for the following groups until c. 349 BCE, the first year of ʿOzmilk's reign. We have tentatively proposed to ascribe Group II.1.1, characterised by a new type (deity riding on seahorse on the obverse), to the period around 425-394. There were apparently no sea-battles during this period, at least in the first stage, just as in the preceding period, if we can have confidence in the lacunary documentation. However, the Tyrian fleet always represented an important part of the Phoenician fleet in the service of the Persians and Tyre had to provide for its maintenance. The second stage of this period was apparently different: after internal troubles which lead to some Tyrians being exiled, the city probably took part in Persian military operations. The anepigraphic Group II.1.1 seems to reflect the evolution of the situation: the coins were initially made with great care, with skilful engraving, larger diameter and smaller thickness. Then the progressive and significant degradation of the coins was probably connected with Tyre's difficulties which were more significant than those endured by Sidon.

Group II.1.2 is the final group before the change in standard from the Phoenician to the 'Attic'. We have tentatively proposed to ascribe it to the period of around 393-358 BCE. The coins of this group, again inscribed, are again debased and there was a major reduction in the volume of coinage produced. The political context was much more troubled than in the preceding period. Several revolts occurred in the Western part of the Persian empire, with repercussions on the city of Tyre because her fleet was always in Persian service and her territory was used as a base to prepare for two campaigns against Egypt, both of which failed. Besides regular war expenses, the Tyrians were also confronted with the expenses caused by the successive Persian defeats. Even if Tyre was not so engaged in revolting against the Persians as king ʿAbdʿaštart I of Sidon was, she was plagued by other substantial difficulties such as the siege of Evagoras in 385-383 and a difficult revolt of slaves, maybe around 354/350.

Group II.2 is clearly distinguished from the preceding group, not by the types which have not varied but by the change of standard from the Phoenician to the 'Attic'. It is more precisely dated: from around 357 to 333/2 BCE. This group reflects an accumulation of Tyrian economic difficulties as it started with a change of standard, following on from a significant decrease in the percentage of silver in the previous series. In similar circumstances, but a few years earlier (365 BCE), Sidon had chosen to devaluate her coinage by around 1.20g for the shekel, while Tyre had changed the standard, which corresponded to a devaluation of about 6.50g, a much bigger change, probably because, at that time, the situation of Tyre was still worse than that of Sidon. The decrease in the volume of production was still more important than previously. The political context of Group II.2 was troubled like in the previous period: an unsettled situation in the Western part of the Persian Empire with, among others, the revolt of ʿAbdʿaštart I of Sidon around 360/359, Mazday's control of Transeuphratene from c. 353, and the failure of a new Persian campaign in Egypt in 351. Another important change occurred during the last series of king ʿOzmilk (II.2.1.14-29) dated from year 3 to 17, that is from around 347 to 333/2. This series was by far the most abundant of all Tyrian coinage. The style is not skilful but less neglected than in the preceding series. In contrast to Sidon where exports of Sidonian coins as merchandise coins seem to have stopped from around 348, Tyrian exports had considerably increased from this date, that is after the suppression of the so-called Tennes' revolt. The fact that King ʿOzmilk started minting coinage in c. 347 with a quite large volume of production, together with the allusions made by classical sources, suggests that Tyre was favoured by the Persians and recuperated some lands taken from Sidon, possibly Sarepta for example. Tyre probably participated in the Persian re-conquest of Egypt in 343/2. The presence of a debased coin and of several plated coins in ʿOzmilk's issues of years 15 to 17 (335-333/2 BCE) could be related to the Persian preparations for war in expectation of Alexander's arrival and to the beginning of the siege of Tyre. King ʿOzmilk was loyal to Darius III and was much involved in these events, but in contrast to the other cities, he had chosen the wrong side. However, he was allowed by Alexander to retain the throne while ʿAbdʿaštart II, the last pro-Persian king of Sidon, was deposed. Possibly the fact that Ozmilk's power was weak had lessened his responsibility with regard to Alexander who only considered the people of Tyre as being responsible for the city's resistance.

A clear sign of the upheavals that affected Tyre at that time is the number of sites with destruction levels dated from the last part of the Persian period, even if not all these cases are linked with violent military events and if some of them are related to the Sidonian troubles: Akko, Tell Keisan, Tell Abu Hawam, Shiqmona, ʿAtlit, Dor, Tel Megadim, Tel Mevorakh, Tel Michal, Mikhmoret, Apollonia-Arṣuf, Jaffa, Megiddo (and also the destruction of Tyre as related by classical sources). Thus, this book has greatly enriched our knowledge of Persian policy towards Tyre. These new conclusions now need to be integrated into the history of the Persian Empire in order to provide a better understanding of the Persians' Western policy.

APPENDIX I

HOARDS CONTAINING TYRIAN COINS

We present here the list of hoards containing Tyrian coins, following the numbering system of our corpus of Phoenician hoards published in 1993,[1] complemented by new discoveries and publications. Where necessary, we have corrected the burial dates, based on the updated chronologies of Sidonian and Tyrian coinages.

– TX: Byblos hoard, 1933-1938.[2]
– TXII: Byblos hoard, 1957.[3]
– TXIII, XIV, XV (?): Byblos hoards, beginning of March 1983, end of 1984/beginning of 1985, 1988 (?).[4] We have presented these three hoards together, all found in Byblos in illicit excavations during the civil war as were unable to assemble any clear information on each of them, being scattered in the Antiquities market. We had the possibility of studying 496 coins, which only represent part of these hoards. The hoard of 400 shekels from Byblos reported to have been found in Beirut in around 1983 probably corresponds to our hoard TXIII.[5] The hoard of the 12 so-called Byblian fractions (one of them being Tyrian) is probably also a part of our hoards TXIII-TXV.[6]
– TXXIII: Qasr Naba hoard, beginning of 1902.[7]
– TXXVI: Khirbet el-Kerak hoard, 1936.[8]

---

1. Elayi-Elayi, *Trésors*.
2. *Ibid.*, pp. 87-90 = *CH* IX, no. 356; *id.*, "Nouveaux trésors de monnaies phéniciennes (*CH* IX)", *Trans* 26, 2003, p. 106. We follow the numbers of our corpus of hoards and we mention, for each hoard, the place and date of discovery.
3. Elayi-Elayi, *Trésors*, pp. 91-92.
4. *Ibid.*, pp. 92-114.
5. *CH* VIII, no. 118; J. Elayi and A.G. Elayi, "Nouveaux trésors de monnaies phéniciennes (*CH* IX)", *Trans* 11, 1996, pp. 98-99.
6. *CH* VIII, no. 120; Elayi-Elayi, *ibid.*, p. 99.
7. Elayi-Elayi, *Trésors*, pp. 133-137 = *CH* VII, no. 32 = *CH* IX, no. 447; cf. Elayi-Elayi, *loc. cit.* (n. 2), p. 113.
8. *Id.*, *Trésors*, pp. 139-147 and 840, fig. 34, for the metrological analysis = *CH* IX, no. 462; *id.*, *loc. cit.* (n. 2), p. 114.

– TXXVII: Palestine (?) hoard, 1943.[9]

Since the most recent coins represented in this hoard are those of ʿAbdʿaš-tart I who reigned from 365 to 352, we propose dating the burial of this hoard from his reign, but probably not at the beginning.

– TXXXIII: Akko hoard, 1962.[10]

– TXXXIV: hoard from the area of Akko, 1966 or earlier.[11]

We have studied the small bronzes of Alexander and we have proposed attributing them to the Tyrian mint.[12]

– TXXXV: Tell Abu Hawam hoard, 15-8-1930.[13]

– TXXXVI: hoard from North Galilee (?), 1983 (?).[14]

By using the photographs presented in *CH* VIII, we were able to study this hoard of 50 Tyrian shekels. In *CH* VIII, it is reported to have been found in 1983 (and not 1985-1990), in North Galilee (and not in the area of Gaza). However, *CH* IX presented it as having been discovered in the area of Gaza in 1985-90, probably on the basis of our previous information given by S. Qedar and others. Since the information given by U. Wartenberg in *CH* VIII seems to be, by far, the most complete, we propose to accept it for the moment. This hoard contains eleven shekels inscribed ʿ*9* (that is about 341 BCE), four inscribed ʿ*10* (340), four inscribed ʿ*12* (338), five inscribed ʿ*13* (337), two inscribed ʿ*14* (336) and twenty-four inscribed ʿ*15* (335). As the coins of series ʿ*15* are the most recent and numerous, we may propose about 335 BCE as a burial date.

– TXXXVII: Safed hoard, Spring 1965.[15]

– TXXXVIII: Damascus hoard, February 1959.[16]

– TXXXIX: unknown provenance, 1987 or slightly earlier.[17]

We wondered whether TXXXIX belonged to the same hoard as TXXXVI as it contains shekels inscribed ʿ*9* to ʿ*15*. However, five of the six shekels are yellowish (low silver content or plated), which could mean that the worst coins had been acquired by Superior Stamp and Coin. This seems curious and, for the moment, we shall consider that there were two hoards.

– TXLIII: hoard from the area of Beirut, Autumn 1966.[18]

---

9. Elayi-Elayi, *Trésors*, pp. 147-148 = *CH* IX, no. 400; *id., loc. cit.* (n. 2), p. 110.
10. Elayi-Elayi, *Trésors*, pp. 163-168 = *CH* IX, no. 382 (without any precision). This hoard entered in the Kadman Numismatic Museum and then was stolen.
11. Elayi-Elayi, *Trésors*, pp. 168-170 = *CH* IX, no. 461; *id., loc. cit.* (n. 2), p. 114.
12. *Id.*, "Une série de petits bronzes d'Alexandre frappés à Tyr", *RN*, 1998, pp. 107-117.
13. *Id., Trésors*, pp. 170-185 = *CH* IX, no. 426 (without any precision); *id., loc. cit.* (n. 2), p. 111; and here above, Chapter VI, for the metrological analysis.
14. *Id., Trésors*, pp. 185-186 = *CH* VIII, no. 149 = *CH* IX, no. 429; *id., loc. cit.* (n. 5), pp. 101-108; and here above, Chapter VI, for the metrological analysis.
15. *Id., Trésors*, pp. 187-189 = *CH* IX, no. 433; *id., loc. cit.* (n. 2), p. 112.
16. *Id., Trésors*, pp. 189-191 = *CH* IX, no. 428; *id., loc. cit.* (n. 2), p. 112.
17. *Id., Trésors*, pp. 191-192 = *CH* IX, no. 431; *id., loc. cit.* (n. 2), p. 112.
18. *Id., Trésors*, pp. 202-206 = *CH* IX, no. 404; *id., loc. cit.* (n. 2), p. 110.

– TXLVI: hoard from the area of Gaza, about 1975.[19]
– TXLVII: alleged Abu Shusheh hoard, about 1930.[20]
– TXLVIII: Wadi Daliyeh hoard, 1962.[21]

The burial date proposed in *CH* IX is 330 BCE. However, since the most recent Tyrian coins and manuscripts are dated from about 335, we propose to keep this date for the burial of the hoard or, more exactly, for the last date attested by the finds.

– TLI: Naplouse hoard, 1968.[22]

This hoard is mistakenly called 'first Naplouse hoard' whereas hoard TL was found much earlier (about 1891) in Naplouse or in the area of Naplouse.

– TLII: Moshav Dalton hoard, 1971 or slightly earlier.[23]

We obtained no further information regarding the exact content of this hoard from G. Foerster, who does not appear to have published it yet.

– TLIII: Jordan hoard, beginning of 1967.[24]

This hoard contained 113 silver coins; among them was a Tyrian shekel (no. 3) belonging to the first series (I.1.1), which was *fleur-de-coin*. Therefore the burial date has to be situated just after the first Tyrian issue. From the analysis of all the coins in this hoard, this date is clearly around 450, a few years earlier or a few years later.[25]

– TLIV: Massyaf hoard, 1961.[26]

This hoard contained 100 silver coins; among them were 14 Sidonian coins (with a Baʿalšillem II double shekel) and 6 Tyrian coins: three shekels (no. 57, 65 and 66), one third of shekel (no. 207) and two fragments (no. 89 and 90). C.M. Kraay and P.R.S. Moorey proposed '425-420 BCE' as a burial date; however A. Destrooper-Georgiades proposed 'around 400' because of the Kition coin. If the Baʿalšillem double shekel is not an intrusion, it was issued between 401 and 373, which is a *terminus post quem* for the burial. The Tyrian coins belong to Series I.2 and are dated from the last part of the third quarter of the 5th century.

– TLV: Aleppo hoard, slightly before 1866.[27]

---

19. *Id., Trésors*, pp. 208-209 = *CH* IX, no. 448; *id., loc. cit.* (n. 2), p. 114.
20. *Id., Trésors*, pp. 209-216 = *CH* IX, no. 434; *id., loc. cit.* (n. 2), p. 112.
21. *Id., Trésors*, pp. 216-218 = *CH* IX, no. 451; *id., loc. cit.* (n. 2), p. 114. See here above, Chapter VII.6.
22. *Id., Trésors*, pp. 231-239 = *CH* IX, no. 440; *id., loc. cit.* (n. 2), p. 113.
23. *Ibid., Trésors*, p. 240.
24. *Ibid.*, pp. 240-241 = *CH* IX, no. 355; *id., loc. cit.* (n. 2), p. 106.
25. See, for example, C.M. Kraay and P.R.S. Moorey, "Two fifth Century Hoards from the Near East", *RN* 10, 1968, pp. 181-235 (about 445); C.G. Starr, *Athenian Coinage 480-449 B.C.*, Oxford 1970, p. 63 (450 or slightly later); H.B. Mattingly, "The Jordan Hoard (IGCH 1482) and Kimon's last Expedition", in *Proceedings of the 10th International Congress of Numismatics*, London 1986, pp. 59-64 (450/449); *id.*, "A new light on the early silver coinage of Teos", *SNR* 73, 1994, p. 8 (454). See here above, Chapter VII.2.
26. *Id., Trésors*, pp. 241-245 = *CH* IX, no. 362; *id., loc. cit.* (n. 2), p. 107.
27. *Id., Trésors*, pp. 245-246 = *CH* IX, no. 360; *id., loc. cit.* (n. 2), p. 107.

— TLVI: hoard from the area of Aleppo, 1989.[28]

This hoard has been published by M.J. Price who proposed 333 as a burial date.[29] The only dated coins are two Tyrian shekels inscribed ʿ10 and ʿ12: the hoard was therefore buried after 338 BCE.

— TLVIII (?): Syrian hoard (?), 1988 or slightly before.[30]

The burial date proposed in *CH* IX ('330 BCE') is not relevant because several coins are much later and it is not sure that these coins, that we have partly published, formed a hoard.

— TLX: Cilician (?) hoard, before 1914.[31]

There are still several uncertainties surrounding this hoard, concerning the provenance and composition. The presence of Phoenician coins in Southern Asia Minor is well-attested. Following the information provided by A. Davesne, several unpublished Phoenician coins, discovered in this area, belong to the Selifke Museum collections. The burial date proposed by E.T. Newell for hoard TLX, and generally accepted, is 'about 380'.[32] However, after the systematic analysis of this corpus, the most recent of the two Tyrian shekels (no. 628) belongs to Series II.1.2 which we have dated around 393-358 BCE.

— TLXI: Cilician hoard, around 1960.[33]

— TLXII: Southern Asia Minor (?) hoard, slightly after 1912.[34]

— TLXIII: Babylon hoard, 1882.[35]

This hoard was found in 1882 during excavations conducted by H. Rassam in Babylon. H. Rassam's original report, written in Abu Habbah (Sippar) on 13 July 1882 and discovered in the archives of the British Museum, confirms the place and date of this find and shows that the silver coins represented only 1% of the weight of the silver contained in this hoard.[36] This hoard was buried in about 385 BCE according to *CH* VIII and about 420-400 according to *CH* IX. However the latest coin seems to be a Tyrian shekel of Series II.1.1 (no. 266), and we have proposed to ascribe this series to about 425-394.

— TLXIV: Tigris hoard, 1810-August 1816.[37]

---

28. *Id., Trésors*, p. 246 = *CH* VIII, no. 158; *id., loc. cit.* (n. 5), pp. 108-109.
29. M.J. Price, "More from Memphis and the Syria 1989 Hoard", in *id. et al.* eds, *Essays in Honour of Robert Carson and Kenneth Jenkins*, London 1993, pp. 31-35.
30. Elayi-Elayi, *Trésors*, pp. 248-249 = *CH* IX, no. 449; *id., loc. cit.* (n. 2), p. 114.
31. *Id., Trésors*, pp. 264-265 = *CH* IX, no. 391; *id., loc. cit.* (n. 2), p. 109.
32. E.T. Newell, "A Cilician Find", *NC*, 1914, pp. 1-33; Elayi-Elayi, *Trésors*, p. 265 (with bibl.).
33. Elayi-Elayi, *Trésors*, pp. 265-266 = *CH* IX, no. 377; *id., loc. cit.* (n. 2), p. 109.
34. *Id., Trésors*, pp. 266-268 = *CH* IX, no. 409; *id., loc. cit.* (n. 2), p. 111.
35. *Id., Trésors*, pp. 268-270 = *CH* VIII, no. 90 = *CH* IX, no. 64; *id., loc. cit.* (n. 5), p. 98; *id., loc. cit.* (n. 2), p. 107.
36. *CH* VIII, p. 88, announces the publication of all the material of this hoard now in the British Museum.
37. *Id., Trésors*, pp. 270-273 = *CH* IX, no. 450; *id., loc. cit.* (n. 2), p. 114. "Chios" has to be corrected in "Cios".

The Phoenician coins of this hoard were several Sidonian coins, some Byblian coins, one Aradian fraction and seven Tyrian shekels of Series II.1.2 (around 393-358 BCE). The date of burial proposed in *CH* IX – 330 BCE – is not argued.

– TLXV: Babylonia hoard, about 1900 (?).[38]
– TLXVI: hoard from Mesopotamia or Babylonia, 1957.[39]
– TLXVIII: Malayer hoard, around 1934.[40]
– TLXIX: hoard of the area of Balkh, 1966.[41]
– TLXXI: Tell el-Maskhuta hoard, 1947.[42]
– TLXXIII: Delta hoard, 1887.[43]

This hoard has been considered as 'archaic' and the burial date proposed on the basis of the Greek coins is 'around 500'. The two Tyrian fractions are considered as intrusive. They belong to Series III.1.2, an unclassified series, but anyway are not earlier than the end of the 5th century.

– TLXXV: Beni Hassan hoard, Winter 1903-1904.[44]

The burial date proposed in *CH* IX – 330 BCE – is groundless. If the Tyrian shekel inscribed ʿ9 is the latest coin, it could give a *terminus post quem* in c. 341.

– TLXXVIII: Phoenicia hoard, 1985.[45]

The Tyrian shekel in this hoard seems to belong to Series II.1.1 dated around 425-394 BCE. The Sidonian double shekel of ʿAbdʿaštart I, year 3, is dated from 363; the double shekel of Mazday, year 16, is dated from 338 and is the latest known coin from this hoard.

– TLXXIX: Phoenicia hoard, 1988.[46]

This hoard, from the Antiquities market, contained at least twelve Tyrian coins briefly presented in *CH* VIII. The three shekels (no. 383, 384 and 385) belong to Series II.1.1 (around 425-394 BCE). The nine small denominations (no. 436 to 440, 457, 488, 540, 724 and 725) are similar to the 25 coins of the hoard TXXXIII, stolen from the Kadman Numismatic Museum, but do not seem to be part of this hoard. They belong to our Series II.1.1.2 and II.1.2.2, dated from around 425-358.

– TLXXXIII: Egypt hoard, before 2006.[47]

---

38. *Id., Trésors*, p. 273.
39. *Ibid.*, pp. 273-274.
40. *Ibid.*, pp. 277-279.
41. *Ibid.*, pp. 279-281.
42. *Ibid.*, pp. 282-286.
43. *Ibid.*, pp. 288-289.
44. *Ibid.*, pp. 290-295 = *CH* VII, no. 32 = *CH* IX, no. 447; *id., loc. cit.* (n. 2), p. 113.
45. *CH* VIII, no. 154; *id., loc. cit.* (n. 5), pp. 110-111.
46. *CH* VIII, no. 156; *id., loc. cit.* (n. 5), pp. 111-112.
47. H. Gitler and O. Tal, *The Coinage of Philistia of the Fifth and Fourth Centuries BC*, Milan-New York 2006, p. 51 (M. Dürr, personal communication).

This unpublished hoard is known as a result of a short mention by H. Gitler and O. Tal in 2006. It is reported to have an Egyptian provenance and to contain Tyrian coins, Athenian, Aeginian and three Philistian coins.

In total, 40 out of the 83 hoards containing Phoenician coins include Tyrian coins, with 46 containing Sidonian coins.[48]

---

48. Elayi-Elayi, *Monnayage de Sidon*, pp. 695-699.

APPENDIX II

FALSE OR DUBIOUS TYRIAN COINS

1*	8.06g	O: deity, beared, riding on seahorse with curled wring, to right; holding reins in right hand and an arched bow in left hand; below, two lines of waves and dolphin, to right; guilloche border? Curious style. R: owl standing to right, head facing; over its left shoulder, crook and flail; ʿ14? in field right; guilloche border? Poinsignon Numismatique, Strasbourg, 30/6/1987, no. 687.
2*	9.04g	Same as 1*. Curious style. R: ʿ15? in field right. Kurpfälzische Münzkabinett, Mannheim, 44, June 1993, no. 54 = Kroha, Kölner Münzkabinett, Köln, 47, 21-22/11/1988, no. 55.
3*	7.80g	Same as 1*. Curious style. R: ʿ15? in field right. Numismatica Ars Classica, Zurich, 2, 21-22/2/1990, no. 232 = Lanz, Munich, 48, 22/5/1989, no. 389 = Elsen, Brussels, 9, 6/2/1988, no. 90 = Superior Galleries, Beverly Hills, 11-12/6/1986, no. 1419.
4*	0.60g	O: dolphin to left; border of dots. R: ram's head to left; border of dots. Abnormal weight (cf. Series III.1.2.f). Y. Meshorer, 'The Mints of Ashdod and Ascalon during the Late Persian Period', *ErIs* 20, 1989, p. 290, no. 16 (attributed to Ashkelon); H. Gitler and O. Tal, 'Coins with the Aramaic Legend *Šhrw* and Other Unrecorded Samarian Issues', *Revue Suisse de Numismatique* 85, 2006, p. 55, no. 16, fig. 5 (attributed to Samaria).

ABBREVIATIONS

The abbreviations used for journals and books are the standard abbreviations of the *Année Philologique* and *International glossary of abbreviations for theology and related subjects* (S. Schwertner, Berlin-New York 1992^2). As for Greek and Latin texts, we conform to the standard abbreviations of Bailly and Gafiot dictionaries.
– *ACFP* = *Atti del Congresso Internazionale di Studi Fenici e Punici*
– *AD* = *Archaiologikon Deltion*
– *AHL* = *Archaeology and History of Lebanon*
– *AI* = Archaeological Institut
– *AJN* = *American Journal of Numismatics*
– AM = Ashmolean Museum
– ANS = American Numismatic Society
– ArchM = Archaeological Museum
– AUB = American University of Beirut
– Babelon, *Perses* = E. Babelon, *Catalogue des monnaies grecques de la Bibliothèque Nationale. Les Perses achéménides*, Paris 1893
– Babelon, *Traité* = E. Babelon, *Traité des monnaies grecques et romaines*, IInd Part, T. 2, Paris 1910
– Baramki, *Coins AUB* = D. Baramki, *The Coins exhibited in the Archaeological Museum of the American University of Beirut*, Beirut 1966
– Baramki, *Coins 1866-1966* = D. Baramki, *The Coins exhibited in the Archaeological Museum of the American University of Beirut*, Centennial Publications 1866-1966, Beirut 1968
– *BES* = *Bulletin of the Egyptian Seminar*
– Betlyon, *Coinage of Phoenicia* = J.W. Betlyon, *The Coinage and Mints of Phoenicia. The Pre-Alexandrine Period*, Chico 1982
– BM = British Museum
– Bishop-Holloway, *Wheaton Collection* = J.D. Bishop and R.R. Holloway, *Wheaton Collection of Greek and Roman Coins*, New York 1981
– *BMC Cyprus* = G.F. Hill, *A Catalogue of the Greek Coins in the British Museum. Greek Coins of Cyprus*, London 1904
– *BMC Lydia* = G.F. Hill, *A Catalogue of the Greek Coins in the British Museum. Greek Coins of Lydia*, London 1902
– *BMC Phoenicia* = G.F. Hill, *A Catalogue of the Greek Coins in the British Museum. Greek Coins of Phoenicia*, London 1910

– BNF = Bibliothèque de France
– Brett, *Greek Coins* = A.B. Brett, *Catalogue of Greek Coins, Museum of Fine Arts*, Boston 1955
– Briend-Humbert, *Tell Keisan* = J. Briend and J.B. Humbert, *Tell Keisan (1971-1976). Une cité phénicienne en Galilée*, Paris 1980
– *BSFN* = *Bulletin de la Société Française de Numismatique*
– *Catalogue De Luynes* = J. Babelon, *Catalogue de la Collection de Luynes, Monnaies grecques III. Asie Mineure et Phénicie*, Paris 1930
– *Catalogue Jameson* = R. Jameson, *Collection Robert Jameson*, Paris 1913-32
– *Catalogue McClean* = *Catalogue of the McClean Collection of Greek Coins III*, Cambridge 1929
– *Catalogue Rosen* = N.M. Wagoner, *Early Greek Coins from the collection of Jonathan P. Rosen*, New York 1983
– *CCEC* = *Cahiers du Centre d'Etudes Chypriotes*
– *CH VIII, IX* = *Coin Hoards*
– Chéhab, *Monnaies* = M. Chéhab, *Monnaies gréco-romaines et phéniciennes du Musée national, Beyrouth, Liban*, Paris 1977
– *DArch* = *Dossiers de l'Archéologie*
– *DISO* = C.-F. Jean and J. Hoftijzer, *Dictionnaire des inscriptions sémitiques de l'ouest*, Leiden 1965
– Dunand, *Byblos I* = M. Dunand, *Fouilles de Byblos I. 1926-1932*, Paris 1937
– Dunand, *Byblos II* = M. Dunand, *Fouilles de Byblos II. 1933-1938*, Paris 1958
– Elayi, ꜥAbdꜥaštart Ier = J. Elayi, *ꜥAbdꜥaštart Ier/Straton : un roi phénicien entre Orient et Occident*, Paris 2005
– Elayi, *Cités phéniciennes* = J. Elayi, *Recherches sur les cités phéniciennes à l'époque perse*, Napoli 1987
– Elayi, *Économie* = J. Elayi, *Économie des cités phéniciennes sous l'Empire perse*, Napoli 1990
– Elayi, *Phénomène monétaire* = J. Elayi, « Le phénomène monétaire dans les cités phéniciennes à l'époque perse », in T. Hackens and G. Moucharte eds, *Numismatique et Histoire économique dans le monde phénico-punique*, Louvain-la-Neuve 1992, pp. 59-76
– Elayi, *Sidon* = J. Elayi, *Sidon, cité autonome de l'Empire perse*, Paris 1990^2
– Elayi-Elayi, *La monnaie* = J. Elayi and A.G. Elayi, *La monnaie à travers les âges*, Paris 1989
– Elayi-Elayi, *Monnayage de Sidon* = J. Elayi and A.G. Elayi, *Le monnayage de la cité phénicienne de Sidon à l'époque perse (V^e-IVe s. av. J.-C.)*, 2 vols, Paris 2004.
– Elayi-Elayi, *Poids phéniciens* = J. Elayi and A.G. Elayi, *Recherches sur les poids phéniciens*, Paris 1997

– Elayi-Elayi, *Trésors* = J. Elayi and A.G. Elayi, *Trésors de monnaies phéniciennes et circulation monétaire (V*^{e}*– IV*^{e} *siècles avant J.-C.)*, Paris 1993
– Elayi-Lemaire, *Graffiti* = J. Elayi and A. Lemaire, *Graffiti et contremarques ouest-sémitiques sur les monnaies grecques et proche-orientales*, Milano 1998
– Elayi-Sayegh, *Beyrouth I* = J. Elayi and H. Sayegh, *Un quartier du port phénicien de Beyrouth au Fer III/Perse. Les objets*, Paris 1998
– Elayi-Sayegh, *Beyrouth II* = J. Elayi and H. Sayegh, *Un quartier du port phénicien de Beyrouth au Fer III/Perse. Archéologie et histoire*, Paris 2000
– FM = Fitzwilliam Museum
– Forrer, *Weber Collection* = L. Forrer, *The Weber Collection*, London 1929
– Gardner, *History of Ancient Coinage* = P. Gardner, *A History of Ancient Coinage 700-300 B.C.*, Oxford 1918
– Head, *A Guide* = B.V. Head, *A Guide to the principal Coins of the Greeks*, London 1959
– Head, *Coinage of Lydia* = B.V. Head, *The Coinage of Lydia and Persia*, London 1877
– Head, *Historia Numorum* = B.V. Head, *Historia Numorum*, Chicago 1967 (1rst edition: Oxford 1887)
– Herzog, *Tel Michal* = Z. Herzog *et al.* eds, *Excavations at Tel Michal, Israel*, Minneapolis-Tel Aviv 1989
– Hill, *Catalog Ward* = G. F. Hill, *Descriptive Catalog of ancient Greek Coins belonging to John Ward* I, London 1901
– *Hunterian Collection* = G. Macdonald, *Catalogue of Greek Coins in the Hunterian Collection*, Glasgow 1899-1905
– IAM = Istanbul Arkeoloji Müzeleri
– *IGCH* = M. Thompson *et al.*, *An Inventory of Greek Coin Hoards*, New York 1973
– IM = Israel Museum
– *INR* = *Israel Numismatic Research*
– INUW = Institut für Numismatik Universität Wien
– Jenkins, *Greek Coins* = G.K. Jenkins, *Ancient Greek Coins*, London 1972
– Jidejian, *Lebanon* = N. Jidejian, *Lebanon and the Greek World*, Beirut 1988
– Jidejian, *Lebanon, its Gods* = N. Jidejian, *Lebanon, its Gods, Legends and Myths illustrated by coins*, Beirut 1985
– *KAI* = H. Donner and W. Röllig, *Kanaanäische und aramäische Inschriften* I-III, Wiesbaden 1966-69
– KHM = Kunst Historisches Museum
– *KI* = M. Lidsbarski, *Kanaanäische Inschriften*, Giessen 1907
– Klein, *Sammlung* = D. Klein, *Sammlung von Griechischen Kleinsilbermünzen und Bronzen*, Milano 1999
– KNM = Kadman Numismatic Museum

– Kraay, *Greek Coins* = C.M. Kraay, *Archaic and Classical Greek Coins*, London 1975
– Kraay-Hirmer, *Greek Coins* = C.M. Kraay and M. Hirmer, *Greek Coins*, London 1966
– KTB = Kültür ve Turizm Bakanligi
– Lapp-Lapp, *Wâdi Ed-Daliyeh* = P. W. and N. Lapp, *Discoveries in the Wâdi Ed-Daliyeh*, *AASOR* 41, Cambridge Ma. 1974
– Le Rider, *Fouilles de Suse* = G. Le Rider, *Suse sous les Séleucides et les Parthes*, MDP XXXVIII, Paris 1965
– Le Rider, *Mission en Susiane* = G. Le Rider, *Mission en Susiane*, MDP XXV, Paris 1934
– MAG = Museum and Art Gallery
– MAN = Museo Arqueológico Nacional
– MBTS = Institut Catholique, Musée Bible et Terre Sainte
– Meshorer-Qedar, *Coinage of Samaria* = Y. Meshorer and S. Qedar, *The Coinage of Samaria in the Fourth Century BCE*, Jerusalem 1991
– Meshorer-Qedar, *Samarian Coinage* = Y. Meshorer and S. Qedar, *Samarian Coinage*, Jerusalem 1999
– Meyers, *Gush Ḥalav* = E.M. Meyers *et al.*, *Excavations at the ancient Synagogue of Gush Ḥalav*, Winona Lake 1990
– MFA = Museum of Fine Arts
– Mildenberg-Hurter, *Dewing Collection* = L. Mildenberg and S. Hurter, *The Arthur S. Dewing Collection of Greek Coins*, New York 1985
– MK = Münzkabinett
– MNK = Muzeum Narodowe w Krakowie
– MNM = Magyar Nemzeti Museum
– Naster, *Collection De Hirsch* = P. Naster, *La Collection Lucien de Hirsch*, Brussels 1959
– NatMus = Nationalmuset
– *NEA* = *Near Eastern Archaeology*
– Newell, *Tyrus* = E.T. Newell, *Tyrus rediviva*, New York 1923
– NFA = Numismatic Fine Arts
– NM = National Museum
– NMM = National Maritime Museum
– *NMN* = *National Museum News*
– Oleson, *Dewing Collection* = J. Oleson, *Greek Numismatic Art. Coins of the Arthur Stone Dewing Collection*, Harvard 1975
– PUL = Princeton University Libraries
– Raynor-Meshorer, *Ancient Meiron* = J. Raynor and Y. Meshorer, *The Coins of Ancient Meiron*, Winona Lake 1968.
– RCC = Royal Coin Cabinet

– Regling, *Sammlung Warren* = K. Regling, *Die Griechischer Münzen der Sammlung Warren*, Berlin 1901
– RM = Rijksmuseum, het Koninklijk Penningkabinet
– RocMus = Rockfeller Museum
– ROM = Royal Ontario Museum
– Schlumberger, *Argent grec* = D. Schlumberger, « L'argent grec dans l'empire achéménide », in R. Curiel and D. Schlumberger, *Trésors monétaires d'Afghanistan*, Paris 1953, pp. 3-54
– *SEAP* = *Studi di Egittologia e di Antichità Puniche*
– *SEL* = *Studi Epigrafici e Linguistici sul Vicino Oriente Antico*
– SM = Staatliche Museum
– SMS = Staatliche Münzsammlung
– *SNG ANS* = *Sylloge Nummorum Graecorum ANS, The Burton Y. Berry Collection*, New York 1961-62
– *SNG Cambridge* = *Sylloge Nummorum Graecorum*, Part 4, Fitzwilliam Museum, Oxford 1940
– *SNG Copenhagen* = *Sylloge Nummorum Graecorum. The Royal Danish Collection*, Copenhagen 1942-77
– *SNG Copenhagen 1987* = *Sylloge Nummorum Graecorum. Fabricius Collection*, Aarrhus University 1987
– *SNG VIII, Hart Collection* = *Sylloge Nummorum Graecorum*, vol. VIII, *The Hart Collection*, Blackburn Museum, Oxford University 1989
– Stern, *Dor Final Report* = E. Stern dir., *Excavations at Dor, Final Report, Volumes IB, Areas A and C: The Finds*, Jerusalem 1995
– Stern, *Dor Ruler* = E. Stern, *Dor Ruler of the Seas. Twelve Years of Excavations at the Israelite-Phoenician Harbor Town on the Carmel Coast*, Jerusalem 1994[2]
– Troxell, *Davis Collection* = H.A. Troxell, *The Norman Davis Collection*, New York 1969
– UOM = Universitetet Oslo Myntkabinettet
– VM = Vatican Museum
– WL = Westfälisches Landesmuseum für Kunst und Kulturgeschichte
– Zeimal, *Monnaies Tadjikistan* = E.B. Zeimal, *Les monnaies antiques du Tadjikistan*, Douchanbe 1983
– Zograf, *Monnaies* = A. N. Zograf, *Monnaies antiques*, Moscow 1951

BIBLIOGRAPHY

We present here a selected bibliography. The other references are mentioned in the footnotes of the different chapters. The references already listed in the 'Abbreviations' are not repeated in the bibliography. The translations of Greek and Latin texts quoted in this book are often those of the Loeb Classical Library, Harvad University Press (LCL).

— ACQUARO, E., 'Iconografie monetali fenicie', *Byrsa* 1, 2003, pp. 1-6.

— AMADASI GUZZO, M.G., 'Cultes et épithètes de Milqart', *Trans* 30, 2005, pp. 9-18.

— AMANDRY, M., 'Manipulations, innovations monétaires et techniques financières dans le monde grec', *Revue de la BN* 44, 1992, pp. 58-63.

— ANSON, E.A., 'The Persian fleet in 334', *CP* 84, 1989, pp. 44-49.

— ARCHI, A. ed., *Circulation of Goods in non-palatial Context in the Ancient Near East*, Rome 1984.

— ARIEL, D.T., 'Coins from Excavations at Tel Nahariya, 1982', *ʿAtiqot* 22, 1993, pp. 125-132.

— AUBET, M.E., *The Phoenician cemetery of Tyre-Al Bass: excavations 1997-1999*, Beirut 2004.

— AUSTIN, R.P., 'Athens and the Satraps' Revolt', *JHS* 64, 1944, pp. 97-100.

— AVIGAD, N., 'Seals and Sealings', *IEJ* 14, 1964, pp. 190-194.

— BADIAN, E., 'The Peace of Callias', *JHS* 107, 1987, pp. 1-39.

— BADIAN, E., 'The King's Peace', in *Georgica. Greek Studies in Honor of G. Cawkwell*, *BICS* Suppl. 58, London 1991, pp. 25-48.

— BALMUTH, M.S., 'The monetary Forerunners of Coinage in Phoenicia and Palestine', in *The Patterns of Monetary Development in Phoenicia and Palestine in Antiquity*, Tel Aviv-Jerusalem 1967, pp. 25-32.

— BALOG, P., 'Notes on ancient and medieval Techniques', *NC* 6th ser. 15, 1955, pp. 195-202.

— BARAG, D., 'The effects of the Tennes rebellion on Palestine', *BASOR* 183, 1966, pp. 6-12.

— BARNETT, R.D., *Assyrian Palace Reliefs and their Influence on the Sculptures of Babylonia and Persia*, London 1960.

— BARRANDON, J.-N., and GUERRA, M.F., 'Méthodes d'analyse appliquées à la numismatique', in C. Morrisson and B. Kluge eds, *A Survey of Numismatic Research 1990-1995*, Berlin 1997, pp. 825-830.

— BASTIEN, P., and HUVELIN, H., 'Orientation des axes de coins dans le monnayage impérial romain', *BSFN* 26, 1971, pp. 130-135.

— BAYNHAM, E., *Alexander the Great. The unique history of Quintus Curtius*, Ann Arbor 1998.

— BELLINGER, A.R., 'An Alexander Hoard from Byblos', *Ber.* 10, 1950-51, pp. 37-49.

— BENDA-WEBER, I., *Zwei autochthone Ethnien Kleinasiens zwischen Orient und Okzident*, Bonn 2005.

— BENZ, F.L., *Personal Names in the Phoenician and Punic Inscriptions*, Rome 1972.

— BÉREND, D., 'Réflexions sur les fractions du monnayage grec', in A. Houghton *et al.* eds, *Studies in Honor of Leo Mildenberg*, Wetteren 1984, pp. 7-30.

— BETLYON, J.W., 'A new Chronology for the Pre-Alexandrine Coinage of Sidon', *ANSMN* 21, 1976, pp. 11-35.

— BETLYON, J.W., 'Canaanite Myth and the Early Coinage of the Phoenician City-States', in M. Silver ed., *Ancient Economy in Mythology: East and West*, Savage/Maryland 1991, pp. 135-161.

— BICKERMAN, E.J., 'Notes sur la chronologie de la XXXe dynastie', in *Mélanges Maspéro* I, Cairo 1934, pp. 77-82.

— BIGWOOD, J.M., 'Ctesias' account of the revolt of Inarus', *Phoenix* 30, 1976, pp. 1-25.

— BIKAI, P.M., *The Pottery of Tyre*, Warminster 1978.

— BIVAR, A.D.H., 'A Rosette Phiale inscribed in Aramaic', *BSOAS* 24, 1961, pp. 189-199.

— BIVAR, A.H., 'A Persian Monument at Athens and its Connections with the Achaemenid State Seals', in *W.B. Henning Memorial Volume*, London 1970, pp. 43-61.

— BLANCO FREIJEIRO, A., et al., *Ancient Mining and Metallurgy in South-West Spain*, London 1982.

— BLOEDOW, E., 'The peaces of Callias', *SO* 67, 1992, pp. 41-68.

— BOGAERT, P.-M., 'Le Chérub de Tyr (Ez 28, 14.16) et l'hippocampe de ses monnaies', in R. Liwak and S. Wagner eds, *Prophetie und geschichtliche Wirklichkeit in alter Israel, Festschrift für S. Herrmann*, Stuttgart el al. 1991, pp. 29-38.

— BOGAERT, R., 'L'essai des monnaies dans l'Antiquité', *RBN* 122, 1976, pp. 8-12.

— BOIG, T., 'The 'Accession Year' in the Late Achaemenid and Early Hellenistic Period', in C. Wunsch ed., *Mining the Archives. Festschrift for Christopher Walker on the Occasion of His 60th Birthday*, Dresden 2002, pp. 25-34.

— BONDÌ, S.F., 'Istituzioni e politica a Sidone dal 351 al 332 av. Cr.', *RSF* 2, 1974, pp. 149-160.

— BONDÌ, S.F., 'Note sull' economia fenicia – I. Impresa privata e ruolo dello Stato', *EVO* 1, 1978, pp. 139-150.

— BONNET, C., 'Le culte de Leucothéa et de Mélicerte, en Grèce, au Proche-Orient et en Italie', *SMSR* 52, 1986, pp. 53-71.

— BONNET, C., *Melqart. Cultes et mythes de l'Héraclès tyrien en Méditerranée*, Leuwen 1988.

— BONNET, C., 'La terminologie phénico-punique relative au métier de lapicide et à la gravure des textes', *SEL* 7, 1990, pp. 111-122.

— BONNET, C., 'Les scribes phénico-puniques', in C. Baurain et al. eds, *Phoinikeia Grammata. Lire et écrire en Méditerranée*, Namur 1991, pp. 147-171.

— BONNET, C., 'Melqart est-il vraiment le Baal de Tyr?', *UF* 27, 1995, pp. 696-701.

— BORDREUIL, P., 'Deux épigraphes phéniciennes provenant des fouilles de Tell Rachidieh', *Annales d'Histoire et d'Archéologie* 1, 1982, pp. 137-140.

— BORDREUIL, P., 'Attestations inédites de Melqart, Baal Ḥamon et Baal Ṣaphon à Tyr (Nouveaux documents religieux phéniciens II)', in C. Bonnet et al. eds, *Religio Phoenicia*, Studia Phoenicia IV, Namur 1986, pp. 77-86.

— BORDREUIL, P., 'Nouvelle inscription phénicienne dédiée à Milqart', in *ACFP* V/1, Palermo 2005, pp. 135-137.

— BOSWORTH, A.B., *A historian commentary on Arrian's history of Alexander* I, Oxford 1980.

— BOSWORTH, A.B., *From Arrian to Alexander. Studies in historical interpretation*, Oxford 1988.

— BOSWORTH, A.B., 'Plutarch, Callisthenes and the peace of Callias', *JHS* 110, 1990, pp. 1-13.

— BOUYON, B., et al., *Systèmes et technologie des monnaies de bronze (4e s. avant J.-C. – 3e s. après J.-C.)*, Wetteren 2000.

— BRAUND, P., and WILKINS, J. eds, *Athenaeus and his world. Reading Greek Culture in the Roman Empire*, Exeter 2000.

— BRIANT, P., *Histoire de l'Empire perse. De Cyrus à Alexandre*, Fayard, Paris 1996 (English translation: *From Cyrus to Alexander. A History of the Persian Empire*, Eisenbrauns, Winona Lake 2002).

— BRIANT, P., 'Numismatique, frappes monétaires et histoire en Asie Mineure achéménide (quelques remarques de conclusion)', in O. Casabonne ed., *Mécanismes et innovations monétaires dans l'Anatolie achéménide. Numismatique et Histoire*, Paris 2000, pp. 265-274.

— BRIANT, P., *Darius dans l'ombre d'Alexandre*, Paris 2003.

— BRIANT, P., and DESCAT, R., 'Un registre douanier de la satrapie d'Egypte à l'époque achéménide (*TAD* C3, 7)', in N. Grimal and B. Menu eds, *Le commerce en Egypte ancienne*, Cairo 1996, pp. 59-104.

— BROWN, J.P., *The Lebanon and Phoenicia I*, Beirut 1969.

— BROWN, T.S., 'Megabysus son of Zopyrus', *AW* 15, 1987, pp. 65-74.

— BRUNT, P.A., 'Persian accounts of Alexander's campaigns', *CQ* 12, 1962, pp. 141-155.

— BUNNENS, G., *L'expansion phénicienne en Méditerranée: essai d'interprétation fondé sur une analyse des traditions littéraires*, Brussels-Rome 1979.

— BURSTEIN, S., 'Prelude to Alexander: the reign of Khababash', *AHB* 14, 2000, pp. 149-154.

— BUTTREY, S., and BUTTREY, T.V., 'Calculating ancient coin production, again', *AJN* 9, 1997, pp. 113-135.

— BUTTREY, T.V., 'Calculating Ancient Coin Production: Facts and Fantasies', *NC* 153, 1993, pp. 335-351.

— CAHILL, J.M., 'Royal Rosettes fit for a King', *BAR* 23/5, 1993, pp. 48-57.

— CAHILL, J.M., 'Rosette Stamp Seal Impressions from Ancient Judah', *IEJ* 45, 1995, pp. 231-252.

— CARREZ-MARATRAY, J.-Y., 'Psammétique le tyran. Pouvoir, usurpation et alliances en Méditerranée orientale au IVe s. av. J.-C.', *Trans* 30, 2005, pp. 37-63.

— CARTER, G.F., 'Simplified Method for Calculating the Original Number of Dies from Die-Link Statistics', *ANSMN* 28, 1983, pp. 195-206.

— CASABONNE, O., 'Le syennésis cilicien et Cyrus: l'apport des sources numismatiques', in P. Briant ed., *Dans les pas des Dix-mille. Peuples et pays du Proche-Orient vus par un Grec*, Toulouse 1995, pp. 147-172.

— CASABONNE, O., 'Présence et influence perses en Cilicie à l'époque achéménide – Iconographie et représentations', *Anatolia Antiqua* 4, 1996, pp. 121-145.

— CASABONNE, O., *La Cilicie à l'époque achéménide*, Paris 2004.

— CAWKWELL, G.L., 'Demosthenes' policy after peace of Philocrates I', *CQ* 13, 1963, pp. 120-138.

— CHEHAB, M., *Fouilles de Tyr*, BMB 33-36, Beirut 1983-1986.

— CHILDS, W.A.P., 'Lycian Relations with Persians and Greeks in the fifth and fourth Centuries reexamined', *AS* 31, 1981, pp. 55-80.

— CHUVIN, P., 'Apollon au trident et les dieux de Tarse', *JSav*, 1981, pp. 305-326.

— CLERMONT-GANNEAU, C., 'Le paradeisos royal achéménide de Sidon', *RB* 30, 1921, pp. 176-182.

— COOPER, D.R., *The Art and Craft of Coinmaking, A History of Minting Technology*, London 1988.

— CORNELIUS, I., 'The lion in the art of the ancient Near East: a study of selected motifs', *JNSL* 15, 1989, pp. 53-79.

— CROSS, F.M., 'The Discovery of the Samaria Papyri', *BA* 26, 1963, pp. 110-121.

— CROSS, F.M., 'Papyri of the Fourth Century B.C. from Dâliyeh', in D.N. Freedman and J.C. Greenfield eds, *New Directions in Biblical Archaeology*, New York 1969, pp. 44-69.

— CROSS, F.M., 'Coins', in Lapp-Lapp, *Wâdī ed-Dâliyeh*, pp. 53-59.

— CULASSO GASTALDI, E., *Le prossenie ateniesi des IV secolo a.c. onorati asiatici*, Alessandria 2003.

— CULICAN, W., 'The iconography of some Phoenician Seals and Seal Impressions', *AJBA* 1, 1968, pp. 50-103.

— CUMONT, F., 'Deux autels de Phénicie', *Syr.* 8, 1927, pp. 163-168.

— DAHOOD, M., 'Some Eblaite and Phoenician Months Names', in *ACFP* I/2, Rome 1983, pp. 595-598.

— DARNELL, J.C., 'The *Kbnt.wt* ships of the late period', in J.H. Johnson ed., *Life in a Multicultural Society. Egypt from Cambyses to Constantine and beyond*, Chicago 1992, pp. 67-89.

— DAVESNE, A., 'La circulation monétaire en Cilicie à l'époque achéménide', *REG*, 1988, pp. 157-168.

— DAVESNE, A., and LE RIDER, G., *Gülnar II. Le trésor de Meydancikkale*, Paris 1989.

— DAVESNE, A., and MASSON, O., 'A propos du trésor des monnaies de Gülnar en Cilicie: problèmes numismatiques et 'graffiti' monétaires', *RA*, 1985, pp. 29-46.

— DE CALLATAŸ, F., 'Calculating ancient coin production: Seeking a balance', *NC* 155, 1995, pp. 289-311.

— DE CALLATAŸ, F., *Les monnaies grecques et l'orientation des axes*, Milan 1996.

— DE CALLATAŸ, F., 'Le volume des émissions monétaires dans l'antiquité', *AIIN* 44, 1997, pp. 53-62.

— DE CALLATAŸ, F., 'Étude de technique monétaire: le rapport 'nombre de coins de revers/nombre de coins de droit' à l'époque hellénistique', *RAHAL* 32, 1999, pp. 91-102.

— DE CALLATAŸ, F., 'La dimension des coins monétaires de tétradrachmes hellénistiques d'après l'étude des monnaies décentrées', in B. Kluge and B. Weisser eds, *XII. Internationaler Numismatischer Kongress, Berlin 1997, Akten I*, Berlin 2000, pp. 244-251.

— DE CALLATAŸ, F., 'Les taux de survie des émissions monétaires antiques, médiévales et modernes. Essai de mise en perspective et conséquences quant à la productivité des coins dans l'Antiquité', *RN* 155, 2000, pp. 87-109.

— DE CALLATAŸ, F., DEPEYROT, G., and VILLARONGA, L., *L'argent monnayé d'Alexandre le Grand à Auguste*, Bruxelles 1993.

— DEBORD, P., *L'Asie Mineure au IVe siècle (412-323 a.c.). Pouvoirs et jeux politiques*, Bordeaux 1999.

— DELAMARE, F., et al., 'A Mechanical Approach to Coin Striking: Application to the Study of Byzantine Gold Solidi', in W.A. Oddy ed., *Metallurgy in Numismatics* 2, London 1988, pp 41-52.

— DELAVAULT, B., and LEMAIRE, A., 'Les inscriptions phéniciennes de Palestine', *RSF* 7, 1979, pp. 1-39.

— DEPUYDT, L., 'Evidence for Accession Dating under the Achaemenids', *JAOS* 115, 1995, pp. 193-204.

— DESIDERI, P., and JASINK, A.M., *Cilicia. Dall' età di Kizzuwatna alla conquista macedone*, Torino 1990.

— DESTROOPER-GEORGIADES, A., 'Chypre et l'Egypte à l'époque achéménide à la lumière des témoignages numismatiques', *Trans* 9, 1995, pp. 149-160.

— DEUTSCH, R., and HELTZER, M., 'Numismatic Evidence from the Sharon Plain', *Trans* 13, 1997, pp. 17-20.

— DEVAUCHELLE, D., 'Réflexions sur les documents égyptiens datés de la deuxième domination perse', *Trans* 10, 1995, pp. 35-43.

— DHENIN, M., 'Quelques remarques sur le travail des graveurs de coins', in G. Depeyrot et al. eds, *Rythmes de la production monétaire, de l'Antiquité à nos jours*, Louvain-la-Neuve 1987, pp. 453-457.

— DIAKONOFF, I.M., 'Slaves, Helots and serfs in early antiquity', *AAH* 22, 1974, pp. 45-78.

— DIEBOLT, J., and NICOLLET PIERRE, H., 'Recherches sur le métal des tétradrachmes à types athéniens', *RSN* 56, 1977, pp. 79-91.

— DOMERGUE, C., *Les mines de la Péninsule Ibérique dans l'Antiquité romaine*, Rome 1989.

— DOTHAN, M., 'Tel Akko', *RB* 82, 1975, pp. 84-86.

— DOTHAN, M., 'Akko: Interim Excavation Report. First Season, 1973/4', *BASOR* 224, 1976, pp. 1-48.

— DOTHAN, M., 'A Phoenician inscription from ʿAkko', *IEJ* 35, 1985, pp. 86-94.

— DUFF, T., *Plutarch's Lives. Exploring Virtue and Vice*, Oxford 1999.

— DUNAND, M., 'Stèle araméenne dédiée à Melqart', *BMB* 3, 1939, pp. 65-76.

— DUSEK, J., *Les manuscrits araméens du Wadi Daliyeh et la Samarie vers 450-432 av. J.-C.*, Leiden-Boston 2007.

— DUS, J., 'Melek ṣōr-Melqart? (Zur Interpretation von Ez 28.11-19)', *ArOr* 26, 1958, pp. 179-185.

— DUSSAUD, R., 'Melqart', *Syr.* 25, 1946-48, pp. 205-230.

— ELAYI, A.G., BARRANDON, J.-N., and ELAYI, J., 'The Devaluation of Sidonian Coins in 365 B.C.E. as Determined by Fast Neutron Activation Analysis and first Bronze Issues', *AJN* 17, 2007, pp. 1-8.

— ELAYI, J., 'The relations between Tyre and Carthage during the Persian Period', *JANES* 13, 1981, pp. 15-29.

— ELAYI, J., 'La révolte des esclaves de Tyr relatée par Justin', *BaghM* 12, 1981, pp. 139-150.

— ELAYI, J., 'Studies in Phoenician Geography during the Persian Period', *JNES* 41, 1982, pp. 83-110.

— ELAYI, J., 'Les cités phéniciennes entre liberté et sujétion', *DHA* 16, 1990, pp. 93-113.

— ELAYI, J., 'Etude typologique des sicles de Tyr au dauphin', *Cahiers Numismatiques* 108, 1991, pp. 11-17.

— ELAYI, J., 'Remarques méthodologiques sur l'étude paléographique des légendes monétaires phéniciennes', in C. Baurain *et al.* eds, *Phoinikeia Grammata. Lire et écrire en Méditerranée*, Namur 1991, pp. 187-200.

— ELAYI, J., 'La domination perse sur les cités phéniciennes', in *ACFP* II/1, Rome 1991, pp. 77-85.

— ELAYI, J., 'Etude paléolographique des légendes monétaires phéniciennes d'époque perse', *Trans* 5, 1992, pp. 21-43.

— ELAYI, J., 'Les sicles de Tyr au dauphin', *NAC* 21, 1992, pp. 37-49.

— ELAYI, J., 'La diffusion des monnaies phéniciennes en Palestine', in Laperrousaz, E., and Lemaire, A. dirs, *La Palestine à l'époque perse*, Paris 1994, pp. 289-309.

— ELAYI, J., 'La place de l'Egypte dans la recherche sur les Phéniciens', *Trans* 9, 1995, pp. 11-24.

— ELAYI, J., 'An Updated Chronology of the Reigns of Phoenician Kings during the Persian Period (539-333 BCE)', *Trans* 32, 2006, pp. 11-43.

— ELAYI, J., 'Remarques méthodologiques sur l'étude iconographique des monnaies phéniciennes', in *Mélanges J.-P. Rey-Coquais, MUSJ* 59, 2006, pp. 47-54.

— ELAYI, J., 'The Tyrian Monetary Inscriptions of the Persian Period', *Trans* 34, 2007, pp. 65-101.

— ELAYI, J., and ELAYI, A.G., 'Systems of Abbreviations used by Byblos, Tyre and Arwad in their pre-Alexandrine Coinages', *JNG* 37-38, 1987-88, pp. 11-22.

— ELAYI, J., and ELAYI, A.G., 'Nouvelles monnaies divisionnaires de Tyr au dauphin avec inscription', *BCEN* 27, 1990, pp. 69-74.

— ELAYI, J., and ELAYI, A.G., 'Les monnaies de Tyr au dauphin et à la rosette', *Annotazioni Numismatiche* 3, 1991, pp. 38-42.

— ELAYI, J., and ELAYI, A.G., 'Nouveaux trésors de monnaies phéniciennes (*CH* VIII)', *Trans* 11, 1996, pp. 95-114.

— ELAYI, J., and ELAYI, A.G., 'La dernière série tyrienne en bronze aux types civiques', *NAC* 27, 1998, pp. 129-139.

— ELAYI, J., and ELAYI, A.G., 'Nouveaux trésors de monnaies phéniciennes (*CH* IX)', *Trans* 26, 2003, pp. 105-117.

— ELAYI, J., and ELAYI, A.G., 'Le monnayage sidonien de Mazday', *Trans* 27, 2004, pp. 155-162.

— ELAYI, J., and LEMAIRE, A., 'Les petites monnaies de Tyr au dauphin avec inscription', *NAC* 19, 1990, pp. 99-116.

— ELAYI, J., and Sapin, J., *Nouveaux regards sur la Transeuphratène*, Brépols, Turnhout 1991 (*Beyond the River. New Perspectives on Transeuphratène*, JSOT.S 250, Sheffield 1998).

— ELAYI, J., and SAPIN, J., *Quinze ans de recherche (1985-2000) sur la Transeuphratène à l'époque perse*, Paris 2000.

— ELGAVISH, Y., 'Shiqmona', *RB* 77, 1970, pp. 386-387.

— EPHʿAL, I., and NAVEH, J., *Aramaic Ostraca of the fourth Century BC from Idumea*, Jerusalem 1996.

— ESTY, W.W., 'Estimating the Size of a Coinage', *NC* 144, 1984, pp. 180-183.

— ESTY, W.W., 'Estimation of the Size of a Coinage: a Survey and Comparison of Methods', *NC* 146, 1986, pp. 185-215.

— FINKIELSZTEJN, G. 'Phanébal, déesse d'Ascalon', in T. Hackens and G. Moucharte eds, *Numismatique et histoire économique phéniciennes et puniques*, Studia Phoenicia IX, Louvain-la-Neuve 1992, pp. 51-58.

— FLEMING, W.B., *History of Tyre*, New York 1915.

— FORBES, R.J., *Studies in Ancient Technology* VIII, Leiden 1964; IX, Leiden 1972.

— FROST, H., 'Recent Observations on the Submerged Harbourworks at Tyre', *BMB* 24, 1971, pp. 103-111.

— FULCO, W.J., 'Monnaies de Tell Keisan 1971-1974', *RB* 82, 1975, pp. 134-139.

— GEIGER, J., *Cornelius Nepos and ancient political biography*, Wiesbaden 1985.

— GERIN, D., 'Techniques of Die-engraving: Some Reflections on Obols of the Arcadian Ligue in the 3rd Century B.C.', in M.M. Archibald and M.R. Cowell, *Metallurgy in Numismatics*, London 1993, pp. 20-25.

— GITLER, H., 'Achaemenid Motifs in the Coinage of Ashdod, Ascalon and Gaza from the Fourth Century BC', *Trans* 20, 2000, pp. 73-87.

— GITLER, H., and TAL, O., *The Coinage of Philistia of the Fifth and Fourth Centuries BC. A Study of the Earliest Coins of Palestine*, Milan-New York 2006.

— GOEDICKE, H., 'Comments of the Satrap Stela', *BES* 6, 1985, pp. 33-54.

— GREENFIELD, J.C., 'A Group of Phoenician City Seals', *IEJ* 35, 1985, pp. 129-134.

— GREENWELL, W., 'On a Find of archaic Greek Coins in Egypt', *NC*, 1890, pp. 1-12.

— GROPP, D.M., *Wadi Daliyeh II. The Samaria Papyri from Wadi Daliyeh*, DJD 28, Oxford 2001.

— GUBEL, E., 'La glyptique et la genèse de l'iconographie monétaire phénicienne', in T. Hackens and G. Moucharte eds, *Numismatique et histoire économique phéniciennes et puniques*, Studia Phoenicia IX, Louvain-la-Neuve 1992, pp. 1-11.

— GUBEL, E., 'Cinq bulles inédites des archives tyriennes de l'époque achéménide', *Sem.* 47, 1998, pp. 53-64.

— GUBEL, E., *Art phénicien. La sculpture de tradition phénicienne*, Paris 2002.

— GUEY, J., and CARCASSONNE, C., 'Coins de droit et de revers. Étude descriptive d'un échantillon', *RN* 6, 1970, pp. 7-32.

— HACKENS, T., 'Terminologie et techniques de fabrication', in *Numismatique antique. Problèmes et méthodes*, Annales de l'Est, Nancy-Louvain 1975, pp. 10-12.

— HALL, E.T., and METCALF, D.M., *Methods of chemical and metallurgical Investigation of ancient Coinage*, London 1970.

— HAMMOND, N.G.L., *Three historians of Alexander the Great*, Cambridge 1983.

— HANSON, R.S., *Tyrian Influence in the Upper Galilee*, Cambridge Ma. 1980.

— HARRISON, C.M., *Coins of the Persian Satraps*, Ann Arbor 1992.

— HAUBEN, H., 'The king of the Sidonians and the Persian imperial fleet', *AncSoc* 1, 1970, pp. 1-8.

— HELTZER, M., 'The Persian invasion to Cyprus and the date of the submission of Evagoras', in *Acts of the third International Congress of Cypriot Studies*, Nicosia 2000, pp. 717-719.

— HOFTIJZER, J., and JONGELING, K., *Dictionary of the North-West Semitic Inscriptions*, Leiden *et al.* 1995.

— HOGLUND, K.G., *Achaemenid Imperial Administration in Syria-Palestine and the Missions of Ezra and Nehemiah*, Atlanta 1992.

— HOMERIN, T.E., 'Echoes of a Thirsty Owl: Death and Afterlife in Pre-Islamic Arabic Poetry', *JNES* 44, 1985, pp. 165-164.

— HUSS, W., 'Der Rätselhäfte Pharao Chababasch', *SEL* 11, 1994, pp. 97-112.

— HVIDBERG-HANSEN, F.O., 'Baᶜal-Malagê dans le traité entre Asarhaddon et le roi de Tyr', *AcOr* 35, 1973, pp. 57-81.

— JENKINS, G.K., 'Coins from the Collection of C.J. Rich', *BMQ* 28, 1964, pp. 88-94.

— JENSEN, L.B., 'Royal Purple of Tyre', *JNES* 22, 1963, pp. 104-118.

— JIDEJIAN, N., *Tyre through the Ages*, Beirut 1969.

— JOANNES, F., 'Métaux précieux et moyens de paiement en Babylonie achéménide et hellénistique', *Trans* 8, 1994, pp. 137-144.

— KAWKABANI, I., 'Les estampilles phéniciennes de Tyr', *AHL* 21, 2005, pp. 1-79.

— KATZENSTEIN, H.J., *The History of Tyre*, Jerusalem 1973.

— KINDLER, A. 'The Mint of Tyre – The Major Source of Silver Coins in Ancient Palestine', *ErIs* 8, 1967, pp. 318-324.

— KLETTER, R., 'Iron Age Hoards of Precious Metals in Palestine – an 'Underground Economy'?', *Levant* 35, 2003, pp. 139-152.

— KLONER, A., 'Flan mould from Kh. Rafi^c', *ʿAtiqot* 11, 1976, pp. 112-113.

— KOFFMAHN, E., 'Sind die altisraelitischen Monatsbezeichnungen mit den kanaanäisch-phönikischen identisch?', *BZ* 10/2, 1966, pp. 197-219.

— KRAAY, C.M., 'Hoards, Small Change and the Origin of Coinage', *JHS* 84, 1964, pp. 76-91.

— KRAAY, C.M., and MOOREY, P.R.S., 'Two Fifth Century Hoards from the Near East', *RN* 10, 1968, pp. 181-235.

— KURZ, O., 'Lion-masks with rings in the West and in the East', in M. Barasch ed., *Studies in Art*, Scripta Hierosolymitana 25, Jerusalem 1972, pp. 22-41.

— LAMBERT, C., 'A Hoard of Phoenician Coins', *QDAP* 1, 1931, pp. 10-20.

— LAMBERT, C., 'Egypto-arabian, Phoenician, and other Coins of the fourth Century B.C. found in Palestine', *QDAP* 2, 1933, pp. 1-10.

— LECLANT, J., 'Relations entre l'Égypte et la Phénicie', in *The Role of the Phoenicians in the Interaction of Mediterranean Civilizations, Archaeological Symposium at the American University of Beirut*, Beirut 1968, pp. 9-31.

— LEMAIRE, A., 'Le monnayage de Tyr et celui dit d'Akko dans la deuxième moitié du IVe siècle av. J.-C.', *RN* 18, 1976, pp. 11-24.

— LEMAIRE, A., 'Le royaume de Tyr dans la seconde moitié du IVe siècle av. J.-C.', in *ACFP* II/1, Roma 1991, pp. 131-150.

— LEMAIRE, A., *Nouvelles inscriptions araméennes d'Idumée au Musée d'Israël*, Paris 1996.

— LEMAIRE, A., *Nouvelles inscriptions araméennes d'Idumée* II, Paris 2002.

— LEMAIRE, A., 'Inscription royale phénicienne sur bateau votif', in M. Heltzer and M. Malul, *T^{e}shûrôt LaAvishur, Studies in the Bible and the Ancient Near East, in Hebrew and Semitic Languages, Festschrift Y. Avishur*, Tel Aviv-Jaffa 2004, pp. 117-129.

— LEMAIRE, A., 'La Transeuphratene en transition', in P. Briant and F. Joannès eds, *La transition entre l'empire achéménide et les royaumes hellénistiques (vers 350-300 av. J.-C.)*, Paris 2006, pp. 405-434.

— LEMAIRE, A., and ELAYI, J., 'Graffiti monétaires ouest-sémitiques', in T. Hackens and G. Moucharte eds, *Numismatique et histoire économique phéniciennes et puniques*, Studia Phoenicia IX, Louvain-la-Neuve 1992, pp. 59-76.

— LENORMANT, F., 'Les graffiti monétaires de l'antiquité', *RN* n.s. 15, 1874-77, pp. 325-346.

— LE RIDER, G., 'Sur la fabrication des coins monétaires dans l'antiquité grecque', *Schweizer Münzblätter* 29, 1958, pp. 4-5.

— LE RIDER, G., 'Contremarques et surfrappes dans l'Antiquité grecque', in *Numismatique antique. Problèmes et méthodes*, Annales de l'Est, Nancy-Louvain 1975, pp. 27-61.

— LE RIDER, G., *La naissance de la monnaie. Pratiques monétaires de l'Orient ancien*, Paris 2001.

— LEUZE, O., *Die Satrapieneinteilung in Syrien und im Zweiströmlande von 520-320*, Halle 1935.

— LEVY, E., 'Les trois traités entre Sparte et le Roi', *BHC* 107, 1983, pp. 221-241.

— LEWIS, D.M., 'The Phoenician fleet in 411', *Historia* 7, 1958, pp. 392-397.

— LIOYD, A.B., 'Were Necho's Triremes Phoenician?', *JHS* 95, 1975, pp. 268-279.

— LIPIŃSKI, E., *Dieux et déesses de l'univers phénicien et punique*, Leuven 1995.

— LIPIŃSKI, E., *Itineraria Phoenicia*, Leuven *et al.* 2004.

— LOCKYEAR, K., 'Hoard structure and coin production in antiquity – an empirical investigation', *NC* 159, 1999, pp. 215-243.

— MACDONALD, G., 'Fixed and Loose Dies in Ancient Coinage', in *Corolla Numismatica. Essays in Honour of B.V. Head*, Oxford 1906, pp. 78-188.

— MACRIDY BEY, T., 'Fouilles exécutées dans le région de Tyr en 1903', *Syr.* 3, 1922, pp. 116-133.

— MATTINGLY, H.B., 'The Jordan Hoard (IGCH 1482) and Kimon's last Expedition', in *Proceedings of the 10th International Congress of Numismatics*, London 1986, pp. 59-64.

— MAZZA, F., et al., *Fonti classiche per la civiltà fenicia e punica* I, Roma 1988.

— MAZZUCATO, C., 'Il murice nelle monete fenicie e puniche', *Byrsa* 2, 2003, pp. 121-130.

— MENDELSOHN, I., *Slavery in the Ancient Near East*, New York 1949.

— MESHORER, Y. 'The Mints of Ashdod and Ascalon during the Late Persian Period', *ErIs* 20, Jerusalem 1989, *Vol. Y. Yadin*, pp. 287-291.

— METCALF, D.M., and ODDY, W.A., *Metallurgy in Numismatics*, London 1980.

— METCALF, D.M., et al., 'Coins from the Excavations at ʿAtlit (Pilgrim's Castle and Its *Faubourg*', ʿ*Atiqot* 37, 1999, pp. 89*-164*.

— MILDENBERG, L., "Those ridiculous arrows'. On the meaning of the die position', *Nomismatika Chronika* 8, 1989, pp. 23-27 (= U. Hübner and E.A. Knauf eds, *Leo Mildenberg. Vestigia Leonis. Studien zur antiken Numismatik Israels, Palästinas und der östlichen Mittelmeerwelt*, Freiburg-Göttingen 1998, pp. 263-264).

— MILDENBERG, L., 'Notes on the Coins Issues of Mazday', *INJ* 11, 1990-91, pp. 9-23 (= Hübner-Knauf eds, *ibid.*, pp. 43-53).

— MILNE, J.G., 'A Hoard of coins from Egypt of the fourth Century B.C.', *RA*, 1905, pp. 257-261.

— MOORE, P., *Quintus Curtius Rufus' 'Historiae Alexandri Magni': A Study in Rhetorical historiography*, Oxford 1995.

— MORHANGE, C., and SAGHIEH-BEYDOUN, M., *La Mobilité des Paysages Portuaires Antiques du Liban*, BAAL Hors-Série II, Beirut 2005.

— MOYSEY, R.A., *Greek Relations with the Persian Satraps: 371-343 B.C.*, Princeton 1974.

— MOYSEY, R.A., 'IG II^2 and the great satrap's revolt', *ZPE* 67, 1987, pp. 93-100.

— MOYSEY, R.A., 'Observations on the Numismatic Evidence relating to the Great Satrapal Revolt of 362/1 B.C.', *REA* 91, 1989, pp. 107-139.

— MOYSEY, R.A., 'Diodorus, the satraps and the decline of the Persian Empire', *AHB* 5, 1991, pp. 113-122.

— MOYSEY, R.A., 'Plutarch, Nepos and the Satrapal Revolt of 362/1 B.C.', *Historia* 41, 1992, pp. 158-166.

— MÜLLER, H.W., *Der 'Armreif' des Königs Ahmose und der Handgelenkschutz des Bogenschützen in Alten Ägypten und Vorderasien*, Mainz 1989.

— NAʾAMAN, N., 'Esarhaddon's Treaty with Baal and Assyrian Provinces along the Phoenician Coast', *RSF* 22, 1994, pp. 3-8.

— NASTER, P., 'La technique des revers partiellement incus de monnaies phéniciennes', in *Centennial Publication of the American Numismatic Society*, New York 1958, pp. 503-511 (= *Scripta Nummaria. Contributions à la méthodologie numismatique*, Louvain-la-Neuve 1983, pp. 22-29).

— NASTER, P., 'Le développement des monnayages phéniciens avant Alexandre, d'après les trésors', in A. Kindler ed., *The patterns of the monetary development in Phoenicia and Palestine in Antiquity, International Numismatic Convention, Jerusalem 1963*, Jerusalem 1967, pp. 3-22 (= P. Naster, *Scripta Nummaria. Contributions à la méthodologie numismatique*, Louvain-la-Neuve 1983, pp. 178-196).

— NASTER, P., 'Le carré creux en numismatique grecque', in *Numismatique antique. Problèmes et méthodes*, Annales de l'Est, Nancy-Louvain 1975, pp. 17-21 (= *id.*, *Scripta Nummaria. Contributions à la méthodologie numismatique*, Louvain-la-Neuve 1983, pp. 45-50).

— NASTER, P. 'Le chien et le murex des monnaies impériales de Tyr', *NAC* 14, 1985, pp. 257-260.

— NAVEH, J., 'Unpublished Phoenician Inscriptions from Palestine', *IEJ* 37, 1987, pp. 25-30.

— NEWELL, E.T., 'A Cilician Find', *NC*, 1914, pp. 1-33.

— NEWELL, E.T., *The Dated Alexander Coinage of Sidon and Ake*, New Haven 1916.

— NICOLET-PIERRE, H., 'Tétradrachmes athéniens en Transeuphratène', *Trans* 20, 2000, pp. 107-119.

— PARISE, N.F., 'Unità ponderali e circolazione metallica nell'Oriente mediterraneo', in T. Hackens *et al.* eds, *A Survey of Numismatic Research 1985-1990*, Brussels 1991, pp. 32-34.

— PECKHAM, J.B., *The Development of the Late Phoenician Scripts*, Cambridge Ma. 1968.

— PELLING, C., *Plutarch and History*, Swansea-London 2002.

— PETIT, T., *Satrapes et satrapies dans l'Empire achéménide de Cyrus le Grand à Xerxès Ier*, Paris 1990.

— PETTINATO, G., 'I rapporti politici di Tiro con l'Assiria alla luce del 'trattato tra Asarhaddon e Baal'', *RSF* 3, 1975, pp. 145-160.

— POIDEBARD, A., *Un grand port disparu: Tyr*, Paris 1939.

— PORADA, E., 'Of Professional Seal Cutters and Nonprofessionally Made Seals', in M. Gibson and R.D. Biggs eds, *Seals and Sealing in the Ancient Near East*, Malibu 1977, pp. 7-14.

— PRICE, M.J., 'On Attributing Alexanders – Some Cautionary Tales', in *Greek Numismatics and Archaeology, Essays in Honour of M. Thompson*, Wetteren 1979, pp. 241-246.

— PRICE, M.J., 'More from Memphis and the Syria 1989 Hoard', in M.J. Price et al. eds, *Essays in Honour of R. Carson and K. Jenkins*, London 1993, pp. 31-35.

— PRITCHARD, J.B., *Sarepta. A preliminary Report on the Iron Age*, Philadelphia 1975.

— RAHE, P.A., 'The military Situation in Western Asia on the eve of Cunaxa', *AJPh* 101, 1980, pp. 79-96.

— RAINEY, A.F., 'The Satrapy 'beyond the River'', *AJBA* 1, 1968-71, pp. 51-78.

— RANSING, G., *The Bow: Some Notes on its Origin and Development*, Acta Archaeologica Ludensia, Lund 1967.

— RAY, J.D., 'Egypt: Dependence and Independence (425-343 B.C.)', in *Achaemenid History I, Sources, Structures and Synthesis*, Leiden 1987, pp. 79-96.

— READE, J., 'A Hoard of silver currency from Achaemenid Babylonia', *Iran* 24, 1986, pp. 79-87.

— RENAN, E., *Mission de Phénicie*, Paris 1864.

— RITNER, R.K., 'Khabbabash and the Satrap stela: a grammatical rejoinder', *ZÄS* 107, 1980, pp. 135-137.

— ROBINSON, E.S.G., 'Athenian Coin Dies from Egypt', *NC* 6th series 10, 1950, pp. 298-299.

— ROBINSON, E.S.G., 'A "silversmith's hoard" from Mesopotamia', *Iraq* 12, 1950, pp. 44-51.

— ROOT, M.C., *The King and Kingship in Achaemenid Art*, Leiden 1979.

— ROUVIER, J., 'L'ère d'Alexandre le Grand en Phénicie', *REG* 12, 1899, pp. 362-381.

— ROUVIER, J., 'Numismatique des villes de la Phénicie: Tyr', *JIAN* 6, 1903, pp. 269-322.

— RUZICKA, S., *Politics of a Persian Dynasty: the Hecatomnids in the Fourth Century*, London 1992.

— RYDER, T.T.B., 'Spartan Relations with Persia after the King's Peace: a Strange Story in Diodorus 15.9', *CQ* 13, 1963, pp. 105-109.

— SADER, H., *Iron Age Funerary Stelae from Lebanon*, Cuadernos de Arqueología Mediterránea 11, Barcelone 2005.

— SALMON, P., *La politique égyptienne d'Athènes, VIe et Ve siècles av. J.-C.*, Brussels 1965.

— SALMON, P., 'Les relations entre la Perse et l'Egypte du VIe au IVe siècle av. J.-C.', in E. Lipiński ed., *The Land of Israel: Cross-Road of Civilizations*, Leuven 1985, pp. 147-148.

— SANTI AMANTINI, L., *Storie Filippiche, Epitome da Pompeo Trogo*, Milan 1981.

— SAVIO, A., 'Ancora sulla numismatica e i problemi quantitativi', *AIIN*, 1997, pp. 45-52.

— SAVIO, A., 'La numismatica e i problemi quantitativi: Intorno al calcolo del volume delle emissioni', *RIN* 98, 1997, pp. 11-48.

— SCANDONE, G., 'Testimonianze egiziane in Fenicia dal XII al IV sec. a.c.', *RSF* 12, 1984, pp. 143-163.

— SCHNEIDER, T., 'Looking for the Source of Tin in the Ancient Near East', *Qad.* 15, 1985, pp. 98-102.

— SCHWABACHER, W., *Griechische Münzkunst*, Mainz 1974.

— SEIBT, O.R., *Griechische Söldner im Achaimenidenreich*, Bonn 1977.

— SELLERS, O.R., *The Citadel of Beth-Zur*, Philadelphia 1933.

— SELLWOOD, D.B., 'Some Experiments in Greek minting Technique', *NC* 7th ser. 3, 1963, pp. 217-231.

— SERVET, J.-M., *Nomismata: Etat et origines de la monnaie*, Lyon 1984.

— SEYRIG, H., 'Antiquités syriennes. Héraclès-Nergal', *Syr.* 24, 1947, pp. 62-80.

— SEYRIG, H., 'Antiquités syriennes. 64 - Sur une prétendue ère tyrienne', *Syr.* 34, 1957, pp. 93-98.

— SHERIDAN, W.W., 'From Cyzicus to Tyre. Numismatic Evidence of an ancient Ship's Trip, circa 400 B.C.', *Numismatist* 8, 1971, pp. 1127-1133.

— SISTI, F., *Arriano, Anabasi di Alessandro* I, Firenze 2001.

— SIX, J.P., 'L'ère de Tyr', *NC* 3rd series 6, 1886, pp. 97-113.

— SIX, J.P., 'Observations sur les monnaies phéniciennes', *NC* New Series 17, 1877, pp. 127-241.

— SIX, J.P., 'Le satrape Mazaios', *NC* 3rd series 4, 1884, pp. 97-159.

— SOLE, L., 'Le emissioni monetali della Fenicia prima di Alessandro-I', *SEAP* 16, 1997, pp. 75-125.

— SOLE, L., 'Le emissioni monetali della Fenicia prima di Alessandro-II', *SEAP* 18, 1998, pp. 81-147.

— SPALINGER, A., 'The Reign of King Chabbash: An Interpretation', *ZÄS* 105, 1978, pp. 142-154.

— SPENCER, D., *The Roman of Alexander: studies in Curtius Rufus*, Cambridge 1997.

— STADTER, P.A., *Arrian of Nicomedia*, Chapel Hill 1980.

— STERN, E. 'The Dating of Stratum II at Tell Abu Hawam', *IEJ* 18, 1968, pp. 213-219.

— STERN, E., 'The Dor Province in the Persian Period in the Light of the Recent Excavations at Dor', *Trans* 2, 1990, pp. 147-156.

— STERN, E., 'Dor à l'époque perse', in Laperrousaz-Lemaire dirs, *La Palestine à l'époque perse*, Paris 1994, pp. 77-115.

— STROGETSKY, V.M., 'The problem of Callias' peace and its significance for the evolution of the Delian League', *VDI*, 1991, pp. 158-168.

— STUCKY, R.A., *Ras Shamra, Leukos Limen. Die Nach-ugaritische Besiedlung von Ras Shamra*, Paris 1983.

— TARN, W.W., *Alexander the Great II, Sources and Studies*, Cambridge 1950.

— TESTART, A., 'Moyen d'échange/moyen de paiement. Des monnaies en général et plus particulièrement des primitives', in *id.* dir., *Aux origines de la monnaie*, Paris 2001, pp. 21-33.

— THOMPSON, H.O., 'The 1972 Excavation of Khirbet Al-Hajjar', *ADAJ* 17, 1972, pp. 47-72

— THOMPSON, H.O., 'The Ammonite Remains at Khirbet al-Hajjar', *BASOR* 227, 1977, pp. 27-34.

— THOMPSON, H.O., 'A Tyrian Coin in Jordan', *BA* 50, 1987, pp. 101-104.

— TONNET, H., *Recherches sur Arrien, sa personalité et ses écrits atticistes* I-II, Amsterdam 1988.

— VAN DER STOCKT, L., 'Plutarch and Dolphins: Love is all you need', in J. Boulogne ed., *Les Grecs de l'Antiquité et les animaux. Le cas remarquable de Plutarque*, Lille 2005, pp. 13-21.

— VARGYAS, P., '*Kaspu ginnu* and the monetary reform of Darius I', *ZA* 89, 1999, pp. 263-284.

— VARGYAS, P., 'Silver and Money in Achaemenid and Hellenistic Babylonia', in *Assyrologia et Semitica, Festschrift für J. Oelsner*, AOAT 252, Neukirchen-Vluyn 2000, pp. 513-521.

— VERKINDEREN, F. 'Les cités phéniciennes dans l'Empire d'Alexandre le Grand', in E. Lipiński ed., *Phoenicia and the East Mediterranean in the First Millennium B.C.*, Studia Phoenicia V, Leuven 1987, pp. 287-308.

— VERMEULE, C.C., 'Some Notes on Ancient Dies and Coining Methods', *Numismatic Circular* 61, 1953, cols 399-402.

— VILLARONGA, L., 'De nuevo la estimaciòn del número original de cuños de una emisión monetaria', *Gacetta Numismatica* 85, 1987, pp. 31-36.

— VISMARA, N., and MARTINI, R., 'Ripostigli con monete della Lycia, di Cyprus e della Phoenicia. Spunti per una discussione', *Trans* 20, 2000, pp. 45-60.

— WALLINGA, H., 'The Ancient Persian navy and its predecessors', in H. Sancisi-Weerdenburg ed., *Achaemenid History I. Sources, Structures and Synthesis*, Leiden 1987, pp. 47-78.

— WALLINGA, H., *Ships and Sea-Power before the great Persian War. The Ancestry of the ancient Trireme*, Leiden *et al.* 1993.

— WATANABE, C.E., 'Symbolism of the Royal Lion Hunt in Assyria', in J. Prosecky ed., *Intellectual Life of the Ancient Near East*, Prague 1998, pp. 439-450.

— WATTS, J.D., *Obadiah. A critic exegetical Commentary*, Grand Rapids 1969.

— WEINFELD, M., 'Ugaritic 'Rider of the Clouds' and ' Gatherer of the Clouds'', *JANES* 5, 1973, pp. 421-426.

— WEISKOPF, M., *The So-Called 'Great Satraps' Revolt', 366-360 B.C.*, Wiesbaden 1989.

— WESTBROOK, R., 'The Female Slave', in V.H. Matthews *et al.* eds, *Gender and Law in the Hebrew Bible and the Ancient Near East*, Sheffield 1998, pp. 214-238.

— WILKINSON, R.H., 'The Representation of the Bow in the Art of Egypt and the Ancient Near East', *JANES* 20, 1991, pp. 83-99.

— WILL, E., 'Fonctions de la monnaie dans les cités grecques de l'époque classique', in *Numismatique antique. Problèmes et méthodes*, Annales de l'Est, Nancy-Louvain 1975, pp. 233-246.

— XELLA, P., *La terra di Baal*, Rome 1984.

— YADIN, Y., *The Art of Warfare in Biblical Lands in the Light of Archaeological Study*, London 1963, pp. 97-103.

— YADIN, Y., *et al.*, *Hazor I*, Jerusalem 1958.

— ZECCHINI, G., *La cultura storica di Ateneo*, Milan 1989.

— ZEUNER, F.E., 'Dolphins on coins of the Classical Period', *BICS* 10, 1963, pp. 97-103.

INDEX OF PUBLIC AND PRIVATE COLLECTIONS

The numbers represent the coin numbers in the catalogue of Chapter I.

1. Public collections

Beirut, National Museum: 2, 64, 90, 193, 377, 691, 1011, 1382
Beirut, American University of Beirut, Museum: 36, 359, 664, 709, 1071, 1170, 1652, 1676, 1702, 1755
Berlin, Staatliche Museum: 17, 18, 29, 55, 63, 194, 256, 274, 278, 335, 340, 378, 380, 412, 413, 485, 620, 671, 681, 686, 768, 835, 843, 860, 868, 1009, 1034, 1157, 1315, 1316, 1443, 1548, 1561, 1609, 1622, 1631
Birmingham, Museum and Art Gallery: 893
Bologne, Archaeological Museum: 421, 617
Boston, Museum of Fine Arts: 13, 355, 655
Brussels, National Museum: 189, 269, 328, 1402
Budapest, Magyar Nemzeti Museum: 342, 800, 873
Cambridge, Fitzwilliam Museum: 39, 77, 211, 268, 295, 330, 370, 407, 1032, 1603
Cambridge, Harvard University: 1738, 1741
Copenhagen, Nationalmuset: 5, 300, 351, 352, 419, 420, 428, 649, 692, 847, 864, 901, 927, 1202, 1415, 1565, 1601, 1634, 1812
Haifa, National Maritime Museum: 907, 993, 1015, 1074, 1206, 1208, 1408, 1513, 1530, 1531, 1571
Istanbul, Istanbul Arkeoloji Müzeleri (Kültür ve Turizm Bakanligi): 255, 293, 319
Jerusalem, Archaeological Institut: 289, 711, 884, 1036, 1138, 1373, 1575
Jerusalem, Israel Museum: 424, 433, 460, 463, 480, 486, 487, 491, 538, 694, 754, 766, 945, 967, 1210, 1517, 1562, 1644, 1649, 1680, 1752, 1761, 1764, 1765, 1768, 1769, 1772, 1774, 1776, 1779, 1780, 1782, 1783, 1786, 1787, 1789, 1791, 1792, 1795, 1796, 1797, 1798, 1799, 1802, 1809
Jerusalem, Rockfeller Museum: 338, 379, 427, 453, 619, 625, 634, 635, 651, 652, 653, 662, 665, 667, 674, 680, 684, 823, 837, 844, 845, 849, 853, 854, 858, 859, 877, 897, 900, 906, 921, 923, 933, 934, 943, 944, 946, 958, 959, 960, 961, 963, 966, 969, 970, 972, 973, 974, 975, 976, 978, 979, 981, 982, 983, 985, 987,

988, 989, 991, 992, 1002, 1005, 1006, 1007, 1010, 1014, 1027, 1028, 1029, 1030, 1035, 1038, 1041, 1042, 1043, 1044, 1047, 1050, 1052, 1053, 1054, 1057, 1058, 1059, 1064, 1065, 1066, 1067, 1068, 1069, 1070, 1072, 1079, 1081, 1085, 1086, 1087, 1088, 1092, 1139, 1141, 1143, 1150, 1154, 1163, 1164, 1165, 1167, 1218, 1238, 1270, 1287, 1411, 1523, 1544, 1586, 1712
Kibboutz Hanita Museum: 230, 1587, 1646, 1715, 1734, 1801
Leiden, Rijksmuseum, Het Koninklijk Penningkabinet: 204, 284, 294, 373, 410, 471, 902, 1352
London, British Museum: 12, 21, 56, 66, 188, 224, 239, 250, 266, 276, 290, 303, 418, 451, 520, 624, 628, 640, 656, 658, 690, 700, 710, 806, 820, 821, 841, 852, 860, 867, 876, 886, 892, 917, 986, 1013, 1149, 1224, 1281, 1286, 1290, 1309, 1396, 1522, 1525, 1542, 1558, 1612, 1618, 1627, 1660, 1669, 1670, 1684
Madrid, Museo Arqueológico Nacional: 372, 912, 1541, 1547, 1564, 1584, 1591, 1593
Munich, Staatliche Münzsammlung: 899, 1640
Münster, Westfälisches Landesmuseum für Kunst und Kulturgeschichte: 894
New York, American Numismatic Society: 4, 10, 15, 19, 23, 25, 27, 32, 41, 53, 72, 79, 190, 191, 206, 228, 245, 247, 271, 273, 280, 282, 302, 308, 339, 343, 344, 347, 348, 356, 366, 367, 402, 406, 462, 472, 473, 475, 615, 627, 650, 654, 659, 669, 672, 685, 695, 762, 803, 829, 831, 836, 838, 856, 857, 871, 890, 918, 926, 977, 1004, 1037, 1040, 1063, 1090, 1145, 1151, 1151, 1159, 1214, 1216, 1229, 1233, 1236, 1346, 1353, 1387, 1390, 1395, 1398, 1410, 1416, 1540, 1543, 1599, 1616, 1621, 1623, 1624, 1638, 1655, 1659, 1661, 1666, 1713, 1751, 1754, 1758, 1775
Nicosia, Archaeological Museum: 1563
Oslo, Universitetet Oslo, Myntkabinettet: 369
Oxford, Ashmolean Museum: 3, 38, 283, 403, 441, 647, 910, 984, 1003, 1162, 1219, 1559, 1560, 1620, 1725
Paris, Bibliothèque de France: 1, 8, 20, 22, 26, 28, 44, 49, 57, 65, 68, 69, 89, 187, 192, 197, 207, 251, 254, 270, 279, 287, 291, 296, 306, 333, 346, 404, 411, 422, 426, 437, 466, 469, 498, 512, 528, 613, 614, 616, 621, 626, 632, 633, 657, 663, 668, 670, 675, 682, 726, 746, 781, 808, 818, 824, 825, 832, 848, 862, 885, 889, 1055, 1148, 1153, 1228, 1271, 1272, 1323, 1354, 1378, 1381, 1549, 1552, 1553, 1610, 1614, 1619, 1626, 1628, 1632, 1633, 1689, 1716, 1718, 1719, 1723, 1731
Paris, Institut Catholique, Musée Bible et Terre Sainte: 638, 1231
Princeton, Princeton University Libraries: 252, 350
Rome, Vatican Museum: 45, 46, 74, 947
Stockholm, Royal Coin Cabinet: 50, 277, 1279
Tehran, National Museum: 93, 110-181, 213, 214-221
Tel Aviv, Kadman Numismatic Museum: 234, 236, 237, 244, 442, 444, 445, 446, 458, 459, 467, 476, 477, 484, 492, 501, 503, 507, 509, 513, 514, 515, 523,

524, 529, 530, 532, 533, 534, 539, 715, 718, 719, 720, 724, 725, 729, 730, 731, 733, 736, 737, 741, 742, 749, 750, 752, 756, 758, 763, 764, 770, 772, 777, 778, 779, 786, 788, 792, 930, 948, 1001, 1062, 1232, 1311, 1374, 1437, 1527, 1528, 1557, 1574, 1579, 1580, 1581, 1595, 1607, 1611, 1629, 1635, 1642, 1643, 1645, 1667, 1683, 1686, 1687, 1691, 1697, 1701, 1726, 1728, 1732, 1733, 1736, 1737, 1739, 1746, 1749, 1759, 1778, 1785, 1803, 1804, 1805
Toronto, Royal Ontario Museum: 326, 382, 1084, 1668
Vienna, Institut für Numismatik Universität Wien: 327
Vienna, Kunst Historisches Museum: 222, 323, 678, 809, 842, 846, 874, 1083, 1239, 1567
Warsaw, National Museum: 869, 1690

2. Private collections

Allotte de la Füye Coll.: 305, 354
Bauer Coll.: 641
Bément Coll.: 5, 53, 281, 313, 804
Benson Coll.: 360
Berry Coll.: 72
Bieder Coll.: 894
Bougon Coll.: 908
Bull Coll.: 819
Bunburry Coll.: 1224
Chandon de Briailles Coll.: 411, 528, 616
Collignon Coll.: 281
Cumberland Clark Coll.: 1451
Cunningham Coll.: 658, 910, 1003, 1560
Dannenberg Coll.: 686
Davis Coll.: 1320
De Behague Coll.: 919
De Granprey Coll.: 1538
De Hirsch Coll.: 189, 269
De Luynes Coll.: 68, 192, 270, 306, 346, 613, 614, 668, 670, 824, 1148, 1153, 1272, 1323, 1549, 1553, 1614, 1633
De Vogüé Coll.: 8, 69, 426, 633, 682, 1378
Dewing Coll.: 88, 371, 374, 875
Fabricius Coll.: 351
Fox Coll.: 18, 274
Gauthier Coll.: 206, 1063
Godard Coll.: 98
Greenwell Coll.: 655
Gunther Coll.: 19

Hart Coll.: 294
Hunterian Coll.: 932
Imhoof-Blumer Coll.: 55
Jameson Coll.: 60, 935
King Gustaf VI Adolf Coll.: 50
Klein Coll.: 227, 435, 1590, 1655
Löbbecke Coll.: 278, 340, 681, 768, 868, 1009, 1157, 1315, 1622
Lockett Coll.: 39, 262, 1289, 1376
Mathey Coll.: 53
McClean Coll.: 209, 295, 330, 407, 802
Montagu Coll.: 246
Moreira Coll.: 1275
Moritz Simon Coll.: 398, 807
Moussaieff Coll., London: 1550
Newell Coll.: 4, 15, 23, 25, 27, 32, 41, 53, 190, 191, 245, 271, 273, 302, 308, 343, 348, 356, 402, 406, 473, 475, 615, 627, 650, 654, 659, 669, 672, 762, 803, 829, 831, 836, 838, 857, 871, 890, 918, 926, 977, 1004, 1037, 1040, 1090, 1145, 1151, 1233, 1236, 1346, 1387, 1390, 1398, 1410, 1416, 1540, 1543, 1599, 1616, 1621, 1623, 1624, 1655, 1659, 1661, 1713, 1751, 1754, 1758, 1775
Norman Coll.: 895
Osborne O'Hagan Coll.: 1240
Parsons Coll.: 641
Petrie Coll.: 282, 1353
Philipsen Coll.: 313, 1176
Pipito Coll.: 1384
Pozzi Coll.: 94, 95, 96, 314, 905
Private Coll.: 16, 31, 48, 59, 182, 305, 316, 401, 545, 798, 1265, 1377, 1421, 1555, 1735, 1742, 1743, 1745, 1747, 1748, 1766
Prokesch-Osten Coll.: 17, 671, 835, 1316
Prosckowsky Coll.: 399
Protassowicki Coll.: 869
Robinson Coll.: 283
Rosen Coll.: 60, 367, 472, 1637, 1638
Rouvier Coll.: 14, 343, 344, 473, 654, 1605, 1661
Sartiges Coll.: 246
Semeran-Siemianowski Coll.: 1690
Seyrig Coll.: 20, 22, 26, 44, 97, 197, 287, 422, 437, 469, 626, 657, 663, 1610, 1619, 1689, 1718, 1719
Shahaf Coll., Haïfa: 331, 447, 448, 449, 454, 455, 456, 468, 470, 474, 489, 490, 500, 525, 535, 536, 618, 646, 666, 676, 721, 759, 761, 767, 769, 773, 775, 780, 793, 794, 971, 1168, 1324, 1556, 1577, 1598, 1615, 1650, 1658, 1688, 1717, 1727, 1753, 1756, 1757, 1762, 1763, 1770, 1771, 1773, 1788, 1790, 1800

Smith-Lessouëf Coll.: 885
Spaer Coll., Jerusalem: 83, 202, 205, 231, 357, 425, 452, 527, 630, 661, 683, 734, 771, 784, 785, 790, 1008, 1221, 1355, 1393, 1554, 1569, 1582, 1585, 1592, 1630, 1681, 1685, 1699, 1721, 1730, 1750, 1760, 1781, 1784
Starcky Coll.: 638, 1231
Suchier Coll.: 834
Traverso-Martini Coll.: 253
Van Rede Coll.: 284, 373
Ward Coll.: 418
Warren Coll.: 250, 396, 655
Weber Coll.: 5, 188, 194, 865, 1202, 1600, 1602, 1612
Webster Coll.: 300, 649
Wheaton Coll.: 673

INDEX OF SALE CATALOGUES

The numbers represent the coin numbers in the catalogue of Chapter I.

Agora, Tel Aviv
1, 14/5/1974: 1647, 1744, 1777
21/5/1975: 304, 1161
Ahlström, Stockholm
35, 9-10/5/1987: 636, 1230
Albrecht-Hoffmann, Münz Zentrum, Köln
23, 12/11/1975: 1223
42, 10-13/11/1980: 1568
43, 27-30/4/1981: 201
50, 23/11/1983: 1017
62, 4-6/11/1987: 1209
74, 11-13/11/1992: 911
Albuquerque, Rouen
41, 16/3/1993: 1436
49, 26/2/1995: 1389
Archaeological Center, Tel Aviv
22, 28/9/1999: 688
Argenor Numismatique, Paris
October 2001: 361
October 2002: 341
Ars Antiqua, London
4, 11-12/12/2003: 1306
Art Gallery of South Australia, North Terrace, Adelaide
731: 1427
Baldwin, London
33, 7/12/2000: 52
34, 13/10/2003: 7, 85, 324, 362, 423, 481, 702, 727, 728, 805, 1433, 1654, 1657, 1707
Ball, Berlin
April 1937: 1535, 1537
Bankhaus Aufhäuser, Munich
13, 7-8/10/1997: 1392

Baranowsky, Milan
25/2/1931: 253
Barré, Saint Malo
30/6/1983: 1303
April 1984: 1303
December 1986: 1428
Berk, Chicago
50, 18/11/1987: 240
57, 29/3/1989: 1215
65, 26/2/1991: 909
70, 16/3/1992: 1046
84, 19/1/1995: 47, 91
87, 13/9/1995: 91
89, 14/2/1996: 91
96, 18/6/1997: 1351
105, 17/11/1998: 375
112, 13/1/2000: 909
135, 10/12/2003: 483
137, 31/3/2004: 60, 1420
Better Auction, Haifa
4-6/7/1972: 1321, 1444
Bonhams, London
1, 21-22/5/1980: 261
Bourgey, Paris
14-15/4/1910: 895
29-31/5/1911: 922
20-21/12/1921: 925
3-5/12/1928: 311
9-10/11/1976: 1385
5-6/12/1977: 78, 325
13-14/11/1980: 1350
7, 29-30/3/1982: 1358
10-11/6/1982: 1350, 1389
7-8/11/1983: 1350
1-2/12/1999: 1204
2-3/4/2001: 345
Brüder Egger, Vienna
26/11/1909: 200, 893
Burgan, Paris
30/6/1987: 1512
Button, Frankfurt/Main
28-29/10/1959: 928

Cahn, Frankfurt/Main
3-4/11/1913: 393
60, 2/7/1928: 1395, 1573
68, 26/11/1930: 398, 807
71, 14/10/1931: 84
84, 29/11/1933: 904
CGB, Paris
31/12/2002: 318
19/6/2003: 1056
Christensen
9/7/1965: 698
7/7/1978: 698
Ciani, Paris
20-22/2/1935: 1538
Classical Numismatic Group, Lancaster-London
9-10/9/1994: 1045
27, 29/9/1993: 687
19/3/1994: 184
33, 15/3/1995: 184
34, 6/5/1995: 687, 1663
38, 6-7/6/1996: 1152
39, 18/9/1996: 797
41, 19/3/1997: 677, 1425
42, 29-30/5/1997: 7, 1031
45, 18/3/1998: 233
46, 26/6/1998: 1372
53, 15/3/2000: 62, 1391
54, 14/6/2000: 297
60, 22/5/2002: 223
63, 21/5/2003: 288
67, 22/9/2004: 324
69, 8/6/2005: 1720, 1729
Coin Galleries, New York
1964: 320, 1277
1965: 1277
1968: 1322
485, 28/3/1977: 1326
10/4/1991: 807
12/2/1992: 249
Comptoir Général Financier, Paris
16/6/2000: 1091
Demirjian, Ridgefield (Connecticut)

Spring 1980: 196
Deutsch, Tel Aviv
11, 4/10/1993: 1439
Dorotheum, Vienna
22-23/9/1992: 1146
Dürr-Michel, Numisart, Geneva
16/11/1998: 272
Elsen, Brussels
40, January 1982: 317
54, April 1983: 1566
7, 21/4/1987: 1363
December 1987: 317
9, 6/2/1988: 3*
10, 27/6/1988: 1363
13, 10/6/1989: 801
147, October 1992: 717, 1200
28, 20/2/1993: 1200
34, 23/4/1994: 717
38, 11/2/1995: 183, 717
28, 20/2/1993: 183
48, 22/2/1997: 776
63, 16/9/2000: 431
70, 15/6/2002: 329
78, 20/3/2004: 75
83, 12/3/2005: 1673
85, 10/9/2005: 443
86, 10/12/2005: 968
Empire Coins, Ormond Beach
4, 9-10/11/1985: 1308
53, 1990: 962
England, Quarryville-London
14, 20/3/1991: 1435
15, 5/6/1991: 1285, 1679
25, 24/3/1993: 1363, 1440
27, 29/9/1993: 1363
Feuardent, Paris
18-19/12/1919: 281
18/6/1924: 922
Florange-Ciani, Paris
1925: 314
17-21/2/1925: 354, 888
17-21/2/1929: 305

Freeman & Sear, Chatsworth
1, 10/3/1995: 260, 1349
2, 31/1/1996: 1217
Freeman & Sear, New York
3/11-1/12/1999: 267
Triton V, 15-16/1/2002: 58
Gadoury, Monte-Carlo
26-27/11/1985: 697
Gadoury, Mulhouse
11-13/10/1981: 364
Gans, NFA, Berkeley
19/4/1960: 641
Gibbons, London
8, Autumn 1975: 263
Glendining, London
18-20/4/1955: 623, 804, 856
4/10/1957: 1388
12, 21-23/2/1961: 39, 416, 1160, 1289, 1376
27/9/1962: 1160
23/5/1963: 249
5/3/1970: 61
11/12/1974: 58, 895
9, 3/6/1976: 78
5/11/1977: 1310
10/12/1986: 30, 262
Gorny, Munich
22, 25-26/5/1982: 1386
32, 12-13/11/1985: 870
36, 8/4/1987: 1694
38, 30/11/1987: 661
40, 7/4/1988: 1423
42, 11/10/1988: 1234
55, 14/5/1991: 1383
58, 9/4/1992: 337
67, 2/5/1994: 307
100, 20/11/1999: 1282
Gorny-Mosch, Giessener Münzhandlung, Munich
113, 18/10/2001: 898
142, 10-11/10/2005: 1524
Hamburger, Frankfurt/Main
17/6/1908: 834
12/6/1930: 399, 1361

Harmer-Rooke
19-20/3/1974: 1356
Hauck & Aufhäuser, Münzen und Medaillen, Deutschland
18, 5-6/10/2004: 227, 435
Helbing, Munich
34, October 1927: 891
8/11/1928: 414, 616, 1452
Hesperia Art Bulletin
10: 1213, 1404
Hess, Frankfurt/Main
224, 18/2/1936: 1536, 1572, 1666
Hess, Lucerne
209, 12/4/1932: 397
15/2/1934: 309, 807
249, 13/11/1979: 261, 1156
Hess-Divo, Zurich
289, 24-25/10/2001: 262
Hess-Leu, Lucerne-Zurich
12-13/4/1962: 924
24, 16/4/1964: 196
31, 6-7/12/1966: 48, 799
Hirsch, Munich
25, 29/11/1909: 313, 1176, 1534
32, 14-15/11/1912: 12, 870
34, 5/5/1914: 48
84, 1973: 1169
151, 24-27/9/1986: 1162
152, 26-29/11/1986: 285, 863
153, 18-20/2/1987: 1278
154, 13-16/5/1987: 1372
156, 25-27/11/1987: 285
158, 4-6/5/1988: 1371
160, 23-25/11/1988: 699, 1372
161, 22-24/2/1989: 33
162, 8-10/5/1989: 368, 712
163, 27-30/9/1989: 1222
164, 29-30/11 and 1/12/1989: 1372
166, 16-19/5/1990: 699
167, 26-29/9/1990: 322
168, 22-24/11/1990: 198, 637, 1077, 1442
169, 20-22/2/1991: 648, 1405, 1414
170, 22-25/5/1991: 1516

171, 25-28/9/1991: 322
172, 27-29/11/1991: 363, 1648
173, 19-22/2/1992: 1405, 1414
175, 23-26/9/1992: 395, 712
176, 19-20/11/19992: 363, 1414
183, 20-24/9/1994: 332
186, 10-12/5/1995: 1672
187, 19-23/9/1995: 1313, 1594
192, 27-29/11/1996: 332
24-26/9/1998: 822
205, 22-25/9/1999: 1664
208, 17-19/2/2000: 840
212, 22-24/11/2000: 1551
233, 12-14/2/2004: 1429
236, 23-25/9/2004: 639, 929, 1429
239, 17-18/2/2005: 1696
242, 22-24/9/2005: 1422, 1441
Jacquier, Kehl/Rhein
22, Spring 1999: 1545, 1589, 1711
23, Autumn 1999: 1545
24, Spring 2000: 1545
25, Autumn 2000: 1545
Kölner Münzen
9-10/4/1974: 1514
Kovacs, San Mateo, California
July 1979: 1604
6, 13/11/1985: 1172, 1273
1988: 450, 461, 1617
Kress, Munich
174, 8-9/3/1979: 376
Kricheldorf, Stuttgart
7, 12-13/11/1959: 285
29, 3-4/3/1975: 1426
Kroha, Kölner Münzkabinett, Köln
47, 21-22/11/1988: 2*
61, 17-18/11/1994: 1407
66, 21-22/4/1997: 1376
Kündig, Münzhandlung, Basel
4, 10/10/1935: 855, 895
8, 22/3/1937: 616
Künker, Osnabrück
11, 8-9/3/1988: 980

24, 10-12/3/1993: 1639
83, 17/6/2003: 1169
94, 27-28/9/2004: 42, 1205, 1673
Kunst und Münzen, Lugano (Asta)
17, June 1977: 1280
Kurpfälzische Münzhandlung, Mannheim
17, 10-13/12/1979: 390
29, 11-13/12/1985: 1207
31, 18-19/12/1986: 1529
32, 1-2/6/1987: 389
42, June 1992: 87
44, June 1993: 2*
46, June 1994: 1326
Lanz, Graz
5, 1/12/1975: 1394
Lanz, Munich
22, 10/5/1982: 1235
26, 5/12/1983: 86
38, 24/11/1986: 1033
48, 22/5/1989: 3*
60, 11/6/1992: 1158
64, 7/6/1993: 257
125, 1-2/11/2005: 840, 1314
Leu, Lucerne
27/3/1956: 60
7, April 1960: 415
31, 6-7/12/1966: 415
36, 17-18/4/1968: 314
Leu, Münzen und Medaillen, Basel
3-4/12/1965: 920
Leu, Zurich
28/5/1974: 67, 246
53, 21-22/10/1991: 185, 1283
54, 28/4/1992: 229
61, 17-18/5/1995: 299
72, 12/5/1998: 1606
79, 31/10/2000: 267, 1312
83, 6-7/5/2002: 47
86, 5-6/5/2003: 1724
Leu, Zurich, and Schulman, Amsterdam
1966: 314, 905
Loudmer-Poulain, Paris

15-16/6/1976: 1389
Malloy, New York
12, 25/4/1978: 1171
13, 8/12/1978: 42, 238, 967
24, 18/3/1988: 541
45, 19/3/1997: 701
Malter, Encino, California
1969: 365, 1357
4, 29/10/1978: 645
27-28/9/1980: 631
27, 10/6/1984: 34
34, 13 and 15/12/1986: 870
29, 1990: 1674
Maly, Lucerne
Nomos 99, 6, Autumn 1975: 186
Markov, New York
11, 2-3/9/2003: 298, 716
Martin, London
12/6/1990: 1725
October 1993: 904
Merzbacher, Munich
15/11/1910: 1175
Monetarium, Schweizerische Kreditanstalt, Zurich
24, December 1977: 1201
28, April 1979: 1358
30, December 1979: 1201
31, April 1980: 42
40, May 1983: 1358
2, 27-28/4/1984: 1073
5, 18-19/4/1986: 1212
45, Spring 1986: 82, 1282
47, Spring 1987: 1282
Spring 1995: 45
Monnaies et Médailles/Münzen und Medaillen, Basel
13, 17-19/6/1954: 77
19, 5-6/6/1959: 50
February 1964: 203
January 1968: 201, 415, 1226, 1348
4, 26-27/11/1974: 400
54, 26/10/1978: 1347
10, 12-13/6/1979: 849
448, September 1982: 931

23-24/6/1983: 807
484, January 1986: 11, 1714
495, January 1987: 1386
581, Nov./Dec. 1994: 1671
583, February 1995: 312
586, May 1995: 457
26, 16-19/9/1996: 1372
32, 20/10/1996: 182, 232
194, 19-22/2/1997: 1227
Müller, Münz Zentrum-Rheinland, Solingen
101, 15-18/12/1999: 693
Müller, Solingen
18, 23-25/9/1976: 713
24, 21-23/9/1978: 517, 522
25, 16-17/2/1979: 516, 1329
31, 4-5/2/1981: 519
53, 26-27/9/1986: 1016
56, 25-26/9/1987: 508
60, 20-21/1/1989: 508
62, 19-20/5/1989: 329
66, 28-29/9/1990: 679
Münzen Auction, Essen
69, 31/5-2/6/1995: 1722
70, 6-8/12/1995: 1722
Münzen und Medaillen, Weil/Rhein
16, 19-20/5/2005: 199
Myers, Ariadne Galleries, New York
1971: 1351
1972: 1515
12, 4/12/1975: 851
February 1976: 1160
9/12/1981: 60
7/12/1982: 81
Myers-Adams, New York
5, 15-16/5/1973: 1446
6, 6/12/1973: 249
Naville, Geneva
1, 1921: 314
7, 23-24/6/1924: 5, 53, 281, 313, 804
December 1928: 265
Noble, Sydney
62, 17-18/11/1999: 248

Numismatica, Vienna
12, 11-14/5/1976: 774
13, 9-11/11/1976: 636, 679, 1673
17, 22-23/6/1977: 1424
21, 20-23/11/1978: 622, 689
Numismatica Ars Classica, New York
Triton II, 1-2/12/1998: 51, 297, 1453, 1519
Numismatica Ars Classica, Zurich
1, 29-30/3/1989: 1426
2, 21-22/2/1990: 3*
27-28/2/1991: 1438
E, 4/4/1995: 40
P, 12/5/2005: 827
Numismatic Art & Ancient Coins, Zurich
4, 17/4/1986: 72, 1695
Numismatic & Ancient Art Gallery, Zurich
11/4/1991: 464
Numismatic Fine Arts, Beverly Hills
18/11/1947: 259
2, 25-26/3/1976: 35
4, 24-25/3/1977: 1201
2, Jan.-Feb. 1979: 42
15/1/1982: 1319
2/12/1985: 48
18, 31/3/1987: 1060
20, 9-10/3/1988: 1276
28, 23/4/1992: 629
Numismatic Fine Arts, Encino
3, 27/3/1976: 1317
7, 6/12/1979: 58
8, 6/6/1980: 655
12/10/1988: 1200, 1546
Numismatic Fine Arts, Los Angeles
26, 14/9/1991: 195
29, 13/9/1992: 185, 1283
33, Spring 1994: 260
Pacific Coast Auction Galleries, Santa Barbara
25-26/9/1986: 1215
Parke, Bern
16-17/10/1968: 392
Peus, Frankfurt/Main
15/3/1954: 1533

267, 12-13/10/1967: 1268
5, July 1968: 1432
10, September 1969: 1703
19, January 1971: 1234
279, 14-17/3/1972: 1327
290, 5-7/10/1976: 1392, 1432
296, 31/10-2/11/1978: 1432
300, 3-4 and 9/11/1987: 83, 258, 315, 1266, 1511, 1636
303, 20-22/10/1981: 317
314, 30631/10, 1 and 4/11/1985: 292
315, 28-30/4 and 2/5/1986: 292
321, 27-29/4 and 2/5/1988: 37, 826
323, 1-4/11/1988: 83, 315, 1328
329, 31/10-5/11/1990: 1288
332, 23-25 and 28/10/1991: 417
361, 6/11/1999: 502, 1678
380, 3/11/2004: 405
Phoenix, Coincraft, London
P96, 1993: 714
P115, 1995: 1445
Platt, Paris
1930: 796
18-19/11/1935: 908, 908
May 1997: 1406
March 1998: 1406
Poinsignon Numismatique, Strasbourg
19/11/1983: 1358
19-20/6/1984: 261
30/6/1987: 1*
Rasmussen, Copenhagen
10-11/3/1970: 399
Ratto, Geneva
26/4/1909: 212, 349, 811
Ratto, Lugano
4/4/1927: 289, 294, 313, 336, 416, 547, 903, 1233
9/10/1934: 301, 1415
Ratto, Milan
15: 294, 310, 336, 1280
Rauch, Vienna
7, 4-5/6/1971: 210, 542, 543, 1447
Reichardt, London
1899: 917

Ritter, Dusseldorf
60, August 2002: 388, 644
63, August 2003: 388
66, May 2004: 388
68, August 2004: 388
75, October 2005: 388
Rollin-Feuardent, Paris
9/5/1910: 887
Rubinger, Antiqua, Woodland Hills
10, 2001: 80, 208, 298, 896
Santamaria, Rome
27/3/1928: 807
Schlessinger, Berlin-Charlottenburg
4/2/1935: 286, 294
Schulman, Amsterdam
16/12/1926: 804
6-8/3/1958: 1225
9-12/3/1959: 1388
18-21/3/1964: 1518
6-8/2/1969: 1362
6-7/4/1971: 990
205, June 1975: 1304
265, 28-29/9/1976: 334
286, 28-30/9/1987: 1325
237, October-November 1988: 1325
Schulman, New York
6-9/5/1974: 1012
Schulten, Köln
18-20/10/1989: 329
Sotheby's, London
7/12/1866: 394
4/5/1908: 1240
3-11/2/1909: 246, 275, 360
19/1/1914: 1451
July 1921: 643, 1376
1/5/1929: 819
16/2/1972: 810
21-22/7/1981: 1203
Sotheby's, New York
21-22/6/1990: 70
19-20/6/1991: 35

Spink, London
14/7/1913: 12
96, 31/3/1993: 73
Spink, Zürich
20, 6/10/1986: 1234
Spink Numismatic Circular
7, September 1992: 1794
10, December 1992: 1677
Stack's, New York
15-16/6/1972: 1147
6/9/1973: 1201
Autumn 1991: 54
Sternberg, Zurich
25-26/11/1976: 740, 787
8, 16-17/11/1978: 839
12, 18-19/11/1982: 417, 1155, 1366, 1606
14, 24-25/5/1984: 1226
22, 20-21/11/1989: 434
June 1998: 822
5, September 1993: 1672
34, 22-23/10/1998: 208, 225, 1318
Superior Coins, New York
8/12/1993: 799
Superior Galleries, Beverly Hills
11-17/6/1986: 75, 1283, 3*
12-14/12/1987: 1306
Superior Galleries, New York
11-12/6/1986: 417
31/5/1989: 408, 1409
Superior Stamp and Coin, Beverly Hills
14-15/10/1971: 1267, 1423
15-18/10/1972: 1267
17-23/6/1974: 60, 391, 994, 1423
12-14/12/1987: 1384
31/5-1/6/1988: 1275
1988: 1360
24/5, Winter 1988/89: 408, 1409
Tradart, New York
1, 13/12/1982: 58
UBS, Basel
29-30/1/2004: 1532

UBS, Zurich
45, 15-17/9/1998: 830
Vecchi, London
1, 13/5/1983: 381
2, 8/10/1984: 1566
12-13/9/1996: 409
12, 5/6/1998: 307
14, 5/2/1999: 223
Védrines, Paris
5/7/1985: 78, 325
Vigne, Paris
September 1986: 354
Vinchon, Paris
17, 1967: 1226
14-15/11/1981: 1307
9-10/12/1983: 1075, 1555
14/4/1984: 919
22-23/5/1995: 358
7/11/2001: 183
Waddell, Gaithersburg
60, Summer 1993: 1675

INDEX OF HOARDS

The numbers represent the coin numbers in the catalogue of Chapter I.

Abu Shusheh hoard TXLVII: 427, 453 ?, 1544, 1712
Akko hoard TXXXIII: 442, 446, 459, 467, 492, 501, 507, 530, 538, 715, 719, 720, 729, 730, 731, 737, 741, 742, 749, 750, 756, 758, 763, 764, 770, 786, 788
Akko hoard TXXXIV: 1761, 1764, 1765, 1768, 1769, 1772, 1774, 1776, 1779, 1780, 1782, 1783, 1786, 1787, 1789, 1791, 1792, 1795, 1796, 1797, 1798, 1799, 1802
Aleppo hoard TLVI: 1237
Babylon hoard TLXIII: 266
Babylonian hoard TLXV: 1539
Balkh hoard TLXIX: 71
Beirut hoard TXLIII: 544, 791, 1708, 1806, 1807, 1808, 1810, 1811
Beni Hassan hoard TLXXV: 326, 382, 1084, 1709-1710
Byblos hoard TX: 92
Byblos hoard TXIII-XV: 239
3rd Byblos hoard: 64
Cilicia hoard TLX: 339, 685
Cilicia hoard TLXI: 254
Damascus hoard TXXXVIII: 1018, 1173, 1174, 1291, 1330, 1331, 1332, 1333, 1334, 1448, 1449, 1450
Delta hoard TLXXIII: 1602, 1612
Gaza hoard TXLVI: 548
Jordan hoard TLIII: 3
Khirbet el-Kerak hoard TXXVI:1411
Lebanon hoard: 264, 297, 353, 386, 387
Malayer hoard TLXVIII: 93-109, 110-181, 213, 214-221
Massyaf hoard TLIV: 57, 65, 66, 89, 90, 207
Naplouse hoard TXXXV: 1094, 1095-1099, 1100-1126,
Naplouse hoard TLI: 430, 432, 434, 466, 479, 498, 512, 545 ?, 549-612, 726, 812-813, 833, 878-883, 914-916, 936-942, 951-957, 964-965, 995-997, 1019-1026, 1187-1199, 1578, 1812, 1813-1814
North Galilee hoard TXXXVI: 1039, 1048, 1051, 1060, 1076, 1078, 1080, 1082, 1089, 1137, 1142, 1144, 1211, 1212, 1269, 1273, 1274, 1284, 1285,

1305, 1306, 1359, 1364, 1365, 1367, 1368, 1369, 1370, 1375, 1379, 1380, 1399, 1400, 1401, 1403, 1412, 1413, 1417, 1418, 1419, 1434
Phoenicia hoard TLXXVIII: 385
Phoenicia hoard TLXXIX: 383-385, 436, 438-440, 457, 488, 540, 722-723
Safed hoard TXXXVII: 814-817, 913, 998-1000, 1127-1136, 1178-1186, 1241-1264, 1292-1302, 1335-1345, 1457-1510, 1520-1521
Samaria hoard TXLIX: 465, 478, 493, 494, 495, 496, 497, 499, 504, 505, 506, 510, 511, 518, 521, 526, 732, 735, 738, 739, 743, 744, 745, 747, 748, 751, 753, 753, 760, 765, 782, 783, 789
South Turkey hoard TLXII: 870
Syrian hoard TLVIII: 828 ?
Tell Abu Hawam hoard TXXXV: 338, 619, 625, 634, 635, 651, 652, 653, 662, 665, 667, 674, 680, 684, 837, 844, 845, 849, 853, 854, 858, 859, 877, 897, 900, 906, 921, 923, 933, 934, 943, 944, 946, 958, 959, 960, 961, 963, 966, 969, 970, 972, 973, 974, 975, 976, 978, 979, 981, 982, 983, 985, 987, 988, 989, 991, 992, 1002, 1005, 1006, 1007, 1010, 1014, 1027, 1028, 1029, 1030, 1035, 1036, 1038, 1041, 1042, 1043, 1044, 1047, 1050, 1052, 1053, 1054, 1057, 1058, 1059, 1064, 1065, 1066, 1067, 1068, 1069, 1070, 1079, 1081, 1082, 1085, 1086, 1087, 1088, 1092, 1093, 1139, 1140, 1141, 1143, 1150, 1154, 1163, 1164, 1165, 1167, 1218, 1270, 1523
Tell el-Maskhuta hoard TLXXI: 370
Tigris hoard TLXIV: 690, 703-708
Wadi Daliyeh hoard TXLVIII: 1430-1431, 1454-1456
Hoard TXXXIX: 1049, 1140, 1360, 1384, 1409, 1414

INDEX OF GEOGRAPHIC NAMES

The name of Tyre is not listed because it is too frequent in the text.

Abu Shusheh, 64, 67, 177, 192, 401
Achzib, 248, 249, 250
Akko, 8, 14, 27, 46, 47, 56, 66, 67, 68, 69, 70, 71, 72, 73, 74, 90, 91, 92, 93, 94, 95, 96, 97, 98, 99, 100, 101, 102, 124, 178, 179, 180, 181, 183, 185, 186, 188, 190, 191, 193, 194, 195, 196, 197, 198, 199, 200, 228, 239, 240, 249, 250, 326, 352, 353, 354, 355, 361, 374, 378, 382, 397, 400, 419, 424
Akshaph, 391
Alep, 146, 151, 376, 401, 402
Alexandrette, 8
Al-Mina, 254
Amrit, 277
Antioch, 22, 301
Aradian. See Arwad
Aradus. See Arwad
Arwad, 7, 9, 19, 205, 208, 223, 250, 251, 252, 253, 254, 263, 266, 271, 281, 284, 295, 296, 303, 308, 321, 330, 331, 332, 333, 335, 338, 345, 363, 364, 365, 369, 374, 377, 378, 379, 382, 385, 389, 403
Ascalon, 7, 8, 267, 405, 422
Ashdod, 374, 405, 422
Aspendus, 342
Atarneus, 382
Athenian. See Athens
Athens, 8, 9, 22, 225, 256, 257, 258, 259, 260, 281, 285, 287, 292, 303, 322, 326, 328, 329, 331, 332, 333, 334, 339, 341, 342, 343, 345, 346, 348, 349, 350, 352, 353, 354, 356, 367, 368, 373, 381, 384, 390, 395, 404, 414
Athienou, 281, 286
ʿAtlit, 117, 130, 148, 174, 176, 179, 397
Babylon, 50, 177, 281, 327, 328, 330, 348, 361, 368, 371, 379, 380, 385, 403
Babylonian. See Babylon
Balkh, 37, 403
Beaumont-sur-Oise, 301
Beer-Sheba, 232

Beirut, 8, 12, 19, 21, 22, 24, 28, 33, 36, 39, 42, 45, 58, 60, 73, 75, 79, 81, 90, 102, 126, 144, 164, 180, 187, 191, 195, 201, 221, 399, 400
Beithir, 319
Beni Hassan, 55, 60, 139, 191, 192, 403
Berytus. See Beirut
Bet-Beṭen, 391
Beth-Shean, 329
Bêt-Zêt. See Bit-Zitti
Bit-Zitti, 391
Byblian. See Byblos
Byblos, 7, 9, 13, 19, 31, 36, 40, 47, 65, 135, 192, 205, 223, 224, 246, 250, 251, 252, 253, 254, 260, 265, 266, 271, 274, 275, 277, 278, 284, 295, 296, 303, 308, 321, 330, 331, 332, 333, 335, 336, 337, 338, 379, 385, 388, 389, 395, 399, 403
Byzantium, 364
Carthage, 281, 306, 359, 362, 387, 389, 390
Carthaginian. See Carthage
Caulonia, 296
Caunus, 339, 346
Cnidus, 346, 348, 350
Corinth, 264, 348, 382
Corinthian. See Corinth
Croton, 296
Cyme, 351
Cythera, 348
Damascus, 24, 130, 146, 156, 159, 173, 372, 376, 400
Daphne, 190
Delos, 267, 365
Demanhur, 225
Dor, 8, 326, 329, 380, 397
Ekron, 329
Elephantine, 328, 345
El-Hofra, 244, 251
En-Gedi, 329
En-Hofez, 329
Enkomi, 286
Erythrae, 281
Eshtemo'a, 329
Eurymedon, 333, 334, 335, 342
Gaza, 75, 91, 95, 99, 101, 182, 193, 374, 376, 391, 400, 401
Gezer, 329, 375
Golgoi, 281

Granicus, 384
Gülnar. See Meydancikkale
Gush Ḥalav, 14, 187
Haifa, 14, 20, 21, 23, 56, 66, 67, 68, 69, 70, 71, 73, 74, 77, 83, 87, 89, 90, 91, 97, 98, 99, 100, 102, 117, 124, 127, 130, 137, 145, 147, 148, 158, 168, 173, 174, 176, 179, 180, 182, 184, 187, 188, 190, 192, 193, 195, 196, 197, 199, 200
Ḥamon. See Umm el-ʿAmed
Hazor, 80
Huelva, 284
Iasos, 263
Ibiza, 281, 284
Idalion, 286
Issos, 385
Jaffa, 326, 380, 397
Jahr el-Bass, 16
Jerusalem, 20, 21, 27, 39, 43, 45, 52, 56, 58, 60, 64, 65, 67, 68, 69, 70, 74, 76, 77, 78, 79, 80, 81, 82, 83, 84, 85, 87, 88, 90, 93, 96, 98, 99, 101, 102, 106, 108, 109, 110, 111, 113, 114, 116, 117, 119, 120, 121, 122, 123, 124, 125, 126, 127, 128, 129, 130, 131, 132, 133, 134, 135, 136, 137, 138, 139, 140, 141, 142, 144, 148, 152, 155, 161, 166, 168, 175, 177, 178, 179, 180, 181, 182, 183, 185, 186, 187, 189, 190, 191, 192, 193, 195, 196, 197, 198, 199, 200, 201, 288, 289, 327, 374, 410, 433
Kabr-Hiram, 15
Kalymna, 296
Kerkouane, 266
Khirbet el-Hajjar, 55
Khirbet el-Kerak, 14, 168, 304, 319, 376, 399, 510
Khirbet el-Qôm, 391
Khirbet Rafiʿ, 288, 289
Kibboutz Ḥanita, 14, 21, 45, 155, 181, 186, 192, 194, 200, 434
Kirmanshah, 280
Kition, 13, 286, 331, 332, 348, 351, 358, 395, 401
Kos, 385
Lapethus, 332
Larnaka. See Kition
Larsa, 329
Malatya, 279
Malayer, 40, 44, 403
Maqqedah. See Khirbet El-Qôm
Massyaf, 35, 36, 37, 39, 43, 401, 455
Megiddo, 329, 397

Meiron, 14, 190, 410
Memphis, 334, 382
Metapontum, 296
Methymna, 263
Meydancikkale, 225, 254
Miṣpe-Yamim, 14
Mikhmoret, 397
Miletus, 339, 341, 384
Moshav Dalton, 14, 376, 401
Mycale, 333, 335, 339
Myriand(r)us, 8
Mytilene, 385
Naplouse, 65, 68, 69, 71, 72, 75, 92, 105, 107, 114, 118, 120, 122, 123, 127, 130, 140, 146, 180, 201, 222, 370, 376, 401, 455
Natanyah, 101
Nesos, 263
Nimrud, 280
Palaetyrus, 349, 350, 361, 387
Paphian. See Paphos
Paphos, 288, 348
Peparethos, 263
Perinthus, 382
Persepolis, 280
Phocaea, 351
Piraeus, 348
Poseidonia, 296
Puig des Molins, 281
Pyrgos, 263
Qadbun, 277
Qana, 15
Qasr Naba, 399
Ras Ibn Hani, 279, 286
Ras Shamra, 241, 279, 281, 329
Safed, 14, 105, 118, 122, 128, 140, 146, 152, 156, 159, 174, 175, 376, 400, 456
Saida. See Sidon
Salamis of Cyprus, 333, 334, 335, 338, 342, 344, 348, 351, 352, 355, 361, 368, 381
Salamis of Greece, 333, 335
Samaria, 47, 68, 69, 70, 71, 72, 73, 93, 94, 95, 96, 97, 98, 101, 102, 288, 289, 329, 405, 410, 456
Samian. See Samos
Samos, 277, 303, 334, 339, 341, 342, 343

Sarafand. See Sarepta
Sardis, 303, 339
Sarepta, 380, 391, 397
Sasa, 14
Sebaste, 102, 149
Seleucia on Tigris, 281
Selifke, 402
Sheshem, 329, 391
Shiqmona. See Sycaminon
Sidon, 7, 8, 9, 13, 14, 15, 211, 223, 233, 236, 237, 250, 251, 253, 268, 271, 284, 285, 295, 296, 301, 302, 308, 310, 312, 314, 319, 321, 322, 324, 325, 326, 327, 330, 331, 332, 333, 335, 337, 340, 343, 345, 346, 347, 348, 349, 352, 355, 356, 358, 361, 365, 368, 369, 370, 371, 372, 373, 376, 377, 378, 379, 380, 381, 385, 386, 387, 388, 389, 390, 393, 396, 397
Sidonian. See Sidon
Sippar, 402
Sirinos, 296
Sousse, 267
Sparta, 341, 342, 343, 344, 345, 346, 348, 349, 350, 354
Spartan. See Sparta
Sulcis, 281
Susa, 56, 358, 368
Sybaris, 296
Sycaminon, 361, 391, 397
Syracusan. See Syracuse
Syracuse, 261, 263, 302, 345
Tamuda, 266
Tarentum, 263, 296
Tarsus, 266, 267, 343, 351, 354, 371, 372, 379
Tawilan, 329
Tel Batash, 286, 329
Tel Megadim, 397
Tel Mevorakh, 397
Tel Michal, 182, 225, 397
Tel Nahariya, 14, 197
Tell Abu Hawam, 14, 56, 76, 77, 78, 82, 83, 84, 85, 87, 88, 90, 108, 109, 110, 111, 113, 116, 117, 119, 120, 121, 122, 123, 124, 125, 126, 127, 128, 130, 131, 132, 133, 134, 135, 136, 137, 138, 139, 140, 141, 142, 144, 149, 153, 175, 209, 304, 318, 320, 376, 397, 400, 456
Tell el-Maʿshuq, 15
Tell el-Maskhuta, 456
Tell es-Samak. See Sycaminon

Tell Halaf, 279
Tell Keisan, 14, 45, 74, 75, 97, 190, 248, 329, 397
Tharros, 281
Theban. See Thebes
Thebes, 328, 337, 356, 368, 382
Til-Barsip, 277
Timnah. See Tel Batash
Tripoli, 7, 377
Tripolis. See Tripoli
Tyre el-Bass, 248, 249, 250
Ugarit. See Ras Shamra
Umm el-ʿAmed, 248, 249, 250, 271, 277, 315
Ushu. See Palaetyrus
Utica, 359
Wadi Daliyeh. See Wâdi Ed-Daliyeh
Wâdi ed-Daliyeh, 171, 174, 374, 376, 380, 401, 456
Zawiya, 281
Zincirli, 279

FIGURES

The figure captions are mentioned under the figures. The coin numbers are those of the catalogue in Chapter I. The inscriptions, graffiti and countermarks are drawn without taking into account the thickness of the strokes.

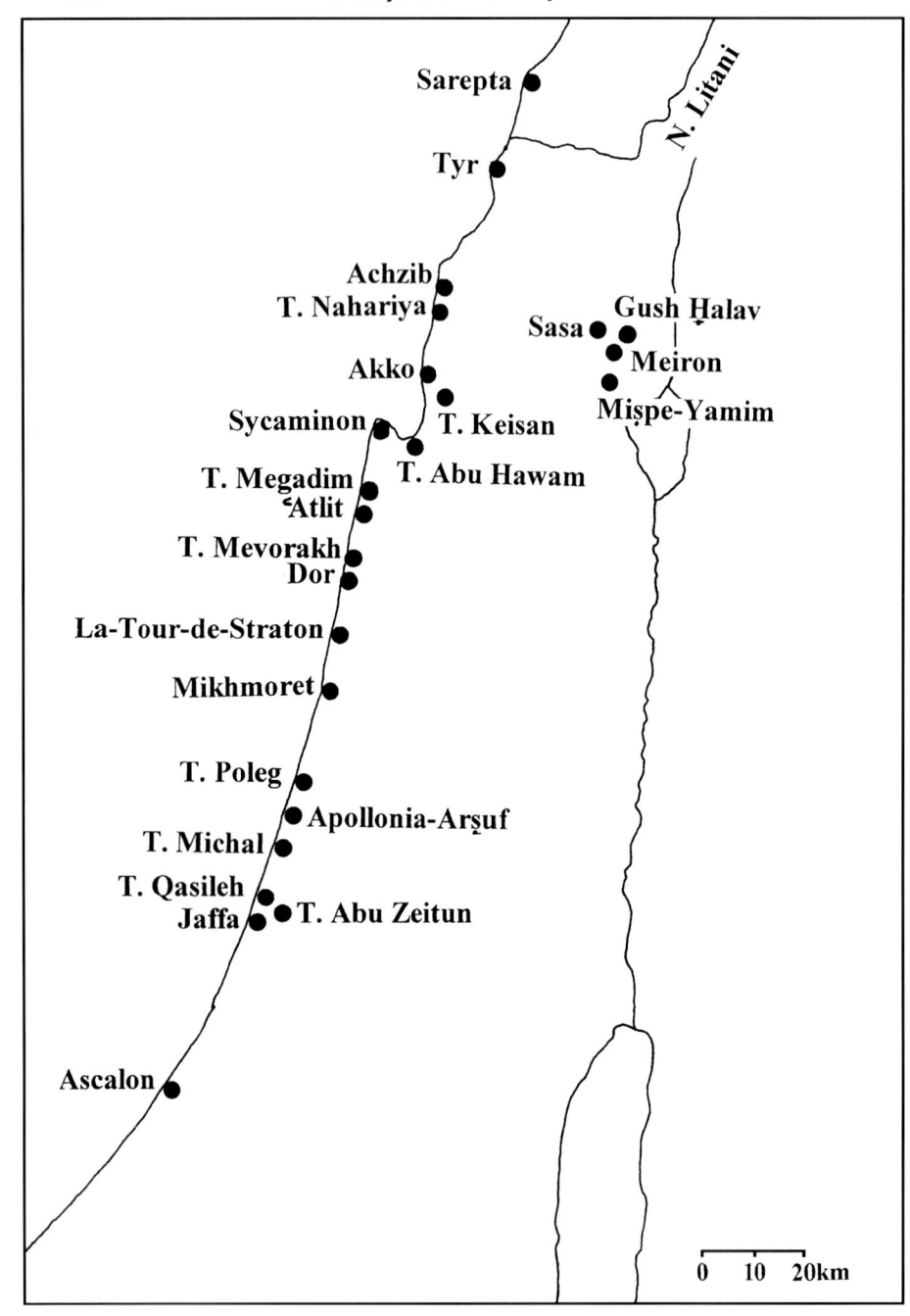

Fig. 1: *The territory of Tyre in the Persian period*

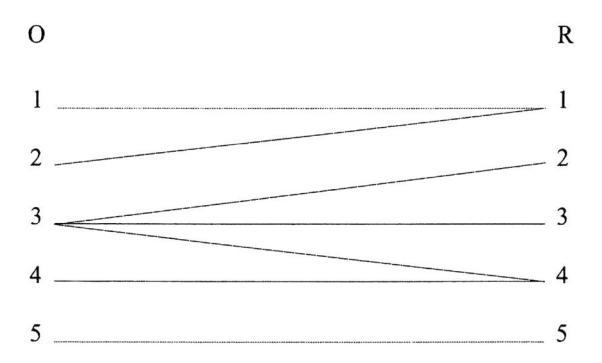

Fig. 2: *Dies of silver shekels (I.1.1)*

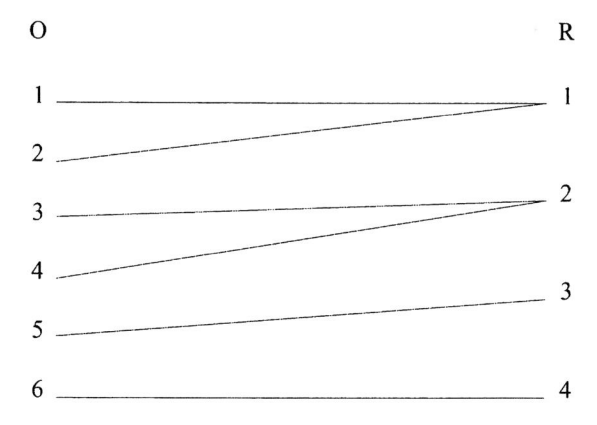

Fig. 3: *Dies of silver quarters of shekel (I.1.2)*

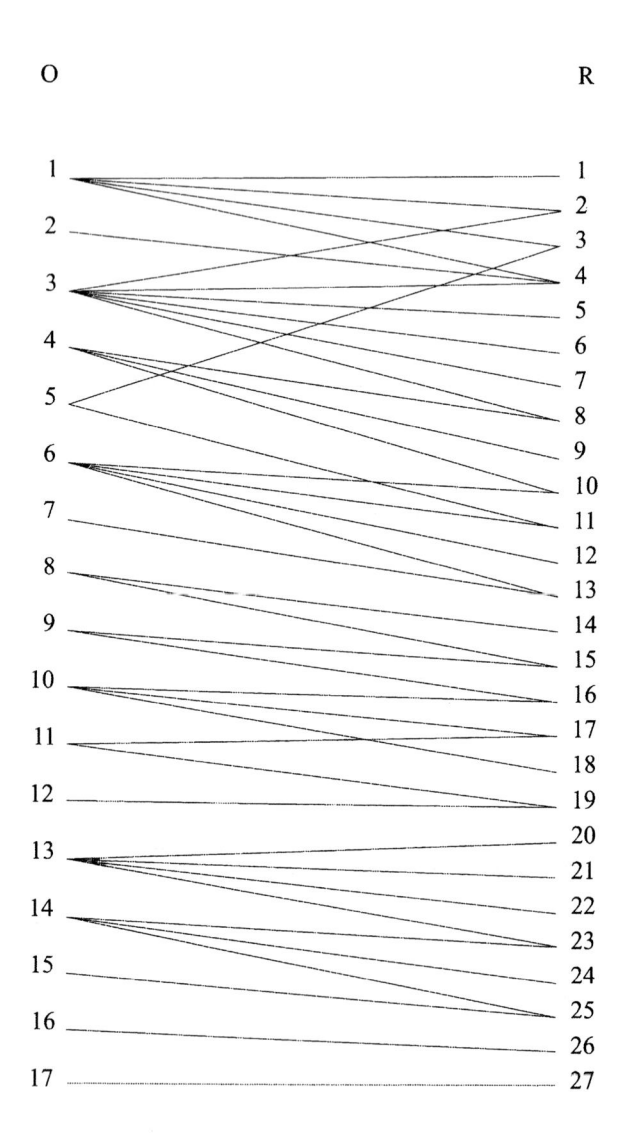

Fig. 4: *Dies of silver shekels (I.2.1)*

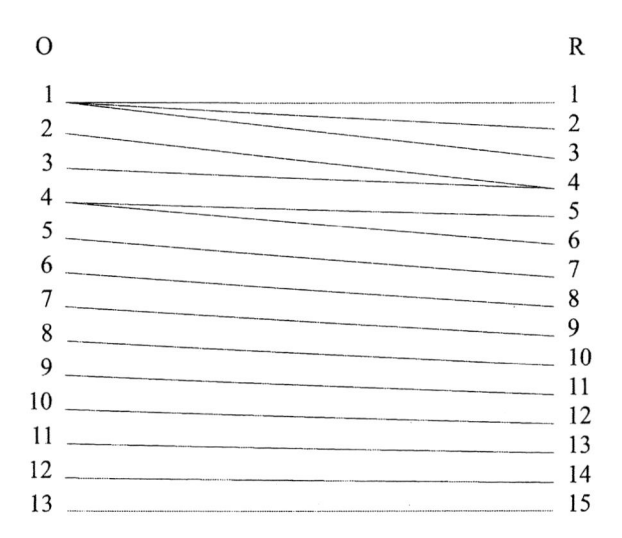

Fig. 5: *Dies of silver quarters of shekel (I.2.2)*

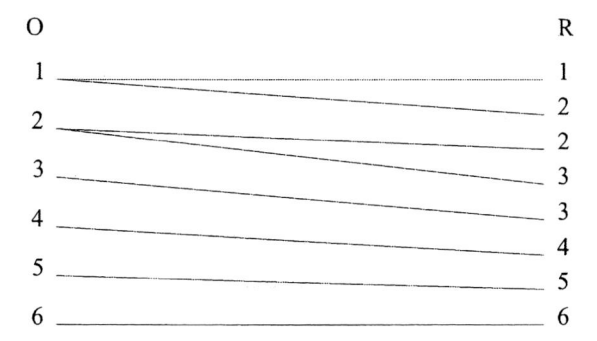

Fig. 6: *Dies of silver sixteenths of shekel (I.2.4)*

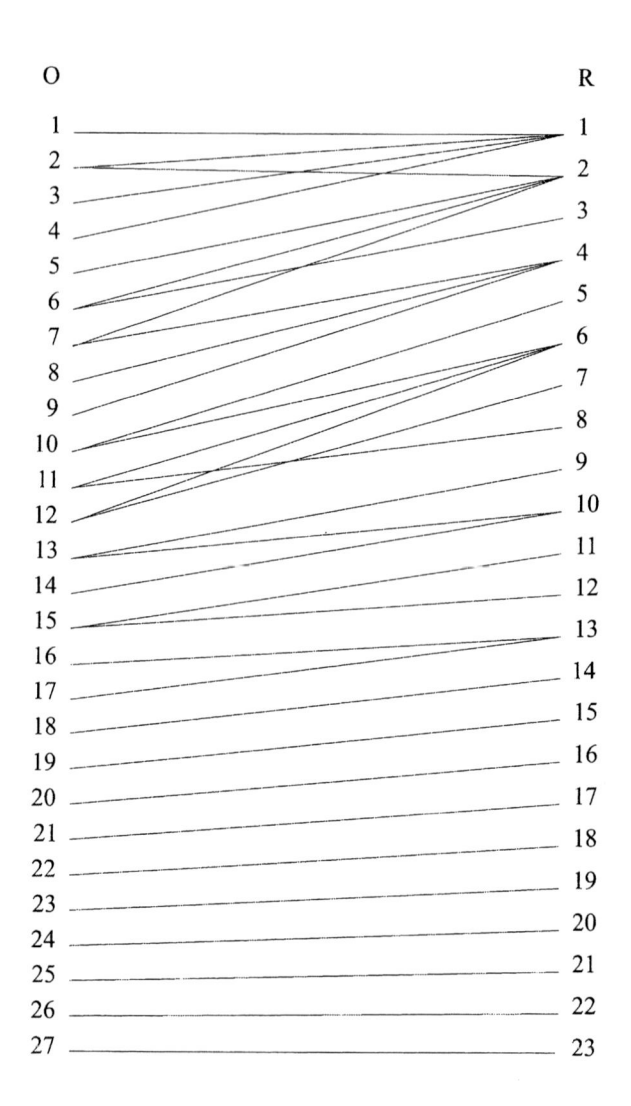

Fig. 7: *Dies of silver shekels (I.1.1.1) (part 1)*

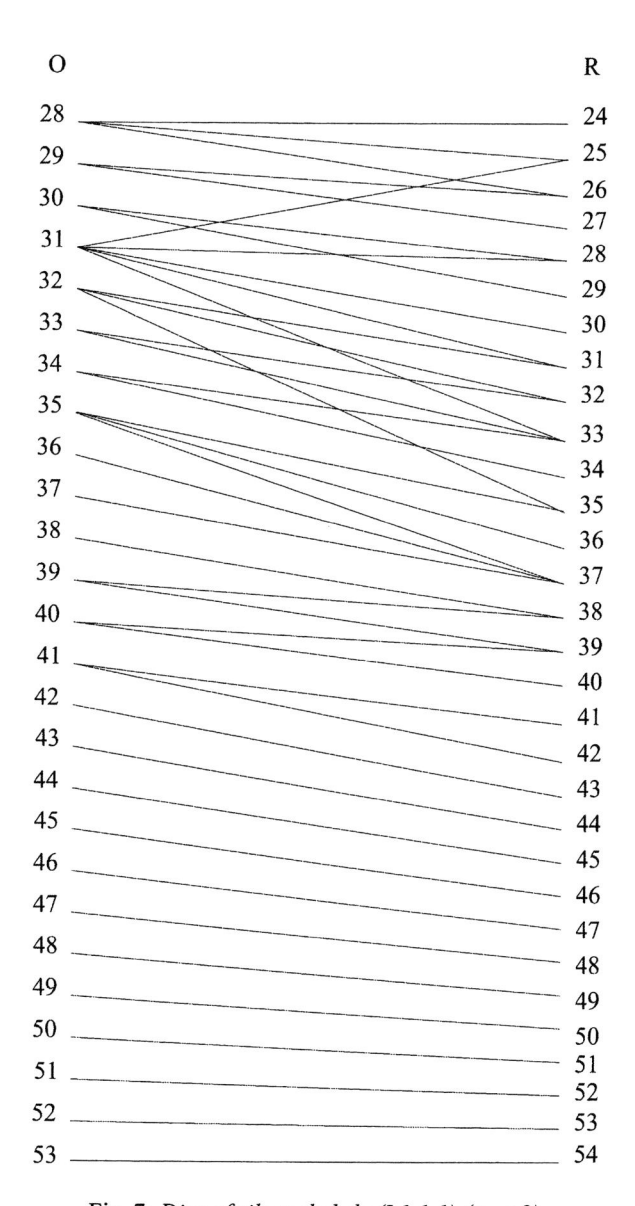

Fig. 7: *Dies of silver shekels (I.1.1.1) (part 2)*

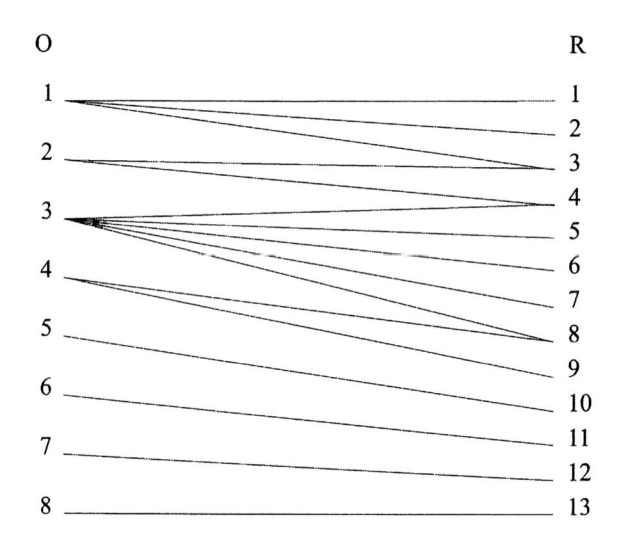

Fig. 8: *Dies of silver fourths of shekel (II.1.1.2)*

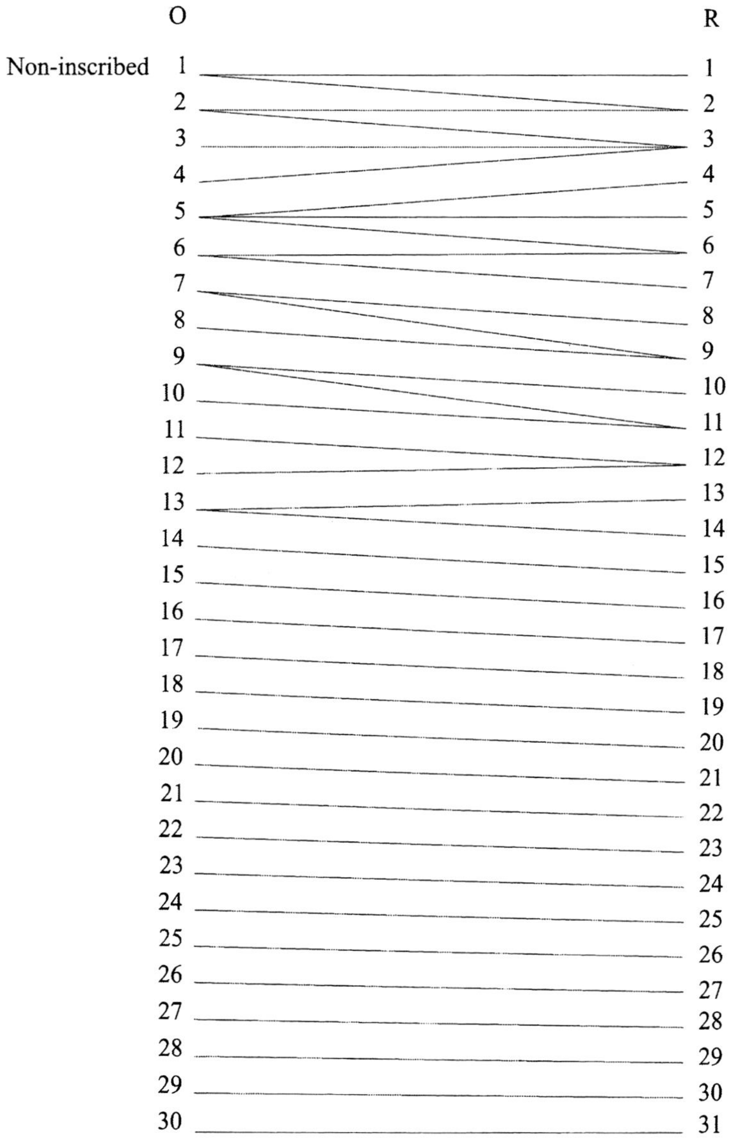

Fig. 9: *Dies of silver sixteenths of shekel (II.1.1.3 and II.1.2.2) (part 1)*

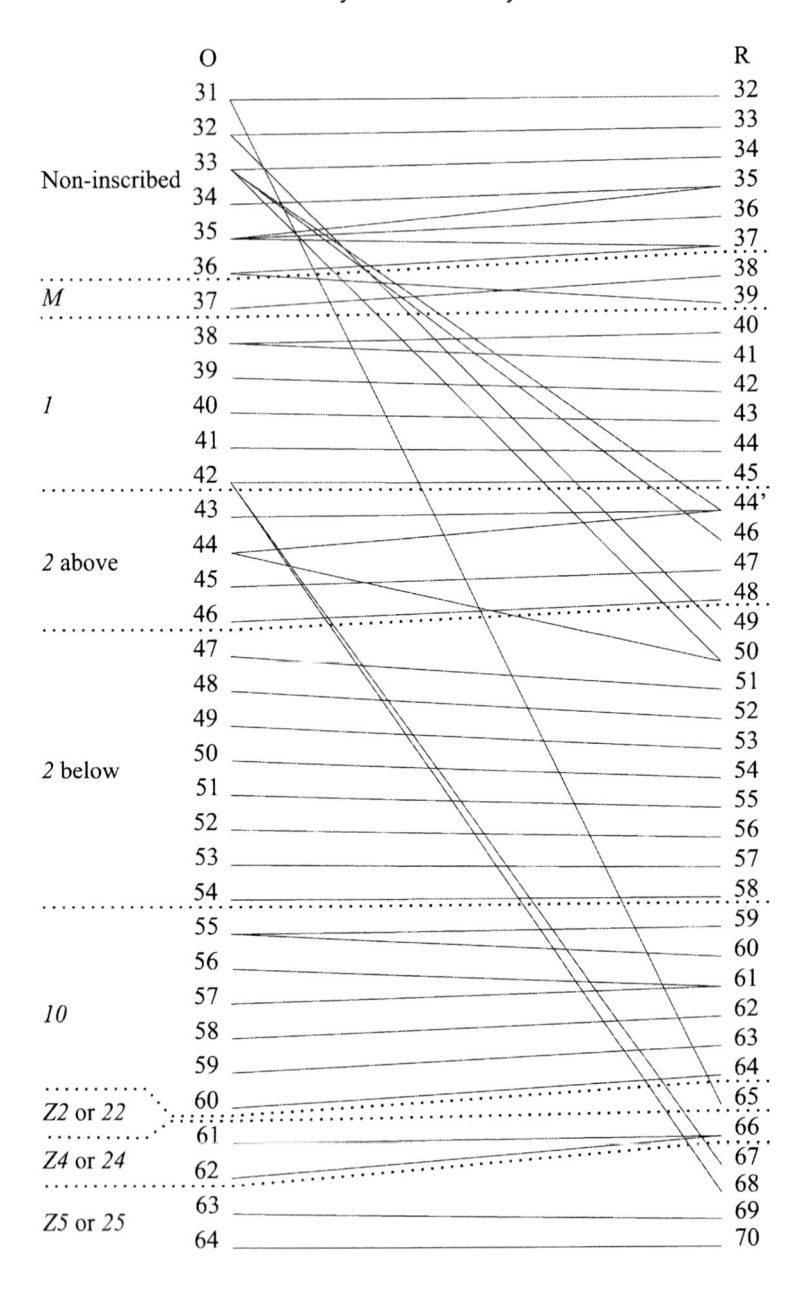

Fig. 9: *Dies of silver sixteenths of shekel (II.1.1.3 and II.1.2.2) (part 2)*

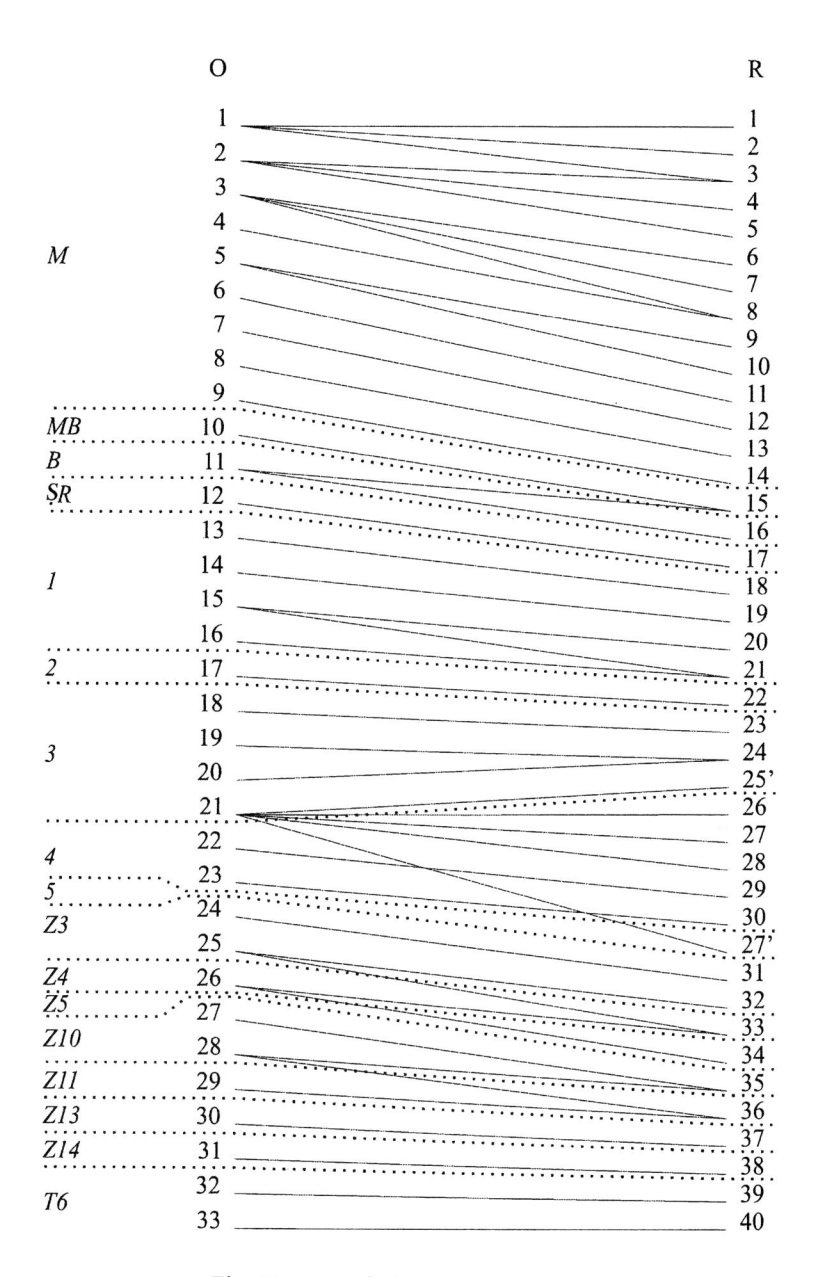

Fig. 10: *Dies of silver shekels (II.1.2.1)*

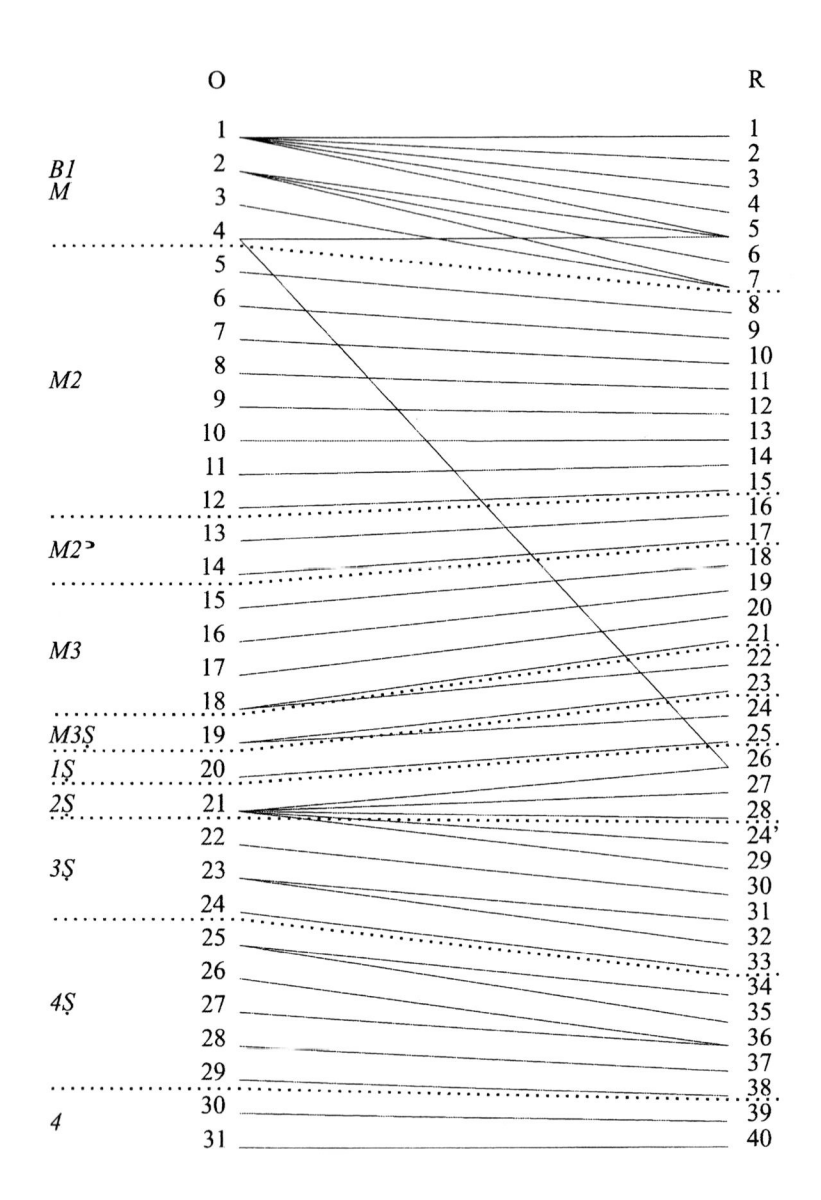

Fig. 11: *Dies of silver shekels (II.2.1.1-13)*

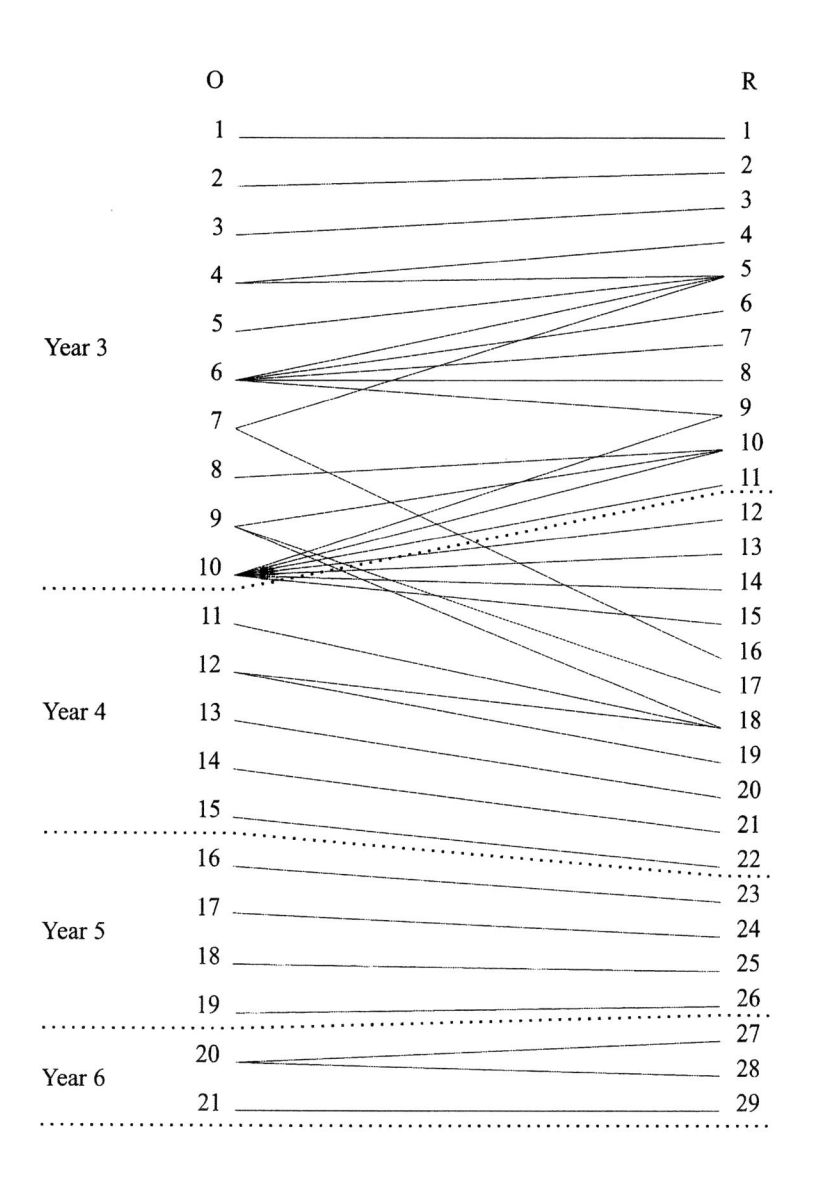

Fig. 12: *Dies of silver shekels (II.2.1.14-29) (part 1)*

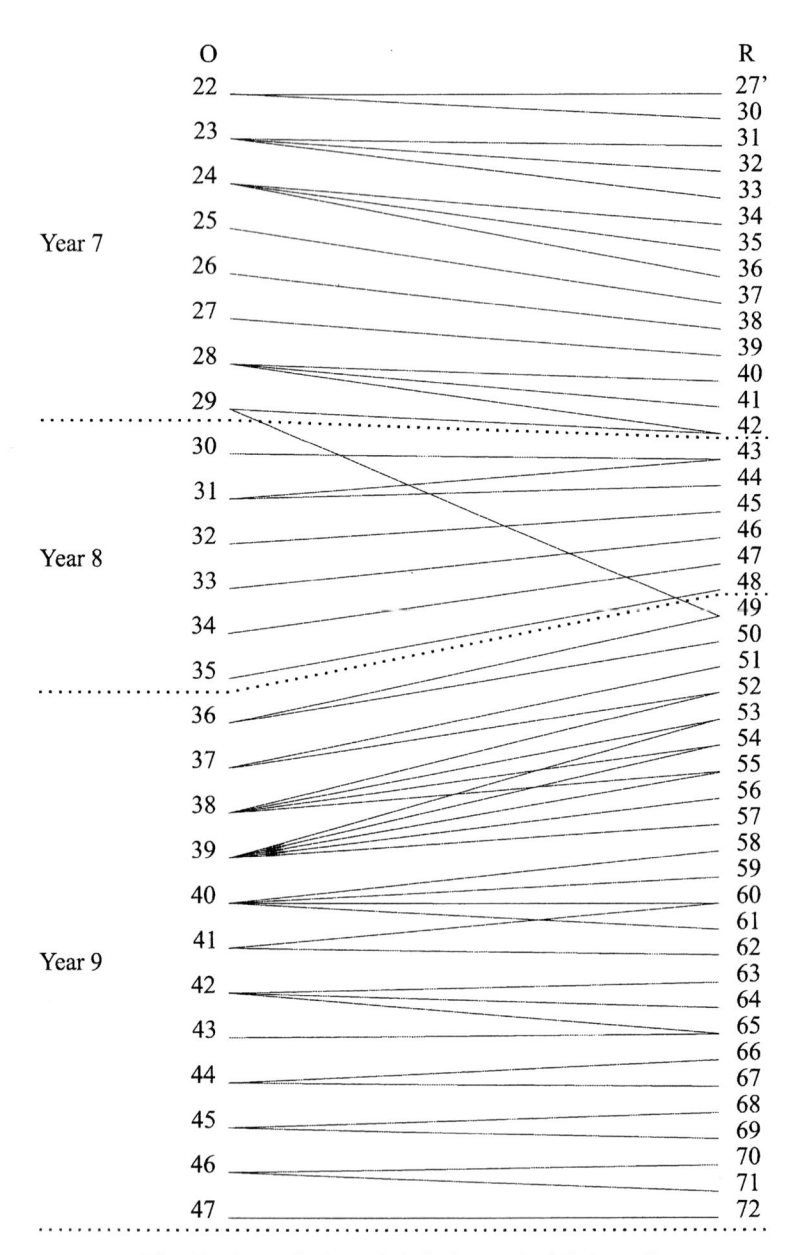

Fig. 12: *Dies of silver shekels (II.2.1.14-29) (part 2)*

The Coinage of Tyre in the Persian period 475

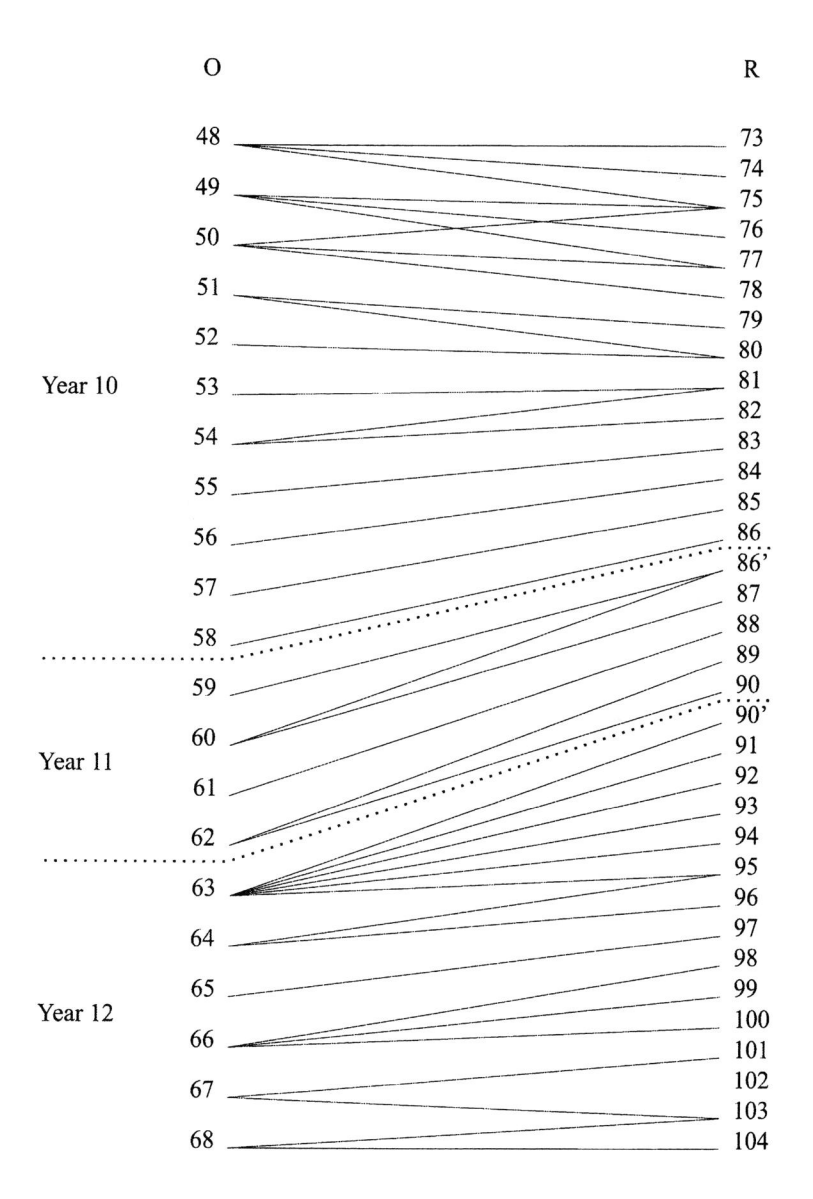

Fig. 12: *Dies of silver shekels (II.2.1.14-29) (part 3)*

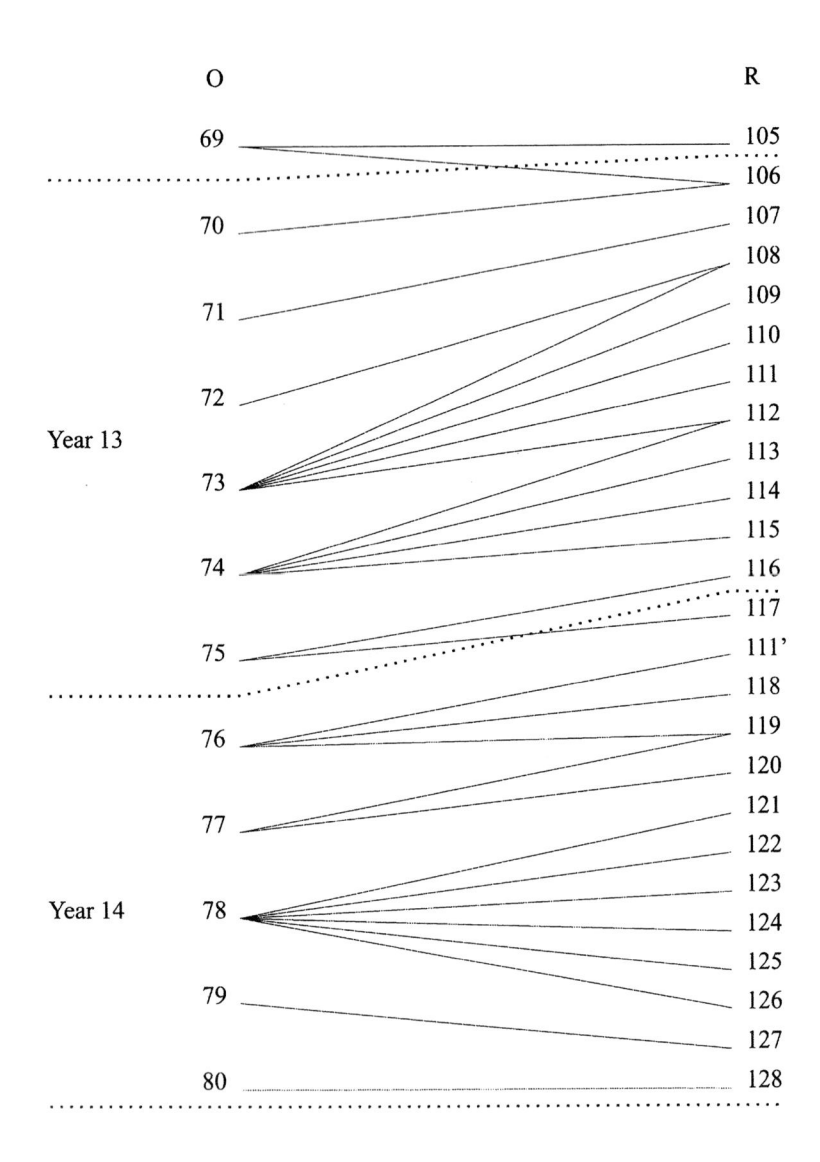

Fig. 12: *Dies of silver shekels (II.2.1.14-29) (part 4)*

The Coinage of Tyre in the Persian period

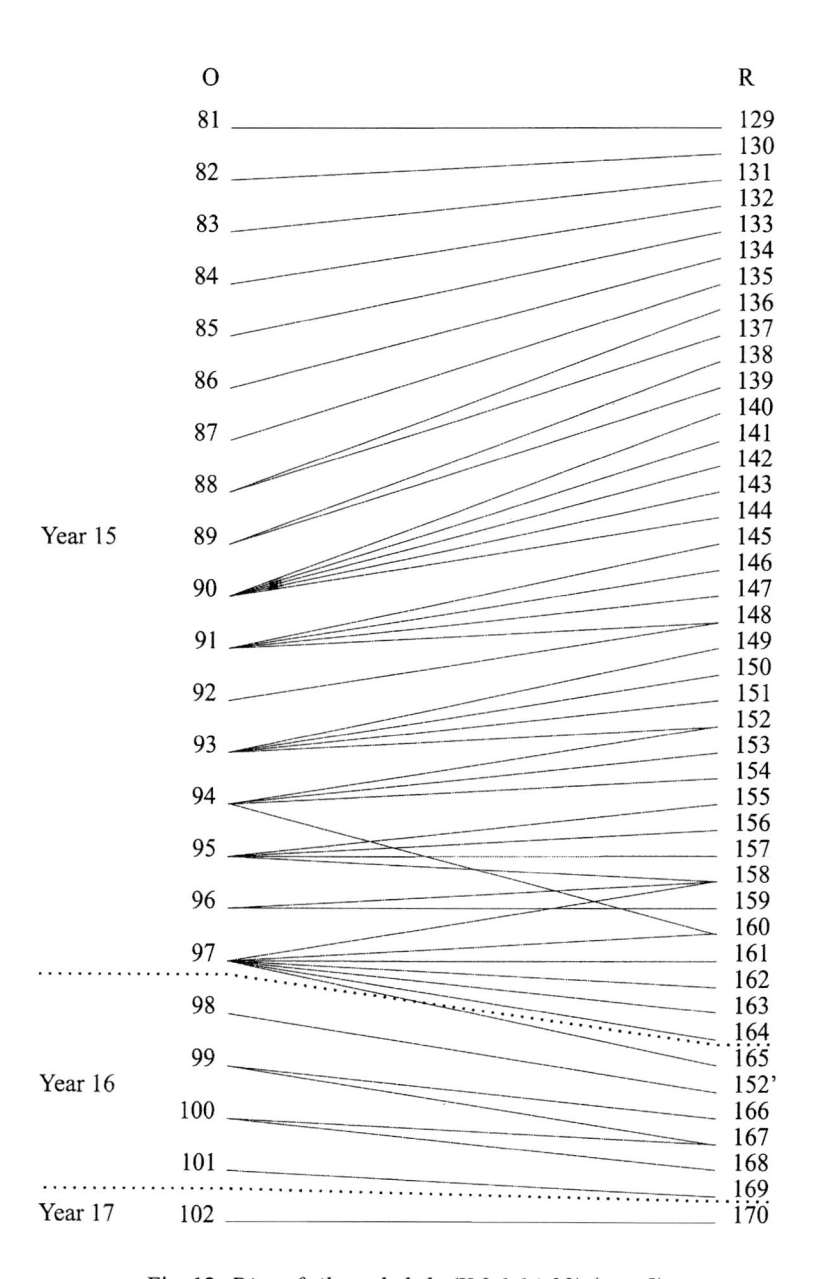

Fig. 12: *Dies of silver shekels (II.2.1.14-29) (part 5)*

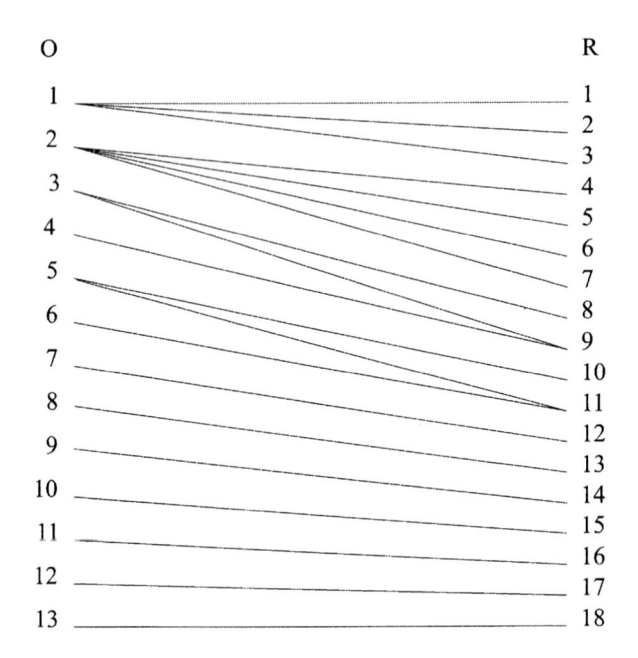

Fig. 13: *Dies of silver sixteenths of shekel (III.1.1.a)*

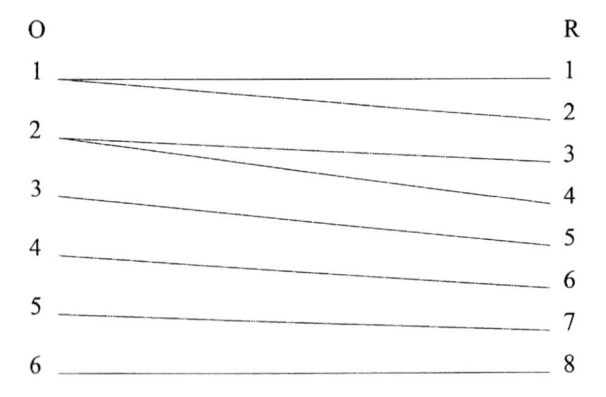

Fig. 14: *Dies of silver halves of sixteenth (III.1.1.f)*

The Coinage of Tyre in the Persian period 479

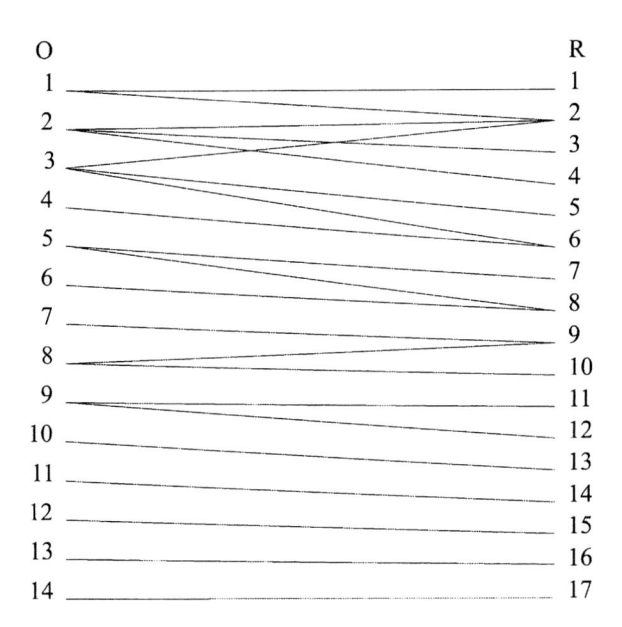

Fig. 15: *Dies of silver sixteenths of shekel (III.1.2.a)*

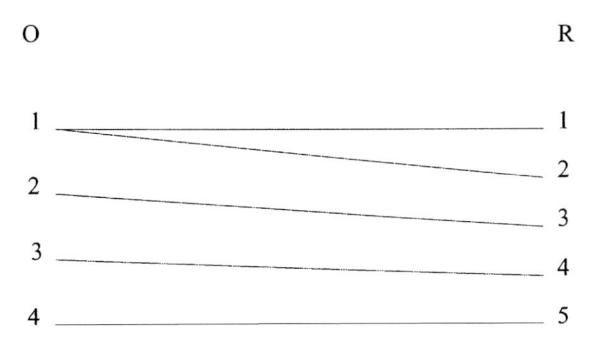

Fig. 16: *Dies of silver sixteenths of shekel (III.1.2.c)*

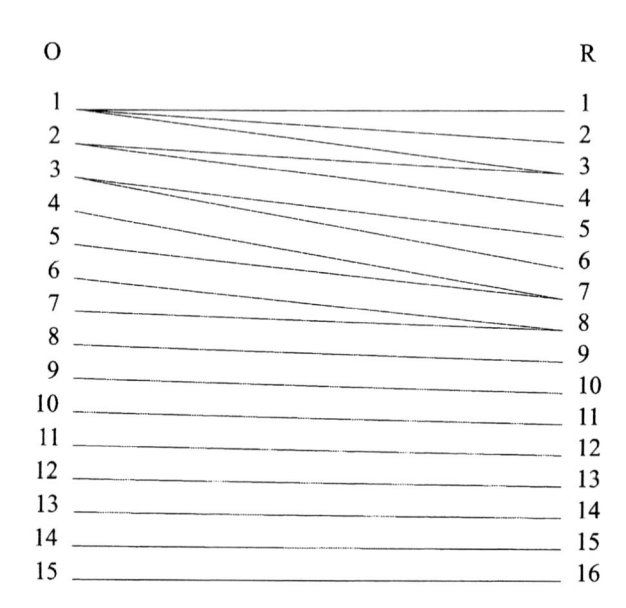

Fig. 17: *Dies of silver sixteenths of shekel (III.1.2.d)*

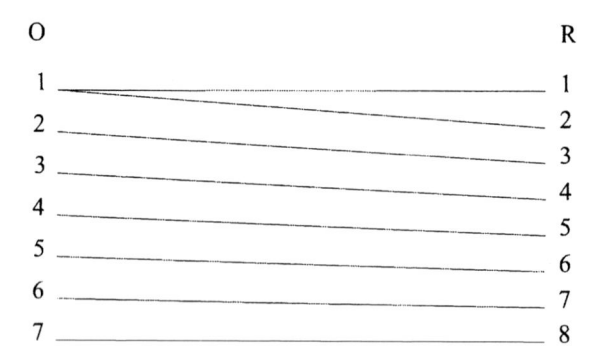

Fig. 18: *Dies of silver halves of sixteenth (III.1.2.f)*

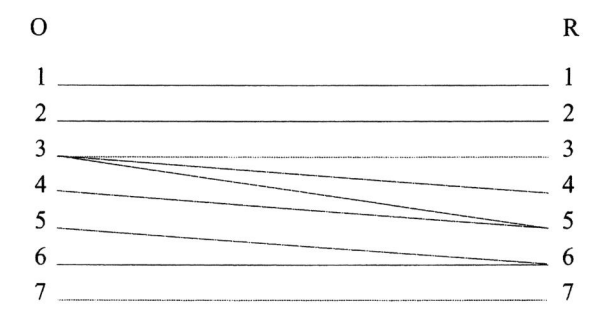

Fig. 19: *Dies of bronze coins (III.2.3)*

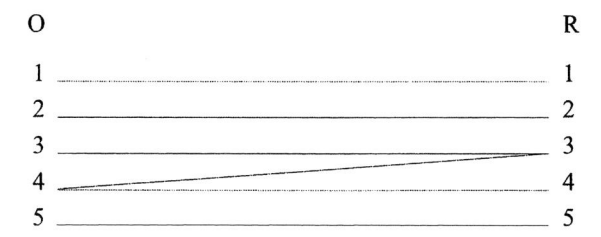

Fig. 20: *Dies of bronze coins (III.2.4)*

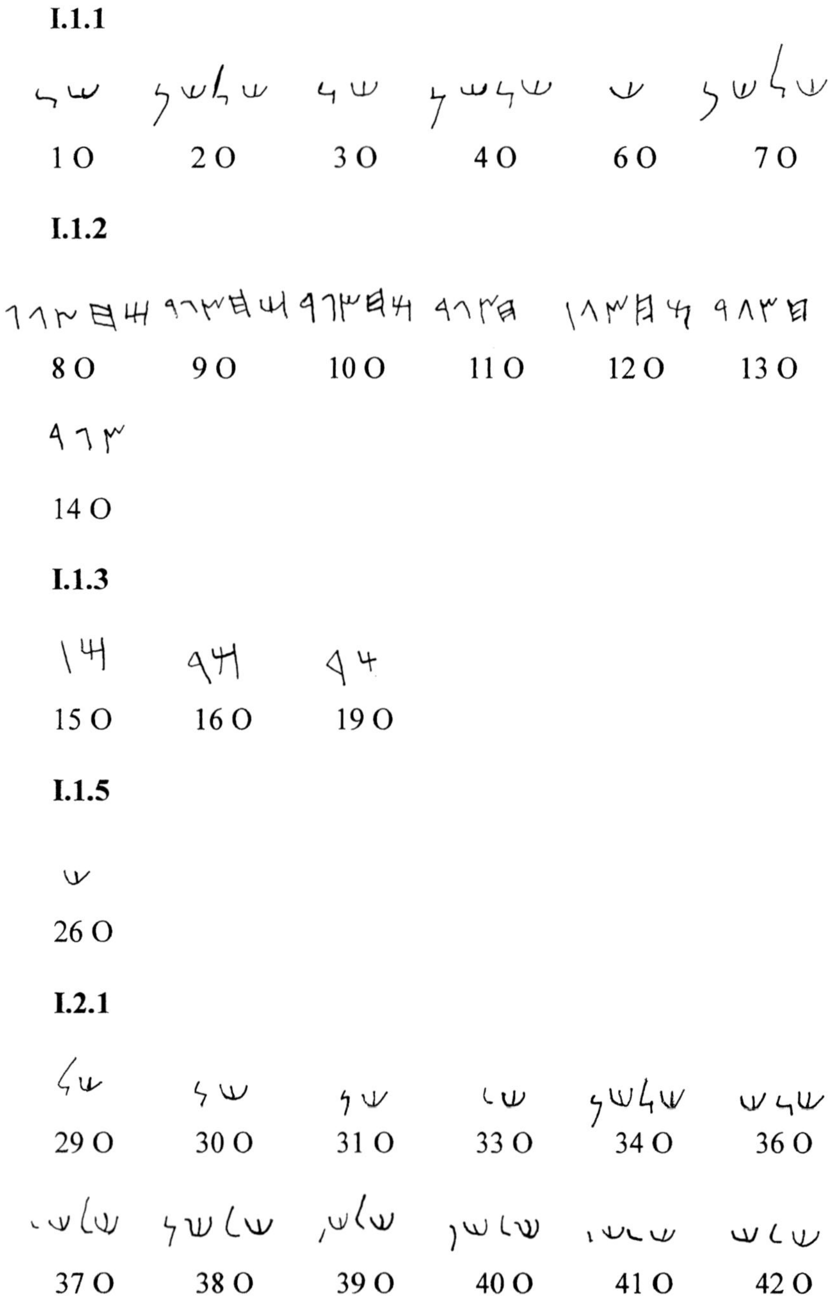

I.1.1

שׁ	שׁלׁשׁ	שׁל	שׁלשׁ	שׁ	שׁלׁשׁ
1 O	2 O	3 O	4 O	6 O	7 O

I.1.2

⨳	⨳	⨳	⨳	⨳	⨳
8 O	9 O	10 O	11 O	12 O	13 O

⨳
14 O

I.1.3

⨳	⨳	⨳
15 O	16 O	19 O

I.1.5

שׁ
26 O

I.2.1

שׁל	שׁל	שׁל	שׁל	שׁלשׁ	שׁלשׁ
29 O	30 O	31 O	33 O	34 O	36 O

שׁלשׁ	שׁלשׁ	שׁלשׁ	שׁלשׁ	שׁלשׁ	שׁלשׁ
37 O	38 O	39 O	40 O	41 O	42 O

Fig. 21: *Tyrian monetary inscriptions*

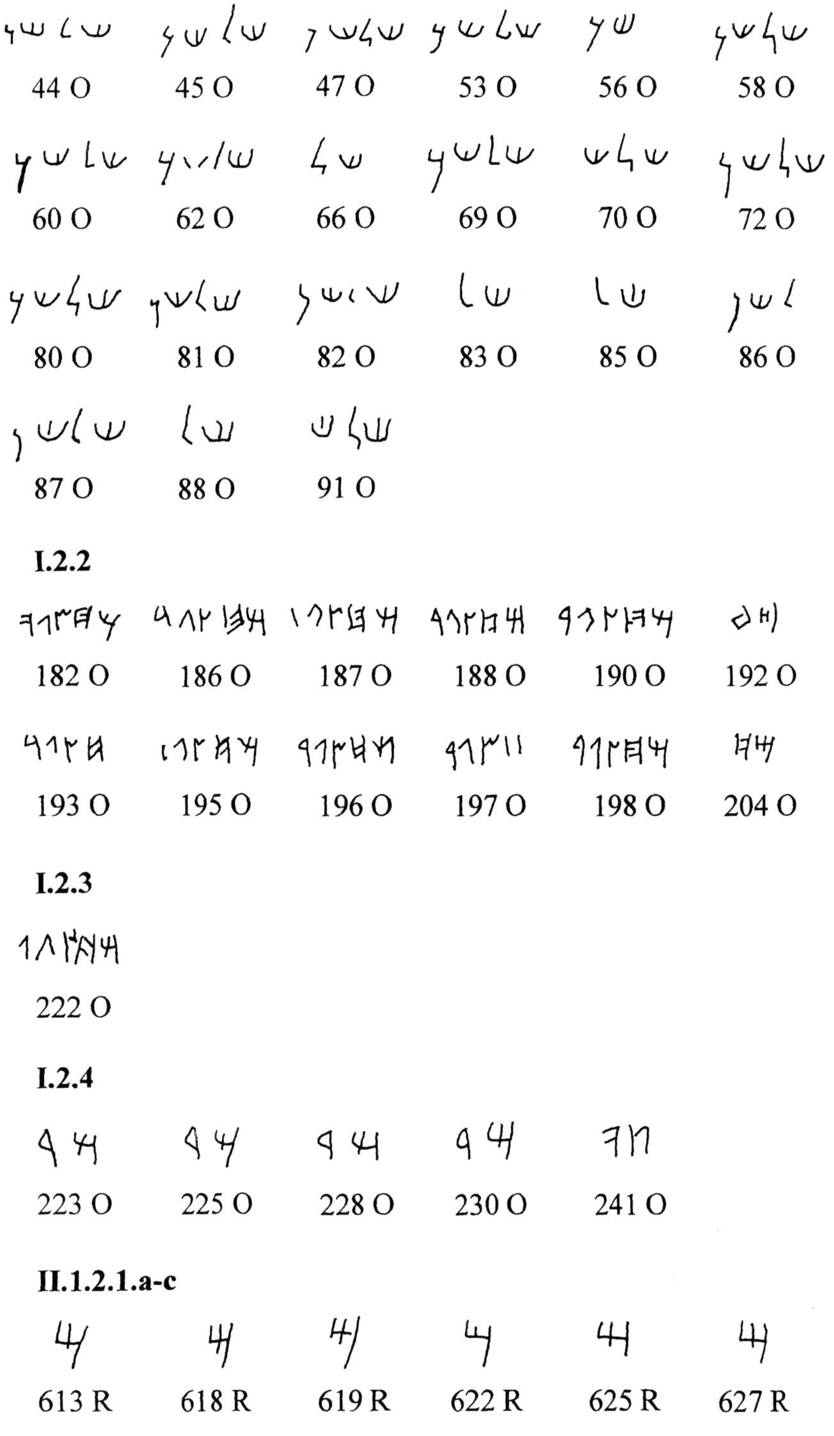

The Coinage of Tyre in the Persian period

שׁלי	שׁלי	שׁלי	שׁלי	שׁי	שׁלי
44 O	45 O	47 O	53 O	56 O	58 O

שׁלי	שׁלי	שׁל	שׁלי	שׁלי	שׁלי
60 O	62 O	66 O	69 O	70 O	72 O

שׁלי	שׁלי	שׁלי	שׁל	שׁל	לשׁי
80 O	81 O	82 O	83 O	85 O	86 O

שׁלי	שׁל	שׁל
87 O	88 O	91 O

I.2.2

עבדמלך	מלכעבד	מלכעבד	מלכעבד	מלכעבד	מל
182 O	186 O	187 O	188 O	190 O	192 O

עבדמ	מלכעב	מלכעב	מלכ	מלכעב	עב
193 O	195 O	196 O	197 O	198 O	204 O

I.2.3

עבדמלך
222 O

I.2.4

עב	עב	עב	עב	עז
223 O	225 O	228 O	230 O	241 O

II.1.2.1.a-c

ע	ע	ע	ע	ע	ע
613 R	618 R	619 R	622 R	625 R	627 R

Fig. 22: *Tyrian monetary inscriptions (continued)*

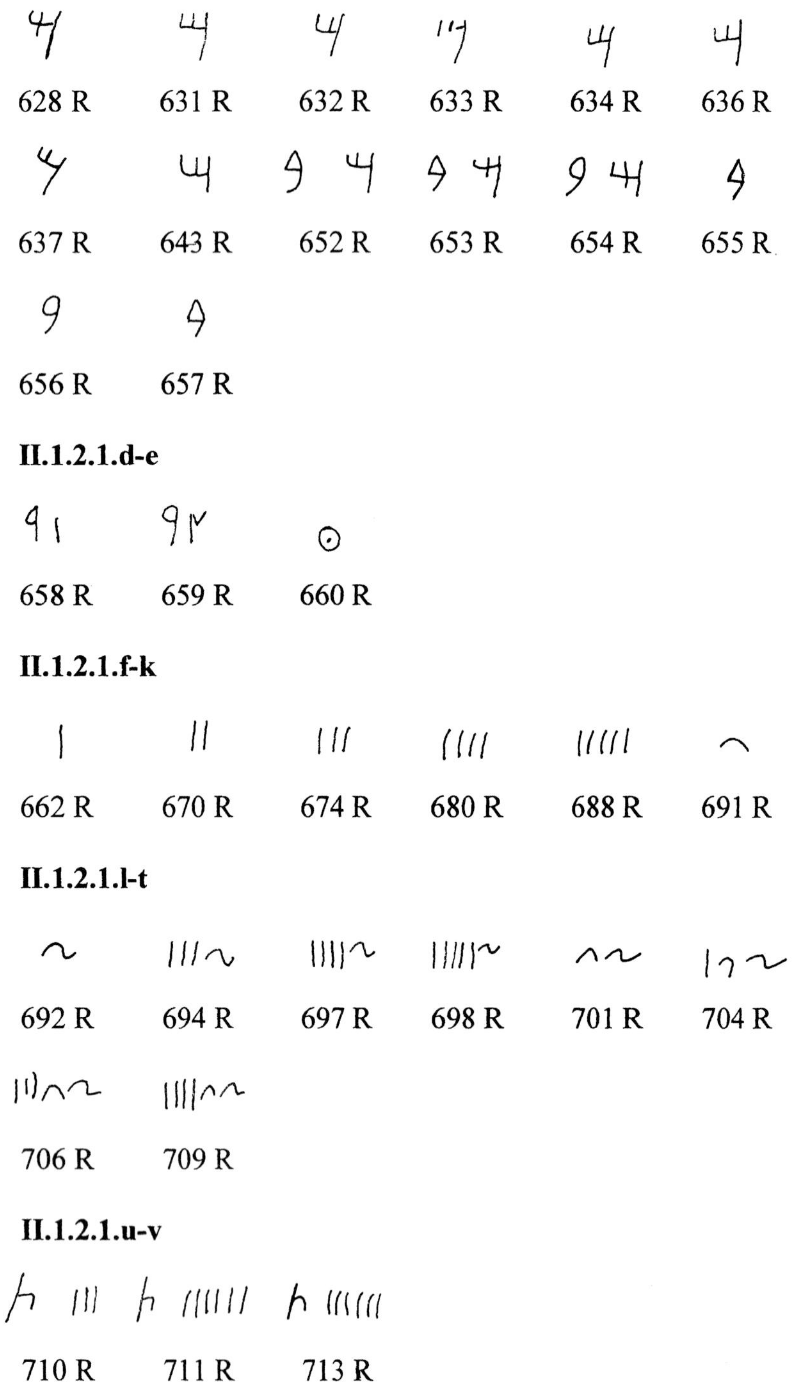

484   J. Elayi and A.G. Elayi

628 R   631 R   632 R   633 R   634 R   636 R

637 R   643 R   652 R   653 R   654 R   655 R

656 R   657 R

II.1.2.1.d-e

658 R   659 R   660 R

II.1.2.1.f-k

662 R   670 R   674 R   680 R   688 R   691 R

II.1.2.1.l-t

692 R   694 R   697 R   698 R   701 R   704 R

706 R   709 R

II.1.2.1.u-v

710 R   711 R   713 R

Fig. 23: *Tyrian monetary inscriptions (continued)*

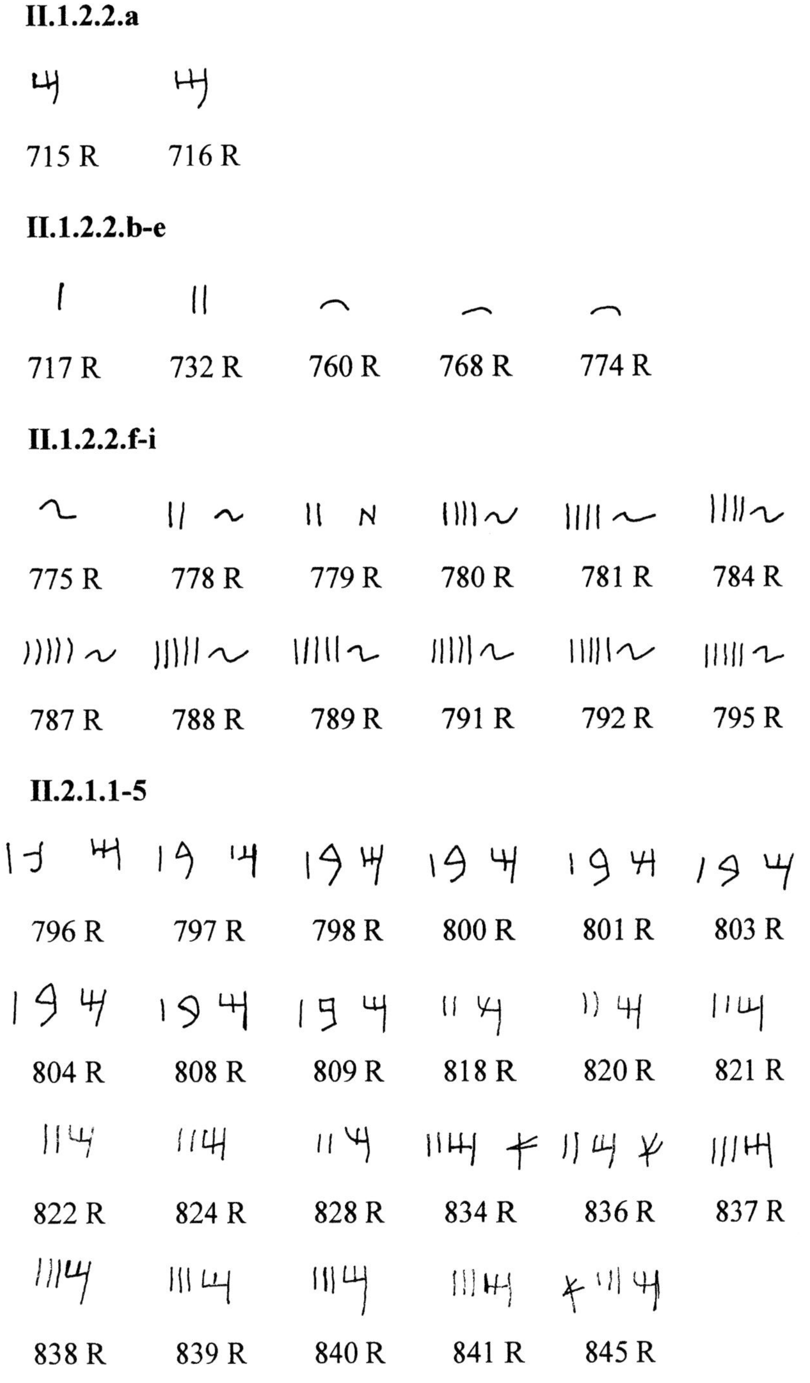

The Coinage of Tyre in the Persian period 485

II.1.2.2.a

↤	⊢⊣
715 R	716 R

II.1.2.2.b-e

l	ll	⌒	⌒	⌒
717 R	732 R	760 R	768 R	774 R

II.1.2.2.f-i

⌒	ll ⌒	ll N	llll ⌒	llll ⌒	llll ⌒
775 R	778 R	779 R	780 R	781 R	784 R

)))))⌒	lllll⌒	lllll⌒	llll⌒	llll⌒	llll⌒
787 R	788 R	789 R	791 R	792 R	795 R

II.2.1.1-5

lϟ ⊬	lϟ ⊬	lϟ ⊬	lϟ ⊬	lϟ ⊬	lϟ ⊬
796 R	797 R	798 R	800 R	801 R	803 R

lϟ ⊬	lϟ ⊬	lϟ ⊬	ll ⊬	l) ⊬	ll⊬
804 R	808 R	809 R	818 R	820 R	821 R

ll⊬	ll⊬	ll ⊬	ll⊬ ⊁	ll⊬ ⊬	lll⊬
822 R	824 R	828 R	834 R	836 R	837 R

lll⊬	lll⊬	lll⊬	lll⊬	⊁ lll⊬
838 R	839 R	840 R	841 R	845 R

Fig. 24: *Tyrian monetary inscriptions (continued)*

II.2.1.6-13

846 R	847 R	849 R	851 R	853 R	858 R
860 R	867 R	868 R	870 R	872 R	873 R

886 R

II.2.1.14-29

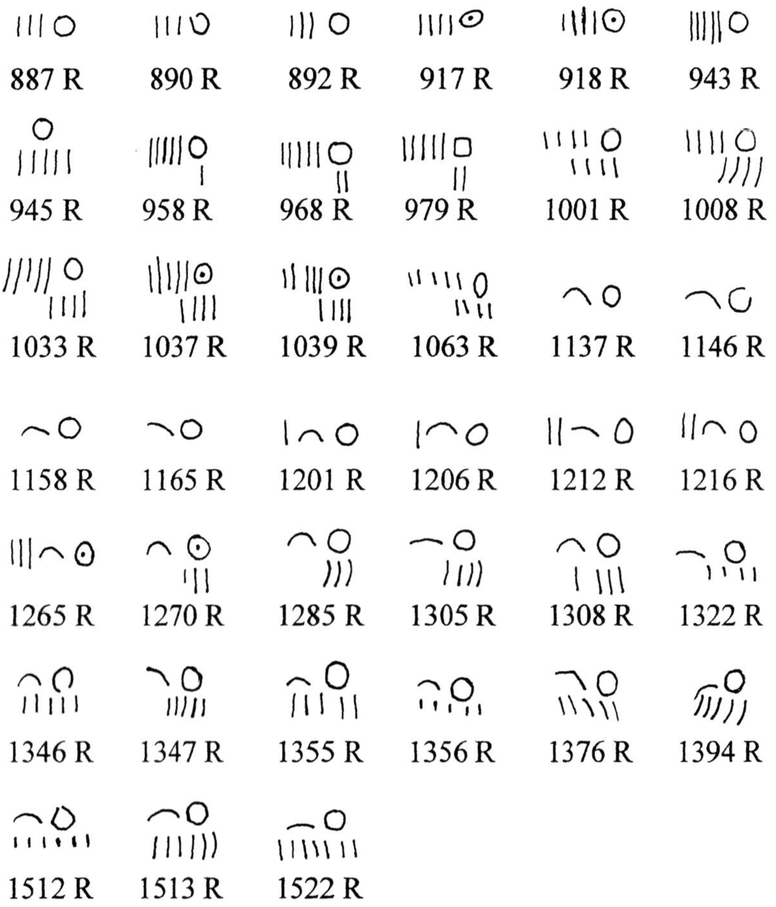

887 R	890 R	892 R	917 R	918 R	943 R
945 R	958 R	968 R	979 R	1001 R	1008 R
1033 R	1037 R	1039 R	1063 R	1137 R	1146 R
1158 R	1165 R	1201 R	1206 R	1212 R	1216 R
1265 R	1270 R	1285 R	1305 R	1308 R	1322 R
1346 R	1347 R	1355 R	1356 R	1376 R	1394 R
1512 R	1513 R	1522 R			

Fig. 25: *Tyrian monetary inscriptions (continued)*

GRAFFITI

| 288 R | 1049 R | 1144 R | 1421 R | 912 R |

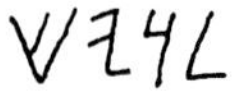

1287 R

COUNTERMARKS

| 1162 O | 329 O |

Fig. 26: *Graffiti and countermarks on Tyrian coins*

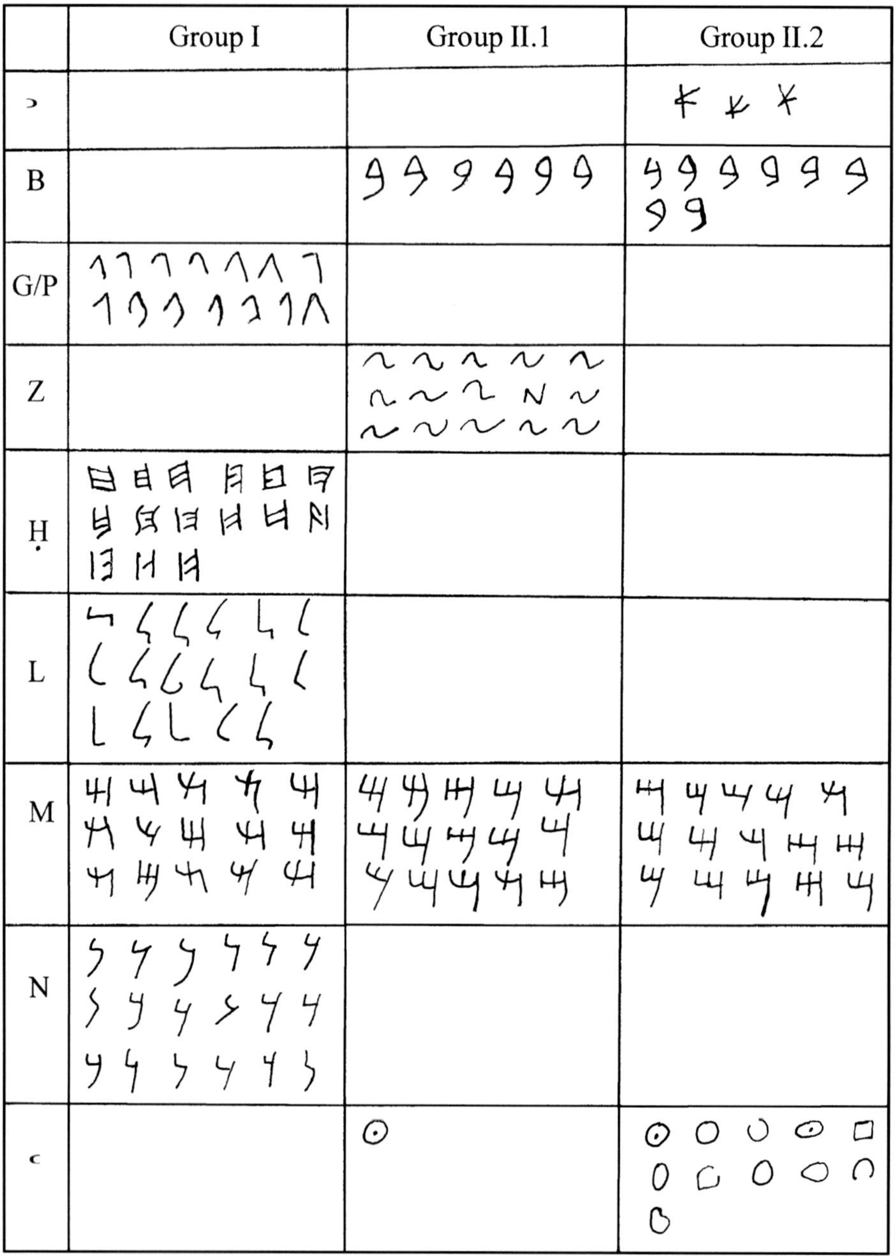

	Group I	Group II.1	Group II.2
ʾ			𐤀 𐤀 𐤀
B		𐤁 𐤁 𐤁 𐤁 𐤁 𐤁	𐤁 𐤁 𐤁 𐤁 𐤁 𐤁 𐤁 𐤁
G/P	𐤂 𐤂 𐤂 𐤂 𐤂 𐤂 𐤂 𐤂 𐤂 𐤂 𐤂 𐤂 𐤂 𐤂		
Z		𐤆 𐤆 𐤆 𐤆 𐤆 𐤆 𐤆 𐤆 𐤆 𐤆 𐤆 𐤆 𐤆 𐤆	
Ḥ	𐤇 𐤇 𐤇 𐤇 𐤇 𐤇 𐤇 𐤇 𐤇 𐤇 𐤇 𐤇 𐤇 𐤇 𐤇		
L	𐤋 𐤋 𐤋 𐤋 𐤋 𐤋 𐤋 𐤋 𐤋 𐤋 𐤋 𐤋 𐤋 𐤋 𐤋		
M	𐤌 𐤌 𐤌 𐤌 𐤌 𐤌 𐤌 𐤌 𐤌 𐤌 𐤌 𐤌 𐤌 𐤌 𐤌	𐤌 𐤌 𐤌 𐤌 𐤌 𐤌 𐤌 𐤌 𐤌 𐤌 𐤌 𐤌 𐤌	𐤌 𐤌 𐤌 𐤌 𐤌 𐤌 𐤌 𐤌 𐤌 𐤌 𐤌 𐤌 𐤌 𐤌 𐤌
N	𐤍 𐤍 𐤍 𐤍 𐤍 𐤍 𐤍 𐤍 𐤍 𐤍 𐤍 𐤍 𐤍 𐤍 𐤍 𐤍 𐤍 𐤍		
ʿ		⊙	⊙ O ʊ ⊙ ▢ 0 ⊂ O ⌒ ∩ ♭

Fig. 27: *Palaeographical chart of the Tyrian monetary inscriptions*

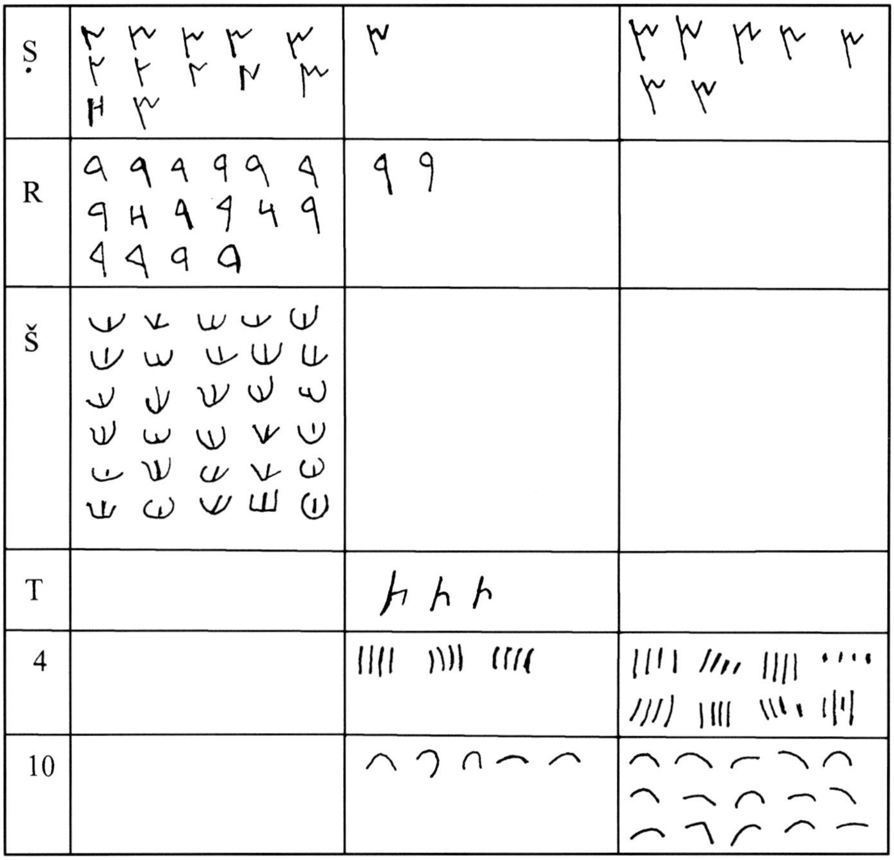

Ṣ	ᴎ ᴎ ᴎ ᴎ ᴎ ᴎ ᴎ ᴎ ᴎ ᴎ ᴎ ᴎ	ᴎ	ᴎ ᴎ ᴎ ᴎ ᴎ ᴎ ᴎ
R	۹ ۹ ۹ ۹ ۹ ۹ ۹ H ۹ ۹ ۹ ۹ ۹ ۹ ۹ ۹	۹ ۹	
Š	ᴗ ᴗ		
T		ⱶ ⱶ ⱶ	
4		‖‖ ‖‖ ‖‖	‖‖ ‖‖ ‖‖ •••• ‖‖ ‖‖ \\\ ‖‖
10		⌒ ⌒ ⌒ ⌒ ⌒	⌒ ⌒ ⌒ ⌒ ⌒ ⌒ ⌒ ⌒ ⌒ ⌒ ⌒ ⌒ ⌒ ⌒ ⌒

Fig. 28: *Palaeographical chart of the Tyrian monetary inscriptions (continued)*

Diameter in mm	Group I.1.1	Group I.2.1	Group II.1.1.1 a-d	Group II.1.2.1 a-v	Group II.2.1 1-13	Group II.2.1 14-29
30						
29						
28			4			
27			6	1		
26		1	12			
25			23	3		
24		6	34	6	2	6
23		2	28	10	12	29
22	1	6	22	16	17	81
21	3	5	12	18	20	74
20	2	4	4	12	6	36
19			1	5	1	2
18			2	1	1	
17				1		
16						

Fig. 29: *Compared diameter of the shekels*

Diameter in mm	Group I.1.2	Group I.2.2	Group II.1.1.2
19			2
18			0
17			3
16			10
15		2	2
14	2	11	2
13	3	6	
12	1		
11	0		
10	0		
9	0		
8	5		

Fig. 30: *Compared diameter of the fourths of shekel*

Diameter in mm	Group I.1.3	Group I.2.4	Group II.1.1.3	Group II.1.2.2. a-i	Group III.1.1. a-c	Group III.1.2. a-d
13						2
12					1	8
11			1	10	15	9
10		1	20	29	12	32
9	5	4	35	16	1	20
8		2	12	1		3
7			1			1
6						

Fig. 31: *Compared diameter of the sixteenths of shekel*

	Shekels AR	1/4 of shekel AR	1/8 of shekel AR	1/16 of shekel AR	1/2 of sixteenth AR	1/10 of sixteenth AR	1/16 of shekel AE	Total by group
Group I.1	7	7		5	6	3		28
Group I.2	153	40	1 ?	16	7			217
Group II.1.1	155	29		183				367
Group II.1.2	102	81						183
Group II.2.1. 1-13	91							91
Group II.2.1. 14-29	653							653
Group III.1.1				115				115
Group III.1.2				79				79
Group III.2							78	78
Total	1161	157	1	398	13	3	78	1811

Fig. 32: *Number of coins preserved by group and denomination*

	Number of coins	%
Silver:		
Shekels	1161	(64.10%)
Quarters of shekel	157	(8.67%)
Eights of shekel	1	(0.06%)
Sixteenths of shekel	398	(21.98%)
Halves of sixteenth	13	(0.72%)
Tenths of sixteenth	3	(0.17%)
Total	1733	
Bronze:		
Sixteenths of shekel	78	(4.31%)
Total	78	

Fig. 33: *Proportion of coins by denomination*

The Coinage of Tyre in the Persian period

AR	Shekels	1/4 of shekel	1/8 of shekel	1/16 of shekel	1/2 of sixteenth	1/10 of sixteenth	Total
Group I.1	5	6		3	3	1	18
Group I.2	17	13	1 ?	6	4		41
Group II.1.1	53	8		36			97
Group II.1.2	33			28			61
Group II.2.1. 1-13	31						31
Group II.2.1. 14-29	102						102
Group III.1.1				16	6		22
Group III.1.2				33	9		42
Total AR	241	27	1	122	22	1	414
AE				1/16 of shekel			
Group III.2				18			18
Total AE				18			18

Fig. 34: *Number of obverse dies by group and denomination*

	Number of obverse dies	%
Silver:		
Shekels	241	(55.79%)
Quarters of shekel	27	(6.25%)
Eights of shekel	1 ?	(0.23%)
Sixteenths of shekel	122	(28.24%)
Halves of sixteenth	22	(5.09%)
Tenths of sixteenth	1	(0.23%)
Total	414	
Bronze:		
Sixteenths of shekel	18	(4.17%)
Total	18	

Fig. 35: *Proportion of obverse dies by denomination*

AR	Shekels	1/4 of shekel	1/8 of shekel	1/16 of shekel	1/2 of sixteenth	1/10 of sixteenth	Total
Group I.1	5	4		3	3	1	16
Group I.2	27	15	1 ?	6	4		53
Group II.1.1	54	13		37			104
Group II.1.2	40			33			73
Group II.2.1. 1-13	36						36
Group II.2.1. 14-29	170						170
Group III.1.1				21	8		29
Group III.1.2				38	10		48
Total AR	332	32	1	138	25	1	529
AE				1/16 of shekel			
Group III.2				18			18
Total AE				18			18

Fig. 36: *Number of reverse dies by group and denomination*

	Number of reverse dies	%
Silver:		
Shekels	332	(60.69%)
Quarters of shekel	32	(5.85%)
Eights of shekel	1 ?	(0.18%)
Sixteenths of shekel	138	(25.23%)
Halves of sixteenth	25	(4.57%)
Tenths of sixteenth	1	(0.18%)
Total	529	
Bronze:		
Sixteenths of shekel	18	(3.29%)
Total	18	

Fig. 37: *Proportion of reverse dies by denomination*

Dates (BCE)	Years of rule	Number of obverse dies
347	3	10
346	4	5
345	5	4
344	6	2
343	7	8
342	8	6
341	9	12
340	10	11
339	11	4
338	12	7
337	13	6
336	14	5
335	15	17
334	16	4
333	17	1
Total		102

Fig. 38: *Number of shekel obverse dies per year of ʿOzmilk's reign*

Groups	Shekels AR	1/4 of shekel AR	1/16 of shekel AR	1/2 of sixteenth AR	1/16 of shekel AE
I.1.1	1.40				
I.1.2		1.16			
I.2.1	2.82				
I.2.2		1.30			
I.2.4			1.33		
I.2.5				1	
II.1.1.1	1.71				
II.1.1.2		2			
II.1.1.3			1.44		
II.1.2.1	1.42				
II.1.2.2			1.17		
II.2.1.1-13	1.54				
II.2.1.14-29	2.05				
III.1.1.a			1.53		
III.1.1.f				1.33	
III.1.2.a			1.57		
III.1.2.c			1.25		
III.1.2.d			1.26		
III.1.2.f				1.14	
III.2.3					1.27
III.2.4					1.20

Fig. 39: *Ratios of the different groups and denominations*

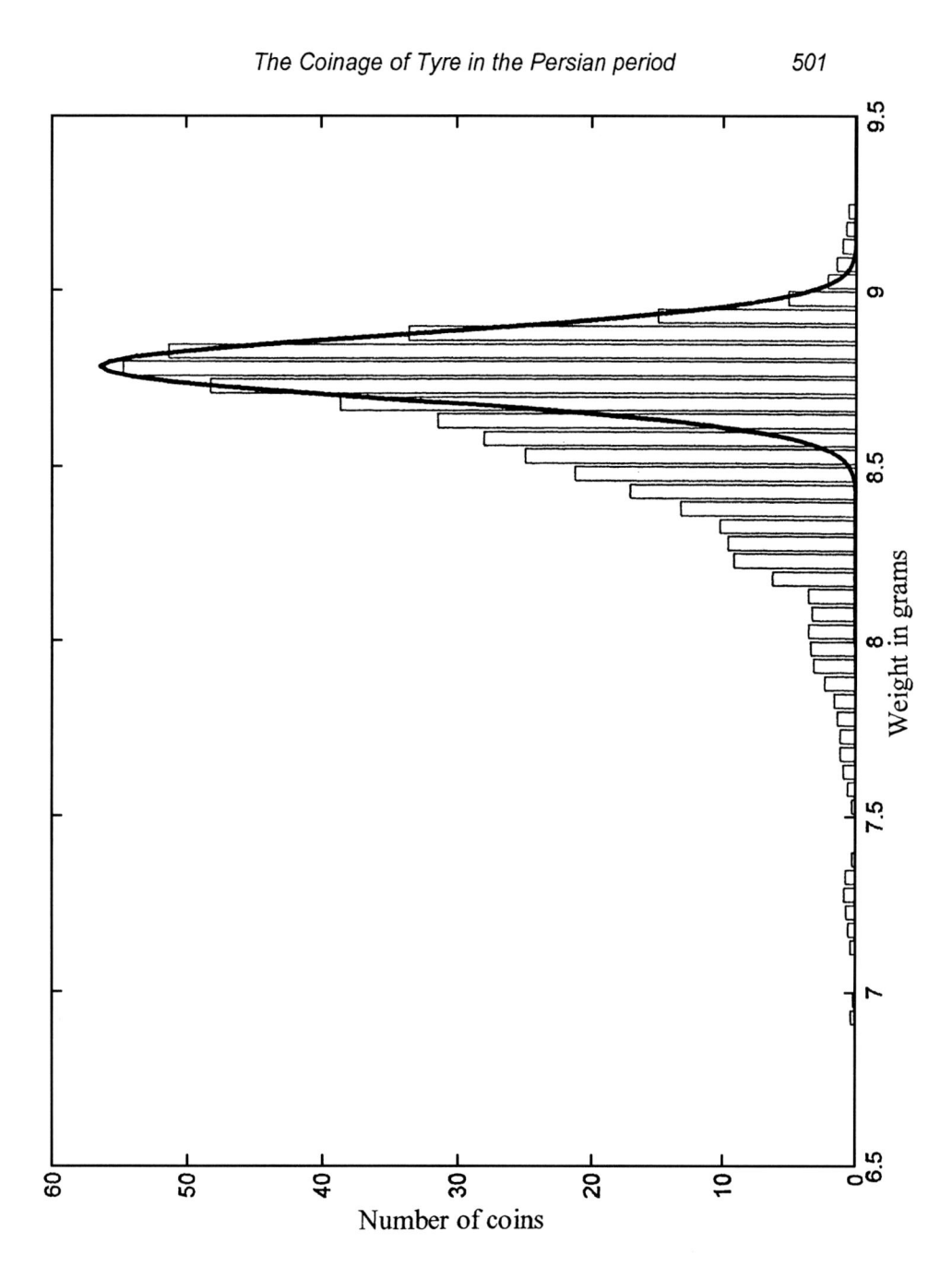

Fig. 40: *Tyrian shekels after the change of standard (step of histogram h= 0.05)*

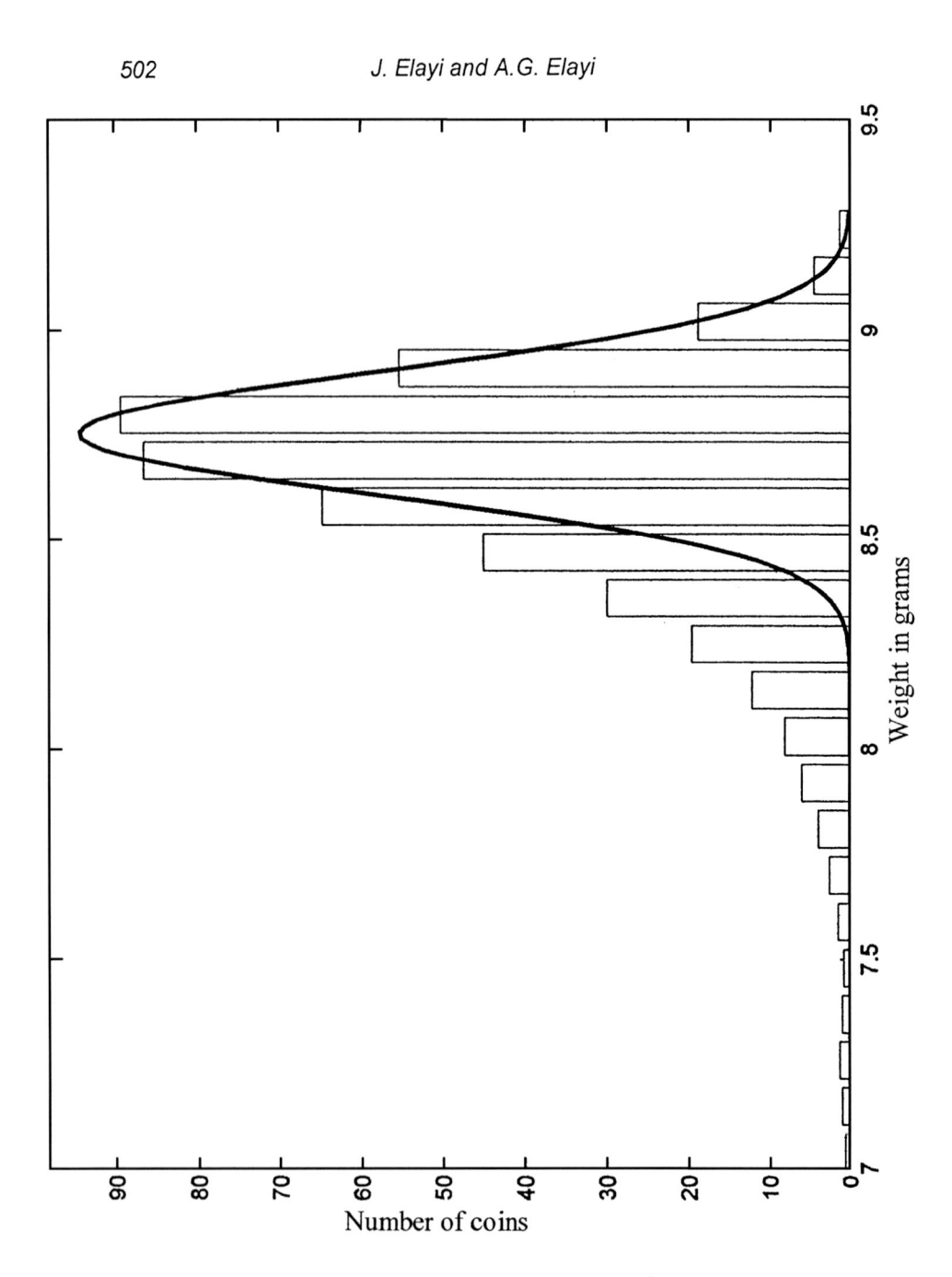

Fig. 41: *Tyrian shekels after the change of standard (step of histogram h= 0.11)*

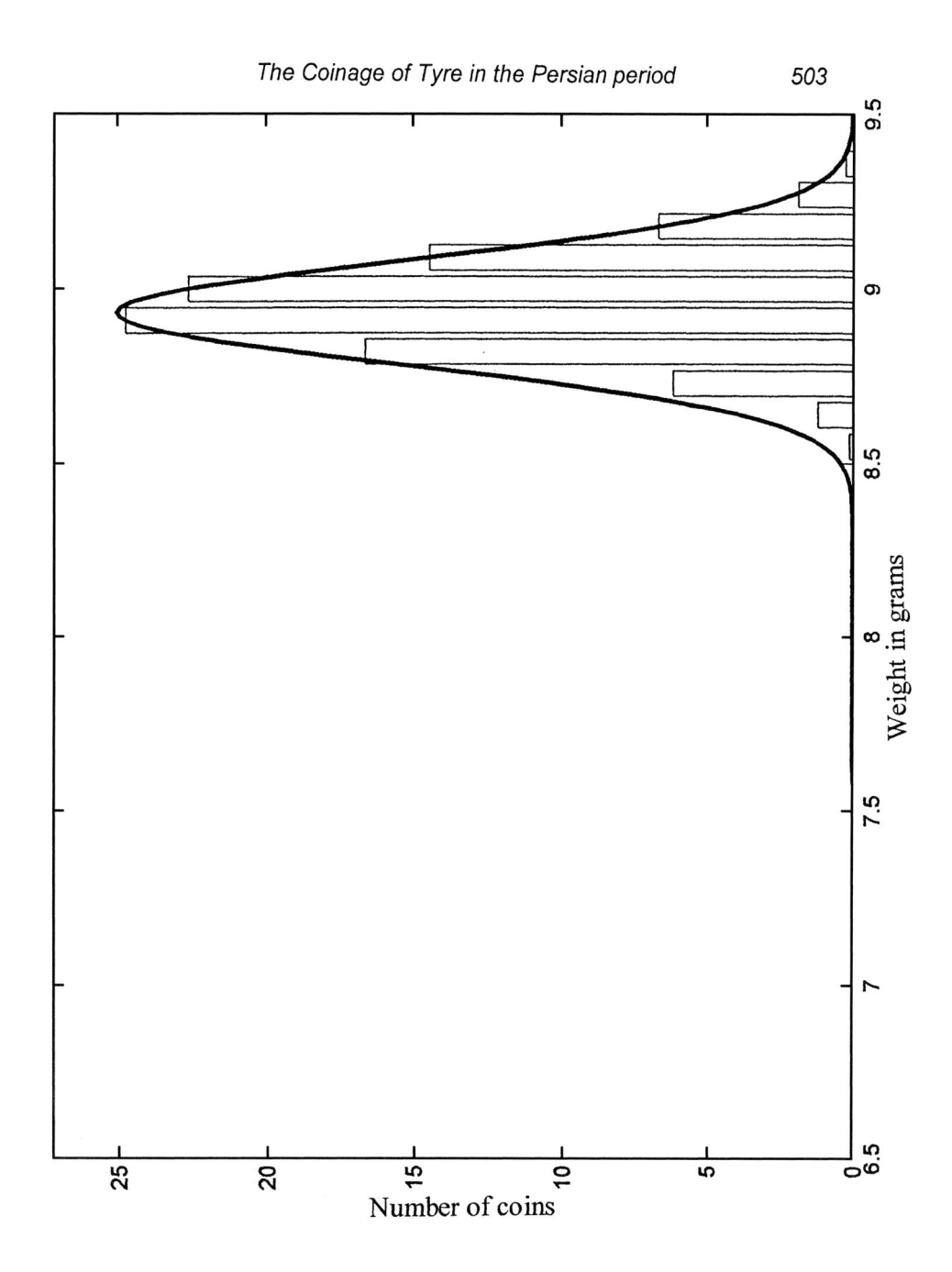

Fig. 42: *Hoard TXXXV before cleaning*

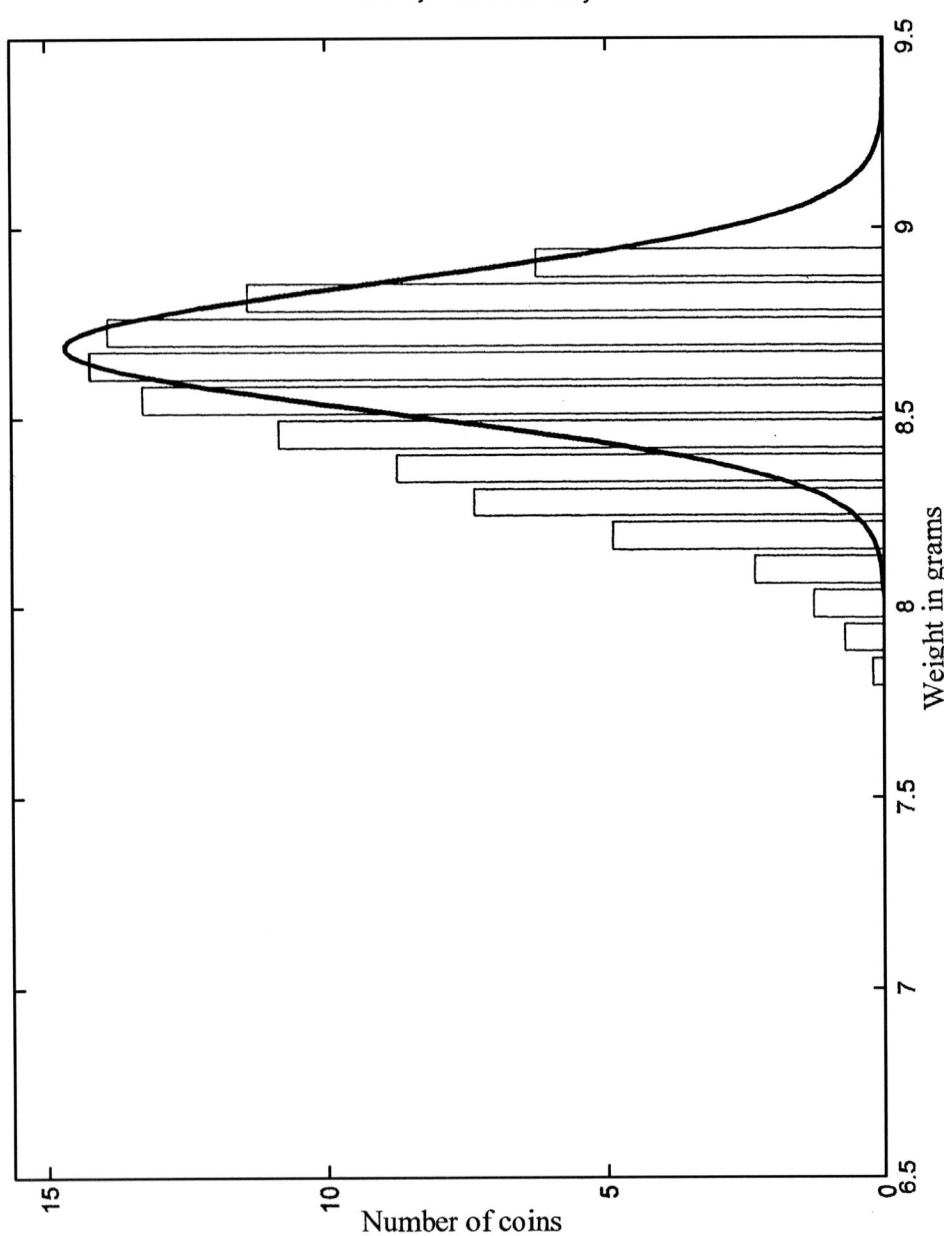

Fig. 43: *Hoard TXXXV after cleaning*

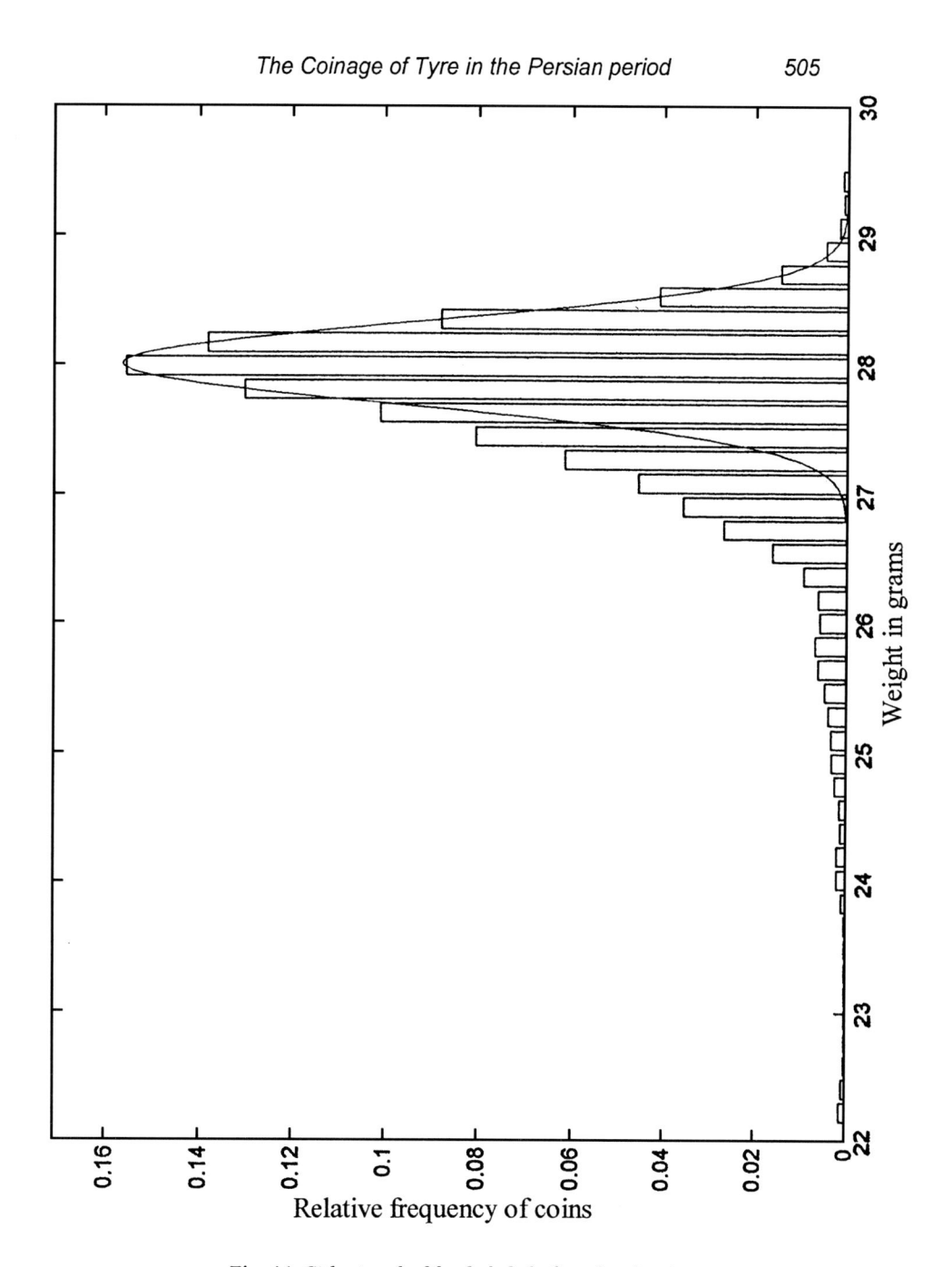

Fig. 44: *Sidonian double shekels before devaluation*

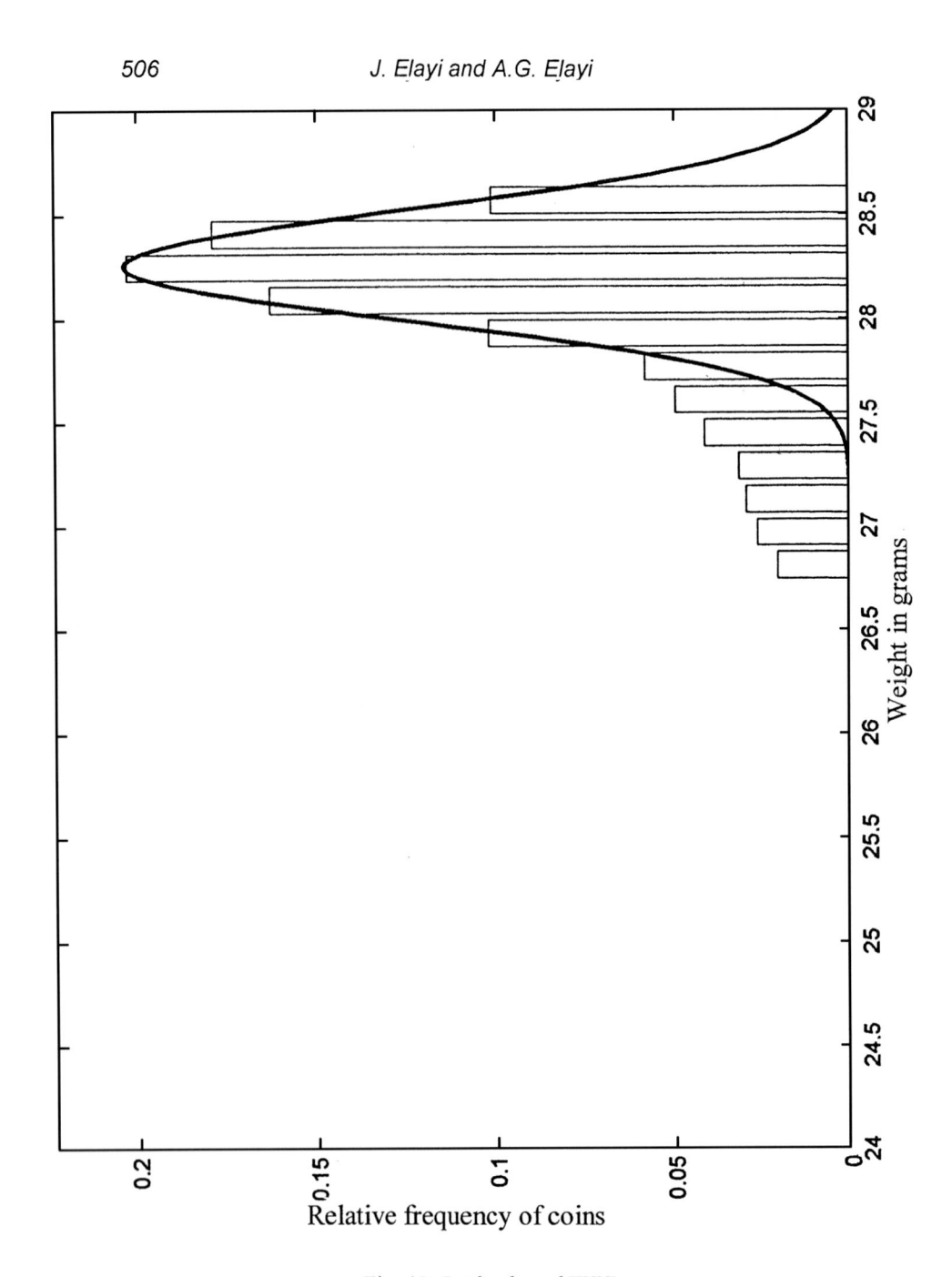

Fig. 45: *Beithir hoard TXXI*

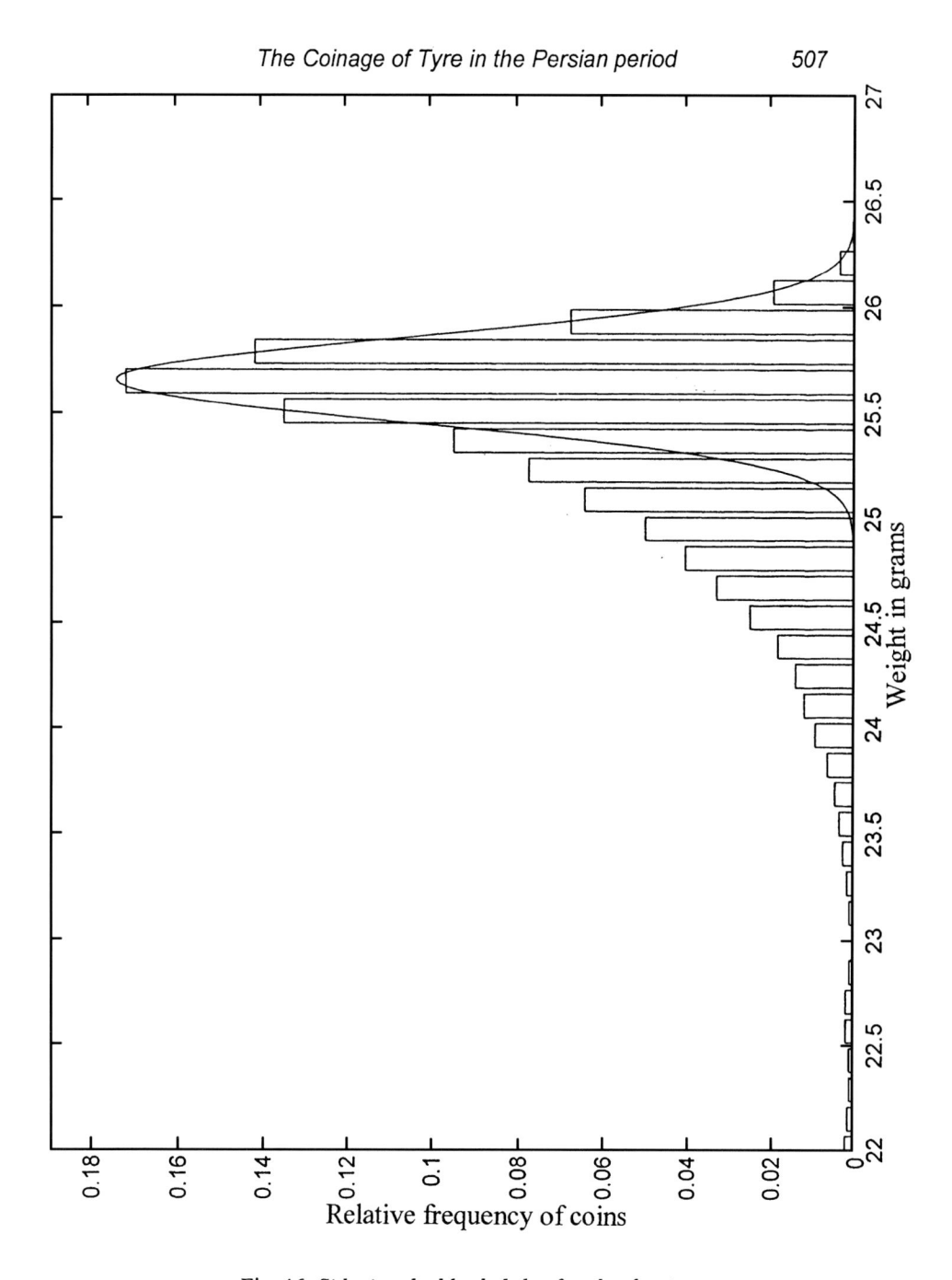

Fig. 46: *Sidonian double shekels after devaluation*

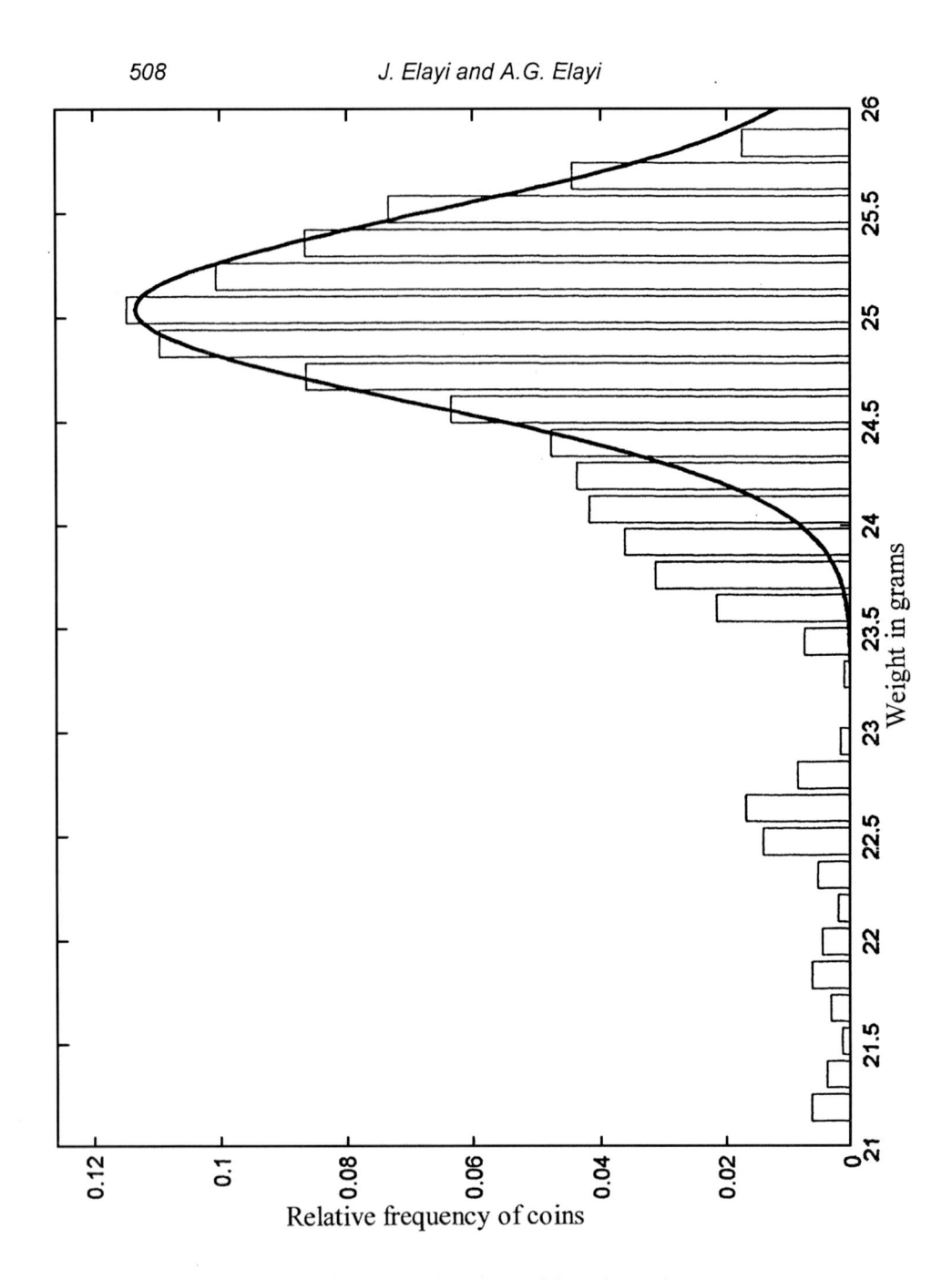

Fig. 47: *Khirbet el-Kerak hoard TXXVI*

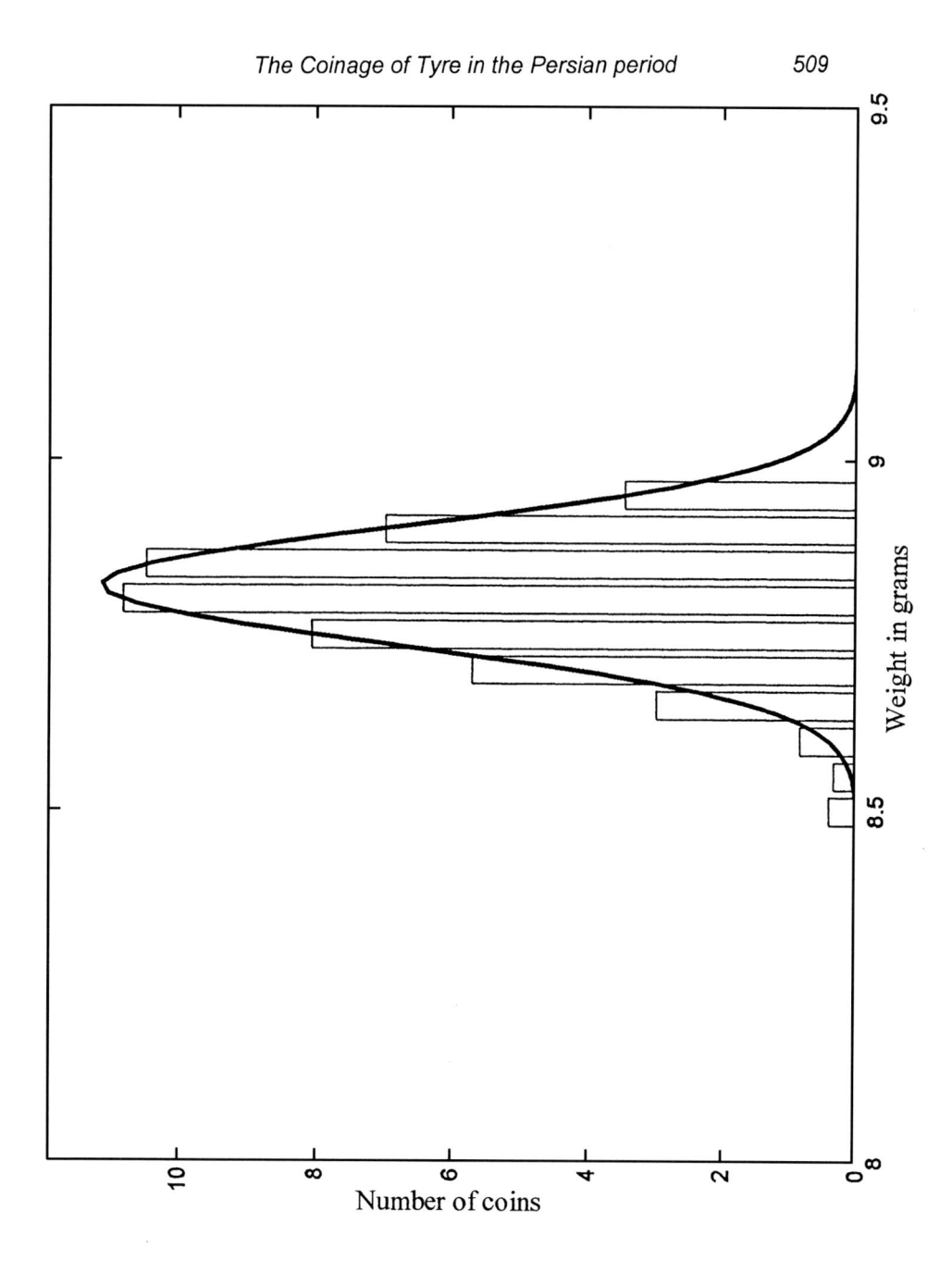

Fig. 48: *Hoard TXXXVI*

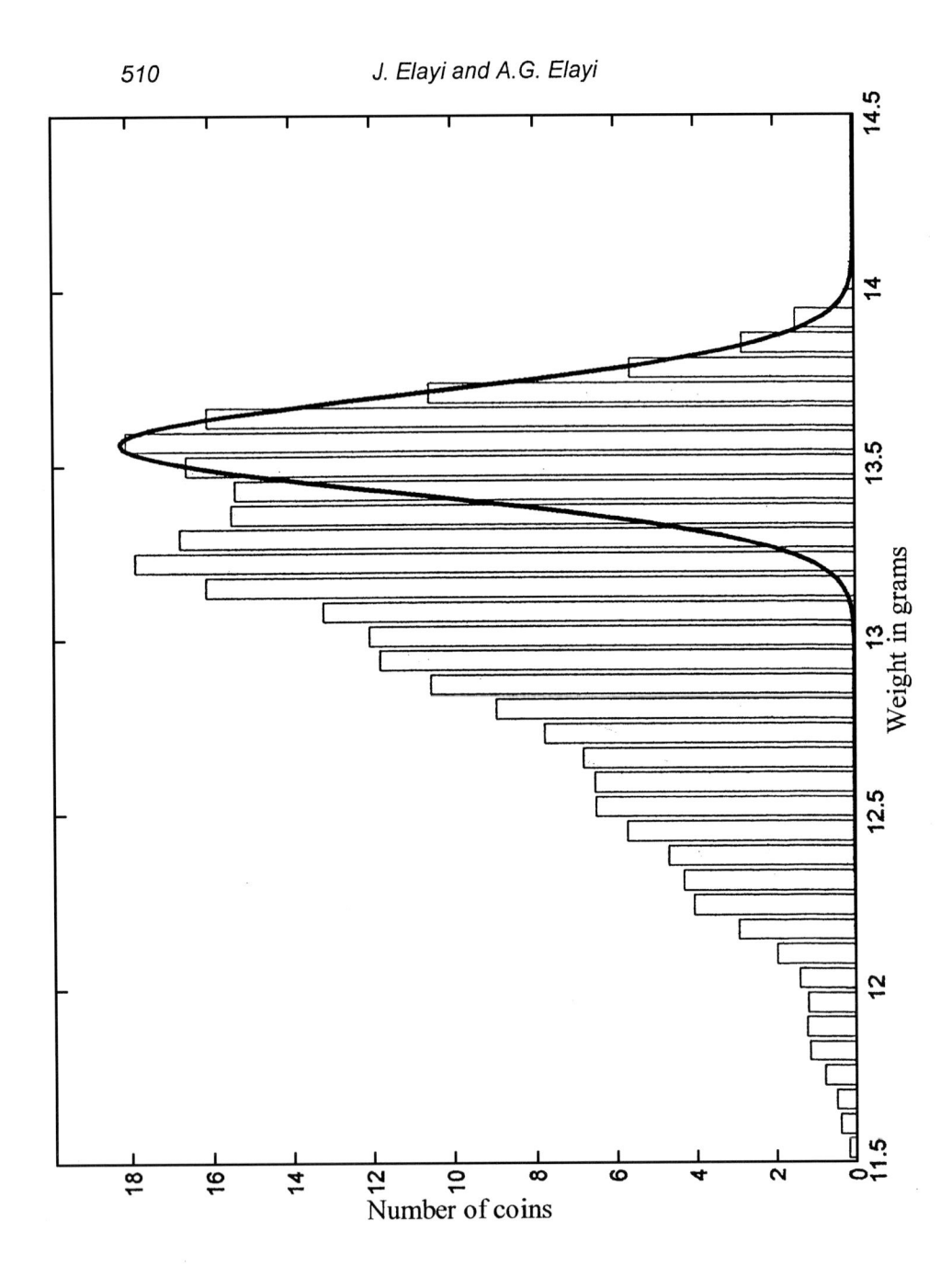

Fig. 49: *Tyrian shekels before the change of standard*

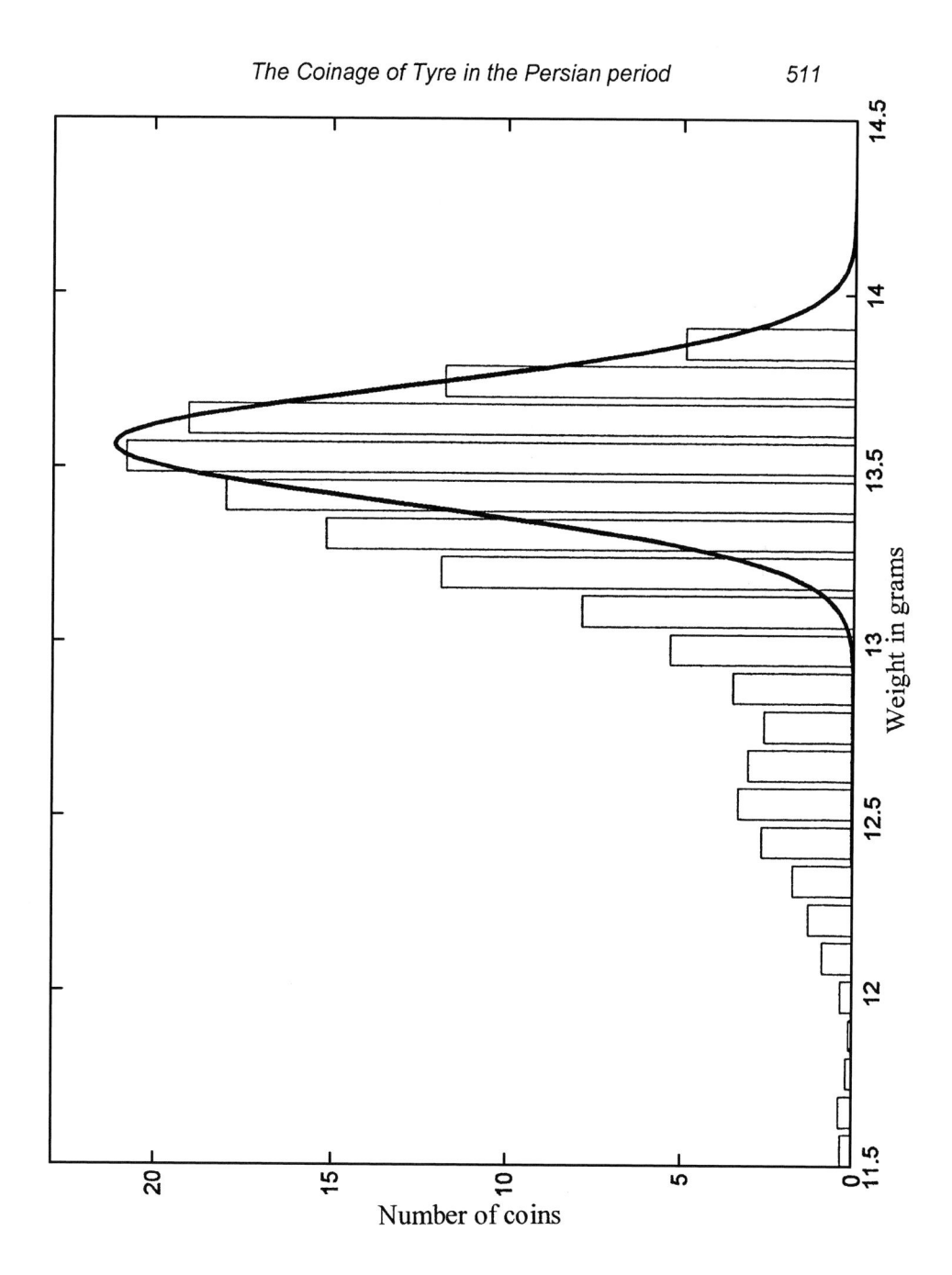

Fig. 50: *Well-preserved Tyrian shekels before the change of standard*

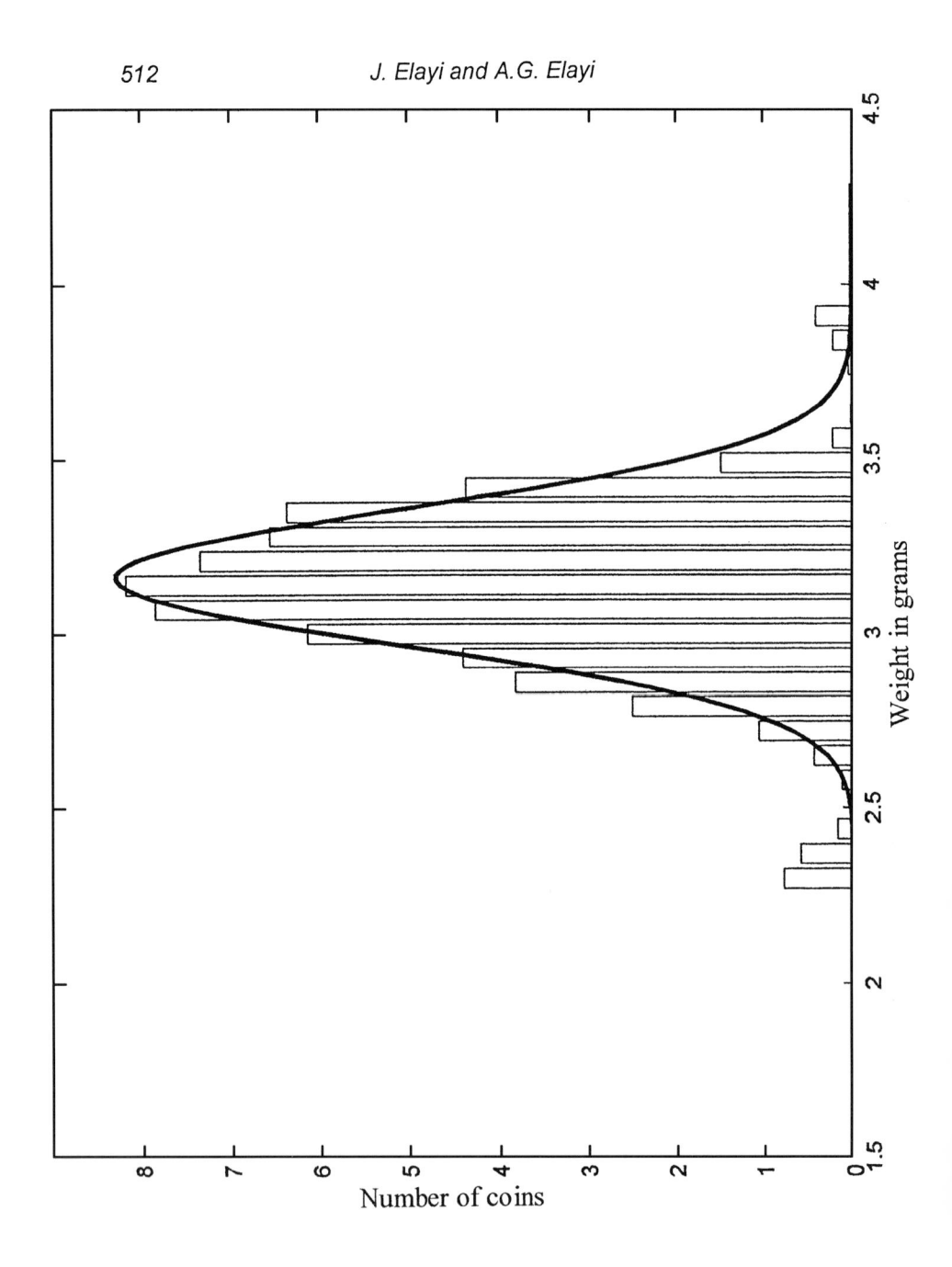

Fig. 51: *Total Tyrian quarters of shekel before the change of standard*

The Coinage of Tyre in the Persian period 513

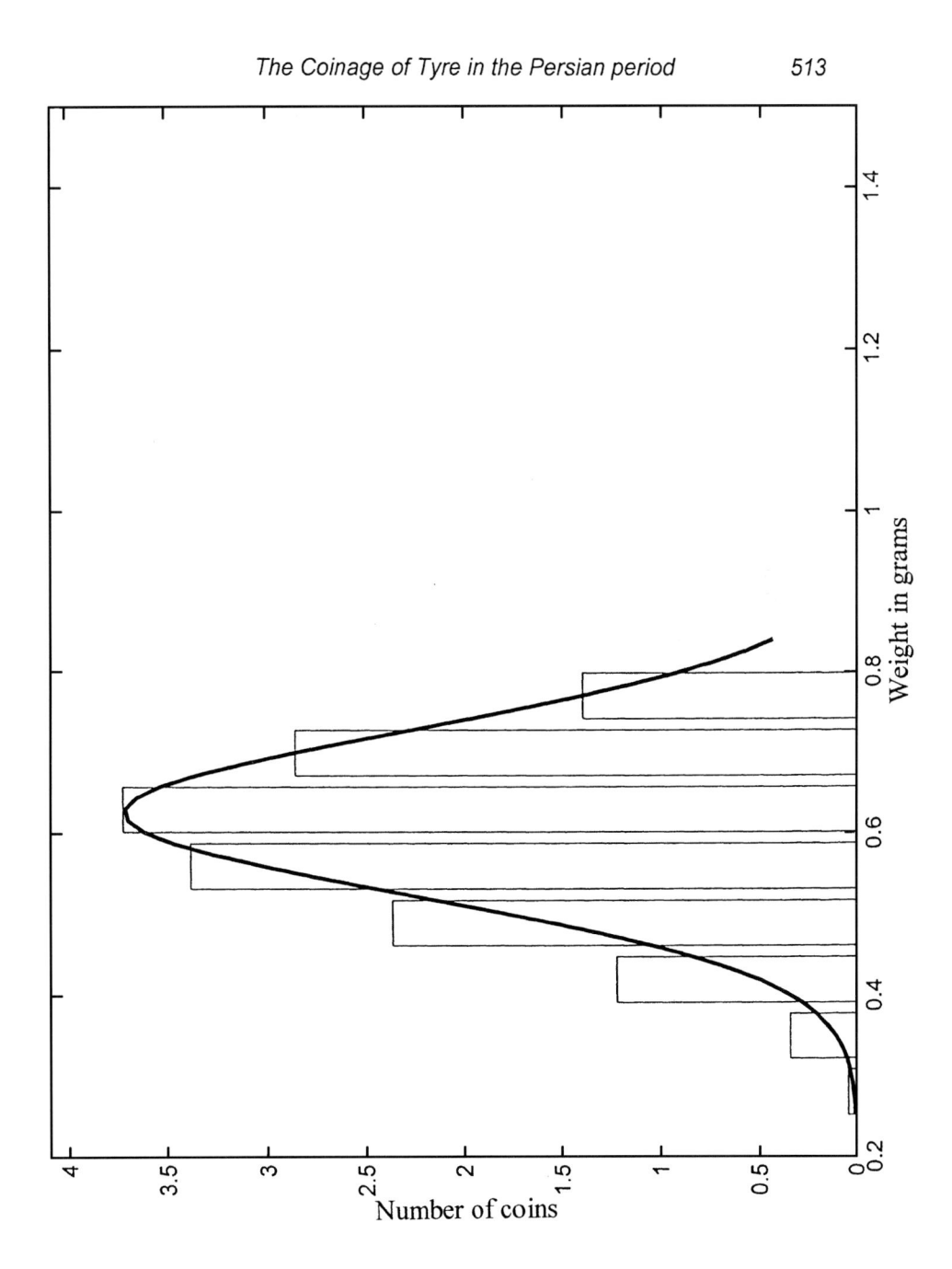

Fig. 52: *Total Tyrian sixteenths of shekel before the change of standard*

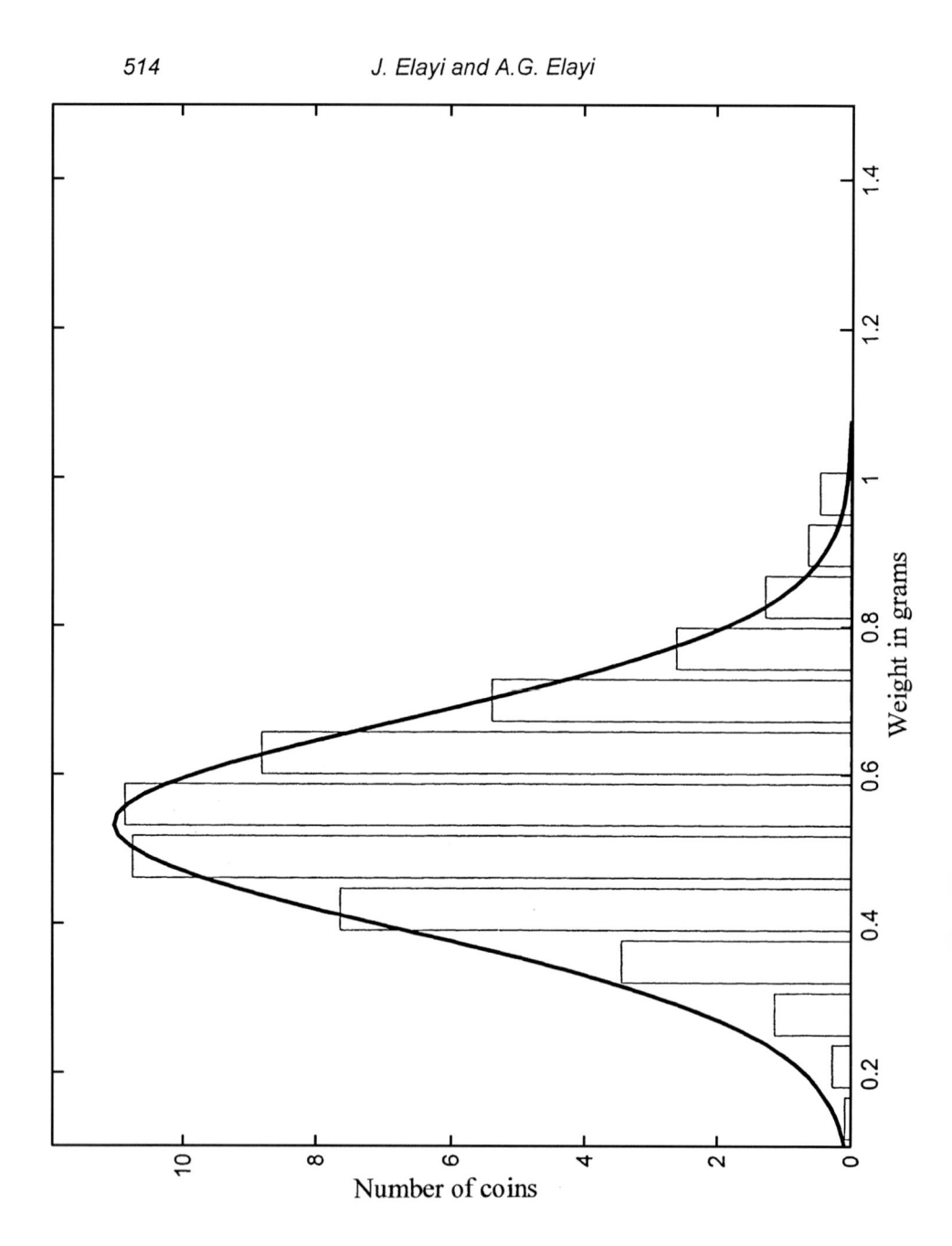

Fig. 53: *Total Tyrian sixteenths of shekel after the change of standard*

The Coinage of Tyre in the Persian period 515

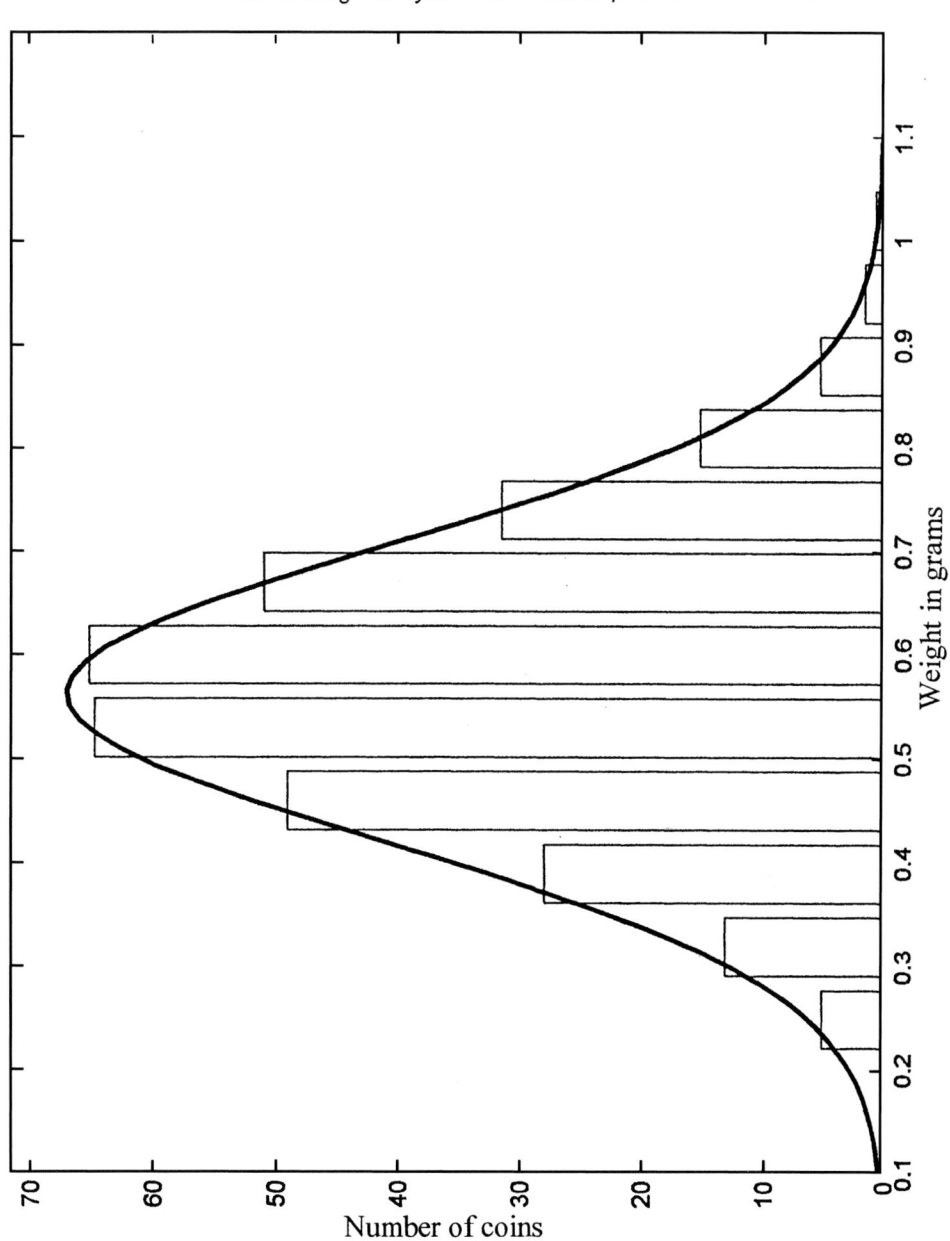

Fig. 54: *Total Tyrian sixteenths of shekel*

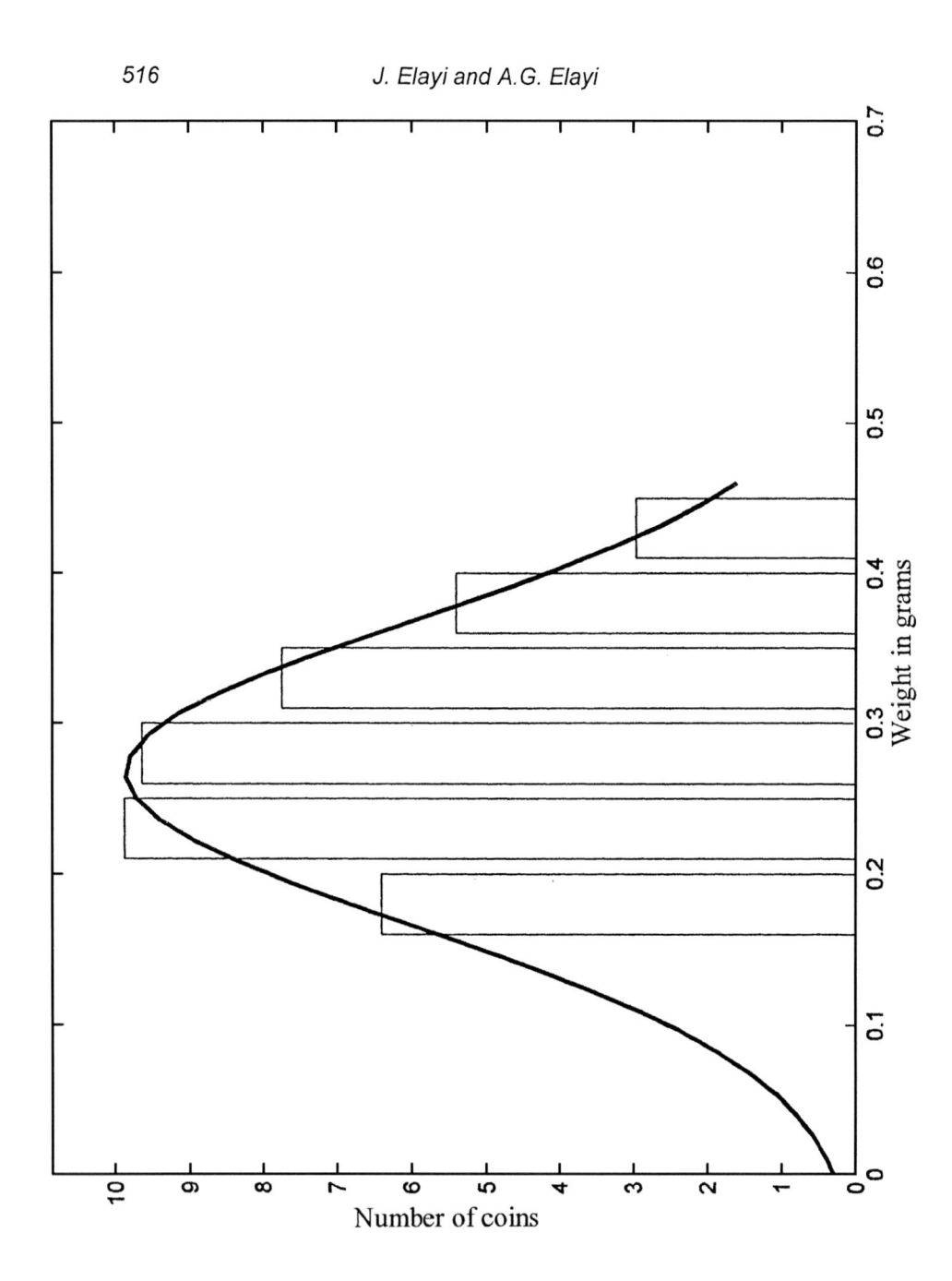

Fig. 55: *Total Tyrian halves of sixteenth*

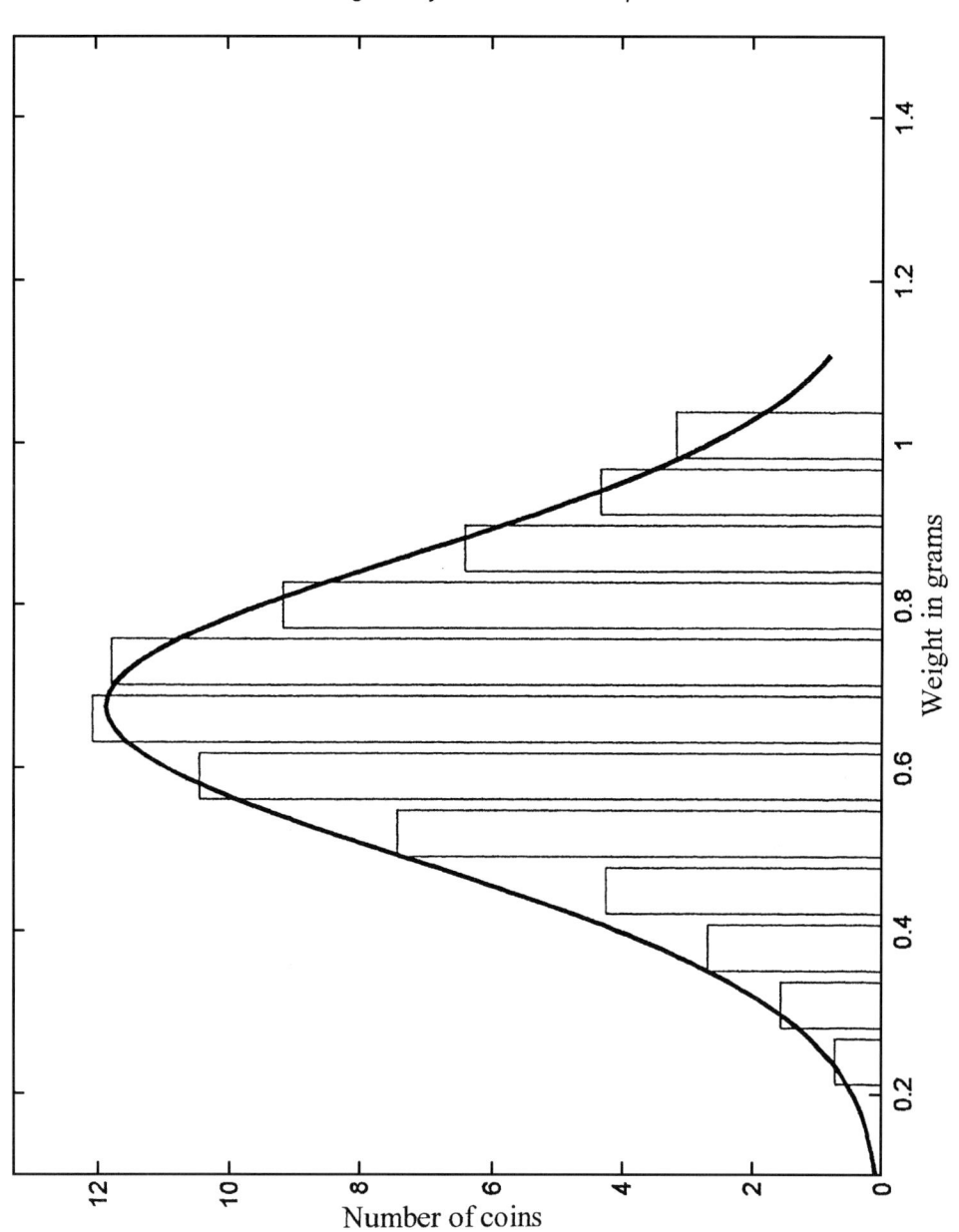

Fig. 56: *Total Tyrian bronze coins*

PLATES

The coin numbers, and the obverse and reverse numbers mentioned in the plates are those of the catalogue of Chapter I. A vertical stroke indicates the change of series. Enlargment, if any, is indicated between brakets after the coin number.

PL. 1

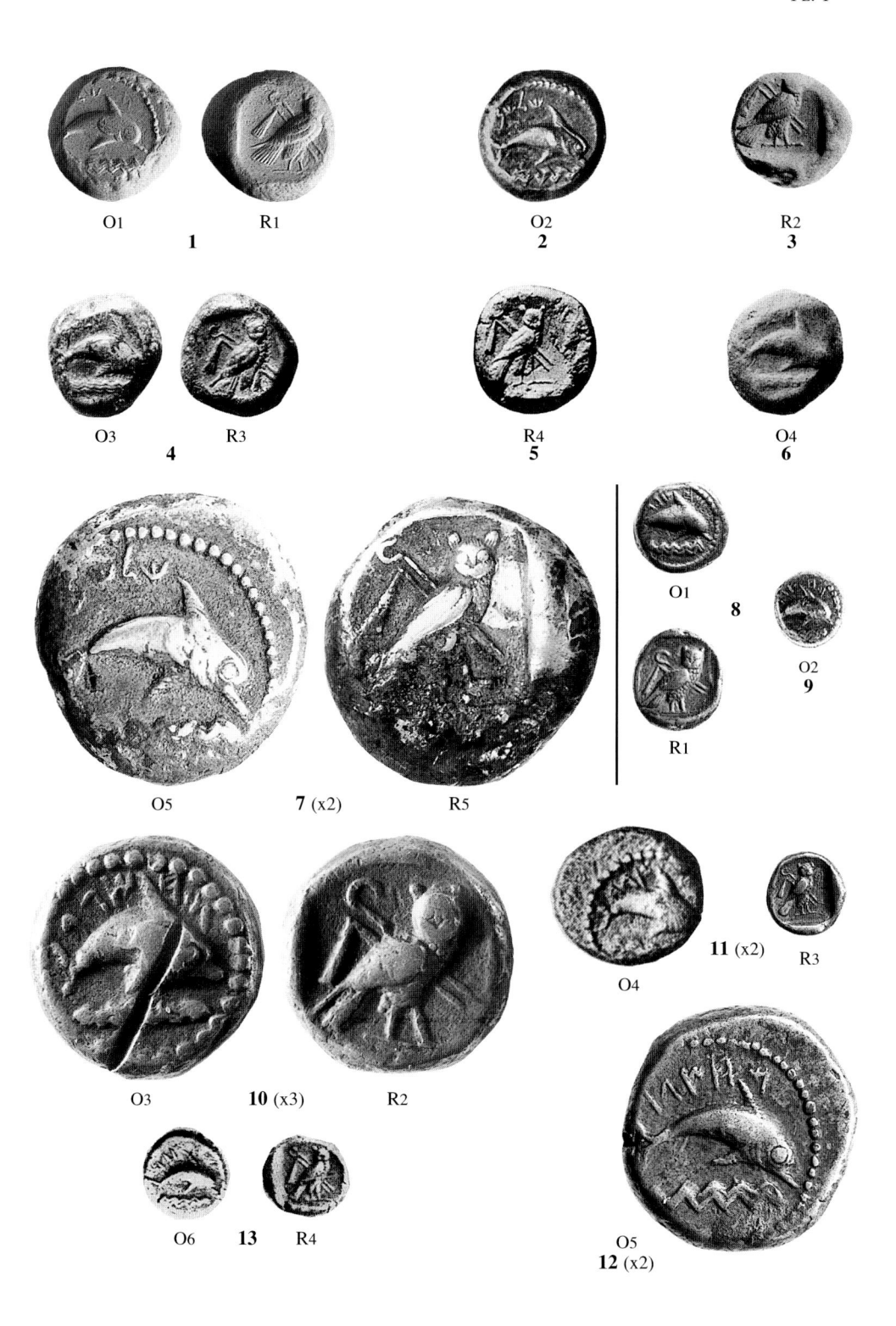

PL. 2

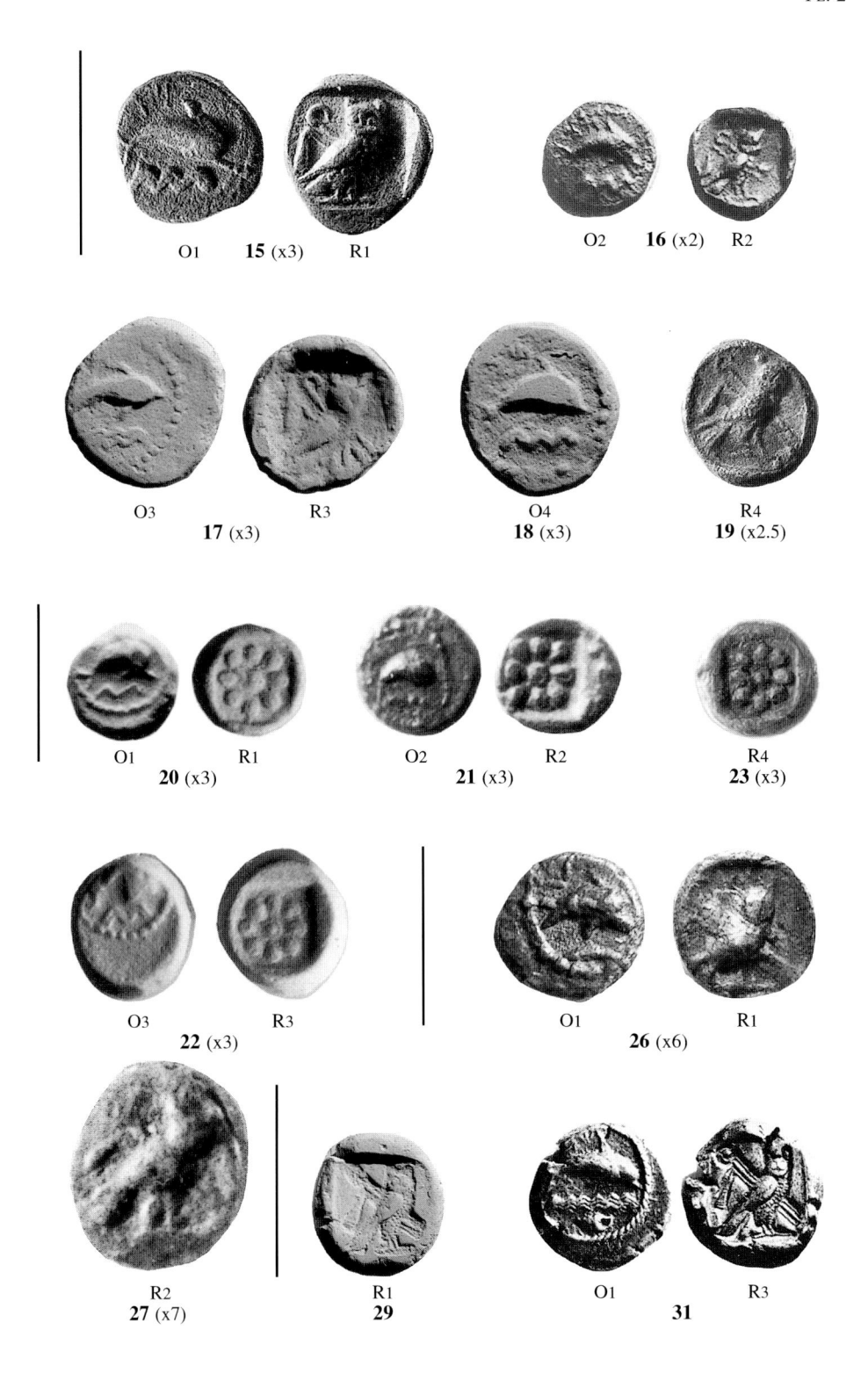

O1 **15** (x3) R1   O2 **16** (x2) R2

O3   R3   O4   R4
   17 (x3)   **18** (x3)   **19** (x2.5)

O1   R1   O2   R2   R4
   20 (x3)   **21** (x3)   **23** (x3)

O3   R3   O1   R1
   22 (x3)   **26** (x6)

R2   R1   O1   R3
27 (x7)   **29**   **31**

PL. 3

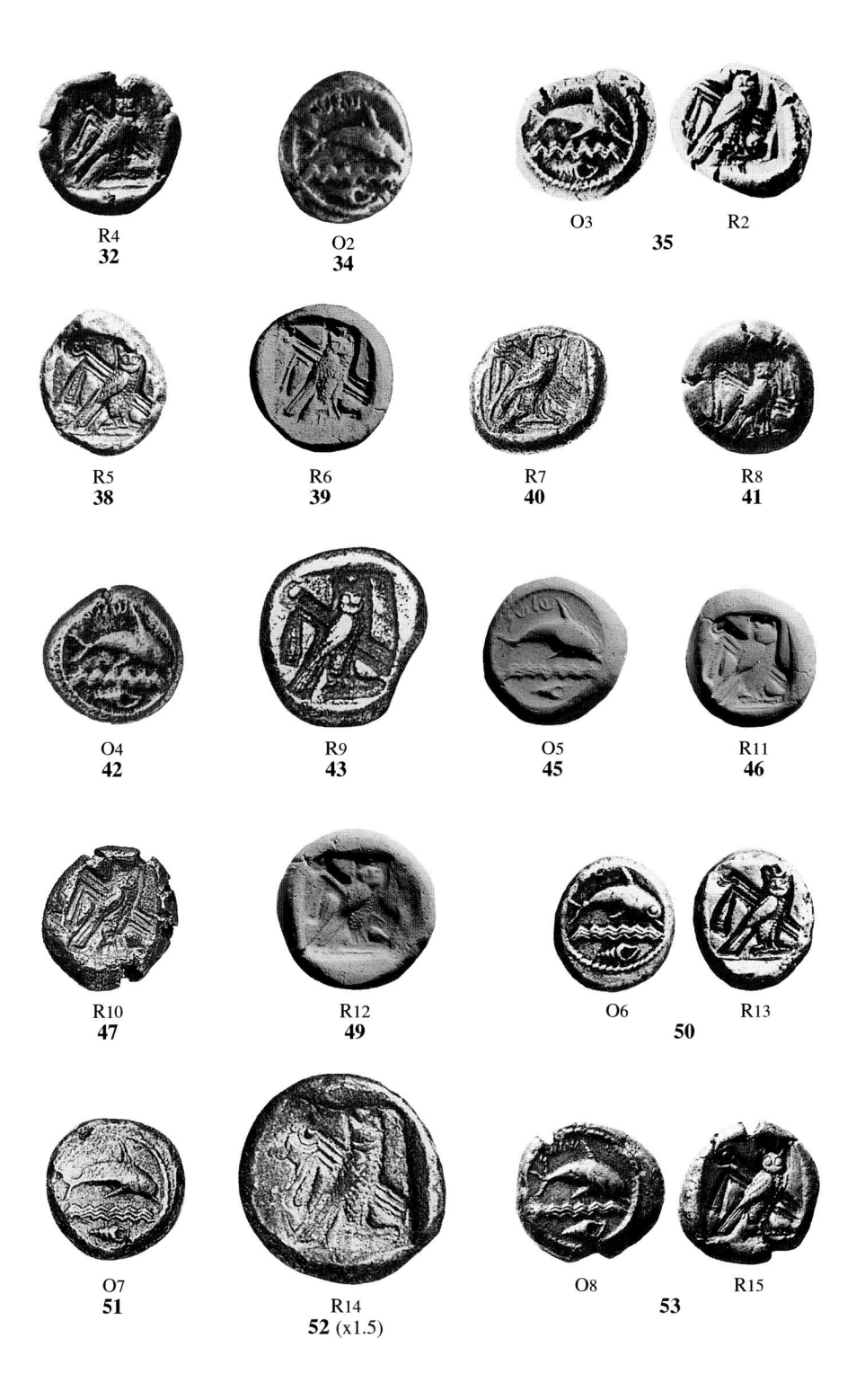

R4
32

O2
34

O3 **35** R2

R5
38

R6
39

R7
40

R8
41

O4
42

R9
43

O5
45

R11
46

R10
47

R12
49

O6 **50** R13

O7
51

R14
52 (x1.5)

O8 **53** R15

PL. 4

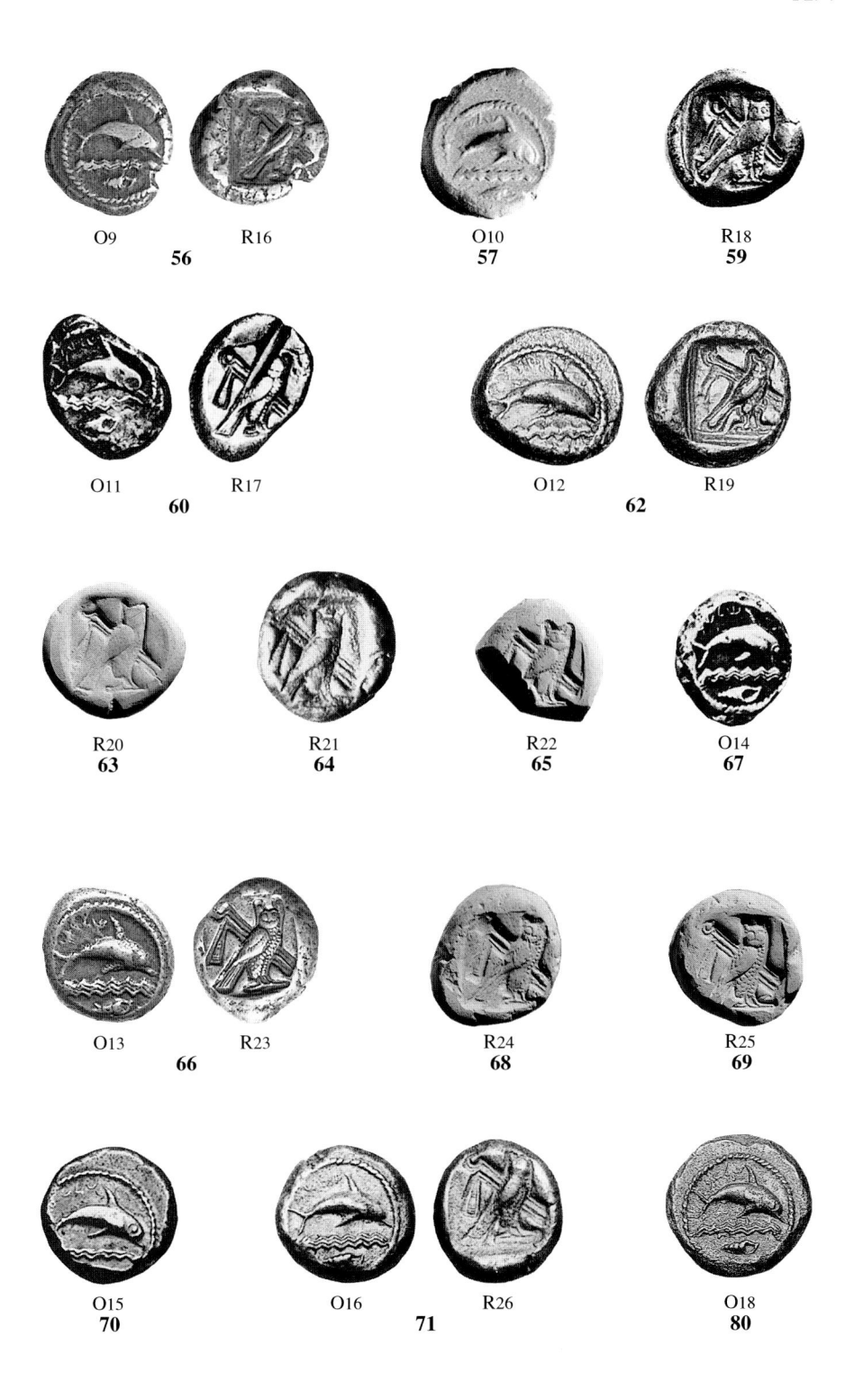

O9	R16	O10	R18
56		**57**	**59**

O11	R17	O12	R19
60		**62**	

R20	R21	R22	O14
63	**64**	**65**	**67**

O13	R23	R24	R25
66		**68**	**69**

O15	O16	R26	O18
70	**71**		**80**

PL. 5

O17　R27
72

R28
83

O1　R1
182 (x2.5)

R2
184

R3
185

O2　R4
186

O3
187

O4　R5
188

R6
189

O5　R7
190 (x2.5)

O7　R9
192

O6　R8
191 (x2.5)

O8　R10
193

PL. 6

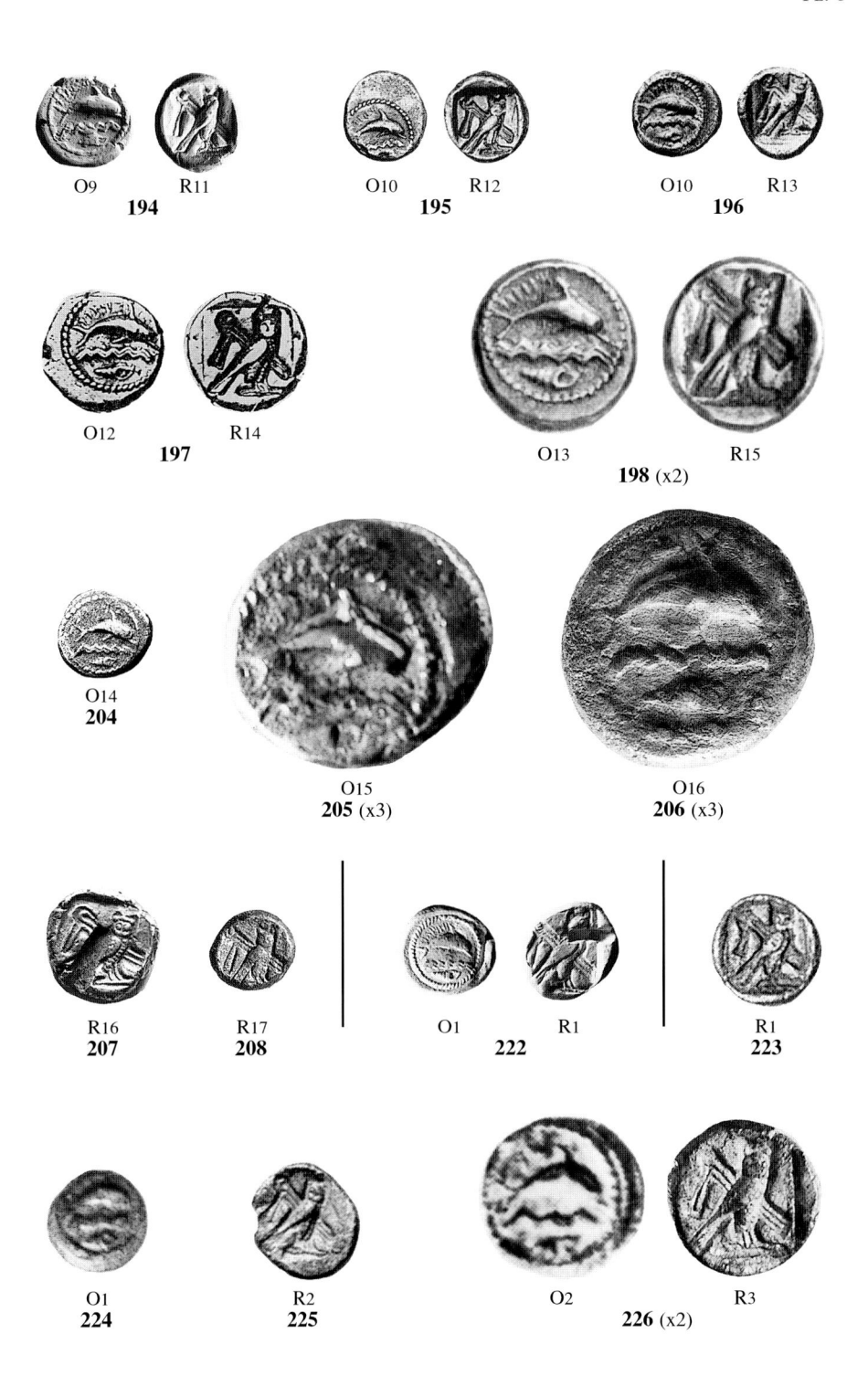

O9   R11
194

O10 R12
195

O10 R13
196

O12   R14
197

O13   R15
198 (x2)

O14
204

O15
205 (x3)

O16
206 (x3)

R16   R17
207 **208**

O1   R1
222

R1
223

O1   R2
224 **225**

O2   R3
226 (x2)

PL. 7

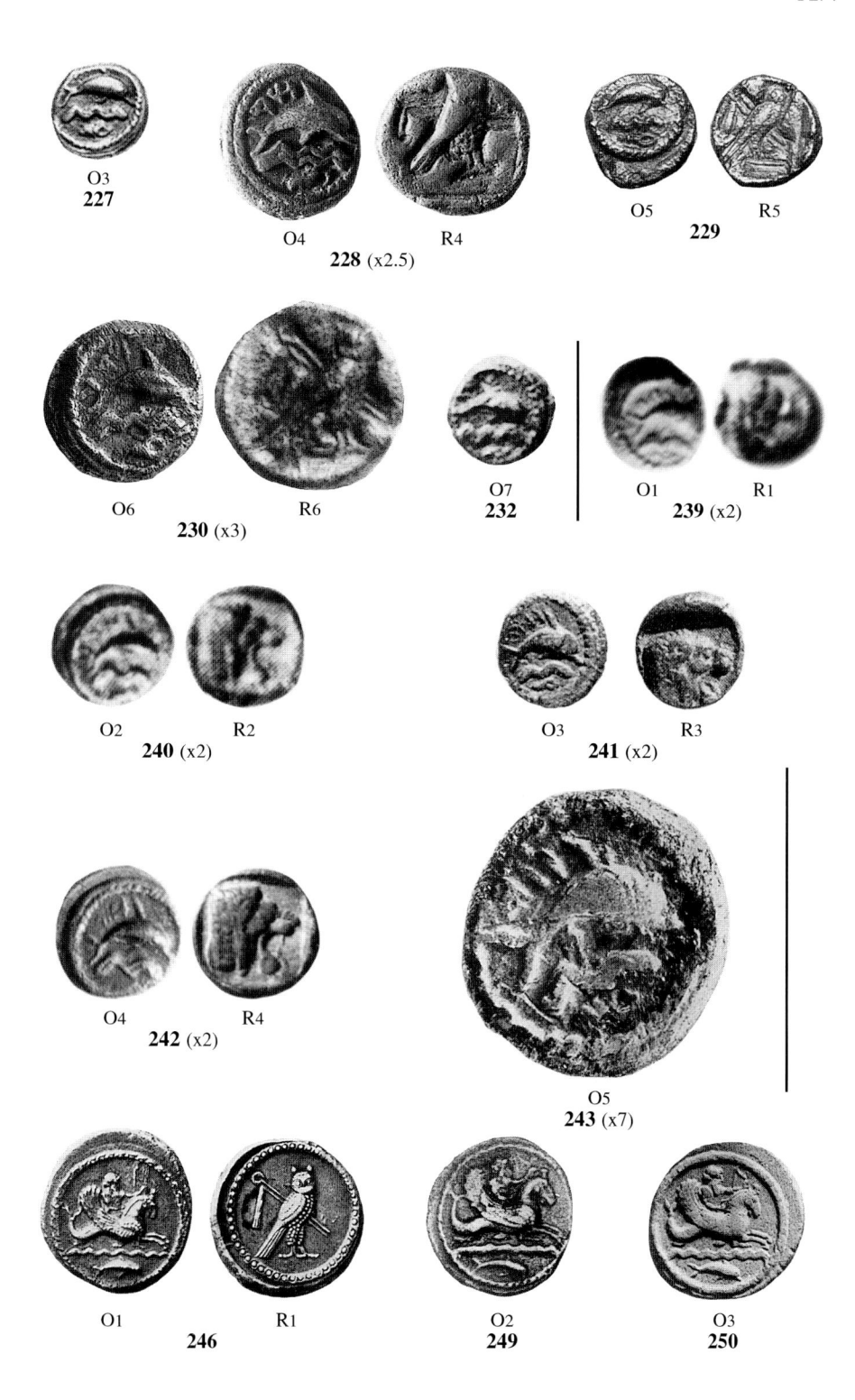

O3
227

O4 R4
228 (x2.5)

O5 R5
229

O6 R6
230 (x3)

O7
232

O1 R1
239 (x2)

O2 R2
240 (x2)

O3 R3
241 (x2)

O4 R4
242 (x2)

O5
243 (x7)

O1 R1
246

O2
249

O3
250

PL. 8

O4
251

O5
252

O6   R2
253

R3
254

O7   R4
256

O8
258

O9
259

R5
260

O10   R6
261

O11   R8
265

O12   R7
267

R9
269

O13   R10
271

O14
272

PL. 9

O15 R11
273

O16 R13
276

R12 O17
274 **278**

O18 R14
279

O19 R15
280

O20 R16
281

O21 R17
282

O22 R18
283

O23 R19
285

O24 R20
286

PL. 10

O25 R21
287

O26 R22
288

O27 R23
289

O28 R24
290

R25
291

O29 R27
294

R29
297

O30 R28
295

R30
300

R31
301

O31 R33
302

O32 R32
305

PL. 11

R35
306

O33 R33
308

O34
309

R34
311

O35
313

R36
315

R37
316

O36
317

O55
321 (x1.5)

R55
323

R56
324

R57
325

R58
326 (x1.5)

R63
327

R39
331

O37 R37
328

O38 R38
329

PL. 12

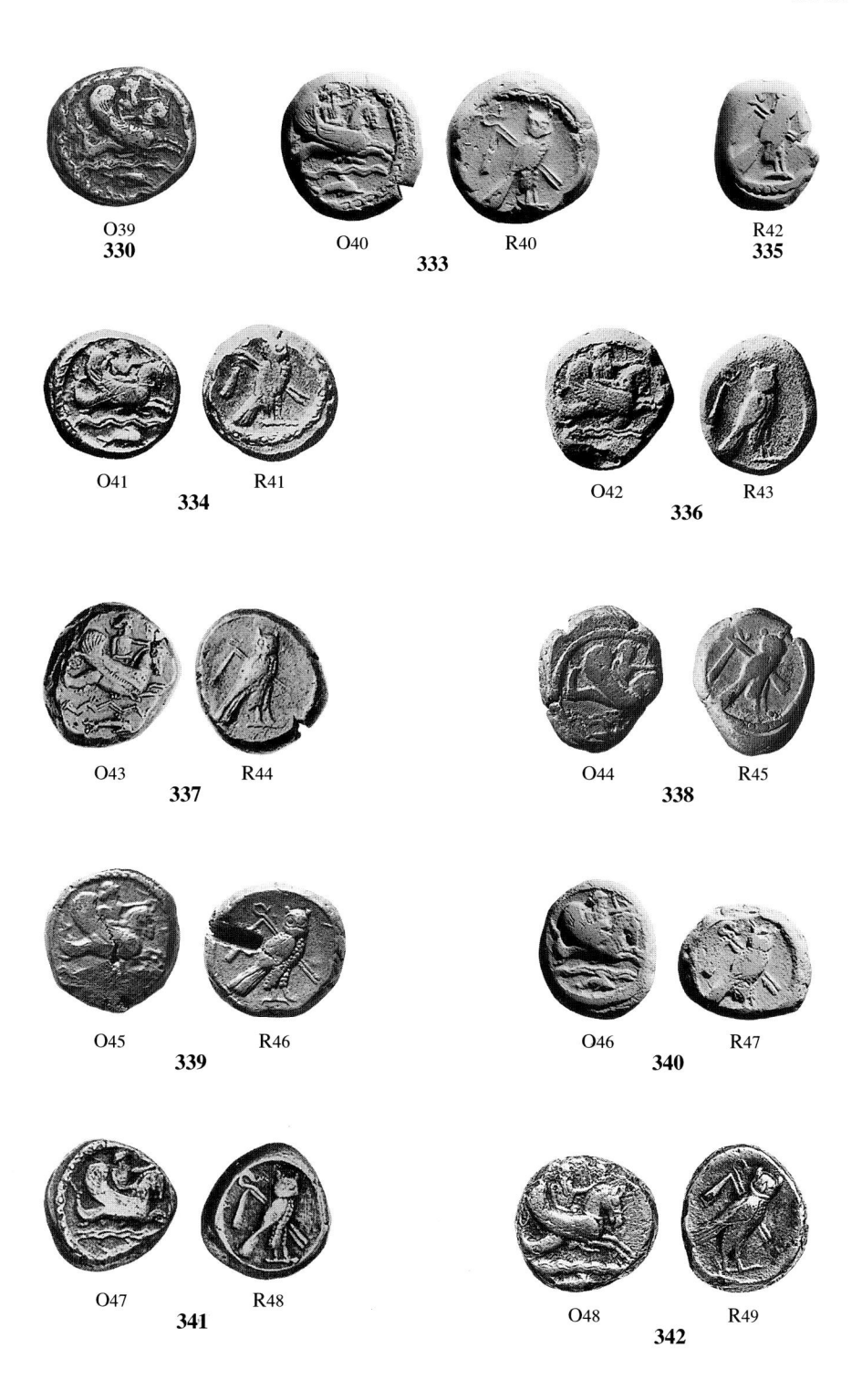

O39
330

O40 R40
333

R42
335

O41 R41
334

O42 R43
336

O43 R44
337

O44 R45
338

O45 R46
339

O46 R47
340

O47 R48
341

O48 R49
342

PL. 13

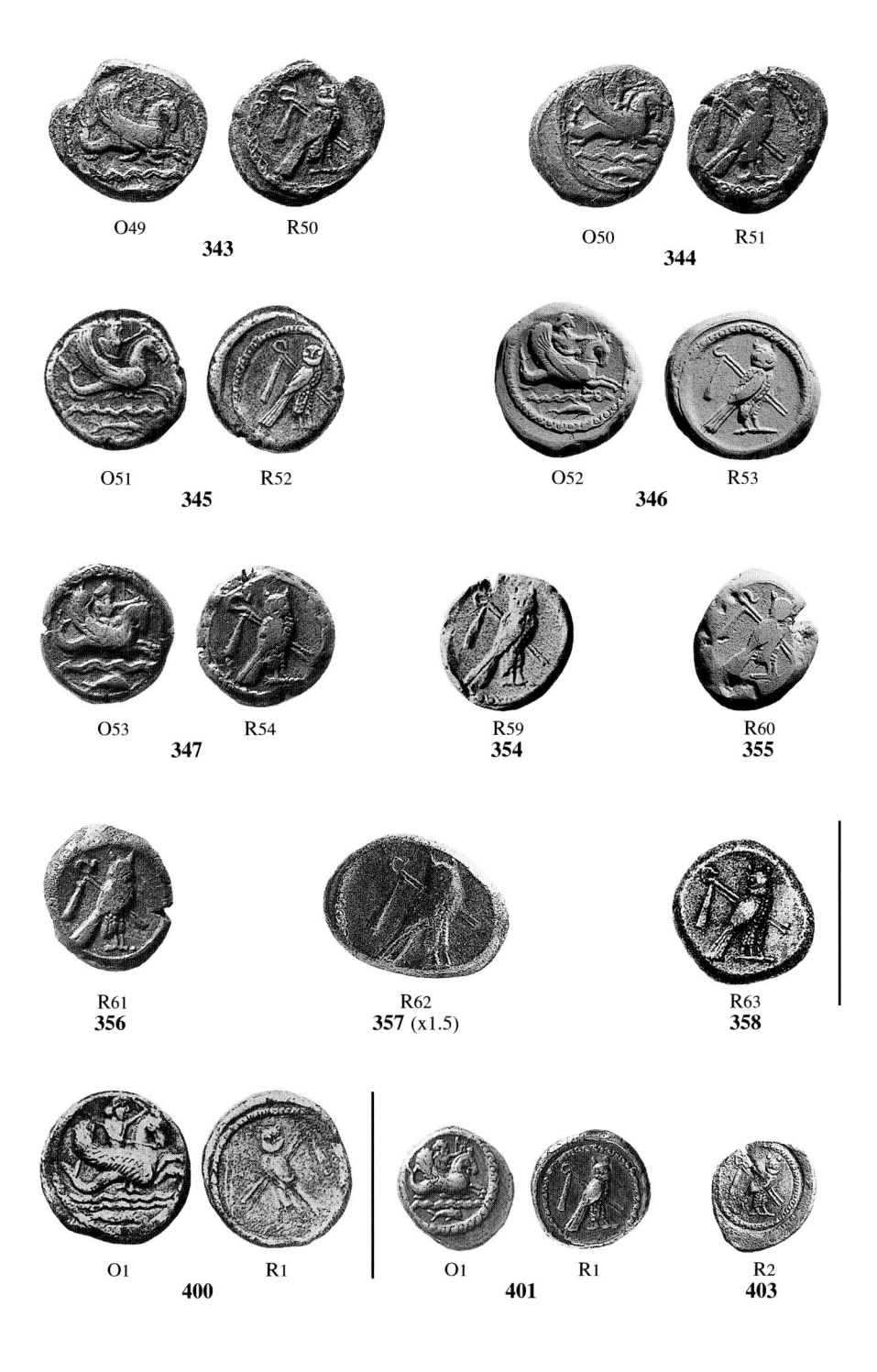

O49 R50
343

O50 R51
344

O51 R52
345

O52 R53
346

O53 R54
347

R59
354

R60
355

R61
356

R62
357 (x1.5)

R63
358

O1 R1
400

O1 R1
401

R2
403

PL. 14

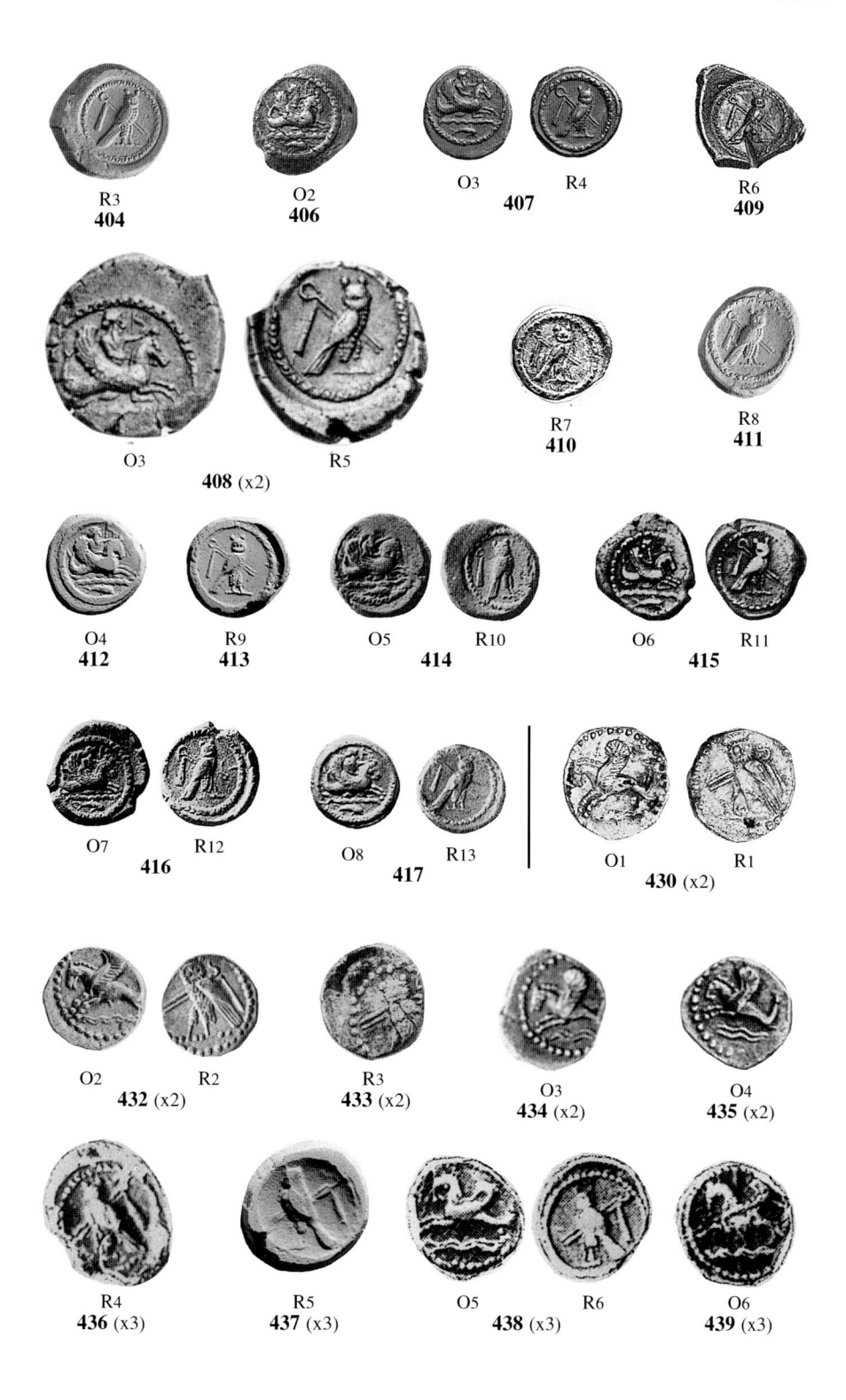

R3	O2	O3	R4	R6
404	**406**	**407**		**409**

O3	R5	R7	R8
	408 (x2)	**410**	**411**

O4	R9	O5	R10	O6	R11
412	**413**	**414**		**415**	

O7	R12	O8	R13	O1	R1
416		**417**		**430** (x2)	

O2	R2	R3	O3	O4
432 (x2)		**433** (x2)	**434** (x2)	**435** (x2)

R4	R5	O5	R6	O6
436 (x3)	**437** (x3)	**438** (x3)		**439** (x3)

PL. 15

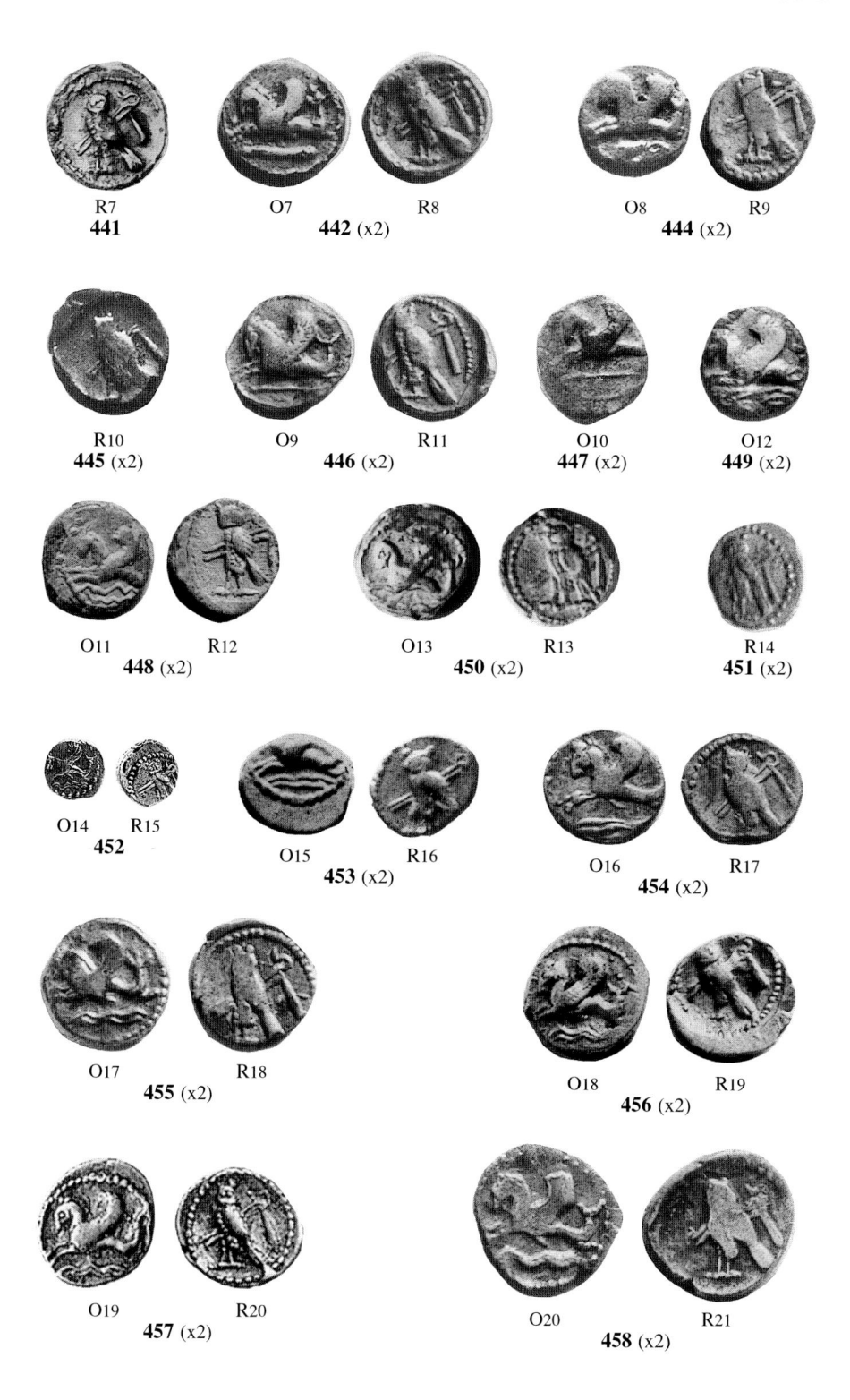

R7
441

O7   R8
442 (x2)

O8   R9
444 (x2)

R10
445 (x2)

O9   R11
446 (x2)

O10
447 (x2)

O12
449 (x2)

O11   R12
448 (x2)

O13   R13
450 (x2)

R14
451 (x2)

O14   R15
452

O15   R16
453 (x2)

O16   R17
454 (x2)

O17   R18
455 (x2)

O18   R19
456 (x2)

O19   R20
457 (x2)

O20   R21
458 (x2)

PL. 16

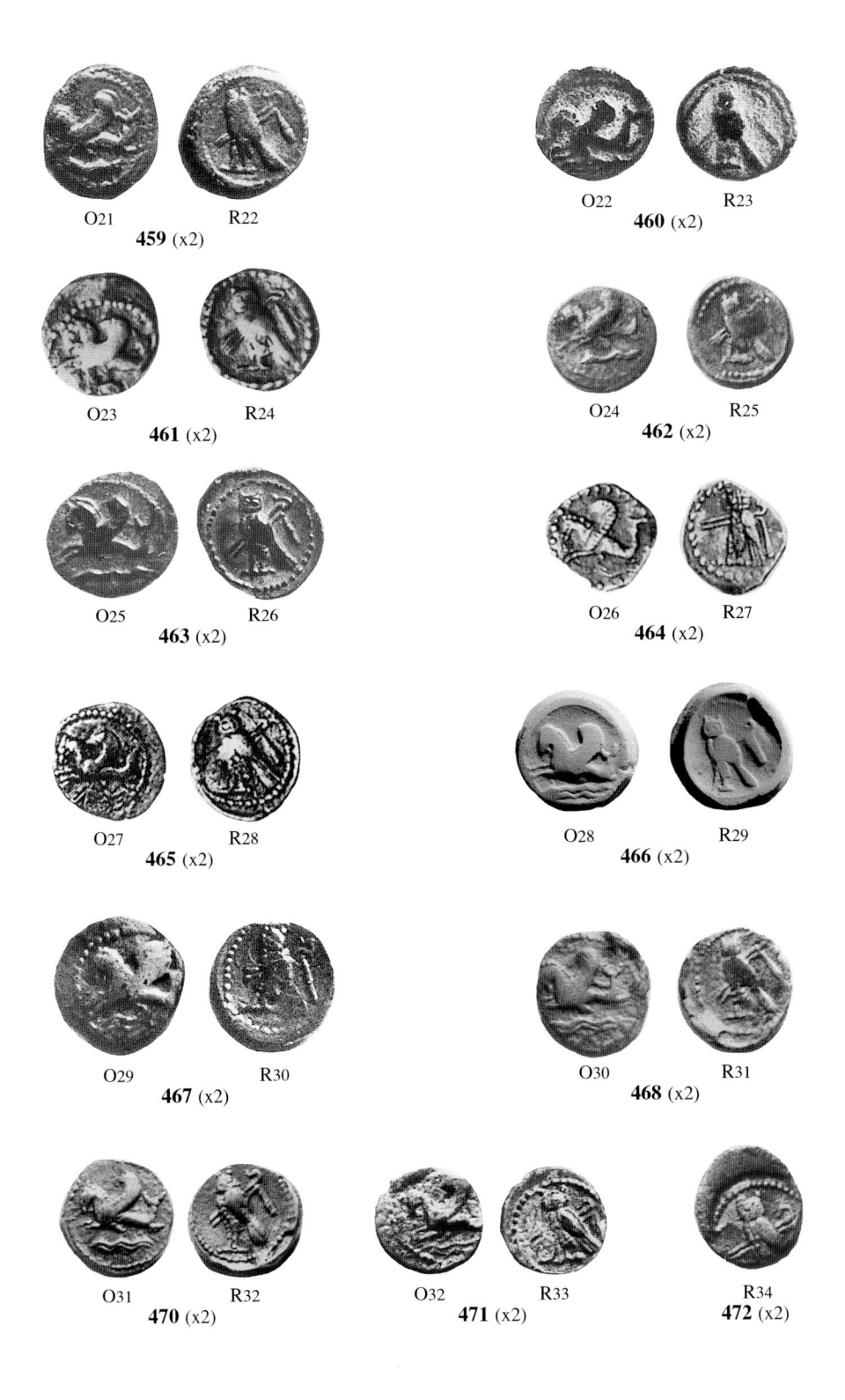

O21　　　R22
459 (x2)

O22　　　R23
460 (x2)

O23　　　R24
461 (x2)

O24　　　R25
462 (x2)

O25　　　R26
463 (x2)

O26　　　R27
464 (x2)

O27　　　R28
465 (x2)

O28　　　R29
466 (x2)

O29　　　R30
467 (x2)

O30　　　R31
468 (x2)

O31　　　R32
470 (x2)

O32　　　R33
471 (x2)

R34
472 (x2)

PL. 17

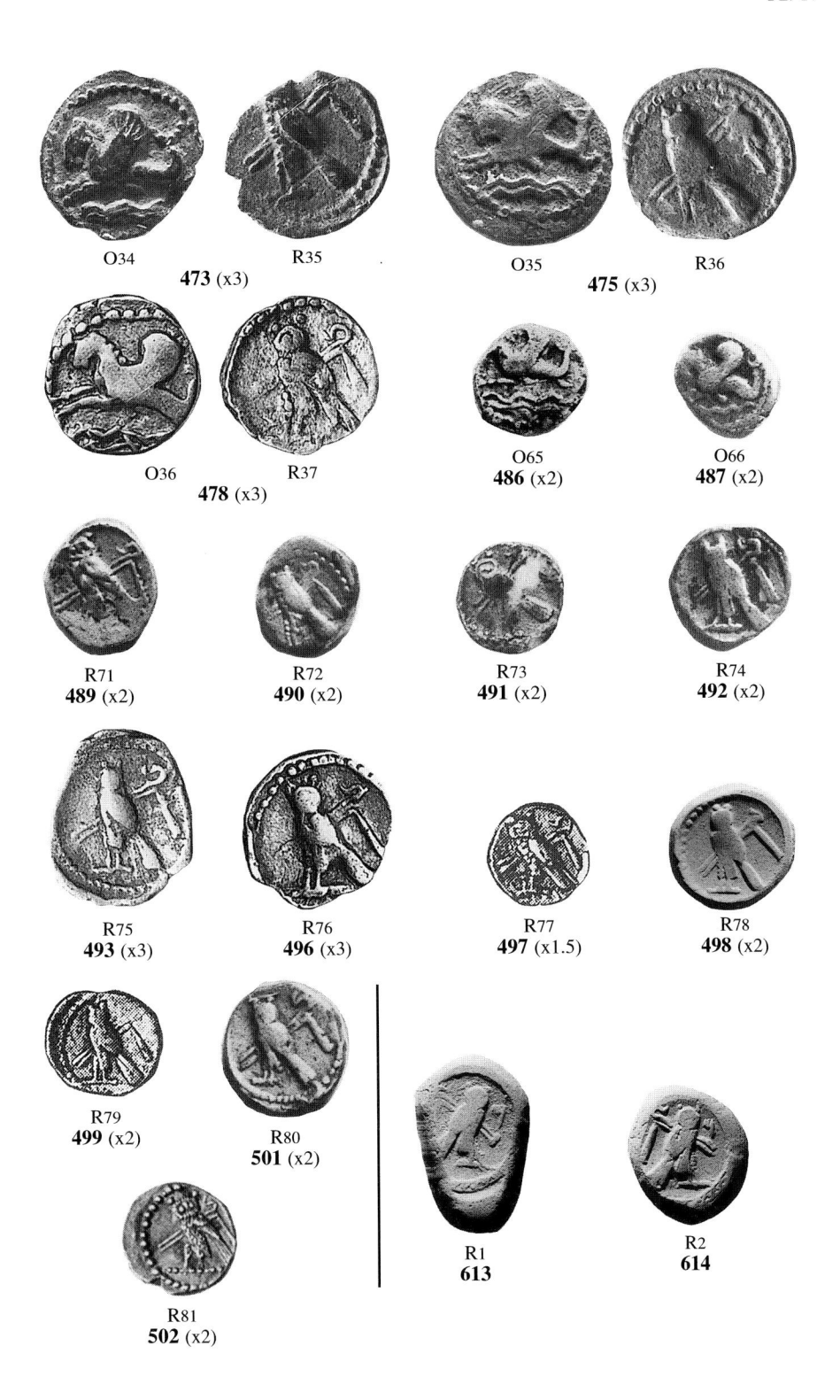

O34   R35
473 (x3)

O35   R36
475 (x3)

O36   R37
478 (x3)

O65
486 (x2)

O66
487 (x2)

R71
489 (x2)

R72
490 (x2)

R73
491 (x2)

R74
492 (x2)

R75
493 (x3)

R76
496 (x3)

R77
497 (x1.5)

R78
498 (x2)

R79
499 (x2)

R80
501 (x2)

R81
502 (x2)

R1
613

R2
614

PL. 18

O1   R3   O2   R4
  615   617

R5   O3   R6   R7
618   619   620

R8   O4   O5   R9   R10
621   622   623   624

O6   R11   O7   R12
  625   626

O8   R13   O9   R14
  627   628

PL. 19

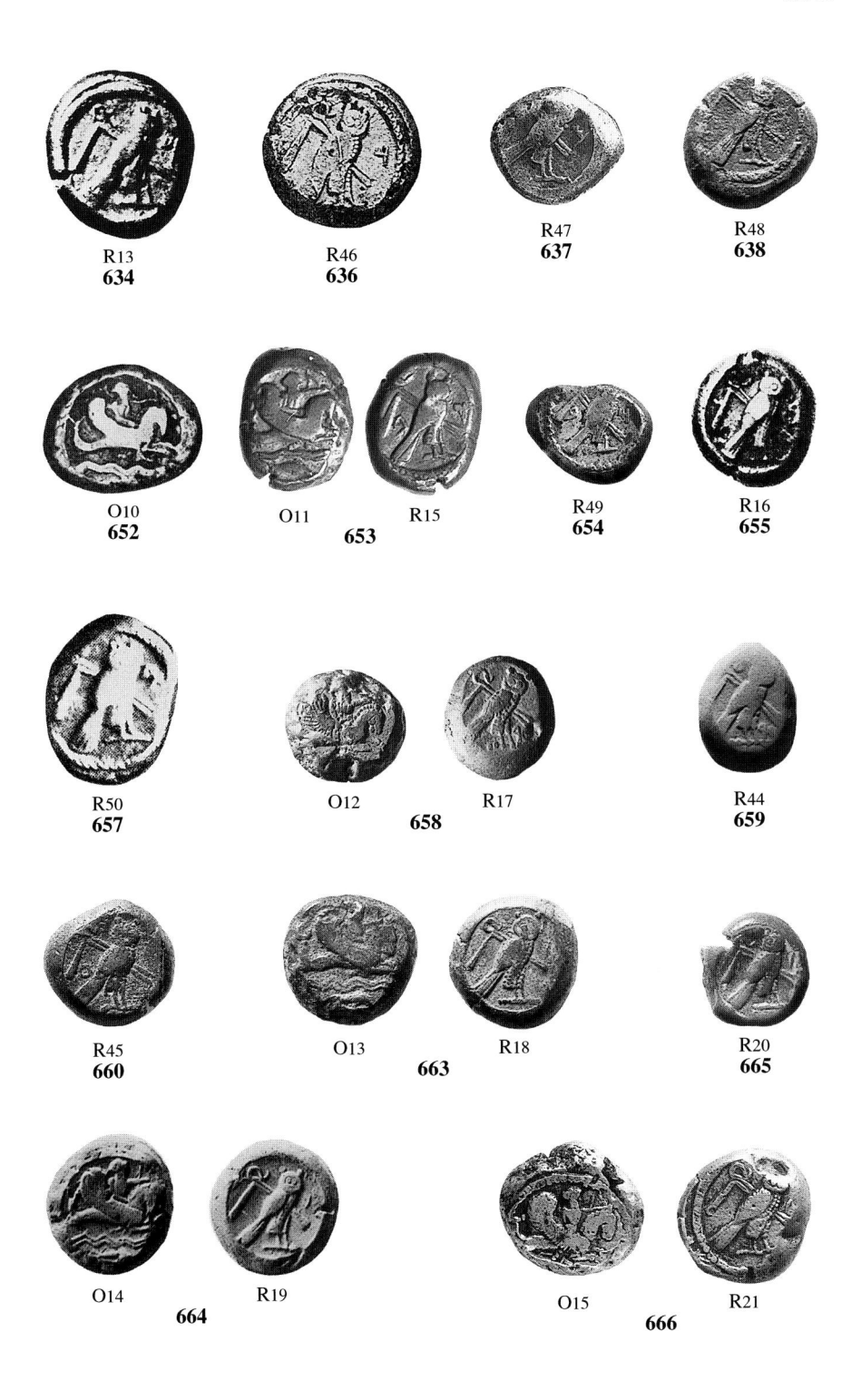

R13
634

R46
636

R47
637

R48
638

O10
652

O11 R15
653

R49
654

R16
655

R50
657

O12 R17
658

R44
659

R45
660

O13 R18
663

R20
665

O14 R19
664

O15 R21
666

PL. 20

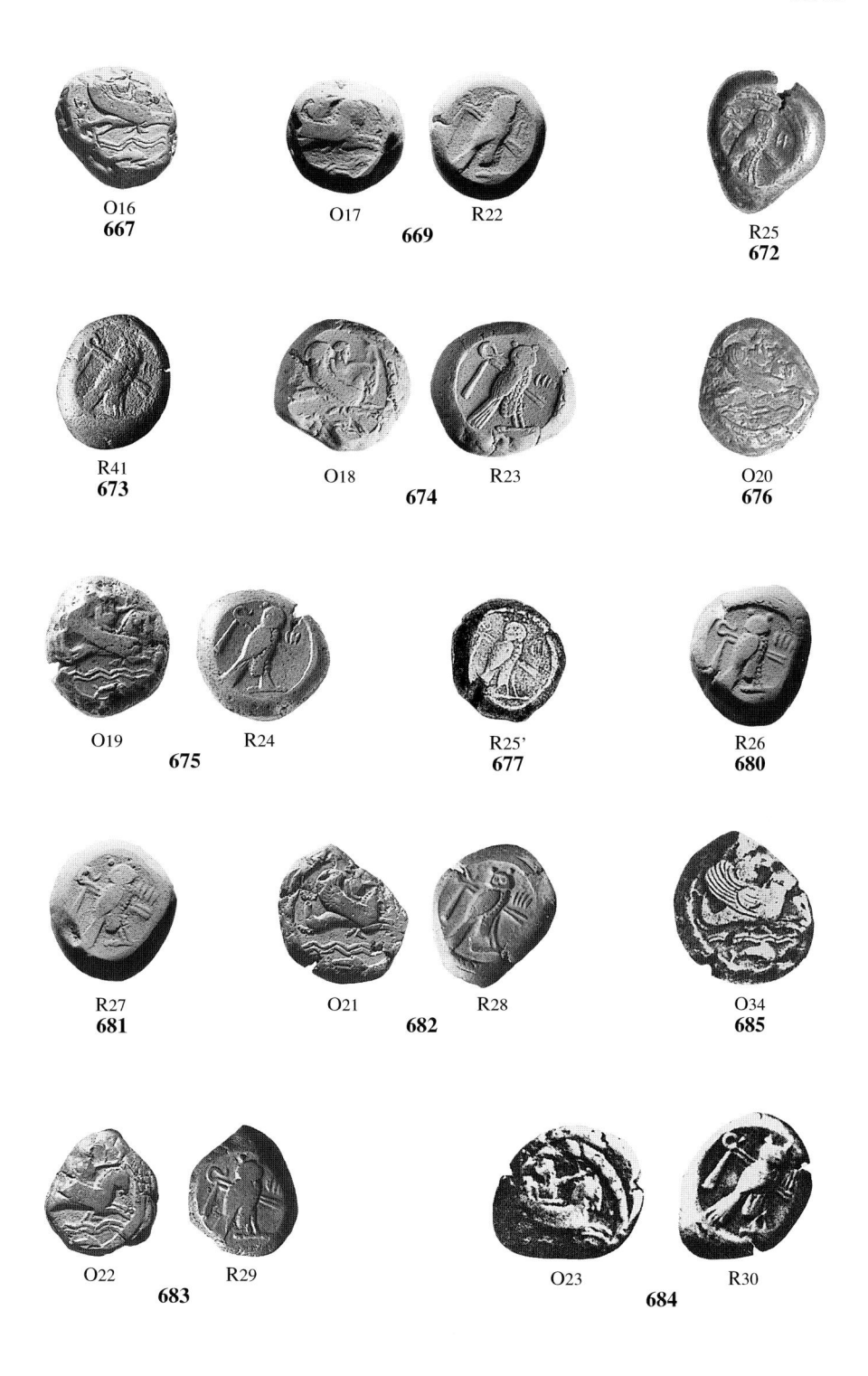

O16
667

O17　　R22
669

R25
672

R41
673

O18　　R23
674

O20
676

O19　　R24
675

R25'
677

R26
680

R27
681

O21　　R28
682

O34
685

O22　　R29
683

O23　　R30
684

PL. 21

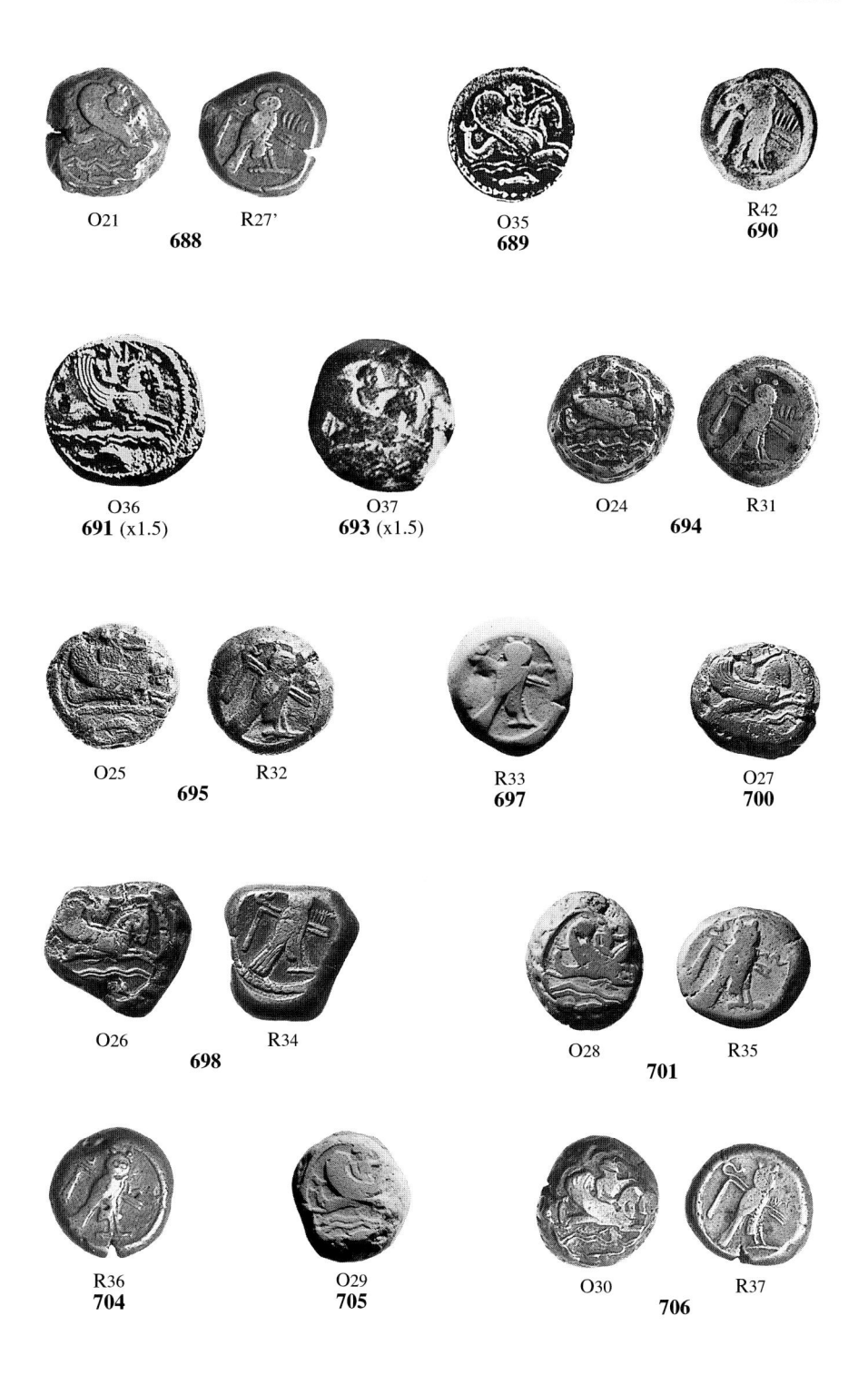

O21 R27'
688

O35
689

R42
690

O36
691 (x1.5)

O37
693 (x1.5)

O24 R31
694

O25 R32
695

R33
697

O27
700

O26 R34
698

O28 R35
701

R36
704

O29
705

O30 R37
706

PL. 22

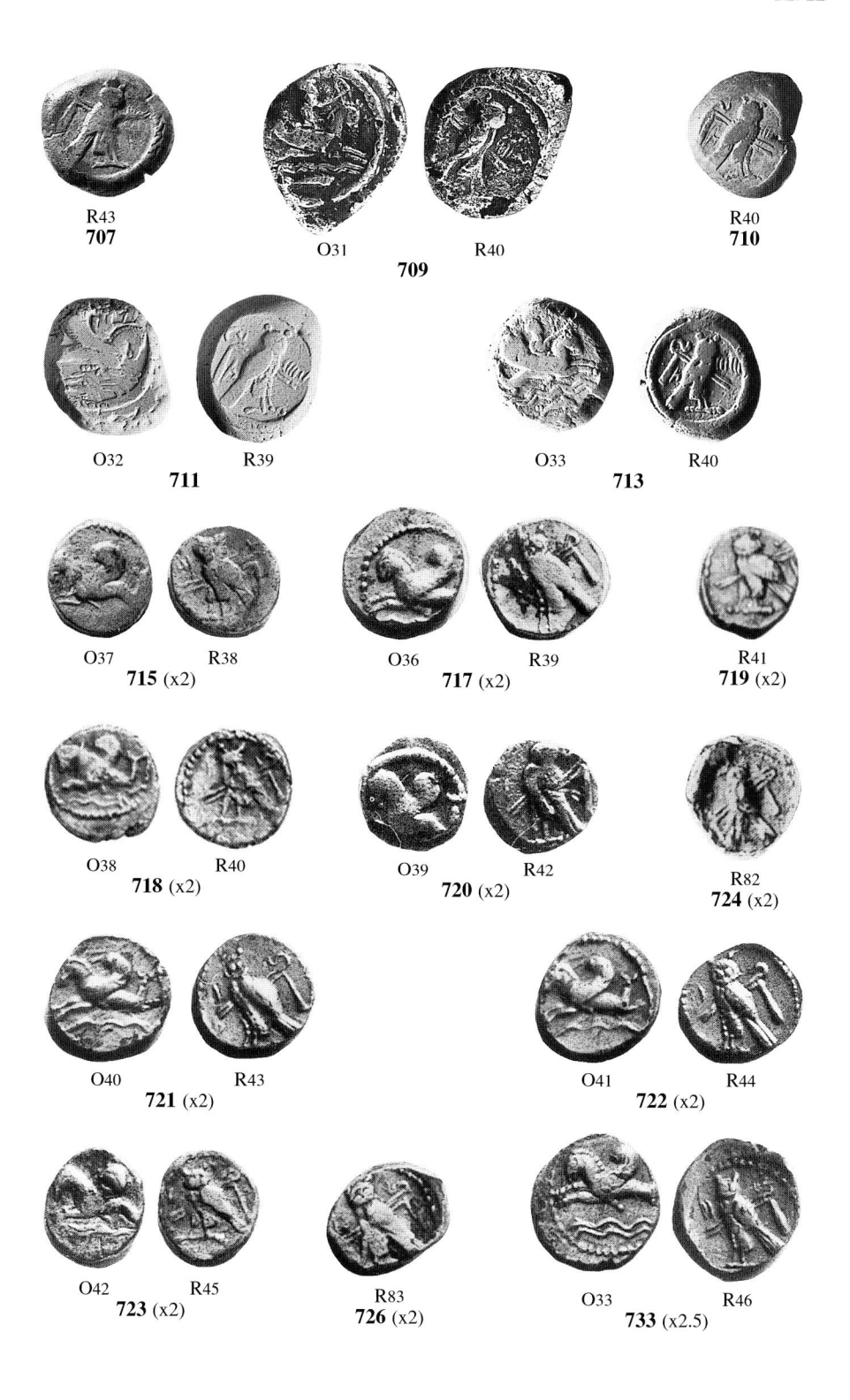

R43
707

O31   R40
709

R40
710

O32   R39
711

O33   R40
713

O37   R38
715 (x2)

O36   R39
717 (x2)

R41
719 (x2)

O38   R40
718 (x2)

O39   R42
720 (x2)

R82
724 (x2)

O40   R43
721 (x2)

O41   R44
722 (x2)

O42   R45
723 (x2)

R83
726 (x2)

O33   R46
733 (x2.5)

PL. 23

O43
734 (x3)

O44
735 (x2)

O45 R47
736 (x2)

O46 R48
737 (x3)

O67
738 (x1.5)

R49
739 (x2)

R50
740 (x2)

O47 R51
742 (x1.5)

O48 R52
743 (x2)

O49 R53
744 (x2)

O50 R54
745 (x2)

O53 R57
748 (x2)

O51 R55
746 (x3)

O52 R56
747 (x3)

PL. 24

O54 R58
749 (x2)

R84
753 (x3)

R85
754 (x2)

R59
760 (x2)

O55 R60
761 (x2)

O56 R61
762 (x3)

O57
763 (x2)

O58 R62
764 (x3)

R86
769 (x2)

O59 R63
765 (x2)

O60 R64
766 (x2)

R87
770 (x2)

R88
775 (x2)

R89
776 (x2)

R65
778 (x3)

O61 R66
780 (x3)

O62
781 (x3)

R90
784 (x3)

R67
787 (x2)

R68
788 (x2)

PL. 25

O63 R69
789 (x2)

O64 R70
790 (x2)

R91
791 (x3)

R92
794 (x2)

R93
795 (x2)

O1 R1
796

R2
798

R3
799

R4
800

O2 R6
803

R7
804

O3 R7
805

O4 R5
806

R41
808

R42
809

O5 R8
818

PL. 26

O6 R9
820

O7 R10
821

O8 R11
822

O9 R12
823 (x1.5)

O10 R13
824

O11 R14
825

O12 R15
826

R43 R44 R45
828 **829** **830**

O13 R16
834

O14 R17
835

O32
836

PL. 27

O15	R18		O16	R19
	837			**838**

O17	R20	O18	R21	R46
	839		**840**	**841**

R22	O19	R23	R47	O20
843		**844**	**845**	**847**

O21	R26	R27	R28
	849	**850**	**851**

R24'	R29	O22	R30
853	**854**		**857**

PL. 28

O23 R31
858

R32
859

R35
862

O24 R33
860

R48
867

O25 R34
868

O26
870

O27 R36
871

O28 R37
872

O29 R38
873

O30 R39
885

O31 R40
886

O1 R1
887

PL. 29

O2　R2
888

O3　R3
889

O4　R4
890

O5　R5
892

O6　R6
894 (x2)

R7　R8　R9　O7
895　**897**　**898**　**899**

O8　R10　O9　O10
900　**901**　**902**

PL. 30

R11
904

O103
906

R171
910

R16
917

R17
918

R12
920

R13
922 (x1.5)

R14
923

R15
924

O11   R18
925

O12
926

R19
927

O13   R20
928

O104
932

O14   R21
929

O15   R22
930

PL. 31

R172 O16 R23 O17 R24
934 **943** **944**

O18 R25 O19 R26 R173
945 **946** **948**

O20 R27 R28 O21 R29
958 **959** **960**

O105 O22 R27' R30
961 **966** **967**

R31 O23 R32 R33
968 **969** **971** (x1.5)

PL. 32

O24	R34	R35	R36
	972	**973**	**974**

O25	R37	O26	R38
	975		**976**

O27	R39	O28	R40	R41
	977		**978**	**979**

O29	R42	R174	R175	R176
	981	**986**	**987**	**988**

R177	O30	R43	O31
991		**1001**	**1003**

PL. 33

R44
1004

O32
1005
R45

O34
1009
R47

O33
1008 (x1.5)
R46

O35
1010
R48

R178
1013

R179
1014

R180
1015 (x1.5)

R49
1027

O36
1028

R50
1031

R51
1032

O37
1034

O38
1035
R52

R53
1036

R54
1037

R55
1038

PL. 34

O39
1044

R56
1045 (x1.5)

R57
1047

R59
1049

O40
1048

R58

R60
1050

R61
1051

O41
1052

R62
1055

O42
1057

R63

R64
1058

R65
1060

O44
1062

R66

R67
1064

O43
1061 (x3)

O45
1066

R68

PL. 35

R69
1069

O46 R70
1070

R71
1071

O47 R72
1072

R181
1087

R182
1088

R183
1089

O48 R73
1137

R74
1141

O49 R75
1143

R76
1144

R77
1145

O50
1148

O51 R80
1150

O52
1151

R53
1152

O54 R81
1154

R82
1155

PL. 36

O55 R83
1156

O56 R84
1157

O57 R85
1158

O58 R86
1159

R78
1163

R79 R184 R185 R186 R187
1164 **1167** **1168** **1169** **1170**

O59 R86'
1200

O60 R87
1202

O61 R88
1204

O62 R89
1206

PL. 37

O63 R90'
1210

R91
1211

R92
1214

R93
1215

O63
1216

O64 R95
1218

R96
1219

O65 R97
1220

O66 R98
1221 (x1.5)

R99
1222

R100
1223

O67 R101
1224

R102
1225

R103
1226

O68 R104
1228

O69 R105
1229

R188
1232

PL. 38

R189	R190	R191	R192	R106
1233	**1234**	**1235**	**1236**	**1265**

O70	O71	R107	O72
1268	**1270**		**1271**

O73	R108	R109
1272 (x2)		**1274**

R110	R111	R112	R113	R114
1278	**1279**	**1281**	**1284**	**1285**

O74	R115	O75	R116	R118
1286		**1287** (x1.5)		**1305**

PL. 39

O76	R119		O77	R120
1306			**1309**	

O78	R121	R122	R123	R124
1311		**1312**	**1314**	**1315**

R125	R126	O79	R127
1316	**1317**	**1318**	

O80	R128	O106	O107	R117
1319		**1321**	**1322**	**1323**

O81	R129	O82	R130
1346		**1347**	

PL. 40

O83   R131
   1348

O84   R132
   1349

O85   R133
   1350

O86   R134
   1352

R137
1355

O87   R135
   1353

O88   R136
   1354

O90
1359

O89   R139
   1358

R141
1360

R142
1361

R143
1362

R144
1363

O91   R147
   1366

R148
1367

O92
1369

PL. 41

R149	O93	R149	R150	R151
1370	**1373**		**1377**	**1378**

R152	R153	R154	O95	R155
1379	**1384**	**1385**	**1387**	

R156	R157	O96	O96	R160
1391	**1392**	**1394**	**1395**	**1397**

O97	R158	R161	R162	R163
1396		**1398**	**1399**	**1400**

R164	O108	R138	R140	R145
1401	**1408**	**1409**	**1410**	**1411**

PL. 42

R146	R196	R197	R198	R199
1412	**1416**	**1417**	**1418**	**1419**

R201	R202
1422	**1423**

R200
1421 (x3)

R203	R204
1424	**1425**

R193	R194	R195	R165	O98
1426	**1427**	**1428**	**1511**	**1512**

O99	R166	R167	O100	R168
1513		**1515** (x1.5)	**1516**	

PL. 43

O101 R169
1517

O102 R170
1522

O1 R1   R2 R3   O2 R4   R5
1540 **1541** **1542** **1543** **1544**

R6   R7   O3 R8   O4   R9
1545 **1546** (x2) **1547**   **1549** (x2)

O5   R10   O6   R11
1550 (x3)   **1552** (x2)

O7 R12   O8 R13   O9 R14   O10 R15
1554 **1555** **1556** **1557**

O11 R16   O12 R17   O13 R18   R19
1558   **1559**   **1560**   **1564**

PL. 44

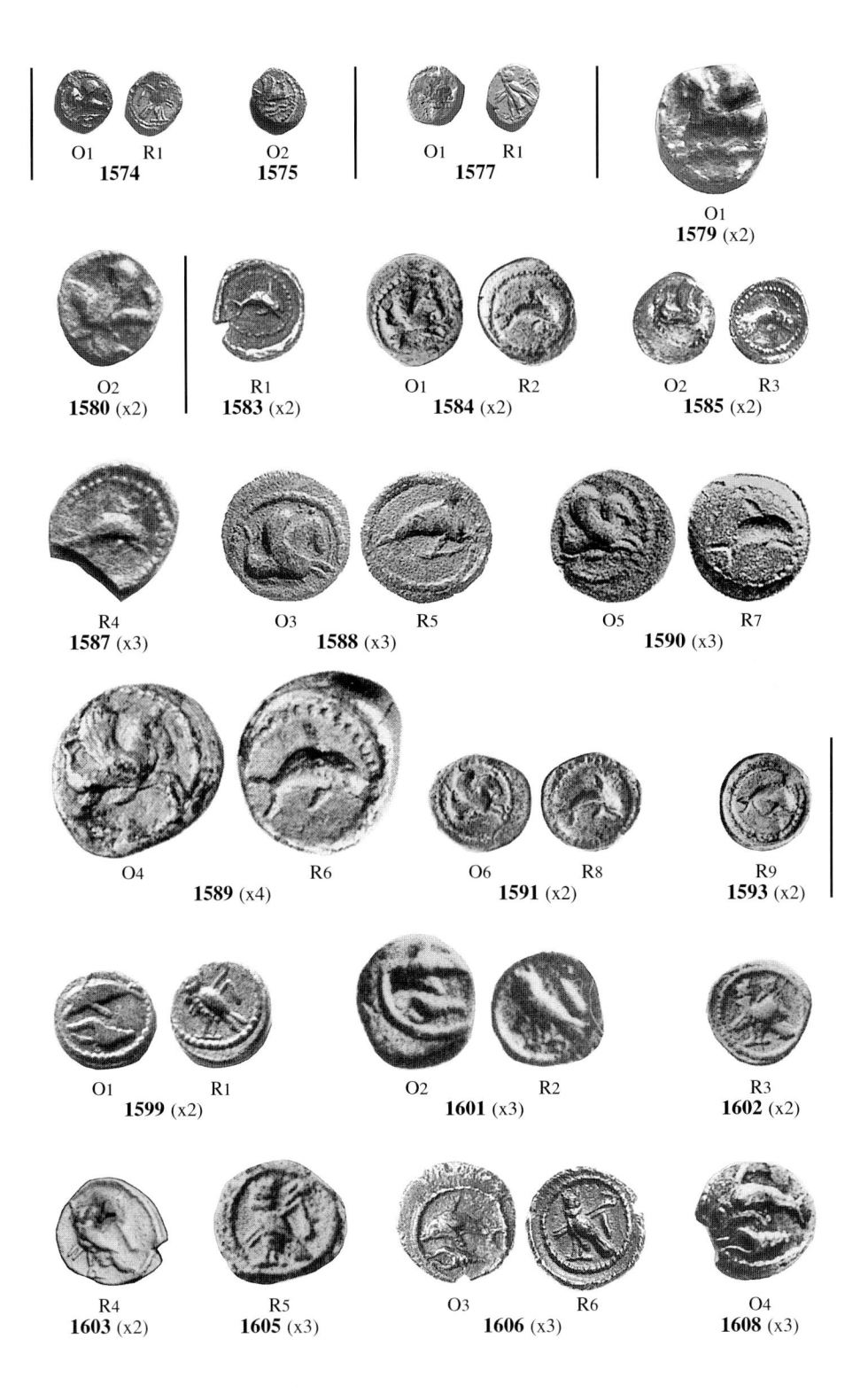

O1 R1	O2	O1 R1	
1574	**1575**	**1577**	

O1
1579 (x2)

O2	R1	O1 R2	O2 R3
1580 (x2)	**1583** (x2)	**1584** (x2)	**1585** (x2)

R4	O3 R5	O5 R7
1587 (x3)	**1588** (x3)	**1590** (x3)

O4 R6	O6 R8	R9
1589 (x4)	**1591** (x2)	**1593** (x2)

O1 R1	O2 R2	R3
1599 (x2)	**1601** (x3)	**1602** (x2)

R4	R5	O3 R6	O4
1603 (x2)	**1605** (x3)	**1606** (x3)	**1608** (x3)

PL. 45

R7
1609 (x1.5)

O5   R8
1610 (x2)

O7   R9
1612 (x2)

O6
1611 (x2)

O8   R10
1614 (x2)

O9   R11
1615 (x2)

R12
1616 (x2)

O10   R13
1617 (x2)

O11   R14
1618 (x2)

O12   R15
1619 (x2)

O13   R16
1620 (x3)

O15
1624 (x3)

O14   R17
1621 (x2)

O16
1625 (x2)

R18
1626 (x2)

R19
1627 (x2)

PL. 46

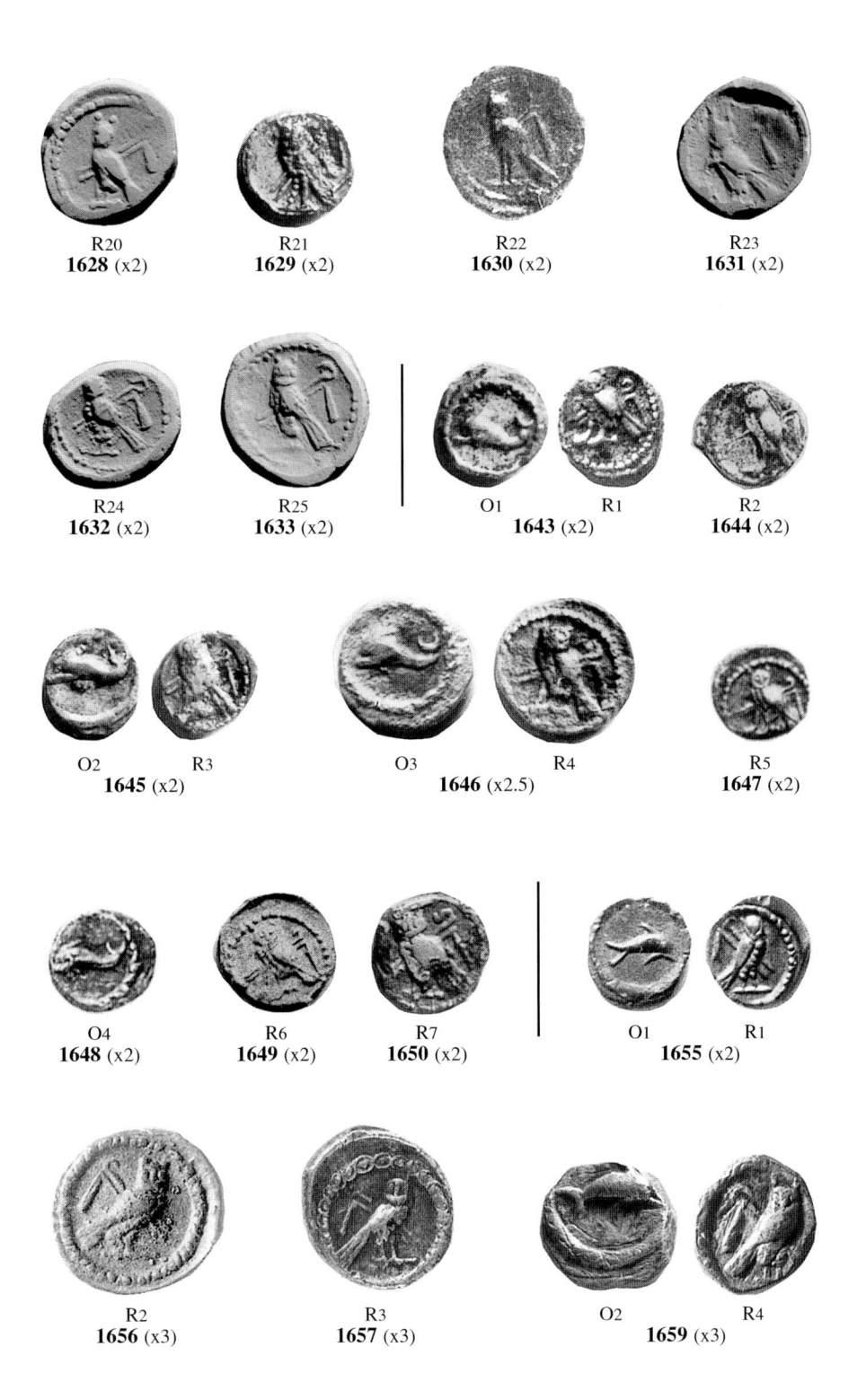

R20
1628 (x2)

R21
1629 (x2)

R22
1630 (x2)

R23
1631 (x2)

R24
1632 (x2)

R25
1633 (x2)

O1　　R1
1643 (x2)

R2
1644 (x2)

O2　R3
1645 (x2)

O3　　R4
1646 (x2.5)

R5
1647 (x2)

O4
1648 (x2)

R6
1649 (x2)

R7
1650 (x2)

O1　　R1
1655 (x2)

R2
1656 (x3)

R3
1657 (x3)

O2　　R4
1659 (x3)

PL. 47

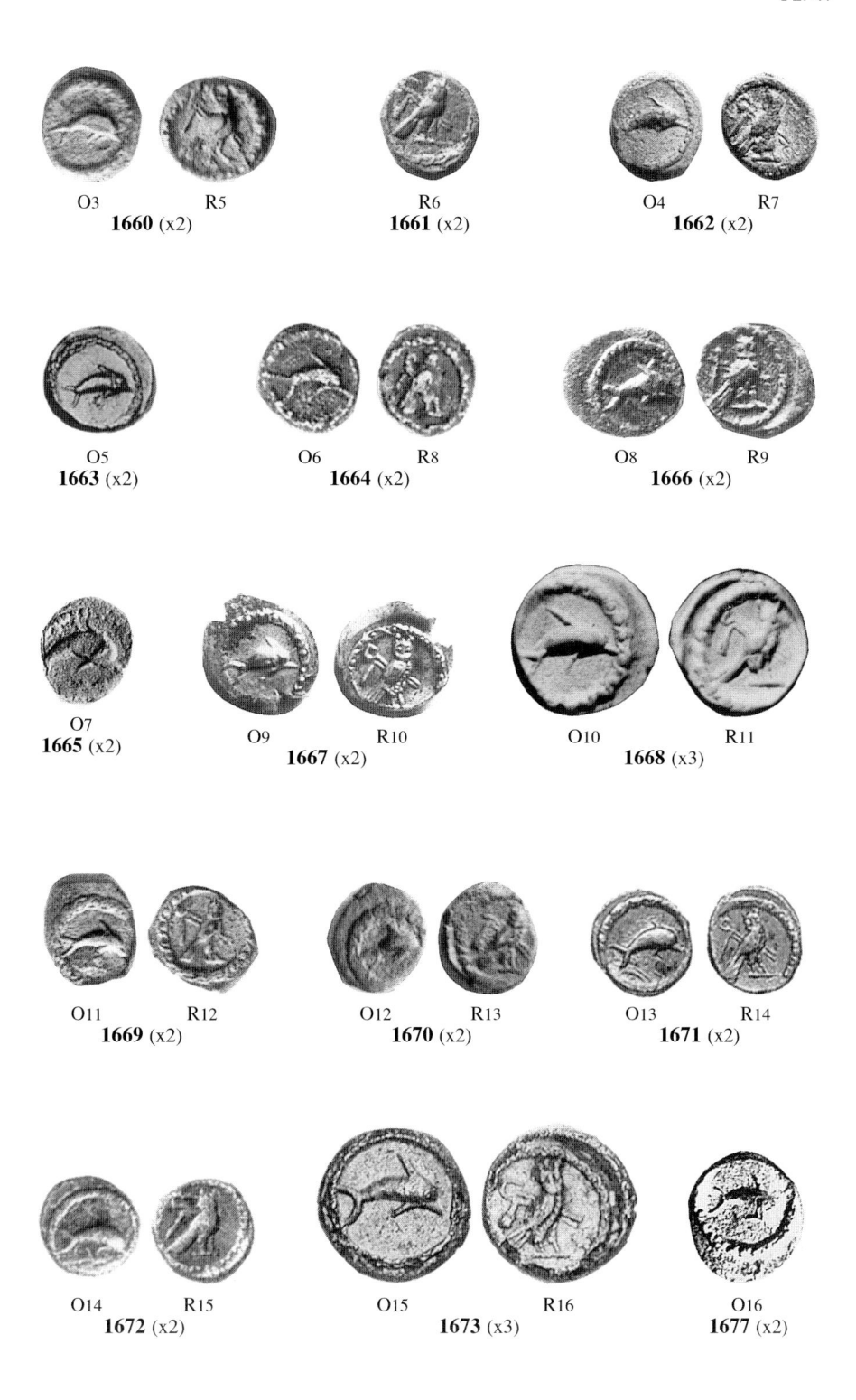

O3   R5
1660 (x2)

R6
1661 (x2)

O4   R7
1662 (x2)

O5
1663 (x2)

O6   R8
1664 (x2)

O8   R9
1666 (x2)

O7
1665 (x2)

O9   R10
1667 (x2)

O10   R11
1668 (x3)

O11   R12
1669 (x2)

O12   R13
1670 (x2)

O13   R14
1671 (x2)

O14   R15
1672 (x2)

O15   R16
1673 (x3)

O16
1677 (x2)

PL. 48

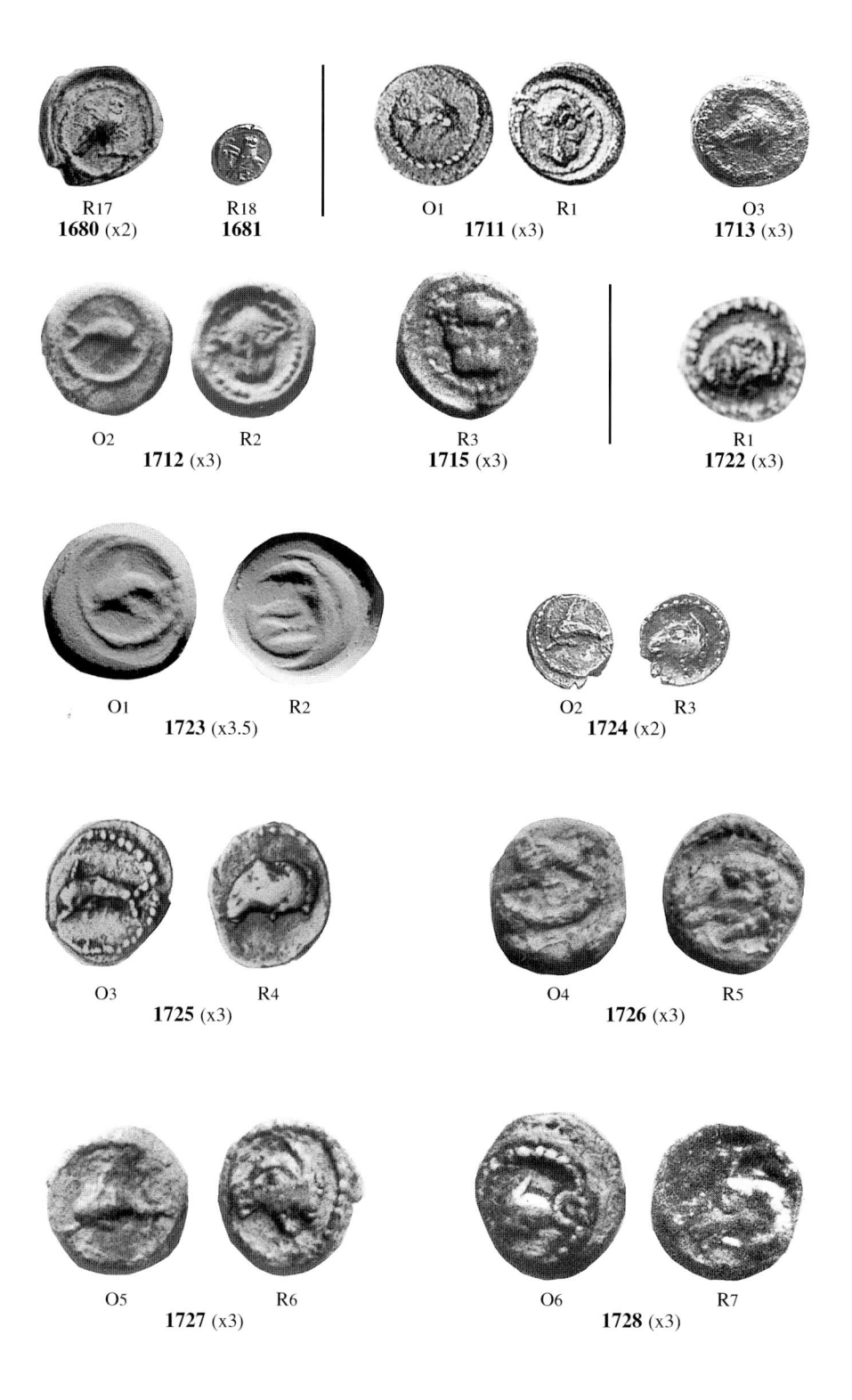

R17
1680 (x2)

R18
1681

O1   R1
1711 (x3)

O3
1713 (x3)

O2   R2
1712 (x3)

R3
1715 (x3)

R1
1722 (x3)

O1   R2
1723 (x3.5)

O2   R3
1724 (x2)

O3   R4
1725 (x3)

O4   R5
1726 (x3)

O5   R6
1727 (x3)

O6   R7
1728 (x3)

PL. 49

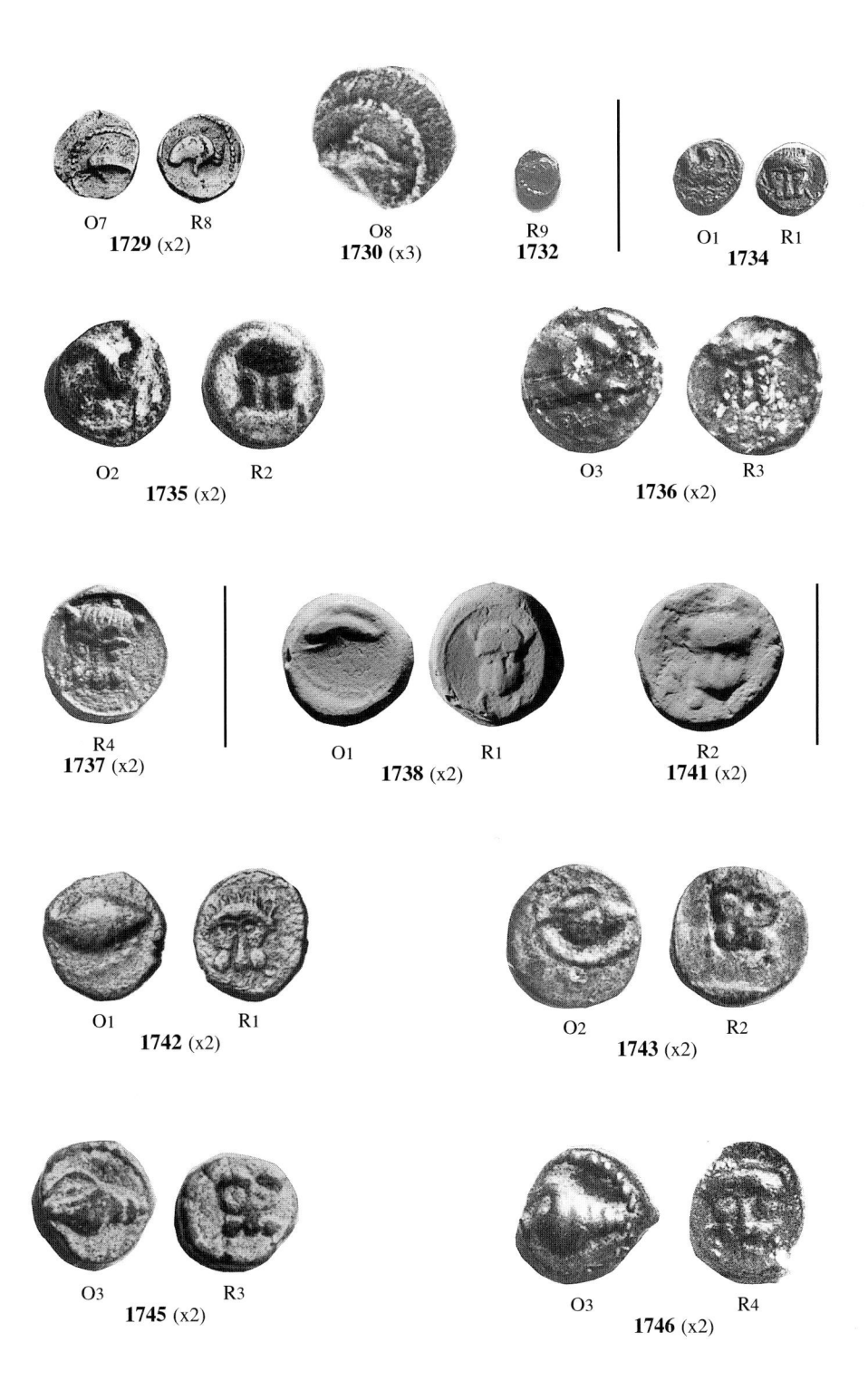

O7 R8
1729 (x2)

O8
1730 (x3)

R9
1732

O1 R1
1734

O2 R2
1735 (x2)

O3 R3
1736 (x2)

R4
1737 (x2)

O1 R1
1738 (x2)

R2
1741 (x2)

O1 R1
1742 (x2)

O2 R2
1743 (x2)

O3 R3
1745 (x2)

O3 R4
1746 (x2)

PL. 50

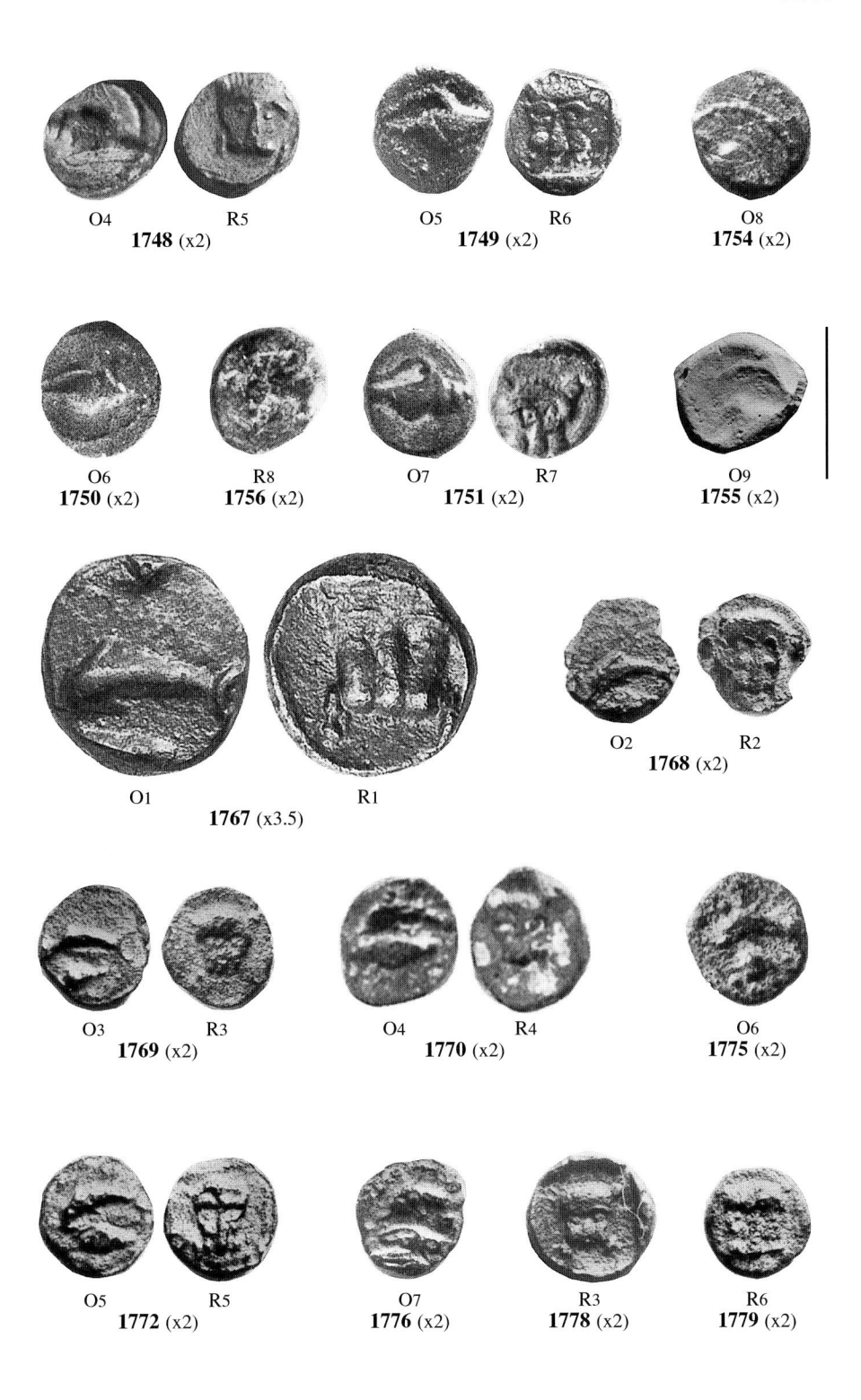

O4 R5
1748 (x2)

O5 R6
1749 (x2)

O8
1754 (x2)

O6
1750 (x2)

R8
1756 (x2)

O7 R7
1751 (x2)

O9
1755 (x2)

O1 R1
1767 (x3.5)

O2 R2
1768 (x2)

O3 R3
1769 (x2)

O4 R4
1770 (x2)

O6
1775 (x2)

O5 R5
1772 (x2)

O7
1776 (x2)

R3
1778 (x2)

R6
1779 (x2)

PL. 51

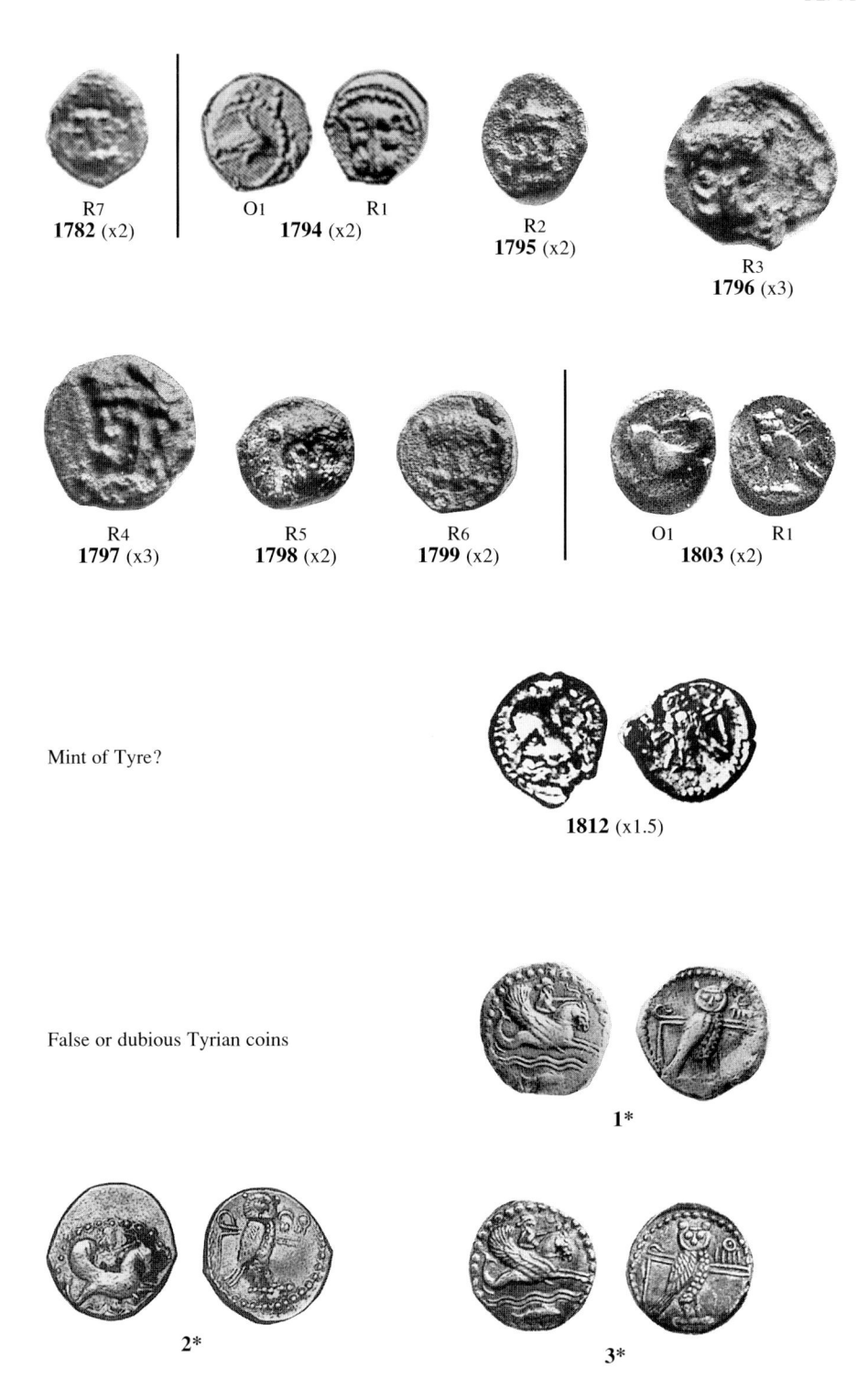

R7
1782 (x2)

O1   R1
1794 (x2)

R2
1795 (x2)

R3
1796 (x3)

R4
1797 (x3)

R5
1798 (x2)

R6
1799 (x2)

O1   R1
1803 (x2)

Mint of Tyre?

1812 (x1.5)

False or dubious Tyrian coins

1*

2*

3*

ORIENTALIA LOVANIENSIA ANALECTA

1. E. LIPIŃSKI, Studies in Aramaic Inscriptions and Onomastics I.
2. J. QUAEGEBEUR, Le dieu égyptien Shaï dans la religion et l'onomastique.
3. P.H.L. EGGERMONT, Alexander's Campaigns in Sind and Baluchistan and the Siege of the Brahmin Town of Harmatelia.
4. W.M. CALLEWAERT, The Sarvāṅgī of the Dādūpanthī Rajab.
5. E. LIPIŃSKI (ed.), State and Temple Economy in the Ancient Near East I.
6. E. LIPIŃSKI (ed.), State and Temple Economy in the Ancient Near East II.
7. M.-C. DE GRAEVE, The Ships of the Ancient Near East (c. 2000-500 B.C.).
8. W.M. CALLEWAERT (ed.), Early Hindī Devotional Literature in Current Research.
9. F.L. DAMEN, Crisis and Religious Renewal in the Brahmo Samaj Movement (1860-1884).
10. R.Y. EBIED, A. VAN ROEY, L.R. WICKHAAM, Peter of Callinicum, Anti-Tritheist Dossier.
11. A. RAMMANT-PEETERS, Les pyramidions égyptiens du Nouvel Empire.
12. S. SCHEERS (ed.), Studia Paulo Naster Oblata I. Numismatica Antiqua.
13. J. QUAEGEBEUR (ed.), Studia Paulo Naster Oblata II. Orientalia Antiqua.
14. E. PLATTI, Yaḥyā ibn ʿAdī, théologien chrétien et philosophe arabe.
15. E. GUBEL, E. LIPIŃSKI, B. SERVAIS-SOYEZ (eds.), Studia Phoenicia I-II.
16. W. SKALMOWSKI, A. VAN TONGERLOO (eds.), Middle Iranian Studies.
17. M. VAN MOL, Handboek Modern Arabisch.
18. C. LAGA, J.A. MUNITIZ, L. VAN ROMPAY (eds.), After Chalcedon. Studies in Theology and Church History.
19. E. LIPIŃSKI (ed.), The Land of Israel: Cross-Roads of Civilizations.
20. S. WACHSMANN, Aegeans in the Theban Tombs.
21. K. VAN LERBERGHE, Old Babylonian Legal and Administrative Texts from Philadelphia.
22. E. LIPIŃSKI (ed.), Phoenicia and the East Mediterranean in the First Millennium B.C.
23. M. HELTZER, E. LIPIŃSKI (eds.), Society and Economy in the Eastern Mediterranean (1500-1000 B.C.).
24. M. VAN DE MIEROOP, Crafts in the Early Isin Period: a Study of the Isin Craft Archive from the Reigns of Išbi-Erra and Šū-Ilišu.
25. G. POLLET (ed.), India and the Ancient World. History, Trade and Culture before A.D. 650.
26. E. LIPIŃSKI (ed.), Carthago.
27. E. VERREET, Modi Ugaritici. Eine morpho-syntaktische Abhandlung über das Modalsystem im Ugaritischen.
28. R. ZADOK, The Pre-Hellenistic Israelite Anthroponomy and Prosopography.
29. W. CALLEWAERT, M. LATH, The Hindī Songs of Nāmdev.
30. A. SHISHA-HALEVY, Coptic Grammatical Chrestomathy.
31. N. BAUM, Arbres et arbustes de l'Égypte ancienne.
32. J.-M. KRUCHTEN, Les Annales des prêtres de Karnak (XXIe-XXIIIe dynasties) et autres textes relatifs à l'initation des prêtres d'Amon.
33. H. DEVIJVER, E. LIPIŃSKI (eds.), Punic Wars.
34. E. VASSILIKA, Ptolemaic Philae.
35. A. GHAITH, La Pensée Religieuse chez Ǧubrân Ḫalil Ǧubrân et Miḫâʾîl Nuʿayma.
36. N. BEAUX, Le Cabinet de curiosités de Thoutmosis III.
37. G. POLLET, P. EGGERMONT, G. VAN DAMME, Corpus Topographicum Indiae Antiquae. Part II: Archaeological Sites.
38. S.-A. NAGUIB, Le Clergé féminin d'Amon thébain à la 21e dynastie.
39. U. VERHOEVEN, E. GRAEFE (eds.), Religion und Philosophie im Alten Ägypten. Festgabe für Philippe Derchain zu seinem 65. Geburtstag.

40. A.R. GEORGE, Babylonian Topographical Texts.
41. A. SCHOORS, The Preacher Sought to Find Pleasing Words. A Study of the Language of Qohelet. Part I: Grammatical Features.
42. G. REININK, H.E.J. VAN STIPHOUT (eds.), Dispute Poems and Dialogues in the Ancient and Mediaeval Near East.
43. C. TRAUNECKER, Coptos. Hommes et dieux sur le parvis de Geb.
44. E. LIPIŃSKI (ed.), Phoenicia and the Bible.
45. L. ISEBAERT (ed.), Studia Etymologica Indoeuropaea Memoriae A.J. Van Windekens dicata.
46. F. BRIQUEL-CHATONNET, Les relations entre les cités de la côte phénicienne et les royaumes d'Israël et de Juda.
47. W.J. VAN BEKKUM, A Hebrew Alexander Romance according to MS London, Jews' College no. 145.
48. W. SKALMOWSKI, A. VAN TONGERLOO (eds.), Medioiranica.
49. L. LAUWERS, Igor'-Severjanin, His Life and Work — The Formal Aspects of His Poetry.
50. R.L. VOS, The Apis Embalming Ritual. P. Vindob. 3873.
51. Fr. LABRIQUE, Stylistique et Théologie à Edfou. Le rituel de l'offrande de la campagne: étude de la composition.
52. F. DE JONG (ed.), Miscellanea Arabica et Islamica.
53. G. BREYER, Etruskisches Sprachgut im Lateinischen unter Ausschluß des spezifisch onomastischen Bereiches.
54. P.H.L. EGGERMONT, Alexander's Campaign in Southern Punjab.
55. J. QUAEGEBEUR (ed.), Ritual and Sacrifice in the Ancient Near East.
56. A. VAN ROEY, P. ALLEN, Monophysite Texts of the Sixth Century.
57. E. LIPIŃSKI, Studies in Aramaic Inscriptions and Onomastics II.
58. F.R. HERBIN, Le livre de parcourir l'éternité.
59. K. GEUS, Prosopographie der literarisch bezeugten Karthager.
60. A. SCHOORS, P. VAN DEUN (eds.), Philohistor. Miscellanea in honorem Caroli Laga septuagenarii.
61. M. KRAUSE, S. GIVERSEN, P. NAGEL (eds.), Coptology. Past, Present and Future. Studies in Honour of R. Kasser.
62. C. LEITZ, Altägyptische Sternuhren.
63. J.J. CLÈRE, Les Chauves d'Hathor.
64. E. LIPIŃSKI, Dieux et déesses de l'univers phénicien et punique.
65. K. VAN LERBERGHE, A. SCHOORS (eds.), Immigration and Emigration within the Ancient Near East. Festschrift E. Lipiński.
66. G. POLLET (ed.), Indian Epic Values. Rāmāyaṇa and its impact.
67. D. DE SMET, La quiétude de l'Intellect. Néoplatonisme et gnose ismaélienne dans l'œuvre de Ḥamîd ad-Dîn al-Kirmânî (X^e-XIe s.).
68. M.L. FOLMER, The Aramaic Language in the Achaemenid Period. A Study in Linguistic Variation.
69. S. IKRAM, Choice Cuts: Meat Production in Ancient Egypt.
70. H. WILLEMS, The Coffin of Heqata (Cairo JdE 36418). A Case Study of Egyptian Funerary Culture of the Early Middle Kingdom.
71. C. EDER, Die Ägyptischen Motive in der Glyptik des östlichen Mittelmeerraumes zu Anfang des 2. Jts. v. Chr.
72. J. THIRY, Le Sahara libyen dans l'Afrique du Nord médiévale.
73. U. VERMEULEN, D. DE SMET (eds.), Egypt and Syria in the Fatimid, Ayyubid and Mamluk Eras I.
74. P. ARÈNES, La déesse Sgrol-Ma (Tara). Recherches sur la nature et le statut d'une divinité du bouddhisme tibétain.
75. K. CIGGAAR, A. DAVIDS, H. TEULE (eds.), East and West in the Crusader States. Context - Contacts - Confrontations I.
76. M. BROZE, Mythe et Roman en Egypte ancienne. Les Aventures d'Horus et Seth dans le papyrus Chester Beatty I.

77. L. Depuydt, Civil Calendar and Lunar Calendar in Ancient Egypt.
78. P. Wilson, A Ptolemaic Lexikon. A Lexicographical Study of the Texts in the Temple of Edfu.
79. A. Hasnawi, A. Elamrani, M. Jamal, M. Aouad (eds.), Perspectives arabes et médiévales sur la tradition scientifique et philosophique grecque.
80. E. Lipiński, Semitic Languages: Outline of a Comparative Grammar.
81. S. Cauville, Dendara I. Traduction.
82. C. Eyre (ed.), Proceedings of the Seventh International Congress of Egyptologists.
83. U. Vermeulen, D. De Smet (eds.), Egypt and Syria in the Fatimid, Ayyubid and Mamluk Eras II.
84-85. W. Clarysse, A. Schoors, H. Willems (eds.), Egyptian Religion. The Last Thousand Years.
86. U. Vermeulen, J.M. Van Reeth (eds.), Law, Christianity and Modernism in Islamic Society.
87. U. Vermeulen, D. De Smet (eds.), Philosophy and Arts in the Islamic World.
88. S. Cauville, Dendara II. Traduction.
89. G.J. Reinink, A.C. Klugkist (eds.), After Bardaisan. Studies on Continuity and Change in Syriac Christianity in Honour of Professor Han J.W. Drijvers.
90. C.R. Krahmalkov, Phoenician-Punic Dictionary.
91. M. Tahtah, Entre pragmatisme, réformisme et modernisme. Le rôle politico-religieux des Khattabi dans le Rif (Maroc) jusqu'à 1926.
92. K. Ciggaar, H. Teule (eds.), East and West in the Crusader States. Context — Contact — Confrontations II.
93. A.C.J. Verheij, Bits, Bytes, and Binyanim. A Quantitative Study of Verbal Lexeme Formations in the Hebrew Bible.
94. W.M. Callewaert, D. Taillieu, F. Laleman, A Descriptive Bibliography of Allama Muhammad Iqbal (1877-1938).
95. S. Cauville, Dendara III. Traduction.
96. K. Van Lerberghe, G. Voet (eds.), Languages and Cultures in Contact: At the Crossroads of Civilizations in the Syro-Mesopotamian Realm.
97. A. Cabrol, Les voies processionnelles de Thèbes.
98. J. Patrich, The Sabaite Heritage in the Orthodox Church from the Fifth Century to the Present. Monastic Life, Liturgy, Theology, Literature, Art, Archaeology.
99. U. Verhoeven, Untersuchungen zur Spähieratischen Buchschrift.
100. E. Lipiński, The Aramaeans: Their Ancient History, Culture, Religion.
101. S. Cauville, Dendara IV. Traduction.
102. U. Vermeulen, J. Van Steenbergen (eds.), Egypt and Syria in the Fatimid, Ayyubid and Mamluk Eras III.
103. H. Willems (ed.), Social Aspects of Funerary Culture in the Egyptian Old and Middle Kingdoms.
104. K. Geus, K. Zimmermann (eds.), Punica — Libyca — Ptolemaica. Festschrift für Werner Huß, zum 65. Geburtstag dargebracht von Schülern, Freunden und Kollegen.
105. S. Cauville, Dendara. Les fêtes d'Hathor.
106. R. Preys, Les complexes de la demeure du sistre et du trône de Rê. Théologie et décoration dans le temple d'Hathor à Dendera.
107. A. Blasius, B.U. Schipper (eds.), Apokalyptik und Ägypten. Eine kritische Analyse der relevanten Texte aus dem griechisch-römischen Ägypten.
108. S. Leder (ed.), Studies in Arabic and Islam.
109. A. Goddeeris, Economy and Society in Northern Babylonia in the Early Old Babylonian Period (ca. 2000-1800 BC).
110. C. Leitz (ed.), Lexikon der ägyptischen Götter und Götterbezeichnungen, Band I.

111. C. LEITZ (ed.), Lexikon der ägyptischen Götter und Götterbezeichnungen, Band II.
112. C. LEITZ (ed.), Lexikon der ägyptischen Götter und Götterbezeichnungen, Band III.
113. C. LEITZ (ed.), Lexikon der ägyptischen Götter und Götterbezeichnungen, Band IV.
114. C. LEITZ (ed.), Lexikon der ägyptischen Götter und Götterbezeichnungen, Band V.
115. C. LEITZ (ed.), Lexikon der ägyptischen Götter und Götterbezeichnungen, Band VI.
116. C. LEITZ (ed.), Lexikon der ägyptischen Götter und Götterbezeichnungen, Band VII.
117. M. VAN MOL, Variation in Modern Standard Arabic in Radio News Broadcasts.
118. M.F.J. BAASTEN, W.Th VAN PEURSEN (eds.), Hamlet on a Hill. Semitic and Greek Studies Presented to Professor T. Muraoka on the Occasion of his Sixty-Fifth Birthday.
119. O.E. KAPER, The Egyptian God Tutu. A Study of the Sphinx-God and Master of Demons with a Corpus of Monuments.
120. E. WARDINI, Lebanese Place-Names (Mount Lebanon and North Lebanon).
121. J. VAN DER VLIET, Catalogue of the Coptic Inscriptions in the Sudan National Museum at Khartoum (I. Khartoum Copt).
122. A. ŁAJTAR, Catalogue of the Greek Inscriptions in the Sudan National Museum at Khartoum (I. Khartoum Greek).
123. H. NIEHR, Ba'alšamem. Studien zu Herkunft, Geschichte und Rezeptionsgeschichte eines phönizischen Gottes.
124. H. WILLEMS, F. COPPENS, M. DE MEYER, P. DILS, The Temple of Shanhûr. Volume I : The Sanctuary, The *Wabet*, and the Gates of the Central Hall and the Great Vestibule (1-98).
125. K. CIGGAAR, H.G.B. TEULE (eds.), East and West in the Crusader States. Context – Contacts – Confrontations III.
126. T. SOLDATJENKOVA, E. WAEGEMANS (eds.), For East is East. Liber Amicorum Wojciech Skalmowski.
127. E. LIPIŃSKI, Itineraria Phoenicia.
128. D. BUDDE, S. SANDRI, U. VERHOEVEN (eds.), Kindgötter im Ägypten der griechisch-römischen Zeit. Zeugnisse aus Stadt und Tempel als Spiegel des Interkulturellen Kontakts.
129. C. LEITZ (ed.), Lexikon der ägyptischen Götter und Götterbezeichnungen, Band VIII.
130. E.J. VAN DER STEEN, Tribes and Territories in Transition.
131. S. CAUVILLE, Dendara V-VI. Traduction. Les cryptes du temple d'Hathor.
132. S. CAUVILLE, Dendara V-VI. Index phraséologique. Les cryptes du temple d'Hathor.
133. M. IMMERZEEL, J. VAN DER VLIET, M. KERSTEN, C. VAN ZOEST (eds.), Coptic Studies on the Threshold of a New Millennium. Proceedings of the Seventh International Congress of Coptic Studies. Leiden, August 27 - September 2, 2000.
134. J.J. VAN GINKEL, H.L. MURRE-VAN DEN BERG, T.M. VAN LINT (eds.), Redefining Christian Identity. Cultural Interaction in the Middle East since the Rise of Islam.
135. J. MONTGOMERY (ed.), 'Abbasid Studies. Occasional Papers of the School of 'Abbasid Studies, Cambridge, 6-10 July 2002.
136. T. BOIY, Late Achaemenid and Hellenistic Babylon.
137. B. JANSSENS, B. ROOSEN, P. VAN DEUN (eds.), Philomathestatos. Studies in Greek Patristic and Byzantine Texts Presented to Jacques Noret for his Sixty-Fifth Birthday.

138. S. Hendrickx, R.F. Friedman, K.M. Ciałowicz, M. Chłodnicki (eds.), Egypt at its Origins. Studies in Memory of Barbara Adams.
139. R. Arnzen, J. Thielmann (eds.), Words, Texts and Concepts Cruising the Mediterranean Sea. Studies on the Sources, Contents and Influences of Islamic Civilization and Arabic Philosophy and Science.
140. U. Vermeulen, J. Van Steenbergen (eds.), Egypt and Syria in the Fatimid, Ayyubid and Mamluk Eras IV.
141. H.T. Davies, Yūsuf al-Shirbīnī's Kitāb Hazz al-Qūḥuf bi-Sharḥ Qaṣīd Abī Shādūf ("Brains Confounded by the Ode of Abū Shādūf Expounded") Volume I: Arabic text.
142. P. Van Nuffelen, Un héritage de paix et de piété. Étude sur les histoires ecclésiastiques de Socrate et de Sozomène.
143. A. Schoors, The Preacher Sought to Find Pleasing Words. A Study of the Language of Qoheleth. Part II: Vocabulary.
144. M.E. Stone, Apocrypha, Pseudepigrapha and Armenian Studies. Collected Papers: Volume 1.
145. M.E. Stone, Apocrypha, Pseudepigrapha and Armenian Studies. Collected Papers: Volume 2.
146. M. Cacouros, M.-H. Congourdeau (eds.), Philosophie et sciences à Byzance de 1204 à 1453. Les textes, les doctrines et leur transmission.
147. K. Ciggaar, M. Metcalf (eds.), East and West in the Medieval Eastern Mediterranean I.
148. B. Michalak-Pikulska, A. Pikulski (eds.), Authority, Privacy and Public Order in Islam.
149. E. Czerny, I. Hein, H. Hunger, D. Melman, A. Schwab (eds.), Timelines. Studies in Honour of Manfred Bietak.
150. J.-Cl. Goyon, C. Cardin (eds.), Proceedings of the Ninth International Congress of Egyptologists. Actes du neuvième congrès international des Égyptologues. Grenoble, 6-12 septembre 2004.
151. S. Sandri, Har-pa-chered (Harpokrates). Die Genese eines ägyptischen Götterkindes.
152. J.E. Montgomery (ed.), Arabic Theology, Arabic Philosophy. From the Many to the One: Essays in Celebration of Richard M. Frank.
153. E. Lipiński, On the Skirts of Canaan in the Iron Age. Historical and Topographical Researches.
154. M. Minas-Nerpel, Der Gott Chepri. Untersuchungen zu Schriftzeugnissen und ikonographischen Quellen vom Alten Reich bis in griechisch-römische Zeit.
155. H. Willems, Dayr al-Barshā Volume 1. The Rock Tombs of Djehutinakht (No. 17K74/1), Khnumnakht (No. 17K74/2), and Iha (No. 17K74/3). With an Essay on the History and Nature of Nomarchal Rule in the Early Middle Kingdom.
156. J. Bretschneider, J. Driessen, K. Van Lerberghe (eds.), Power and Architecture. Monumental Public Architecture in the Bronze Age Near East and Aegean.
157. A. Camplani, G. Filoramo (eds.), Foundations of Power and Conflicts of Authority in Late Antique Monasticism.
158. J. Tavernier, Iranica in the Achaemenid Period (ca. 550-330 B.C.). Lexicon of Old Iranian Proper Names and Loanwords, Attested in Non-Iranian Texts.
159. P. Kousoulis, K. Magliveras (eds.), Moving Across Borders. Foreign Relations, Religion and Cultural Interactions in the Ancient Mediterranean.
160. A. Shisha-Halevy, Topics in Coptic Syntax: Structural Studies in the Bohairic Dialect.
161. B. Lurson, Osiris, Ramsès, Thot et le Nil. Les chapelles secondaires des temples de Derr et Ouadi es-Seboua.
162. G. del Olmo Lete (ed.), Mythologie et Religion des Sémites occidentaux.

163. N. Bosson, A. Boud'hors (eds.), Actes du huitième congrès international d'études coptes. Paris, 28 juin - 3 juillet 2004.
164. A. Berlejung, P. Van Hecke (eds.), The Language of Qohelet in Its Context. Essays in Honour of Prof. A. Schoors on the Occasion of his Seventieth Birthday.
165. A.G.C. Savvides, Byzantino-Normannica. The Norman Capture of Italy and the First Two Invasions in Byzantium.
166. H.T. Davies, Yūsuf al-Shirbīnī's Brains Confounded by the Ode of Abū Shādūf Expounded (Kitāb Hazz al-Qūḥuf bi-Sharḥ Qaṣīd Abī Shādūf). Volume II: English translation, introduction and notes.
167. S. Arguillère, Profusion de la vaste sphère. Klong-chen rab-'byams (Tibet, 1308-1364). Sa vie, son œuvre, sa doctrine.
168. D. De Smet, Les Épîtres sacrées des Druzes. Rasā'il al-Ḥikma. Volumes 1 et 2.
169. U. Vermeulen, K. D'Hulster (eds.), Egypt and Syria in the Fatimid, Ayyubid and Mamluk Eras V.
170. W.J. van Bekkum, J.W. Drijvers, A.C. Klugkist (eds.), Syriac Polemics. Studies in Honour of Gerrit Jan Reinink.
171. K. D'Hulster, J. Van Steenbergen (eds.), Continuity and Change in the Realms of Islam. Studies in Honour of Professor Urbain Vermeulen.
172. B. Midant-Reynes, Y. Tristant, J. Rowland, S. Hendrickx (eds.), Egypt at its Origins 2.
173. J.H.F. Dijkstra, Philae and the End of Ancient Egyptian Religion. A Regional Study of Religious Transformation (298-642 CE).
174. I. Uytterhoeven, Hawara in the Graeco-Roman Period. Life and Death in a Fayum Village.
175. P. Kousoulis (ed.), Ancient Egyptian Demonology. Studies on the Boundaries between the Demonic and the Divine in Egyptian Magic.
176. A. Karahan, Byzantine Holy Images – Transcendence and Immanence. The Theological Background of the Iconography and Aesthetics of the Chora Church.
177. J. Nawas (ed.), 'Abbasid Studies II. Occasional Papers of the School of 'Abbasid Studies, Leuven, 28 June - 1 July 2004.
178. S. Cauville, Dendara. Le temple d'Isis. Volume I: Traduction.
179. S. Cauville, Dendara. Le temple d'Isis. Volume II: Analyse à la lumière du temple d'Hathor.
180. M. Zitman, The Necropolis of Assiut.
181. E. Lipiński, Resheph. A Syro-Canaanite Deity.
182. C. Karlshausen, L'iconographie de la barque processionnelle en Égypte au Nouvel Empire.
183. U. Vermeulen, K. D'Hulster (eds.), Egypt and Syria in the Fatimid, Ayyubid and Mamluk Eras VI.
184. M. Immerzeel, Identity Puzzles. Medieval Christian Art in Syria and Lebanon.
185. D. Magee, J. Bourriau, S. Quirke (eds.), Sitting Beside Lepsius. Studies in Honour of Jaromir Malek at the Griffith Institute.
186. A. Stevenson, The Predynastic Egyptian Cemetery of el-Gerzeh.
187. D. Bumazhnov, E. Grypeou, T.B. Sailors, A. Toepel (eds.), Bibel, Byzanz und Christlicher Orient. Festschrift für Stephen Gerö zum 65. Geburtstag.
188. J. Elayi, A.G. Elayi, The Coinage of the Phoenician City of Tyre in the Persian Period (5th-4th Century BCE).